# Business Communication
## Developing Leaders for a Networked World

Third Edition

Peter W. Cardon

*University of Southern California*

Mc
Graw
Hill
Education

BUSINESS COMMUNICATION: DEVELOPING LEADERS FOR A NETWORKED WORLD, THIRD EDITION

Published by McGraw-Hill Education, 2 Penn Plaza, New York, NY 10121. Copyright © 2018 by McGraw-Hill Education. All rights reserved. Printed in the United States of America. Previous edition © 2016 and 2014. No part of this publication may be reproduced or distributed in any form or by any means, or stored in a database or retrieval system, without the prior written consent of McGraw-Hill Education, including, but not limited to, in any network or other electronic storage or transmission, or broadcast for distance learning.

Some ancillaries, including electronic and print components, may not be available to customers outside the United States.

This book is printed on acid-free paper.

5 6 7 8 9 0 LMN 21 20 19

ISBN 978-1-259-69451-6
MHID 1-259-69451-8

Chief Product Officer, SVP Products & Markets: *G. Scott Virkler*
Vice President, General Manager, Products & Markets: *Michael Ryan*
Vice President, Content Design & Delivery: Betsy Whalen
Managing Director: *Susan Gouijnstook*
Brand Manager: *Anke Weekes*
Director, Product Development: *Meghan Campbell*
Marketing Manager: *Michael Gedatus and Necco McKinley*
Marketing Coordinator: *Brittany Bernhold*
Product Developer: *Kelly I. Pekelder*
Digital Product Analyst: *Kerry Shanahan*
Director, Content Design & Delivery: *Terri Schiesl*
Program Manager: *Mary Conzachi*
Content Project Managers: *Christine Vaughan and Evan Roberts*
Buyer: *Susan K. Culbertson*
Design: *Egzon Shaqiri*
Content Licensing Specialists: *DeAnna Dausener and Ann Maie Jannette*
Cover Images: *©Shutterstock/VLADGRIN; ©Shutterstock/Mario7*
Compositor: *MPS Limited*
Typeface: *10.5/12 STIX General*
Printer: *LSC Communications*

All credits appearing on page or at the end of the book are considered to be an extension of the copyright page.
Social media icons/infographic interior image: *VLADGRIN/Getty Images*

Library of Congress Control Number: 2016962089.

The Internet addresses listed in the text were accurate at the time of publication. The inclusion of a website does not indicate an endorsement by the authors or McGraw-Hill Education, and McGraw-Hill Education does not guarantee the accuracy of the information presented at these sites.

mheducation.com/highered

# Dedication

To my daughters: Camilla Jean and Audrey Mei. Your Mom and I love spending every day with you. You make me the happiest Dad in the world!

—Peter W. Cardon

# About the Author

Courtesy of Peter Cardon

**Peter W. Cardon,** MBA, PhD, is a professor in the Department of Business Communication at the University of Southern California. He also serves as Academic Director for the MBA for Professionals and Managers program. He teaches a variety of courses in the MBA and undergraduate business programs, including management communication, intercultural communication, and new media and communication. With approximately 50 refereed articles, Pete is an active contributor to the latest research in intercultural communication, social networking, team collaboration, and leadership communication. He is proud to engage in a discipline that helps so many business professionals and students reach career and personal goals.

Pete is an active member of the Association for Business Communication (ABC). He previously served as the president of ABC. He currently serves as an Editorial Review Board member for the *International Journal of Business Communication (IJBC)* and *Business and Professional Communication Quarterly (BPCQ)*.

Prior to joining higher education, Pete worked as a marketing director at an international tourism company that focused on the markets of Brazil, South Korea, Japan, and Taiwan. Before that position, he was an account manager in a manufacturing company.

Pete is a strong advocate of global business ties. Having worked in China for three years and consulted in and traveled to nearly 50 countries, he has worked extensively with clients, customers, colleagues, and other partners across the world. To help students develop global leadership skills, he has led student groups on company tours and humanitarian projects to mainland China, Hong Kong, Macao, Taiwan, South Korea, Mexico, and the Dominican Republic.

# Brief Contents

**Bonus Content** Mc Graw Hill Education create™   Mc Graw Hill Education connect

Available only at www.mcgrawhillcreate.com/cardon or in the e-book within McGraw-Hill Connect®.

# Developing Leaders for a Networked World

Welcome to the third edition of *Business Communication*. This learning program develops leaders for a networked world. Through the author's **practitioner and case-based approach**, students are more likely to read and reflect on the text. They are better positioned to understand why **credibility** is essential to efficient and effective business communication in today's rapidly changing business communication environment. Cardon's integrated solution, including the **results-driven technology** and content, provides a contemporary yet traditional view into the business communication field, allowing instructors to teach bedrock communication principles while also staying up to date with cultural and **technological** changes. Students are empowered to build strong relationships through effective writing, master foundation concepts, and practice their communication skills anytime and anywhere—transforming them into leaders for a networked world.

The content of this textbook is organized around the traditional business communication topics such as routine messages, persuasive messages, bad-news messages, reports, and presentations. Beyond the basics, it adds unique and modern topics that instructors want and need in their courses.

## Credibility

Since professional success depends on managing and working within professional relationships, this textbook uses credibility or trust as a central principle throughout. Principles of relationship-building such as personal credibility, emotional intelligence, and listening hold a prominent role throughout the book. This product begins with a discussion of credibility and refers to it throughout the book

## Effective Writing Builds Relationships

Effective writing in the workplace is essential to building connections and a professional brand. Cardon's three-stage writing process drives excellence in critical thinking, collaboration, and productivity in work relationships. With more examples of internal messages, Cardon develops the skills used early in a career.

## Enhanced Coverage of Technology

This book adopts a more visionary and reliable view of the communication technologies of tomorrow. While nearly all textbooks refer to use of social media, they focus on a thin slice of social media activities that involve marketing and customer relations. This book, by contrast, takes a larger view of social media use that includes team communication and communication with external partners. It prepares students for communication in the evolving workplace that involves truly networked communication. Cardon also addresses the need for students to develop an online professional persona that builds personal credibility.

## Business Focus

The business case–based approach allows students to learn how communications can build rich and productive relationships between professionals. Each chapter opens with a short business case and, unlike any other product on the market, weaves examples from the case throughout the chapter and into the model documents, engaging readers in the story behind each business message.

## Forward-Looking Vision Built on Tradition

The book stays true to core business communication principles established over many decades. Yet it also goes beyond traditional coverage by its inclusion of the latest communication practices facilitated by communication technologies and its enhanced coverage of increasingly important business communication topics such as:

Interpersonal communication (Chapters 2, 3, and 4), social media and technology (Chapters 7 and 8), crisis communication and public relations (Bonus Chapter), oral communication (throughout the book), and business plans and business proposals (Bonus Appendix).

## Why Does This Matter?

Each chapter begins with a section that states the compelling reasons the content is crucial to career success. These first few paragraphs are intended to gain buy-in among students. A QR code located at the beginning of these sections allows students to view a short video clip of the author reinforcing this message.

## Chapter Takeaways

The chapter takeaway is provided in a visual format. With graphics and lists, it quickly engages students with key chapter content and serves as a reference for applying the principles to their oral and written communication.

## Learning Exercises

Each chapter contains a multitude of engaging learning exercises. These exercises are organized into discussion exercises, evaluation exercises, application exercises, and language and mechanics check to help students develop expertise in business communication.

## Required=Results

©Getty Images/iStockphoto

## McGraw-Hill Connect®
## Learn Without Limits

Connect is a teaching and learning platform that is proven to deliver better results for students and instructors.

Connect empowers students by continually adapting to deliver precisely what they need, when they need it, and how they need it, so your class time is more engaging and effective.

73% of instructors who use **Connect** require it; instructor satisfaction **increases** by 28% when **Connect** is required.

# Analytics

## Connect Insight®

Connect Insight is Connect's new one-of-a-kind visual analytics dashboard—now available for both instructors and students—that provides at-a-glance information regarding student performance, which is immediately actionable. By presenting assignment, assessment, and topical performance results together with a time metric that is easily visible for aggregate or individual results, Connect Insight gives the user the ability to take a just-in-time approach to teaching and learning, which was never before available. Connect Insight presents data that empowers students and helps instructors improve class performance in a way that is efficient and effective.

# Mobile

Connect's new, intuitive mobile interface gives students and instructors flexible and convenient, anytime–anywhere access to all components of the Connect platform.

### Connect's Impact on Retention Rates, Pass Rates, and Average Exam Scores

| | without Connect | with Connect |
|---|---|---|
| Retention Rates | 70.1% | 89.9% |
| Course Pass Rates | 72.5% | 85.2% |
| Average Exam Scores | 71.0% | 80.1% |

Using **Connect** improves retention rates by **19.8%**, passing rates by **12.7%**, and exam scores by **9.1%**.

### Impact on Final Course Grade Distribution

| | without Connect | | with Connect |
|---|---|---|---|
| A | 22.9% | | 31.0% |
| B | 27.4% | | 34.3% |
| C | 22.9% | | 18.7% |
| D | 11.5% | | 6.1% |
| F | 15.4% | | 9.9% |

Students can view their results for any **Connect** course.

# Adaptive

## THE **ADAPTIVE** READING EXPERIENCE DESIGNED TO TRANSFORM THE WAY STUDENTS READ

> More students earn **A's** and **B's** when they use McGraw-Hill Education **Adaptive** products.

## SmartBook®

Proven to help students improve grades and study more efficiently, SmartBook contains the same content within the print book, but actively tailors that content to the needs of the individual. SmartBook's adaptive technology provides precise, personalized instruction on what the student should do next, guiding the student to master and remember key concepts, targeting gaps in knowledge and offering customized feedback, and driving the student toward comprehension and retention of the subject matter. Available on tablets, SmartBook puts learning at the student's fingertips—anywhere, anytime.

> Over **8 billion questions** have been answered, making McGraw-Hill Education products more intelligent, reliable, and precise.

STUDENTS WANT

Mc Graw Hill Education **SMARTBOOK®**

**95%** of students reported **SmartBook** to be a more effective way of reading material.

**100%** of students want to use the Practice Quiz feature available within **SmartBook** to help them study.

**100%** of students reported having reliable access to off-campus wifi.

**90%** of students say they would purchase **SmartBook** over print alone.

**95%** of students reported that **SmartBook** would impact their study skills in a positive way.

Mc Graw Hill Education *Findings based on 2015 focus group results administered by McGraw-Hill Education

www.mheducation.com

# Grammar and Mechanics

## LearnSmart Achieve

Put responsible writing into practice. LearnSmart Achieve develops and improves editing and business writing skills. This adaptive learning system helps students learn faster, study more efficiently, and retain more knowledge for greater success. Visit bit.ly/meetLSAchieve for a walkthrough.

## Grammar Quizzes

Students may not think grammar and mechanics are the most exciting topics, but they need to master the basics. Our grammar quizzes within Connect assess students' grammar and mechanics. With a total of 150 auto-graded questions, these are great to use as pre- and post-tests in your courses.

# Application

## Presentation Capture

Skill practice inside and outside the classroom. Presentation Capture gives instructors the ability to evaluate presentations and students the freedom to practice their presentation skills anytime and anywhere. With its fully customizable rubrics, instructors can measure students' uploaded presentations against course outcome and give students specific feedback on where improvement is needed.

## Application Exercises

Each chapter contains exercises that allow students to

- Apply concepts to real-world video cases.
- Analyze a case and apply chapter concepts.
- Quiz knowledge on grammar and usage.
- Demonstrate problem-solving skills through complex examples and diagrams.
- Assess student's values, skills, and interests via self-assessments.
- Demonstrate knowledge about business models and processes.

Students receive immediate feedback and can track their progress in their own report. Detailed results let instructors see at a glance how each student performs and easily track the progress of every student in their course.

# Keeping Up with What's New

The third edition of *Business Communication: Developing Leaders for a Networked World* continues to provide results-driven, technology-focused, case-based, and forward-looking content to help business students develop professional credibility for the workplace of tomorrow.

In an increasingly networked world, students will need better interpersonal skills than ever before; they will need better team skills than ever before; they will need better writing skills, especially adapted to new technologies; and they will need stronger presentation skills. This third edition contains the following changes to help students succeed:

## Chapter 1 (Credibility)

- The FAIR model of ethical business communication has been expanded with more clarification in text, a current example in the business world (Apple), and several end-of-chapter exercises.
- The *caring* section now includes content about givers and takers. This is based on Adam Grant's work, which has received significant attention in academic circles and business popular press during the past few years.

## Chapters 2 and 3 (Interpersonal and Team Communication)

- Additional content about a *giver-versus-taker* mentality is included in the emotional intelligence section.
- A section on short-term teams and quick trust is added to help student teams perform better.
- Personality differences (based on the motivational values model) are included in sections about team dynamics and team effectiveness.
- A *getting-to-know-you* exercise is added to help student teams learn about each other and function more effectively in teams.

## Chapter 4 (Intercultural Communication)

- A section on generational differences is added with related end-of-chapter exercises.
- A section on gender differences is added with related end-of-chapter exercises.

## Chapters 5 and 6 (The Writing Process)

- The AIM planning model has been visually updated to make the concepts of audience, information, and message more recognizable throughout the book.
- The examples are updated, and additional end-of-chapter exercises are provided.

## Chapters 7 and 8 (Technology and Communication)

- The sections on instant messaging and phone conversations are updated.
- The sections on social collaboration tools are updated and expanded.
- A new section about using social tools for learning and developing professional expertise is added.
- The section about managing an online professional reputation is expanded with an additional focus on LinkedIn.

**Chapters 9, 10, and 11 (Business Messages: Routine, Persuasive, and Bad-News Messages)**

- Examples of all types of messages are updated.
- Additional exercises are added at the end of each chapter, including a new case for each chapter.

**Chapters 12 and 13 (Business Reports and Proposals)**

- Examples of reports are revised and updated.
- Additional exercises are added at the end of each chapter, including a new case.

**Chapters 14 and 15 (Presentations)**

- Examples are updated in each chapter.
- Additional exercises are added, including a new case.

**Chapter 16 (Employment Communication)**

- A new section about using LinkedIn strategically is provided.
- Examples of résumés are updated.
- Additional exercises are added, including a new case.

# Appreciation

Thank you to all the reviewers and other business communication instructors who gave advice for the third edition. I've made dozens of changes and updates to meet the needs of today's business students based on the recommendations of these reviewers and advisory board members. Each of these instructors is at the forefront of best practices in business communication. Again, I express my appreciation for their advice and time to help improve this learning program. A special thank you to Jennifer Loney and Suzanne Buck for their ongoing support.

## Reviewers and Advisory Board Members Supporting Development of the Third Edition

Nicky Adams, University of Dayton

Angel Alexander, Piedmont Technical College

Kathryn Archard, University of Massachusetts–Boston

Traci L. Austin, Sam Houston State University

Melissa Bakeman-Daly, California State University–San Bernardino

Fiona Barnes, University of Florida

Judith Haywood Bello, Lander University

Linda Blake Walsh, University of Tennessee

Yvonne Block, College of Lake County

Julie E. Boto, Liberty University

Pamela Bourjaily, University of Iowa

Shanti Bruce, Nova Southeastern University

Suzanne Buck, University of Houston

Debra D. Burleson, Baylor University

Dana Burton, The University of Alabama in Huntsville

Kevin Michael Caporicci, University of Southern California

Maria Colman, University of Southern California

Debbie Cook, Utah State University

Jan Robin Costello, Georgia State University

C. Brad Cox, Midlands Technical College

Jeanne Craig, Indiana Wesleyan University

Brittany T. Cuenin, Lander University

Andrea Deacon, University of Wisconsin–Stout

Nicole Dilts, Angelo State University

Lucía Durá, The University of Texas at El Paso

Sandra Ehrlich-Mathiesen, University of Alaska–Anchorage

Donna R. Everett, Morehead State University

Stevina Evuleocha, California State University–East Bay

Jodie Ferise, University of Indianapolis

Melissa Gavin, University of Wisconsin–Platteville

Kenneth Green, University of South Dakota

Susan Hall Webb, University of West Georgia

Jeanette Heidewald, Indiana University–Bloomington

Nancy Hicks, Central Michigan University

Melanie A. Hicks, Liberty University

Dini M. Homsey, University of Central Oklahoma

Christina Iluzada, Baylor University

William T. Jones, State University of New York at Canton

Erin Kilbride-Vincent, Indiana University

Erin Kramer, Owens Community College

Robert Lambdin, University of South Carolina–Columbia

Dr. Janet L. Lear, University of Nebraska at Kearney

Joyce Lopez, Missouri State University

Becky Mahr, Western Illinois University

Molly Mayer, University of Cincinnati

Dr. John Meis, Thomas University

Elizabeth Metzger, University of South Florida

Annie Laurie I. Meyers, Northampton Community College

Karl Mitchell, Queens College–CUNY

Gregory H. Morin, University of Nebraska–Omaha

Farrokh Moshiri, California State University, Fullerton

Bill Moylan, Shidler College of Business, University of Hawaii–Manoa

Chynette Nealy, University of Houston Downtown

Christina Anne Nelson, Indiana University–Purdue University Indianapolis

Cathy Onion, Western Illinois University

Iswari P. Pandey, California State University–Northridge

Audrey Parajon, Wilmington University

Michael Pennell, University of Kentucky

Melinda Phillabaum, Indiana University–Purdue University Indianapolis

Anita Satterlee, Liberty University

Allyson D. Saunders, Weber State University

Steven Sedky, Santa Monica College

Stephen Soucy, Santa Monica College

Kathleen Standen, Fullerton College

Cecil V. Tarrant III, Western Illinois University

Elvira Teller, California State University–Dominguez Hills

Erik Timmerman, University of Wisconsin–Milwaukee

Anne Tippett, Monroe Community College

Elizabeth Tomlinson, West Virginia University

Angelika L. Walker, University of Nebraska at Omaha

Carol Watson, Indiana University–Bloomington

Leigh Ann Whittle, Elon University/Liberty University

Elisabeth C. Wicker, Bossier Parish Community College

Donald J. Wood, Winston-Salem State University

## Event Participants Supporting Development of the Third Edition

Kevin Michael Caporicci, University of Southern California

Marilyn Chalupa, Ball State University

Maria Colman, University of Southern California

Jennifer D'Alessandro, Niagara County Community College

Debra Gosh, Cleveland State University

Mary Groves, University of Nevada, Reno

Jeanette Heidewald, Indiana University–Bloomington

Jo Mackiewicz, Iowa State University

Marla Mahar, Oklahoma State University–Stillwater

Becky Mahr, Western Illinois University

Lisa O'Laughlin, Delta College

Anita Satterlee, Liberty University

Steven Sedky, Santa Monica College

Stephen Soucy, Santa Monica College

Erik Timmerman, University of Wisconsin–Milwaukee

Emil Towner, Saint Cloud State University

Doris Wright, Troy University

## Reviewers and Event Participants Supporting the Development of Previous Editions

I extend my deepest thanks to the many business leaders and professionals, business communication scholars and instructors, and colleagues and friends who have contributed their valuable ideas. I especially appreciate the efforts of reviewers and other colleagues who reviewed iterations of the previous editions of this product. With each round of reviews, reviewers provided excellent and influential feedback to improve and refine the content. Thank you to each of the following experts in the business communication field who have contributed to the development of this learning program!

Angel Alexander, Piedmont Technical College

Melody Alexander, Ball State University

Laura L. Alderson, University of Memphis

Dianne Anderson, Texas Tech University

Delia Anderson-Osteen, Texas Tech University

Kathryn Archard, University of Massachusetts–Boston

Eve Ash, Oklahoma State University–Stillwater

Carolyn Ashe, University of Houston–Downtown

Beverly Augustine, Elgin Community College

Kathie Bahnson, Boise State University

Lisa Bailey, University of South Carolina

Melissa Bakeman, California State University–San Bernardino

Rod Barker, Mount Hood Community College

Mary Barton, California State University–Chico

Jim Beard, University of Arkansas–Fort Smith

Roxanne Bengelink, Kalamazoo Valley Community College

Cynthia Bennett, Albany State University

Magdalena Berry, Missouri State University

Shavawn Berry, Arizona State University

Danielle Blesi, Hudson Valley Community College

Erin Blocher, University of Missouri–Kansas City

Yvonne Block, College of Lake County

Pamela Bourjaily, University of Iowa

Mary Bowers, Northern Arizona University

Sandy Braathen, University of North Dakota

Sheryl Broedel, University of North Dakota

Paula E. Brown, Northern Illinois University

Shanti Bruce, Nova Southeastern University

Suzanne Buck, University of Houston

Michael Buckman, University of Texas at Arlington

Debra Burleson, Baylor University

Amy Burton, Northwest Vista College

Cheryl Byrne, Washtenaw Community College

Kim Campbell, Sydow University of Alabama

Donna Carlon, University of Central Oklahoma

Deborah Casanova, California State University–Dominguez Hills

Marilyn Chalupa, Ball State University

Barbie Chambers, Texas Tech University

Elizabeth Christensen, Sinclair Community College

G. Jay Christensen, California State University–Northridge

Miriam Coleman, Western Michigan University

Anthony M. Corte, University of Illinois at Chicago

David Covington, North Carolina State University

Barbara Cox, Saddleback College

Rosemarie Cramer, Community College of Baltimore

Tena Crews, University of South Carolina

Michelle Dawson, Missouri Southern State University

Andrea Deacon, University of Wisconsin–Stout

Sandra Dean, Jacksonville University

Patrick Delana, Boise State University

Linda Didesidero, University of Maryland–University College

Nicole Dilts, Angelo State University

Jack Doo, California State University

Heidi Eaton, Elgin Community College

Sandra G Ehrlich, University of Alaska–Anchorage

Daniel Emery, University of Oklahoma

Joyce Anne Ezrow, Arundel Community College

Anne Finestone, Santa Monica College

Melissa Fish, American River College

Kathe Kenny Fradkin, Portland State University

Marla Fowler, Albany Technical College

Heidi Fuller, American River College

Jan Gabel-Goes, Western Michigan University

David Gadish, California State University

Anthony Gatling, University of Nevada–Las Vegas

Jorge Gaytan, North Carolina A&T State University

Robert Goldberg, Prince George's Community College

Connie Golden, Lakeland Community College

Terri Gonzales-Kreisman, Delgado Community College

Douglas Gray, Columbus State Community College

Germaine Gray, Texas Southern University

Diana J Green, Weber State University

Mary Groves, University of Nevada–Reno

Kari Guedea, Edmonds Community College

Elizabeth Guerrero, Texas State University

Karen Gulbrandsen, University of Massachusetts–Dartmouth

Lynda Haas, University of California–Irvine

Frances Hale, Columbus State Community College

Susan E. Hall, University of West Georgia

Melissa Hancock, Texas Tech University

Patricia L. Hanna-Garlitz, Bowling Green State University

Jeanette Heidewald, Indiana University–Bloomington

K. Virginia Hemby, Middle Tennessee State University

Ronda G. Henderson, Middle Tennessee State University

Candy Henry, Westmoreland County Community College

Kathy Hill, Sam Houston State University

Dini Homsey, University of Central Oklahoma

Matthew Houseworth, University of Central Missouri

Sally Humphries, Georgia College & State University

Sandie Idziak, The University of Texas at Arlington

Sandra Jackson, California State University–Northridge

Jack Janosik, Cleveland State University

Elaine Jansky, Northwest Vista College

Norma Johansen, Scottsdale Community College

Kenneth E. Jones Jr., Northeastern State University–Broken Arrow

Susan M. Jones, Utah State University

Marguerite P. Joyce, Belhaven University

Brian Keliher, Grossmont College

Kayla Kelly, Tarleton State University

Stephanie Kelly, North Carolina A&T State University

Beth Kilbane, Lorain County Community College

Mary Catherine Kiliany, Robert Morris University

Stephen Kirk, East Carolina University

Jack Kleban, Barry University, Miami Shores, Florida Atlantic University

Lisa Kleiman, Boise State University

David Koehler, DePaul University

Erin Kramer, Owens Community College

Melinda G. Kramer, Prince George's Community College

Gary Lacefield, University of Texas at Arlington

Linda LaMarca, Tarleton State University

Robert Lambdin, University of South Carolina

Elizabeth A. Lariviere, University of Akron

Marianna Larsen, Utah State University

Newton Lassiter, Florida Atlantic University

Cheryl Law, Tarrant County College

Lisa D. Lenoir, Stephens College

Paula Lentz, University of Wisconsin–Eau Claire

Jeffrey S. Lewis, Metropolitan State College of Denver

Jere Littlejohn, University of Mississippi

Jennifer Loney, Portland State University

Susan Long, Portland Community College

Joyce Lopez, Missouri State

Eunice Madison, Purdue University Calumet

Marla Mahar, Oklahoma State University–Stillwater

Anna Maheshwari, Schoolcraft College

Joan Mansfield, University of Central Missouri

Kenneth R. Mayer, Cleveland State University

Molly Mayer, University of Cincinnati

Elaine McCullough, Ferris State University

Sheryl McGough, Iowa State University

David A. McMurrey, Austin Community College

Daniel McRoberts, Northcentral Technical College

Jacqueline Meisel, California State University–Northridge

Marcia Metcalf, Northern Arizona University

Elizabeth Metzger, University of South Florida

Michelle Meyer, Joliet Junior College

Jack Miao, Southern Methodist University

Julianne Michalenko, Robert Morris University

Angelina Misaghi, California State University–Northridge

Shawna Moffitt, University of South Carolina

Kathaleena Edward Monds, Albany State University

Gregory H. Morin, University of Nebraska–Omaha

Rodger Morrison, Troy University

Farrokh Moshiri, University of California, Riverside

Gwen Moultrie, Midlands Technical College

Elwin Myers, Texas A&M University–Corpus Christi

Chynette Nealy, University of Houston–Downtown

Darryl Neher, Indiana University–Bloomington

Ashley Keller Nelson, Tulane University

Grace Noyes, Texas Tech University

Keith Nyquist, Northern Illinois University

Ephraim Okoro, Howard University

Lisa O'Laughlin, Delta College

Lori Oldham, San Diego City College

Jo Ann Oravec, University of Wisconsin–Whitewater

Delia (Joy) O'Steen, Texas Tech University

Mary Padula, Borough of Manhattan Community College

Ranu Paik, Santa Monica College

Anita Pandey, Morgan State University

Audrey Parajon, Wilmington University

Robyn E. Parker, Plymouth State University

Beverly Payne, Missouri Western State University

Michael Pennell, University of Kentucky

Delissa Perez, Northwest Vista College

Debra Ann Petrizzo-Wilkins, Franklin University

Melinda Phillabaum, Indiana University–Purdue University Indianapolis

Evelyn Pitre, University of North Texas

Greg Rapp, Portland Community College

Rob Rector, Delaware Technical and Community College

Phyllis Annette Reed, University of Texas at San Antonio

Teeanna Rizkallah, California State University–Fullerton

Betty Robbins, University of Oklahoma

Sherry J. Roberts, Middle Tennessee State University

Cassie Rockwell, Santa Monica College

Wayne Rollins, Middle Tennessee State University

Kara Romance, Indiana University of Pennsylvania

Juli Rosenbaum, Baylor University

Sia Rose-Robinson, George Mason University

S. E. Rouse, The University of Southern Mississippi

Sharon Rouse, The University of Southern Mississippi

Tim Rowe, State University of New York Fredonia

David Russell, Iowa State University

Joyce Russell, Rockingham Community College

Terry Sanders, Macon State College

Ronit Sarig, California State University–Northridge

Danielle Scane, Orange Coast College

Juliann C. Scholl, Texas Tech University

Nicola S. Scott, George Mason University

Mary Shannon, California State University–Northridge

Mike Shaw, Montana State University–Bozeman

Nelda Shelton, Tarrant County College

Michael Shurman, University of South Florida

Lucia Sigmar, Sam Houston State University

Joyce Monroe Simmons, Florida State University

Jeanetta Sims, University of Central Oklahoma

Jean Smith, Kentucky State University

Patricia Smith, Northcentral Technical College

Rachel V. Smydra, Oakland University

Kipp Snow, Anne Arundel Community College

Kim Snyder, South Texas College

Stephen Soucy, Santa Monica College

Rita Soza, MiraCosta College

Bob Sprague, California State University–Chico

Nicole St. Germaine, Angelo State University

Kathy Standen, Fullerton College

Jo Ann Starkweather, Northeastern State University

Jan Starnes, University of Texas at Austin

Erica Steakley, California State University–Northridge

Susan Stehlik, New York University

Natalie Stillman-Webb, University of Utah

Thomas Stoffer, Ferris State University

Kevin Swafford, Bradley University

Stephen Takach, University of Texas at San Antonio

Cecil Tarrant, Western Illinois University

Sandra Thompson, University of West Georgia

Susan Timm, Elgin Community College

Allen D. Truell, Ball State University

Kathleen L. Voge, University of Alaska–Anchorage

Jie Wang, University of Illinois at Chicago

Melvin Washington, Howard University

Kristin Watson, Metropolitan State University of Denver

McClain Watson, University of Texas at Dallas

Marlea Welton, Santa Monica College

Juli White, Arizona State University

Raholanda White, Middle Tennessee State University

Jo Wiley, Western Michigan University

Karin A. Wilking, Northwest Vista College

Anita Williams, Oklahoma City Community College

Linda S. Williams North Georgia College & State University

Tom Williams, University of Houston, Victoria

Linda Willis, Georgia State University

Kadi Wills, Northwest Vista College

Bennie J. Wilson, University of Texas at San Antonio

Doris N. Wright, Troy University

Robert Yale, University of Dallas

Caroline Yarbrough, Delgado Community College

Diane Youngblood, Greenville Technical College

Lydia Yznaga, Northwest Vista College

Ann Zeman, Bellarmine University

Jensen Zhao, Ball State University

I also recognize the entire editorial and marketing teams at McGraw-Hill that have made this book possible: Kelly Pekelder, Anke Weekes, Michael Gedatus, Christine Vaughan, Egzon Shaqiri, Joni Thompson, John Weimeister, and all of the talented McGraw-Hill publisher's representatives. It has been such a pleasure to work with these incredibly talented and skilled professionals who have shaped the content and design of this textbook and consulted with instructors around the globe. When I signed with McGraw-Hill, I was proud to be aligned with such a well-respected publisher. After working for nearly a decade with these talented and quality-driven professionals, my respect has grown. I can see the focus they place on producing learning materials that have real impact on the lives of students.

I want to thank my family. My wife, Natalie, is a beautiful and inspired person. She and I are on a wonderful journey together, and she has embraced this book as part of our journey. My daughters energize me in so many ways. Camilla inspires me by her eye for beauty, her sense of wonderment, and her joy in building things. Audrey inspires me by her spontaneous expressions of happiness, her sense of fun, and her love of people. I'm also blessed to have the best parents. They understand and support me. I love them and hope to be like them.

Finally, I'd like to thank several people who have been instrumental in influencing my career direction and success. First, I recognize the influence of my dissertation advisor, James Calvert Scott. He contributed decades of research and teaching to the business communication field and selflessly devoted thousands of hours to my development. Without his influence, I would not have become part of the business communication community. Second, I want to thank Pat Moody, former dean of the College of Hospitality, Retail, and Sport Management at the University of South Carolina; Lucy Lee, former director of the Center for Management Communication at the University of Southern California; and Marion Philadelphia, current director of the Department of Business Communication at the University of Southern California. These three women are the most inspiring and caring leaders I've worked for. They have had a lasting influence on my work.

**Peter W. Cardon**
**Academic Director, MBA.PM Program**
**Professor, Department of Business Communication**
**Marshall School of Business**
**University of Southern California**
**Twitter: @petercardon**
**Pinterest: pinterest.com/cardonbcom**
**LinkedIn: www.linkedin.com/in/petercardon**

# Contents

## 8  Social Media for Business Communication  230

## Part 5    Reports and Presentations

**12  Research and Business Proposals and Planning for Business Reports 368**

**13  Completing Business Proposals and Business Reports 404**

**Bonus Content**

Available only at www.mcgrawhillcreate.com/cardon or in the e-book within McGraw-Hill Connect®.

**Bonus Chapter**  Crisis Communications and Public Relations Messages  BC-1

**Bonus Appendix**  Creating Proposals and Business Plans  BA-1

# Introduction to Business Communication

**Chapter 1** —— Establishing Credibility

PART ONE

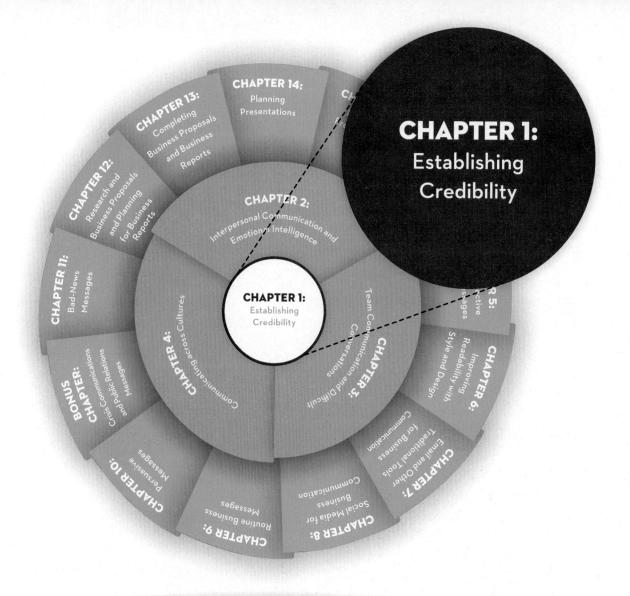

CHAPTER 14:
Planning
Presentations

CHAPTER 13:
Completing
Business Proposals
and Business
Reports

CHAPTER 12:
Research and
Business Proposals
and Planning
for Business
Reports

CHAPTER 11:
Bad-News
Messages

BONUS
CHAPTER:
Crisis Communications
and Public Relations
Messages

CHAPTER 10:
Persuasive
Messages

CHAPTER 9:
Routine Business
Messages

CHAPTER 8:
Social Media for
Business
Communication

CHAPTER 7:
Email and Other
Traditional Tools
for Business
Communication

CHAPTER 6:
Improving
Readability with
Style and Design

CHAPTER 5:
Creating Effective
Business Messages

CHAPTER 3:
Team Communication and
Conversations for Business

CHAPTER 2:
Interpersonal Communication and
Emotional Intelligence

CHAPTER 4:
Communicating across Cultures

CHAPTER 1:
Establishing
Credibility

**CHAPTER 1:**
Establishing
Credibility

 **ESTABLISHING CREDIBILITY**

 **PRINCIPLES OF INTERPERSONAL COMMUNICATION**

 **PRINCIPLES FOR & TYPES OF BUSINESS MESSAGES**

## Learning Objectives

After studying this chapter, you should be able to do the following:

**LO1.1** Explain the importance of establishing credibility for business communications.

**LO1.2** Describe how competence, caring, and character affect your credibility as a communicator.

**LO1.3** Define and explain business ethics, corporate values, and personal values.

**LO1.4** Explain the FAIR approach to ethical business communications.

In most business situations, others make judgments about what you say, write, and do based on your credibility. **Credibility** is your reputation for being trustworthy—trustworthy to perform your work with excellence; to care about those you work with and for; to live by high ethical, corporate, and personal values; and to deliver on your promises. In short, your credibility is the degree to which others believe or trust in you. In this book, we often use the terms *trust* and *credibility* interchangeably.

Business communications occur in the context of working relationships, all of which depend on trust.[1] Credibility has always been important to business relationships, yet its importance has grown in recent years with an increasingly interdependent, knowledge-based workplace.[2] As one of the foremost thinkers on trust in the workplace, Stephen M. R. Covey made this observation:

> *Contrary to what most people believe, trust is not some soft, illusive quality that you either have or you don't; rather, trust is a pragmatic, tangible, actionable asset that you can create—much faster than you probably think possible. . . . It is the key leadership competency of the new global economy.*[3]

The importance of credibility as a basis for effective communication is universal. As Victor K. Fung, chairman of the Li and Fung Group centered in Hong Kong, China, stated, "A good leader is probably no different in any culture in the sense that a good leader must have credibility. That is something one establishes . . . based on the way one handles [oneself] . . . and by [an] established track record."[4] Fung's comments illustrate an important point that we will explore in detail: Credibility emerges from several sources, including abilities and achievements as well as interpersonal skills and traits.

In this chapter, we discuss the ways that business executives and the business community establish trust. Then, we focus on three components of credibility: competence, caring, and character.[5] First, however, you will read a short scenario about choosing a mentor. Each potential mentor has credibility but for different reasons.

**Hear Pete Cardon explain why this matters.**

**Can't scan? Try ScanLife at your app store or visit bit.ly/cardon1**

**LO1.1** Explain the importance of establishing credibility for business communications.

---

## CHAPTER CASE: WHOM DO YOU TRUST AS YOUR MENTOR?

 Luis

 Sally

 Tom

**WHO'S INVOLVED**

Assume you were hired about a month ago. Your company has a practice of assigning a mentor to new employees during their first six months. You've been told that mentors can have a major impact on your opportunities: your team assignments, your projects, and your overall career development. You've gotten to know

**THE SITUATION**

some of your new colleagues, and your boss has asked you which one you would like to be your mentor. Read through your impressions of your colleagues below, and consider who would make the best mentor for you.

**LUIS**

Luis has worked at your company for one year. Everyone enjoys working with him. He is always cheerful and happy to see those around him. He consistently finds out what his colleagues need and goes out of his way to help out. Everyone thinks Luis is fun. He likes to go out for a drink after work and gets everyone laughing. Luis is well known for being well connected within your company. One thing that every colleague says about him is that he's honest. He continues to make some rookie mistakes, however, and he has done sloppy work several times when he was up against tight deadlines.

**SALLY**

Sally has worked at your company for three years. She has a reputation of being a star performer. In fact, she's generally assigned the most important projects for that reason. Colleagues know that when she promises something, she makes it happen. A lot of colleagues think she's excessively critical of others when they fall short of her expectations. A colleague complained to one of the managers, "Sally never gives me a chance to develop my skills. She just takes over the project."

**TOM**

Tom has worked at your company for four years. He consistently receives excellent ratings on his quarterly performance reviews. He is intensely loyal to his team members, and he does everything he can to make sure they succeed. Recently, one of his team members lost a client because she missed several deadlines. When Tom's boss asked why they lost the client, Tom protected his teammate by saying that the client preferred the services of a competitor.

**TASK**

Luis, Sally, and Tom are like most people—they have some strengths and some weaknesses. As you read this chapter, you will find that each of them lacks complete credibility but for different reasons. Now, choose your mentor. Whom do you trust to help you succeed in your new position?

## The Role of Trust in the Post-Trust Era

Do you operate from a position of trust or credibility? That is one of the first things you should consider as you communicate. In the business world, you often start from a deficit of trust. As a result, one of your first goals should be to gain trust or credibility from colleagues, clients, customers, and other contacts.[6]

Given the major business scandals over the past decade (i.e., Enron, Adelphia Communications, WorldCom), trust in businesses and business executives has dropped to all-time lows. As depicted in Figure 1.1, the trust extended by the general public to business executives is far lower than the trust extended to members of other selected professions.[7]

The public also increasingly views companies with less trust. Approximately 85 percent of senior executives surveyed believe that public trust in business has gone down. Approximately 62 percent of survey respondents across 20 countries said their trust in corporations had gone down following the economic crises of 2008 and 2009.[8]

A deficit of trust also exists within companies. Various surveys show that employees often do not trust their own business leaders. Just 51 percent of employees trust senior management, and only 36 percent of employees believe their company leaders act with honesty and integrity. Furthermore, approximately 76 percent of employees have seen illegal or unethical conduct in the past 12 months at their jobs.[9] As future

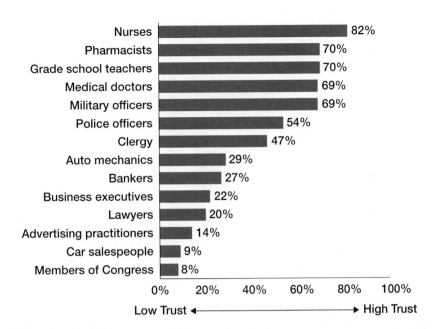

**FIGURE 1.1**

How Will You Overcome Public Perceptions to Build Credibility?

A Look at Trust in Various Professions

*Note:* Based on the percentage of American adults who considered members of these occupations "very high" or "high" in honesty and ethical standards in a November 2013 Gallup poll. Available at www.gallup.com/poll/166298/honesty-ethics-rating-clergy-slides-new-low.aspx.

business managers and leaders, you will often find yourself in charge of employees who are accustomed to not trusting those in leadership positions.

A strong predictor of cheating in the workplace is cheating in school. Sadly, recent research has found that cheating is so pervasive that some use the label a *global cheating culture.* Among high school students, 80 percent of high-performing students admit to having cheated, and 50 percent do not believe cheating is wrong. Other research about high school students found that more than 70 percent had engaged in serious cheating, and 50 percent had plagiarized assignments from the Internet. In a study of more than 50,000 undergraduate students in the United States, more than 70 percent admitted to serious cheating. Nearly 80 percent stated that Internet plagiarism was not a serious offense.[10]

Perhaps most concerning is that business students are among the worst offenders. When asked in anonymous surveys if they had cheated to get into graduate school, many students admitted to having done so: 43 percent of liberal arts students, 52 percent of education students, 63 percent of medical students, 63 percent of law students, and 75 percent of business students. Think about that! Three-quarters of graduate-level business students admitted to some form of cheating to get into their programs. In another study involving hypothetical ethical dilemmas, convicts in minimum-security prisons scored as high on unethical behavior as MBA students.[11] In yet another study of 6,226 undergraduate business students in 36 countries, American business students viewed cheating no differently than did students from countries considered high in corruption.[12]

Michael Maslansky, a leading corporate communications expert, has labeled this the post-trust era. In the **post-trust era**, the public overwhelmingly views businesses as operating against the public's best interests, and the majority of employees view their leaders and colleagues skeptically. Regarding the post-trust era, Maslansky said, "Just a few years ago, salespeople, corporate leaders, marketing departments, and communicators like me had it pretty easy. We looked at communication as a relatively linear process. . . . But trust disappeared, things changed."[13]

Most of these perceptions about business leaders as untrustworthy are not necessarily fair. Daniel Janssen, former chairman of the board of directors of Solvay (a Belgian chemicals company operating in more than 50 countries), explained the dilemma:

> Executives of large companies today are generally perceived as efficient and competent, but also self-interested and ungenerous. However, I think that people who form this opinion are underestimating something of which they lack knowledge. Many executives, in top management and also at other levels, are incredibly generous and not at all self-interested. They do their job and they do it with respect for the common interest. But it is true that capitalism is too often marked by its dark and greedy side.[14]

**FIGURE 1.2**

The Three Components of Credibility

You will often find yourself needing to establish credibility in this post-trust era. As a future manager and executive, you can control your reputation as a credible communicator by focusing on three well-established factors: competence, caring, and character. Research has shown that these three factors almost entirely account for whether a person is considered credible in professional situations. As depicted in Figure 1.2, credibility is like a three-legged stool. Without any one element, it is compromised.

## The Role of Competence in Establishing Credibility

**LO1.2** Describe how competence, caring, and character affect your credibility as a communicator.

**connect**

Visit http://connect. mheducation.com for an exercise on this topic.

**Competence** refers to the knowledge and skills needed to accomplish business tasks, approach business problems, and get a job done. Most people will judge your competence based on your track record of success and achievement.

In her memoir, Meg Whitman, current CEO of HP, explains how as a young professional she gained credibility and displayed competence within her organization: "I just focused on delivering results," she said. "You have to excel at the tasks you're given and you have to add value to every single project, every conversation where someone seeks your input."[15]

People develop competence in many ways: through study, observation, and, most important, practice and real-world business experiences. Your entire business program is likely centered on developing competence in a certain business discipline and/or industry. You may already have significant business experience. If you're a novice, seeking internships and jobs related to your discipline will help you develop competence.

How you communicate directly affects the perceptions others have of your competence. Throughout this book, you will find an emphasis on two traits associated with competence: a focus on action and an emphasis on results.

A *focus on action* implies that you seize business opportunities. Meg Whitman emphasized this action-oriented approach to work: "The way I usually put it is, the price of inaction is far greater than the cost of making a mistake. You do not have to be perfect to be an effective leader, but you cannot be timid."[16] She also described an *emphasis on results:*

> I don't believe that all a company needs to do is declare that it has values and then say, "Trust us, we know what's best." To be a success, you must identify a goal with a measurable outcome, and you must hit that goal—every day, every month, every year. Trying is important. But trying is not the same as achieving success. . . . [Some] people expect to advance in their careers regardless of results and are surprised when it doesn't happen. They feel entitled. Their attitude is: "Because I'm here, because I'm me, you owe me."[17]

In the opening scenario in which you chose a mentor, Luis is weakest in competence. While he is strong at caring for others and displaying good character, many people will question his ability to accomplish tasks well. He has less experience than his colleagues and sometimes performs sloppy work. Yet, many people would choose him as their mentor because they trust his ability to find out about their career needs and trust he knows how to connect them to others in the company.

In summary, you demonstrate competence by taking an active role in your business and by getting results. How you communicate your plan of action and the results of those actions will determine how others perceive your competence and your credibility.

## The Role of Caring in Establishing Credibility

Your colleagues, clients, and even your customers will trust you far more if they know you care about them. As Mahatma Gandhi once stated, "The moment there is suspicion about a person's motives, everything he does becomes tainted." This statement applies in nearly all business circumstances: People distrust individuals who are perceived as unconcerned about the interests of others or disinterested in causes above and beyond themselves. In the business world, **caring** implies understanding the interests of others, cultivating a sense of community, and giving to others and showing generosity. In the past, caring was seldom discussed as integral to business. Now, it is among the most important abilities for business leaders and managers. In fact, a recent study of business managers found that caring is considered among the top 3 skills or abilities (from a list of 18 skills or abilities) for managers of nearly any business discipline.[18]

### Understanding the Interests of Others

Meg Whitman, when she was CEO of eBay, observed how important recognizing the needs of others is. She explained:

> Connecting with people's hopes and dreams is a dynamic I perceived in the eBay community. Both buyers and sellers so often loved eBay because it connected them to their aspirations—perhaps the desire of amassing a great collection, or the dream of financial stability from successfully building an online business.[19]

Your ability to gain credibility strongly depends on your ability to show that you care for the needs of others. Furthermore, your ability to show you care puts you in a rare position as a business leader. After all, less than half (42 percent) of employees believe their managers care about them. Even worse, less than one-third (29 percent) of employees believe their managers care about whether they develop skills.[20]

Effective communicators gain trust by connecting with others—that is, seeking to understand others' needs, wants, opinions, feelings, and aspirations. Virtually every aspect of communication you will focus on in this book relies on this other-orientation.

### Cultivating a Sense of Community

The most effective business leaders in today's corporate environment have generally risen to their positions because of their sense of community and teamwork. Meredith Ashby and Stephen Miles recently interviewed hundreds of prominent and accomplished business leaders to answer questions such as *What are the burning issues for corporate leaders today?* and *How do companies identify, attract, develop, and retain the best and brightest people in the workplace?* Here is what they learned from these CEOs:

> Most defined their main responsibility as chief executive to be that of inspiring, influencing, setting the direction for, facilitating, coaching, mentoring, and developing their employees. The word "control" was rarely used; instead, they spoke emphatically

about the importance of a strong team orientation. Their role was to identify and empower a team, not command it. Indeed, many of them characteristically used the term "we" rather than "I" in discussing success within the organization. Instead of thinking in terms of individual accomplishment, most tended to think in terms of what their management teams had achieved.[21]

Throughout this textbook, you will see techniques for communicating your "we" and "you" orientation rather than a "me" orientation. Speaking about "our needs" or "your needs" as opposed to "my needs" engenders trust and helps you come up with solutions that achieve mutual benefit.

### Giving to Others and Showing Generosity

Recent research has shown that most professionals can broadly be characterized as *givers* and *takers*. Givers are those professionals who go out of their way to help colleagues, respond to their requests and needs, and generously support others in the workplace. Takers are those professionals who frequently ask for favors from colleagues yet infrequently volunteer to help their peers in return.

Dozens of studies in recent years show that organizations with more generous and giving employees perform better. Companies with higher percentages of givers achieve higher profitability, higher productivity, and higher customer satisfaction. In addition, these companies experience lower employee turnover rates. These studies also show that givers are more likely than takers to be rated as top performers. (However, givers are also more likely than takers to be rated the lowest performing employees. In Chapter 2, you'll learn more about strategies to be a giver *and* maintain top performance.)[22] Particularly early in your career, you'll find that gaining a reputation for helping your colleagues will open up many professional opportunities and enhance your professional credibility.

In the opening scenario, Sally is weakest in caring. While she is strong at getting the job done and communicating honestly, she often does not seem to act in the best interests of others. She may even be indifferent to the growth of her colleagues. Yet, many people would choose her as a mentor because they could learn from the best and likely participate on the most important projects.

## The Role of Character in Establishing Credibility

**Character** refers to a reputation for staying true to commitments made to stakeholders and adhering to high moral and ethical values. Character has always been important in business relationships, especially long-term, collaborative relationships. It is becoming even more important—especially for leaders—in an increasingly open, transparent, connected, and interdependent workplace. David Pottruck, chairman of HighTower Advisors, explained it this way:

> The twenty-first-century leader is surely different from the leaders of the last two decades. The Internet has placed real power in the hands of people around the world. It has increased the possibilities for millions to do the work that enlivens them. There will be little loyalty to people or to organizations that are not worthy. No longer do pension plans and benefits create chains that hold people in one spot. To create loyalty in such an environment, the new leader will understand how to create a compelling culture, one that will allow people to contribute their best. He or she will then communicate meaning and trustworthiness in every word and action. Culture, character, and communication are the cornerstones of today's new leadership.[23]

Character is central in creating trust. Consider the recent research, depicted in Figure 1.3.[24] Business executives were asked what the most important determinants of trust in workplace projects were. Overwhelmingly, character-based traits—that is, honesty, ethical behavior, and willingness to exchange information—ranked at the top.

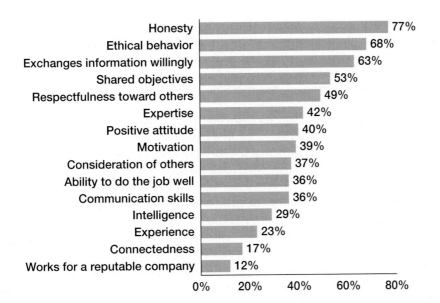

**FIGURE 1.3**

What Determines Trust in Individuals in the Workplace?

For Collaboration on Work-place Projects

*Source:* The Economist Intelligence Unit.

In the following sections, we focus on sevearl topics closely related to character: business ethics, corporate and personal values, open and honest communication, a stakeholder view of accountability, and fairness in business communication.

## Business Ethics

**Ethics** are "rules of conduct or moral principles that guide individual or group behavior."[25] **Business ethics** are the commonly accepted beliefs and principles in the business community for acceptable behavior. At a minimum, business ethics involve adhering to laws; safeguarding confidential or proprietary information; avoiding conflicts of interest and misuse of company assets; and refraining from accepting or providing inappropriate gifts, gratuities, and entertainment.[26]

As far as corporate communications, the dominant business ethic in recent years is transparency. **Transparency** involves sharing all relevant information with stakeholders. As defined by Transparency International, transparency "is a principle that allows those affected by administrative decisions, business transactions or charitable work to know not only the basic facts and figures but also the mechanisms and processes. It is the duty of civil servants, managers and trustees to act visibly, predictably and understandably."[27]

In recent years, perhaps in large part due to public scandals, employees of companies in the United States have observed higher ethical behavior within their companies and generally view their upper managers as ethical. For example, in a recent Ethics Resource Center survey of 3,010 employees across the United States, 80 percent of employees said they were satisfied with the information they received from top management about what was going on in the company, 74 percent trusted that top management would keep its promises and commitments, and 89 percent stated that top management actively encouraged employees to do the right thing. Furthermore, 82 percent of employees believed that top managers would be punished and held accountable if they were caught violating the organization's ethical standards.[28] For the foreseeable future, transparency is expected to remain the dominant business ethic related to communications.

You will soon be in leadership positions within your organization. You can create a transparent workplace by being accessible, acknowledging the concerns of others, and following through when you don't have immediate answers. Trust-building behaviors include extending trust, sharing information, telling it straight, providing opportunities, admitting mistakes, and setting a good example by following rules.[29]

**LO1.3** Define and explain business ethics, corporate values, and personal values.

**connect**

Visit http://connect. mheducation.com for an exercise on this topic.

You likely will need to analyze ethical dilemmas in your business program, while training for your job, and once you are on the job. You probably recognize that "making the right choice" is not always obvious. In such situations, where the law and ethical principles do not provide a clear answer, transparency is key: Decision making needs to be open, documented, and based on the collective conscience of your work team and affected stakeholders.

Often, employees fail to speak up when they observe potentially unethical behavior. Business professionals remain silent for four basic reasons: (1) They assume it's standard practice, (2) they rationalize that it's not a big deal, (3) they say to themselves it's not their responsibility, or (4) they want to be loyal.

Prepare now to speak up constructively when you observe unethical behavior. It's part of your job. You can challenge rationalizations with questions such as these:

> *If this is standard, why is there a policy against it?*
> *If it is expected, are we comfortable being public about it?*
> *I may be new here, so I might not understand our policy clearly. But, shouldn't we . . . ?*[30]

When you frame your concerns in terms of benefits to your team or organization, your colleagues and other contacts will often respond appropriately. Over the long run, you will be rewarded for having a reputation of speaking up when ethical dilemmas arise.[31]

## Corporate and Personal Values

**Corporate values** are the stated and lived values of a company. The Society for Human Resource Management espouses corporate values as the essence of business ethics. It defines business ethics as "organizational values, guidelines, and codes," and it emphasizes "behaving within those boundaries when faced with dilemmas in business or professional work."[32]

Most organizations have created a written **code of conduct** or code of ethics. Publicly traded companies are required by the Sarbanes-Oxley Act of 2002 to have a code of ethics available to all employees and to ensure that it is enacted. eBay's culture of trust is embodied in its *Code of Business Conduct & Ethics*. It encourages employees that "beyond complying with the law. . . [they] can *Do the Right Thing*." It encourages them to "be open, honest and direct and conduct business with integrity" and "encourage open communication free from the threat of retaliation." The 78-page document helps employees know how to live up to eBay's corporate values.[33] (See eBay's *Code of Business Conduct & Ethics* at https://www.ebayinc.com/assets/Uploads/eBay-CodeofEthics-external-080615.pdf.)

Aligning **personal values**—those values that individuals prioritize and adhere to—with corporate values is an important element of character. After all, if one is living corporate values that do not match one's personal values, then there is a lack of integrity. Paul Polman, CEO of Unilever, was recently interviewed about the importance of corporate values:

> One thing I've learned over the course of my career is that if your values—your personal values—are aligned with the company's values, you're probably going to be more successful in the long term than if they are not. Because if they aren't, it requires you to be an actor when you go to work or to have a split personality.[34]

## Open and Honest Communication

In Tamar Frankel's excellent book on the role of honesty in American business culture, she chronicles the increasing abuses of honesty, including health care fraud, insurance fraud, check fraud, consumer fraud, identity theft, and student cheating, to name a few. She concludes her work with an appeal for more honesty:

> The goal of honesty is not to reduce competitive ardor but to channel it in less destructive ways. Honesty encourages competition on the merits and prohibits competition by cheating. Honesty brings better quality of products and services and less shoddy products and fake services. If businesses do not compete on fraud, they can be more successful in gaining and retaining customers.[35]

Frankel's point about honesty at an institutional level also applies on a personal level. By staying honest in all situations and avoiding cutting corners in any manner, you allow yourself to perform based solely on merit. Over the long run, complete honesty not only forges your character, it helps you develop and maximize your competencies.

Nothing short of complete honesty is demanded in business for several reasons. First, the price of dishonesty on financial performance can be devastating. Over her corporate career, Meg Whitman became adept at identifying when executives were avoiding reality: "At some companies, board meetings are mainly a mind-numbing series of *happy PowerPoints*. From the agenda and the demeanor of the CEO, you would think that all is sweetness, light, and ice cream."[36] Her comment points to three important issues. First, by avoiding open and honest communication of business problems, employees doom a business to poor financial performance. Second, dishonesty is among the primary reasons for lower employee morale. Nearly six in ten employees say that they've left an organization because of lack of trust—the key reasons being lack of communication and dishonesty.[37] Finally, dishonesty can be reason for dismissal. In some cases, dishonesty can destroy careers and even result in criminal charges.

Some business executives and managers view slight deviations from the truth in small matters as inconsequential. Often, they feel, these small lies are expressed with no ill will and without much impact on important business matters. Yet, experienced executives and management consultants have observed how damaging even minor dishonesty can be. Drs. Dennis S. Reina and Michelle L. Reina focus on this point in their book *Trust and Betrayal in the Workplace:*

> There was a time, many years ago, when we too assumed that what broke the delicate fiber of trust in relationships were large acts that had significant impact. However, our research and work over the last fifteen years have taught us differently. What gradually erodes trust and creates a climate of betrayal in our workplaces today are small, subtle acts that accumulate over time. When we don't do what we say we will do, when we gossip about others behind their backs, when we renege on decisions we agreed to, when we hide our agenda and work it behind the scenes, and when we spin the truth rather than tell it, we break trust and damage relationships.[38]

Today, most organizational cultures are moving to flatter, more open communication structures. However, you will also find yourself in many situations where confidentiality is mandated. Companies often direct employees to maintain confidentiality about information that can harm profitability, productivity, and employees within the organization if it is disclosed. In some cases, confidentiality is required by legal considerations, such as laws regarding medical records, disclosure of insider information, or copyrights. In other cases, you may need to protect intellectual property. When Apple rolled out the iPhone, employees underwent a code of silence for months when they could not even talk about their work to family members. In fact, until the release of the iPhone, many Apple employees could not even speak about certain iPhone features to Apple employees in other divisions.[39]

## A Stakeholder View of Accountability

A sense of accountability implies an *obligation* to meet the needs and wants of others. It also involves an *enlarged vision* of those affected by your business activities. It takes a **stakeholder** view that includes all groups in society affected by your business.

In a commencement speech to business students at UCLA, Robert Eckert, then CEO of Mattel, spoke about trust and, in particular, the sense of accountability that is needed among business executives and managers. He concluded his speech this way:

> You are the future leaders of business. And when it comes to trust, your leadership style affects those you are leading. . . . As you go to work, your top responsibility should be to build trust. To perform every day at the highest standards. Not just for yourself, but for

your team, for your supervisor, for the consumer, for the company's shareholders, for the rest of us in business. . . . It's day one of the next chapter of your life, and I'm putting my trust in each of you.[40]

Thus, a sense of accountability involves a feeling of responsibility to stakeholders and a duty to other employees and customers. By placing a rationale for accountability in your communications, you will generate substantial trust and goodwill from others.

**LO1.4** Explain the FAIR approach to ethical business communications.

**connect**

Visit http://connect. mheducation.com for an exercise on this topic.

## Fairness in Business Communications

Generally, others' perceptions of your character—your unquestioned adherence to personal and corporate values—are largely determined by your communications. Moreover, your colleagues, clients, and customers will gauge your communications based on a judgment of how fair they are.

Thus, in all your communications, you should consider whether you are being fair to others. For routine communications, you make this calculation quickly. For important, less straightforward, and perhaps even controversial communications, you should spend a significant amount of time evaluating the best way to be fair. You might consider talking to your supervisor, peers, and other trusted individuals to appraise the situation. Meg Whitman explained this principle based on her experience at eBay:

> Ultimately the character of a company, like the character of a person, is an accumulation of many, many moments when the choices are not necessarily clear and we make the best decisions we can. But over time the logic and reasoning that we use to make those decisions, the moral compass to follow in making those decisions, is the essence of our authentic self, our character.[41]

One way to evaluate your communications is to use the *FAIR test* (see Figure 1.4). The FAIR test helps you examine how well you have provided the *facts*; how well you have granted *access* to your motives, reasoning, and information; how well you have examined *impacts* on stakeholders; and how well you have shown *respect*. As you respond to questions such as those posed in Figure 1.4, you ensure that your communications are fair to yourself and others.

Applying the FAIR test is especially important for high-stakes messages. Consider how Tim Cook, CEO of Apple, responded to a February 2016 court order to force Apple to bypass the security functions of the iPhone of one of the San Bernardino terrorists. Explaining that Apple should focus on the privacy and security of its customers, he resisted the court order and wrote a letter to Apple customers and spoke repeatedly to the media to defend Apple's position.[42]

This was clearly a polarizing and divisive situation, with roughly 51 percent of Americans thinking Apple should follow the court order and unlock the iPhone while about 38 percent thought Apple should resist the order to unlock the iPhone.[43] Most tech companies and advocacy groups, such as the American Civil Liberties Union (ACLU) and the Reform Government Alliance, lined up behind Apple. Yet, government agencies and law enforcement groups tended to oppose Apple's position. The top two members of the Senate Intelligence Committee, one a Republican and the other a Democrat, sided with the FBI.[44]

Accurately portraying the *facts* in such a complex situation is challenging. Tim Cook, in an open letter to customers and in media interviews, explained Apple's position that it should protect customers' privacy and security and provided what he viewed as the technical and legal facts of the case. Cook suggested that to comply with the court order, Apple would have to create a backdoor that could be used to violate the privacy and security of any iPhone user. He explained that Apple's position of protecting customers was the moral high ground. Some questioned whether Apple was accurately portraying the government's request. For example, Bill Gates and other experts suggested that the government's request was for a particular case (helping unlock a single phone) rather than creating a solution that would make all other phones

**FIGURE 1.4**

The FAIR Test of
Ethical Business
Communication

*Are Your Communications FAIR?*

**Facts** (How *factual* is your communication?)

- Have you presented the facts correctly?
- Have you presented all the relevant facts?
- Have you presented any information that would be considered misleading?
- Have you used the facts in a reasonable manner to arrive at your conclusions and recommendations? Would your audience agree with your reasoning?

**Access** (How *accessible or transparent* are your motives, reasoning, and information?)

- Are your motives clear, or will others perceive that you have a hidden agenda?
- Have you fully disclosed how you obtained the information and used it to make your case?
- Are you hiding any of the information or real reasons for making certain claims or recommendations?
- Have you given stakeholders the opportunity to provide input in the decision-making process?

**Impacts** (How does your communication *impact* stakeholders?)

- Have you considered how your communication impacts all stakeholders?
- Have you thought about how your communication will help or even hurt others?
- How could you learn more about these impacts?

**Respect** (How *respectful* is your communication?)

- Have you prepared your communication to recognize the inherent dignity and self-worth of others?
- Would those with whom you are communicating consider your communication respectful?
- Would a neutral observer consider your communication respectful?

vulnerable or less secure. In other words, some experts thought Tim Cook was exaggerating the nature of the FBI's request.[45]

Providing *access* to your real motivations and explaining how you made your decisions can also prove challenging in complicated and emotionally charged situations. Cook explained to customers and the media that Apple's motivation was to protect its customers' privacy and security. Most people viewed Cook as a sincere champion of digital privacy. Yet, some questioned Apple's stated motivations. For example, a *Los Angeles Times* journalist noted that Apple's defiant approach in the United States differed markedly from its approach in China, where it complied with a variety of government requests that made iPhone users' data less secure. The journalist noted that Apple's primary motivation could be profitability. In North America and Europe, where Apple had relatively flat sales, defying the government was less risky politically and financially. On the other hand, Apple's top market for iPhones was China and sales in China were booming. Taking a strong position in China would be much riskier to Apple. Some observers noted that Apple was unwilling to so defiantly stand on principle in the Chinese market.[46]

Evaluating *impacts* requires a stakeholder view. Tim Cook argued that resisting the court order served the privacy and security interests of its customers and the public at large. Yet, some people felt Tim Cook was not taking national security concerns seriously enough and wasn't paying enough attention to the needs of victims. A group of victims of the crime joined a collective lawsuit to force Apple to help unlock the iPhone of one of the terrorists.[47] The FBI Director specifically stated that the FBI's primary goal was to get justice for the victims of this crime and was not seeking to create a precedent to force tech companies to reduce privacy.[48]

With such a divisive issue, showing *respect* to those with different views is particularly important. In Tim Cook's open letter to customers, he attempted to show respect for the FBI and those with similar views to the FBI. He used phrases such as "We have great respect for the professionals at the FBI, and we believe their intentions are good" and "While we believe the FBI's intentions are good, it would be wrong for the government to force us to build a backdoor into our products." Yet, some observers thought the tone of some comments unnecessarily attacked the motives and integrity of FBI professionals, such as the following statement: "The FBI may use different words to describe this tool, but make no mistake: Building a version of iOS that bypasses security in this way would undeniably create a backdoor. And while the government may argue that its use would be limited to this case, there is no way to guarantee such control."[49]

Applying the FAIR test to Tim Cook's letter and media interviews shows the complicated process of developing messages that accurately provide *facts*, grant *access* to motivations and information, consider the *impacts* on all stakeholders involved, and show *respect* for all parties involved. In Exercises 1.15 and 1.16 at the end of the chapter, you can see additional resources to evaluate Tim Cook's communications in this situation.

Returning to the opening chapter scenario, Tom is weakest in character. While he performs at a high level and displays commitment and interest in those around him, he is not always honest. Many professionals will find it hard to consider him credible for this reason. Yet, some people would choose him as a mentor because they believe he will act in their interests and he can help secure important projects.

## High-Trust Relationships, Ease of Communication, and Improved Work Outcomes

*Establishing credibility allows you to communicate more easily and more influentially.* Extensive research has shown that high-trust relationships lead to more efficient and superior work outcomes.[50] In terms of ease of communication, credibility leads to less resistance from others, increased willingness to cooperate, and less likelihood of miscommunication:

> In low-trust work environments, people tend to assume the negative regarding others' actions. In higher-trust work environments, people tend to give others the benefit of the doubt and assume the positive, until proven otherwise.[51]

In high-trust relationships, since individuals willingly and freely give the benefit of the doubt, communication is simpler, easier, quicker, and more effective.[52] As Dr. Stephen R. Covey, among the most respected management writers of the past three decades, stated regarding trust:

> It simply makes no difference how good the rhetoric is or even how good the intentions are; if there is little or no trust, there is no foundation for permanent success. . . . What we are communicates far more eloquently than anything we say or do. We all know it. There are people we trust absolutely because we know their character. Whether they're eloquent or not, whether they have the human relations techniques or not, we trust them, and we work successfully with them.[53]

When business leaders and managers are considered credible, the positive effects on company performance are dramatic. One recent study of 32,000 employees examined the relationship between employee engagement and profitability. **Engagement** is a measure of how much employees are connected emotionally to their work, how willing they are to expend extra effort to help their organizations meet their goals, and how

**TABLE 1.1**

The Impact of Leaders' Credibility on Employee Engagement

| | Percentage of Employees Who Agree in Highly Engaged Companies | Percentage of Employees Who Agree in Disengaged Companies |
|---|---|---|
| Employees have trust and confidence in the job leaders are doing (competence). | 79 | 16 |
| Senior leadership has sincere interest in employees' well-being (caring). | 74 | 18 |
| Senior management does a good job developing future leaders (caring). | 65 | 17 |
| Manager acts in ways consistent with his/her words (character). | 77 | 29 |
| Manager coaches employees to improve performance (caring). | 73 | 21 |
| Organization conducts business activities with honesty and integrity (character). | 84 | 27 |

*Source:* Towers Watson, 2012 *Global Workforce Study: Engagement at Risk: Driving Performance in a Volatile Global Environment* (New York: Towers Watson, 2012). Based on a 2012 survey of 32,000 employees in global large and midsize organizations.

much energy they have to reach those goals. The study showed that companies with highly engaged employees were nearly three times as profitable as companies with low engagement among employees. A key influence on this employee engagement was the credibility of business leaders. For example, in highly engaged companies, 77 percent of employees said their managers act consistently with what they say, whereas just 29 percent say the same in disengaged companies (see Table 1.1 for more examples of how competence, caring, and character of leaders and managers vary within highly engaged and disengaged companies).[54]

## How You Can Improve Your Communication Skills

This textbook is designed to help you improve your skills in a variety of professional settings so that you can become a credible and trusted communicator. Overall, you may feel that you excel at some communication skills but not others. For example, you may feel more confident in your presentation skills than your writing skills, or vice versa. Regardless of your present skill level, this textbook gives you opportunities to deliberately and consciously elevate your communication skill set. It also gives you tools to continue developing your communication abilities over the course of your career.

Figure 1.5 provides an overview of the topics we will cover in this textbook. Chapter 1 focused on the credibility of the communicator, since at the core of all communication is the issue of trust (explored further in the Communication Q&A with Melvin Washington). The techniques and skills covered in the rest of this textbook are of little use if you are not considered credible.

Once you have established yourself as a credible communicator, the techniques and skills in other chapters can greatly increase your communication effectiveness and career opportunities. Thus, later chapters focus on core principles, such as the interpersonal communication process, emotional intelligence, active listening, teamwork, and intercultural communication (the middle ring in Figure 1.5). These chapters lay out principles that also are important for written communication. For example, we discuss the listening-centered approach to communication, which is critical to effective writing.

**FIGURE 1.5**

Overview of Book

 **ESTABLISHING CREDIBILITY**

 **PRINCIPLES OF INTERPERSONAL COMMUNICATION**

 **PRINCIPLES FOR & TYPES OF BUSINESS MESSAGES**

You will also find chapters about planning and preparing written messages: routine messages, persuasive messages, email messages, and bad-news messages. And you will learn about conducting business research, writing business reports, and delivering presentations. You will work at developing résumés and preparing for job interviews.

As you read this book, you will be invited often to reflect about what you are reading. Try to apply what you read to your current challenges and your past experiences. Envision what you want to accomplish in your career. Imagine yourself communicating in business situations. Mentally evaluate your strengths and weaknesses. Turn off your phone and television. Reflect. You will be rewarded often during your career for staying aware of your communication skills and striving for consistent progress.[55]

# COMMUNICATION Q&A

## CONVERSATIONS WITH CURRENT BUSINESS PROFESSIONALS

**Pete Cardon: How important is trust in the workplace?**

**Melvin Washington:** When people trust you, they listen and respond. It really does not matter whether the communication is internal or external. When you have the reputation of being an honest and trustworthy manager, people will listen. They may not agree with every suggestion or policy you bring to the table, but they will respond with objectivity and honesty.

A business environment is analogous to a team sport. Each team member is trusted to do his or her part. At Anheuser-Busch, I was responsible for forecasting the sales of hundreds of products for an array of market segments. The distributorships trusted me to provide the correct information in order to provide an adequate supply of product to each region. Similarly, I depended on and trusted the sales team to provide me with accurate information, enabling me to forecast future sales correctly. Reliable information was the key to success. In other words, we depended on and, most of all, trusted each other to accomplish our corporate goals.

One aspect of trust is confidentiality. If a trust is betrayed, it may never be regained. It does not matter whether you're the best employee the company has ever hired, if you can't be trusted, you can't be tolerated. A manager at one of the past distributorships where I was employed was an extremely competent employee. She was what you would call a "go-to person." Her performance reviews were among the best in the company. However, she couldn't be trusted. She did not know how to keep matters confidential and constantly repeated information that was told to her in private. Hence, many of the employees ignored her, and it became increasingly difficult for her to function effectively on the job. Eventually, she became incompatible within the company climate and resigned from the job.

**PC: How important is trust when working with customers and clients?**

**MW:** In the business world, customers and clients are our lifeblood, and trust holds our business relationships together. Customers trust us to be competent and to look out for their interests. As business communicators, we must be careful to build and maintain that trust. In fact, if customers and clients do not trust us, many times they will not be honest with us.

During my tenure as a sales representative, I had a prospective customer who declined to speak with me. He did not carry any of our products in his establishment even though his store was in a market where the sale of our products had skyrocketed. After several attempts, however, he finally consented to a meeting. When I asked him why he did not want to do business with our company, he told me one of our past sales representatives had been untrustworthy. Apparently, this representative had promised him some incentives for promoting our product, which he never received. The merchant was willing to lose money by not selling our product because of a broken trust years before.

**PC: How important is credibility for leaders?**

**MW:** Credibility has to do with followers believing in their leaders. It is about leaders being trustworthy and following through on their promises. Also, employees are more willing to follow a leader who exhibits genuine care for them. Many managers are perceived as credible during the infancy of business relationships, but as the relationships continue, their honesty comes into question.

*Melvin Washington has worked in senior management positions for over 20 years at Anheuser-Busch and ARA Services. He has supervised hundreds of employees in operations and supply logistics roles. He currently is a professor of marketing at Howard University.*

Courtesy of Melvin Washington

# Chapter Takeaway for *Establishing Credibility*

**LO1.1 Explain the importance of establishing credibility for business communications. (pp. 3–6)**

You often operate from a deficit of trust when conducting business. In the **post-trust era**, skepticism is high. By establishing credibility, your colleagues, clients, customers, and other contacts will respond far more favorably to your communications.

**LO1.2 Describe how competence, caring, and character affect your credibility as a communicator. (pp. 6–9)**

At the heart of effective business communication is **credibility**. It is a reflection of your competence, caring, and character.

**Competence** relates to your proven set of skills and knowledge to accomplish business tasks. Others will judge you by your track record of success.

**Caring** shows that you will act in the interests of others, cultivate a sense of community, and demonstrate accountability to others.

**Character** shows that you will adhere to high personal, corporate, and business values. You can be counted on to do the right thing.

**LO1.3 Define and explain business ethics, corporate values, and personal values. (pp. 9–12)**

**Business ethics** are the commonly accepted beliefs and principles in the business community for acceptable behavior. **Corporate values** are those values that are the stated and lived values of a company. They are often provided in a formal code of conduct. **Personal values** are those values prioritized and adhered to by individuals.

**LO1.4 Explain the FAIR approach to ethical business communications. (pp. 12–17)**

**FAIR TEST**

**Facts:** How *factual* is your communication?
**Access:** How *accessible* or *transparent* are your motives, reasoning, and information?
**Impacts:** How does your communication *impact* stakeholders?
**Respect:** How *respectful* is your communication?

See *example questions for the FAIR test* in Figure 1.4.

# Key Terms

business ethics, 9

caring, 7

character, 8

code of conduct, 10

competence, 6

corporate values, 10

credibility, 3

engagement, 14

ethics, 9

personal values, 10

post-trust era, 5

stakeholder, 11

transparency, 9

# Discussion Exercises

*Note*: Check with your instructor to see how she or he would like you to approach these exercises. Sometimes, you will work individually; other times, you'll work in teams.

**1.1 Chapter Review Questions** (LO1.1, LO1.2, LO1.3, LO1.4)

Answer each of the following questions with one to three paragraphs:

A. Explain the importance of establishing credibility in business communications.

B. Explain the three components of credibility: competence, caring, and character. How do they interrelate?

C. Define and explain business ethics, corporate values, and the relationship between them.

D. Explain the FAIR approach to evaluating ethical business communications.

E. Describe how credibility impacts communication efficiency and effectiveness.

**1.2 Communication Q&A** (LO1.1, LO1.2, LO1.3, LO1.4)

Read the Communication Q&A with Melvin Washington, and write a one- or two-paragraph response to each of the following questions:

A. What points does Melvin Washington make about the impact of competence in establishing credibility?

B. What points does he make about the impact of caring in establishing credibility?

C. What points does he make about the impact of character in establishing credibility?

D. Which of his comments or experiences do you view as particularly insightful or helpful? Why that one?

**1.3 Character and Rules** (LO1.2)

As a former chair of the U.S. Federal Reserve once said, "Rules cannot take the place of character." In two to three paragraphs, explain what you think he meant by this statement.

**1.4 Transparency** (LO1.3)

As Drs. Dennis S. Reina and Michelle L. Reina explained in their book *Trust and Betrayal in the Workplace,* "Some leaders assume that . . . they are obligated to tell employees only what they specifically need to do their job. This couldn't be further from the truth."[56] In three to five paragraphs, explain the meaning of this statement. Why might leaders provide information about their activities and decision making, even when employees may not be directly affected?

**1.5 Gather Information from Websites about Ethics in Business** (LO1.3)

Read at least three blogs or articles about trust and/or ethics from a reputable organization or other source. Choose an issue that interests you, and in four to five paragraphs, summarize key findings related to that issue. Consider the following options for gathering information:

- Ethics and Compliance Initiative (www.ethics.org)
- Institute of Business Ethics (www.ibe.org.uk)
- Society of Corporate Compliance and Ethics (www.corporatecompliance.org)
- *Business Ethics* magazine (http://business-ethics.com)
- International Business Ethics Institute (www.business-ethics.org)
- Edelman website about trust (www.edelman.com/trust)

**1.6 Watch Interviews with Business Executives about Corporate Values** (LO1.2, LO1.3)

Watch at least three videos of interviews with executives talking about corporate values. In four to five paragraphs, summarize what you learned. Consider the following options for gathering information:

- Go to CNBC's online video section (www.cnbc.com, select Video link) and search for CEO interviews about corporate values or corporate culture.
- Go to YouTube and search with terms such as *corporate values, core values,* and *corporate culture*. Select videos of business executives and managers speaking about corporate values. Choose videos that are five minutes or longer.
- See Meg Whitman and Rajiv Dutta talking about building corporate values at eBay: www.businessweek.com/managing/content/mar2009/ca20090327_626373.htm.

**1.7 Learn about Corporate Citizenship** (LO1.3)

In recent years, companies have increasingly focused on their social responsibility. Many companies refer to the actions they take to help or give back to society as *corporate citizenship*. Learn about corporate citizenship from at least three reliable organizations or sources. In four to five paragraphs, summarize what you've learned. Consider the following options for gathering information:

- Boston College Center for Corporate Citizenship (www.bcccc.net/index.cfm?pageId=2053)
- *Forbes* Special Section on Corporate Citizenship (www.forbes.com/leadership/citizenship/)

- World Economic Forum special section on Corporate Global Citizenship (http://web.worldbank.org/archive/website00818/WEB/OTHER/GLOBAL-3.HTM)
- Santa Clara University Markkula Center for Applied Ethics (www.scu.edu/ethics/)

### 1.8  Identify Specific Approaches to Corporate Citizenship (LO1.3)

Choose a company and analyze its corporate citizenship measures. In four to five paragraphs, explain the company's major corporate citizenship initiatives and how they reflect its core values. Generally, you can find a corporate citizenship page at a company's website by navigating within sections with titles such as "About Us," "Company Overview," "Public Relations," "Media," and so on. If you are unsure which company you would like to learn about, consider the following:

- Boeing (www.boeing.com/companyoffices/aboutus/community/)
- Citigroup (www.citigroup.com/citi/citizen/)
- Accenture (www.accenture.com/us-en/company/citizenship/Pages/index.aspx)
- IBM (www.ibm.com/ibm/ibmgives/)

### 1.9  Business Ethics and Changing Values (LO1.3)

David Pottruck, former president and co-CEO of the Charles Schwab Corporation, explained the following regarding ethics and law:

> At Schwab, we are constantly looking for new ways to express our values without compromising them. For example, we built the company on the principle of "no conflict of interest." For many years, we defined that principle as "we will not give investment advice," because we equated advice with the old-line practice of selling hot stocks to maximize brokerage commissions. When we found that our customers were demanding advice from us, we realized that our business model, one that did not compensate brokers for sales, made it possible for us to give advice and continue to avoid conflict. We changed our practice to give the customers what they wanted, expert advice that is "objective, uncomplicated and not driven by commission," and at the same time we strengthened our commitment to our values. We feel that was a highly responsible change.[57]

In three to five paragraphs, discuss whether you think corporate and personal values can and/or should change over time. Specifically discuss Pottruck's statements.

# Evaluation Exercises

### 1.10  Compare Two Individuals' Credibility (LO 1.1, LO 1.2)

Think about two people—one whom you trust implicitly and another whom you do not trust. Ideally, these should be two people you currently work with or have worked with in the past. Compare them in the following ways: (a) competence, (b) caring, (c) character, (d) openness of communication, and (e) ease of communication. Write four to five paragraphs. Conclude with several general statements about the impact of credibility on communication efficiency and effectiveness.

### 1.11  Assess Credibility (LO 1.1, LO 1.2)

Think about four people: (a) a person who lacks complete credibility because he or she lacks competence, (b) a person who lacks credibility because he or she lacks caring, (c) a person who lacks credibility because he or she lacks character, and (d) a person with complete credibility. Compare and contrast these four individuals in terms of communication effectiveness in the workplace.

### 1.12  Evaluate a Communication Event (LO 1.1, LO 1.2)

Choose two communication events (conversations, email exchanges, and so on) that you were involved in—one in which you had credibility from the perspective of others and one in which you did not. If possible, choose communication events that occurred in the workplace. Respond to the following items about these two events:

A. Provide an overview of each communication event.

B. Explain the results of each event in terms of ease of communication and accomplishment of workplace objectives.

C. Explain why in one situation others granted you credibility but not in the other.

D. For the situation in which you had less perceived credibility, think about how you might have better established trust. Write down three ways you could have done so before the communication event occurred.

### 1.13  Examine Personal Credibility (LO 1.2)

Think about a specific professional context, and respond to each of the following questions. For the context, you can use a current or previous job. Or you could use a professional or student activity in which you participated. Ideally, you will select a context with challenging cooperation issues.

A. How much do/did others trust you in this situation?

B. How credible are/were you in terms of competency, caring, and character (from the perceptions of others)?

C. Do you think you are/were being perceived inaccurately in any ways? Why?

D. Have you done/did you do anything that may have broken trust in any way?

E. Have you kept/did you keep all your agreements? Explain.

F. List three things you need to do or should have done to better establish credibility.

### 1.14  Apply the FAIR Test (LO 1.4)

Choose a recent communication event (conversation, email exchange, and so on) that you were involved in, observed, or heard about. If possible, choose a communication event that occurred in the workplace and that involved a challenging ethical problem. Analyze the communication event with the FAIR test of ethical business communication. Devote at least one paragraph to each aspect of the test: (a) **facts** (how *factual* was the communication?); (b) **access** (how *accessible* or *transparent* were the motives, reasoning, and information?); (c) **impacts** (how did the communication *impact* stakeholders?); (d) **respect** (how *respectful* was the communication?). See Figure 1.4 for more information about the FAIR test.

**1.15 Apply the FAIR Test to a Customer Letter** (LO 1.4)

Using the FAIR test, evaluate Tim Cook's open letter to customers (published as "A Message to our Customers" on February 16, 2016, on the Apple website: www.apple.com/customer-letter/). Address each aspect of the FAIR test: (a) **facts** (how *factual* was the communication?); (b) **access** (how *accessible* or *transparent* were the motives, reasoning, and information?); (c) **impacts** (how did the communication *impact* stakeholders?); (d) **respect** (how *respectful* was the communication?). See Figure 1.4 for more information about the FAIR test.

Consider using other sources to help you evaluate Tim Cook's letter. You can find a variety of online information. Some online articles you might consider include the following:

- **Examples of various views of Apple's position:** "Apple v. Washington over Encryption" in *The New York Times*, available at http://www.nytimes.com/2016/02/19/opinion/apple-vs-washington-over-encryption.html?_r=0
- **The view of an editorial board:** "Why Apple Is Right to Challenge an Order to Help the F.B.I." by *The New York Times* Editorial Board, *The New York Times*, available at www.nytimes.com/2016/02/19/opinion/why-apple-is-right-to-challenge-an-order-to-help-the-fbi.html
- **The international complications of the issue:** "While It Defies U.S. Government, Apple Abides by China's Orders—and Reaps Big Rewards" by David Pierson in the *Los Angeles Times*, available at http://www.latimes.com/business/technology/la-fi-apple-china-20160226-story.html
- **Public opinion polls:** "More Support for Justice Department Than for Apple in Dispute over Unlocking iPhone," by the Pew Research Center, available at www.people-press.org/2016/02/22/more-support-for-justice-department-than-for-apple-in-dispute-over-unlocking-iphone/

- **The views of other tech companies:** "Bill Gates Says Apple-FBI Fight Is Not Black and White," by Charle Riley in *CNN Money*, available at money.cnn.com/2016/02/23/technology/bill-gates-apple-fbi-encryption/
- **The Apple approach to privacy:** "The Most Personal Technology Must Also Be the Most Private," available at http://www.apple.com/privacy/approach-to-privacy/
- **A public relations perspective of Apple's actions:** "The Optics of Apple's Encryption Fight," by Kaveh Wadell in *The Atlantic* (online), available at http://www.theatlantic.com/technology/archive/2016/02/why-apple-is-fighting-the-fbi/463260/
- **Reactions by victims of the terrorism:** "Anger, Praise, for Apple for Rebuffing FBI over San Bernardino's Killer's Phone" by Greg Botelho, Lorenza Brascia, and Michael Martinez on the *CNN* website, available at http://www.cnn.com/2016/02/18/us/san-bernardino-shooter-phone-apple-reaction/index.html

**1.16 Apply the FAIR Test to a Media Interview** (LO 1.4)

Using the FAIR test, evaluate a *Wall Street Journal* interview with Tim Cook ("Tim Cook Defends Apple's Encryption Policy" on YouTube: (https://www.youtube.com/watch?v=BZmeZyDGkQ0) about resistance to a U.S. court order to help unlock a terrorist's iPhone. Address each aspect of the FAIR test: (a) **facts** (how *factual* was the communication?); (b) **access** (how *accessible* or *transparent* were the motives, reasoning, and information?); (c) **impacts** (how did the communication *impact* stakeholders?); (d) **respect** (how *respectful* was the communication?). See Figure 1.4 for more information about the FAIR test. Use other online materials as needed to help you evaluate the fairness of the interview (you might consider some of the options listed in Exercise 1.15).

# Application Exercises

**1.17 Personal Mission Statement and Code of Conduct** (LO 1.3)

Write your own mission statement, including a code of conduct. Consider the following steps as you create the statement:

- Find several companies you admire. Use their code of conduct statements to help you craft your personal statement. Make sure you've personalized the statement to capture your deepest values and goals.
- Go to a career development website. These websites often contain articles and blogs about creating personal statements. For example, see the following:
  - "The Five-Step Plan for Creating Personal Mission Statements" by Randall S. Hansen (www.quintcareers.com/creating_personal_mission_statements.html)
  - "Writing a Personal Mission Statement" by Rodger Constandse (www.timethoughts.com/goalsetting/mission-statements.htm)
  - "Example Mission Statement," by Nightingale-Conant Sites (www.nightingale.com/example-mission-statement/)

- Go to a consultant website specializing in mission statements. Usually, these websites provide free resources for developing your own statement. In some cases, you will be required to create a username and password, but the online assistance is free. For example, see FranklinCovey's step-by-step guide (www.franklincovey.com/msb/).

**1.18 Statement of Career Aspirations** (LO 1.3)

When asked "What's your career advice for young people?" Vineet Nayar, former CEO of HCL Technologies, a $5 billion IT services company centered in India, said the following:

When you come out of college, you're raw. You have energy. You want to experiment. You want to learn. You have hopes. You have aspirations. You want to be Oprah Winfrey. You want to be Steve Jobs. You want to be Bill Gates. You want to be all that. Slowly, over time, you lose it. And by looking in the mirror every day as you get older, you fool yourself that you're OK. There has to be another way of looking in the mirror and revisiting what you really want to do. So I would say, maybe at the end of college, write it down honestly, in 100 words or whatever it is, and put it in a box. I call it the magic box. Revisit it once a year or once every two years and say, how honest are you to that? Don't let anybody run your life. That, in my mind, is very, very important. You should be in control of your life.[58]

Think about what Nayar's comments mean for you. In approximately 100 to 200 words, describe your deepest career aspirations. Include several statements about your guiding philosophy and the core personal values that drive your ambitions. Explain who you want to be in the future. Write the statement assuming that you will return to it in five, ten, or more years to see what progress you have made with your self-determined career aims.

# Language Mechanics Check

**1.19** **Review the comma rules C1 through C4 in Appendix A. Then, rewrite each sentence to add commas where needed.**

A. Financial advisors who have CFA certification can provide better advice.

B. Janice and Jim Atkinson who are certified financial advisors pay attention to your unique investment situation.

C. Janice received her CFA certification at the same time that I did.

D. Janice Atkinson president of Atkinson Financial will speak at the next Chamber of Commerce event.

E. Level 1 of the CFA exam focuses on ethical standards and Level 2 focuses on security valuation and portfolio management.

F. Janice spent almost three months preparing on her own for the CFA exam but still didn't pass it on her first try.

G. As a result she took a workshop in portfolio management from one of the top local experts.

H. Janice received her CFA certification last year the same time that I did.

I. Janice specializes in retirement planning and Jim specializes in tax preparation.

J. Jim not Janice prepares all their slide decks.

# Endnotes

1. Dennis S. Reina and Michelle L. Reina, *Trust and Betrayal in the Workplace* (San Francisco: Berrett-Koehler Publishers, 2006): 5.

2. Stephen R. Covey, "Foreword," Stephen M. R. Covey, *The Speed of Trust* (New York: Free Press, 2006).

3. Ibid., 2.

4. Ibid., 55.

5. These categories capture the dimensions of trust/credibility established by various scholars and experts. Various terms used in the scholarly literature include competence, benevolence, integrity, and intent. For sample works, see the following: Lisa C. Abrams, Rob Cross, Eric Lesser, and Daniel Z. Levin, "Nurturing Interpersonal Trust in Knowledge-Sharing Networks," *Academy of Management Executive* 17, no. 4 (2003): 64–77; Penelope Sue Greenberg, Ralph H. Greenberg, and Yvonne Lederer Antonucci, "Creating and Sustaining Trust in Virtual Teams," *Business Horizons* 50 (2007): 325–333; Covey, *The Speed of Trust;* Reina and Reina, *Trust and Betrayal in the Workplace.*

6. Reina and Reina, *Trust and Betrayal in the Workplace.*

7. Art Swift, "Honesty and Ethics Rating of Clergy Slides to New Low: Nurses Again Top List; Lobbyists Are Worst," retrieved April 1, 2014, from www.gallup.com/poll/166298/honesty-ethics-rating-clergy-slides-new-low.aspx.

8. Sheila Bonini, David Court, and Alberto Marchi, "Rebuilding Corporate Reputations," *McKinsey Quarterly,* no. 3 (2009).

9. Covey, *The Speed of Trust.*

10. Victoria L. Crittenden, Richard C. Hanna, and Robert A. Peterson, "The Cheating Culture: A Global Societal Phenomenon," *Business Horizons* 52 (2009): 337–346; D. McCabe, "Classroom Cheating among Natural Science and Engineering Majors," *Science and Engineering Ethics* 3, no. 4 (1996): 433–445; D. McCabe, *Levels of Cheating and Plagiarism Remain High* (Clemson, SC: Center for Academic Integrity, 2005); D. Callahan, *The Cheating Culture: Why More Americans Are Doing Wrong to Get Ahead* (New York: Harcourt, 2004).

11. Covey, *The Speed of Trust.*

12. Crittenden et al., "The Cheating Culture: A Global Societal Phenomenon"; McCabe, "Classroom Cheating among Natural Science and Engineering Majors"; McCabe, *Levels of Cheating and Plagiarism Remain High*; Callahan, *The Cheating Culture: Why More Americans Are Doing Wrong to Get Ahead.*

13. Michael Maslansky, *The Language of Trust* (New York: Prentice Hall, 2010): 6.

14. Patrick de Cambourg, *Corporate Accountability and Trust: Thoughts from 12 Top Managers* (Paris: Economica, 2006): 37.

15. Meg Whitman, *The Power of Many: Values for Success in Business and in Life* (New York: Crown Publishers, 2010): 81, 85.

16. Ibid., 45–46.

17. Ibid., 132.

18. Caring was listed as *conscientiousness* in a survey of important skills and abilities for business managers in the following study: Graduate Management Admission Council, *Alumni Perspectives Survey: 2014 Survey Report* (Reston, VA: GMAC, 2014).

19. Whitman, *The Power of Many: Values for Success in Business and in Life:* 179.

20. Covey, *The Speed of Trust.*

21. Meredith D. Ashby and Stephen A. Miles, *Leaders Talk Leadership: Top Executives Speak Their Minds* (New York: Oxford University Press, 2002): 5.

22. Adam Grant, "In the Company of Givers and Takers," *Harvard Business Review*, April 2013: 90–97.

23. Ashby and Miles, *Leaders Talk Leadership: Top Executives Speak Their Minds*: 55.

24. Economist Intelligence Unit, *The Role of Trust in Business Collaboration* (London: The Economist and Cisco Systems, 2008).

25. Ethics Resource Center, "Definitions of Values," retrieved June 24, 2010, from www.ethics.org/resource/definitions-values.

26. Peter J. Eide, "Introduction to the Human Resources Discipline of Ethics and Sustainability," retrieved June 25, 2010, from www.shrm.org/hrdisciplines/ethics/Pages/EthicsIntro.aspx.

27. Transparency International, "What Is 'Transparency?'" retrieved June 24, 2010, from www.transparency.org/news_room/faq/corruption_faq.

28. Patricia J. Harned and Michael G. Oxley, *2009 National Business Ethics Survey: Ethics in the Recession* (Arlington, VA: Ethics Resource Center, 2009).

29. Ken Blanchard Companies, *Building Trust* (Escondido, CA: Author, 2010).

30. Mary C. Gentile, "Keeping Your Colleagues Honest," *Harvard Business Review*, March 2010: 116.

31. Ibid., 114–117.

32. Eide, "Introduction to the Human Resources Discipline of Ethics and Sustainability."

33. eBay, *Code of Business Conduct & Ethics*, available at https://www.ebayinc.com/assets/Uploads/eBay-CodeofEthics-external-080615.pdf.

34. Adam Bird, "McKinsey Conversations with Global Leaders: Paul Polman of Unilever," retrieved July 15, 2012, from www.mckinsey-quarterly.com/McKinsey_conversations_with_global_leaders_Paul_Polman_of_Unilever_2456.

35. Tamar Frankel, *Trust and Honesty: America's Business Culture at a Crossroad* (Oxford: Oxford University Press, 2006): 206.

36. Whitman, *The Power of Many: Values for Success in Business and in Life*: 92.

37. Ken Blanchard Companies, *Building Trust.*

38. Reina and Reina, *Trust and Betrayal in the Workplace:* 7.

39. Lyle Sussman, "Disclosure, Leaks, and Slips: Issues and Strategies for Prohibiting Employee Communication," *Business Horizons* 51: 331–339.

40. UCLA Anderson School of Management, "Robert Eckert of Mattel Shares Insight with Class of 2004 Commencement Address," June 18, 2004, retrieved June 5, 2010, from www.anderson.ucla.edu/x3704.xml.

41. Whitman, *The Power of Many: Values for Success in Business and in Life*: 99.

42. Eric Lichtblau and Katie Benner, "Apple Fights Order to Unlock San Bernadino Gunman's iPhone," *The New York Times* (online), February 17, 2016, www.nytimes.com/2016/02/18/technology/apple-timothy-cook-fbi-san-bernardino.html.

43. Pew Research Center, "More Support for Justice Department than for Apple in Dispute over Unlocking iPhone," Pew Research Center website, February 22, 2016, www.people-press.org/2016/02/22/more-support-for-justice-department-than-for-apple-in-dispute-over-unlocking-iphone/.

44. Charles Riley, "Bill Gates Says Apple-FBI Fight Is Not Black and White," *CNN Money*, February 23, 2016, money.cnn.com/2016/02/23/technology/bill-gates-apple-fbi-encryption/.

45. Ibid.; Joe Rago, "The FBI vs. Apple," *The Wall Street Journal* (online), February 19, 2016, www.wsj.com/articles/the-fbi-vs-apple-1455840721.

46. David Pierson, "While It Defies U.S. Government, Apple Abides by China's Orders—and Reaps Big Rewards," *Los Angeles Times*, February 26, 2016, http://www.latimes.com/business/technology/la-fi-apple-china-20160226-story.html.

47. Dan Levine, "San Bernardino Victims to Oppose Apple on iPhone Encryption," *Reuters* (online), www.reuters.com/article/us-apple-encryption-victims-exclusive-idUSKCN0VV00B.

48. Horia Ungureanu, "San Bernardino Victims Side with Government, Legally Opposing Apple in Encryption Debacle," *Tech Times*, www.techtimes.com/articles/135562/20160223/san-bernardino-victims-side-with-government-legally-opposing-apple-in-encryption-debacle.htm.

49. Tim Cook, "A Message to Our Customers," February 16, 2016, Apple website, www.apple.com/customer-letter/.

50. Covey, *The Speed of Trust.*

51. Reina and Reina, *Trust and Betrayal in the Workplace*: 36.

52. Covey, *The Speed of Trust.*

53. Stephen R. Covey, *The 7 Habits of Highly Effective People: Restoring the Character Ethic* (New York: Simon and Schuster, 1989): 22–23.

54. Towers Watson, *2012 Global Workforce Study: Engagement at Risk: Driving Performance in a Volatile Global Environment* (New York: Towers Watson, 2012).

55. Stewart D. Friedman, "Be a Better Leader, Have a Richer Life," *Harvard Business Review*, April 2008: 1–13; Peter F. Drucker, "Managing Oneself," *Harvard Business Review*, January 2005: 16–28.

56. Reina and Reina, *Trust and Betrayal in the Workplace*: 37.

57. Ashby and Miles, *Leaders Talk Leadership: Top Executives Speak Their Minds*: 53.

58. Adam Bryant, "He's Not Bill Gates, or Fred Astaire," *Corner Office* (blog), *The New York Times*, February 13, 2010, www.nytimes.com/2010/02/14/business/14cornerweb.html.

# Principles of Interpersonal Communication

PART

TWO

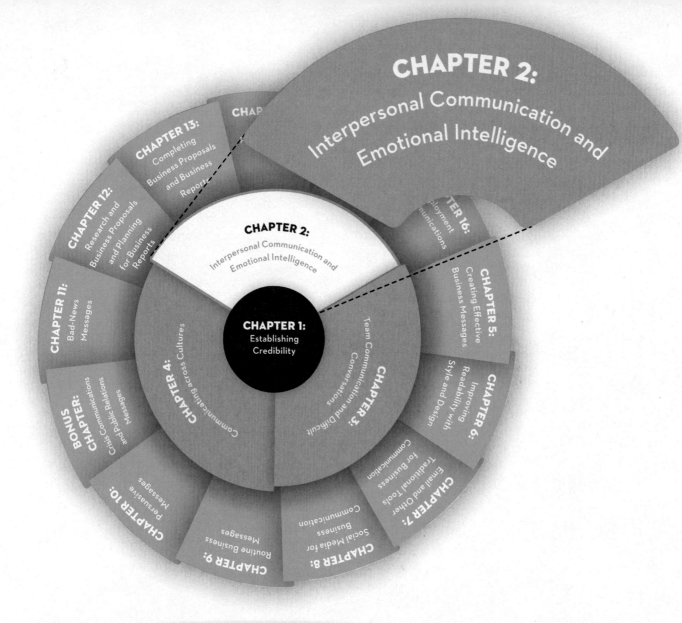

CHAPTER 2:
Interpersonal Communication and
Emotional Intelligence

CHAPTER 1:
Establishing
Credibility

CHAPTER 13:
Completing
Business Proposals
and Business
Reports

CHAPTER 12:
Research and
Business Proposals
and Planning
for Business
Reports

CHAPTER 11:
Bad-News
Messages

BONUS
CHAPTER:
Crisis Communications
and Public Relations
Messages

CHAPTER 10:
Persuasive
Messages

CHAPTER 9:
Routine Business
Messages

CHAPTER 8:
Social Media for
Business
Communication

CHAPTER 7:
Email and Other
Traditional Tools
for Business
Communication

CHAPTER 6:
Improving
Readability with
Style and Design

CHAPTER 5:
Creating Effective
Business Messages

CHAPTER 3:
Team Communication,
Conversations, and Difficult
Conversations

CHAPTER 4:
Communicating across Cultures

 **ESTABLISHING CREDIBILITY**

 **PRINCIPLES OF INTERPERSONAL COMMUNICATION**

 **PRINCIPLES FOR & TYPES OF BUSINESS MESSAGES**

 **Learning Objectives**

After studying this chapter, you should be able to do the following:

**LO2.1** Describe the interpersonal communication process and barriers to effective communication.

**LO2.2** Explain how emotional hijacking can hinder effective interpersonal communication.

**LO2.3** Explain how self-awareness impacts the communication process.

**LO2.4** Describe how self-management impacts the communication process.

**LO2.5** Explain and evaluate the process of active listening.

**LO2.6** Describe and demonstrate effective questions for enhancing listening and learning.

**LO2.7** Explain strategies to sight-read the nonverbal communication of others.

**LO2.8** Identify common communication preferences based on motivational values.

**LO2.9** Explain how extroversion-introversion impacts interpersonal communication.

**LO2.10** Explain the role of civility in effective interpersonal communication and the common types of incivility in the workplace.

In nearly any poll of skills needed for career success, employees identify interpersonal skills as the most important. For example, consider the results of a recent Gallup poll of working adults, depicted in Table 2.1.[1] More than any other item in the survey, respondents recognized "skill in dealing with people" as the most critical.

Consider also the remarks of Linda Hudson, former president and CEO of BAE Systems:

> I find new business school graduates come in here thinking that, first of all, they're going to run the company overnight. Many of them are convinced they've never made a mistake. They're not accustomed to encountering the kinds of roadblocks or disappointments that often come with the way decisions get made in a corporate environment, and they have almost no people skills. So I think an important part of teaching business ought to be focused more on realistic expectations and the people-skill part of business. . . . We give them all the book smarts, but we don't tend to give them the other skills that go along with business.[2]

In this chapter, we provide an overview of the interpersonal communication process, including an explanation of emotional intelligence, which is a foundation of effective interpersonal communication.

Read the following short case about budget cuts at Eastmond Networking. Throughout the chapter, you'll find effective and ineffective examples of interpersonal communication that are based on this case.

**Hear Pete Cardon explain why this matters.**

Can't scan? Try ScanLife at your appstore or visit bit.ly/cardon2

**TABLE 2.1**

### Skills That Determine Success

| Skills | Percentage* |
|---|---|
| 1. Skill in dealing with people | 87 |
| 2. Critical-thinking skills | 84 |
| 3. Basic use of computers | 65 |
| 4. Writing ability | 57 |
| 5. Basic mathematics | 56 |
| 6. Advanced use of computers | 44 |
| 7. Physical strength | 33 |
| 8. Scientific knowledge | 27 |
| 9. Advanced mathematics | 23 |
| 10. Artistic skill | 23 |
| 11. Knowledge of history | 19 |

*Percentage of American adults who rated skills as "critical" or "extremely important" to career success.
*Source:* "Which Skills Hold the Secret to Success at Work?" by Linda Lyons, Gallup.

## CHAPTER CASE: HARD DECISIONS AT EASTMOND NETWORKING

**WHO'S INVOLVED**

**Latisha Jackson, summer intern**
- Hired for a summer internship to develop a corporate wellness program
- Double majoring in business administration and health education

**Jeff Brody, personnel director**
- Worked as the head of personnel at Eastmond Networking for the past five years

**Lisa Johnson, finance manager**
- Has held current position for three years
- Specializes in developing budgets and financial forecasts

**Steve Choi, summer intern**
- Hired for a summer internship
- Majoring in human resource management

## SITUATION 1: BUDGET CUTS

Jeff Brody recently hired Latisha Jackson as a summer intern to help develop a corporate wellness program. During Latisha's interview, Jeff explained that he had seen a recent segment on a business network about how wellness programs could save companies money. He said, "Our company president is asking us to identify some low-cost options that can improve morale. So as far as I'm concerned, if we can provide a wellness program with little cost—maybe around $200 to $300 per year for each employee—and it improves morale, it would be worth it."

Typically, corporate wellness programs focus on nutrition, exercise, stress management, disease management, and even life enrichment. Because Latisha was a dual major in business administration and health education, this internship exactly matched her interests. Plus, she was passionate about physical fitness and even led a daily Zumba class.

She accepted the internship at minimum wage. She had been offered another summer internship in sales that offered $15 per hour plus commissions and bonuses. But she turned down the sales position to focus on her real passion: promoting health in the workplace. She thought she was making the right choice, but she had believed the same thing for an internship the previous summer. That internship turned out to be a disaster; the company was disorganized and provided her with few of the exciting professional opportunities that were promised.

During Latisha's first week of work, the company president informed Jeff that he would need to make 10 to 15 percent cuts in his department budget immediately. Furthermore, the company president told him to avoid any *nonessential* work functions or initiatives.

Just after receiving this news, Jeff saw Latisha enter her office down the hall. He knew how excited she was about developing the wellness program. Yet he knew that if anything could be classified as nonessential, it would be her project. He dreaded what he was about to do—tell her that they had to postpone any work on the wellness program and that she would be reassigned to other tasks.

Jeff went to Latisha's office and said, "Latisha, can I have a minute with you?"

"Sure," she responded. "Come on in." Jeff hoped the conversation would go well.

## SITUATION 2: CHANGES IN PERFORMANCE REVIEWS

Eastmond Networking holds performance evaluations for employees once per year. Jeff sees the results of the company's internal, anonymous employee survey each year. Each year, he notices that employees do not like the performance evaluations. They think the evaluations are not fair and do not help them improve. Jeff has talked to several human resources (HR) directors and learned that many companies now use continuous performance reviews with a lot of success. To help transition to continuous performance reviews, he has asked the following employees to help out: Lisa Johnson, finance manager; Steve Choi, intern; and Latisha Jackson, intern.

TASK

1
Overcome barriers to communication.

2
Manage emotions to engage in constructive communication.

## Understanding the Interpersonal Communication Process

For the most part, we engage in interpersonal communication instinctively. By the time we are adults, we have engaged in hundreds of thousands of interpersonal interactions. We often take the interpersonal communication process for granted, rarely thinking about its building blocks and how they influence the quality of our communications. However, consciously becoming aware of these basic elements can help you improve your interpersonal communication skills and work more effectively with others. The **interpersonal communication process**, depicted in Figure 2.1, is the process of sending and receiving verbal and nonverbal messages between two or more people. It involves the exchange of simultaneous and mutual messages to share and negotiate meaning between those involved.[3]

Each person involved in interpersonal communication is both encoding and decoding meaning. **Meaning** refers to the thoughts and feelings that people *intend* to communicate to one another. **Encoding** is the process of converting meaning into messages composed of words and nonverbal signals. **Decoding** is the process of interpreting messages from others into meaning.

In the interpersonal communication process, communicators encode and send messages at the same time that they also receive and decode messages. When Communicator A wants to express an idea, she encodes it as a verbal (i.e., language) and nonverbal (i.e., gestures, expressions) message. Communicator B simultaneously decodes the verbal and nonverbal message and ascribes meaning to it. Whereas the verbal communication process typically involves turn-taking, with Communicator A and Communicator B alternating between sending messages, the nonverbal communication in face-to-face communication is typically constant. Furthermore, the processing

**LO2.1** Describe the interpersonal communication process and barriers to effective communication.

**connect**

Visit **http://connect. mheducation.com** for an exercise on this topic.

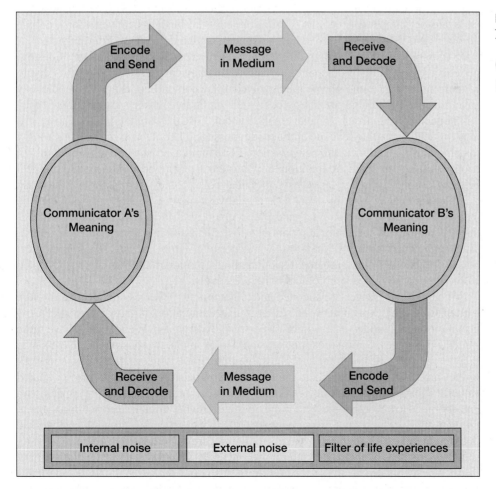

**FIGURE 2.1**

The Interpersonal Communication Process

of messages in the form of encoding and decoding occurs continuously. One goal of interpersonal communication is to arrive at **shared meaning**—a situation in which people involved in interpersonal communication attain the same understanding about ideas, thoughts, and feelings. In practice, many barriers interfere with achieving shared meaning, including external noise, internal noise, and lifetime experiences.

**Noise** causes distortion to or interruption of messages. Four types of noise affect the quality of message delivery: physical noise, physiological noise, semantic noise, and psychological noise. **Physical noise** is external noise that makes a message difficult to hear or otherwise receive. Examples include loud sounds nearby that interrupt verbal signals or physical barriers that prevent communicators from observing nonverbal signals. Physical noise can also be a function of the medium used. A poor signal for a phone conversation or blurry video feed for a teleconference are examples of physical noise. The other three types of noise are distortions or interruptions of messages that are caused by *internal* characteristics of communicators.

**Physiological noise** refers to disruption due to physiological factors. Examples include hearing problems, illness, memory loss, and so on. Conversely, a communicator may have a difficult time sending a message due to physiological constraints such as stuttering, sickness, or other temporary or permanent impairments.

**Semantic noise** occurs when communicators apply different meanings to the same words or phrases. For example, two people may have different ideas about what an *acceptable profit margin* means. One manager may have a figure in mind, such as 10 percent. Another may think of a range between 20 and 30 percent. Semantic noise can be most difficult to overcome when strong emotions are attached to words or phrases. For example, a term such as *downsize* may invoke positive emotions for a manager who associates this term with frugality and wise cash management. However, another manager may view this term with negative emotions and associate it with callousness and disloyalty on the part of the corporation. In nearly all business conversations, people throw around words and phrases that they understand and interpret differently.

**Psychological noise** refers to interference due to attitudes, ideas, and emotions experienced during an interpersonal interaction. In many cases, this noise occurs due to the current conversation—the people involved or the content. For example, people may have preexisting feelings or stereotypes ("he's unreliable," "she's calculating," "they will not defend us in front of management") about those they are talking to. Those feelings influence how they encode and decode messages. People also may react strongly to comments made during the conversation. For example, a listener can't stop thinking about an inaccurate statistic mentioned by a speaker or the upside of a potential deal being discussed. In many cases, psychological noise comes from sources other than the interpersonal interaction. People nearly always begin a conversation affected by moods. Perhaps they are stressed and preoccupied with thoughts of upcoming deadlines. Perhaps a person is unhappy about a lost client and has a lingering sour mood. The demanding impacts of day-to-day business activities can create psychological noise for many reasons. In the next section about emotional intelligence, we focus on methods of managing psychological noise effectively.

All outgoing messages are encoded and all incoming messages are decoded through a **filter of lifetime experiences**. This filter is an accumulation of knowledge, values, expectations, and attitudes based on prior personal experiences. When people have more shared experiences, communication is easier.[4] For example, two business managers who grew up in the same community at the same time, got engineering degrees, and work in the same company likely share enough common background in the form of shared values and experiences that they can quite easily sort through noise as they speak with one another. However, people who grew up in different communities or cultures and at different times, who have far different educational backgrounds, and who have worked in different industries are far more likely to filter incoming messages differently. As a result, they are more likely to encounter noise and are less equipped to deal with the noise.

The short conversation between Jeff and Latisha in Figure 2.2 illustrates the interpersonal communication process. Notice the sender's intended messages and how they

**FIGURE 2.2**

## The Interpersonal Communication Process in a Short Conversation

Jeff Brody sat down, shifted uncomfortably, and sighed. Latisha Jackson turned down the radio volume, but Jeff could still hear the weather report.

"Latisha, you've done a great job for us." Shrugging his shoulders, he continued, "My hands are tied, though, and we need to abandon the wellness program initiative. I'm being forced to cut our budget immediately. There's simply no room for new projects that cost additional money."

Latisha looked stunned. "I thought we went through this already. We all know that this will help the employees and save money. Doesn't the company care about that?"

"Hey," Jeff said. "Don't overreact. Look, it's not about caring. It's about surviving so we can try not to lay anyone off."

"Are you saying I don't have an internship anymore?"

"Of course you have an internship," he said, exasperated. "We'll find some other great projects for you to work on. I'm going to schedule a time this afternoon with Jenn and you. We can all talk about some new tasks for you."

"OK," Latisha said, "well, whatever you want. I'll see you this afternoon then."

As Jeff got up, Latisha couldn't hide a look of displeasure. And, Jeff couldn't hide his frustration that Latisha didn't understand his predicament.

**Jeff encodes**: Thanks for your great work. Unfortunately, you will need to work on a different project.

**Latisha decodes**: Jeff thinks other projects are more important. This is an excuse.

**Latisha encodes**: The health initiative will help our employees and save money. Don't *you* care?

**Jeff decodes**: Latisha thinks I don't care about her project.

**Jeff encodes**: Of course I care. This is the reality of business. I'm doing my best to keep everyone's job.

**Latisha decodes**: Jeff thinks he has to fire people to save money.

**Latisha encodes**: Is my job safe?

**Jeff decodes**: She doesn't trust me.

**Jeff encodes**: You have great talents, and we want you to help on an important project.

**Latisha decodes**: Jeff probably wants to help but has no idea what I can do for the company.

**Latisha encodes**: I'll do whatever you want me to.

**Jeff decodes**: Latisha doesn't want to work on other projects.

**Physical noise**: Radio weather report is on.

**Psychological noise**: Jeff is worried about budget cuts in his department. He is also worried about disappointing Latisha. Latisha becomes disappointed and feels like she's in another dead-end internship.

**Physiological noise**: Jeff is physically tired from lack of sleep. He is also physically stressed from work.

**Semantic noise**: Jeff views the word *surviving* neutrally. He views it as a normal process that companies go through from time to time. Latisha perceives *surviving* as a panic word. She also views it as an excuse word to justify giving bad news.

**Filter of lifetime experiences**: Latisha has been disappointed by a lot of supervisors. For example, in her last internship, her supervisors repeatedly promised great opportunities and projects. She ended up doing menial database entry of personnel records. Jeff has been through ups and downs for companies. He has always tried to protect his employees during downturns and has always figured out how to do it. He has found that in each crisis, he is more effective when he avoids rash decisions.

are encoded and decoded. Also notice the noise factors and filters and consider how they interfere with achieving shared meaning. Consider that this short conversation is between two well-meaning people who are both caught up in a frustrating but relatively straightforward situation. Both want to help the other. Yet, as you read the conversation, you will notice they do not understand one another completely and become agitated. Many business conversations are far more challenging than this one.

## Emotional Hijacking

**LO2.2**  Explain how
 emotional hijacking
can hinder effective
interpersonal
communication.

**connect**

**Visit** http://connect.
mheducation.com for an
exercise on this topic.

The ability to manage effective interpersonal communication depends on emotional intelligence. **Emotional intelligence** involves understanding emotions, managing emotions to serve goals, empathizing with others, and effectively handling relationships with others.[5] Business managers with high emotional intelligence are more effective at influencing others, overcoming conflict, showing leadership, collaborating in teams, and managing change.[6] Furthermore, research has shown emotional intelligence leads to better outcomes in business reasoning and strategic thinking.[7] You may see emotional intelligence referred to as **EQ**, which stands for *emotional quotient,* a play on the term IQ, *intelligence quotient.* We use both terms in this book.

Recently, EQ has been shown to be the single best predictor of workplace performance. About 90 percent of high performers in the workplace are high in EQ, whereas only 20 percent of low performers are high in EQ. On average, people with high EQs make $29,000 more per year than those with low EQs.[8]

Emotional intelligence comes into play in many business circumstances. It is especially important during moments of stress. Recent research showed that out of 200 common positions, business executives held the second most stressful job (just behind firefighters).[9] Emotional intelligence contributes to one's ability to communicate clearly and constructively, overcome nerves before a presentation, gain the courage to talk to someone about bad news, respond well to disappointment and failure, motivate team members to move toward a common goal, and many other situations. In short, emotional intelligence allows business managers and executives to think clearly about business objectives without letting their emotions get the best of them.

Business leaders increasingly emphasize the need for emotional intelligence in today's demanding business environment. Richard Anderson, CEO of Delta Air Lines, recently described the kind of qualities he's looking for in employees more so now than five or ten years ago:

> I think this communication point is getting more and more important. People really have to be able to handle the written and spoken word. . . . You've got to have not just the business skills, you've got to have the emotional intelligence. It's not just enough to be the best person operating an H-P calculator. You have to have the emotional intelligence to understand what's right culturally, both in your company and outside your company.[10]

In the upcoming pages, you will learn strategies for developing your emotional intelligence. In general, emotional intelligence is developed through conscious effort and attention to your feelings and interactions with others. Common approaches to improving emotional intelligence include reflecting on emotions and behavior, keeping a journal, and practicing interpersonal skills in social situations.[11]

In this section, we first focus on emotional hijacking. Then, we discuss four domains of emotional intelligence—self-awareness, self-management, empathy, and relationship management. Finally, we'll suggest strategies for improving your emotional intelligence in each of these domains to achieve more effective interpersonal communication in the workplace.

Some people might wonder why emotional intelligence is so critical for business managers and executives, especially those in finance, accounting, and quantitatively driven disciplines and positions. After all, competence in many types of business decision making is primarily based on logic and reason. The primary reason that emotional intelligence is so critical is physiological: People are hardwired to experience emotions before reason. All signals to the brain first go through the limbic system, where emotions are produced, before going to the rational area of the brain (see Figure 2.3).[12]

In other words, you feel all your incoming messages before you reason about them. Furthermore, one function of the limbic system is protection. This part of the brain creates a fight-or-flight response when incoming messages appear as threats. For example, people may experience **emotional hijacking**, a situation in which emotions control our behavior, causing us to react without thinking. The impacts of emotions last long after they've subsided.[13]

Emotional hijacking prevents you from engaging in effective interpersonal communication. It can lead to unwanted behaviors: You may misrepresent your ideas, confuse the facts, say things to others that you later regret, display frustration or anger, remain silent when you would prefer to be heard, fail to listen to others, or disengage from working relationships that are in your best interest.

In the conversation between Jeff and Latisha (see Figure 2.2), both are in danger of emotional hijacking. Latisha is living the experience in the context of past disappointments with supervisors. She further panics when she perceives that her job may be in danger. All her thoughts are influenced by the emotions generated in the limbic system. Jeff similarly is at risk of emotional hijacking. He easily becomes agitated because he thinks Latisha does not trust him or understand his motives. Furthermore, he still has lingering stress from his conversation just minutes earlier with the company president, who informed him that he needed to cut nonessential work activities.

**FIGURE 2.3**

Neuropathways of Signals Entering the Brain

Rational Part of Brain

Emotional Part of Brain (Limbic System)

Sensory Signals Enter through the Spinal Cord

## Self-Awareness

The most-used EQ test for business professionals shows that emotional intelligence can be divided into four domains: self-awareness, self-management, empathy, and relationship management. Throughout this section, we refer to statistics based on this particular measure of EQ.[14]

**Self-awareness** is the foundation for emotional intelligence. It involves accurately understanding your emotions as they occur and how they affect you. One prominent researcher defines self-awareness as "ongoing attention to one's internal states."[15] People high in self-awareness understand their emotions well, what satisfies them, and what irritates them. Understanding your emotions as they occur is not always easy. In fact, research indicates that just 36 percent of people can accurately identify their emotions as they occur.[16]

Self-awareness is particularly important for stressful and unpleasant situations. People high in self-awareness have the ability to be self-reflective when they experience strong or even distressful emotions. Often, this involves the ability to explicitly identify feelings as they occur. For example, a person who becomes angry with a colleague can simultaneously think, "I'm feeling anger right now."[17]

High self-awareness includes the ability to manage events that stir strong—often fight-or-flight—responses. Events that cause strong emotional reactions are called **triggers**.[18] As you become more aware of your triggers or tendencies, you can adjust your interpersonal communication to avoid dysfunctional behaviors caused by emotional hijacking, such as blaming others as a defense mechanism or not speaking up when you're nervous.

Adele Lynn, one of the foremost experts on the role of emotional intelligence in workplace performance, explained the benefit of emotional intelligence.

> I'm sure you know people who go through life and never seem to learn from their mistakes, or they don't see how one experience is connected to another. Self-awareness will help

**LO2.3** Explain how self-awareness impacts the communication process.

**connect**

Visit **http://connect. mheducation.com** for an exercise on this topic.

**TABLE 2.2**

Low versus High Self-Awareness Thoughts

| Low Self-Awareness Thoughts | High Self-Awareness Thoughts |
|---|---|
| **Jeff:** Latisha needs to learn how to trust people. She's not being fair to me and she needs to understand the constraints I'm facing. | **Jeff:** I'm bothered that she doesn't trust my motives. Typically, I feel disrespected when others don't trust my motives. Sometimes, I lash out in these circumstances. |
| Jeff ignores and deflects his feelings to focus on what he perceives as Latisha's misperceptions. | Jeff recognizes that he feels distrusted and disrespected by what Latisha said. He also recognizes that he often says things he later regrets in these situations. |
| **Latisha:** This is ridiculous. Jeff promised me that I'd be working on the health care initiative. How can he go back on his word so quickly? | **Latisha:** I feel afraid and confused. Jeff doesn't seem to care if I have challenging work. I've felt this way before at other jobs. I wonder how my past experiences are impacting how I'm judging Jeff. |
| Latisha overreacts to Jeff's words and actions because she is not aware of how past disappointments are affecting how she is judging Jeff. | Latisha notices that how she feels about Jeff is affected by previous, similar events. She knows she should be careful not to let those events make her rush to judgment. |

prevent this from happening to you, but only if you keep building on your lessons. This linking of life experiences into ever-increasing lessons is the foundation of wisdom. It is the quintessential difference in living one year of experiences thirty times versus thirty years of experience.[19]

In the conversation between Jeff and Latisha, more self-awareness would help both of them manage their feelings and thoughts. If Jeff is self-aware, he says to himself, "I'm feeling bothered that she doesn't trust me and thinks I don't care." Similarly, Latisha is self-aware if in the moment, she says to herself, "I feel afraid and confused. Jeff doesn't seem to care if I have challenging work. I've felt this way before at other jobs. I wonder how my past experiences are impacting how I'm judging Jeff." Table 2.2 shows differences in low versus high self-awareness in the encounter between Jeff and Latisha.

Also, read through Table 2.3 to learn more about self-awareness and strategies for developing it. You'll notice that this table also contains information about self-management, empathy, and relationship management. After reading about each element of EQ, consider going back to the table for additional information about these dimensions of EQ.

## Self-Management

**LO2.4**  Describe how self-management impacts the communication process.

**Self-management** is the "ability to use awareness of your emotions to stay flexible and to direct your behavior positively."[20] It involves the discipline to hold off on current urges to meet long-term intentions. Excellent self-managers know how to use both positive and negative emotions to meet personal and business goals.[21]

Most strong emotions can impair rational communication and behavior. For example, anger is an intense emotion tied to a physical sense of endangerment. Most people have impulses to verbally attack or defend themselves during a rush of intense emotion. While intense emotions often last just moments, their impacts last far longer. For example, when you experience anger, the resulting adrenal and cortical excitation creates less intense reactions to this sense of endangerment that can last hours

**TABLE 2.3**

Emotional Intelligence Dimensions, Related Impacts on Interpersonal Communication, and Strategies for Improvement

| EQ Dimension | Impact on Interpersonal Communication | Strategies for Improvement |
|---|---|---|
| Self-awareness | **Low self-awareness**<br>• Unaware of own emotional states and related impacts on communication.<br>• Unaware of triggers that lead to emotional hijacking and making judgmental, rash, or unfair comments.<br>• Unaware of strengths and weaknesses of own communication abilities.<br><br>**High self-awareness**<br>• Aware of own emotional states and related impacts on communication.<br>• Aware of triggers and related tendencies to say the wrong thing.<br>• Aware of strongest communication skills. | • Constantly evaluate your feelings and moods; attempt to understand your feelings as they occur.<br>• Think about your last reactions to the following experiences: joy, anger, self-doubt, frustration.<br>• Ask yourself how certain emotions alter or distort your thinking.<br>• Identify your triggers and make plans to handle them effectively.<br>• Reflect on personal strengths, weaknesses, and values. |
| Self-management | **Low self-management**<br>• Unable to control impulses.<br>• Frequently vent frustrations without a constructive work purpose.<br>• Spend a higher percentage of work conversations on small talk, gossip, and non-work-related issues.<br>• React defensively and with a me-first attitude when threats are perceived.<br><br>**High self-management**<br>• Control emotional impulses that are not aligned with work and relationship goals.<br>• Discuss frustrations in the context of solving problems and improving relationships.<br>• Spend a higher percentage of work conversations on work-related topics with a focus on solutions.<br>• When threats are perceived, seek to de-escalate interpersonal tensions and resolve issues at hand. | • Engage in relaxation techniques to clear your mind.<br>• Examine strategies for overcoming impulses that compete with achieving your long-range goals.<br>• Focus on how to improve for your next effort rather than dwelling on disappointments of the current failure.<br>• Practice expressing positive emotions more frequently and in situations where you normally do not.<br>• Talk to a trusted colleague who is an effective self-manager.<br>• Sleep on it.<br>• Practice self-talk and visualize yourself responding effectively to challenging interpersonal issues. |
| Empathy | **Low empathy**<br>• Fail to listen carefully to others.<br>• Direct conversations to topics that are important to self.<br>• Avoid volunteering to help others with their work assignments.<br>• Engage in a me-first approach to work with colleagues.<br><br>**High empathy**<br>• Attempt to understand the feelings, perspectives, and needs of others.<br>• Direct conversations to topics that focus on the needs of others and self.<br>• Volunteer advice or help to others as appropriate.<br>• Show a sincere interest in others: their efforts, their ideas, and their successes. | • Always attempt to place yourself in the position of others: think about the emotions and thoughts others are experiencing.<br>• Anticipate how others will react during business conversations and meetings.<br>• Listen to others, even when you disagree, without interrupting or judging.<br>• Pay attention to nonverbal behavior.<br>• Practice asking good questions.<br>• Think about group dynamics and the related impacts on each team member.<br>• Give others your undivided attention and time.<br>• Get to know others. |

**TABLE 2.3**

(*Continued*)

| EQ Dimension | Impact on Interpersonal Communication | Strategies for Improvement |
|---|---|---|
| Relationship management | **Low relationship management**<br>• Focus exclusively on the task at hand without paying attention to rapport-building.<br>• Remain silent to avoid discussions about differences of opinions, or attempt to silence the dissenting opinions of others.<br>• Provide indirect and vague feedback and ideas to others.<br>• Disregard feedback and constructive criticism.<br>• Discourage dissent.<br>• Respond to others only when it's convenient.<br><br>**High relationship management**<br>• Build rapport with others to focus on collaboration.<br>• Speak out constructively about differences of opinion.<br>• Provide direct and constructive feedback to others.<br>• Accept and even welcome feedback and constructive criticism.<br>• Encourage contrarian views.<br>• Respond to others when it's convenient for them. | • Attend work-related social outings.<br>• Keep records of people in your network and keep track of their skills, interests, hobbies, birthdays, and other important dates.<br>• Maintain regular contact with colleagues and others in your work network.<br>• Devote time to conversations on a range of topics.<br>• Greet others by name.<br>• Live up to your promises.<br>• Collaborate more effectively with others.<br>• Build up the courage to have a difficult conversation.<br>• Speak up in meetings or work conversations when you ordinarily do not; or, encourage others who rarely speak up to voice their thoughts and feelings. |

and days. An individual may ignore this less intense reaction yet still feel a sour mood for a period of time. Furthermore, research shows that anger builds on anger. Thus, people are more vulnerable to being provoked to anger during this period. Strong self-managers realize that they are still vulnerable for several days following feelings of anger and learn to heighten their levels of self-awareness during these time periods.[22]

People can quickly control moderate negative emotions. For example, an individual who tries to understand **mitigating information** can short-circuit moderate anger almost immediately. Mitigating information involves favorable explanations for why others have behaved in a certain way. See Table 2.4 for examples of low and high self-management and the use of mitigating information.

A common misperception of many business professionals is that venting negative feelings helps people cope with anger. Study after study has shown that venting is temporarily satisfying—but it rarely makes anger go away, especially when the venting is intended as retaliation. Physiologically, venting continues to arouse the brain with feelings of anger. Thus, venting is considered one of the least effective strategies for de-escalating anger.[23]

Typically, other strategies should be pursued to deal with intense anger. These strategies include removing oneself temporarily from the anger-inducing situation, going on a walk, breathing deeply, or enjoying some entertainment (e.g., TV, movies, reading). Also, writing about the feelings of frustration, anger, and hostility can help you articulate your feelings, review the events rationally, and challenge and reappraise the feelings. Typically, excellent self-managers experiment with ways of cooling down so that they find tried-and-true solutions to overcoming intense emotions. Generally, however, this cooling down is typically not effective when the time is used to relive the anger-inducing events.[24]

**TABLE 2.4**

Low versus High Self-Management Thoughts and the Use of Mitigating Information

| Low Self-Management Thoughts | High Self-Management Thoughts |
|---|---|
| **Jeff:** If Latisha is going to treat me like I'm the bad guy, then maybe I should just turn her over to someone else so I don't have to worry about her. | **Jeff:** Latisha is probably reacting this way because she cares so much about a health initiative, which helps the employees of this company. She is eager to contribute. |
| Jeff assumes the worst about Latisha's comments, thus allowing his frustration with her to grow. He considers an action that is extreme. | Jeff assumes a positive explanation for Latisha's actions (*mitigating information*), thus short-circuiting his feelings of frustration and perhaps moderating anger. |
| **Latisha:** There's no way I can change anything. Jeff will assign me to another project and that's that. I'm stuck in another dead-end internship. | **Latisha:** I want to express to Jeff my desire to work on a meaningful project. We can discuss how my approach to the health initiative could be applied to another project. And we could discuss how I can still spend some time working on the health initiative in the planning process—in a way that does not require cash commitments during this budget crunch. |
| This thought process reflects *pessimism*. Latisha neither thinks of other options available to her for the health initiative nor assumes that other work tasks will provide her with rewarding challenges. | This thought process reflects *optimism*. Latisha considers how she can approach Jeff and constructively discuss options that are good for her and the company. |

Self-management involves far more than corralling anger. It involves responding productively and creatively to feelings of self-doubt, worry, frustration, disappointment, and nervousness. It also includes tempering oneself when experiencing excitement and elation. In short, self-management helps you avoid knee-jerk reactions that may compromise your ability to meet your business and career objectives.[25]

A major distinction between those high in self-management and those low in self-management is **optimism** versus **pessimism**. Optimists view failures as events that can be changed in the future. They view these failures as temporary setbacks and learning experiences. Pessimists, by contrast, view failures as indications of their own incompetence or inability. They dwell on the past rather than looking to the future. Under duress or disappointment, optimists form a plan of action, whereas pessimists focus on the permanence of their situation and their inability to overcome the disappointment. One study showed that among insurance sales workers, optimists outperformed pessimists by 37 percent in sales. Furthermore, pessimists were twice as likely as optimists to quit.[26]

## Empathy

Whereas the first two dimensions of emotional intelligence primarily deal with identifying and managing one's own emotions, the final two dimensions—empathy and relationship management—involve understanding others and managing your interactions with them effectively. **Empathy** is the "ability to accurately pick up on emotions in other people and understand what is really going on with them."[27] Empathy also includes the desire to help others develop in their work responsibilities and career objectives.[28] In this chapter, we focus on two communication skills that will help you develop your empathy: listening and sight-reading nonverbal communication. In nearly each chapter thereafter, we discuss types of business communication with a constant focus on understanding and relating to the needs of others (empathy).

## Active Listening

**LO2.5** Explain and evaluate the process of active listening.

**Visit** http://connect. mheducation.com for an exercise on this topic.

Dozens of studies have shown that listening is ranked among the most important communication skills.[29] For example, 7,674 business school alumni who graduated between 2000 and 2010 were asked to rank the most important communication skills for success in the business world (see Table 2.5). They ranked listening skills second, only slightly behind the broad ability to work with others. They valued listening skills more highly than presentation skills, writing skills, and a dozen or so other types of communication skills.[30]

Listening requires hard work. And it requires more than simply hearing. It requires one's full attention and all senses. In fact, great listeners respond physically to others. Research indicates that brain activity in excellent listeners mimics that of the speakers. In some cases, the listener's brain shows activity before that of the speaker. In other words, the best listeners anticipate how a speaker thinks and feels.[31]

In recent years, management and communication scholars have increasingly emphasized this notion with the term **active listening**. Michael Hoppe of the Center for Creative Leadership has defined active listening as "a person's willingness and ability to hear and understand. At its core, active listening is a state of mind. . . . It involves bringing about and finding common ground, connecting to each other, and opening up new possibilities."[32] Hoppe breaks down active listening into six skills: (1) paying attention, (2) holding judgment, (3) reflecting, (4) clarifying, (5) summarizing, and (6) sharing.

**Paying Attention**   This first step involves devoting your whole attention to others and allowing them enough comfort and time to express themselves completely. As others speak to you, try to understand everything they say from *their* perspective. Michael Mathieu, CEO of the video advertising company YuMe, recently recommended that business managers pay better attention to those with whom they interact:

> Be connected, and have conversations with people. Don't be distracted, and the little nuances of life will show up, and you will hear things. I'm not immune. I have to do a lot of

**TABLE 2.5**

## Most Important Communication Skills

### According to Recent Business Graduates (2000–2010)

| Skills | Percentage |
|---|---|
| 1.  Ability to work with others | 93 |
| **2.  Listening skills** | **90** |
| 3.  Ability to influence others | 89 |
| 4.  Diplomacy and tact | 87 |
| 5.  Managing expectations | 80 |
| 6.  Leadership skills | 78 |
| 7.  Presentation skills | 74 |
| 8.  Networking skills | 70 |
| 9.  Writing skills | 69 |
| 10.  Meeting management | 68 |
| 11.  Ability to give constructive feedback | 65 |
| 12.  Managing organizational politics | 65 |
| 13.  Negotiation skills | 65 |
| 14.  Cross-cultural sensitivity | 52 |
| 15.  Mentoring skills | 45 |

*Source:* Alumni Perspectives Survey, 2009–2010.
*Note:* Percentage of employees who rated skill extremely or very important to their current job.

things, and I try to slow down sometimes. I try to be present so I can enjoy the richness and quality of interactions with people. Most people can't multitask without losing something in each of those tasks.[33]

Paying attention requires active nonverbal communication. Your body language, including appropriate eye contact, should show you are eager to understand the other person. Lean forward. Keep an open body position. Sit up straight. Nod to show you are listening. Smile as appropriate. Pay attention to the speaker's nonverbal behaviors. Avoid any distractions, such as taking calls or checking your phone. Become comfortable with silence. To hear people out inevitably requires a few breaks in the flow of the conversation.[34] In the next section, "Sight-Reading Nonverbal Communication and Building Rapport," you will focus more on your ability to recognize the nonverbal communication of others.

**Holding Judgment**   People will share their ideas and feelings with you only if they feel safe. Holding judgment is particularly important in tense and emotionally charged situations. One of the best ways to make others feel comfortable expressing themselves fully is to demonstrate a learner mind-set rather than a judger mind-set.

In a **learner mind-set**, you show eagerness to hear others' ideas and perspectives and listen with an open mind. You do not have your mind made up before listening fully. When you disagree, you stay open to the possibility of finding common ground and mutually beneficial solutions. Under the learner mind-set, difference of opinion is considered normal, even healthy, and potentially solution-producing.[35]

In a **judger mind-set**, people have their minds made up before listening carefully to others' ideas, perspective, and experiences. Judgers view disagreement rigidly, with little possibility of finding common ground unless the other person changes his or her views. Judging often involves punishing others for disagreement. At its extreme, the judger mind-set involves ascribing negative traits to others and labeling them in undesirable terms. For example, judgers often enter conversations with thoughts such as "she's not creative" or "he's unreliable." Not surprisingly, the judger mind-set stifles conversation.[36]

Holding judgment does not mean that you agree with everything you hear. It also does not mean you avoid critiquing the ideas of others. Rather, it's a commitment to hearing the entire version of others' ideas and experiences. It's a commitment to listen fully before reacting. And, it's a mind-set of rewarding others for opening up, especially when you disagree with them. Niki Leondakis, chief operating officer of the Kimpton Hotels, explained how she moved away from a judger mind-set to a learner mind-set over the course of her career:

> When I was a younger manager, my anxiety about what wasn't right drove me to confront things quickly. The faster I confronted it, the more quickly it could get fixed . . . and while that's a good thing, the manner in which I did it frequently left people feeling defensive. So by listening first and trying to understand how we got here and their story, I think it allows them to then hear my point of view. And then we can move into solutions. When people feel judged right out of the gate, it's hard for them to open up and listen and improve.[37]

You can create an environment in which others open up and you can listen more effectively with **learner statements**, which show your commitment to hearing people out. In effective learner statements, you explicitly state your desire to hear differing opinions with statements such as "I have a different perspective, so I want to understand how you see this." By contrast, people who make **judger statements**, which show they are closed off to hearing people out, shut down honest conversations.[38]

Recall Jeff Brody, the personnel director from the opening case. He is hoping to transition from annual performance reviews to continuous performance reviews. Throughout this section on listening, you will see parts of a conversation between Jeff

| Active-Listening Components |
| :--- |
| • Paying attention |
| • Holding judgment |
| • Reflecting |
| • Clarifying |
| • Summarizing |
| • Sharing |

**TABLE 2.6**

## Judger Statements versus Learner Statements

| Judger Statements | Learner Statements |
|---|---|
| *Lisa:* You're basing your conclusions on just a few people you've talked to. Why aren't you concerned about finding out more about the costs? | *Lisa:* I don't know much about continuous feedback systems. What have you learned from the people you've talked to? |
| This statement implies Jeff is not concerned about costs and isn't open to learning more. This will likely lead to defensiveness. | This statement is neutral and shows a desire to learn about Jeff's experiences and thoughts. This positions Lisa well to ask tough questions later on in a constructive manner. |
| *Jeff:* I spend a lot of time talking to HR directors and know which ones are best at helping their employees stay engaged and productive. Don't you think HR professionals would know more about this than people with a finance background? | *Jeff:* I've learned several things from HR directors about continuous feedback systems. . . . I need to learn more about the financial implications. Based on what I've told you, what are your thoughts about the cost-effectiveness? |
| This statement begins with an *I'm right, you're wrong* message. It directly calls into question the competence of the listener. Many listeners would become defensive. | This statement reflects a learning stance and shows a cooperative approach moving forward. |

and Lisa Johnson, the finance manager. Lisa is skeptical that continuous performance reviews are cost-effective and practical. Notice the distinctions between judger statements and learner statements in this conversation in Table 2.6.

**Reflecting** Active listening requires that you reflect on the ideas and emotions of others. To make sure you really understand others, you should frequently paraphrase what you're hearing. As Table 2.7 shows, good reflecting statements begin with phrases such as "It sounds like you think . . ."; "So, you're not happy with . . ."; or "Let me make sure I understand. . . ."[39]

**Clarifying** Clarifying involves making sure you have a clear understanding of what others mean. It includes double-checking that you understand the perspectives of

**TABLE 2.7**

## Reflecting Statements

| Types of Effective Reflecting Statements | Example |
|---|---|
| It sounds to me like . . . | *Lisa:* It sounds to me like you think we should replace annual performance reviews with continuous performance reviews because continuous reviews improve employee performance and morale. |
| So, you're not happy with . . . | *Jeff:* So, you're not happy with this transition unless we carefully evaluate all of the costs, is that right? |
| Is it fair to say that you think . . . | *Lisa:* Is it fair to say that you think we should make this change even if we don't know all the costs? |
| Let me make sure I understand . . . | *Jeff:* Let me make sure I understand your view. Are you saying that we can understand the costs better by . . . ? |

**TABLE 2.8**

Clarifying Statements

| Types of Effective Clarifying Statements | Example |
|---|---|
| What are your thoughts on . . . ? | *Lisa:* What are your thoughts on considering other ways of conducting annual reviews more effectively? |
| Could you repeat that? | *Jeff:* Could you repeat what you just said about evaluating the costs of continuous reviews? |
| I'm not sure I understand . . . | *Lisa:* I'm not sure I understand why the problems with our current annual review process mean that we should move away from annual reviews. Do you know of companies that are using annual reviews more effectively than we are? |
| Could you explain how . . . ? | *Jeff:* Could you explain how you would calculate the costs of a continuous review system? |
| What might be your role in . . . ? | *Lisa:* What roles will Steve and Lisa have in helping us understand what employees think of the current review process? |

others *and* asking them to elaborate and qualify their thoughts. It is more than simply paraphrasing. It involves trying to connect the thoughts of others so you can better understand how they are making conclusions. As Table 2.8 shows, good clarifying questions are open-ended and start with learner-oriented phrases such as, "What are your thoughts on . . . ?" or "Could you explain how. . . ?"[40]

**Summarizing**   The goal of summarizing is to restate major themes so that you can make sense of the *big issues* from the perspective of the other person. Ideally, you can show that you understand the major direction of the conversation. You can summarize with statements that begin with phrases such as "So, your main concern is . . ." or "It sounds like your key points are . . . ," as shown in Table 2.9.[41]

**Sharing**   Active listening also involves expressing your own perspectives and feelings. If you do not share your own ideas completely, your colleagues do not know

**TABLE 2.9**

Summarizing Statements

| Types of Effective Summarizing Statements | Example |
|---|---|
| So, your main concern is . . . | *Jeff:* So, your two main concerns are that moving to a continuous review process will be costly and impractical. The software and time needed in the process will cost far more than what we invest in an annual review process. Also, it may be difficult to get all employees to participate often in this process. Is that right? |
| It sounds like your key points are . . . | *Lisa:* It sounds like you have a few key points. Continuous feedback systems improve morale and performance at each of the companies you've learned about. Also, your contacts at these companies think evaluating the costs of the software is easy, but evaluating the costs of time invested by employees is not possible. Is that correct? |

what you really think. This is not fair to them or to you. It is even arguably dishonest. Michael Hoppe of the Center for Creative Leadership explains:

> Being an active listener doesn't mean being a sponge, passively soaking up the information coming your way. You are an active party to the conversation with your own thoughts and feelings. Yet active listening is first about understanding the other person, then about being understood.[42]

As a related point, business leaders often use the term *silence is agreement*. In other words, many organizational cultures expect all employees to state their ideas. If they don't say anything, they are presumed to agree. Because it can be so challenging to give others enough comfort and space to express themselves fully, some listeners avoid talking and inadvertently send signals that they agree. One key to active listening is allowing others to open up completely with their work-related ideas and then also to foster dialogue, which includes providing your respectful views.

## Recognizing Barriers to Effective Listening

Active listening is not easy, especially in certain corporate cultures and in the face of time constraints.[43] As you read about the following barriers to listening, consider which are most challenging to you.

**Lack of Time**   Not surprisingly, pressing deadlines give most managers the sense that they do not have time for listening. Furthermore, when talking to others, managers are often preoccupied with thoughts of other projects. In other words, managers may feel overwhelmed with internal noise. However, the best managers understand that listening pays strong dividends over time and that they need to schedule time for listening to others each day.

**Lack of Patience and Attention Span**   Some people simply do not have long attention spans or for other reasons feel impatient. Patience and attention span can be improved with conscious, consistent effort. Highly self-aware communicators frequently ask themselves questions such as the following: *Did I allow others enough time to express themselves? In which situations or with which people (triggers) do I feel most impatient? What strategies help me focus my attention when I'm feeling impatient?*

**Image of Leadership**   Some executives and managers think that listening too much shows indecisiveness and thus threatens their authority. To preserve a command-and-control approach to leading, they speak more and listen less. This view of listening is rarely effective, especially in today's increasingly flat organizations. Yet, the image of strong leaders who do most of the talking is difficult to overcome for some business professionals.

**Communication Technology**   Technology continues to create new and better opportunities for people to communicate with one another. However, most communication technologies make listening more difficult due to fewer and less rich visual and nonverbal cues. Typically, using communication tools such as mobile phones and email can facilitate a listening-centered approach to communication, supplemented with significant face-to-face, rich communication. On the other hand, relying too heavily on communication technology can reduce effective listening.

**Fear of Bad News or Uncomfortable Information**   Once bad news and other forms of unpleasant information are out in the open, managers are generally responsible for creating solutions and responding to the morale needs of fellow employees. Listening fully to the feedback, concerns, and perspectives of colleagues and clients can make work more complicated. Astute business executives and managers recognize that they *need* information—even bad or unpleasant news—to lead an organization to its best potential performance. Conversely, when you do not listen, you may inadvertently encourage others to cover mistakes and weaknesses that harm the organization.[44]

In addition to barriers that prevent listening from occurring in the first place, other behaviors can disrupt a conversation and prevent real learning. **Nonlistening behaviors** are those actions that prematurely deflect attention from speakers or prevent them from completely expressing their ideas and feelings. Such behaviors may display lack of caring and signal that the conversation is not equitable and reciprocal. Some common nonlistening behaviors in the workplace are defending, "me too" statements, giving advice, and judging.[45]

**Defending**  Instinctively, all of us engage in self-protective behaviors. Often, the comments of others in the workplace call into question our credibility, including our performance, competence, concern for others, or even ability to honor our commitments. When we feel threatened, we often become defensive. In other words, we are emotionally hijacked. Defensive comments end listening for several reasons. First, others often perceive them as threats or escalations. Thus, they may lead to self-protectiveness from all parties involved in a conversation and reduce trust and goodwill. These cycles of escalation close conversations off from complete and honest exchange of information. In some cases, people even attack others in an effort to protect themselves. Second, they shift attention away from the speaker to the listener—meaning the person who has made the defensive comment. This premature shift in focus is a *me-centered* maneuver that disrupts the listening process.

Figure 2.4 displays defensive and nondefensive replies to a potentially upsetting comment. Avoiding defensiveness requires a high level of self-awareness and self-management. It requires understanding the triggers that make you feel threatened in a professional environment. It also requires understanding how to manage these emotions so that you can maintain your roles as an active listener and a problem solver.

**"Me Too" Statements**  As you listen to other people share their ideas and experiences—their stories—you often think about similar ideas and experiences of your own—your stories. This often leads to "me too" comments. We take the other

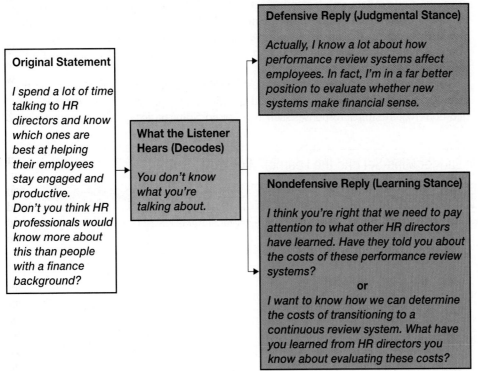

**FIGURE 2.4**

Defensive and Nondefensive Replies

**Original Statement**

*I spend a lot of time talking to HR directors and know which ones are best at helping their employees stay engaged and productive.*
*Don't you think HR professionals would know more about this than people with a finance background?*

**What the Listener Hears (Decodes)**

*You don't know what you're talking about.*

**Defensive Reply (Judgmental Stance)**

*Actually, I know a lot about how performance review systems affect employees. In fact, I'm in a far better position to evaluate whether new systems make financial sense.*

**Nondefensive Reply (Learning Stance)**

*I think you're right that we need to pay attention to what other HR directors have learned. Have they told you about the costs of these performance review systems?*
**or**
*I want to know how we can determine the costs of transitioning to a continuous review system. What have you learned from HR directors you know about evaluating these costs?*

person's story and respond with our story, in an effort to empathize and share. Sometimes, however, this shifts attention away from their story to your story. To listen effectively, be careful about prematurely drawing attention away from the stories of others.

**Giving Advice**   In leadership roles, your job is often to tell others what to do and how to do it. Also, many of your bosses and colleagues will give you advice. Giving advice to others in a competitive work environment is inevitable and often desirable. However, during conversations, premature or heavy-handed advice can abruptly end dialogue and result in resistance. When you provide advice too soon, you give the impression of wanting to end the conversation. When you provide excessive advice, you challenge the autonomy and decision making of others and make them feel *micromanaged*. To avoid giving advice that cuts off listening, give others enough time to fully explain themselves. Once you talk about options and solutions, make sure that it is a "we" conversation rather than just your ideas for what others should do.

**LO2.6** Describe and demonstrate effective questions for enhancing listening and learning.

**Judging**   Judging is one of the worst nonlistening behaviors. It not only ends listening for the current conversation but often leaves lingering animosity. Once people have displayed a judger mind-set, others may be unwilling to open up to them in the future. People who feel that their leaders are judgers might say, "He's really not interested in what I have to say," or "She's already made up her mind."[46]

## Asking the Right Questions

Listening involves a cluster of communication skills. A crucial one is the ability to ask the right questions. In a recent survey of 2,181 accountants, the most sought-after interpersonal skill was *listening,* ranked 4.51 on a scale from 1 (not important) to 5 (essential). Following *listening* were closely related skills: *asks appropriate questions when talking with customers* (4.22) and *asks appropriate questions when talking with supervisors* (3.97). Next on the list of 14 skills was a cluster of presentation skills, such as *organizes presentations effectively* (3.86), *establishes rapport with audience* (3.59), and *maintains eye contact* (3.58). In other words, the ability to ask questions was valued more highly than presentation skills.[47]

On the most fundamental level, good questions reflect the learner mind-set, and poor questions reflect a judger mind-set. The ability to ask good questions creates a culture of learning. Good questions are not good in and of themselves, however. Unless you truly listen to the answers and even encourage other perspectives and dissent, you may not achieve learning. Notice examples of questions in Table 2.10 that reflect judger and learner mind-sets.[48]

To ask questions that facilitate the most learning, frame and structure your questions carefully. Generally speaking, most good questions are open-ended. In contrast, closed questions require simple responses such as *yes* or *no*. Some basic types of learning-centered

**TABLE 2.10**

Questions That Reflect the Judger Mind-Set and the Learner Mind-Set

| Judger Mind-Set | Learner Mind-Set |
|---|---|
| How come this doesn't work? | How is this useful or beneficial? |
| Who is responsible for this mess? | What can we do about this? |
| Why can't you get it right? | Going forward, what can we learn from this? |
| Can't you try a better approach? | What are you trying to accomplish? |
| Why don't you focus on helping customers? | How will customers react? |
| Are you sure this approach will really meet your goals and objectives? | How well does this approach meet your goals and objectives? |

**TABLE 2.11**

## Types of Effective Questions

| Types of Questions | Examples |
| --- | --- |
| Rapport-building | How was your trip to the human resources conference? <br> What did you learn about at the last Chamber of Commerce event? <br><br> These questions, when asked sincerely, provide an opportunity for asker and listener to bond through understanding one another. They also break the ice for a substantive conversation about the business issues at hand. |
| Funnel | So, how do you think we should go about researching what our employees think about performance reviews? → How do you think we can capture the employees' perspectives about continuous review systems? → What types of survey questions will help us understand their thoughts about continuous review systems? → Could you give me a word-by-word example of how you'd capture that in a survey question? <br><br> These questions progressively break down a problem into manageable pieces, starting with a large, open-ended question and moving to increasingly specific and tactical questions. Once broken into smaller pieces, the asker and listener are more likely to achieve shared meaning and move toward finding solutions. |
| Probing | How often do you receive complaints about the annual performance review process? What concerns do supervisors have? What ideas do employees have for making the review process fairer? Do you ever hear supervisors or employees talk about how to make the process more goal-oriented? Other than the frequency of reviews, what are some other explanations for why employees make these complaints? <br><br> These iterations of questions about the causes, consequences, and scope of group guest complaints attempt to look at the problem from every angle. This approach is effective at identifying root causes and best solutions. |
| Solution-oriented | How can we find out which software vendors offer the most attractive performance review features? What are your ideas for ensuring that employees provide continuous feedback to one another? What are some best practices in making performance reviews candid and honest yet also rewarding and productive? <br><br> These questions form the basis for identifying options about how to move forward. Ideally, solution-oriented questions are open, we-oriented, and offer help to others. |

questions include rapport-building questions, funnel questions, probing questions, and solution-oriented questions. See Table 2.11 for examples of each type of question.[49]

**Rapport-building questions** are intended to create bonds between people. They can break the ice and gradually ease people into conversations about shared business interests. They tend to be casual and social and steer clear of divisive or offensive topics. Questions about current work projects, interests, and experiences are generally appropriate. As you will notice in the team communication section in the next chapter, however, time devoted to building rapport should be limited. Too much time spent on this purpose can be counterproductive.

**Funnel questions** move from general to specific. They are intended to increasingly deconstruct a business issue so that a team can tackle or approach it in pieces. This approach involves starting with broad and open questions and moving to more specific and closed ones.

**Probing questions** are intended to analyze a business problem from every angle to uncover its root causes. Such questions can ensure that no explanation is overlooked, thus leading to a reliable understanding. The classic, institutionalized example of probing questions is the *Five Whys* approach at Toyota, in which employees were encouraged to ask at least five iterations of questions to understand manufacturing quality issues. Ultimately, this approach led to world-class quality standards that businesses around the world have studied.

**TABLE 2.12**

Types of Counterproductive Questions

| Types of Questions | Examples |
|---|---|
| Leading | Wouldn't you agree that employee engagement and productivity should be our priorities? I'm sure you think it's a good idea to keep costs under control, right? |
| | These questions are meant to lead the listener to agree with or adopt the perspective of the asker. Many listeners will resent feeling pressured into the views of others. Also, this approach will not lead to a learning conversation. |
| Disguised statements | Why do you insist on focusing on costs instead of benefits? Don't you think you're jumping to conclusions by paying attention to the opinions of only a few of your close contacts? |
| | These are not real questions. They are statements that say you are close-minded on this issue. This flaw-finding approach will cause many listeners to become defensive and/or avoid sharing their real thoughts. Many listeners will view disguised statements as underhanded and manipulative because they are often attempts to get the listeners to acknowledge their own faults. |
| Cross-examination | Just now, you said annual reviews don't work because they don't happen often enough. Yet, last week, you said the real reason our annual reviews fail is not because of how often they occur but because they don't involve setting goals. So, what's the real reason annual reviews don't work? |
| | This cross-examination question will put most listeners on the defensive. It may score points for the asker, but it will move the conversation away from learning and toward a battle of messages. |

**Solution-oriented questions** focus on how to overcome business problems. They focus on what *should* be done to accomplish business objectives. Solution-oriented questions are among the most difficult ones in which to maintain a learner mind-set. Nearly all of us have strong preconceptions about what *should* be done. Staying flexible and open to mutually developed solutions begins with open, solution-oriented questions.

## Avoiding the Wrong Questions

Not all questions are good ones. Most poor questions fall into the category of the judgmental mind-set and can actually lead to less listening. Poor questions include leading questions, disguised statements, and cross-examination questions. Table 2.12 provides examples.

**Leading questions** are intended to guide people to your way of thinking. These questions are often perceived as dishonest or manipulative. Business professionals are notorious for asking leading questions in sales. In fact, some sales training programs even recommend using leading questions to build desire for products and services. However, recent research indicates that even for sales, the best questions are open ones that focus on learning customers' real wants and needs.[50]

**Disguised statements** are opinions presented in question form. Disguised statements almost always end a learning conversation when they are used to point out flaws.

**Cross-examination questions** are intended to find contradictions in what others have said or done. Like disguised statements, they can abruptly end learning conversations when they repeatedly call into question the credibility of others.

## Avoiding the Traps of Empathy

In Chapter 1, you learned about the distinction between *givers* and *takers*. Givers frequently help others out in the workplace, whereas takers often accept help but infrequently reciprocate. The highest performers are most often givers. Yet, the weakest performers are also most often givers. In other words, some givers manage their generosity in a way that improves their own performance and those around them while other givers help others at the expense of their individual performance.

Givers are generally motivated by empathy. They perform best when they address three potential barriers to performance associated with empathy: *timidity, availability,* and *emotional concern for others.* Givers are often timid or less assertive about asking for help because they don't want to impose on others. By learning to frame their own requests as acts on the behalf of others, givers can be more assertive with their requests. Many givers make themselves available to all requests, often at the expense of getting their own work done. Givers should learn to set boundaries on when and what they choose to help others with. Due to a strong emotional concern for others, givers often say "yes" to takers. Givers can avoid being manipulated by takers by spending more time analyzing the needs of all parties involved. By staying self-aware about your natural impulses for timidity, availability, and/or emotional concern for others, you can manage your empathy in a way that most helps others *and* yourself. [51]

## Sight-Reading Nonverbal Communication and Building Rapport

By various estimates, nonverbal communication accounts for 60 to 80 percent of meaning in various face-to-face business situations, including in conversations, meetings, and negotiations.[52] Gestures, expressions, tone, and other nonverbal signals convey seriousness or sarcasm, enthusiasm or disinterest, caring or lack of concern, attentiveness or boredom, and many other messages. Compared to verbal communication, however, the meaning of nonverbal communication is less precise. It is almost entirely understood on a subconscious level and developed instinctively. Rarely, if ever, do people consciously attempt to improve their ability to understand the nonverbal communication of others.

**LO2.7** Explain strategies to sight-read the nonverbal communication of others.

Among the foremost authorities on nonverbal communication in the workplace is David Givens of the Center for Nonverbal Studies. He has spent decades examining nonverbal behavior in the workplace. He has observed, "Perhaps even more than written memos, text messages, and e-mail, nonverbal signs have the power to inspire or intimidate, to arouse sympathy, allegiance, anger, or fear."[53] He further explains that people can learn **sight-reading**, which he defines as "intelligent observation [of nonverbal communications] . . . it is the act of anticipating intentions and moods through the perceptive examination of nonverbal cues."[54]

Throughout this section, we focus on meaning that can be conveyed through various nonverbal signals. As you read through this section, focus on how you can listen to others better in two ways: (1) by understanding the meanings of others' nonverbal signals and (2) by helping others feel more comfortable sharing their perspectives and feelings with you because of the welcoming nonverbal signals that you send to them.

**Learning to Sight-Read**   Research clearly shows that people are not good at masking their feelings—nearly all people reveal their real emotions through nonverbal behavior. However, research also shows that most people are not consistently effective at decoding the nonverbal signals of others. In other words, nonverbal signals are always present and important in face-to-face communications, but few people can reliably interpret them.[55]

Recently, Malcom Gladwell, in his book *Blink: The Power of Thinking without Thinking*, revealed much of the research about how expert sight-readers can quickly understand the impacts of nonverbal communication. For example, in a study of physicians and patients, researchers videotaped hundreds of interactions. They found that with just 40-second video clips, they could reliably predict whether doctors got sued simply by the intonation and pitch of the doctors' voices. Whether the doctors made mistakes or what they said was not predictive of who got sued. Rather, how the doctors spoke to the patients did impact who got sued. Those doctors whose voice displayed dominance, hostility, and indifference got sued.[56]

Generally, you should pay close attention to nonverbal signals and attempt to decode their meanings. Yet, always make sure to suspend a certain level of judgment and avoid rigid conclusions. Consider the following guidelines as you develop your sight-reading:[57]

- *Consciously practice each day.* Consider taking 15 minutes each day to watch people's nonverbal behaviors. Learn to understand the meaning of various nonverbal signals from those you interact with frequently.
- *Pay attention to congruence.* Nonverbal messages are most important when they are not congruent, or consistent, with verbal messages. Listeners instinctively place more value on nonverbal messages when nonverbal messages are incongruent with verbal messages.
- *Sight-read in clusters, not in isolation.* You can easily misinterpret nonverbal signals if you are simply looking at single behaviors. For example, arms crossed on the chest, crossing legs, clenching fists, and pointing fingers are signs of defensiveness. However, in isolation, these signals may have other meanings. Arms crossed on the chest may mean someone is cold or crossing legs may be nothing more than a comfortable sitting position. Taken together, various nonverbal signals help you more reliably decode the message.
- *Sight-read in context.* Use the situation at hand to help understand nonverbal signals. Pointing fingers during an argument likely indicates blaming, whereas pointing fingers at others during a sales presentation more than likely indicates a desire to get input from others.

**Paying Attention to Nonverbal Cues**  Sight-reading is the process of decoding the nonverbal signals that others send as you communicate with them. To engage in active listening and dialogue, it's also important for you to send the right nonverbal signals. Ideally, you can send nonverbal signals that show sincerity, interest, affirmation, and other traits that show your esteem and respect for others.

One key to effective nonverbal communication to make others more comfortable talking to you is to synchronize your body language with theirs. **Synchronizing** body language involves adopting some of your counterpart's body language to make the conversation more natural for them and to show empathy to them. You'll often find that others are more expressive nonverbally than you are. In these cases, you may need to be more expressive than usual to match your counterpart's preferred communication style. Or, you may find that they are less expressive nonverbally. In these cases, you may want to tone down your nonverbal communication. In any case, keeping your body language in sync with others creates a more natural conversation for you and your conversation partners. The primary goal of synchronizing is to not overwhelm or underwhelm others with your nonverbal language.[58]

© Rob Daly/AGE Fotostock

As you synchronize, attempt to convey emotions appropriate to the conversation. For most business situations, you should try to express positive or neutral emotions. In some situations, you may express sad or disappointing expressions to show empathy for the setbacks others have experienced. Keep in mind that people naturally mimic one another's emotions and that the emotions you express can impact others. For example, researchers have shown that people who view a smiling face often mimic that mood with changes in their own facial muscles. Conversely, when people view angry faces, they often reflect that mood with slight changes in their own facial muscles that exhibit some signs of anger. Dr. Daniel Goleman calls this natural synchronizing of nonverbal signals the *coordination of moods.* He further stated, "Coordination of moods is the essence of rapport."[59]

In the remainder of this section, we will focus on the nonverbal signals sent by various body parts and actions. As you read these sections, think about the related nonverbal signals that you send or how you could try to understand others better by looking for certain types of body language.

**Eyes** Among the most influential body parts in sending nonverbal signals are the eyes. Eyes can reveal a lot about the feelings of others. This is one reason many of the best poker players wear sunglasses, aware that they may involuntarily send signals about the strength of their poker hands as well as their intentions.

Typically, people who achieve eye contact build emotional connections to one another. They are more likely to build rapport and empathy. In most situations, the more eye contact, the better. Of course, intense stares and deep gazes can make others uncomfortable. So, you should be aware of what others would consider visual intrusiveness. Most people are far better at resolving differences when making eye contact during face-to-face conversations.[60]

The eyes make many involuntary movements that are associated with various feelings. For example, large, dilated pupils show emotional excitement. By contrast, small, constricted pupils show little emotional engagement. Thus, dilated pupils can show interest and approval, whereas constricted pupils can show disinterest and boredom. Of course, extremely dilated pupils are not necessarily positive—they can also indicate extreme emotions such as anger.[61]

Another involuntary eye movement is CLEM (conjugate lateral eye movement). **CLEM** is a rapid sideward shift of the eye. It shows that a person is giving your ideas careful consideration and is thus generally positive. It indicates processing and reflection. Whereas CLEM is a rapid sideways movement of the eyes, longer sideways glances are often associated with discomfort. Your ability to distinguish between the rapid sideways glances (CLEM) and longer sideways glances can provide insight into how engaged and comfortable other people are with your ideas.[62]

You can often notice discomfort in others by observing their blinking rates. The average blinking rate is around 20 blinks per minute. Faster-than-normal blinking often indicates emotional distress. Thus, you may be able to observe the comfort level of others based on how much eye contact they give to you or others. Avoiding eye contact sometimes indicates insecurity, nervousness, and even deception. Closely related, squinting slightly is often associated with skepticism and suspicion.[63]

You should generally avoid using your eyes to show disapproval, especially when your goal is to hear people out. When people abruptly look away to indicate disapproval or disinterest, this sends a message of strong displeasure with others and their ideas. This action, called **visual cutoff**, can quickly end dialogue, especially when a superior visually cuts off subordinates. Visual cutoff is especially harsh when accompanied with sideways head movements and sighs. Similarly, intense glares to show displeasure with others and their ideas can be intimidating.[64]

As you sight-read the eyes of others, make sure to do so flexibly. Be particularly careful about judging the truthfulness of what others say based solely on the eyes. A frequently perpetuated myth is that liars can't look you straight in the eye. In actuality, pathological liars can look people in the eyes and lie. There are also other explanations, including nervousness, personality, and cultural differences.[65]

© Image Source/Getty Images

**Smiles and Nods** Generally, you should attempt to be lively, smile a lot, and look interested. As you nod to show interest and sometimes agreement, you signal that you are interested and welcome the thoughts of others.[66] Sincere, genuine smiles are an excellent way to help others trust your intentions. Research has shown that positive emotional expressions such as smiles cause customers to have more positive feelings about transactions, be more satisfied with the products and services, and even feel more loyal to companies.[67] However, unless smiles are genuine and sincere, they may not generate goodwill. Smiles can convey many meanings, including sarcasm and mocking. They can also be displayed in moments of fear, embarrassment, and forced compliance.[68]

**Hands and Arms** Among the most symbolic shows of friendship, camaraderie, shared purpose, openness, hospitality, and greeting in the business world is the handshake. In introductions, handshakes can create emotional connections between people and help people build rapport quickly. Typically, handshakes should last for two to three seconds. Make the handshake firm but avoid bone-crushing or limp handshakes.

© Caia Images/Glow Images

Make sure that as you shake hands, you have eye contact to strengthen the emotional bond you build through handshakes.

As you shake hands, remember that holding your hand straight up and down is a show of equality. Handshakes can show dominance when the palm faces down. One study of 350 business executives found that 88 percent of male executives attempted the dominant position (compared to 31 percent of women executives). Attempt to use the handshake as a show of respect and equality to others.[69]

Hands and arms can be used as gestures to create an open and inviting atmosphere for discussion in a variety of ways. Extended and opened palms send the same positive and inviting messages as handshakes. Also, open and extended hands reduce the physical distance between people, thus increasing emotional connection. As nonverbal communication expert David Givens stated, "In business those who reach out with hands have an advantage over those who keep hands to themselves, concealed in pockets, folded in laps, or hiding beneath desks."[70]

Hands and arms sometimes contribute to an unwelcome and unfriendly atmosphere for dialogue. Typically, palms-down gestures are less inviting to others. Table pounding is an extreme version of a palms-down gesture that is used for emphasis. It emphasizes speaking points and shows confidence and conviction. However, when done too frequently, it can make others uncomfortable and less open about their true thoughts and feelings. One of the most serious gestures is the halt hand, which involves holding the palm straight up toward others. It sends a strong message of *stop*. Withholding hand gestures, especially for people who typically use them, may suggest deceit.[71]

Hands often signal discomfort or nervousness. Placing the hands behind the head often shows uncertainty or conflicted feelings. Most self-touching gestures (i.e., playing with hair, touching the face, biting nails, rubbing or pinching skin) are displays of anxiety, confusion, or uncertainty. These self-touching gestures comfort the body as it copes with fight-or-flight impulses. Other self-touching gestures such as holding or hugging oneself are signs of deeper distress.[72]

Hands may also communicate defensiveness. Hands in pockets, fistlike gestures, pointing fingers, and other fidgeting often are part of strong self-protective urges. Placing the hands on the hips with elbows pointing away from the body is often a show of extreme defensiveness, even aggressiveness. Kids generally know they're in trouble when they see their parents do this. This nonverbal display is usually associated with annoyance, disagreement, or anger. In some cases, it is perceived positively in the workplace. For example, it may display an eagerness to move forward on a project. However, since this stance is so often perceived negatively, be careful about placing your hands on your hips because of the way others may decode your messages.[73]

Interestingly, research has shown that how well hands are groomed impacts how accurately others decode nonverbal signals. Research in board meetings has shown that executives are less able to correctly interpret gestures of meeting participants when they have "physically distressed" hands, which includes scars, dryness, dry cuticles, unkempt nails, roughness, or dirtiness. In other words, well-groomed hands allow people to better understand gestures, whereas poorly groomed hands hinder others' ability to correctly interpret your nonverbal signals.[74]

**Touch** Touching others, including with handshakes, can create an instant bond and establish rapport. It can build loyalty between strangers and even increase honest exchange of information. Touch has been explored extensively in customer service interaction. For example, one such study showed that waiters and waitresses who touch customers on the hand or elbow receive between 22 and 36 percent more in tips. Another recent experiment examined how touch impacts truthfulness. In the study, money was purposefully left in a public location. When people found the money, the researchers, acting like strangers, approached the people to ask if they'd seen any money. Without any physical touch in these interactions, people who found the money admitted to having found the money and returned it 23 percent of the time. When the researchers touched the people on the arm for a few seconds while asking, people who found the money returned the money 68 percent of the time. Of course, in this same experiment, touching for more than three seconds resulted in a more negative reaction.[75] North American culture is typically considered a nontouch culture compared to other cultures around the world. However, even in this nontouch environment, it makes sense to use brief touch such as handshakes to make connections with others.[76]

# RELATIONSHIP MANAGEMENT

**Relationship management** is the "ability to use your awareness of emotions and those of others to manage interactions successfully."[77] In this chapter we introduce the following principles for managing relationships effectively: adapting communication to the preferred styles of others and ensuring civility in the workplace. In each subsequent chapter, we discuss many ways of expressing your ideas to manage your work relationships effectively.

## Adapting Communication to the Preferred Styles of Others

People have many preferences for communicating. You can benefit from constantly learning about the many ways people differ in preferences. In this section, you will learn about just a few aspects of personality—motivational values and level of extroversion-introversion—that impact communication preferences in the workplace. While there are many other ways of examining differences in communication styles, understanding motivational values and level of extroversion-introversion can dramatically improve your ability to recognize the communication preferences of others and adapt accordingly.

**LO2.8** Identify common communication preferences based on motivational values.

**connect**

Visit **connect.mheducation. com** for an exercise on this topic.

Differences in Communication Preferences Based on Motivational Values   Many communication styles can be traced to motives and values. Relationship Awareness Theory[78] explains how professionals often act and communicate differently from one another based on a fairly constant set of motives and values. People have a blend of three primary motives: nurturing (identified as *blue* in this model), directing (identified as *red*), and autonomizing (identified as *green*). A person's **motivational value system (MVS)** is a blend of these primary motives and refers to the frequency with which these values guide their actions. (These MVSs can be depicted on a triangle. For example, see Figure 3.4 in Chapter 3.)

Professionals with a **blue MVS** are most often guided by motives to protect others, help others grow, and act in the best interests of others. About 30 percent of business managers are strongly aligned with blue motivations. Professionals with a **red MVS** are most often guided by concerns about organizing people, time, money, and other resources to accomplish results. About 46 percent of business managers are strongly aligned with red motivations. Professionals with a **green MVS** are most often concerned about making sure business activities have been thought out carefully and that the right processes are put into place to accomplish things. About 16 percent of business managers are strongly aligned with green motivations. **Hubs** are professionals who are guided almost equally by all three of these MVSs. Among business professionals, roughly 43 percent are hubs.[79]

An important premise of Relationship Awareness Theory is that each of the primary values—nurturing, directing, and autonomizing—can be expressed by strengths. People gain a sense of self-worth by acting in ways consistent with their blend of values. While each person's motivational values generally lead to strengths, these strengths may be perceived by others as weaknesses when overdone or misapplied.

In Table 2.13, you can see how blues, reds, greens, and hubs differ in various ways. Take several minutes to view this table and see how people with these MVSs differ as far as what they prefer in work environments, what makes them feel satisfied and rewarded, what triggers conflict for them, and how their overdone strengths may be perceived as weaknesses. Think about which style best matches you. You might also

**TABLE 2.13**

## Motivational Value Systems

| | Blues (Altruistic and Nurturing) | Reds (Assertive and Directing) | Greens (Analytical and Autonomizing) | Hubs (Flexible and Cohering) |
|---|---|---|---|---|
| **Primary concerns** | Protection, growth, and welfare of others | Task accomplishment; use of time, money, and any other resources to achieve desired results | Assurance that things have been properly thought out; meaningful order being established; self-reliance and self-dependence | Flexibility; welfare of the group; sense of belonging in the group |
| **Preferred work environment** | Open, friendly, helpful, considerate; being needed and appreciated; ensuring others reach their potential | Fast-moving, competitive, creative, progressive, innovative, verbally stimulating; potential for personal advancement and development | Clarity, logic, precision, efficiency, organized; focus on self-reliance and effective use of resources; time to explore options | Friendly, flexible, social, fun; consensus-building; encouraging interaction |
| **People feel best when . . .** | Helping others in a way that benefits them | Providing leadership and direction to others | Pursuing their own interests without needing to rely on others | Coordinating efforts with others in a common undertaking |
| **People feel most rewarded when . . .** | Being a warm and friendly person who is deserving of appreciation for giving help | Acting with strength and ambition, achieving excellence, and leading and directing others | Working with others in a fair, clear, logical, and rational manner | Being a good team member who can be loyal, direct when necessary, and knows when to follow rules |
| **People want to avoid being perceived as . . .** | Selfish, cold, unfeeling | Gullible, indecisive, unable to act | Overly emotional, exploitive of others | Subservient to others, domineering, isolated |
| **Triggers of conflict** | When others compete and take advantage; are cold and unfriendly; are slow to recognize helpful efforts on their behalf | When others are too forgiving and don't fight back; don't provide clear expectations about rewards | When others don't take issues seriously; push their help on them; do not weigh all the facts when making a decision | When others are not willing to consider alternatives; insist on one way of doing things; restrict ability to stay flexible and open to options |
| **Overdone strengths** | *Strength* / *Overdone*<br>Trusting / Gullible<br>Devoted / Subservient<br>Caring / Submissive | *Strength* / *Overdone*<br>Confident / Arrogant<br>Persuasive / Abrasive<br>Competitive / Combative | *Strength* / *Overdone*<br>Fair / Unfeeling<br>Analytical / Nit-picking<br>Methodical / Rigid | *Strength* / *Overdone*<br>Flexible / Wishy-washy<br>Option-oriented / Indecisive<br>Tolerant / Uncaring |

*Sources:* Elias Porter, *Strength Deployment Inventory* (Carlsbad, CA: Personal Strengths Publishing, 2014); Tim Scudder and Debra LaCroix, *Working with SDI: How to Build Effective Relationships with the Strength Deployment Inventory* (Carlsbad, CA: Personal Strengths Publishing, 2013). You can learn more about this inventory at personalstrengths.com.

**TABLE 2.14**

## Words and Phrases That Resonate with Professionals of Various MVSs

| MVS | Verbs | Nouns | Modifiers | Phrases |
|-----|-------|-------|-----------|---------|
| Blues | Feel, appreciate, care, help, thank, include, support | Satisfaction, well-being, people, cooperation | Thoughtful, loyal, sincere, respectful, maybe | Serve everyone's best interests, look out for everyone |
| Reds | Compete, win, lead, challenge, dominate | Achievement, results, success, performance, goals, advantage | Challenging, rewarding, passionate, definitely, quickly | Make it happen, take charge, go for it |
| Greens | Think, analyze, evaluate, identify, organize | Process, principles, standard, schedules, accountability, details | Fair, careful, accurate, objective, correct, efficient, risky | Take our time, get it right, make sure it's fair |
| Hubs | Brainstorm, decide together, play, experiment, meet | Options, flexibility, teamwork, fun, consensus, compromise | Balanced, open, flexible, friendly, inclusive, committed | Let's work together, let's try this out |

think about which style you might clash with the most. In Table 2.14, you can see some of the words that resonate most with various MVSs. Of course, all people use these words at times. But, you will often be able to recognize others' motivational values by noting *how often* they use these and synonymous words and phrases.

In Figures 2.5 and 2.6, you will notice two brief conversations. These conversations, which are somewhat simplified due to space, demonstrate some common differences

**FIGURE 2.5**

## A Conversation between a Hub and a Green

Jeff explained, "Lisa, I'd like you, Steve, and Latisha to help work with me to implement a continuous performance review system. Our current system of annual performance reviews is really outdated."

**Jeff encodes:** Let's work as a team to improve our performance feedback system.

Lisa was silent for several seconds. "I think we need to step back and really make sure we're making the right decision here. Have you taken the time to carefully compare annual reviews and continuous reviews? Can you share some of that information with me?"

**Lisa decodes:** Jeff is rushing to a decision too quickly and thinks I'm on board.

**Lisa encodes:** This might be a good idea but let's weigh our options first.

Jeff was surprised Lisa wasn't enthusiastic. After all, it was Lisa who always loved data, and continuous feedback provided more information to everyone. "Well, I think it's a no-brainer. I've talked to quite a few HR directors who've had a lot of success with continuous performance reviews—never heard a bad thing yet. I guess we could gather some more information to make sure we're doing the right thing. Maybe we could do an employee survey, or we could find some industry surveys of how companies are implementing performance reviews, or maybe we could even attend a conference about performance reviews and talk to people there to figure out how we should go about this. What do you think we should do at this point?"

**Jeff decodes:** Lisa doesn't like this idea. I wonder what's wrong.

**Jeff encodes:** I want to work with you and figure out how to move forward. Here are some additional ways of learning our options. I want your input.

**Lisa decodes:** Jeff doesn't really know what he wants to accomplish.

**Lisa encodes:** Let's be really thorough about this decision.

Lisa responded, "All those ideas might help. Let's think first about our objectives for the new system and then think about some ways of gathering information to decide whether the new system meets those objectives more so than annual reviews . . ."

**Jeff decodes:** This approach is time-consuming and far too cautious.

**FIGURE 2.6**

## A Conversation between a Red and a Blue

*Steve:* We should aim to get the survey done within the next few days. Jeff and Lisa will be really impressed if we get the results quickly. As soon as you get the questions ready and send out the link to employees, I can take over and do the statistics.

*Latisha:* I feel like we should include the employees first to find out what kinds of questions we should ask in the survey. Maybe we could hold a few focus groups. If the employees see us do this, they'll feel included in the process and become more committed to our efforts.

*Steve:* You don't need to worry so much about what the employees think about us. Sending them a survey shows we're interested in their input. If you're not comfortable doing the questions, I can do that part of the project.

*Latisha:* Steve, it's in everyone's best interests to involve the employees more in this process. They need to feel like partners with us as we gather the information.

**Steve encodes:** Let's get results quickly.

**Latisha decodes:** Steve is being bossy and isn't thinking about how to include the employees.

**Latisha encodes:** First, let's think about how to include the employees in the process.

**Steve decodes:** Latisha needs to just take charge. That will take too long.

**Steve encodes:** Let's just make this happen and not complicate the task.

**Latisha decodes:** Steve is too assertive. He doesn't understand you have to win people's hearts to make changes.

**Latisha encodes:** We REALLY need to involve everyone more.

**Steve decodes:** Latisha probably doesn't know how to create the survey questions on her own.

between reds, blues, greens, and hubs. In the first conversation, Jeff, a hub, talks with Lisa, a green. Jeff talks with Lisa about transitioning from annual performance reviews to continuous performance reviews. One of Jeff's strengths as a hub is flexibility. Yet, Lisa views him as wishy-washy and indecisive in this case because he appears too flexible in making a decision. One of Lisa's strengths as a green is her careful analysis and caution. Yet, Jeff perceives her as nit-picking and rigid when he presents an idea he's enthusiastic about.

In the next conversation (Figure 2.6), Latisha and Steve talk about setting up an online survey to get input from employees about performance review systems. One of Latisha's strengths as a blue is her ability to think about the needs and feelings of others. Yet, in this case, Steve views her as lacking in initiative and subservient to others. Two of Steve's strengths as a red are his focus on action and his desire to lead positive change. Yet, in this case, Latisha perceives him as combative and bossy.

**LO2.9** Explain how extroversion-introversion impacts interpersonal communication.

**Differences in Communication Preferences Based on Extroversion-Introversion**   One element of personality that plays a major role in workplace communication is professionals' level of extroversion-introversion. Generally, **introverts** tend to get much of their stimulation and energy from their own thoughts, feelings, and moods. **Extroverts** tend to get much of their stimulation and energy from external sources such as social interaction. Whereas most introverts need time to recharge after social interactions, extroverts thrive on social interactions and feel more energized. Introverts are often more quiet, reserved, and thoughtful, whereas extroverts are often more outspoken, charismatic, and spontaneous. Introverts often feel less comfortable around unfamiliar people and situations, whereas extroverts often relish meeting new people and entering unfamiliar environments. Similarly, introverts are more likely to feel discomfort in public speaking and speaking up in meetings, whereas extroverts are more likely to enjoy engaging with an audience while public speaking and making frequent comments in meetings. Introverts typically prefer one-to-one or small group conversations, whereas extroverts typically prefer conversations in larger groups and social events. Introverts tend to speak only once they have clarified their own thoughts privately, whereas extroverts often want to think out loud, using speech as a way of refining their ideas. Introverts usually dislike small talk and prefer extended, deep conversations, whereas extroverts usually prefer lively and varied conversations that include small talk. Introverts are more likely to want to do much of their work alone, whereas extroverts are more likely to want to do much of their work in groups.[80]

Recently, Susan Cain drew attention to the evolving research about extroversion and introversion in the workplace in her best-selling book *Quiet: The Power of Introverts in a World That Can't Stop Talking*. She documented the "Extroversion Ideal," in which the workplace tends to be structured to favor extroverts, especially in North America.[81] In the past, extroverts have been perceived as better leaders and received more promotions and opportunities. In fact, one study showed that roughly 96 percent of managers and leaders display extroverted personalities. In many workplaces, there has been bias against introverts. For example, roughly ten years ago, research showed that 65 percent of executives thought introversion was a barrier to effective leadership.[82] One of the major barriers of businesses drawing from the skills and talents of introverts is the common misunderstanding that extroversion is prosocial and introversion is antisocial. Rather, introverts and extroverts are each social in different ways. One expert characterized introverts as "social in quieter ways."[83]

In the past ten years, a variety of research has debunked the idea that introverts are less effective at leading. This research has shown that extroverts and introverts each possess many leadership qualities and essential professional traits. For companies to succeed in today's increasingly collaborative work environment, they must find ways to tap into the strengths of extroverts and introverts, especially since estimates suggest that roughly one-third to one-half of professionals are introverts. Take several minutes to review Tables 2.15 and 2.16. The first table shows some of the strengths of introverts and extroverts. Consider how people can accomplish much more by uniting these strengths. The next table gives advice for how introverts can work more effectively with extroverts and vice versa.

**TABLE 2.15**

## Strengths of Introverted and Extroverted Professionals

| Strengths of Introverted Professionals | Strengths of Extroverted Professionals |
|---|---|
| • Asking thoughtful and important questions<br>• Listening to the ideas of others<br>• Giving people space to innovate<br>• Developing insights to deal with uncertain situations<br>• Improving the listening environment in meetings<br>• Networking among close-knit professional groups<br>• Making lasting impressions in social tasks that require persistence<br>• Taking time to reflect carefully<br>• Providing objective analysis and advice<br>• Excelling in situations requiring discipline | • Stating views directly and charismatically<br>• Gaining the support of others<br>• Organizing people to innovate<br>• Inspiring confidence in uncertain situations<br>• Driving important conversations at meetings<br>• Networking at large social events with potential clients and other contacts<br>• Making strong first impressions that often lead to future partnerships<br>• Acting quickly to gain advantages<br>• Acting pragmatically in the absence of reliable information<br>• Excelling in competitive situations |

# TECHNOLOGY TIPS

## MOBILE PHONES

Mobile phones have transformed business communication: Most business professionals carry at least one phone at all times for calls, texting, Internet use, scheduling, and much more. In many ways, mobile phones increasingly serve as a communication center for business professionals. Keep in mind the following guidelines for mobile phone use:

*Speak in person for important matters.* The advantage of using mobile phones for calls, texts, emails, and other messages is convenience. For important requests and other business matters, meet in person if possible. You can generally influence others more easily in a rich, face-to-face environment; they are far more likely to say "yes" in person.

*Avoid using your mobile phone if possible during meetings.* Multitasking with your phone while talking with others sends a strong signal that you are not paying full attention to them, which disrupts a listening-centered approach to communication. Younger professionals are more accepting of mobile phone use in meetings; however, even the majority of 21- to 30-year-old business professionals say you should never answer calls or write or send texts during meetings. The majority of professionals over 31 years of age say you shouldn't even glance at your phone to check the time while meeting with others.

*If you need to use your phone during a meeting, do so discreetly and acknowledge your distracting behavior.* If a must-answer call comes in during a meeting, quietly leave the room and make sure you apologize for any distraction. If appropriate, ask permission before taking the call.

*Leave professional, brief but complete, and friendly voice mails.* Make sure you keep voice mail messages to the point. Be brief about your requests but provide enough information for others to respond to your requests. If you must leave a lengthier message, make sure you leave your name and contact information at the beginning and the end of the message. Never leave an unfriendly voice mail message. Also, pay special attention to your greetings and leave pleasant closings. Finally, let people know your availability for a return call.

*Speak with a pleasant, enthusiastic voice.* Although others cannot see you, your nonverbal behaviors are often reflected in your voice. Consider sitting up straight or standing up, breathing deeply, intonating clearly, gesturing, and even smiling as you would if you were in person. These nonverbal actions will often carry through in a pleasant, professional voice and help you avoid a monotone. From time to time, consider listening to your recorded voice to pick up on ways in which you can speak more professionally and energetically.

*Plan for your phone calls.* Avoid simply winging calls. Like other forms of business communication, think ahead about your key discussion topics and points. Consider writing a few notes about these items or even plan an agenda. Also, let the person know how long you expect to take for the phone call.

*Set expectations and boundaries about how you use your mobile phone.* Talk to those you work with about how rapidly you hope for return calls, what you consider appropriate contact hours, and what types of messages you prefer to receive by phone as opposed to other communication channels (i.e., email, face-to-face). Conversely, ask others about their preferences.

© BananaStock/Jupiterimages

**TABLE 2.16**

Working Effectively with Introverts and Extroverts

| Introverts can work more effectively with extroverts by . . . | Extroverts can work more effectively with introverts by . . . |
|---|---|
| • Making sure their extroverted colleagues have enough time to interact with team members.<br>• Engaging in small talk and light topics during conversations.<br>• Speaking up more quickly than feels natural.<br>• Offering personal information more often.<br>• Expressing their preference to respond to questions later on.<br>• Giving them more opportunities to interact with others.<br>• Shortening their emails.<br>• Telling people they're shy or uncomfortable speaking up; requesting that others ask or call on them to speak up.<br>• Appreciating extroverts for their many strengths.<br>• Teaming up with extroverts to complement one another's strengths. | • Making sure their introverted colleagues have enough time to prepare for presentations or meetings.<br>• Allowing conversations to have fewer and more in-depth topics.<br>• Pausing more often and allowing longer periods of silence.<br>• Spending less time talking about personal interests.<br>• Expressing their preference to discuss things immediately.<br>• Giving them more opportunities to be alone and recharge.<br>• Lengthening their emails.<br>• Telling people they have a hard time not sharing their views; requesting that others signal them when they're talking too much.<br>• Appreciating introverts for their many strengths.<br>• Teaming up with introverts to complement one another's strengths. |

## Maintaining Civility

An outgrowth of emotional intelligence for interpersonal business communication is the notion of civility. Civility is a show of respect for the dignity and importance of others. It includes an orientation toward achieving honest, open, and respectful dialogues and validating the worth of others and their work efforts. In every instance, you should find ways to maintain civil communication in the workplace, especially for situations in which you disagree with others. Even when others treat you poorly—which will undoubtedly occur—responding civilly potentially de-escalates an ugly situation and shows your character and caring.

By contrast, incivility is "rudeness and disregard for others in a manner that violates norms for respect."[84] Unfortunately, incivility seems to be on the rise in the workplace.[85] In this section about civility, we first focus on the prominence and consequences of incivility. Then, we discuss common types and causes of incivility in the workplace. We conclude with strategies for maintaining civility.

**LO2.10** Explain the role of civility in effective interpersonal communication and the common types of incivility in the workplace.

### Incivility in Society and the Workplace

Many Americans perceive society as increasingly rude and disrespectful. A recent survey of more than 2,000 people in the United States illustrated the extent to which they perceive rudeness in society.[86] Consider the following findings from this research:

- Seventy-nine percent of respondents felt that a lack of respect is a serious problem for our society and that we should try to address it.
- Eighty-eight percent of respondents said that they often or sometimes come across people who are rude and disrespectful.
- Seventy-three percent believe that Americans treated each other with more respect in the past.
- Thirty-seven percent say they are so affected by rudeness that they have thought about moving to another community.

One place respondents cite for lack of respect is retail stores. For example, 46 percent of respondents claim to have gotten such bad service sometime during the past year that they left the store. Among those making $75,000 or more (those from whom stores might lose the most business), 57 percent had received such bad service sometime during the past year that they left the store. Nearly four out of five respondents (77 percent) agreed that it is all too common to see employees act as if the customer is not even there. One danger for stores is that customers who feel disrespected may never say anything. Approximately 65 percent of respondents stated they hardly ever complained when getting bad service. On the other hand, 74 percent of respondents agreed that they often saw customers being rude or disrespectful to retail employees or customer service representatives.[87]

In the interactions among colleagues in the workplace, incivility is also common. Nearly four in ten respondents (39 percent) said they have colleagues who are rude or disrespectful. More than three in ten respondents (31 percent) said that their workplace supervisors are rude or disrespectful. About 30 percent of respondents said they *often* experienced rudeness at the workplace, and another 38 percent said they *sometimes* experienced rudeness in the workplace. The majority of respondents admitted that they are rude themselves; 61 percent agreed with the statement, "I'm so busy and pressed for time that I'm not as polite as I should be, and I feel sorry about it later on." As the researchers of this study concluded, "Few people can count on being consistently treated with respect and courtesy as they go about their daily lives. The cumulative social costs—in terms of mistrust, anger, and even rage—are all too real to ignore."[88]

Perhaps the foremost experts on workplace incivility are Christine Pearson and Christine Porath. They have examined the nature and consequences of incivility in hundreds of organizations in North America over the past decade, finding that roughly one-quarter to one-half of employees experience incivility on a *weekly* basis. Furthermore, the consequences are devastating to organizational performance. Incivility erodes organizational culture and can escalate into conflict. It lowers individuals' productivity, performance, motivation, creativity, and helping behaviors. It also leads to declines in job satisfaction, organizational loyalty, and leadership impact.[89] Employees who are targets of incivility respond in the following ways:

- Half lose work time worrying about future interactions with instigators of incivility.
- Half contemplate changing jobs.
- One-fourth intentionally cut back work efforts.
- Approximately 70 percent tell friends, family, and colleagues about their dissatisfaction.
- About one in eight leave their jobs: turnover expense per job is estimated at $50,000.

The cost to companies is not always easy to quantify. However, some companies have started civility initiatives that include cost estimates of incivility. For example, Cisco recently started a Global Civility Program. The company estimated its annual loss due to incivility was $71 million, based on lost productivity, turnover, and absenteeism.[90]

You will soon find yourself in business leadership positions. One primary cost of incivility is business leaders' time. By one estimate, business executives spend 13 percent of their time, or what amounts to seven weeks per year, managing the fallout of disputes among employees.[91]

## Types and Causes of Workplace Incivility

People show disrespect and rudeness to others in almost limitless ways. Table 2.17 includes common types of workplace incivility.[92] This list is by no means exhaustive, but it does contain broad categories. Generally, incivility occurs when a person ignores others, fails to display basic courtesies, fails to recognize the efforts of others, fails to respect the time and privacy of others, and fails to recognize the basic worth and dignity of others. As you read through the list, think about whether you have witnessed or engaged in some of these types of incivility. These actions make people

**TABLE 2.17**

Common Types of Incivility

| Common Types of Incivility in the Workplace |
| --- |

**Ignoring others**
 Not responding to calls or emails in a timely manner
 Taking credit for the work of others
 Not responding when others greet you
 Withholding important information from colleagues
 Not inviting colleagues to participate in important decisions
 Overruling the decisions of others without providing any reasons
 Not acknowledging the presence of others
 Leaving some colleagues out of work social functions

**Treating others without courtesy**
 Not using basic terms of courtesy such as please and thank you
 Using a bossy or domineering tone, expression, or words
 Copying the boss on emails as a power play
 Interrupting others frequently
 Not using titles such as *Mr.* and *Ms.* as appropriate

**Disrespecting the efforts of others**
 Diminishing the ideas or efforts of others
 Providing vague and ambiguous feedback
 Blaming others unfairly

**Disrespecting the time of others**
 Disrupting a meeting
 Interrupting meetings or demanding an immediate meeting
 Setting deadlines without sufficient notice
 Sending too much email
 Flagging all email as important
 Calling colleagues on weekends or after work hours

**Disrespecting the privacy of others**
 Taking up too much space or being messy in shared space
 Being too noisy (especially in cubicles/shared work spaces)
 Telling offensive jokes
 Asking intrusive questions about the personal lives of others
 Forwarding private or sensitive emails

**Disrespecting the dignity and worth of others**
 Not greeting others warmly
 Delivering bad news by email
 Talking behind the backs of others and gossiping
 Criticizing or reprimanding a person in front of others
 Making condescending or demeaning comments to others
 Attacking the character of others
 Attacking others based on political, religious, or other beliefs
 Giving others a dirty look or the silent treatment
 Insulting or yelling at others
 Insulting others due to gender, ethnicity, or sexual orientation
 Harassing others

feel undervalued and unwelcome. They also lead to less collegiality and cooperation among co-workers.

The final category in Table 2.17—disrespecting the dignity and worth of others—is among the most serious types of incivility. Many of these actions involve direct attacks on the identity and inherent worth of others. Verbal insults or even non-verbal expressions such as glares can send strong messages that show you do not value or respect others. Even without mean intentions, jokes about traits such as gender, ethnicity, or sexual orientation can create a hostile working environment for colleagues.

Of course, people of different personalities and cultures vary in their level of sensitivity to the behaviors listed in Table 2.17. Instigators of incivility are sometimes unaware of how much they impact others. Your responsibility, however, is to be sensitive to how others perceive your behaviors.

The world is increasingly interconnected. This is especially the case in the business world. Ironically, an increasingly interconnected world may be a force that removes many people from enduring, fairly permanent communities and creates a new kind of anonymity. P. M. Forni, founder of The Civility Initiative, highlighted the relationship between anonymity and incivility:

> Every day we encounter legions of strangers who will remain strangers. Soulless extras in our life stories, they hardly seem to warrant a nod of acknowledgment—let alone a kind word. In fact, we can easily get away with being rude to them. Gone are the days when the fear of being ostracized was an incentive to be civil: The cohesive social texture which allowed that motivation disappeared long ago. Anonymity gives us the feeling we can act with impunity.[93]

## Maintaining Civil Communications

Forni, one of the leading voices on improving civility in society and the workplace, recommended eight guiding principles:[94]

1. Slow down and be present in life.
2. Listen to the voice of empathy.
3. Keep a positive attitude.
4. Respect others and grant them plenty of validation.
5. Disagree graciously and refrain from arguing.
6. Get to know people around you.
7. Pay attention to small things.
8. Ask, don't tell.

You may already use these strategies in your everyday life. The workplace, however, presents additional challenges. Intense competition and deadlines create pressures that make many of these strategies more difficult. Also, as you advance into higher leadership positions, these pressures can increase rapidly. Making a conscious effort to build emotional intelligence will help you maintain respectful communications even under moments of intense pressure.

One of the best ways of keeping your emotional intelligence high and maintaining the habit of communicating respectfully is to get to know people around you and humanize your work. While this approach may seem time-consuming, it will help you develop the types of work relationships that make communication easier, even for difficult conversations. Consider the comments of Joseph Plumeri, former chairman and CEO of the insurance broker Willis Group:

> I spend 25 percent to 30 percent of my time calling my associates—whether they had a family problem or pulled off a great deal and brought in a new client, or saved a client. Two-minute phone call, or handwritten note. I can't begin to tell you how important that stuff is.[95]

In the opening case, Jeff and Latisha are each confronted with an uncomfortable situation. In the sections about the interpersonal process and emotional intelligence, you read examples of how they could have confronted this uncomfortable situation in less effective and more effective ways. If Jeff and Latisha make personal commitments to stay civil at all times, they are each more likely to communicate effectively and productively. Furthermore, a commitment to civility will help each of them build their emotional intelligence.

**COMMUNICATION Q&A**

### CONVERSATIONS WITH CURRENT BUSINESS PROFESSIONALS

**Pete Cardon: How important are interpersonal communication skills in terms of getting promoted?**

**Shane Stowell:** To become a successful business executive, you must master a set of interpersonal communication skills early in your career. However, many business professionals believe this set of skills will take care of itself as they progress down their career path. In today's market, two individuals can have similar educational pedigrees and comparable business acumen, but the clear distinction used in the promotional decision is whether or not someone has exceptional interpersonal communication skills.

**PC: How do employers assess interpersonal communication skills?**

**SS:** In today's job market, human resources departments and hiring executives are using very sophisticated methods to better understand their candidates and maximize the value they receive for the investment they make in the hiring process. They often use multiple interviews to look for consistency of interaction styles. They look online to see if they can discern your judgment and character. They want to know how you might handle and react to stressful situations and solve real-world problems, so they create scenarios in the interview to test these skills. Finally, they rely on psychological measurement and assessment to help them understand personality style and how you will match the core values of the organization.

**PC: Do employers pay attention to emotional intelligence? In what ways does emotional intelligence lead to better business performance?**

**SS:** Successful organizations want to make sure you can help them move the business forward long term. The intangible leadership skills of wisdom, self-awareness, insight, integrity, executive maturity, fortitude, and a willingness to be vulnerable at the right time are critical leadership skills in today's global business climate. In its simplest form, emotional intelligence is at the core of all of these "softer" leadership skills. Awareness of how you impact others and how others impact you in an interaction should be a skill you actively develop.

**PC: Businesspeople have so many choices of communication channels today. What are a few tips for how executives and managers should choose the right communication channel?**

**SS:** Even in the midst of all of these options, the core components of clarity of message, respect for another person's time, openness to collaboration, and good listening skills are still the foundation of all communications. One word of advice would be to find a form of communication that allows for as much interpersonal interaction as possible. For instance, if given the choice between a conference call and a videoconference, I would select the videoconference in order to maximize your ability to use your core emotional intelligence skills.

*Shane Stowell* is a partner at RHR International LLP, a business consulting firm that specializes in improving the assessment, selection, and development of senior-level executives. Before joining RHR, Stowell owned and ran a variety of businesses and earned a doctorate degree in psychology.

Courtesy of Shane Stowell

# Chapter Takeaway for *Interpersonal Communication and Emotional Intelligence*

**LO2.1 Describe the interpersonal communication process and barriers to effective communication. (pp. 29–32)**

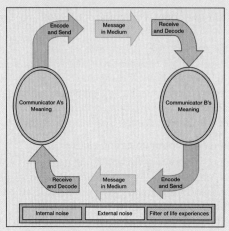

See an *example of the interpersonal communication process* in Figure 2.2.

**LO2.2 Explain how emotional hijacking can hinder effective interpersonal communication. (pp. 32–33)**

People are hardwired to experience emotions before reason. All signals to the brain first go through the limbic system, where emotions are produced, before going to the rational area of the brain. **Emotional hijacking** occurs when emotions control our behavior, causing us to react without thinking. During emotional hijacking, we often make statements that are rash, unintentional, and nonanalytical.

**LO2.3 Explain how self-awareness impacts the communication process. (pp. 33–34)**

See *examples of low versus high self-awareness thoughts* in Table 2.2, a *summary of EQ impacts on communication* in Table 2.3, and *strategies for improving EQ* in Table 2.3.

**LO2.4 Describe how self-management impacts the communication process. (pp. 34–37)**

See *examples of low versus high self-awareness thoughts* in Table 2.4.

**LO2.5 Explain and evaluate the process of active listening. (pp. 38–44)**

| Barriers to Active Listening | | Nonlistening Behaviors |
|---|---|---|
| • Lack of time<br>• Lack of patience and attention span | • Image of leadership<br>• Communication technology<br>• Fear of bad news | • Defending<br>• "Me too" statements<br>• Giving advice<br>• Judging |

See an *example of defensive and non-defensive replies* in Figure 2.4.

**LO2.6 Describe and demonstrate effective questions for enhancing listening and learning. (pp. 44–47)**

| Types of Good Questions | Types of Poor Questions |
|---|---|
| • Rapport-building<br>• Funnel<br>• Probing<br>• Solution-oriented | • Leading questions<br>• Disguised statements<br>• Cross-examination Questions |

See *examples of good questions* in Table 2.11 and *poor questions* in Table 2.12.

**LO2.7 Explain strategies to sight-read the nonverbal communication of others. (pp. 47–51)**

| **Strategies for Developing Abilities in Sight-Reading** |
| --- |
| • Consciously practice each day. |
| • Pay attention to congruence. |
| • Sight-read in clusters, not in isolation. |
| • Sight-read in context. |

**LO2.8 Identify common communication preferences based on motivational values. (pp. 51–54)**

See a *summary of concerns, preferred work environments, and other preferences for each MVS* in Table 2.13. See *words and phrases that resonate with professionals of each MVS* in Table 2.14. See *examples of conversations between professionals of different MVSs* in Figures 2.5 and 2.6.

**LO2.9 Explain how extroversion-introversion impacts interpersonal communication. (pp. 54–57)**

**LO2.10 Explain the role of civility in effective interpersonal communication and the common types of incivility in the workplace. (pp. 57–61)**

**Guiding principles:** (1) Slow down and be present in life; (2) listen to the voice of empathy; (3) keep a positive attitude; (4) respect others and grant them plenty of validation; (5) disagree graciously and refrain from arguing; (6) get to know people around you; (7) pay attention to small things; (8) ask, don't tell. (*Source:* P. M. Forni's *The Civility Solution*)

See *examples of incivility* in Table 2.17.

# Key Terms

active listening, 38
blue MVS, 51
CLEM, 49
cross-examination questions, 46
decoding, 29
disguised statements, 46
emotional hijacking, 33
emotional intelligence (EQ), 32
empathy, 37
encoding, 29
extrovert, 54
filter of lifetime experiences, 30
funnel questions, 45
green MVS, 51
hub, 52

interpersonal communication process, 29
introvert, 54
judger mind-set, 39
judger statements, 39
leading questions, 46
learner mind-set, 39
learner statements, 39
meaning, 29
mitigating information, 36
motivational value system (MVS), 51
noise, 30
nonlistening behaviors, 43
optimism, 37
pessimism, 37
physical noise, 30

physiological noise, 30
probing questions, 45
psychological noise, 30
rapport-building questions, 45
red MVS, 51
relationship management, 51
self-awareness, 33
self-management, 34
semantic noise, 30
shared meaning, 30
sight-reading, 47
solution-oriented questions, 46
synchronizing, 48
triggers, 33
visual cutoff, 49

# Discussion Exercises

**2.1 Chapter Review Questions** (LO2.1, LO2.2, LO2.3, LO2.4, LO2.5, LO2.6, LO2.7, LO2.8, LO2.9, LO2.10)

A. What barriers are there to achieving shared meaning? Explain these barriers in terms of the interpersonal communication model.

B. List ten words that could easily be perceived differently. Choose words that create semantic noise because of generational differences, occupational differences, cultural differences, or other kinds of differences.

C. Why is emotional intelligence so important in logical business tasks?

D. What are the four domains of emotional intelligence? Describe three related communication competencies for each domain (see Table 2.3).

E. What do you think are the five best strategies for developing emotional intelligence? Explain your rationale. (See Table 2.3 for help.)

F . Explain how optimism and pessimism affect self-management.

G. What are some concrete examples of people using a message-centered approach to conversations compared to people using a listening-centered approach?

H. What are some signs of a judger mentality in conversations? How about a learner mentality?

I. The active listening process contains six steps. What steps do you think are most critical? Explain.

J. How can image of leadership be a barrier to active listening? Provide some concrete examples.

K. Do you think fear of bad news is a common barrier to active listening among supervisors? Explain your viewpoint and provide some examples.

L. A common statement in classrooms is *there's no such thing as a bad question*. In the context of the workplace, in what ways would you agree and disagree with this statement? How would you qualify this statement?

M. What strategies can professionals use to interpret the nonverbal communication of others? How reliable do you think interpretations of nonverbal communication can be? Explain.

N. What are the motivational value systems (MVSs) explained in this chapter? What do you view as the two most important strengths and one most significant weakness of each style? Explain.

O. Which strategies do you think are most important for extroverts to work effectively with introverts? Which strategies do you think are most important for introverts to work effectively with extroverts? Explain.

P. Consider the common types of incivility shown in Table 2.17. Which five types of incivility do you think are most common? Most serious? Name five other behaviors you view as common forms of incivility in the workplace, school, or society.

Q. What are three things you can do to create a culture of civility and candor in the workplace? Explain.

**2.2 Communication Q&A Discussion Questions** (LO2.2, LO2.3, LO2.4, LO2.5)

Read the Communication Q&A in this chapter. For each question, write a one- or two-paragraph answer.

A. What does Shane Stowell say about the role of emotional intelligence in determining career success and gaining promotions?

B. According to Stowell, what are the key benefits of strong interpersonal skills in the workplace?

C. What approaches do companies use to assess your interpersonal communication skills and emotional intelligence?

D. What principles does he describe as important in determining a choice of communication channel?

**2.3 The Personal Part of Employees** (LO2.2, LO2.3, LO2.4, LO2.10)

In response to the question "How do you hire?," Kasper Rorsted, CEO of Henkel, a consumer and industrial products company based in Düsseldorf, Germany, had this to say:

I want to know who you are, who you've worked for, what kind of successes you've had, what are the failures or missteps in your career. But what I try to spend a lot of time on is trying to understand the person I'm speaking to. Did you work in an ice cream parlor when you were young? Do you have sisters? Do you have brothers? Why are you now living here? I'm trying to figure out who's actually behind the person, and what are the value sets that drive you as a person.

Then I always ask the question, what would you do if you won 10 million bucks? Would you leave? Would you retire? Do you want to do charity work? Will you stay?

I never look at grades from university. I look at what they've done, but I look very much at what they've done outside work. How do they spend their time? Who do they relate to? Have they moved? Have they been put in situations in their personal and professional lives that were not very straightforward?

I'm concerned about people who have come through their career with "A" grades throughout their entire life, and have never really had any setbacks and have always been in environments where they knew the environment.

Also, do they say goodbye and hello to the person who stands in front of the building, and do they say hello to the person who sweeps the floor? How do they act as a person? The personal part is, for me, equally important to the professional part. Because I think you can get a lot of people who are professionally very good, but I think the personal part and the value part are the difference between a good manager or leader and a great leader.[96]

Respond to the following questions:

A. When Rorsted says he is looking to find out about the *personal part*, not just the professional part, of a job applicant, what does he mean?

B. How does what Rorsted describes as the personal part of an employee relate to emotional intelligence? How about civility?

C. Rorsted explains that he wants to know how people have responded to setbacks. How does this relate to emotional intelligence?

D. He distinguishes between a good manager and a good leader. In two or three paragraphs, describe some characteristics that would distinguish a good leader from a good manager in terms of interpersonal communication, emotional intelligence, and/or civility.

### 2.4 Listening and Caring (LO2.5, LO2.6)

Tachi Yamada of the Bill & Melinda Gates Foundation recently stated the following:

A second key lesson was from a doctor named Marcel Tuchman. He was the most compassionate person I have ever met in my life—I mean, full of human kindness. And every time he met somebody, you had the sense that he cared more about them than anything else in the world. So what I learned from him is that when you actually are with somebody, you've got to make that person feel like nobody else in the world matters. I think that's critical. So, for example, I don't have a mobile phone turned on because I'm talking to you. I don't want the outside world to impinge on the conversation we're having. I don't carry a Black-Berry. I do my e-mails regularly, but I do it when I have the time on a computer. I don't want to be sitting here thinking that I've got an e-mail message coming here and I'd better look at that while I'm talking to you. Every moment counts, and that moment is lost if you're not in that moment 100 percent.[97]

Based on Yamada's comments and your own experiences, answer the following questions:

A. What do you think Yamada means by the statement, "*that moment is lost if you're not in that moment 100 percent*"? How does this relate to listening? Do you think this is a reasonable expectation in the workplace?

B. What kinds of electronic gadgets and communication tools can take focus away from a conversation? What are some principles for making sure these gadgets and tools are not distracting?

C. Do you believe kindness is an important principle of listening and communicating in business? Can kindness be developed? How?

### 2.5 Civility and Assertiveness (LO2.1, LO2.2, LO2.3, LO2.4, LO2.10)

Think of three business (or school) situations that require assertiveness. Describe how you can be assertive and also civil at the same time.

# Evaluation Exercises

### 2.6 Describe a Miscommunication from a Movie or TV Episode (LO2.1)

Think about a recent movie or TV episode you observed. Select a scene that involved a miscommunication. Ideally, it should include a conversation that might occur in a workplace. Based on this conversation, do the following:

A. Summarize the conversation in one paragraph.

B. Analyze the conversation in terms of the following components of the interpersonal communication process: encoding, decoding, physical noise, physiological noise, psychological noise, semantic noise, and filter of lifetime experiences.

C. Describe at least three strategies the characters in the conversation could have adopted to increase shared meaning and avoid miscommunication. Describe these strategies in terms of reducing noise and adapting to the filters of others.

### 2.7 Assess a Recent Miscommunication (LO2.1)

Think about a recent miscommunication you had with someone. Ideally, select an in-depth conversation that occurred in the workplace or at school. Based on this conversation, do the following:

A. Summarize the conversation in one paragraph.

B. Analyze the conversation in terms of the following components of the interpersonal communication process: encoding, decoding, physical noise, physiological noise, psychological noise, semantic noise, and filter of lifetime experiences.

C. Describe at least three strategies you could have adopted to increase shared meaning and avoid miscommunication.

Describe these strategies in terms of reducing noise and adapting to your and your counterpart's unique filters.

### 2.8 Analyze a Case of Emotional Hijacking at School or Work (LO2.2)

Think about a recent situation at school or work in which you observed a serious instance of emotional hijacking. Based on this situation, do the following:

A. Briefly explain what happened. Who was involved and what were they doing? You can write about yourself and/or others.

B. Explain the cause and nature of the emotional hijacking. For example, explain what the emotions were and what caused them.

C. Explain the impacts of the emotional hijacking. How did it affect an interaction? How did it affect performance?

D. Describe how the emotional hijacking could have been avoided or lessened.

E. Write a set of self-awareness and self-management thoughts that would be considered effective and ineffective in this situation (see Tables 2.2 and 2.4).

### 2.9 Identify Your Triggers (LO2.2)

In three to five paragraphs, describe three triggers that could lead to emotional hijacking for you. For each trigger, explain one or two strategies you can use to calm down and communicate constructively.

**2.10 Assess Your Emotional Intelligence** (LO2.3, LO2.4, LO2.5, LO2.6, LO2.7, LO2.8, LO2.9)

Respond to the items below as you assess your emotional intelligence and develop a plan to raise your EQ. Ideally, choose situations from work or school. You may want to use Table 2.3 from the chapter as a guide.

A. Identify one strength and one weakness you have in terms of self-awareness. Describe a situation in which you showed low self-awareness and a situation in which you showed high self-awareness. Choose two strategies for improving your self-awareness.

B. Identify one strength and one weakness you have in terms of self-management. Describe a situation in which you showed low self-management and a situation in which you showed high self-management. Choose two strategies for improving your self-management.

C. Identify one strength and one weakness you have in terms of empathy. Describe a situation in which you showed low empathy and a situation in which you showed high empathy. Choose two strategies for improving your empathy.

D. Identify one strength and one weakness you have in terms of relationship management. Describe a situation in which you showed low relationship management and a situation in which you showed high relationship management. Choose two strategies for improving your relationship management skills.

**2.11 Describe the Communication Skills of a Person with High EQ** (LO2.3, LO2.4, LO2.5, LO2.6, LO2.7, LO2.8, LO2.9)

Think of someone you have worked with extensively and who you think has high emotional intelligence. Describe at least two communication skills this person has that demonstrate each of the four EQ domains: self-awareness, self-management, empathy, and relationship management. Also, in two or three paragraphs, describe one challenging interpersonal situation this person handled effectively due to high EQ.

**2.12 Describe the Listening Skills of an Excellent Listener and a Poor Listener** (LO2.5, LO2.6)

Think of two people with whom you have worked at school or work–one an excellent listener and the other a poor listener. Describe and contrast these two individuals in terms of their ability to actively listen: paying attention, holding judgment, reflecting, clarifying, and sharing. Explain how each person made you feel as he or she listened, or didn't listen, to you. Explain two or three ways in which you want to emulate the excellent listener in the workplace.

**2.13 Assess Your Active Listening Skills** (LO2.5, LO2.6)

Think about how well you listen in *high-pressure* environments or when you're busy. Explain how well you do at each of the following active listening skills: paying attention, holding judgment, reflecting, clarifying, and sharing. For each skill, take approximately two paragraphs to explain how well you do these skills and think of strategies to help you improve.

**2.14 Write a Listening Journal** (LO2.5, LO2.6)

For a length of time specified by your instructor (one week, two weeks, one month), write daily in a journal about your listening skills. Each day, describe one interaction you had and discuss whether you actively listened. Explain how well you did at each of the following active listening skills: paying attention, holding judgment, reflecting, clarifying, and sharing. For each of these interactions, describe the nonverbal behavior of others and the nonverbal behavior you exhibited to show your interest. Also, analyze how effectively you asked questions. Conclude your daily journal with a summary of lessons you have learned and five goals for improving your active listening.

**2.15 Evaluate the Nonverbal Actions of Others** (LO2.7)

For a length of time specified by your instructor (one week, two weeks, one month), write observations about nonverbal communications during one conversation each day. For each of these conversations, explain your observations of nonverbal communication from the following: eye contact and movement, smiles and nods, other facial expressions, gestures, posture, and touch. Conclude your daily journal with a summary of lessons you have learned and five goals for improving your sight-reading.

**2.16 Describe Nonverbal Behavior from a Movie or TV Episode** (LO2.7)

Think about a recent movie or TV episode you watched. Select a scene that involves interesting nonverbal communication—ideally, one that might occur in the workplace. Based on this scene, do the following:

A. Summarize the scene in approximately a paragraph.

B. Analyze the nonverbal communication. Explain how various body parts sent signals, including the eyes, mouth, shoulders, arms, and hands.

C. Describe how you can mimic or avoid three aspects of this nonverbal behavior in the workplace and why you would want to do so.

**2.17 Evaluate the Motivational Value Systems of Yourself and Others** (LO2.8)

Explain which MVS best matches you. Then, identify three others (could be family members, friends, colleagues, classmates, or others) who match the other three MVSs described in this chapter. Explain the characteristics that lead you to believe these MVSs match you and these others. Then, explain how knowing these differences will help you communicate more effectively with each of these three people.

**2.18 Analyze an Episode of Incivility at Work** (LO2.10)

Think of a situation you have observed at work or at school that was uncivil. In one or two paragraphs, describe the event. Then, in two or three paragraphs, explain how each person involved in the encounter contributed to the uncivil event. Analyze the event in terms of noise, filters, and emotional intelligence. In two paragraphs, explain how the person who was most responsible for the incivility could have behaved to make the situation productive for everyone.

**2.19 Assess Your Civility** (LO2.10)

Look at Table 2.17 in the chapter and think about various types of incivility: ignoring others, treating others without courtesy, disrespecting the time of others, disrespecting the privacy of others, and disrespecting the dignity and worth of others. Read through examples of behaviors associated with each type of incivility. In three or four paragraphs, describe three aspects of civility you will exemplify in your professional life and how you will avoid inadvertently communicating disrespectfully to others.

# Application Exercises

**2.20 Create a Presentation about Avoiding Miscommunication in the Workplace (LO2.1)**

Individually or in teams, develop a five- to ten-minute presentation about how to avoid miscommunication in the workplace. Use terms such as *noise, filter, encoding,* and *decoding* to explain miscommunication. Provide several specific scenarios that have happened or could happen in the workplace. Provide a simple set of recommendations that your audience will find compelling, insightful, and easy to remember.

**2.21 Create a Presentation about EQ as a Basis for Effective Interpersonal Communication** (LO2.2, LO2.3, LO2.4, LO2.5, LO2.6, LO2.7, LO2.8, LO2.9)

Individually or in teams, develop a five- to ten-minute presentation about the importance of EQ for effective communication in the workplace. Describe each of the four dimensions of emotional intelligence. Provide several specific scenarios that have happened or could happen in the workplace. Provide a simple set of recommendations that your audience will find compelling, insightful, and easy to remember.

**2.22 Listening Exercise (LO2.5, LO2.6)**

Form groups of three. You will complete this exercise three times, with each person rotating roles each time. The roles are asker, listener, and observer. Choose a time period (two minutes, three minutes, or five minutes) to complete the exercise. The asker will choose a topic to learn about from the listener (e.g., professional interests, reasons for choosing major, challenges at work or in school right now). The asker will devote the time to learning about the other person through asking questions. The observer will take notes about how effective the asker's asking, listening, and nonverbal communication skills are. Once the exercise is complete, the observer will facilitate a three- to five-minute debriefing by explaining his/her observations and asking both the asker and the listener about their observations.

**2.23 Create a Presentation about Civility in Today's Workplace** (LO2.10)

Individually or in teams, develop a five- to ten-minute presentation about maintaining civil communications in the workplace. Provide several scenarios that have happened or could happen in the workplace. Provide a simple set of recommendations that your audience will find compelling, insightful, and easy to remember.

# Language Mechanics Check

**2.24 Review the comma rules C5 through C7 in Appendix A. Then, rewrite each sentence to add commas where needed.**

A. To utilize big data companies should hire data scientists.

B. You should consider hiring professionals trained in statistics social media analytics and management theory.

C. She is the first competent data scientist we've hired since starting this important expensive initiative.

D. Under her leadership our company has increased revenue because of our focus on big data.

E. By hiring the right data scientists companies can make better use of marketing resources and target the right customers.

F. Using this software will help us identify expertise among employees evaluate which employees require training and predict which employees are likely to leave the firm within two years and take their knowledge with them.

G. The business school now offers a valuable exciting major in data analytics.

H. To qualify for the program you must hold a 3.0 GPA.

I. You must hold a 3.0 GPA to qualify for the program.

J. Under the leadership of a new dean the program grew rapidly.

# Endnotes

1. Linda Lyons, "Which Skills Hold the Secret to Success at Work?" Gallup online, August 19, 2003, retrieved from www.gallup.com/poll/9064/Which-Skills-Hold-Secret-Success-Work.aspx.

2. Adam Bryant, "Fitting In, and Rising to the Top," *Corner Office* (blog), *The New York Times,* September 19, 2009, www.nytimes.com/2009/09/20/business/20corner.html.

3. This model is based on the transactional model of communication: Paul Watzlawick, Janet H. Beavin, and Don D. Jackson, *Pragmatics of Human Communication: A Study of International Patterns, Pathologies, and Paradoxes* (New York: Norton, 1967); D. C. Barnland, "A Transactional Model of Communication," in K. K. Sereno and C. D. Mortensen, eds., *Foundations of Communication Theory* (New York: Harper & Row, 1970): 83–102; Uma Narula, *Handbook of Communication: Models, Perspectives, Strategies* (New Delhi, India: Atlantic Publishers, 2006); Richard West and Lynn H. Turner, *Understanding Interpersonal Communication: Making Choices in Changing Times,* 2nd ed. (Boston: Wadsworth Cengage Learning, 2009).

4. West and Turner, *Understanding Interpersonal Communication: Making Choices in Changing Times.*

5. Most discussion in this section, including this definition, comes from the following sources: Daniel Goleman, *Working with Emotional Intelligence* (New York: Bantam Dell, 2006); Daniel Goleman, *Emotional Intelligence: Why It Can Matter More Than IQ* (New York: Bantam Books, 1995); Adele B. Lynn, *The EQ Difference: A Powerful Plan for Putting Emotional Intelligence to Work* (New York: AMACOM, 2005); Travis Bradberry and Jean Greaves, *Emotional Intelligence 2.0* (San Diego: TalentSmart, 2009).

6.  Sue Campbell Clark, Ronda Callister, and Ray Wallace, "Undergraduate Management Skills Courses and Students' Emotional Intelligence," *Journal of Management Education* 27, no. 1 (2003): 3–23.

7.  Roderick Gilkey, Ricardo Caceda, and Clinton Kilts, "When Emotional Reasoning Trumps IQ," *Harvard Business Review,* September 2010: 27; Robert Kelley and Janet Caplan, "How Bell Labs Creates Star Performers," *Harvard Business Review,* July/August 1993: 128–139.

8.  Bradberry and Greaves, *Emotional Intelligence 2.0.*

9.  "America's Most Stressful Jobs 2010," retrieved April 14, 2011, from www.cnbc.com/id/36715336/America_s_Most_Stressful_Jobs_2010.

10.  Adam Bryant, "He Wants Subjects, Verbs and Objects," *Corner Office* (blog), *The New York Times,* April 25, 2009, www.nytimes.com/2009/04/26/business/26corner.html.

11.  Clark et al., "Undergraduate Management Skills Courses and Students' Emotional Intelligence."

12.  Bradberry and Greaves, *Emotional Intelligence 2.0.*

13.  Goleman, *Emotional Intelligence: Why It Can Matter More Than IQ*; Lynn, *The EQ Difference: A Powerful Plan for Putting Emotional Intelligence to Work*; Dan Ariely, "The Long-Term Effects of Short-Term Emotions," *Harvard Business Review,* January/February 2010: 38.

14.  Bradberry and Greaves, *Emotional Intelligence 2.0.*

15.  Goleman, *Emotional Intelligence: Why It Can Matter More Than IQ:* 46.

16.  Lynn, *The EQ Difference: A Powerful Plan for Putting Emotional Intelligence to Work;* Bradberry and Greaves, *Emotional Intelligence 2.0.*

17.  Goleman, *Emotional Intelligence: Why It Can Matter More Than IQ.*

18.  Bradberry and Greaves, *Emotional Intelligence 2.0.*

19.  Lynn, *The EQ Difference: A Powerful Plan for Putting Emotional Intelligence to Work:* 46.

20.  Bradberry and Greaves, *Emotional Intelligence 2.0:* 32.

21.  Lynn, *The EQ Difference: A Powerful Plan for Putting Emotional Intelligence to Work.*

22.  Goleman, *Emotional Intelligence: Why It Can Matter More Than IQ.*

23.  Ibid.

24.  Ibid.

25.  Lynn, *The EQ Difference: A Powerful Plan for Putting Emotional Intelligence to Work.*

26.  Goleman, *Emotional Intelligence: Why It Can Matter More Than IQ.*

27.  Bradberry and Greaves, *Emotional Intelligence 2.0:* 38.

28.  Goleman, *Emotional Intelligence: Why It Can Matter More Than IQ.*

29.  Michael Purdy and Deborah Borisoff, *Listening in Everyday Life: A Personal and Professional Approach* (Lanham, MD: University Press of America, 1997).

30.  Sabeen Sheikh, *2010 Graduate Management Admission Council Alumni Perspectives Survey* (McLean, VA: GMAC, 2010).

31.  Uri Hasson, "I Can Make Your Brain Look Like Mine," *Harvard Business Review,* December 2010: 32–33.

32.  Michael H. Hoppe, *Active Listening: Improve Your Ability to Listen and Lead* (Greensboro, NC: Center for Creative Leadership, 2006): 6, 12.

33.  Adam Bryant, "Want the Job? Tell Him the Meaning of Life," *Corner Office* (blog), *The New York Times,* June 19, 2010, www.nytimes.com/2010/06/20/business/20corner.html.

34.  Hoppe, *Active Listening: Improve Your Ability to Listen and Lead.*

35.  Michael Marquardt, *Leading with Questions: How Leaders Find the Right Solutions by Knowing What to Ask* (San Francisco: Jossey-Bass, 2005): 77–78.

36.  Marilee Adams, *Change Your Questions, Change Your Life: 7 Powerful Tools for Life and Work* (San Francisco: Berrett-Koehler, 2004); Marquardt, *Leading with Questions: How Leaders Find the Right Solutions by Knowing What to Ask:* 78.

37.  Adam Bryant, "O.K., Newbies, Bring Out the Hula Hoops," *Corner Office* (blog), *The New York Times,* June 12, 2010, www.nytimes.com/2010/06/13/business/13corner.html.

38.  Hoppe, *Active Listening: Improve Your Ability to Listen and Lead.*

39.  Ibid.

40.  Ibid.

41.  Ibid.

42.  Ibid., 18.

43.  Paul J. Donoghue and Mary E. Siegel, *Are You Really Listening? Keys to Successful Communication* (Notre Dame, IN: Ave Maria Press, 2005); Hoppe, *Active Listening: Improve Your Ability to Listen and Lead.*

44.  Donoghue and Siegel, *Are You Really Listening? Keys to Successful Communication.*

45.  Ibid.

46.  Hoppe, *Active Listening: Improve Your Ability to Listen and Lead.*

47.  David S. Christensen and David Rees, "An Analysis of the Business Communication Skills Needed by Entry-Level Accountants," *Proceedings of the 2002 Mountain Plains Management Conference.* Available at www.mountainplains.org/articles/2002/general/Communication%20Skills4_MPJ_.pdf.

48.  John Baldoni, "Are You Asking the Right Questions?" *Harvard Management Communication Letter,* March 2003: 3–4.

49.  Baldoni, "Are You Asking the Right Questions?": 3–4; Douglas Stone, Bruce Patton, and Sheila Heen, *Difficult Conversations: How to Discuss What Matters Most* (New York: Penguin, 2000); Dale Carnegie Training, *The 5 Essential People Skills: How to Assert Yourself, Listen to Others, and Resolve Conflicts* (New York: Simon & Schuster, 2009); Adams, *Change Your Questions, Change Your Life: 7 Powerful Tools for Life and Work*; Marquardt, *Leading with Questions: How Leaders Find the Right Solutions by Knowing What to Ask.*

50.  Michael Maslansky, *The Language of Trust* (New York: Prentice Hall, 2010).

51.  Adam Grant, "In the Company of Givers and Takers," *Harvard Business Review*, April 2013: 90–97.

52.  Allan Pease and Barbara Pease, *The Definitive Book of Body Language* (New York: Bantam Dell, 2006); Pearn Kandola, *The Psychology of Effective Business Communications in Geographically Dispersed Teams* (San Jose, CA: Cisco, 2006).

53.  David Givens, *Your Body at Work: A Guide to Sight-Reading the Body Language of Business, Bosses, and Boardrooms* (New York: St. Martin's Griffin, 2010): xvi.

54.  Ibid., 2.

55.  Nick Morgan, "The Truth Behind the Smile and Other Myths: Reading Body Language Is Important, But the Clues May Be Misleading," *Harvard Management Communication Letter,* August 2002: 4.

56.  Malcom Gladwell, *Blink: The Power of Thinking without Thinking* (New York: Barclay Books, 2007).

57.  Pease and Pease, *The Definitive Book of Body Language.*

58. Givens, *Your Body at Work: A Guide to Sight-Reading the Body Language of Business, Bosses, and Boardrooms*; Beverly Langford, *The Etiquette Edge: The Unspoken Rules for Business Success* (New York: American Management Association, 2005).

59. Goleman, *Emotional Intelligence: Why It Can Matter More Than IQ*: 117.

60. Nick Morgan, "Are You Standing in the Way of Your Own Success?" *Harvard Management Communication Letter*, 2003: 3.

61. Givens, *Your Body at Work: A Guide to Sight-Reading the Body Language of Business, Bosses, and Boardrooms*.

62. Ibid.

63. Ibid.

64. Ibid.

65. Morgan, "The Truth Behind the Smile and Other Myths: Reading Body Language Is Important, But the Clues May Be Misleading": 3–4.

66. Morgan, "Are You Standing in the Way of Your Own Success?": 3.

67. S. Douglas Pugh, "Service with a Smile: Emotional Contagion in the Service Encounter," *Academy of Management Journal* 44, no. 5 (2001): 1018–1027.

68. Morgan, "The Truth Behind the Smile and Other Myths: Reading Body Language Is Important, But the Clues May Be Misleading": 3–4.

69. Pease and Pease, *The Definitive Book of Body Language*.

70. Givens, *Your Body at Work: A Guide to Sight-Reading the Body Language of Business, Bosses, and Boardrooms*: 52.

71. Ibid., 52.

72. Ibid., 52.

73. Ibid., 52.

74. Ibid., 52.

75. Pease and Pease, *The Definitive Book of Body Language*.

76. Morgan, "Are You Standing in the Way of Your Own Success?": 3.

77. Bradberry and Greaves, *Emotional Intelligence 2.0*: 44.

78. Relationship Awareness Theory was developed by the psychologist Elias H. Porter. There are many other psychological assessments and tools for assessing differences in communication styles. Each assessment has various advantages. Nearly all of these assessments can help professionals and students develop emotional intelligence to work more effectively with others. I chose this tool because it contains the following advantages: (1) the assessment has 96 percent face validity: in other words, people who use the instrument believe it explains their relating styles extremely well; (2) it is a comparatively simple and practical tool; and (3) it distinguishes between situations where things are going well and situations involving conflict and discomfort.

79. These figures are based on my administration of the Strengths Deployment Inventory (SDI) to full-time working professionals enrolled in part-time MBA programs at the University of Southern California. Among roughly 750 SDI tests of these managers, the breakdown is as follows: hubs, 43 percent; blue-reds, 22 percent; red, 17 percent; red-greens, 7 percent; blue-greens, 6 percent; greens, 3 percent; and blues, 2 percent. These figures are similar to those provided by Personal Strengths for all professionals: hubs, 39 percent; blues, 17 percent; blue-reds, 13 percent; blue-greens, 13 percent; reds, 10 percent; red-greens, 4 percent; and greens, 6 percent.

80. Susan Cain, *Quiet: The Power of Introverts in a World That Can't Stop Talking* (New York: Crown Publishers, 2012); Nancy Ancowitz, *Self-Promotion for Introverts: The Quiet Guide to Getting Ahead* (New York: McGraw-Hill, 2009); Douglas R. Conant, "Are You an Introverted Boss?" Harvard Blog Network, April 4, 2011, retrieved from http://blogs.hbr.org/2011/04/are-you-an-introverted-boss/; Adam M. Grant, Francesca Gino, and David A. Hofmann, "The Hidden Advantages of Quiet Bosses," *Harvard Business Review*, July 2010: 28.

81. Cain, *Quiet: The Power of Introverts in a World That Can't Stop Talking*.

82. Grant et al., "The Hidden Advantages of Quiet Bosses": 28.

83. HBR IdeaCast, "The Power of the Introvert in Your Office," HBR Blog Network, retrieved April 4, 2014, from http://blogs.hbr.org/2012/07/the-power-of-the-introvert-in/.

84. Christine M. Pearson and Christine L. Porath, "On the Nature, Consequences and Remedies of Workplace Incivility: No Time for 'Nice'? Think Again," *Academy of Management Executive* 19, no. 1 (2005): 8.

85. Ronald J. Alsop, "Social Disgraces," *Workforce Management*, January 2011: 34.

86. Steve Farkas, Jean Johnson, Ann Duffett, and Kathleen Collins, *Aggravating Circumstances: A Status Report on Rudeness in America* (New York: Public Agenda), retrieved November 25, 2009, from www.publicagenda.org/files/pdf/aggravating_circumstances.pdf.

87. Ibid.

88. Ibid., 24.

89. Pearson and Porath, "On the Nature, Consequences and Remedies of Workplace Incivility: No Time for 'Nice'? Think Again": 7–18.

90. Christine M. Pearson and Christine L. Porath, *The Cost of Bad Behavior: How Incivility Is Damaging Your Business and What to Do about It* (New York: Penguin Group, 2009).

91. Ibid.

92. These types of workplace incivility are adopted and modified from a variety of sources, including the following: Pearson and Porath, *The Cost of Bad Behavior: How Incivility Is Damaging Your Business and What to Do about It*; P. M. Forni, *The Civility Solution: What to Do When People Are Rude* (New York: St. Martin's Press, 2008); Lorraine A. Krajewski, "Workplace Incivility: A Research Study," Presentation at the 2010 Annual Convention of the Association for Business Communication, October 27, 2010, Chicago.

93. Forni, *The Civility Solution: What to Do When People Are Rude*: 24.

94. Ibid., 29.

95. Adam Bryant, "On Passion and Playing in Traffic," *Corner Office* (blog), *The New York Times*, December 5, 2009, www.nytimes.com/2009/12/06/business/06corner.html.

96. Adam Bryant, "No Need to Hit the 'Send' Key. Just Talk to Me," *Corner Office* (blog), *The New York Times*, August 28, 2010, www.nytimes.com/2010/08/29/business/29corner.html.

97. Adam Bryant, "Talk to Me. I'll Turn Off My Phone," *Corner Office* (blog), *The New York Times*, February 27, 2010, www.nytimes.com/2010/02/28/business/28corner.html.

**ESTABLISHING CREDIBILITY**

 **PRINCIPLES OF INTERPERSONAL COMMUNICATION**

 **PRINCIPLES FOR & TYPES OF BUSINESS MESSAGES**

## ⟨⟨⟨ Learning Objectives

After studying this chapter, you should be able to do the following:

**LO3.1** Explain the principles of team communication in high-performing teams.

**LO3.2** Describe and demonstrate approaches to planning, running, and following up on meetings.

**LO3.3** Explain the principles of effective virtual team communication.

**LO3.4** Describe strategies for effective group writing.

**LO3.5** Explain basic principles for handling difficult conversations.

Organizations of all types have increasingly recognized that teams deliver more innovation and better business results. You can expect that in your career you will spend a significant amount of your time in teams. In fact, about 54 percent of professionals spend about one-third of their work time in a team setting. Another 34 percent say they spend about half of their work time in a team setting. Yet, just 3 percent of these professionals say they've been trained to work in teams.[1]

Your ability to contribute to and lead teams will provide you with many career opportunities. In fact, excellent team players are often fast-tracked for better positions. Aside from the many career benefits of teams, working in teams can be energizing. It allows you to bond with your colleagues, learn from others, share your ideas, and celebrate together when your team hits big milestones. Working in teams isn't always easy. It requires that you give up some of your independence. It can be discouraging when team members don't work together well. However, with an understanding of principles for effective teamwork, discipline, and hard work, you're well positioned to succeed in teams. As you read this chapter, think about how you can improve your team communication skills and facilitate productive teamwork.

**Hear Pete Cardon explain why this matters.**

**bit.ly/cardon3**

## CHAPTER CASE: LISTENING AND COMMUNICATING IN TEAMS AT THE PRESTIGIO HOTEL

**WHO'S INVOLVED**

Nancy Jeffreys, director of marketing

Kip Yamada, marketing associate

**The Prestigio** Marketing Team

### The Marketing Team Prepares for a Meeting

The marketing team is about to hold its biweekly meeting. Team members intend to discuss plans for upcoming market research, assess progress on an ongoing initiative to improve customer service, examine ways to use blogs and wikis to improve communication within the team, and finalize plans for a Valentine's Day marketing campaign.

**SITUATION 1**

### Nancy and Kip Hold Grudges from a Prior Disagreement

Nancy and Kip have ignored one another as much as possible in recent months. Problems started when Kip authorized refunds to ten business travelers totaling nearly $4,000. The business travelers complained that they were charged standard hotel rates over several months rather than at discounted rates as advertised on the hotel website. The travelers, however, were not incorrectly charged. Rather, they had not read the fine

**SITUATION 2**

(Nancy Jeffreys character): © Photodisc/Getty Images; (Kip Yamada character): © John A Rizzo/Pixtal/SuperStock

print on the website, which restricted discounts on weekends. Kip authorized the refunds because he felt the travelers were frequent guests who deserved special considerations.

Nancy was furious when she found out that Kip had given the refunds without first checking with her. She called him into her office and scolded him for not speaking to her first. Kip abruptly said, "So much for the famous Prestigio customer service," and left her office. Since then, Nancy had complained to co-workers that Kip didn't understand the business side of running a hotel. Kip complained that Nancy didn't relate to hotel guests and that the hotel was losing business because of it.

**TASK**

**1**

How will the marketing team work together effectively to implement a cohesive marketing approach? (See the team communication section.)

**2**

How will Nancy and Kip discuss their differences and work productively together again? (See the chapter section on difficult conversations.)

## Principles of Effective Team Communication

**LO3.1** Explain the principles of team communication in high-performing teams.

**connect**

Visit http://connect. mheducation.com for an exercise on this topic.

Teams can take many forms. Some teams are formally and permanently organized and titled (such as the *marketing team*). Other teams are temporarily formed for completing a project or an activity (i.e., project team, committee). The most common functions of teams are handling special projects, completing the work of particular departments, developing internal systems innovations, creating customer service innovations, developing product innovations, engaging in employee development, and reducing time to market for products and services.[2]

In a recent survey, business professionals cited ineffective communication (66 percent) as the biggest barrier to team effectiveness. Other major barriers included lack of effective chartering and goal setting (56 percent), lack of clarity and understanding of roles (47 percent), low morale (44 percent), low productivity (42 percent), and lack of trust (36 percent). Similarly, when ranking the most frustrating aspects of being part of a team, business professionals cite the following: ineffective use of meeting time (54 percent), ineffective communication among team members (50 percent), lack of accountability (47 percent), individuals who don't complete assignments (44 percent), and lack of preparation in meetings (41 percent).[3] All of these factors in turn relate to communication competencies.

Your teams will perform far better if they follow the basic principles of team communication, all of which depend on a strong listening-centered approach. Work in teams is among the most researched aspects of work performance, and hundreds of studies have supported each of the following principles:

*Teams should focus first and foremost on performance.* The most basic ingredient of excellent teams is a focus on high performance. Make sure that your team has a sense of urgency and direction to achieve excellence.[4] One signal that teams are sufficiently focused on performance is how often teams talk directly about work priorities. Out of every 100 comments team members in high-performing groups make, 60 to 70 directly relate to work—goals, coordination, roles, task clarification, and other project-related issues. Of the 100 comments, team members make about 15 to 20 supportive statements, intended to show goodwill and encouragement. And, they make 10 to 15 statements that are primarily social.[5] By contrast, team members in lower-performing groups make far fewer work-related and supportive statements. They typically replace these statements with social statements that may help team members bond socially but not around work issues.

**FIGURE 3.1**

Stages of Development in High-Performance Teams

*Source:* Adapted from Susan A. Wheelan, *Creating Effective Teams: A Guide for Members and Leaders* (Thousand Oaks, CA: Sage, 1999), which examines hundreds of scholarly studies on teamwork.

*Teams go through four natural stages to reach high performance.*[6] Nearly all high-performing teams go through four stages before they maximize their performance. In best-case scenarios, work teams take roughly six to seven months to reach this level (see Figure 3.1).[7] Typically, leaders become less directive and more consultative as the team progresses through the stages:

1. *Forming* (months 1 and 2). In the **forming** stage, team members focus on gaining acceptance and avoiding conflict. In some ways, this stage is a honeymoon period in which team members get to know one another.

2. *Storming* (months 2 and 3). In the **storming** stage, team members open up with their competing ideas about how the team should approach work. This stage is typically the least productive, since team members are attempting to make sense of uncertain roles, goals, and accountabilities.

3. *Norming* (months 4 and 5). In the **norming** stage, the team arrives at a work plan, including the roles, goals, and accountabilities.

4. *Performing* (months 6 and 7). In the **performing** stage, teams operate efficiently toward accomplishing their goals. They have evolved to a level where they can transform disagreement and conflict into consensus for future action.

*Effective teams build a work culture around values, norms, and goals.* Organizations and teams constantly attempt to foster unity and high performance. **Team culture** refers to a set of shared perceptions and commitment to collective values, norms, roles, responsibilities, and goals.[8] Typically, teams rapidly develop such shared perceptions and commitment during the norming stage. Only at the performing stage do these shared perceptions and commitments lead to high productivity.

High-performing teams avoid simply going with the flow. Rather, they frequently, explicitly, and openly discuss the set of values, norms, and goals they share. This process is critical, since team members often attach different meanings to the same goals. Open discussion helps team members avoid misinterpreting each other's motivations and actions.

One way that high-performing teams ensure they develop and live up to shared values, norms, and goals is to create a team charter. The team charter provides direction to the team in how it functions to meet shared objectives. Common elements of team charters include purpose or mission statements, values, goals, team member roles (including leadership), tasks, ground rules, communication protocol, meeting protocol, decision-making rules, conflict resolution, and feedback mechanisms. For short-term teams and groups, such as those that operate for school projects, you should make sure your charter also includes contact information for each team member as well as deadlines for task completion.[9]

In Figure 3.2, you can see an abbreviated team charter created by the Prestigio marketing team. It contains many features common to team charters. As you develop team charters, you should view this as an important agreement with your team members.

**FIGURE 3.2**

Team Charter for the
Prestigio Marketing
Team

---

**Prestigio Marketing Team Charter**

**Mission Statement:** We provide marketing for Prestigio that matches its mission of outstanding guest service, superior financial results, and sustainability.

**Values:** Excellence in all work, creativity, honesty, sharing and collaboration, professional growth.

**Goals:** (a) To become the premier resort destination for sustainable conferences in this region; (b) to increase revenue annually by 12 percent; and (c) to maintain 95 percent guest satisfaction among business travelers and reach 85 percent guest satisfaction among conference attendees.

**Team Member Roles/Responsibilities**

| Team Member | Position | Responsibilities |
|---|---|---|
| Andrea Garcia | General manager | Oversee all marketing initiatives. |
| Nancy Jeffreys | Director of marketing | Lead marketing efforts for non-convention guests. |
| Barbara Brookshire | Director of conventions | Lead marketing efforts for convention guests. |
| Kip Yamada | Marketing associate | Develop campaigns for business travelers. |
| Jeff Anderton | Marketing assistant | Conduct market research and analytics. |
| Kailey Chang | Marketing assistant | Create concepts and graphics for campaigns. |

**Communication Protocol**

- We will post project updates, recommendations, and relevant experiences to our team blog. Team members should post roughly twice per week.
- We will respond to direct messages from each other (emails, phone calls) within four hours.
- We recognize the value of each team member's ideas. We will discuss differences of opinion with one another immediately, directly, and respectfully.

**Meetings**

- We will hold meetings on the 1st and 3rd Wednesdays of each month at 10:00 a.m.
- We will rotate facilitators for each meeting. The facilitator will ensure agenda items are covered with the input of all team members.
- The facilitator should create the agenda. By the Monday preceding each meeting, the facilitator should make a call for agenda items. The facilitator should distribute the final agenda as a blog post by Tuesday at noon on the day before each meeting.
- We will rotate note-takers for each meeting.
- The note-taker should post minutes to the team blog by the end of the day on Tuesday. The note-taker will create calendar entries for all action items.

**Decision Making**

We aim for consensus. If we do not achieve consensus, decisions will be based on a majority vote of the general manager, the director of marketing, and the director of conventions.

**Feedback**

- After each major marketing initiative, we will evaluate each team member's performance.
- In June and December each year, we will evaluate team performance and communication.
- We are dedicated to professional growth. We will constantly help one another reach our professional goals.

---

From time to time, your team should evaluate the team charter itself and modify it to better meet the needs of your team.

*Effective teams meet often.* Most groups underperform because they do not spend enough time meeting. Frequent meetings are necessary to establish shared perceptions of roles, goals, and accountabilities. (See the next section on managing meetings.) Also, meetings force team members to meet deadlines. Teams that do not meet often may never reach the performing stage. Or they regress from the performing stage to an even less productive stage. Similarly, effective teams prioritize first meetings and actions. They recognize that the initial series of meetings often set the tone and build a foundation for high performance for an entire project.

*Effective teams embrace differing viewpoints and conflict.* High-performing teams embrace conflict. They see differences of opinion as natural and as a path to creativity and innovation. So, they encourage one another to share their ideas, even when those ideas differ from their own.

One way teams can welcome new ideas is to embrace diversity. Increasingly, research shows that diversity brings better business returns. Diversity comes in two forms: inherent and acquired. **Inherent diversity** involves traits such as age, gender, ethnicity, and sexual orientation. **Acquired diversity** involves traits you acquire through experience, such as customer service experience, retail experience, or engineering experience. Having both types of diversity is called **2-D diversity**. Companies with 2-D diversity are about 45 percent more likely to report a growth in market share during the past year and about 70 percent more likely to have captured a new market. The following behaviors help drive acquired diversity: (1) making sure everyone is heard, (2) making it safe to let team members express novel ideas, (3) giving team members decision-making authority, (4) sharing credit, (5) giving useful feedback, and (6) putting feedback into action. In short, these behaviors drive an innovative, "speak-up culture."[10]

Ensuring that teams are innovative requires discipline because team cultures can easily develop groupthink. In the past decade, businesses have increasingly encouraged teamwork and developed open-space environments where team members stay together for longer periods. However, for teams to function well, most team members need periods of time to work independently and without interruption. The most innovative teams balance time in teams with time for independent work to capture a diversity of strong ideas.[11]

In the final section of this chapter, we will discuss further principles for handling differences of opinion and even conflict. Here, we present two principles that team members use to embrace and respond to differing viewpoints: disassociation and association. **Disassociation** is a process by which professionals accept critique of their ideas without taking it personally and becoming defensive. On the other hand, **association** is the psychological bonding that occurs between people and their ideas. Because the purpose of most meetings and team communication is to increase agreement about roles, goals, and accountabilities and to increase the group's sense of purpose, team members should seek association by the end of a meeting or team communication. Generally, high-performing teams go through repeated cycles of disassociation and association. That is, they suspend attachment to ideas in the initial discussion phase and then attach themselves to ideas as they commit to mutually developed goals and related action items (see Figure 3.3).[12]

One particularly effective approach of developing excellent team communication is for all team members to take assessments of personality and communication styles. After taking the assessments, team members typically share their results with one another. The major value of these types of assessments is to create explicit conversations about styles and preferences.

In the last chapter, you learned about the motivational value system (MVS). You learned how individuals with blue MVSs tend to focus most on nurturing, those with red MVSs focus most on directing, those with green MVSs focus most on autonomizing, and those with hub MVSs focus equally on these motivational values. In this model, the colors are also connected with approaches to conflict. Blue is associated with an *accommodating* approach in which meeting the needs of others is the first concern. These individuals tend to avoid conflict if possible. Red is associated with *asserting* one's viewpoints and interests. These individuals tend to embrace conflict and enjoy trying to win an argument. Green is associated with taking a step back and

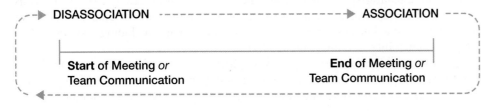

**FIGURE 3.3**

The Cycle of Disassociation and Association in Team Communication

**FIGURE 3.4**

The Strengths Deployment Inventory Triangle Displaying Motivational Value Systems

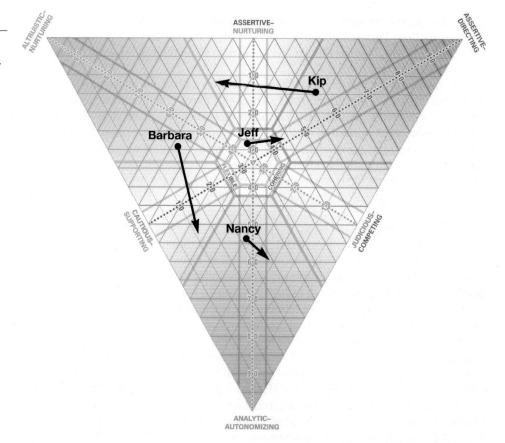

cautiously *analyzing* the situation. These individuals tend to want to discuss differences of opinion after having time to carefully think through their positions. Each approach to conflict is valid. However, team members with different approaches to conflict can easily misinterpret the motives and intentions of one another.[13]

Team members who take this assessment can plot their personalities and approaches to conflict on a triangle. The dot depicts the MVS in routine situations, whereas the arrow depicts approaches to conflict. By taking the assessment, the Prestigio team can rapidly see how their values and preferred communication styles in routine and conflict situations compare to one another (see Figure 3.4). A variety of personality assessments are available to help you and your team members share your preferences of communicating in routine interactions and in conflict situations.

*Effective teams provide a lot of positive feedback and evaluate their performance often.* High-performing teams consistently provide feedback—most of which should be positive—to one another. They may measure aspects of individual and team performance. They may evaluate performance for projects or initiatives or for certain periods of time. Many teams take time at each meeting to briefly evaluate their performance. Several keys to effective evaluation include the following: (a) the process should be primarily positive and goal-driven and rarely punitive; (b) the process should involve clear expectations; and (c) all team members should participate.[14]

You will notice that in the Prestigio marketing team's charter (see Figure 3.2), there are several ways of providing feedback to one another. One way they do this is by completing a team assessment several times per year. In Figure 3.5, you can see an abbreviated example of this team assessment. Common areas of emphasis on team assessments are a focus on results, communication climate (including conflict resolution), accountability, commitment, and trust.

*Effective teams feel a common sense of purpose.* This sense of purpose feeds the team's morale, dedication, and ability to negotiate roles and accountabilities. Thus, high-performing teams frequently discuss their purposes. They also commit to bonding socially and showing concern for one another.[15]

FIGURE 3.5

Sample Team Assessment for the Prestigio Marketing Team

**Prestigio Team Assessment**

Assess your team on a scale from 1 (never) to 5 (always).

| Our team . . . | 1<br>(Never) | 2<br>(Rarely) | 3<br>(Sometimes) | 4<br>(Usually) | 5<br>(Always) |
|---|---|---|---|---|---|
| Focuses on high performance. | 1 | 2 | 3 | 4 | 5 |
| Sets high goals and standards. | | | | | |
| Follows the team charter. | | | | | |
| Gives each team member a chance to participate. | | | | | |
| Engages in open and candid conversation. | | | | | |
| Holds high-value meetings. | | | | | |
| Handles differences of opinion constructively. | | | | | |
| Develops creative solutions together. | | | | | |
| Helps team members grow professionally. | | | | | |
| Trusts one another. | | | | | |

## Developing Quick Trust and Working in Short-Term Teams

Many teams are created to accomplish projects in short periods of time, often in just a few weeks up to a few months. Short-term teams face unique challenges. They are often comprised of people who don't know each other well. They must quickly coordinate their efforts to meet pressing deadlines. They need to reach a high level of performance rapidly. Developing trust is particularly challenging given the short duration of these teams. As a result, developing quick trust is critical.

*Get to know each other.* Most short-term teams are so focused on accomplishing the tasks at hand that they don't take enough time to get to know one another. This is a mistake. Investing 30 minutes to an hour getting to know one another in a social but professional manner helps build the trust the team needs to effectively coordinate its efforts.

One of the fastest ways to increase trust, particularly among teammates who don't know one another, is through self-disclosure. **Self-disclosure** is sharing information about yourself, such as your goals, aspirations, views and values, and experiences. Teammates often bond emotionally and learn about one another's strengths by opening up or self-disclosing to each other. Yet, too much self-disclosure and the wrong types of self-disclosure in professional settings can often backfire.[16] See Exercise 3.7 in the end-of-chapter exercises for ideas about getting to know each other quickly.

*Hold an effective launch meeting.* Short-term teams rely on a well-organized, thorough launch meeting. One of the primary barriers to success for short-term teams is not exploring all options. Because the team is under pressure to meet quick deadlines, team members often feel rushed to decide on a direction, create a plan, and start making progress. By spending an extra hour or two in the launch meeting to explore all options carefully, short-term teams generally choose a better direction from the start of a project and ultimately save time by better coordinating their efforts on a strong choice of direction.

*Commit to working together and separately.* Team members on high-performing teams do a lot of work together and independently. Short-term teams often quickly delegate independent work and then attempt to tie the individual pieces together near the end of the project. By setting up a regular meeting schedule, short-term teams can ensure they spend enough time together to produce excellent work.

*Set up a deliverable schedule and evaluate performance regularly.* Short-term teams often produce poor or mediocre work because the first time they produce shared work is close to final deadlines. Forward-looking short-term teams set up internal deadlines for deliverables across a project so they can evaluate and improve their joint work.

## Managing Meetings

Meetings are one of the primary forums for teams to share and listen to one another's ideas. Because of the increasing importance of teams in the workplace, employees increasingly participate in project and interdepartmental teams. Meetings are an opportunity for teams to coordinate their efforts and increase productivity. Done well, they can be invigorating and produce new insights.[17]

At their best, problem-solving meetings provide incredible return on investment. For example, NorTel evaluated its return on investment on a series of 12 two-day meetings with the express purpose of reducing manufacturing costs. Altogether, the company invested $500,000, but calculations indicated that it saved $91 million due to solutions developed during the meetings.[18]

Yet, meetings have many trade-offs. The biggest drawback is that they take a lot of time. A survey of 150 financial executives found that, on average, they spent 7.8 hours per week in meetings. Over the course of a year, this amounted to 2.3 months of work. Ten years prior in this same survey, financial executives had averaged 6.0 hours per week in meetings, amounting to 1.8 months per year.[19]

Bad meetings are more than just a waste of time. They can create division, lower morale, and decrease productivity.[20] Thus, managers who run effective meetings help their teams work more productively and have better career opportunities.[21] As you prepare to lead and participate in meetings, consider all phases of successful meetings: preparing for them, running them, and following up afterward.

**LO3.2** Describe and demonstrate approaches to planning, running, and following up on meetings.

Visit **http://connect. mheducation.com** for an exercise on this topic.

### Planning for Meetings

As with other communication responsibilities, running effective meetings starts with planning. For routine meetings, you should spend 30 to 60 minutes preparing.[22] For especially important and nonroutine meetings, you may need to spend at least several hours or days planning.

**Essential Questions** Planning for meetings requires strategy, scheduling, and coordination. At a minimum, you should answer the following questions in your preparations:[23]

- What is the purpose of the meeting? What outcomes do I expect?
- Who should attend?
- When should the meeting be scheduled?
- What roles and responsibilities should people at the meeting have?
- What will be the agenda?
- What materials should I distribute prior to the meeting?
- When and how should I invite others?
- What logistical issues do I need to take care of (reserving rooms, getting equipment, printing materials)?

As you answer these questions, keep in mind your purpose and ensure that your plans focus on productive outcomes. Also, think about how scheduling will impact productivity. Generally, you should avoid meetings, especially brainstorming meetings, during the least productive times of the day (usually the afternoon). Typically, most employees are at their best performance in the morning (see Figure 3.6).[24] As far as timing during the week, Tuesdays are overwhelmingly considered the most productive days (57 percent of employees think so). By contrast, Fridays are the least productive days (just 3 percent of employees think they are the most productive).[25]

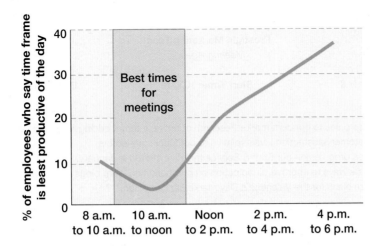

**FIGURE 3.6**

Least Productive Parts of the Workday

*Source:* Adapted from Accountemps, "Accountemps Survey: Employee Output Is Weakest Late in the Day," August, 17, 2010, retrieved November 20, 2010, from http://accountemps.rhi.mediaroom.com/least_productive.

In addition, think about the materials you should send ahead of time. Often, you will make requests of various meeting participants before the meeting to help them prepare. Plan to send materials sufficiently far in advance to give people enough time to do required preparation.

As you plan, consider the type of meeting you want. Meetings can be broadly categorized as coordination meetings or problem-solving meetings. **Coordination meetings** primarily focus on discussing roles, goals, and accountabilities. **Problem-solving meetings** typically involve brainstorming about how to address and solve a particular work problem. In actuality, nearly all meetings involve both coordination and problem solving. However, coordination meetings typically include many agenda items with a reasonable expectation of accomplishing each item in the allocated time. Problem-solving meetings, by contrast, involve more fluid issues that are less easily classified as discrete agenda items and that are less easily given time allotments. For especially difficult issues (i.e., periods of transition such as with mergers), some teams commit to meeting at the same time each day and without a preset agenda until they clearly define the issues at hand.[26]

**Creating and Distributing the Agenda** Agendas provide structure for meetings. For most meetings, preparing and distributing an agenda ahead of time allows each meeting participant to form expectations and prepare.[27]

Most agendas should include items to be covered, time frames, goals and/or expected outcomes, roles, and materials needed. You can foster more effective meetings by getting others involved in the agenda-creation process. For example, at least several days in advance, ask meeting participants for agenda items they want included. Typically, you should send out the final agenda at least one day in advance. Sending out the agenda ahead of time and inviting team members to provide agenda items increases buy-in from meeting participants. You can also consider assigning roles. For example, you might assign someone as a facilitator, a note-taker (minutes), a timer, and so on.[28]

As you develop the agenda, pay attention to the ordering of items so that it flows much like you would expect other written communications to flow from point to point. Also, consider placing those agenda items of most importance near the beginning. This way, if items take longer than expected and you are forced to shelve some items, you have addressed the highest-priority items.[29] See Figure 3.7 for an agenda for the Prestigio marketing team.

## Running Effective Meetings

If you've planned and prepared well for the meeting, you are in a great position to carry out your meeting objectives. Ideally, you've provided clear expectations for meeting participants—what they should have done before the meeting and what they can expect in terms of content and length of the meeting. Once the meeting arrives, you have several options for achieving productive outcomes.

> **Agenda Components**
>
> - Agenda items
> - Time frames*
> - Goals/expected outcomes
> - Roles
> - Materials needed
>
> *optional

**FIGURE 3.7**

Sample Meeting
Agenda

---

**Prestigio Marketing Team**
*Meeting Agenda*

**Date:** November 9          **Start Time:** 10 a.m.          **End Time:** 11 a.m.

**Purposes:**
1. Discuss plans to conduct market research about (a) Internet pricing for groups and (b) customer satisfaction levels relative to our local competitors.
2. Discuss progress on our Staff & Service Initiative started in January.
3. Examine ways to improve participation on our marketing team blogs and wikis.
4. Finalize plans for the Valentine's Day marketing campaign.

**Desired Outcome:**
Create action items to complete within the next month (by December 15). At our December 15 meeting, we will develop our annual marketing plan, which will include priorities for improving guest satisfaction and pricing.

**Agenda Item 1: Internet Pricing for Groups (20 minutes)**
- Summary of findings from Internet pricing survey for groups (Jeff)          5 min.
- Industry standards for Internet pricing for conference groups (Barbara)          5 min.
- Group discussion of findings and options          10 min.
- Develop action items          5 min.

**Agenda Item 2: Improving Customer Satisfaction (20 minutes)**
- Summary of findings from customer satisfaction research on external websites (Jeff)          5 min.
- Group discussion of findings and options          10 min.
- Develop action items          5 min.

**Agenda Item 3: Enterprise Social Software**
- Discuss goals for increased use of wikis and discussion forums (Andrea)          5 min.

**Agenda Item 4: New Promotions**
- Valentine's Day hotel promotions (Nancy)          5 min.

**Summarize Action Items**          3 min.

**Participants:** Andrea Garcia, Nancy Jeffreys, Barbara Brookshire, **Kip Yamada (note-taker)**, Jeff Anderton

---

**Create Tradition, Culture, and Variety**   Most meetings at Starbucks Coffee start with a customer story.[30] Many manufacturing companies start meetings with safety stories. You can create traditions that take only moments or minutes but that reinforce the core values of your organization. These types of traditions create a common sense of purpose (one of the key ingredients of effective teamwork) and are a light way to open people up at the start of meetings.[31]

**Set Expectations and Follow the Agenda**   Take a few moments to explain the purpose of the meeting and what you hope to accomplish. You may also want to set some ground rules, such as your expectations for others to participate, how much time to take with comments, or how to deal with differences of opinion. Part of the ground rules may involve assigning the roles of facilitator, timer, and note-taker. They may also include protocol for use of mobile phones and other potentially disruptive electronic equipment. You may also point out whether certain issues are considered confidential and shouldn't be discussed outside the meeting.[32]

For most meetings, keep the discussion focused on agenda items and stick to allotted times. Some meeting participants may become uninterested or annoyed if they perceive the meeting as unstructured or off schedule.[33]

**Encourage Participation and Expression of Ideas** Each meeting should have a facilitator. The **facilitator** acts from a neutral position to get each person to participate in the conversation and ensure that each agenda item is properly discussed. Facilitators should acknowledge, check for understanding, paraphrase and summarize, not judge, ask for elaboration, and get everyone involved. Sometimes, this may require using explicit phrases such as "I'd like each person to take two minutes to. . . ." For routine meetings, the facilitator is often the organizer.[34]

The issue of neutrality for facilitating is critical. If others view the facilitator as predisposed toward certain positions or perspectives, they are less likely to express their real thoughts. This is especially the case when the facilitator is a person of higher authority.

Making your meetings "safe" for each team member requires conscious effort. After all, in surveys of nearly 2.5 million employees, just 15 percent of respondents agreed that *work teams function in a safe, "win–win" work environment,* and just 17 percent agreed that *work teams have mutual understanding and creative dialogue.*[35] As a meeting leader, encourage debate but defuse any comments that are perceived as noncollegial. The art of encouraging discussion but avoiding arguments takes time. In meetings, it requires that you initially foster disassociation but end with association. Research has shown that teams that have more dissent during meetings reach higher-quality decisions. By opening discussion to all available information and options, teams tend to adopt the best options more often and become more committed to the decisions.[36]

In problem-solving meetings, the leader must establish a pattern for discussion and debate. Generally, the first focus is getting agreement on the definition of the problem. Then, the focus switches to the history of the problem and its current impacts. Third, participants consider the causes and future consequences if the problem is not solved. Finally, the group is ready to brainstorm options for addressing the problem.[37]

**Build Consensus and a Plan of Action** The primary purpose of meetings is to create a plan of action. When all the ideas have been stated, the team must evaluate the alternatives and create an action plan. For important decisions, the group should attempt to build consensus around a decision-making approach that prioritizes factors such as timelines, financial resources, and so on. You may find it difficult to build consensus on the bigger issues. Start by building consensus on smaller ones.[38]

**Closing the Meeting** One priority should be to end the meeting on time. Before ending the meeting, summarize what you have accomplished. In just a few minutes, you can recap action items that the team has agreed on. Make sure the roles and assignments are clear for each of these action items, to establish accountabilities for follow-up.[39]

After a meeting ends (even for those you do not lead), you should mentally evaluate your performance. Consider these questions:[40]

- How much information, analysis, and interpretation did I provide?
- Did I communicate my ideas even if they conflicted with someone else's?
- Did I participate in the implementation of the timeline? Did I meet deadlines?
- Did I facilitate the decision-making process? Or did I just go with the flow?

**Dealing with Difficult People** Inevitably, you will work on teams with disruptive members. They may consistently display a negative attitude, refuse to participate, interrupt others, make irrelevant comments, make condescending remarks about other participants or their ideas, or dominate with excessively lengthy comments. One of the best ways to prevent such behaviors is to provide strong leadership with a clear agenda, goals, and roles. If the problem persists, pull that team member aside. Talk about the disruptive behaviors, and explain how the behavior impacts group performance.

**Meeting Follow-up/ Minutes Components**

- Date and time
- Team members present
- Meeting roles
- Key decisions
- Key discussion points (optional)
- Open issues (optional)
- Action items and deadlines

Consider making specific and polite but firm requests such as the following: "At the next meeting, please give people more time to explain themselves."[41]

## Following Up after Meetings

Follow up by distributing the minutes of the meeting (as a memo, in an email, in a meetings folder on the corporate intranet, or as part of a team blog or wiki). Minutes of the meeting should include the date and time, team members present, decisions, key discussion points, open issues, and action items and related deadlines. You can also include names of people who were invited but were absent and the assigned roles (i.e., note-taker). The minutes serve as a record of what your team accomplished. Figure 3.8 provides an example of meeting minutes.

**FIGURE 3.8**

Sample Meeting Minutes

---

**Prestigio Marketing Team**
*November 9 Meeting Minutes*

**Date:** November 9          **Start Time:** 10 a.m.          **End Time:** 11 a.m.

**Agenda Item 1: Internet Pricing for Groups**
*Discussion:* Jeff presented survey findings about conference attendees' purchases of Internet service while here. The group agreed that Internet-service purchases are far too low and that less use for lower-income groups suggests high price sensitivity.

| Action Items | Responsibility | Completion Time |
|---|---|---|
| • Develop and conduct survey that identifies price points at which conference guests are willing to purchase Internet service. | Barbara, Jeff | December 15 |
| • Develop price sensitivity estimates and related revenue impacts. | Barbara | December 15 |

**Agenda Item 2: Improving Customer Satisfaction**
*Discussion:* Jeff presented customer satisfaction ratings of Prestigio and three local competitors. The group agreed that our customer satisfaction ratings have improved, particularly in relation to competitors. We are most concerned about the areas of cleanliness, business center, and meeting rooms.

| Action Items | Responsibility | Completion Time |
|---|---|---|
| • Develop plans to improve the equipment and furnishings of the business center. | Andrea | December 15 |
| • Develop plans for improving cleanliness and meeting rooms. | Nancy, Andrea | January 15 |

**Agenda Item 3: Enterprise Social Software**
*Discussion:* Andrea encouraged the group to log on to the new enterprise social platform throughout the day, share documents, use wikis, and stay aware of progress on shared projects.

| Action Item | Responsibility | Completion Time |
|---|---|---|
| • Use a wiki to collaborate on a joint project with another member of the marketing team. | All members of marketing team | December 15 |

**Agenda Item 4: New Promotions**
*Discussion:* Nancy introduced her plans for Valentine's promotions, including a price special and advertising campaign designed to cater to local-area couples.

| Action Item | Responsibility | Completion Time |
|---|---|---|
| • Negotiate TV and print ad campaign details with ad agency. | Nancy, Kip | December 1 |

**Participants:** Andrea Garcia, Nancy Jeffreys, Barbara Brookshire, **Kip Yamada (note-taker)**, Jeff Anderton

## ⏻ TECHNOLOGY TIPS

### ONLINE MEETINGS

Business professionals increasingly use online meetings for many purposes: to bring together work teams that have members in different locations, allow marketers and account representatives to show their products and services to customers and clients, provide training to employees, give manufacturers and suppliers a forum to work out quality issues from a distance, and deliver many other opportunities.

© Steve Cole/Getty Images

Online meetings allow you to conduct a meeting in a true, multimedia format. Typically, they are appropriate when people are far away, when the group is large (25 or more), when you feel too emotional or nervous for a face-to-face meeting, when you've already established trust with meeting participants, or when the agenda is fairly routine. Consider face-to-face meetings if possible when trust is not yet established or when discussing sensitive topics such as bad news or big changes.

*Learn about the many functions of meeting software and its limitations.* There are many software platforms for online meetings, including commercial options such as WebEx and GoToMeeting as well as platforms developed in-house. These software platforms include many functions, such as video calling, picture and drawing windows, screen sharing, virtual breakout rooms, instant polls, email, chats, slide shows, electronic whiteboards, discussion boards, shared folders, and a variety of online resources. Learn about each of these tools, experiment with them, and make sure you use them to accomplish the key objectives of your meetings.

Although online meetings provide an increasingly rich communication environment, they rarely attain the connection that face-to-face meetings do. You often encounter a lack of visual cues and thus are less able to develop trust and rapport. Also, participants can easily detach from the meeting and focus on other things going on in their own offices. So, you confront more difficulty directing or monitoring the behavior of meeting participants. Another limitation is that many meeting participants may not know how to use the meeting software well. Similarly, you may encounter technology failures. Most of these limitations can be overcome by using the many features of meeting software. Your job is to know how to use these features naturally so that you can employ them while orchestrating an effective meeting.

*Prepare.* Typically, you should follow roughly the same process for online meetings as face-to-face meetings: preparing an agenda, encouraging everyone to express their ideas, creating action items, and so on (see the discussion of effective meetings in the team communication section). However, since you are using meeting software with participants in many locations, you need extra time to plan how you will coordinate and keep people engaged. Consider assigning roles such as producer and moderator. Also, you should rehearse for important meetings and make sure technical details are functioning correctly before the meeting.

*Discuss ways of documenting and distributing the discussion.* Typically, face-to-face meetings are fairly straightforward to document: One person records the action items and/or minutes. This written document can be distributed to everyone on the team in a single format and serves as a reminder of important goals and action items and eventually a standard for follow-up. By contrast, online meetings generally involve many types of media. Plan how you will document the meeting and make it available to meeting participants later. A variety of software applications are available to document decisions, to-do items, and deadlines.

If you are the team leader, make sure your team members follow through on action items. Follow up as soon as possible on those issues you were not able to resolve during the meeting. If each participant knows you will follow up, they will perceive the meeting as important. If you do not follow up, team members are more likely to view the meeting as a waste of time.

Also, as a team leader, you will likely hold online meetings from time to time. Online meetings have become increasingly popular with improved technology and more dispersed teams. Principles of face-to-face meetings apply well to online meetings. However, online meetings present other challenges and benefits, the topic we discuss in the Technology Tips box.

# Working in Virtual Teams

**LO3.3** Explain the principles of effective virtual team communication.

Organizations increasingly rely on virtual teams to complete projects, initiatives, and a variety of other tasks. These virtual teams generally consist of team members located at various offices (including home offices) and rely almost entirely on virtual technologies to work with one another. One recent survey showed that about 80 percent of professionals in multinational companies report working on a team that is located in different locations. In fact, 64 percent of these professionals work with team members located in other countries. Of those in virtual teams, roughly 46 percent have never met their teammates in person, and another 30 percent meet in person about once per year.[42] In practice, nearly all teams, including teams located in the same office, rely on virtual technologies for a substantial amount of their communication.

Virtual teams are often created because they cost less, are more convenient, and help assemble experts who are not located in the same office. Many times, virtual teams can be more productive and effective than co-located, in-person teams (we'll call these *traditional teams*). However, virtual teams present a variety of unique challenges. Compared to professionals in traditional teams, virtual team members are more likely to experience the following challenges: feeling isolated, not feeling connected to team members, not being able to read nonverbal cues, managing conflict, making decisions, and expressing opinions (introverts generally feel more comfortable expressing opinions in virtual teams; extroverts generally feel more comfortable expressing opinions in traditional teams). Virtual teamwork is further complicated by issues such as time zone differences, language differences, and communication technologies.[43] In addition to the principles for working effectively in traditional teams, consider the following tips when working in virtual teams.[44]

## Focus on Building Trust at Each Stage of Your Virtual Team

Compared to traditional teams, virtual teams typically find it more challenging to maintain trust over the duration of their work together. One way of ensuring trust within the team is living up to the characteristics most sought after in virtual teammates. Professionals in virtual teams rank the following characteristics as most important among virtual teammates: willingly sharing information, being proactively engaged, and collaborating.[45] Typically, you can take actions across the entire life cycle of a virtual team that bolster your credibility and help establish trust within your virtual team with a focus on competence, caring, and character (compared to traditional teams, research has shown that virtual teams far less often go through the storming stage).[46] In Table 3.1, you can see various strategies for displaying competence, caring, and character at each stage of virtual teamwork to build and maintain trust within the team.[47]

## Meet in Person If Possible

The most effective, long-term virtual teams meet in person at the beginning of projects to help the team members build rapport. These kickoffs for virtual teams help team members do the tricky work of forming and norming. Not only are these stages of teamwork more natural for most professionals to accomplish in person, these meetings generally force team members to take enough time together to clearly articulate goals and objectives, values, responsibilities, communication protocol, and other elements of a team charter.

## Get to Know One Another

For all teams, this is important. For virtual teams, this is even more important. Especially in the early stages, forming and norming, virtual team members should schedule plenty of time to bond with one another. This social cement pays off later on with stronger and more aligned teamwork. Throughout the duration of projects, virtual teams should find ways to communicate spontaneously and even socialize in virtual

**TABLE 3.1**

Maintaining Trust over the Life of a Virtual Team Project

| Stage of Project | Elements of Trust | Key Actions to Foster Trust |
|---|---|---|
| Forming | Competence | • Asking and responding to questions about one another's professional accomplishments, strengths, and weaknesses |
| | Caring | • Showing interest in teammates<br>• Expressing a desire to work with teammates |
| | Character | • Making commitments to high team performance<br>• Discussing shared values for a team charter |
| Norming | Competence | • Demonstrating strong performance in early deliverables<br>• Preparing well for initial meetings |
| | Caring | • Sharing information, offering to help teammates, and staying accessible to teammates<br>• Responding promptly to the requests of teammates |
| | Character | • Living up to commitments in the team charter |
| Performing | Competence | • Completing all tasks with excellence |
| | Caring | • Encouraging and supporting teammates to complete tasks near final deadlines when the pressure is highest |
| | Character | • Ensuring all team outcomes are fair to team members and stakeholders |

environments. Colleagues who work in the same location often rely on informal, *watercooler* conversations to get to know each other better and discuss emerging opportunities in a relaxed environment. Effective virtual teams find ways to establish *virtual watercoolers*, where teammates regularly and spontaneously interact. Many tools exist to help virtual teams do this (we discuss some of these tools in Chapter 8 about social media for business communication).

## Use Collaborative Technologies

Over the past 25 years, virtual teams have relied primarily on phone calls, teleconferences, and email to communicate with one another. Some, but not most, virtual teams have also used videoconferences. In the past five years, however, there are far more social collaboration tools that allow virtual team members to communicate and collaborate more efficiently (we discuss some of these tools in Chapter 8 about social media for business communication). However, the many collaboration technologies available create a challenge for many professionals. In fact, 43 percent of virtual team members feel "confused and overwhelmed" by the many choices.[48] Virtual team members should schedule time to agree about which communication technologies to use and ensure team members who are less confident with these tools get training.

## Choose an Active Team Leader

The primary obstacle to virtual team performance is the lack of regular communication. Team leaders should ensure frequent contact and communication to keep the team moving toward its goals. One strategy many virtual teams use is to periodically rotate team leaders. This helps energize the team and keeps team leaders from burning out. This strategy also helps develop leadership skills of team members.

### Run Effective Virtual Meetings

Professionals in virtual teams report that the primary challenge of virtual team meetings is not enough time to build relationships (90 percent). They also cite the following major challenges: the need to make decisions too quickly (80 percent); differing leadership styles (77 percent), unclear decision-making rules (76 percent), and lack of participation (75 percent).[49] Consider the following tips to make your virtual meetings more productive:[50]

- *Start the meeting with social chat.* One long-time expert and observer of virtual teams, Keith Ferrazzi, recommends the "Take 5" strategy—for the first five minutes of the meeting, each person takes a turn to share how he or she is doing.

- *Start with a contentious question.* Opening meetings with energetic and lively conversation causes virtual team members to embrace the meeting.

- *Ask "what do you think about" questions.* Virtual teams—perhaps more than traditional teams—are able to profit from diversity. Make sure your team is capturing the perspectives of all team members.

- *Make sure each team member is involved.* Some team members are more comfortable and outspoken using virtual technologies. Make sure all team members get opportunities to share their views. You might even consider protocols for taking turns in your discussions.

- *Articulate views precisely.* Most virtual teams focus on efficiency in meetings. This forces you to prepare carefully ahead of time and state your views precisely when you have the chance.

- *Take minutes in real time.* In real-time virtual meetings, you can take minutes—particularly those related to decisions—in real time so that meeting participants can comment on and correct information during the meeting. This practice often leads to more accurate recollections of the meeting, more buy-in from team members, and a higher likelihood that action items get accomplished.

- *Focus on your teammates and avoid multitasking.* Up to 90 percent of virtual team members admit they multitask during virtual team meetings.[51] Many new collaboration tools allow teammates to participate in several conversations at a time during an online meeting. Also, most virtual teams report heavily using IM and texting during virtual team meetings. In many cases, this allows side conversations that help the meeting operate more efficiently. However, there are several risks. First, this may distract focus from participating in the larger meeting. Second, it can lead to cliquish subgroups.[52] Make sure you focus sufficiently on your teammates.

- *Use video when possible.* Using video has many benefits. First and foremost, it allows virtual team members to better interpret one another's verbal and nonverbal cues. Also, this real-time conversation generally leads to faster decision making. Finally, an important but often unintended consequence of videoconferences is that virtual team members are less likely to multitask. Most virtual team members think video communication makes the most sense but rarely actually do it. One recent survey of professionals in virtual teams showed that 72 percent believed video would make team communication more effective. Yet, only 34 percent of virtual team members used video to communicate with one another.[53]

## Group Writing

**LO3.4** Describe strategies for effective group writing.

You will undoubtedly have many opportunities to co-create or co-author business reports and other documents during your career. The emphasis on teams in today's workplace is one reason group writing is becoming more prevalent. Many new technologies make this process easier and more efficient than at any time in the past. Yet, creating a strong, precise, and coherent document with many writers is challenging. As you write with teams or other groups, consider applying the following tips.

## Start Right Away

One of the major obstacles to nearly all good writing is not starting soon enough. Developing ideas well near a deadline is rarely successful. This is even more problematic when many members of a team have competing views about the direction of a writing project close to a deadline.

## Work Together at the Planning Stage

In Chapter 5 about developing business messages, we will discuss the three stages of writing: planning, drafting, and reviewing. For all strong writing, planning is the most important stage—it's the stage where you carefully think about audiences and their needs, develop compelling ideas that are well-reasoned, and think about how to frame your message for the most impact. Planning is even more important for group writing. As the group plans together, it should develop clear and specific purposes and goals, clarify and define the basic problems and issues together, prioritize finding certain pieces of information, identify subject-matter experts, and delegate roles for researching and writing. Generally, you should spend a significant amount of time together (*at least* one to two hours for student team writing projects) before delegating independent work. When team members work independently during the planning stage, they often waste time and energy working with different purposes, goals, and expectations.

## Make Sure Your Roles and Contributions Are Fair

Early in the process, your group should clearly discuss the roles and expectations you have for one another—make sure part of this conversation involves splitting up contributions and time commitments equally. You might consider placing this in a team charter.

## Stay Flexible and Open

As a group, it's important to remain open to change during the course of a writing project. As you start gathering information and drafting initial findings and conclusions, you may recognize that earlier decisions about purpose, direction, major points, and roles aren't strong or practical. Instead of staying silent and forging ahead with the writing project, groups should constantly reevaluate whether they need to modify their original plans.

## Meet in Real Time Consistently and Ensure the Writing Reflects the Views of the Group

You can accomplish a lot of coordinated writing working separately. However, you'll inevitably need to make some hard decisions as the writing project evolves. These tough decisions are often difficult to manage without holding real-time conversations about the direction and content of your project.

## Discuss How You Will Edit the Document Together

Make sure all team members discuss and agree about the technologies you'll use as you draft your document. Some people prefer sharing offline word processing files (in programs such as Microsoft Word) with one another. Some people prefer cloud-based documents (such as those on Google Drive) that can be edited in real time by all members of the group. Pay attention to version control (so that some members aren't simultaneously editing different versions of the same document). Discuss how your team will use comments and track changes within the document. Also, be clear about rules for overwriting one another's work. Most programs allow backtracking to find former versions of the document. However, overwriting the work of others, without talking to them first, can lead to frustration.

Finally, make sure your group is clear about the purposes of each round of revisions. Generally, you should first revise with a focus on the strength of your ideas and how well these ideas match the needs of your audience. Then, you should focus on how smoothly the various sections of your paper flow together. Next, you should consider issues such as formatting, ease of reading, and language mechanics.

### Consider a Single Group Member to Polish the Final Version and Ensure a Consistent Voice

Many groups use this strategy effectively. Make sure you choose the right person for this role. Also, avoid viewing this as a single person's work. Consider having the whole group together for this process so that as your designated writer polishes the document, each group member is present to offer input and confirmation.

## Managing Difficult Conversations

**LO3.5**  Explain basic principles for handling difficult conversations.

Business professionals routinely—often on a daily basis—encounter difficult conversations, especially when working in teams and collaborating with others. Difficult conversations are approached with apprehension, nervousness, anxiety, and even fear. Douglas Stone, Bruce Patton, and Sheila Heen of the Harvard Negotiation Project have spent three decades training business professionals to confront difficult conversations. They define difficult conversations as follows:

> Any time we feel vulnerable or our self-esteem is implicated, when the issues at stake are important and the outcome is uncertain, when we care deeply about what is being discussed or about the people with whom we are discussing it, there is potential for us to experience the conversation as difficult.[54]

Difficult conversations often center on disagreements, conflict, and bad news. Common types of difficult conversations for entry-level business professionals include receiving a bad performance review, having ideas rejected, critiquing a colleague, giving feedback to a boss, correcting someone, approaching rule breakers about their behavior, talking to a slacker on a group project, and dealing with office politics.[55]

Many people prefer to avoid difficult conversations because they want to avoid hurting the feelings of others, want to avoid conflict, or for other reasons. Many business professionals believe that honesty during moments of conflict may backfire and hurt their careers. However, this is not necessarily the case. Those business managers and executives who approach difficult conversations in a timely, honest, and caring manner typically accomplish much more professionally. After working with corporate clients for nearly three decades, one research team concluded that the most influential people are those who can effectively handle difficult conversations:[56]

> As it turns out, you don't have to choose between being honest and being effective. You don't have to choose between candor and your career. People who routinely hold crucial conversations and hold them well are able to express controversial and even risky opinions in a way that gets heard. Their bosses, peers, and direct reports listen without becoming defensive or angry.[57]

In this section, we briefly present basic, tried-and-true principles for handling difficult conversations in the workplace. You will notice that these principles rely on active listening with a learner mind-set. You can see several examples of how to put these principles into practice (see Table 3.2 and Figure 3.9). These examples relate to Kip and Nancy from the opening case. Kip and Nancy hold strong grievances toward one other because of a past disagreement about issuing refunds to business travelers. They avoid one another when possible. Their poor working relationship hinders productivity and makes work less pleasant for them and their team.

### Embrace Difficult Conversations and Assume the Best in Others

Most people back away from uncomfortable or unpleasant conversations. This is particularly the case when we feel we have a lot to gain but risk heavy losses if it doesn't go right. For these reasons, difficult conversations are often emotionally challenging.[58] Successful people in the workplace do not evade difficult conversations. Those who regularly tackle them with skill and tact improve work performance for themselves and others.

One way to embrace difficult conversations is to view conflict as an opportunity.[59] That is, the exchange of perspectives and competing ideas reflects open and honest

**TABLE 3.2**

## Ineffective and Effective Approaches to Difficult Conversations

| Approaches | Ineffective Examples | Effective Examples |
|---|---|---|
| Initiating the conversation <br>© Photodisc/Getty Images<br><br>© John A Rizzo/ Pixtal/SuperStock | **Nancy:** I want to go over your mishandling of the refunds several months ago. I have some ideas for how we can avoid this kind of problem in the future.<br><br>This approach starts with blame. Worse yet, it frames the conversation as Nancy's story. | **Nancy:** Kip, let's talk about how the refunds to business travelers were handled a few months ago. First, I want to apologize for speaking so harshly without hearing your side first. Since then, I feel like we haven't worked well together. I think we can figure out a better way to make sure we're on the same page, and I also think we can figure out ways to avoid misleading our customers.<br><br>When you authorized the refunds, I never heard all of the details. Do you mind telling me about some of the customers who were upset and what you did to address their concerns?<br><br>This approach is effective for several reasons. Nancy apologizes for her harsh words. She declares her intent: to work together better and come up with solutions. Nancy expresses her intent of discussing solutions that take into account both hers and Kip's perspectives (shared story). She invites Kip to tell his story. |
| Disagreeing diplomatically | **Nancy:** Look, you clearly overstepped your authority. You refunded $4,000, but you are authorized to refund $500. Simply because the computer system is set up on a per-customer basis doesn't mean you can authorize such large refunds. You definitely should have talked to me about these refunds prior to approval.<br><br>Nancy does not recognize Kip's explanation or feelings as having any merit, which places Kip on the defensive and could lead him to resentment. Nancy projects a tone of blame by consistently using you-statements. | **Nancy:** Thanks for telling me how you felt. I can see that you were looking out for the interests of the guests and our long-term success here at the Prestigio. I do want to explain why I thought you should have consulted with me prior to making the refunds. We developed the weekend special together, so I think you were clear about the policies. In the reservation system, it's true that I've allowed you to refund up to $500 per traveler. However, I think you should have talked to me about these large refunds as soon as you started refunding more than one traveler for the same reason. I view you as overstepping your authority because you refunded nearly $4,000.<br><br>Nancy validates Kip's perspective by understanding how he *felt*. She explains why she thinks he overstepped his authority with a variety of I-statements. |
| Avoiding exaggeration and either/or approaches | **Kip:** I can never approach you with customer issues. You're always fixated on following the pricing policies to a tee, even when the guests have no way of knowing the costs they're incurring. You never try to understand the guest's perspective. Your approach is not working, and it's losing us money.<br><br>Kip repeatedly exaggerates the frequency of Nancy's actions with words such as never and *always*. He takes an either/or approach by saying Nancy's approach doesn't work. | **Kip:** I'm hesitant to bring up customer issues with you. I think you sometimes take a tough approach to guests, even when they have legitimate complaints. I can think of several cases in which guests have stopped coming here after you denied their claims. In each case, I agreed with their reasoning and understood why they were not aware of costs they were incurring. In the end, I think we end up losing revenues when we deny refunds to our guests who feel unfairly charged.<br><br>Kip states his real feelings of frustration and explains his point of view. By using phrases such as *sometimes* and *I think*, he avoids a right-versus-wrong comparison between his and Nancy's approaches. |

**FIGURE 3.9**

Sample Approach to a
Difficult Conversation

*Nancy:* Kip, let's talk about how the refunds to business travelers were handled a few months ago. First, I want to apologize for speaking so harshly without hearing your side first. Since then, I feel like we haven't worked as well together. I think we can figure out a better way to make sure we're on the same page, and I also think we can figure out ways to avoid misleading our customers.

When you authorized the refunds, I never heard all of the details. Do you mind telling me about some of the customers who were upset and what you did to address their concerns?

| Nancy initiates difficult conversation |

*Kip:* Well, I guess I think you overreacted. You were upset that I didn't get your permission before issuing the refunds. But I thought I was acting within my authority. In our reservation system, I'm cleared to authorize refunds of up to $500. So, I didn't see a need to get your permission when I'm already cleared in the system. And, I felt that you didn't even give me time to explain myself.

| Kip's story |

But that's not the whole story. I'm hesitant to bring up customer issues with you. I think you sometimes take a tough approach to guests, even when they have legitimate complaints. I can think of several cases in which guests have stopped coming here after you denied their claims. In each case, I agreed with their reasoning and understood why they were not aware of costs they were incurring. In the end, I think we end up losing revenue when we deny refunds to our guests who feel unfairly charged.

*Nancy:* Thanks for telling me how you felt. I agree that at the time I should not have snapped at you. I do want to explain why I thought you should have consulted with me prior to making the refunds. We developed the weekend special together, so I think you were clear about the policies. In the reservation system, it's true that I've allowed you to refund up to $500 per traveler. However, I think you should have talked to me about these large refunds as soon as you started refunding more than one traveler for the same reason. I view you as overstepping your authority because you refunded nearly $4,000. Now, I understand your perspective. I also know that you were acting with the best interests of our customers and the hotel in mind.

| Nancy's story |

*Kip:* So, I think you're saying that you felt I overstepped my authority because, cumulatively, I was refunding far more than $500 for the same complaint, even though it was for different customers. Is that right?

*Nancy:* That's right. Now, I think the key is to figure out how we can work better together in the future. It sounds to me like there are several issues. First, we need to make sure we always hear one another out immediately instead of letting hard feelings fester. I think this issue would have been resolved right away if I had listened to you right away. Second, I think we should discuss the process for handling major guest complaints. Finally, but I think most importantly, we should reevaluate what we believe constitutes a reasonable complaint and under what circumstances we provide refunds. I think it's safe to say that we view this differently. Kip, do you have suggestions for how we should manage this situation in the future?

| Nancy and Kip's shared story |

*Kip:* Well, I think there are several basic cases where we should refund our guests. For example . . .

_____ *Nancy and Kip continue to talk about shared approaches and solutions.*_____

communication. If there is no conflict, employees are likely not voicing their true perspectives. Generally, colleagues tend to respect one another more when they know they can safely disagree.

To make a difficult conversation safe, follow the advice of Jacqueline Kosecoff, CEO of Prescription Solutions:

> Assume positive intent. It's one of the ways to . . . keep communication on the high road. Perhaps somebody was misunderstood, or they misheard something. You have to go back and ask for the context, and it's very likely to be simply a misunderstanding. And if you listen, it can be resolved. And it tends to, I think, breed a lot more trust and respect among us.[60]

### Adopt a Learning Stance and Commit to Hearing Everyone's Story

Earlier in the chapter, we distinguished between the judger and learner mind-sets. In emotionally charged, high-stakes conversations, approaching the conversation with a learner mind-set will often lead to productive outcomes. You can do this by avoiding the message-delivery stance.[61] Because difficult conversations typically involve unresolved problems, each person should participate in a joint process of understanding the problems and creating solutions. The message-delivery stance implies that you have nothing to learn from the other person involved in the conversation. In sensitive situations, others will resist your attempts to impose solutions.

The learning stance involves a commitment to understanding others' **stories**— their retrospective versions of interpersonal interactions or their explanations of business successes and failures. In difficult conversations, invite others to describe their views and feelings of disputed events. When people have the opportunity to share their stories, they are often less resistant to change and more accommodating of the views of others. Sharing stories with one another can lead to shared interpretations of events, empathy, and new ways of viewing workplace relationships and business possibilities.[62]

One major benefit of allowing all people involved in a difficult conversation to share their views is buy-in. Research has shown that when everyone involved shares their ideas, they tend to be more committed to the ultimate decision of the group, even when their ideas are not adopted. When they remain silent, they tend not to commit to the decision of the group.[63]

### Stay Calm and Overcome Noise

Few business professionals prepare for difficult conversations. And because emotions run high during such conversations, they often do not go well. Participants face a lot of internal noise, and this muddies rational thinking: They are nervous about the outcome of the encounter for themselves and others, and they often feel incapable of constructively expressing all their thoughts and emotions.

During these difficult encounters, high emotional intelligence is crucial. Self-awareness is the foundation. When you feel angry or defensive, you need to ask yourself, "What do I really want?" and "How is what I'm feeling affecting how I'm responding?" By consciously asking yourself these questions, you are redirecting activity to the rational part of your brain. This de-escalates physical threats and allows you to respond more rationally.

While you should pay a lot of attention to your own emotions, intentions, and goals, you must also focus on those with whom you are speaking. They are likely experiencing similar emotions. Apply your active listening skills to feel and show empathy. If someone gets angry, view this as an opportunity. Do not return the anger, but rather help the other person channel the anger appropriately and rationally. Consider asking your conversational partner to sit down or offer a drink. As you summarize his or her thoughts and feelings, you defuse strong emotions and make the conversation constructive and rational.[64]

---

**Principles of Difficult Conversations**

- Embrace difficult conversations.
- Assume the best in others.
- Adopt a learning stance.
- Stay calm/ overcome noise.
- Find common ground.
- Disagree diplomatically.
- Avoid exaggeration and either/or approaches.

---

**Components of Difficult Conversations**

*Steps*
1. Start well/declare your intent.
2. Listen to their story.
3. Tell your story.
4. Create a shared story.

### Find Common Ground

Finding common ground seems like obvious advice, but it's not easy to do during emotionally charged moments when you feel attacked. Finding common ground will help you and others accomplish two things. Emotionally, it lessens the perceived distance between you, and it may even lead to bonding. Rationally, it helps you analyze the issues at hand in a way that will likely lead to mutually acceptable solutions. You can find common ground in a number of areas, including facts, conclusions, feelings, goals, and values.

### Disagree Diplomatically

Difficult conversations involve different perspectives. To create a learning conversation rather than a defensive and judgmental one, find ways to disagree diplomatically. By disagreeing well, you lessen the resistance that others have to you and your views. Typically, you can disagree diplomatically by validating the views and feelings of others and using I-statements. **Validating** others means that you recognize their perspectives and feelings as credible or legitimate. It does not necessarily mean that you agree. **I-statements** begin with phrases such as *I think*, *I feel*, or *I believe*. During disagreements or difficult conversations, I-statements soften comments to sound more conciliatory and flexible and less blaming and accusatory (see examples in Table 3.2).

### Avoid Exaggeration and Either/Or Approaches

As you navigate difficult conversations, avoid making them overly simplistic. Usually, you are encountering complex business and relationship issues. Also, by simplifying your story, you often inadvertently cause others to become defensive because you are in effect disputing their story or challenging their identity.

Two ways of oversimplifying your approach to difficult conversations is by exaggerating and by applying either/or approaches. If you find yourself using superlatives such as *always*, *never*, *most*, or *worst*, you might be exaggerating. By choosing other words, you're more likely to present your story accurately and also validate others. Applying an either/or approach to most business communication is ineffective. For difficult conversations, it usually translates into a right-versus-wrong approach. Approaching a difficult conversation with an *I'm right, you're wrong* approach inevitably dooms the conversation. See examples of exaggeration and either/or approaches in Table 3.2.

### Initiate the Conversation, Share Stories, and Focus on Solutions

Initiating a difficult conversation is stressful. You may have avoided bringing up the issue because you are nervous about how the conversation will affect your working relationships with others, or you are worried about costs to your career. Starting well is crucial. The opening moments of a difficult conversation offer a great opportunity to frame or orient the conversation for problem solving. In the opening moments, consider declaring your intent—your sincere desire to understand and find a solution that works for each of you. One obstacle to holding difficult conversations is that one or more people involved tend to judge the motives of others unfairly. Declaring your intent can reduce the likelihood of unfairly judging motives. See Table 3.2 for examples of initiating a conversation.[65]

When you initiate a difficult conversation, a common learning stance is to listen to the story of others first, then share your story, and then create a shared story.[66] When you invite others to share their perspectives and versions of events first, they recognize your sincere interest in understanding and cooperating with them. By telling your story, you allow others to see another version of reality and empathize with you. Finally, together you create a shared story. A **shared story** involves combining yours and others' experiences, perspectives, and goals into a shared approach to work. The *their story–your story–shared story* process requires a substantial time commitment, but it is well worth it. Figure 3.8 presents a simplified example of this process.

# COMMUNICATION Q&A

## CONVERSATIONS WITH CURRENT BUSINESS PROFESSIONALS

**Peter Cardon: What is your role leading teams?**

**Peter Ernandes:** I am an international supply chain manager at Northrop Grumman Aerospace. It is my challenge to rely on the skill set of my cross-functional team to accurately assess business opportunities and formally communicate our expectations and conditions to new business partners.

**PC: Why are teams so important in today's workplace?**

**PE:** Teams are the standard of any working environment today. I feel one reason for this is the pace of the current working environment. The only way to deal with the new pace of demand is to break up responsibilities and collaborate appropriately. I also feel that working in teams of "co-located" team members is a quickly fading model of teams. It is because of these two factors that using tools and technology which facilitate communication with one another is that much more vital.

**PC: What are some keys to making teams work well?**

**PE:** The key to driving success in teams, first and foremost, is a commitment to understanding that teams are a collection of people, not machinery or software. Culture, experience, and personality can be polarizing elements of a team. However, those same differences, channeled properly, often foster the most triumphant accomplishments, effectively trumping any output a perfectly coded algorithm can create. Respect and communication are each essential components of the commitment I mentioned earlier.

*Peter Ernandes is a senior associate at PwC with an emphasis on finance strategy and operations. He was an international supply manager at Northrop Grunman Aerospace at the time of the interview.*

Courtesy of Peter Erandes

If a team starts off with an understanding that each team member is unique, it creates an environment where open dialogue can take place. Whenever possible, I lay this foundation as an expectation in my teams.

**PC: How do you make sure meetings are productive and fun?**

**PE:** Forging a fun and productive environment depends on the maturity of the team. Newly formed teams are much more productive, in my opinion, when they start tasks early and meet often. This allows for two things: (1) time for each team member to assess the strengths and shortcomings of one another and (2) time to adjust for the unexpected. Challenges will most certainly occur at this stage with the newness of dealing with one another, as members might feel hesitant expressing their "true" opinions on the task at hand. Communication at this stage is critical to ensure all members are focused on the same goal and have an understanding of how to accomplish the task at hand. Fun is not hard to create given the newness of the team and the task.

As a team matures, the environment shifts. Members learn to trust one another for various tasks, and less up-front communication is usually needed. But, that is not to say that it shouldn't take place. When meetings are absolutely necessary, I push for longer ones, allocating a portion of the time for individuals just to catch up with one another. I also try to promote off-site meetings as much as I can so that people can engage with one another over food and drinks. Final word on this: All teams are different; therefore, what is productive for one group of individuals might not work in other scenarios or arrangements.

**PC: What communication tools do you use to help your teams meet their goals?**

**PE:** Communication tools are essential to effective collaboration. However, tools need to be used as the situation dictates, and not as a plug-and-play template. I have used a variety of tools like Google Hangouts, Prezi, SlideShare, and Google Drive. I feel when these tools are used appropriately, all are quite effective and allow for a collaborative environment which facilitates communication. But, I pick and choose when to use these tools. The culture of the aerospace environment is one comprised of an older workforce, and a flashy Prezi sometimes does not communicate the message a PowerPoint would. Therefore maintaining a tool belt of communication tools and knowing which one is appropriate given your team or audience is a fundamental skill to hone through one's professional career.

**PC: For young professionals, what concluding advice would you give about developing skills to communicate effectively in teams?**

**PE:** I pull on my life experiences when developing strategies to effectively communicate in my professional setting. I grew up in an environment of noise and chaos. So I learned that the most effective form of communication was listening appropriately, and timing when I could contribute something that would be regarded as "valuable." So, the first bit of advice is to listen more than you speak. Secondly, whenever engaging with teams, there is a lesson to be learned. Oftentimes, we get so caught up in the task at hand that we fail to give ourselves time to reflect on the moment and what was learned. If young professionals take a moment to reflect on their experiences, they will find they are developing and adopting a variety of tools, internal and external, which will help them grow as individuals.

# Chapter Takeaway for *Team Communication and Difficult Conversations*

## LO3.1 Explain the principles of team communication in high-performing teams. (pp. 72–78)

### Characteristics of High-Performing Teams

- Teams should focus first and foremost on performance.
- Teams go through natural stages to reach high performance.
- Effective teams build a work culture around values, norms, and goals.
- Effective teams meet often.
- Effective teams embrace differing viewpoints and conflict.
- Effective teams provide a lot of positive feedback and evaluate their performance often.
- Effective teams feel a common sense of purpose.

Stages of Development in High-Performance Teams

## LO3.2 Describe and demonstrate approaches to planning, running, and following up on meetings. (pp. 78–83)

### Items in an Agenda

- Agenda items
- Time frames*
- Expected outcomes
- Roles
- Materials needed

*optional

### Items in Minutes

- Date and time
- Team members present
- Meeting roles
- Key decisions
- Key discussion points*
- Open issues*
- Action items and deadlines

*optional

See *examples of an agenda* in Figure 3.7 and *minutes* in Figure 3.8.

## LO3.3 Explain the principles of effective virtual team communication. (pp. 84–86)

### Principles for Virtual Team Communication

- Focus on building trust at each stage of your virtual team.
- Meet in person if possible.
- Get to know one another.
- Use collaborative technologies.
- Choose an active team leader.
- Run effective virtual meetings.

## LO3.4 Describe strategies for effective group writing. (pp. 86–88)

### Tips for Group Writing

- Start right away.
- Work together at the planning stage.
- Make sure your roles and contributions are fair.
- Stay flexible and open.
- Meet in real time consistently and ensure the writing reflects the views of the group.
- Discuss how you will edit the document together.
- Consider a single group member to polish the final version and ensure a consistent voice.

## LO3.5 Explain basic principles for handling difficult conversations. (pp. 88–93)

### Principles for Difficult Conversations

- Embrace difficult conversations.
- Assume the best in others.
- Adopt a learning stance.
- Stay calm/overcome noise.
- Find common ground.
- Disagree diplomatically.
- Avoid exaggeration and either/or approaches.

### Steps in Difficult Conversations

1. Start well.
2. Listen to their story.
3. Tell your story.
4. Create a shared story.

See *examples of less effective and more effective statements in difficult conversations* in Table 3.2. See an *example of a difficult conversation* in Figure 3.9.

# Key Terms

acquired diversity, 75

association, 75

coordination meetings, 79

disassociation, 75

facilitator, 81

forming, 73

inherent diversity, 75

I-statements, 92

norming, 73

performing, 73

problem-solving meetings, 79

self-disclosure, 77

shared story, 92

stories, 91

storming, 73

team culture, 73

2-D diversity, 75

validating, 92

# Discussion Exercises

**3.1  Chapter Review Questions** (LO 3.1, LO 3.2, LO 3.3, LO 3.4, LO 3.5)

A. Research shows that under ideal conditions, most teams reach high performance in six to seven months. How can a student team that must complete a project in a few weeks to a few months go through the stages of team development more quickly and reach peak performance?

B. In what ways can teams form a common sense of purpose? Provide examples from your experience.

C. Explain how creating and following an agenda is beneficial. Are there situations in which an agenda is not beneficial? Explain.

D. Explain the three strategies of virtual teams that you think are most important.

E. Explain the three strategies of effective group writing that you think are most important.

F. Explain what is meant by concluding a difficult conversation with a shared story.

**3.2  Communication Q&A Discussion Questions** (LO 3.1, LO 3.2)

A. What are some reasons that Peter Ernandes provides for a shift toward more teamwork?

B. What does Ernandes say about the keys to making teams work well? Which point do you think is most important? Explain.

C. What does he say about the nature of communication at different stages of the team?

D. What does he say about how to select the right communication tools?

E. What do you think is the best advice Ernandes gives? Explain.

**3.3  Speaking Up in Meetings** (LO 3.1, LO 3.2, LO 3.5)

Barbara J. Krumsiek of the Calvert Group recently talked about the style of meetings that take place in her organization:

> I think it can be a little jarring actually for people who are used to perhaps a little more civility. I think we're civil, but we're direct. I don't like meetings if my direct reports leave the room and turn to somebody and say, "Can you believe someone said that?" And so I try to explain to them by example that if you find yourself doing that when you leave the room, or shaking your head, or kicking yourself for not having said something, or thinking that there were real problems with what somebody said, next time you have to say it in the room. You have to, or you will not be the most impactful member of this team. When I first got to Calvert, there was a lot of that. And I had one of my direct reports send me an email, complaining about something somebody else said. I just got back to them and said, "I'm not going to read this because I don't see the person you're talking about CC'd on it. So if you CC them on it and send it back to me, I will deal with it." Well, I never had to get it back, because once the person really dealt with it, it was fine.[67]

Based on Krumsiek's comments, answer the following:

A. What types of expectations are there for meetings at the Calvert Group?

B. What does Krumsiek say about the nature of directness and civility at meetings? Does this imply the meetings are not civil?

C. How does Krumsiek deal with complaints about other team members?

D. What are three principles from Krumsiek's comments that you can apply to how you approach team communication?

**3.4  Brainstorming at Meetings** (LO 3.1, LO 3.2, LO 3.5)

Susan Docherty, former president and managing director of General Motors, described how she and her team communicate at meetings:

> I love to brainstorm with my team around the table in my office. I like to use a big whiteboard for ideas, because when you make things visual, you encourage the team to get up there at the whiteboard and put their thoughts out there. It's one thing to say that you're inclusive, but it's a whole other thing to be inclusive. And when people come into my office, they feel welcome. My door is open. They can bring ideas. They begin to understand that, as a leader, I want to be collaborative. I don't have all the answers or all the best ideas, nor do I want to. The whiteboard also keeps great ideas in front of us, not buried in

an email and not buried in a stack of papers on our desks. And it enables everybody to own what we've got to get done. People will grab a marker and put up there that we're going to do a deep dive to figure something out, and they put their name beside it. And there are lots of times where we put something on the board, and it requires a couple of people to get together to go work on it.[68]

Based on Docherty's comments and your own experiences, answer the following:

A. What strategies can you use for making meetings more visual? What are the benefits of making meetings visual?

B. What strategies can you use to make meetings more inclusive?

C. What does it mean for "everybody to own what we've got to get done"? What are a few approaches you can take to help make this happen for work teams?

### 3.5  *Being Friendly* versus *Being Friends* for Difficult Conversations (LO 3.5)

Kasper Rorsted, chief executive of Henkel, the consumer and industrial products company based in Düsseldorf, Germany, recently talked about the first time he had to be someone else's boss:

> [I first became someone else's boss] in 1989, right when I got promoted from being a sales rep in the Digital Equipment Corporation to being a sales manager at the age of 27. I had about 20 people at that point in time. All but two of them were older than I was. When you're 27, you're inexperienced, so you don't know what to fear. I didn't know what I probably should have known. The first time I realized it was serious was when, after about six months, I had to lay somebody off. And then suddenly you move from the sunny side of the deal to the real deal. I remember I was sleeping very poorly for almost a week. He had a family.
>
> So one of the lessons I learned from that, which I've been very aware of since, is to be friendly, but not a friend. I had grown up in the company and I knew everybody, so I was more a friend. But then I had to start having honest conversations with people about how they performed, and that taught me a lesson. I've always been friendly but never been friends anymore. When we have parties, I'm the one who will leave early.[69]

Based on Rorsted's comments, answer the following questions:

A. What do you think Rorsted means that he could "be friendly, but not a friend" once he became a boss and had to have difficult conversations with others?

B. Do you agree with his perspective about being friendly versus being friends? Do you think being friends makes having honest conversations in the workplace more difficult? Explain.

C. How can a person prepare for the difficult conversations necessary as one becomes a boss or supervisor?

### 3.6  **Evaluating a Prior Team's Performance** (LO 3.1, LO 3.2, LO 3.3, LO 3.5)

Think about a recent team or group project you were part of. Evaluate your team's performance in the following ways:

A. How well did your team set goals up front?

B. How well did your team establish norms, values, roles, and accountabilities?

C. To what degree did your team move through various stages of team development (forming, norming, storming, and performing)?

D. How effective were your meetings? Explain.

E. How well did all team members participate? Explain reasons for participation and nonparticipation.

F. How well did your team handle differences of opinion?

G. If you were to start the project over again, what three pieces of advice would you give to your team to drive higher performance?

### 3.7  **Getting to Know Each Other** (LO 3.1)

In your newly formed short-term team, share responses to questions about your personal, academic, and professional backgrounds and goals. Take turns responding to questions such as the following:

A. *Personal background and interests*:

- Who is a person you admire and would most want to meet? Why would you want to meet this person? What would you ask this person?
- What's your favorite movie? Why?
- What are some of your hobbies?
- What place do you want to travel to the most? Why?
- What's the craziest thing you've ever done? What is your biggest pet peeve? What's your idea of fun?
- Where were you born? What is unique about that city?

B. *Academic background*:

- What's the favorite class you've taken? What did you enjoy about it?
- What electives would you recommend? Why?
- What's your major? Why did you choose it?

C. *Professional background and goals*:

- What's the best job you've had? What did you enjoy about it?
- What was the best team you've worked on? Why was this team so successful?
- What was the worst team you've worked on? Why was this team unsuccessful?
- What companies or organizations would you want to work at? Why?
- What's your idea job? Why?

# Evaluation Exercises

**3.8  Evaluating a Prior Group Writing Project** (LO 3.1, LO 3.2, LO 3.3, LO 3.4, LO 3.5)

Think about a recent team or group project you were part of. Evaluate your team's performance in the following ways:

A. How well did your team set goals and purposes for your writing project up front?

B. How did your team establish roles for the project? Was the rationale for these roles appropriate?

C. Did your team ever change direction during the project? Did you not change direction but wanted to? Explain how flexible your team was over the course of the project.

D. How effective were your meetings? Explain.

E. How well did all team members participate? Explain reasons for participation and nonparticipation.

F. How well did your team handle differences of opinion?

G. If you were to start the project over again, what three pieces of advice would you give to your team to create a better final report?

**3.9  Describe a Difficult Conversation from a Movie or TV Episode** (LO 3.5)

Think about a recent movie or TV episode you watched. Select a scene that involves an interesting but difficult conversation. Ideally, select one that might occur in the workplace. Based on this scene, do the following:

A. Summarize the scene in one paragraph.

B. Analyze the difficult conversation. Explain how well the characters involved applied effective principles for communicating.

C. Describe how you can apply two strategies from the scene as you approach difficult conversations in the workplace.

**3.10  Assess a Recent Difficult Conversation** (LO 3.5)

Think about a recent difficult conversation you had. Ideally, select a conversation that occurred in the workplace or at school. Based on this conversation, do the following:

A. Summarize the conversation in one paragraph.

B. Evaluate your and others' performance in terms of assuming the best in one another, staying calm, finding common ground, disagreeing diplomatically, avoiding exaggeration and either/or approaches, and sharing all stories (including a shared story).

C. Describe three ways you would approach the conversation differently if you did it over again.

D. Assuming you had the conversation again, what are three questions you would ask to invite a learning stance?

**3.11  Create a Team Charter** (LO 3.1)

For a team project you're currently working on, create a team charter. Consider using categories such as the following: purpose or mission statements, values, goals, team member roles (including leadership), tasks, ground rules, communication protocol, meeting protocol, decision-making rules, conflict resolution, and feedback mechanisms. Feel free to add your own categories as you and your team deem appropriate.

**3.12  Create a Team Assessment** (LO 3.1)

For a team project you're currently working on, create a team assessment. You can use ratings and/or open-ended questions. Consider including items such as the following: focus on results, communication climate (including conflict resolution), accountability, commitment, and trust. Feel free to add other categories as you and your team deem appropriate.

# Application Exercises

**3.13  Creating an Agenda** (LO 3.2)

Create an agenda for a recent meeting you had or a meeting that you will have soon (it could be a work or school agenda). Feel free to make up details if necessary. Prepare the agenda with agenda items, time frames, goals, roles, and materials needed.

# Language Mechanics Check

**3.14  Review the comma rules C8 through C10 in Appendix A. Then, rewrite each sentence to add or remove commas where needed.**

A. You must apply for this credit card offer by July 1.

B. You must apply for this credit card offer by July 1 2015.

C. You must apply for this credit card offer by July 1 2015 in order to be eligible.

D. You can apply for the credit card anytime between July 1 and July 31.

E. Please come to my office on Tuesday July 5.

F. In 2015 22 of our engineers will visit our China branch.

G. The president, of our university, was a successful entrepreneur.

H. The president of our university, a successful entrepreneur, will lead, the delegation.

I. The president, owner of three companies, believes that entrepreneurship is the key, to success.

J. The president, went out to dinner, after giving the keynote address.

# Endnotes

1. Ken Blanchard Companies, *The Critical Role of Teams* (Escondido, CA: Author: 2006).

2. Ibid.

3. Ibid.

4. Jon R. Katzenbach and Douglas K. Smith, *The Wisdom of Teams: Creating the High-Performance Organization* (New York: Harper-Collins, 2003); Jon R. Katzenbach and Douglas K. Smith, "The Discipline of Teams," *Harvard Business Review,* July/August 2005: 162–171.

5. Susan A. Wheelan, *Creating Effective Teams: A Guide for Members and Leaders* (Thousand Oaks, CA: Sage, 1999).

6. Wheelan, *Creating Effective Teams: A Guide for Members and Leaders*; Bruce Tuckman, "Developmental Sequence in Small Groups," *Psychological Bulletin* 63, no. 6 (1965): 384–399. The terms *forming, storming, norming,* and *performing* are among the most commonly used terms for stages in team development. They are used in close approximation to Susan Wheelan's stages of dependency and inclusion, counterdependency and fight, trust and structure, and work.

7. Wheelan, *Creating Effective Teams: A Guide for Members and Leaders.*

8. Ibid.

9. John T. Byrd and Michael R. Luthy, "Improving Group Dynamics: Creating a Team Charter," *Academy of Educational Leadership Journal* 14, no. 1 (2010): 13–26; Janet Hillier and Linda M. Dunn-Jensen, "Groups Meet . . . Teams Improve: Building Teams That Learn," *Journal of Management Education* 37, no. 5 (2012): 704–733.

10. Silvia Ann Hewlett, Melinda Marshall, and Laura Sherbin, "How Diversity Can Drive Innovation," *Harvard Business Review,* December 2013: 30.

11. Susan Cain, *Quiet: The Power of Introverts in a World That Can't Stop Talking* (New York: Crown Publishers, 2012); Susan Cain, "The Rise of the New Groupthink," *The New York Times,* January 13, 2012.

12. Richard T. Watson and Cliff Saunders, "Managing Insight Velocity: The Design of Problem Solving Meetings," *Business Horizons* 48 (2005): 285–295.

13. Elias Porter, *Strength Deployment Inventory* (Carlsbad, CA: Personal Strengths Publishing, 2014); Tim Scudder and Debra LaCroix, *Working with SDI: How to Build Effective Relationships with the Strength Deployment Inventory* (Carlsbad, CA: Personal Strengths Publishing, 2013): 7.

14. Hillier and Dunn-Jensen, "Groups Meet . . . Teams Improve: Building Teams That Learn."

15. Richard Benson-Armer and Tsun-Yan Hsieh, "Teamwork across Time and Space," *McKinsey Quarterly*, no. 4 (1997).

16. Lynn Offermann and Lisa Rosh, "Building Trust through Skillful Self-Disclosure," HBR Blog, June 13, 2012, available at https://hbr.org/2012/06/instantaneous-intimacy-skillfu/.

17. Tom Krattenmaker, "How to Make Every Meeting Matter," *Harvard Management Communication Letter,* May 2003: 3–5.

18. Watson and Saunders, "Managing Insight Velocity: The Design of Problem Solving Meetings": 285–295.

19. Accountemps, "Survey Finds Executives Waste More Than Two Months a Year in Unnecessary Business Discussion," June 8, 2000, retrieved January 10, 2010, from http://accountemps.rhi.mediaroom.com/index.php?s=189&item=336.

20. Barbara J. Streibel, *The Manager's Guide to Effective Meetings* (New York: McGraw-Hill, 2003).

21. Kim Ribbink, "Run a Meeting to Fast-Track Your Career," *Harvard Management Communication Letter,* October 2002: 3–4.

22. Krattenmaker, "How to Make Every Meeting Matter."

23. Ribbink, "Run a Meeting to Fast-Track Your Career."

24. Accountemps, "Accountemps Survey: Employee Output is Weakest Late in the Day," August 17, 2010, retrieved November 20, 2010, from http://accountemps.rhi.mediaroom.com/least_productive.

25. Accountemps, "Second Day of the Week Remains Most Productive, Survey Shows," February 7, 2008, retrieved January 10, 2010, from www.accountemps.com/PressRoom?id=2121.

26. Marty Linsky, "The Morning Meeting: Best-Practice Communication for Executive Teams," *Harvard Management Communication Letter,* Spring 2006: 3–5.

27. *New York Times Corner Office* (blog), "Meetings," retrieved June 15, 2010, from http://projects.nytimes.com/corner-office/Meetings.

28. Christina Bielaszka-DuVernay, "Is Your Company as Dull and Unproductive as Its Meetings?" *Harvard Management Communication Letter,* Summer 2004: 3–5.

29. Streibel, *The Manager's Guide to Effective Meetings.*

30. Terrence L. Gargiulo, *Stories at Work: Using Stories to Improve Communication and Build Relationships* (Westport, CT: Praeger, 2006).

31. Susan Bixler and Lisa Scherrer Dugan, *How to Project Confidence, Competence, and Credibility at Work: 5 Steps to Professional Presence* (Avon, MA: Adams Media, 2001).

32. Streibel, *The Manager's Guide to Effective Meetings.*

33. Bixler and Dugan, *How to Project Confidence, Competence, and Credibility at Work: 5 Steps to Professional Presence.*

34. Ribbink, "Run a Meeting to Fast-Track Your Career"; Streibel, *The Manager's Guide to Effective Meetings*; Bielaszka-DuVernay, "Is Your Company as Dull and Unproductive as Its Meetings?"; Janice Obuchowski, "Your Meeting: Who's in Charge?" *Harvard Management Communication Letter,* Spring 2005: 3–5.

35. Stephen R. Covey, *The 8th Habit: From Effectiveness to Greatness* (New York: Free Press, 2004).

36. S. Schulz-Hardt, F. C. Brodbeck, A. Mojzisch, R. Kerschreiter, and D. Frey, "Group Decision Making in Hidden Profile Situations: Dissent as a Facilitator for Decision Quality," *Journal of Personality and Social Psychology* 91, no. 6 (2006): 1080–1093.

37. Bielaszka-DuVernay, "Is Your Company as Dull and Unproductive as Its Meetings?": 3–5.

38. Ribbink, "Run a Meeting to Fast-Track Your Career"; Krattenmaker, "How to Make Every Meeting Matter": 3–5; Bielaszka-DuVernay, "Is Your Company as Dull and Unproductive as Its Meetings?"

39. Streibel, *The Manager's Guide to Effective Meetings.*

40. Lisa Gueldenzoph Snyder, "Teaching Teams about Teamwork: Preparation, Practice, and Performance Review," *Business Communication Quarterly,* March 2009: 77–78.

41. Obuchowski, "Your Meeting: Who's in Charge?"

42.  RW³, *The Challenge of Working in Virtual Teams: Virtual Teams Report—2010* (New York: RW³, 2010).

43.  Ann Majchrzak, Arvind Malhotra, Jeffrey Stamps, and Jessica Lipnack, "Can Absence Make a Team Grow Stronger?" *Harvard Business Review* 82, no. 5 (2004): 131–137; Sue Greenberg, Ralph H. Greenberg, and Yvonne Lederer Antonucci, "Creating and Sustaining Trust in Virtual Teams," *Business Horizons* 50 (2007): 325–333; RW³, *The Challenge of Working in Virtual Teams: Virtual Teams Report—2010*; Keith Ferrazzi, "Five Ways to Run Better Virtual Meetings," *HBR Blog Network,* May 3, 2012.

44.  Majchrzak et al., "Can Absence Make a Team Grow Stronger?"; Ferrazzi, "Five Ways to Run Better Virtual Meetings"; Michael Watkins, "Making Virtual Teams Work: Ten Basic Principles," *HBR Blog Network,* June 27, 2013; Gregory R. Berry, "Enhancing Effectiveness on Virtual Teams: Understanding Why Traditional Skills Are Insufficient," *Journal of Business Communication* 48 (2011): 186–206.

45.  RW³, *The Challenge of Working in Virtual Teams: Virtual Teams Report—2010.*

46.  Berry, "Enhancing Effectiveness on Virtual Teams: Understanding Why Traditional Skills Are Insufficient."

47.  The table is inspired by the work of Greenberg et al., "Creating and Sustaining Trust in Virtual Teams."

48.  Majchrzak et al., "Can Absence Make a Team Grow Stronger?"

49.  RW³, *The Challenge of Working in Virtual Teams: Virtual Teams Report—2010.*

50.  Majchrzak et al., "Can Absence Make a Team Grow Stronger?"; RW³, *The Challenge of Working in Virtual Teams: Virtual Teams Report—2010;* Ferrazzi, "Five Ways to Run Better Virtual Meetings"; Watkins, "Making Virtual Teams Work: Ten Basic Principles."

51.  Majchrzak et al., "Can Absence Make a Team Grow Stronger?"

52.  Ibid.

53.  Keith Ferrazzi, "How Virtual Teams Can Create Human Connections Despite Distance," *HBR Blog Network,* January 31, 2014.

54.  Douglas Stone, Bruce Patton, and Sheila Heen, *Difficult Conversations: How to Discuss What Matters Most* (New York: Penguin, 2000): xv.

55.  Kerry Patterson, Joseph Grenny, Ron McMillan, and Al Switzler, *Crucial Conversations: Tools for Talking When Stakes Are High* (New York: McGraw-Hill, 2002); Laura L. Myers and R. Sam Larson, "Preparing Students for Early Work Conflicts," *Business Communication Quarterly* 68, no. 3 (2005): 306–317.

56.  Patterson et al., *Crucial Conversations: Tools for Talking When Stakes Are High.*

57.  Ibid., 9–10.

58.  Ibid.

59.  Renee Evenson, "Effective Solutions for Team Conflict," *Toastmasters* online, July 2009, www.toastmasters.org/Toastmasters Magazine/ToastmasterArchive/2009/July/EffectiveSolutions.aspx.

60.  Adam Bryant, "The Divine, Too, Is in the Details," *Corner Office* (blog), *The New York Times,* June 20, 2009, www.nytimes.com/2009/06/21/business/21corner.html.

61.  Stone et al., *Difficult Conversations: How to Discuss What Matters Most.*

62.  Ann C. Baker, *Catalytic Conversations: Organizational Communication and Innovation* (Armonk, NY: M. E. Sharpe, 2010).

63.  Patterson et al., *Crucial Conversations: Tools for Talking When Stakes Are High.*

64.  Patterson et al., *Crucial Conversations: Tools for Talking When Stakes Are High*; Evenson, "Effective Solutions for Team Conflict"; Richard Bierck, "Managing Anger," *Harvard Management Communication Letter,* November 2001: 4–5.

65.  Stephen M. R. Covey, *The Speed of Trust* (New York: Free Press, 2006).

66.  Evenson, "Effective Solutions for Team Conflict."

67.  Adam Bryant, "It's Not a Career Ladder, It's an Obstacle Course," *Corner Office* (blog), *The New York Times,* May 22, 2010, www.nytimes.com/2010/05/13/business/23corner.html.

68.  Ibid.

69.  Adam Bryant, "No Need to Hit the 'Send' Key. Just Talk to Me," *Corner Office* (blog), *The New York Times,* August 28, 2010, www.nytimes.com/2010/08/29/business/29corner.html.

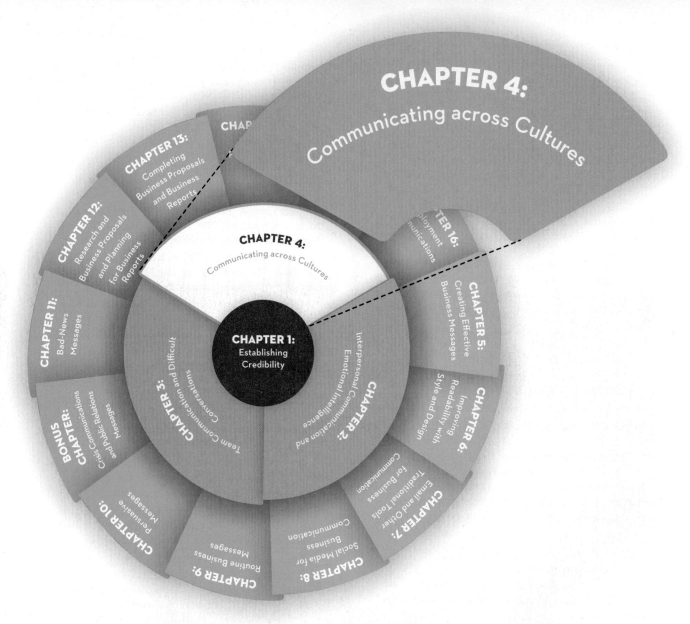

CHAPTER 4:
Communicating across Cultures

 ESTABLISHING CREDIBILITY     PRINCIPLES OF INTERPERSONAL COMMUNICATION     PRINCIPLES FOR & TYPES OF BUSINESS MESSAGES

 **Learning Objectives**

After studying this chapter, you should be able to do the following:

**LO4.1** Describe characteristics of cultural intelligence, its importance for global business leaders, and approaches to developing it.

**LO4.2** Explain the major cultural dimensions and related communication practices.

**LO4.3** Name and describe key categories of business etiquette in the intercultural communication process.

**LO4.4** Identify how generational, gender, and other group differences affect workplace communication.

You are living in one of the most exciting times because of opportunities to work and interact with people from across the globe. Only a few decades ago, few businesspeople worked closely with members of other cultures. Now, however, global business connections have increased rapidly, and you will undoubtedly work across cultures throughout your career. For example, you will probably have some chances to travel internationally for work assignments. More frequently, however, you are likely to work across cultures by collaborating with work teams in India, videoconferencing or emailing with customers or suppliers in China, or working in a culturally diverse office in your hometown. The possibilities are immense!

Throughout this chapter, you will see a variety of national cultures compared. The countries selected for this chapter are among the most important trading partners for the United States. In terms of trade volume, countries such as China (including Taiwan), Canada, Mexico, Japan, the United Kingdom, and Germany dominate. (See Table 4.1 for the most important trading partners of the United States.) Of course, you will likely work with business professionals, clients, or customers from many other national backgrounds. Your business discipline, company, and industry will factor into the national cultures with which you most frequently interact. At the end of the chapter, you'll also read about how generation, gender, and other group identities affect communication in ways similar to culture.

Carlos Ghosn, CEO of Nissan and Renault, explained the necessity of learning to work and communicate effectively across cultures:

> Companies are going global, but the teams are being divided and scattered all over the planet. If you're head of engineering, you have to deal with divisions in Vietnam or China, and you have to work across cultures. You have to know how to motivate people who think very differently than you, who have different kinds of sensitivities, so I think the most important message is to get prepared to deal with teams who are multicultural, who do not think the same way.[1]

Read the following case about Carlos Ghosn. Throughout the chapter, you will read more advice from him and other business executives.[2]

**Hear Pete Cardon explain why this matters.**

bit.ly/cardon4

### TABLE 4.1

Top Trading Partners of the United States

| Country | Total Trade (billions of U.S. dollars) | Percentage of Total Trade |
|---|---|---|
| China | $45.4 | 16.5% |
| Canada | 42.0 | 15.3 |
| Mexico | 40.5 | 14.8 |
| Japan | 14.3 | 5.2 |
| Germany | 11.9 | 4.4 |
| South Korea | 9.1 | 3.3 |
| United Kingdom | 7.6 | 2.8 |
| France | 5.5 | 2.0 |
| Taiwan | 5.4 | 2.0 |
| India | 5.2 | 1.9 |
| Italy | 4.4 | 1.6 |
| Belgium | 3.9 | 1.4 |
| Ireland | 3.9 | 1.4 |
| Brazil | 3.8 | 1.4 |

*Note:* Based on January 2016 trade figures from the U.S. Census Bureau.

**CHAPTER CASE:** CARLOS GHOSN AND WORKING ACROSS CULTURES AT NISSAN

Carlos Ghosn

**WHO'S INVOLVED**

**President and CEO of Nissan and Renault**

- Held many international management positions: Michelin in France, 1978–1985; Michelin in Brazil, 1985–1989; Michelin in the United States, 1989–1996; Renault in France, 1996–present; Nissan in Japan, 1999–present.
- Speaks six languages: Arabic, Portuguese, Spanish, French, English, and Japanese.
- Born in Brazil, grew up in Lebanon, and moved to France for university studies.
- Industry analysts comment that Ghosn "epitomizes a new breed of borderless global managers. . . . These executives are multilingual, have worked around the world, and seem impervious to jet lag."[3]

In March 1999, Carlos Ghosn was asked to lead the turnaround at the struggling Japanese carmaker Nissan. The company was $23 billion in debt, had suffered declines in domestic market share for 27 straight years, was unprofitable on 43 of the 46 products it sold, and had lost money for seven of the prior eight years. Many viewed Ghosn, who was nicknamed *Le Cost-Killer* and renowned for his turnaround abilities, as the best hope to fix the crisis. Yet, many industry analysts thought the situation was impossible. They also wondered how a foreigner could succeed in the Japanese work environment.

**THE SITUATION**

Within 18 months, Nissan was restored to profitability and has sustained annual profitability for all but one year (during the recent worldwide recession) since then. Within five years of Ghosn's arrival in Japan to run Nissan, the debt of $23 billion had been turned into a $7 billion surplus. It now sells and markets cars in nearly every country in the world and runs manufacturing facilities in nearly 20 countries. Nissan has developed some of the most innovative cars, including the Nissan Leaf, the first zero-emissions car. Ghosn credits much of this turnaround at Nissan to his ability to work across cultures and to build on the best parts of each culture involved.

**QUESTIONS TO CONSIDER AS YOU READ**

- What types of attitudes do business professionals need to communicate effectively across cultures?
- How can business students learn about and prepare to work with members of other cultures?
- How can understanding cultural dimensions help business professionals work cross-culturally?
- What advantages accrue to companies with a global mentality?
- What is the value of global leaders?
- How do generational, gender, and other group identities affect business communication?

# Developing Cultural Intelligence

Companies depend on business professionals who can manage across cultures. Companies such as Coca-Cola sell more products abroad than they do locally. In fact, Coca-Cola sells more drinks in Japan alone than in the United States. In Chapter 2, you read about emotional intelligence (EQ), your ability to manage emotions in interpersonal situations. Similarly, **cultural intelligence (CQ)** is a measure of your ability to work with and adapt to members of other cultures. Like EQ (but unlike IQ), CQ can be developed and improved over time with training, experience, and conscious effort.[4]

Business professionals with high CQ understand differences and similarities between and among cultures. **Culture** includes the shared values, norms, rules, and behaviors of an identifiable group of people who share a common history and communication system. There are many types of culture, such as national, organizational, and team. We discuss principles of intercultural communication in this chapter primarily in the context of national cultures, which tend to be more permanent and enduring than other types of culture. The norms and values of national cultures are instilled in young members through a shared language, shared history and traditions, school systems, and political and economic systems. At the end of the chapter, we also briefly discuss norms and values associated with generations, gender, and other groups.

When working with members of other cultures at the home office or abroad, business professionals with high CQ are skilled at forming goals, discussing and succeeding on joint projects, resolving differences, and negotiating mutually beneficial outcomes. They understand new markets and can develop global plans for marketing and supply chain management. When people with high CQ encounter unfamiliar situations, they implement a variety of the skills displayed in Table 4.2 and discussed throughout the chapter.[5]

Developing cultural intelligence is more than possessing favorable attitudes toward members of other groups. It also requires developing skills and knowledge. In this section, we focus briefly on several characteristics of cultural intelligence.

## Respect, Recognize, and Appreciate Cultural Differences

Cultural intelligence is built on attitudes of respect and recognition of other cultures. This means that you view other cultures as holding legitimate and valid views of and approaches to managing business and workplace relationships. Ghosn, when first sent to Japan from France to turn around Nissan, demonstrated this view of cultures:

> People who try to impose one system onto another only wind up destroying it. This has never been our strategy. If Renault had wanted to do that, they would have picked anyone but me, because I'm completely convinced of the opposite course. Nissan had to be changed from the inside. If you're French and you come to Japan, you have no chance, zero, of budging the system an inch. I'm convinced of this. My conviction is both human

**LO4.1** Describe characteristics of cultural intelligence, its importance for global business leaders, and approaches to developing it.

**connect**

Visit **http://connect. mheducation.com** for an exercise on this topic.

**TABLE 4.2**

Cultural Intelligence in the Workplace

| **Characteristics of High Cultural Intelligence** |
| --- |

- Respect, recognize, and appreciate cultural differences.
- Possess curiosity about and interest in other cultures.
- Avoid inappropriate stereotypes.
- Adjust conceptions of time and show patience.
- Manage language differences to achieve shared meaning.
- Understand cultural dimensions.
- Establish trust and show empathy across cultures.
- Approach cross-cultural work relationships with a learner mind-set.
- Build a co-culture of cooperation and innovation.

and professional, and it's bolstered by the experience of having lived on several continents. Right from the beginning, I told them: "You're not missionaries. You've come here not to change Japan but to straighten out Nissan with the men and women of Nissan. We're the ones who have to assimilate with them—it's not up to them to adapt to us."[6]

In recent years, many public and educational campaigns have focused on embracing diversity. In this book, we refer to **diversity** as the presence of many cultural groups in the workplace. Business professionals with high cultural intelligence embrace diversity as a moral imperative and as a means to achieve higher performance. A great deal of research has examined the role of cultural diversity in the workplace. These studies have shown that a mix of cultural groups in terms of national culture, ethnicity, age, and gender leads to better decision making.[7] Nissan, like many companies, has recognized the moral and business value of diversity and explicitly states this on its website:

> At Nissan, we believe that diversity is a source of strength. . . . Nissan is committed to diversity to ensure that we meet the diverse needs of our customers and achieve sustainable growth for all stakeholders. Each and every employee will respect diversity and take full advantage of it. . . . We believe that embracing and leveraging this cultural diversity gives us a competitive advantage.[8]

## Be Curious about Other Cultures

As a college student, you are in a stage of life that gives you unique opportunities to acquire cross-cultural experiences. Consider the following options: studying abroad, learning a language, developing friendships with international students on campus, and taking an interest in and learning about a particular culture.[9]

**Study Abroad**   Living in another culture is perhaps the best approach to learning about one. It allows you to immerse yourself in another way of living—to observe and experience up close how members of another cultural group communicate, work in groups, manage relationships, celebrate successes, and deal with disappointments. When asked "What's your best career advice to young graduates?" Quintin E. Primo III, co-founder and chief executive of Capri Capital Partners, responded in the following way:

> Leave the country. Get out of here. That's what I tell everybody—just go. I don't care where you go, just go. Because the world is changing. It is no longer acceptable to speak only English if you are 25 and younger. . . . You have little chance of being successful if you speak only one language. If you don't understand Islam, you're in trouble because Islam comprises somewhere between 1.6 billion and 1.8 billion people, and there are markets that are untapped that need to be tapped. So you've got to get out of your front door, get out of the comfort and quiet of your home, and your safety zone, and step into a pool of risk where you have no idea what the outcome is going to be. Out of it all, you will have a much broader understanding of the world's cultures, and you will have a much clearer idea of how the world perceives our culture, and all the value, and the benefits, and the beauty of our culture. There is nothing more important. I don't care where you went to business school. I don't care whether your grades were good or bad. You have to leave the country.[10]

As freshmen, most university students express a desire to study abroad and even believe that they will have an opportunity to do so before they graduate. However, just 3 to 5 percent of university students actually do.[11] So, if you want to study abroad, make it a priority. Plan for it now. Furthermore, consider choosing locations and programs that are most important for your career. Typically, business recruiters value study-abroad programs that are at least one semester long, involve the development of business skills, and include language study. Also, business recruiters are more impressed with study-abroad programs located in countries that are considered strategically important business partners. Whereas most students choose locations in Western Europe and Australia, recruiters see more value in countries such as China, Japan, Brazil, Mexico, or India. Of course, this varies by discipline and industry. For example, if you are going into the fashion design industry, experience in Italy or France would be extremely valuable.

When you study abroad, learn all you can about adapting to the culture. However, avoid developing strong preconceptions and remain flexible. When you arrive in your chosen destination, open yourself completely to the experience. As Ghosn said about entering the Japanese culture, "I did not try to learn too much about Japan before coming, because I didn't want to have too many preconceived ideas. I wanted to discover Japan by being in Japan with the Japanese people."[12]

**Learn a Language**   Although English is considered the global business language and business managers in other parts of the world increasingly speak it well, you can benefit from learning another language for a variety of reasons. It gives you many insights into how people of other cultures think. It helps you appreciate the richness of other cultures. It fosters tremendous goodwill with others. And you may find yourself in situations where your language ability allows smoother communication than relying on English.

Ghosn, who now speaks six languages, commented on the reasons and the benefits: "Learning languages quickly became one of my passions. The study of language is the best way of understanding the connections between people and cultures."[13] Of course, learning languages takes a lot of time. Also, it requires forcing oneself into authentic and sometimes uncomfortable situations. Ghosn was determined to learn English while studying in Paris. So, twice each month, he invited Americans living in France to dinner to practice his English.[14]

**Develop Friendships with International Students on Your Campus**   Your university likely has hundreds or even thousands of international students. This presents you with a rare opportunity to experience the world. You can learn more about other cultures by befriending international students than you can by taking a group tour of another country. Also, you can help these students feel at home. One reason you can learn so much from international students is that they are experiencing the challenges of living in and adapting to a new culture. During your career, you are most likely to interact with business professionals who are the current generation of international students.

**Take an Interest in a Culture and Routinely Learn about It**   Each culture has its own complexity. Ideally, you should seek an in-depth understanding of one culture. Once you've done this, you can more quickly adapt to and learn other cultures. One of the best ways to gain an in-depth understanding is to take an inquisitive approach—asking questions and seeking the answers to how other cultures view knowledge; how they reason and approach problems; how they work, worship, and view the world; how they view time, and so on.[15] You can routinely learn about cultures of interest in some of the following ways:[16]

- *Watch films, television, documentaries, news, and other video of the culture.* It's increasingly easy to access video of other cultures. This allows you to observe many aspects of the culture in context with visual and auditory cues.
- *Follow the business culture of a country.* Many websites contain global business news sections with both text and videos. For example, consider the following: *Bloomberg Businessweek,* CNBC, *Time,* Foreign Exchange, and CIBERweb.
- *Take courses and attend events related to particular cultures.* Your university offers numerous opportunities, including taking courses about international and intercultural topics and attending symposia that feature international speakers.
- *Make friends with people who live in other cultures and communicate online.* You might try to make friends abroad and communicate frequently via email, chat, and online calls. One of the most common means of communicating internationally is via online call services such as Skype. Read the Technology Tips box about online calls.

## Avoid Inappropriate Stereotypes

When Ghosn moved to Japan, he selected a team of roughly 20 executives from Renault in France to join him. As he selected his team, he was adamant that each team member must be open to the Japanese:

> However competent a candidate may have been, however motivated, if I sensed that he or she was even slightly close-minded about cultural differences, that person was excluded. . . . I wanted competent, enthusiastic, open-minded people capable of engaging in a real dialogue.[17]

We naturally develop stereotypes, or generalizations, to try to understand the attitudes and behavior of people we do not know, especially those of different cultures. It is an attempt by the brain to group and categorize in complex situations. Stereotypes can make interactions less complicated since they serve as a starting point for understanding the motives and values of others. For example, people may have a stereotype of tax accountants as credible, professional, competent, helpful, and detail-oriented. This stereotype allows people to go to a tax accountant's office with the assumption that the professional will help them and provide excellent service. Similarly, people who work across cultures often form stereotypes of how members of that culture communicate and approach work problems. These stereotypes can be productive as long as they are only a starting point, they are flexible, and they are primarily positive.[18]

Stereotyping about cultures can also be dysfunctional, counterproductive, and even hurtful. People tend to form two types of stereotypes when interacting with members of other cultures: *projected cognitive similarity* and *outgroup homogeneity effect*.[19] **Projected cognitive similarity** is the tendency to assume others have the same norms and values as your own cultural group. This occurs when people project their own cultural norms and values to explain the behaviors they see in others. Take the case of an American interviewing a Japanese man for a new position. The Japanese man might downplay his own achievements and give credit to the teams he has worked on. The American interviewer, based on the American cultural lens, may think the man lacks self-confidence and independence or initiative. The Japanese applicant, by contrast, is most likely displaying Japanese norms and values associated with modesty, politeness, and collectivism.

**Outgroup homogeneity effect** is the tendency to think members of other groups are all the same. Psychologically, this approach minimizes the mental effort needed to get to know people of other groups. Practically speaking, it is counterproductive to developing effective working relationships with members of other cultures. The reality is that all cultures contain a lot of diversity—individuals of many backgrounds, worldviews, interests, and approaches to life. In the "Individualism and Collectivism" section of this chapter, we will illustrate more about the nature of diversity.

Negative stereotyping can easily emerge from popular culture. Research has shown that television depictions of particular cultural groups as criminal, cruel, backward, or dishonest affect the stereotypes viewers have of those cultures.[20] Similarly, viewing members of other cultures through a political lens based on news stories about the political relations between countries often leads to unjustified negative stereotyping.

While you should be careful about forming negative or rigid stereotypes of members of other cultures, you should also be aware of stereotypes that others may have of you. Many people you interact with will have already formed some impressions of your cultural background and what to expect from you. Members of other cultures often form stereotypes of Americans based on news stories as well as popular culture (i.e., films, television shows, music). Typically, most people around the world hold mixed views of Americans (see Table 4.3). Even in countries where the majority of adults view Americans as dishonest or greedy, they also view Americans as hardworking and inventive.[21]

## Adjust Your Conceptions of Time

One frustration that most people experience when communicating and working across cultures is dealing with time. This is because people have a lifetime of experiences,

**TABLE 4.3**

Perceptions That Members of Various Cultures Have about Americans

|  | Hardworking | Inventive | Honest | Greedy | Rude |
|---|---|---|---|---|---|
| **Canada** | 77% | 76% | 42% | 62% | 53% |
| **China** | 44 | 70 | 35 | 57 | 44 |
| **France** | 89 | 76 | 57 | 31 | 36 |
| **Germany** | 67 | 56 | 52 | 49 | 12 |
| **India** | 81 | 86 | 58 | 43 | 27 |
| **Jordan** | 78 | 68 | 37 | 63 | 64 |
| **Netherlands** | 84 | 69 | 46 | 67 | 26 |
| **Russia** | 72 | 56 | 32 | 60 | 48 |
| **Spain** | 74 | 53 | 45 | 58 | 39 |
| **UK** | 76 | 64 | 57 | 62 | 35 |

*Source:* Pew Global Attitudes Project.

*Note:* Red shading indicates a majority of adults in a country have a negative view. Green shading indicates a majority of adults in a country have a positive view.

related to their particular culture, that form their expectations for when things should happen during any given process.

People high in CQ show patience. They understand that most tasks take longer when working across cultures because more time is needed to understand one another and cooperate effectively. Furthermore, many cross-cultural work projects are conducted across great distances. Naturally, this requires additional time due to the communication tools and organizational decision-making processes.

Guy McLeod, president of Airbus China, explained why business managers arriving in China need to adapt their pace: "When people have just arrived, they want to change things. But making quick moves in the wrong way isn't the right thing to do. You need to have patience, patience, patience. It is one of the clichés you hear in China, but it is true. You need to make a long-term strategy and stick to it."[22]

Also, people of various cultures conceptualize time differently. What seems *fast* in one culture may seem *slow* in another. One recent study ranked pace of life in various cultures by measuring walking speed over a distance of 60 feet, the average time for a postal worker to complete one request, and the accuracy of clocks in public. Countries such as Germany, Japan, and Italy were considered fast-paced cultures, whereas countries such as China, Brazil, and Mexico were considered slow-paced ones (see Figure 4.1).[23] The point is that cultures establish expectations about what is considered timely, late, rushed, and hectic. Cultures also differ in their priorities related to focusing on the present versus focusing on the future (as discussed in the "Future Orientation" section in the upcoming pages). As you can see, you will need to adjust your sense of time to coordinate effectively with members of other cultures.

A final time consideration relates to adjustment. You need time to get accustomed to and proficient in working with other cultures. When traveling to a new culture or taking an international assignment, you should allot time for adjusting. Ghosn noted the difficulties he and his family had when they moved to Japan:

> The language barrier was huge. When you first get to Japan, you're really constrained, because you feel dependent on other people for everything. . . . The culture's different. The customs are different. . . . As time passed, however, our family got its bearings.[24]

**FIGURE 4.1**

Pace of Life across Cultures

### Manage Language Differences

English is increasingly considered the global business language. Many global companies such as Nissan, which are composed primarily of non-native English-speaking business professionals, have adopted policies of conducting meetings in English. Yet, even with the strong push for English as a business language, many professionals around the business world speak limited English. Also, many forms of English exist—that of the United Kingdom, Australia, Singapore, and India, to name just a few places. Thus, standard English is a matter of interpretation. As you conduct business across cultures with those who have limited English ability, consider the following advice:[25]

- *Avoid quickly judging that others have limited communication proficiency.* Many non-native English speakers take time to warm up. The first moments—or in some cases days or weeks—of your interactions with them are not representative of their real language abilities. Many business professionals have studied English for years yet infrequently have opportunities to speak it in an authentic encounter.
- *Articulate clearly and slow down.* Many Americans inadvertently run their words together. Make sure you pronounce each word distinctly and slow your pace slightly.
- *Avoid slang and jargon.* Slang and jargon can be particularly confusing to members of other cultures. For example, Americans are well known for using sports slang in business (e.g., striking out, throwing a curve ball, hitting a home run). Use as much literal language as you can.
- *Give others time to express themselves.* Allow those with limited English ability enough time to process their thoughts into English. You will often find that non-native English speakers, given time, express their thoughts with a more precise, creative, and even accurate use of English words than native English speakers.
- *Use interpreters as necessary.* In some situations, you will rely on interpreters. Spend some time in advance getting to know the interpreter's abilities and preferences for facilitating an exchange. During interpretation, focus on the person you are communicating with rather than the interpreter. That is, focus on the person with whom you are trying to build rapport.

Ghosn made several excellent points about overcoming language barriers:

> Of course there are frustrations that always exist with language barriers: where you don't operate in an environment of spontaneous communication; where you have to go through a translator (you know that when you go through a translator, about 40 percent of your intended meaning is lost); where you're not sure that what you want to get across to people, on the shop floor or in meetings with customers, is actually being communicated the way you intended it. *These are what I consider small frustrations;* if you accept these and other things that perhaps are part of the fact that people don't think or act the same way in France or in Japan, it is easier to deal with such things as language barriers. When you have taken the time to understand that, and when you are really motivated and mobilized by a very strong objective, then the cultural differences can become seeds for innovation as opposed to seeds for dissention.[26]

## Understanding Cultural Dimensions

**LO4.2** Explain the major cultural dimensions and related communication practices.

In this section, we describe recent research on cultural norms and values among businesspeople throughout the world. This research, conducted by the GLOBE group (which includes dozens of business researchers around the world), is based on surveys and interviews of about 20,000 business leaders and managers in 62 countries.[27]

The GLOBE group found that cultures can be grouped into eight dimensions. **Cultural dimensions** are fairly permanent and enduring sets of related norms and values and are classified as (1) individualism and collectivism, (2) egalitarianism and hierarchy, (3) performance orientation, (4) future orientation, (5) assertiveness, (6) humane orientation, (7) uncertainty avoidance, and (8) gender egalitarianism. By understanding these eight dimensions, you can get a good sense of the underlying motivations and goals that impact acceptable behaviors within a culture.

Although cultures constantly evolve, usually over decades or generations, the cultural dimension that changes most rapidly is individualism and collectivism. As prosperity and economic development rise, individualism typically increases as well.

We describe each of the eight cultural dimensions, along with related communication practices, focusing on norms, meaning the range of expected and acceptable behaviors in each culture. You will notice that rankings are provided for each cultural dimension, and these rankings include the United States as well as the top ten trading partners of North America.[28] You can find rankings for other countries included in the GLOBE study in the online resources.

## Individualism and Collectivism

Most intercultural communication scholars identify individualism and collectivism as the most influential cultural dimension. This dimension deals with the level of independence and interdependence that people in a society possess and encourage. **Individualism** refers to a mind-set that prioritizes independence more highly than interdependence, emphasizing individual goals over group goals, and valuing choice more than obligation. By contrast, **collectivism** refers to a mind-set that prioritizes interdependence more highly than independence, emphasizing group goals over individual goals, and valuing obligation more than choice.

Individualists view themselves as distinct and separate from their family members, friends, and colleagues. They pursue their own dreams and goals, even when it means spending less time with family members and friends. They enter friendships and relationships primarily based on common interests. They also leave relationships when they are no longer mutually satisfying, beneficial, or convenient. Decision making tends to be based on an individual's needs.[29]

On the other hand, collectivists view themselves as interdependent—forming an identity inseparable from that of their family members, friends, and other groups. They tend to follow the perceived dreams and goals of the group as a matter of duty and obligation, even when it means sacrificing their own hopes and ambitions. They form permanent and lifetime relationships. They also tend to stay in contact with and work through extended networks built on family relationships, schoolmates, and hometowns. Decisions are made by groups.[30] Figure 4.2 displays country rankings for individualism and collectivism in society. Of the countries we are considering here, China has the highest ranking for collectivism and the Netherlands has the lowest. Japan, which many people think of as highly collectivist, falls in the middle of this group. Table 4.4 shows communication practices normally associated with high individualism and high collectivism.

**connect**

Visit http://connect.mheducation.com for an exercise on this topic.

**FIGURE 4.2**

Individualism and Collectivism across Cultures

| Collectivism in Society | |
|---|---|
| China | 82 |
| S Korea | 77 |
| Mexico | 74 |
| Taiwan | 68 |
| Hong Kong | 64 |
| Brazil | 58 |
| Italy | 53 |
| Japan | 43 |
| France | 41 |
| USA | 26 |
| Germany | 24 |
| UK | 21 |
| Netherlands | 11 |
| Individualism in Society | |

**TABLE 4.4**

Communication Practices in High-Individualist and High-Collectivist Cultures

| High Individualism | High Collectivism |
|---|---|
| • Discuss individual rewards and goals | • Discuss group rewards and goals |
| • Emphasize opportunities and choices | • Emphasize duties and obligations |
| • Spend less time in group decision making | • Spend more time in group decision making |
| • Socialize infrequently with colleagues outside of work | • Socialize frequently with colleagues outside of work |
| • Network in loosely tied and temporary social networks | • Network in tightly knit and permanent social networks |
| • Communicate directly to efficiently deal with work tasks and outcomes | • Communicate indirectly to preserve harmony in work relationships |

**FIGURE 4.3**

Individualism and
Collectivism within
Companies

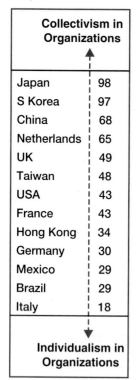

| Collectivism in Organizations |
| --- |
| Japan | 98 |
| S Korea | 97 |
| China | 68 |
| Netherlands | 65 |
| UK | 49 |
| Taiwan | 48 |
| USA | 43 |
| France | 43 |
| Hong Kong | 34 |
| Germany | 30 |
| Mexico | 29 |
| Brazil | 29 |
| Italy | 18 |

Individualism in
Organizations

Traditionally, North American and Western countries have been far more individualist than Asian, Latin American, and other countries. However, some countries have increasingly become individualist, such as Japan. Generally, as countries increase the standard of living, they develop more individualist tendencies.

A major distinction in individualism and collectivism can be made between norms and values in *society* versus norms and values in *organizations*. All companies tend to promote both individualist and collectivist values. For example, encouraging self-initiative and individual accountability are individualist values. Encouraging teamwork and team incentives are collectivist values. In practice, many companies in individualist countries have attempted to adopt more team-oriented strategies in recent decades. Thus, highly individualist countries such as the United States exhibit many collectivist characteristics within organizations. Figure 4.3 displays country rankings for individualism and collectivism within companies. In many cases these rankings differ from norms and values in society at large.

One key to Ghosn's success with Nissan was his ability to work within the Japanese mind-set of collectivism.[31] He immediately formed cross-functional teams to develop solutions and goals. As Ghosn said, "One of the striking things about Japanese industry is the quality of teamwork. . . . In France, people aren't naturally inclined to teamwork. In Japan, on the other hand, people are quite comfortable working in teams."[32]

Cultures that exhibit extremely high collectivism within organizations tend to have a family-centered culture. Many Asian organizations adopt this family-oriented approach to running a company. As Ernst Behrens, president of Siemens China, explained, "The Chinese—and Asians generally—enter into employment with a different understanding than we have in Europe. For us, the company certainly is important, but mainly as an employment base. To the Chinese, the company is more like a family. The idea is, 'I am giving myself to Siemens. Now you have to take care of me.'"[33]

As you read through this section on cultural dimensions and view the continuums with rankings for each country, note that cultures are more than a spot on a scale. For example, Figure 4.4 shows how the United States, which is considered to have one of the most individualist cultures, and China, which is considered among the most collectivist cultures, overlap to some extent on this dimension (the triangular area enclosed by the intersection of the red and blue curves). In other words, some Chinese individuals behave in more individualist ways than some American individuals. However, by and large, most Chinese are more collectivist than most Americans. Furthermore, norms within a culture typically evolve to reflect what *most* people value. Even within cultures, there is great variety. Research in the United States has shown that individualism and collectivism vary significantly by region, with the Mountain West region the most individualist and the Deep South the most collectivist.[34] By constantly reminding yourself that variety exists within cultures, you are less likely to typecast people (outgroup homogeneity effect).

**FIGURE 4.4**

Variety in Individualist
and Collectivist Norms
in the United States,
Japan, and China

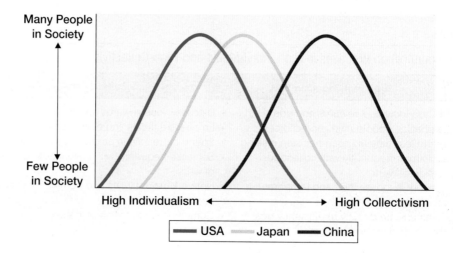

**TABLE 4.5**

Communication Practices in Egalitarian and Hierarchical Cultures

| Egalitarianism | Hierarchy |
|---|---|
| • Decision making is more decentralized.<br>• Protocol based on status is less important and is reserved for unusually formal business situations.<br>• Subordinates speak more openly with leaders even during disagreements.<br>• Subordinates do not take responsibility for the mistakes of leaders.<br>• Leaders are approached directly. | • Decision making is more centralized.<br>• Protocol (use of titles, seating arrangements) based on status is extremely important.<br>• Subordinates defer to leaders during disagreements.<br>• Subordinates take blame for and save face for leaders at all times.<br>• Leaders are approached through intermediaries. |

## Egalitarianism and Hierarchy

All cultures develop norms for how power is distributed. In **egalitarian** cultures, people tend to distribute and share power evenly, minimize status differences, and minimize special privileges and opportunities for people just because they have higher authority. In **hierarchical** cultures, people expect power differences, follow leaders without questioning them, and feel comfortable with leaders receiving special privileges and opportunities. Power tends to be concentrated at the top.

In egalitarian organizations, leaders avoid command-and-control approaches and lead with participatory and open management styles. Competence is highly valued in positions of authority. People of all ranks are encouraged to voice their opinions. Status symbols for leaders are discouraged. Salary ranges between the top and the bottom of the organization are quite narrow. By contrast, in hierarchical organizations, leaders expect employees to fall in line with their policies and decisions by virtue of their authority. Employees are discouraged from openly challenging leaders. Status symbols are common. Salary differences between the top and the bottom of the organization are extreme.[35] Figure 4.5 displays country rankings for hierarchy and egalitarianism. Table 4.5 presents communication practices normally associated with hierarchy and egalitarianism.

## Performance Orientation

**Performance orientation (PO)** is "the extent to which a community encourages and rewards innovation, high standards, and performance improvement."[36] Of all cultural dimensions, societies cherish this one the most, especially in business. Yet many cultures are still developing a performance orientation.[37] To some degree, the distinctions between high-PO and low-PO cultures are captured in the phrase *living to work versus working to live.*

The cultures of Far Eastern Asia, Western Europe, and North America are particularly high in performance orientation. For example, professionals in higher-PO cultures often perceive members of lower-PO cultures as not prioritizing results, accountability, and deadlines. By contrast, members of lower-PO cultures often perceive members of higher-PO cultures as impatient and even obsessed with short-term results.

Some cultures that are midrange-PO cultures such as China and India are rapidly developing performance orientations in work culture. Each of these countries has implemented major economic reforms in recent decades and is achieving stunning economic growth. These countries increasingly have companies and workforces that adopt norms and policies promoting innovation, improvement, and accountability systems. Figure 4.6 displays country rankings for performance orientation. Table 4.6 presents communication practices normally associated with high and low performance orientation.

**FIGURE 4.5**

Hierarchy and Egalitarianism across Cultures

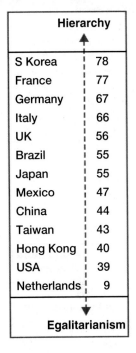

| Hierarchy | |
|---|---|
| S Korea | 78 |
| France | 77 |
| Germany | 67 |
| Italy | 66 |
| UK | 56 |
| Brazil | 55 |
| Japan | 55 |
| Mexico | 47 |
| China | 44 |
| Taiwan | 43 |
| Hong Kong | 40 |
| USA | 39 |
| Netherlands | 9 |

Egalitarianism

**FIGURE 4.6**

Performance Orientation across Cultures

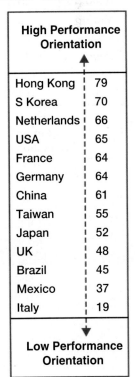

| High Performance Orientation | |
|---|---|
| Hong Kong | 79 |
| S Korea | 70 |
| Netherlands | 66 |
| USA | 65 |
| France | 64 |
| Germany | 64 |
| China | 61 |
| Taiwan | 55 |
| Japan | 52 |
| UK | 48 |
| Brazil | 45 |
| Mexico | 37 |
| Italy | 19 |

Low Performance Orientation

**TABLE 4.6**

Communication in High and Low Performance Orientation Societies

| High Performance Orientation | Low Performance Orientation |
|---|---|
| • Emphasize results more than relationships<br>• Prioritize measurable goals and objectives in meetings and communications<br>• View feedback as essential to improvement<br>• Explicitly talk about financial incentives<br>• Value statements of individual accountability<br>• Expect urgency in communications and emphasize deadlines | • Emphasize relationships more than results<br>• Discuss goals and objectives casually without mechanisms for measuring them<br>• View feedback as judgmental and uncomfortable<br>• De-emphasize financial incentives; consider this motivation inappropriate<br>• Value expressions of loyalty and sympathy<br>• Show a relaxed view of time and view overemphasis on deadlines as pushy |

**FIGURE 4.7**

Time Orientation across Cultures

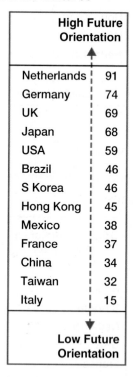

| High Future Orientation | |
|---|---|
| Netherlands | 91 |
| Germany | 74 |
| UK | 69 |
| Japan | 68 |
| USA | 59 |
| Brazil | 46 |
| S Korea | 46 |
| Hong Kong | 45 |
| Mexico | 38 |
| France | 37 |
| China | 34 |
| Taiwan | 32 |
| Italy | 15 |
| Low Future Orientation | |

Hallmarks of high performance orientation are competition and discipline. These attributes are often instilled through school systems, as Ghosn explained about his upbringing in the Jesuit education system:

> In their educational philosophy, discipline is very important, and competition equally so. There's a constant challenge, a grading system that encourages students to outdo one another. After all, the Jesuit order was the first multinational company in the world. . . . I learned a lot from the Jesuits, and by the time I graduated I had a firm sense of discipline and organization, along with a taste for competition and a job well done.[38]

## Future Orientation

**Future orientation (FO)** involves the degree to which cultures are willing to sacrifice current wants to achieve future needs. Cultures with low FO (or present-oriented cultures) tend to enjoy being in the moment and spontaneity. They are less anxious about the future and often avoid the planning and sacrifices necessary to reach future goals. By contrast, cultures with high FO are imaginative about the future and have the discipline to carefully plan for and sacrifice current needs and wants to reach future goals.[39]

In future-oriented societies, many organizations create long-term strategies and business plans. Furthermore, they use these strategies and plans to guide their short-term business activities. By contrast, in present-oriented societies, organizations are less likely to develop clear long-term strategies and business plans. Moreover, they rarely focus short-term activities on long-term plans, even when they exist. Future orientation within organizations is a strong predictor of financial performance. High-FO cultures plan extensively for crises and unforeseen contingencies, whereas low-FO cultures take events as they occur.[40] Figure 4.7 displays country rankings for future orientation. Table 4.7 presents communication practices normally associated with high and low future orientation.

**TABLE 4.7**

Communication Practices in High and Low Future Orientation Cultures

| High Future Orientation | Low Future Orientation |
|---|---|
| • Emphasize control and planning for the future<br>• Focus more on intrinsic motivation<br>• Frequently discuss long-term strategies as part of business communications<br>• Use flexible and adaptive language<br>• Often mention long-term rewards and incentives<br>• Appreciate visionary approaches to business problems | • Emphasize controlling current business problems<br>• Focus more on extrinsic motivation<br>• Rarely discuss long-term strategies as part of communications<br>• Use inflexible and firm language<br>• Often mention short-term rewards and incentives<br>• Prioritize proven and routine approaches to problems |

## Assertiveness

The level of directness in speech varies greatly across cultures, and this can lead to miscommunication, misinterpretation of motivations, and hard feelings. The cultural dimension of **assertiveness** deals with the level of confrontation and directness that is considered appropriate and productive.[41] Typically, North Americans and Western Europeans are the most assertive in business situations, whereas Asians tend to be less assertive. The mentality of "say it how it is," "cut to the chase," and "don't sugarcoat it" is emblematic of high assertiveness.

Members of highly assertive cultures often view members of less assertive cultures as timid, unenthusiastic, uncommitted, and even dishonest, since they withhold or temper their comments. On the other hand, members of less assertive cultures often view members of highly assertive cultures as rude, tactless, inconsiderate, and even uncivilized.[42]

In particular, businesspeople notice differences in levels of assertiveness when a yes or no answer is expected. In less assertive cultures, the answer is sometimes vague; people are expected to read between the lines. As Guy McLeod, president of Airbus China, stated, "In Europe or the States, 'yes' means 'yes,' so we can work together toward a common goal. Here, 'yes' doesn't always mean 'yes,' and 'no' doesn't always mean 'no.' . . . One piece of advice I give people about China: Everything is difficult, but everything is possible."[43] Figure 4.8 displays country rankings for assertiveness. Table 4.8 presents communication practices normally associated with high and low assertiveness.

## Humane Orientation

**Humane orientation (HO)** is "the degree to which an organization or society encourages and rewards individuals for being fair, altruistic, friendly, generous, caring, and kind."[44] In high-HO cultures, people demonstrate that others belong and are welcome. Concern extends to all people—friends and strangers—and nature. People provide social support to each other and are urged to be sensitive to all forms of unfairness, unkindness, and discrimination. Companies and shareholders emphasize social responsibility, and leaders are expected to be generous and compassionate.

In low-HO cultures, the values of pleasure, comfort, and self-enjoyment take precedence over displays of generosity and kindness. People extend material, financial, and social support to a close circle of friends and family. Society members are expected to solve personal problems on their own. Companies and shareholders focus primarily on financial profits, and leaders are not expected to be generous or compassionate.[45] Figure 4.9 displays country rankings for humane orientation. Table 4.9 presents communication practices normally associated with high and low humane orientation.

**FIGURE 4.8**

Assertiveness across Cultures

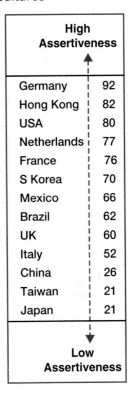

| High Assertiveness | |
|---|---|
| Germany | 92 |
| Hong Kong | 82 |
| USA | 80 |
| Netherlands | 77 |
| France | 76 |
| S Korea | 70 |
| Mexico | 66 |
| Brazil | 62 |
| UK | 60 |
| Italy | 52 |
| China | 26 |
| Taiwan | 21 |
| Japan | 21 |
| Low Assertiveness | |

**TABLE 4.8**

Communication Practices in High- and Low-Assertiveness Cultures

| High-Assertiveness Cultures | Low-Assertiveness Cultures |
|---|---|
| • Emphasize direct and unambiguous language<br>• Uncomfortable with silence and speak up quickly to fill the silence<br>• Prioritize resolving issues over showing respect to others<br>• Typically express more emotion<br>• Use tough, even dominant, language<br>• Stress equity and use competitive language<br>• Value unrestrained expression of thoughts and feelings | • Emphasize indirect and subtle language<br>• View silence as communicative and respectful<br>• Prioritize showing respect over resolving issues<br>• Typically express less emotion<br>• Use tender and pleasant language<br>• Stress equality and use cooperative language<br>• Value measured and disciplined expression of thoughts and feelings |

**FIGURE 4.9**

Humane Orientation
across Cultures

**TABLE 4.9**

Communication Styles in High and Low Humane Orientation Cultures

| High Humane Orientation | Low Humane Orientation |
|---|---|
| • Express greetings, welcome, concern, and appreciation in most interactions | • Express greetings and welcome in formal interactions |
| • Consider taking time to talk about feelings as critical | • Consider taking time to talk about feelings as inefficient |
| • Volunteer to help others | • Help others when asked |
| • Smile and display other nonverbal signs of welcome frequently | • Smile and display other nonverbal signs of welcome infrequently |

Ghosn enjoyed the humane orientation encountered while working in the United States and Japan:

> Those were perhaps the most important years of my professional education. I had to learn how to be an American CEO, which is much different from being a Brazilian-style boss or a European CEO. . . . My education in America was extremely rich: the market, the competition, the mingling of cultures. . . . The United States is a very good training school for learning about customers, and about everything to do with marketing tools and communication.[46]

He similarly was grateful to the Japanese during his stay there:

> The Japanese are very courteous people, sensitive to the feelings of others. They'll never speak to you unpleasantly. When they don't think much of you, they keep quiet. But when they think a lot of you, they tell you. . . . But in any case, during those first months I was spared harsh criticism and negative comments. This was a big help. I didn't need anyone making my task more difficult.[47]

**FIGURE 4.10**

Uncertainty Avoidance
across Cultures

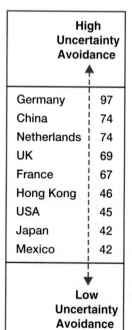

## Uncertainty Avoidance

**Uncertainty avoidance (UA)** refers to how cultures socialize members to feel in uncertain, novel, surprising, or extraordinary situations. In high-UA cultures, people feel uncomfortable with uncertainty and seek orderliness, consistency, structure, and formalized procedures. People in high-UA cultures often stress orderliness and consistency, even if it means sacrificing experimentation and innovation. They prefer that expectations are clear and spelled out precisely in the form of instructions and rules. People in high-UA cultures prefer tasks with sure outcomes and minimal risk. They also show more resistance to change and less tolerance for breaking rules.[48]

In low-UA cultures, people feel comfortable with uncertainty. In fact, they may even thrive, since they prefer tasks that involve uncertain outcomes, calculated risks, and problem solving and experimentation. They often view rules and procedures as hindering creativity and innovation. Members of low-UA cultures develop trust more quickly with people from other groups and tend to be more informal in their interactions. They also show less resistance to change, less desire to establish rules to dictate behavior, and more tolerance for breaking rules.[49] Figure 4.10 displays country rankings for uncertainty avoidance. Table 4.10 presents communication practices normally associated with high and low uncertainty avoidance.

## Gender Egalitarianism

**Gender egalitarianism** deals with the division of roles between men and women in society. In high gender-egalitarianism cultures, men and women are encouraged to occupy the same professional roles and leadership positions. Women are

**TABLE 4.10**

Communication Styles in High and Low Uncertainty Avoidance Cultures

| High Uncertainty Avoidance | Low Uncertainty Avoidance |
|---|---|
| • Document agreements in legal contracts<br>• Expect orderly communication: keep meticulous records, document conclusions drawn in meetings<br>• Refer to formalized policies, procedures, and rules as basis for decision making<br>• Verify with written communication<br>• Prefer formality in the majority of interpersonal business interactions | • Rely on the word of others they trust rather than contractual arrangements<br>• Expect casual communication: less concerned with documentation and maintenance of meeting records<br>• Feel unbound by formalized policies, procedures, and rules when discussing work decisions with others<br>• Verify with oral communication<br>• Expect informality in most interpersonal business interactions |

included equally in decision making. In low gender-egalitarianism cultures, men and women are expected to occupy different roles in society. Typically, women have less influence in professional decision making. However, in societies where gender roles are highly distinct, women often have powerful roles in family decision making.[50]

Traditionally, nearly all cultures afforded low professional status to women. In recent decades, however, women have increasingly gained opportunity and status in many cultures. When Ghosn arrived at Nissan, only 1 percent of managers were women. He quickly made it a goal to increase the number of female managers. Now, 7 percent of managers at Nissan are women, and the goal is to reach 10 percent by 2017.

Gender egalitarianism relates not only to equal professional opportunity for men and women, but also to expectations and customs about how men and women should communicate. Growing up, for example, Ghosn was accustomed to letting women walk through doors first. Yet, in Japan, the tradition is for men to enter doors and elevators first. Ghosn discussed how entering elevators in Japan before women remained uncomfortable for a long time due to his expectations about gender roles.[51] In Table 4.11, you will find communication practices normally associated with high and low gender-egalitarianism cultures.

## Business Values around the World

To this point, we have discussed *norms,* or what cultures actually do. The GLOBE group also surveyed business professionals about *values,* or what they prefer for workplace culture. Refer to Table 4.12 to see which dimensions each culture prioritizes as their ideal work arrangements. Business cultures around the world show many convergences in terms of values—as a result of globalization and increased development. Business cultures, in particular, have converged more rapidly than other parts of society.

**TABLE 4.11**

Communication Practices in High and Low Gender-Egalitarianism Cultures

| High Gender Egalitarianism | Low Gender Egalitarianism |
|---|---|
| • Provide equal professional opportunities to men and women<br>• Expect men and women to have the same communication and management styles<br>• Avoid protocol that draws attention to gender | • Provide more professional leadership opportunities to men<br>• Expect men and women to communicate in distinct masculine and feminine ways<br>• Prefer protocol that draws attention to gender |

**TABLE 4.12**

Preferred Priorities for Work Cultures around the World

| Brazil | China | France |
|---|---|---|
| 1. Performance orientation | 1. Performance orientation | 1. Performance orientation |
| 2. Future orientation | 2. Assertiveness | 2. Humane orientation |
| 3. Organizational collectivism | 3. Humane orientation | 3. Collectivism |
| 4. Humane orientation | 4. Uncertainty avoidance | 4. Future orientation |
| 5. Collectivism | 5. Collectivism | 5. Organizational collectivism |
| 6. Uncertainty avoidance | 6. Future orientation | 6. Uncertainty avoidance |
| 7. Assertiveness | 7. Organizational collectivism | 7. Assertiveness |
| 8. Hierarchy | 8. Hierarchy | 8. Hierarchy |

| Germany | Hong Kong | Italy |
|---|---|---|
| 1. Performance orientation | 1. Performance orientation | 1. Performance orientation |
| 2. Humane orientation | 2. Future orientation | 2. Future orientation |
| 3. Collectivism | 3. Humane orientation | 3. Collectivism |
| 4. Organizational collectivism | 4. Collectivism | 4. Humane orientation |
| 5. Future orientation | 5. Assertiveness | 5. Organizational collectivism |
| 6. Uncertainty avoidance | 6. Uncertainty avoidance | 6. Uncertainty avoidance |
| 7. Assertiveness | 7. Organizational collectivism | 7. Assertiveness |
| 8. Hierarchy | 8. Hierarchy | 8. Hierarchy |

| Japan | Mexico | Netherlands |
|---|---|---|
| 1. Assertiveness | 1. Performance orientation | 1. Performance orientation |
| 2. Humane orientation | 2. Collectivism | 2. Humane orientation |
| 3. Collectivism | 3. Future orientation | 3. Collectivism |
| 4. Future orientation | 4. Uncertainty avoidance | 4. Future orientation |
| 5. Performance orientation | 5. Humane orientation | 5. Organizational collectivism |
| 6. Uncertainty avoidance | 6. Organizational collectivism | 6. Uncertainty avoidance |
| 7. Organizational collectivism | 7. Assertiveness | 7. Assertiveness |
| 8. Hierarchy | 8. Hierarchy | 8. Hierarchy |

| South Korea | United Kingdom | United States |
|---|---|---|
| 1. Future orientation | 1. Performance orientation | 1. Performance orientation |
| 2. Humane orientation | 2. Collectivism | 2. Collectivism |
| 3. Collectivism | 3. Humane orientation | 3. Humane orientation |
| 4. Performance orientation | 4. Future orientation | 4. Future orientation |
| 5. Uncertainty avoidance | 5. Organizational collectivism | 5. Assertiveness |
| 6. Organizational collectivism | 6. Uncertainty avoidance | 6. Organizational collectivism |
| 7. Assertiveness | 7. Assertiveness | 7. Uncertainty avoidance |
| 8. Hierarchy | 8. Hierarchy | 8. Hierarchy |

*Source:* Based on a GLOBE study of work values among business managers in 62 countries.
*Notes:* Performance orientation is the most valued dimension in nearly all work cultures (in green shade).
Hierarchy is the least valued dimension in all work cultures (in red shade).
Humane orientation is highly valued among most cultures (in light blue shade).

## TECHNOLOGY TIPS

### ONLINE CALLS

Business professionals frequently use online calls—voice and video—to communicate conveniently and inexpensively. Online calls use VoIP (voice over IP) technology to allow people to speak with one another over Internet connections. Well-known software packages for online calls include Skype and Vonage.

Skype is the most commonly used online call system for businesses. Skype now has more than 1 billion users, so it may be particularly important for your international dealings. It has caught on for business use for international calls because it is so inexpensive (free for PC-to-PC calls) and convenient. Furthermore, it is often more convenient than mobile phones because many business professionals have phones without international plans. Consider the following when making online calls.

*Understand the limitations of online calls.* Online calls often provide excellent audio and video quality. However, they are generally less predictable than landline calls. Network outages, heavy traffic creating bandwidth problems, and even power failures threaten call quality. Most software for online calls contains components of online-meeting software packages, such as videoconferencing, file transfer, and screen sharing. These additional features are useful but sometimes contribute to lower audio quality due to bandwidth limitations. Test your equipment and be aware of its limitations before making important calls.

*Be sensitive to those who share work space with you.* If you work in cubicles or an open office, you may inadvertently distract your colleagues from their work when making online calls. Online calls are typically louder for two reasons. First, you are broadcasting the voices of those with whom you are speaking. Second, you will find that you often project your voice more loudly on online calls than on phones.

*Spend time setting up the camera, look professional, and tidy up your work area.* Most online calls allow video. If possible, take advantage of this option to add nonverbal cues to your conversation. Take time to set up the camera so that it displays your image in an appealing manner rather than at an odd angle. Also, pay attention to your work space. During lengthy online video calls, the person you are talking with will certainly notice your surroundings. Some will make judgments about your professionalism based on how you maintain your desk and office space.

© Klaus Tiedge/Blend Images LLC

You will notice that nearly all cultures value performance orientation. Note also that all cultures place the lowest priority on hierarchy. In other words, business professionals across the world nearly universally want to focus on performance in an egalitarian, participatory work environment. Furthermore, nearly all cultures value a humane orientation, thus demonstrating that results-focused communication remains critical, but members of most cultures will increasingly expect this strong performance orientation to be framed in a caring manner. As you conduct business across cultures, stay aware of these trends.

## Building and Maintaining Cross-Cultural Work Relationships

Thus far, we have focused on aspects of cultural intelligence primarily related to understanding other cultures. In this section, we focus on the process of building relationships and co-creating success with members of other cultures. This process may involve communicating and working in entirely new ways for you and those of other cultures.

## Establish Trust and Show Empathy

As in any other business relationships, trust is critical in cross-cultural work relationships. And as in other relationships, you can establish your credibility through competence, caring, and character. These aspects of credibility take more time to demonstrate and convey when working across cultures. People from other cultures may interpret behavior differently, so consider how each aspect of credibility is earned in other cultures. Similarly, allow members of other cultures to show their credibility and learn to interpret how they display competence, caring, and character in their cultures.

Business managers often start relationships from a position of needing to earn the trust of others. This is further complicated when working across cultures, where the beliefs that *most people are fair* or *most people can be trusted* may be less prominent than in North America (see Figures 4.11 and 4.12). China, Canada, the United States, the Netherlands, and Saudi Arabia are considered to be high-trust cultures, meaning that their citizens are more conditioned to trust. In contrast, Mexico, Brazil, and France are considered to be low-trust cultures.[52]

One way of establishing trust is to show empathy. After three decades of working across cultures and a full decade heading Nissan, Ghosn reflected on its importance: "I think one of the basics of transcultural leadership is empathy. I would say even though the term today is not very popular, love the country and love the culture you are in. And try to learn about its strengths, don't focus on the weaknesses, and make sure that all the people you are transferring with you are of the same opinion."[53]

**FIGURE 4.11**

## Perceptions of Trust across Cultures

*Note:* % of adults who agree that *most people can be trusted.*

| High-Trust Societies ▲ | |
|---|---|
| China | 53 |
| Netherlands | 45 |
| Japan | 41 |
| Canada | 40 |
| USA | 38 |
| Germany | 34 |
| UK | 30 |
| Italy | 29 |
| S Korea | 29 |
| Spain | 27 |
| Mexico | 19 |
| France | 19 |
| Brazil | 9 |
| ▼ Low-Trust Societies | |

**FIGURE 4.12**

## Expectations of Fair Play across Cultures

*Note:* % of adults who agree that *most people are fair.*

| High Expectations of Fair Play ▲ | |
|---|---|
| Japan | 57 |
| China | 55 |
| USA | 49 |
| Netherlands | 40 |
| Mexico | 30 |
| Taiwan | 29 |
| Brazil | 26 |
| UK | 25 |
| S Korea | 24 |
| Hong Kong | 23 |
| Italy | 20 |
| France | 17 |
| Germany | 1 |
| ▼ Low Expectations of Fair Play | |

Developing empathy is more than showing you care. It also involves understanding members of other cultures as individuals and in terms of business goals and competencies. As you read on, you will notice that trust and credibility across cultures are built on many levels, chief of which is a vision of shared business potential.

## Adopt a Learner Mind-Set

Developing strong cross-cultural relationships requires a learner mind-set. With the learner mind-set, you expect that members of other cultures possess unique types of knowledge and unique approaches to problem solving that will be helpful for shared business interests. You expect that they will be full partners in the decision-making process. Ghosn exemplified this attitude when entering the Japanese environment: "I was bound and determined to become assimilated. When I signed on for this Japanese adventure, I told myself that Japan was going to be a part of me, just as Nissan was going to be a part of me. But assimilation doesn't mean that you lose your individuality or your originality."[54]

Although Ghosn did not know much about Japanese culture before he moved to Japan, he had a deep and profound respect for Japanese innovations in the car industry:

> The Japanese left an indelible mark on the automobile industry by extending the boundaries of the factory management system. . . . It was at Toyota that "lean production" was born. The system would be copied and adapted, more or less successfully, by the automobile industry worldwide, beginning with Toyota's competitors in Japan. . . . The Japanese aren't champions of theory. Their strong suit is to start from a simple, pragmatic observation and try to create a solution from that. I haven't seen very many theoretical solutions produced in Japan.[55]

The opposite of the learner mind-set when working with other cultures is the judger mind-set. In cross-cultural working relationships, the judger mind-set is often referred to as **ethnocentrism**. It is the belief that your own culture is superior—that it provides better approaches for solving work problems or dealing with work relationships and contains a better knowledge base to conceptualize work. In all interpersonal relationships, the judger mind-set is damaging. In cross-cultural relationships, it is particularly damaging because most people have a great deal of self-respect and self-esteem tied to their cultural identities.[56]

## Build a Co-culture of Cooperation and Innovation

When working across cultures, people generally adopt a unique set of communication and collaboration practices. These practices combine aspects of each culture. Over time, these practices, norms, and values form a **co-culture** that combines elements of each culture. One of the best signs that your cross-cultural working relationships are going well is when you have become comfortable enough with one another to form a co-culture. Doing so requires a mind-set that you are creating something new—a belief that you will adopt the best practices of the other culture and vice versa, as Ghosn explained:

> In cross-border acquisitions or alliances, cultural differences can be viewed as either a handicap or a powerful seed for something new. From the beginning, I said that I viewed cultural differences as an opportunity to innovate in achieving the pragmatic business objectives we had before us. This is risky when you say it before you even start. It's been 15 months since I arrived at Nissan. And now, six months after the start of the revival plan, *I can tell you that today cultural differences are seen more as an object of cross-fertilization and innovation in the way we are doing things, than as a motive for frustration or reason to disagree.* This is because of one thing—the Nissan Revival Plan. When the Renault people came to Japan, the management of Nissan had from the beginning a very strong consciousness about the severity of the situation. There was

no room for bickering or fighting or infinite discussions about whose method or whose process we were going to adopt.[57]

Business managers high in cultural intelligence recognize that developing effective co-cultures requires creating something new. This is one reason that seasoned executives select people for international assignments who can handle uncertainty. As Ekkehard Rathgeber, former president of Direct Group Asia, explained, "My belief is: If you pick the wrong person, no matter how much training you give, it won't work. You need to find a person who is very determined and can handle the ambiguity you find every day in China. . . . You must be very open to new things, excited by new things—not someone who wants to preserve his own culture and identity."[58]

Creating a co-culture involves abandoning some—not all—cultural norms and values from each culture. At Nissan, Ghosn replaced some elements of Japanese culture that were not serving the needs of the company. For example, he introduced merit pay increases rather than seniority pay increases and broke up the keiretsu supplier network (the traditional approach to Japanese partnerships between companies based on shared ownership and loyalty). As Ghosn explained, however, these changes were aligned with Nissan's business interests, implemented with the collectivist approach of cross-functional teams (CFTs), and accommodated various Japanese preferences for work:[59]

> I knew that if I had tried simply to impose the changes from the top, I would have failed. Instead, I decided to use as the centerpiece of the turnaround effort a set of cross-functional teams. I had used CFTs in my previous turnarounds and had found them a powerful tool for getting line managers to see beyond the functional or regional boundaries that define their direct responsibilities. . . . Inside Nissan, though, people recognized that we weren't trying to take the company over but rather were attempting to restore it to its former glory. We had the trust of employees for a simple reason: We had shown them respect. . . . We have been able to exploit the uniquely Japanese combination of keen competitiveness and sense of community that has driven the likes of Sony and Toyota—and Nissan itself in earlier times.[60]

Business leaders know that an effective co-culture has been built when corporate culture includes aspects of each culture and delivers results. Ghosn explained this sense of co-culture at Nissan:

> We spend all of our time collaborating. We're crossing cultures and experiences. In my opinion, that's an advantage for the future. Nissan is building a culture that's well adapted to this new world. At the top levels of the company, we can't think in specifically Japanese or French terms any longer. . . . I'm convinced that if General Motors and Ford are having difficulties today, it's because they haven't become truly global corporations. They have remained too American. They realize most of their profits are in the United States. . . . What we're on our way to understanding is that tomorrow's winners, at least those in the automobile industry, will be those that are truly global, capable of according importance to all markets. Tomorrow's company will be the one that assumes a global character without losing its identity.[61]

## Learning the Etiquette of Another Culture

**LO4.3** Name and describe key categories of business etiquette in the intercultural communication process.

Following the rules of etiquette in other cultures is one way of gaining favorable first impressions and showing respect. This is especially the case as you get to know potential partners or clients. On exploratory trips, you will participate in meetings and social engagements—banquets and meals, refreshments during meetings, and plenty of small talk. These are opportunities for members of each culture to get to know one another in a nonthreatening, casual environment.

## COMMUNICATION Q&A

### CONVERSATIONS WITH CURRENT BUSINESS PROFESSIONALS

**Pete Cardon: How important is it for business leaders to understand other cultures?**

**Nipul Patel:** It is extremely important. We live in a connected society. Social media (Facebook, Twitter, LinkedIn, etc.) are increasingly connecting cultures across the globe. Successful business leaders must understand the needs, wants, and desires of people in the cultures they want to conduct business with.

**PC: What are a few of the major differences in how people communicate to conduct business in India and the United States?**

**NP:** Some differences have gotten smaller over time. However, there are still big differences. The American business climate has a contract-based business approach. Even a simple rental contract requires many pages and goes through many revisions by many legal professionals. From the Indian perspective this contract-based approach shows distrust. In my opinion, it hinders the openness that must exist in conducting business transactions. In India, the majority of transactions are still conducted on a handshake basis. The value of one's word is still a major aspect of doing business overseas. We are in the process of establishing a business venture in Thailand and Bangladesh. I see many similarities in conducting business in India and those countries. Although the formalities involved in doing business in the United States protect both buyer and seller, trust is an ingredient for a successful recipe. In India if you don't get this trust, you have no chance of getting any deals with anyone.

**PC: What can business students do right now to increase their knowledge of other cultures?**

**NP:** Business students should learn as much about other cultures as possible. I would encourage every aspiring business student to study in another country for at least a semester, if not more. Studying abroad allows you to experience the culture firsthand. It is significantly different than just taking a course or two in a foreign language. Although it is extremely important to learn the language, it is more important to learn the culture, traditions, and overall business climate of another country.

**Nipul Patel** *spends about nine months each year in the United States running the restaurants and convenience stores that he owns in Indiana. He lives in India for about three months per year to manage his real estate company and focus on various venture capital interests.*

Photo courtesy Nipul Patel

---

You have many sources for learning about the appropriate customs and etiquette of other cultures. In Table 4.13, you will find examples from Brazil, Russia, India, and China (often called the *BRIC* countries because of their expected strategic importance for business during the 21st century).[62] This table includes the types of customs and etiquette you should become aware of before traveling to another country for business, including appropriate versus taboo topics of conversation, conversation style, punctuality and meetings, dining, touching and proximity, business dress, and gift giving.

## Generation, Gender, and Other Group Identities

Like culture on a global level, generational groups, gender, and other group identities can impact workplace communication. Often, members of these groups have been *socialized* in certain ways—they grew up with similar societal expectations and interacted with others as children and adults in ways that shaped what they came to view as acceptable and appropriate. The way members of these groups have been socialized often creates shared values, shared identities, and similar communication patterns in the workplace.

**connect**

Visit http://connect.
mheducation.com for an
exercise on this topic.

**LO4.4** Identify how generational, gender, and other group differences affect workplace communication.

**TABLE 4.13**

Etiquette and Customs in the BRIC Countries

| | Brazil | Russia | India | China |
|---|---|---|---|---|
| **Appropriate Topics of Conversation** | Personal topics, soccer, weather, traffic, cultural events | Politics, Russian culture and history, art (if you know a lot about it), current events, books, films | Family and personal life, politics, cricket, films, economic reforms | Chinese history, art, calligraphy, Chinese food |
| **Private or Taboo Topics of Conversation** | Politics, poverty, crime, security, deforestation, corruption | Personal life, religion, comparing Moscow and St. Petersburg, comparing Russia to developing countries | Religion, Pakistan, poverty, slums, caste system | Taiwan, Tibet, Tiananmen Square, human rights |
| **Punctuality and Meetings** | Meeting times are relaxed and often start 10 to 15 minutes late. | Meetings are scheduled far in advance. Time is viewed flexibly. | Meetings are scheduled far in advance. Time is viewed flexibly. | Meetings begin on time; arrive at social events on time. |
| **Dining** | Meals (lunch and dinner) are an important part of building relationships. Careful attention to etiquette: Food is never touched with the hands. Begin meal with the toast: "Saúde." | Meals (dinners) are often used to finish a deal. Seating arrangements follow protocol. Continental style of using utensils. Hands should always stay above the table. Drinking alcohol is an important part of socializing. | Meals are important to show hospitality to visitors. | Extravagant meals and banquets are an essential part of building relationships. Toasting is an important part of meals. Individual meals rarely served; rather, dishes for the group are provided on a lazy Susan (rotating tray). |
| **Touching and Proximity** | Frequent and extended touching: handshakes, embraces between friends, kissing on cheeks between women as a greeting, touching arms, standing close to one another during conversation | Touching reserved for greetings and handshakes | People stand closer (2 to 2½ feet apart) to one another than in North America. | Handshakes and slight bows during greetings. Touching is rare. People commonly sit side by side rather than facing one another during meetings. |
| **Conversation Style** | Animated, lively, expressive, lots of interruptions, loud, spontaneous | Calm, deliberate, careful, metaphorical and symbolic, philosophical, frank | Agreeable, friendly, conflict-avoiding | Modest, reserved, cautious display of emotion, indirect about disagreements |
| **Business Dress** | Formal business attire is important. Should be stylish, fashionable. For women, dress should be feminine. | Brand-name, expensive suits | Men: suit and tie except in warmer climates where more casual. Women: salwar suit. Conservative dress is important. | Conservative suits. Bright colors are avoided. High heels are avoided. |
| **Titles** | Titles are used only in formal situations. | First names are appropriate only after a relationship is well established. | Titles are typically used unless directed otherwise. | Titles are generally used in the workplace. |
| **Gift Giving** | Gifts generally are not expected on first meeting. A better alternative is to buy a meal. | Gifts are appreciated. Cheap gifts should be avoided. Good gifts include chocolates, dessert items, fine wine. | Gift giving is a sign of friendship. Expensive and leather gifts should be avoided. | Gift giving is common in first meetings. Gifts should be presented with two hands. Expensive gifts are avoided. |

## Working across Generations

Over the past decade, at least four generations have worked together in the workplace. Now, you enter a workplace with up to five generations (see Figure 4.13). Professionals work across generations more so now for several reasons. Many workers are retiring later. More importantly, changes in technology and workplace cultures are dramatically affecting how often professionals of different generations interact. Technology allows easier access to colleagues and customers of all ages. Similarly, workplace cultures are moving to more flat, team-based structures that reduce the layers within organizations that, in the past, often separated colleagues by age.

Working with colleagues, clients, and customers of all ages presents many opportunities and challenges. Some of the challenges of working across generations involve distinct differences in working styles.[63] Other challenges are related to power and resources. Older professionals often hold positions with more power and clout, which some researchers suggest is the primary cause of conflict across generations. These challenges may be exacerbated when younger professionals hold leadership positions over older professionals. Many experts note that differences across generations are often a matter of life stages. For example, younger professionals are naturally eager to learn more and gain rapid advancement in their careers, whereas older professionals may feel more established and secure in their careers.[64] Yet other challenges are based on misperceptions and stereotyping. Savvy professionals with high CQ learn to see the best in the experiences and insights of professionals of all generations.

The *Silent Generation* or **Traditionalists** were born between 1925 and 1945. Traditionalists grew up during the Depression and World War II. Radio and telephones were emerging communication technologies during this time. Strong parental authority was the norm in most families. Traditionalists tend to be financially conservative, disciplined, patient, and respectful of authority. They believe in logic, hold a sense of right and wrong, and feel less comfortable with ambiguity. In the workplace, they are typically viewed as hardworking, loyal, and dedicated. They hold respect for titles and feel comfortable with command-and-control approaches to leadership and management.[65]

■ **connect**

**Visit http://connect. mheducation.com** for an exercise on this topic.

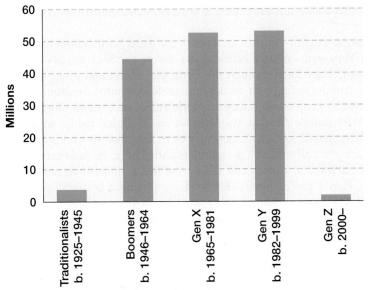

**American Workforce by Generations**

**FIGURE 4.13**

Five Generations in the American Workforce

*Source:* Richard Fry, "Millennials Surpass Gen Xers as the Largest Generation in the U.S. Labor Force," *Pew Research Center* website, May 11, 2015, available at http://www.pewresearch.org/ fact-tank/2015/05/11/millennials- surpass-gen-xers-as-the-largest- generation-in-u-s-labor-force/1c.

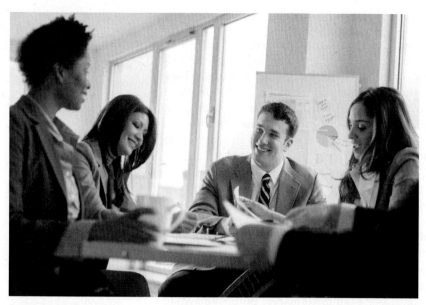

© mediaphotos/Getty Images

*Baby Boomers* or **Boomers** were born between 1946 and 1964. Boomers grew up during a prosperous World War II era. They also experienced major political and social changes, including the protest movements to the Vietnam War, the Civil Rights movement, the sexual revolution, Watergate, and the King and Kennedy assassinations. Most families were nuclear families with mothers staying at home. Families often gathered around the TV to watch shows together. Boomers are often considered optimistic, free spirited, and experimental. In the workplace, they hold a strong work ethic—in fact, the term *workaholic* was created for this generation. They hold strong loyalty to employers, and they prefer a professional work environment. Many Boomers have retired or are currently near retirement. Yet, they still comprise roughly 28 percent of the American workforce.[66]

**Gen X** refers to those who were born between 1965 and 1981. Gen Xers grew up during rapid globalization with growing and intense worldwide competition. Corporate downsizing was common. They also saw the end of the Cold War. They were the first generation to use desktop computers and home video games as children or teenagers. They experienced the rapid proliferation of entertainment options, including MTV and movie channels, on cable TV. The home environment shifted significantly during this era. With more women entering the workforce and more single-parent families, children from this generation were often called *latchkey kids* because they frequently let themselves into their homes after school and had less parental supervision and attention. Gen Xers are known as independent, confident, self-reliant, responsibility driven, results focused, and less formal. In the workplace, they work hard but attempt to maintain a balance with personal lives. Compared with prior generations, they seek more continuous feedback, they're less loyal to employers, they're not impressed by titles, and they're willing to put in extra time to get the job done. Gen X professionals prioritize open communication. Gen X professionals comprise roughly 34 percent of the workforce.[67]

*Millennials, Digital Natives,* or **Gen Y**ers were born between 1981 and 1999. Most Gen Yers were children or teenagers during the 9/11 attacks and the conflicts that followed. They lived through the Great Recession and often saw their parents or friends' parents struggle in an unpredictable economic environment. They grew up connected to people and information via social media and other online communication. With mobile devices, they had access to digital media with amazing convenience. Compared to Gen Xers, most Gen Yers had far more involved parents. Gen Yers are generally viewed as optimistic, adaptable, inclusive, sociable, friendly, collaborative, loyal to causes and issues, confident, impatient, and entitled. In the workplace, Gen Y professionals seek to strike a balance between work and lifestyle, want flexibility in work hours, enjoy working in teams, want to make an impact, seek continuous feedback and instant results, are less loyal to employers, prioritize a friendly and casual workplace, and enjoy multitasking. Gen Y comprise roughly 35 percent of the workforce.[68]

As you navigate your early professional life, understanding how other professionals view Gen Y professionals will help you play to your strengths and overcome

**TABLE 4.14**

Perceived Strengths and Weaknesses of Millennials in the Workplace

|  | Boomers | Gen X | Gen Y |
|---|---|---|---|
| Tech savvy | 27 | 77 | 85 |
| Adaptability | 36 | 67 | 69 |
| Diversity | 42 | 68 | 69 |
| Enthusiastic | 38 | 64 | 68 |
| Entitled and concerned primarily about individual promotion | 32 | 51 | 68 |
| Entrepreneurial | 55 | 71 | 68 |
| Brand ambassador | 39 | 65 | 67 |
| Collaboration | 54 | 70 | 63 |
| Lacking relevant experience | 14 | 15 | 59 |
| Relationship builder | 71 | 72 | 54 |
| Flexibility | 53 | 63 | 47 |
| Communication skills | 72 | 71 | 42 |
| Hardworking | 73 | 69 | 39 |
| Decision making | 74 | 70 | 38 |

*Note:* Based on 2013 survey of 1,215 professionals. Numbers refer to the percentage of respondents who agreed that professionals of each generation exhibited these traits.

*Source:* EY, "Survey Shows Younger Mangers Rise in the Ranks," 2013, EY website, available at http://www.ey.com/Publication/vwLUAssets/EY-Survey_shows_younger_managers_rising_in_the_ranks/$FILE/Executive-Summary-Generations-Research.pdf.

possible misperceptions. In Table 4.14, you'll notice common perceptions professionals hold toward various generations. For example, you'll see most professionals regard Gen Y professionals as tech savvy, adaptable, enthusiastic, and entrepreneurial. They also see Gen Y professionals as strong brand ambassadors. Yet, most professionals also regard Gen Y professionals as entitled and inexperienced. These perceptions are common over time—every generation entering the workforce faces these stereotypes. Less than half of professionals view Gen Y employees as hardworking, strong in communication skills, and effective in decision making.[69] One common misperception is that Millennials don't want to talk face-to-face. In fact, Millennials prefer face-to-face communication as much as members of other generations.[70] Your credibility will grow as you disprove some of these common stereotypes and misperceptions.

*Post-Millennials* or **Gen Z**ers were born in 2000 or after. They amplify many of the traits associated with Gen Yers. For example, they are growing up even more connected, even more reliant on mobile devices, more focused on visual media, and even more accustomed to collaborative platforms.[71] Some Gen Z individuals have already entered the workforce. They are the smallest portion of the American workforce at roughly 1 percent. However, within five to ten years, they'll likely comprise up to 10 percent of the workforce. Members of each generation, particularly those entering the workforce, face stereotypes developed by members of other generations. Gen Y professionals have already formed stereotypes of Gen Z professionals. On the positive side, many Gen Y professionals consider Gen Z employees open-minded (41 percent) and creative (38 percent). On the negative side, many Gen Y professionals consider Gen Z employees lazy (45 percent), self-centered (37 percent), and easily distracted (35 percent).[72]

While work styles may vary across generations, keep in mind that media accounts of generational differences are often hyped or exaggerated.[73] As you work with colleagues, clients, and customers of all ages, consider the following tips:

*Focus on individuals and their professional goals.* This tip spans nearly all communication—people want to be recognized and respected for who they are on an individual level. While national, generational, gender, and other identities matter to most people, no one wants to be defined or stereotyped by these identities. Learning about others' individual goals and interests is the best way to understand them.

*Recognize the similarities across generations.* Members of various generations have far more similarities than differences in the workplace. For example, members of each generation are fairly aligned in what they consider the most important aspects of workplace culture. Members of each generation rank fairness, being ethical, and being straightforward as the most important aspects of workplace culture.[74] They also expect virtually the same traits of their leaders: credible, good listeners, forward-looking, and supportive. The Center for Creative Leadership has found that members of each generation hold quite similar life values, with strong importance attached to family, love, integrity, achievement, and happiness.[75] It's also worth noting that many childhood experiences occur in cycles and affect people of various generations in quite similar ways. For example, the two most financially conservative generations are the Traditionalists and the Gen Yers. Not surprisingly, the Traditionalists grew up during the Great Depression and the Gen Yers grew up during the Great Recession.[76]

*Pay attention to preferred approaches to communicating.* Members of various generations grew up with slightly different communication patterns that they carry throughout their lives. Communication technologies are often used quite differently by each generational group. Not surprisingly, Boomers and Gen Xers are most comfortable with phone calls, and Gen Yers are most comfortable with texting. Gen Xers are particularly comfortable on PCs and laptops, whereas Gen Yers are more comfortable on tablets and other mobile devices. (We discuss technology in more detail in Chapters 7 and 8.) Beyond technology, however, members of various generations may differ in a variety of ways: word choice, turn-taking in meetings, choice of humor, and many other ways. Pay attention to these differences and enjoy fitting in!

*Observe appropriate formality and attire.* Professionals of various generations often hold distinct views of formality, etiquette, and attire. While some of these differences may seem more about style and less about substance, noticing, appreciating, and even adopting some of these practices can show respect and a touch of class in the eyes of others.

## Gender and Communication Patterns

Visit http://connect.
mheducation.com for an
exercise on this topic.

While some communication patterns of men and women in the workplace have converged over the past decades, differences still exist. Overall, women tend to be more relationship oriented, collaborative, and interconnected in thinking, whereas men tend to be more independent, competitive, and linear in thinking. These differences are somewhat similar to some of the cultural dimensions you read about at the beginning of the chapter. For example, a relational, group-oriented focus tends to describe a collectivist approach to work, and an independent, competitive focus tends to describe an individualist approach to work. In Figure 4.14, you'll notice several differences about the relationship between gender and collectivism that hold in nearly all societies. First, differences in national cultures are typically far greater than those of gender within societies. Second, women tend to be more relationship-oriented in individualist and collectivist societies. Third, there is significant overlap between men and women within societies. This suggests women and men may have general tendencies, but you can easily find many exceptions on an individual level.

One of the foremost experts on gendered communication in the workplace, Dr. Deborah Tannen, has spent the past half century exploring the ways women and men speak in the workplace. She has also studied how boys and girls grow up, and she has shown that the way men and women speak is often rooted in how they socialized and played as children. She has shown that the relational approach of women

**FIGURE 4.14**

Gender in Individualist and Collectivist Societies

*Source:* Chart created by author based on dozens of research studies that demonstrate women tend to exhibit more collectivist, relational attitudes and behaviors in collectivist and individualist societies.

influences a variety of speech patterns in the workplace.[77] In this section, we explore speech patterns most often associated with women (see Table 4.15 for an overview). Historically, these speech patterns were not considered the dominant speech patterns in the workplace. Increasingly, these speech patterns are recognized and recommended as important ways to help professionals, teams, and organizations succeed.

**TABLE 4.15**

Speech Patterns More Common among Women than Men

| | **Pattern More Common among Women than Men** | **Benefits** | **Risks** |
|---|---|---|---|
| **Asking Questions** | Asking lots of questions | Opening up conversations; giving others a chance to speak; generating knowledge; gaining answers | Speaker appears to know less than others |
| **Apologizing** | Apologizing often | Expressing sympathy for others; smoothing over awkward situations; admitting mistakes and taking responsibility for them | Speaker appears to unnecessarily take responsibility or appears to lack authority |
| **Sharing Credit** | Using "we" rather than "I" when talking about accomplishments | Avoiding self-promotion and recognizing the contributions of others; maintaining a team orientation | Speaker doesn't get enough credit for individual accomplishments |
| **Giving Feedback** | Mentioning weaknesses only after citing strengths | Buffering criticism, maintaining high morale, and showing appreciation | Person receiving feedback doesn't recognize the importance of improving |
| **Avoiding Verbal Opposition** | Avoiding directly challenging others' ideas; hedging when stating one's own views | Allowing others to state their ideas freely; adopting flexible views of one another's ideas | Others conclude that speaker has weak ideas and lacks confidence |
| **Being Indirect to Subordinates** | Speaking indirectly rather than bluntly when talking to subordinates | Placing everyone on the same level and not coming across as commanding, domineering, or bossy | Subordinates conclude that manager lacks assertiveness and clear thinking |
| **Complimenting** | Showing genuine appreciation for the actions of others | Maintaining an enjoyable working relationship and showing others they're valued | Being known first and foremost as "nice" at the expense of being considered results driven |

*Sources:* The table is primarily adapted from Deborah Tannen, "The Power of Talk: Who Gets Heard and Why," *Harvard Business Review,* September–October 1995, 138–148. Tannen's work primarily focused on risks or unintended consequences of the various speech patterns. In the subsequent decades, many of these speech patterns have become much more in favor. In fact, many of these patterns are often recommended as the preferred approaches to teamwork, collaboration, and other forms of workplace communication. This adapted table also includes information from other sources, including the following: Deborah Tannen, *You Just Don't Understand: Women and Men in Conversation* (New York: William Morrow Paperbacks, 2007); Barbara Annis and John Gray, *Work with Me: The 8 Blind Spots between Men and Women in Business* (New York: St. Martin's Press, 2013); Sheryl Sandberg, *Lean In: Women, Work, and the Will to Lead* (New York: Knopf, 2013).

© Blend Images - JGI/Jamie Grill/
Getty Images

Asking questions and listening are key leadership abilities. The frequency and purposes of questioning tend to differ slightly between women and men. Women tend to *ask questions* more than men do. In fact, in research about brainstorming meetings of about one hour in length, North American women ask about 19 questions compared with 15 questions for North American men. In similar meetings, East Asian women tend to ask about 11 questions compared with about 6 questions for East Asian men.[78] Whereas men are more likely to ask questions primarily to seek information, women are more likely to also ask questions to build consensus, to show concern, to offer feedback, or to ask for support. Because men view questions primarily as information seeking, they often miss the relational purposes women use for some questions. In the workplace, about 72 percent of men say they think women ask too many questions, and about 80 percent of women prefer to ask questions even when they know the answer.[79]

Women also apologize more than men do for several reasons. Women are more likely to view apologies as expressions of sympathy, whereas men are more likely to view apologies as expressions of responsibility.[80] With a relational focus, women generally have lower thresholds for rudeness, so they're more likely to offer an apology as a matter of politeness or to ease an awkward situation.[81] Women are also more likely to admit mistakes. Increasingly, employees respect leaders who can admit mistakes. A recent survey of 3,500 business professionals in 13 countries found that admitting mistakes was the third most important leadership ability—just slightly behind leading by example and communicating in an open, transparent way.[82] Still, apologies can be misinterpreted depending on how much others see them as statements of responsibility versus statements of politeness.

A variety of other speech patterns are more common among women. Women are more likely to *share credit* rather than state their individual contributions, *give feedback* by stating strengths first and then suggesting improvements, *avoid verbal opposition*, and *offer compliments*. Generally, women are more likely to be *indirect* to subordinates and *speak less* in meetings so they avoid sounding bossy. In fact, women who are more assertive and speak up more often are often judged more negatively (by men and women), whereas men are judged more positively for these same actions.[83] Recently, Sheryl Sandberg, COO of Facebook, has been a public advocate for overcoming this type of bias. She explained:

> The data show that success and likeability are positively correlated for men and negatively correlated for women. Which means that as women get more successful, they are liked less—both by men and by other women. That's because we want people to conform to our stereotypes. And when they don't, we don't like them as much. We expect men to have leadership qualities, to be assertive and competent, to speak out. We expect women to have communal qualities, to be givers and sharers, to pursue the common good. The problem is, we want to promote and hire people who are both competent and liked. And that's just much easier for men.[84]

As you work with others, you'll often notice people use these various speech patterns in different ways. Consider the following tips:

*Notice when professionals use these speech patterns for task-based versus relationship-based reasons.* While gender often plays a role in these speech patterns, many other factors are at play and you can easily think of some exceptions. Regardless, by observing the purposes behind asking questions, apologizing, indirectly offering feedback, and these other speech patterns, you can better understand the intentions of others.

*Purposefully and consciously adopt your own style.* Most professionals adopt these speech patterns without any thought. Take note of how you use these speech patterns. Be willing to experiment with alternative ways of speaking in the workplace. Find the mix of speech patterns that fits your personality, helps you work well with others, and helps you succeed.

*Do your part to overcome biases.* Women continue to be underrepresented in leadership positions. The reasons for this are complex and hard to pinpoint. Bias is likely a factor in many cases. For example, research shows that women continue to be judged less positively than men when they're assertive and direct.[85]

## Displaying Cultural Intelligence with Other Groups

Professionals hold identities in many groups and generally adopt some of the shared values and norms of these groups.[86] Regional differences may impact communication. Phrases such as *Southern hospitality* or a *New York minute* often reflect distinct approaches to working with others and getting things done. Similarly, professionals who grew up in rural, suburban, and urban areas often gain lifelong attitudes and behaviors related to sense of community, pace of life, and communication patterns. Ethnicity likewise affects many professionals' values, attitudes, and identities in the workplace. Occupational groups often hold distinct ways of approaching work. For example, engineers and marketers are often socialized into distinct ways of discussing, approaching, and solving problems. Even companies have distinct cultures, which are influenced by many factors, including industry and size. For example, a small tech start-up in Silicon Valley likely has a markedly different culture than that of a large, established bank in New York City. The longer people work in companies, the more they adopt the ways of doing things in those organizations. Your ability to identify the norms and values associated with various groups will help you throughout your career as you work with others.

# Chapter Takeaway for *Communicating across Cultures: Global, Generational, and Gender Communication Patterns*

**LO4.1 Describe characteristics of cultural intelligence, its importance for global business leaders, and approaches to developing it. (pp. 103–108)**

| Principles of High Cultural Intelligence | |
|---|---|
| • Respect, recognize, and appreciate cultural differences.<br>• Possess curiosity about and interest in other cultures.<br>• Avoid inappropriate stereotypes.<br>• Adjust conceptions of time and show patience.<br>• Manage language differences to achieve shared meaning. | • Understand cultural dimensions.<br>• Establish trust and show empathy across cultures.<br>• Approach cross-cultural work relationships with a learner mind-set.<br>• Build a co-culture of cooperation and innovation. |

**LO4.2 Explain the major cultural dimensions and related communication practices. (pp. 108–120)**

| Cultural Dimensions |
|---|
| **Individualism** refers to a mind-set that prioritizes independence more highly than interdependence, emphasizes individual goals over group goals, and values choice more than obligation. |
| **Collectivism** refers to a mind-set that prioritizes interdependence more highly than independence, emphasizes group goals over individual goals, and values obligation more than choice. |
| **Egalitarianism** refers to cultures that distribute and share power evenly, minimize status differences, and minimize special privileges and opportunities for people just because they have higher authority. |
| **Hierarchy** refers to cultures that expect power differences, follow leaders without questioning them, and feel comfortable with leaders receiving special privileges and opportunities. |
| **Performance orientation** refers to cultures that encourage and reward innovation and set high standards of performance. |
| **Future orientation** involves the degree to which cultures are willing to sacrifice current wants to achieve future needs. |
| **Assertiveness** deals with the level of confrontation and directness that is considered appropriate and productive within a culture. |
| **Humane orientation** refers to cultures that encourage and reward individuals for being fair, friendly, generous, and kind. |
| **Uncertainty avoidance** refers to how cultures socialize members to feel in uncertain, novel, surprising, or extraordinary situations. |
| **Gender egalitarianism** deals with the division of roles between men and women in society. |

See *rankings of countries along these cultural dimensions* in Figures 4.2 through 4.10. See *related communication practices* in Tables 4.4 through 4.12. See a *comprehensive set of rankings* for 62 cultures in the online resources.

**LO4.3 Name and describe key categories of business etiquette in the intercultural communication process. (pp. 120–121)**

| Etiquette and Customs | |
|---|---|
| • Appropriate topics of conversation<br>• Private or taboo topics<br>• Punctuality and meetings<br>• Dining<br>• Touching and proximity | • Conversation style<br>• Business dress<br>• Titles<br>• Gift giving |

See *examples of etiquette and customs across the BRIC countries* in Table 4.13.

**LO4.4 Identify how generational, gender, and other group differences affect workplace communication. (pp. 121–129)**

| Generations |
|---|
| Traditionalists were born between 1925 and 1945. |
| Boomers were born between 1946 and 1964. |
| Gen X individuals were born between 1965 and 1981. |
| Gen Y individuals were born between 1982 and 1999. |
| Gen Z individuals were born in 2000 or after. |

See Table 4.14 for perceived strengths and weaknesses of Gen Y according to current professionals.

| Speech Patterns More Common among Women | |
|---|---|
| • Asking questions<br>• Apologizing<br>• Sharing credit<br>• Giving feedback | • Avoiding verbal opposition<br>• Being indirect to subordinates<br>• Complimenting |

See Table 4.15 for description of *benefits and risks of these speech patterns*.

# Key Terms

assertiveness, 113

Boomers, 124

co-culture, 119

collectivism, 109

cultural dimensions, 108

cultural intelligence (CQ), 103

culture, 103

diversity, 104

egalitarian, 111

ethnocentrism, 119

future orientation (FO), 112

Gen X, 124

Gen Y, 124

Gen Z, 125

gender egalitarianism, 114

hierarchical, 111

humane orientation (HO), 113

individualism, 109

outgroup homogeneity effect, 106

performance orientation (PO), 111

projected cognitive similarity, 106

Traditionalists, 123

uncertainty avoidance (UA), 114

# Discussion Exercises

**4.1 Chapter Review Questions** (LO 4.1, LO 4.2, LO 4.3, LO 4.4)

A. As you choose a culture or cultures to learn about, which do you think would be most helpful for your career? Why?

B. Explain what cultural intelligence is. How is it similar to and different from emotional intelligence?

C. What does it mean to embrace diversity in the context of conducting business across cultures?

D. How can you learn about another culture? Map out a plan for learning about a culture of interest.

E. How can stereotypes be productive and counterproductive? How does popular culture impact stereotypes of cultures?

F. What strategies can you use to overcome language barriers?

G. Describe each of the cultural dimensions and related communication practices.

H. Explain what is meant by a co-culture. Explain how a co-culture of communication practices might take form in a business setting.

I. Based on what you've learned from Carlos Ghosn's comments and your own experiences, how can you show respect for other cultures while also attempting to change some aspect of the culture?

J. Think of a culture of interest to you. Describe several things you could learn from that culture to enrich your life, deepen your business expertise, and improve your communication skills.

K. Describe what you think are the defining events in each of the generations. Explain how you think these events had long-lasting impacts on members of each of these generations.

L. Choose three of the speech patterns from the section about gender. Explain how these speech patterns may differ between individuals who view them primarily as task based versus those who view them primarily as relationship based?

**4.2  Communication Q&A Discussion Questions** (LO 4.1, LO 4.2, LO 4.3)

Read the Communication Q&A section in this chapter. Based on Nipul Patel's comments and your own experiences, respond to the following questions:

A. Patel speaks about the importance of trust in doing business in India. Based on his comments, how might you feel about doing business in India? Would you be able to adapt your level of trust and distrust?

B. What does Patel recommend for business students who want to learn about other cultures?

C. If you had the chance to speak with Patel before a trip to India for business, what five questions would you ask him?

**4.3  Leadership Lessons Learned through International Experiences** (LO 4.1)

Robert W. Selander, former president and CEO of MasterCard, was asked, "What are the most important leadership lessons you have learned?" He responded by describing some of his international experiences. He explained how English ability isn't necessarily reflective of managerial competence:

> I was out visiting a branch [in Brazil] . . . [Since] he was struggling with his English, the coin sort of dropped that this guy really knows what he's talking about. He's having a hard time getting it out. . . . I realized this was probably the best branch manager I'd seen, but it would have been very easy for me to think he wasn't, because he couldn't communicate as well as some of the others who were fluent in English.[87]

Based on Selander's comments and your own experiences, respond to the following questions:

A. In what ways might you misjudge the competence of others based on language skills?

B. What are several strategies to overcoming language barriers?

C. How can you improve your ability to be a good listener for those with limited English abilities?

# Evaluation Exercises

**4.4  Evaluate Your Cross-Cultural Stereotypes** (LO 4.1)

Think about a culture of interest to you. Do the following:

A. Describe five preconceptions or stereotypes you have about the culture.

B. Conduct some research and find out how correct you are. Use books or articles written by experts on the culture. Or find a friend from that country or someone with a lot of experience working there and ask about the accuracy of your preconceptions and stereotypes.

C. Report your findings. For each preconception, describe causes and accuracy. Explain what this might mean about the way one develops impressions, holds preconceptions, and thinks in stereotypes of other cultures.

**4.5  Evaluate Your Speech Patterns** (LO 4.4)

Based on the speech patterns described in Table 4.15, do the following for three of these speech patterns:

A. Explain how you use this speech pattern compared to others you know.

B. Evaluate the degree to which you hold task-based versus relationship-based purposes when you use this speech pattern.

C. Describe how others could potentially misinterpret your approach to this speech pattern.

# Application Exercises

**4.6  Analyze, Explain, and Make a Presentation about Your Own Business Culture** (LO 4.2)

Review the GLOBE rankings for the eight cultural dimensions for your culture. Also, go to a website that describes business etiquette in your country (e.g., www.executiveplanet.com). Assume you are going to train a group of business professionals from another country about doing business in your country. Also, assume the business professionals have read about the GLOBE rankings and learned about etiquette in your country. Create a presentation that includes the following:

A. Explain the five key norms and values that drive business culture in your country. Give at least one example of related communication behavior for each of the five key norms and values.

B. Describe the accuracy of the GLOBE rankings and information about business etiquette.

C. Explain three cases that involve exceptions to the rule. For example, if you say that performance orientation is one of the key norms and values, you could explain a few cases where views toward performance are more relaxed.

D. Provide three final tips for working effectively with members of your own culture that you won't find in books.

**4.7  Analyze the Cultural Dimensions of a Country** (LO 4.2)

Choose a country of interest to you. (The GLOBE study rankings for 62 countries are provided in the online resources that accompany this book.) Analyze the country in terms of the following cultural dimensions:

- Individualism and collectivism.
- Egalitarianism and hierarchy.
- Performance orientation.
- Future orientation.
- Assertiveness.
- Humane orientation.

- Uncertainty avoidance.
- Gender egalitarianism.

In conclusion, describe five communication practices you think may be key when working with members from this country.

### 4.8 Analyze the Etiquette of a Business Culture (LO 4.3)

Choose a country of interest to you. Go to the Executive Planet website (www.executiveplanet.com) or other website with cross-cultural comparisons of business etiquette. Read all the information about this country's business culture and then do the following:

A. Write about the five most intriguing aspects of the culture.

B. Write about the five aspects of etiquette you would observe when interacting with members of this culture.

C. Choose three relevant cultural dimensions (underlying sets of norms and values) and explain how they impact business etiquette in this country.

D. Write five questions about business etiquette you would like to ask a person from the country you chose.

### 4.9 Read News Stories Written by and for Members of Another Culture (LO 4.1, LO 4.2)

Read three online newspaper articles from a country of interest. You should be able to find an online English-language newspaper for your chosen country fairly easily. Go to these websites:

- www.world-newspapers.com
- www.onlinenewspapers.com
- www.refdesk.com/paper.html

After reading the three newspaper articles, write the following for each article:

A. *Article information:* article name, source (magazine name), date/edition, pages, web address if available.

B. *Summary:* a short summary of the article.

C. *Cultural lessons:* one paragraph that describes one or two aspects of culture that are illustrated by the article.

D. *Implications for business communication:* Explain how these aspects of the culture would impact conducting business with members of this culture.

### 4.10 Read a Magazine Article about Global Business (LO 4.1, LO 4.2)

Read a magazine article about global business that includes issues about cross-cultural differences. Consider the following online sources for an article:

- www.businessweek.com/global-economics
- www.time.com/business
- edition.cnn.com/BUSINESS/

After reading the three articles, write the following for each:

A. *Article information:* article name, source (magazine name), date/edition, pages, web address if available.

B. *Summary:* a short summary of the article.

C. *Cultural lessons:* one paragraph that describes one or two aspects of culture that are illustrated by the article.

D. *Implications for business communication:* Explain how these aspects of the culture would impact conducting business with members of this culture.

### 4.11 Interview a Professional with International Experience (LO 4.1, LO 4.2, LO 4.3)

Interview someone you know who has worked extensively with members of other cultures. Spend an hour or two asking this person about his/her experiences. Report what this person had to say about five of the following ten areas:

- Etiquette.
- Preferred communication channels.
- Working in teams.
- Conducting meetings.
- Approaches to resolving differences of opinion.
- Negotiation style.
- Cultural values and norms.
- Adjusting to living in another country.
- Approaching conflicts or disagreements.
- Persuasion.

### 4.12 Interview an International Student (LO 4.1, LO 4.2)

Interview an international student at your university. Report about the interview in five of the following ten areas:

- Business in the student's country.
- Popular entertainment in the country.
- Changes occurring in the culture.
- Challenges in adapting to the food.
- Challenges in adapting to housing.
- Challenges in adapting to transportation.
- Experiences making friendships with Americans.
- Experiences working in teams with American students.
- Experiences working with American professors.
- Observations about American culture.

Conclude your report with three recommendations you have for people doing business with members of that culture.

### 4.13 Interview Professionals from Several Generations (LO 4.4)

Interview at least two professionals from at least two generations. Ask them about their views of similarities and differences between professionals of various generations. Consider asking questions such as the following:

- What do you see as some of the differences in how people of various age groups use technology? (You might consider being specific about various types of communicating and computing, such as texting, calling, voice mail, email messages, word processing, and so on.)
- What are some differences in word choice across the generations?
- How do members of various generations approach meetings differently?
- How do members of various generations view etiquette and formality differently?
- What do you think members of the various generations can learn from each other?
- What do you see as the main similarities across generations?

Write a short report of your findings. Conclude your report with three recommendations for working effectively across generations.

# Language Mechanics Check

**4.14 Review the comma rules C1 through C10 in Appendix A. Then rewrite each sentence to add commas where needed.**

A. China where most of our manufacturing is located offers advantages such as quality price and speed.

B. We manufacture in a location where we get superior quality and price.

C. To get the best quality we often need to locate our factories in Western Europe.

D. Between July 2014 and July 2020 we get tax breaks at our Poland factory.

E. We need to remit tax payments for this quarter between July 1 2015 and July 15 2015.

F. Often we relocate factories to gain tax advantages.

G. To gain tax advantages we often relocate factories.

H. Vietnam not China is the new destination for low-cost manufacturing.

I. Vietnam offers a low-cost highly educated workforce.

J. We also are considering opening factories in Malaysia Indonesia and the Philippines.

# Endnotes

1. Richard M. Smith, "In the Driver's Seat," *Newsweek,* June 20, 2008.

2. John P. Millikin and Dean Fu, "The Global Leadership of Carlos Ghosn at Nissan," *Thunderbird International Business Review* 47, no. 1 (2005): 121–137; Carlos Ghosn, "Saving the Business without Losing the Company," *Harvard Business Review,* January 2002; Renault Nissan, "Alliance Facts & Figures 2009," retrieved April 26, 2011, from www.nissan-global.com/EN/DOCUMENT/PDF/ALLIANCE/HANDBOOK/2009/Alliance_FactsAndFigures_2009.pdf; Carlos Ghosn, "How I Work," *Fortune,* March 20, 2006; Alex Taylor III, "The Nissan Leaf Battery-Powered Car," *Fortune,* March 1, 2010: 90–98; Alex Taylor III, "The Man Who Vows to Change Japan Inc.," *Fortune,* December 20, 1999.

3. Alex Taylor III, "The Man Who Vows to Change Japan Inc."

4. P. Christopher Earley and Elaine Mosakowski, "Cultural Intelligence," *Harvard Business Review,* November 2004: 139–146; David Livermore, "CQ: The Test of Your Potential for Cross-Cultural Success," Forbes Leadership Blog, retrieved April 9, 2011, from www.forbes.com/2010/01/06/cq-cultural-intelligence-leadership-managing-globalization.html (January 10, 2010).

5. M. Javidan, R. M. Steers, and M. A. Hitt, "Putting It All Together: So What Is a Global Mindset and Why Is It Important?" in *The Global Mindset,* ed. M. Javidan, R. M. Steers, and M. A. Hitts (Oxford: Elsevier, 2007); Lillian H. Chaney and Jeanette S. Martin, *Intercultural Business Communication* (Upper Saddle River, NJ: Prentice Hall, 2011); Livermore, "CQ: The Test of Your Potential for Cross-Cultural Success"; Earley and Mosakowski, "Cultural Intelligence."

6. Carlos Ghosn and Philippe Riés (translated from French by John Cullen), *Shift: Inside Nissan's Historic Revival* (New York: Currency Doubleday, 2005): 90.

7. Susan A. Wheelan, *Creating Effective Teams: A Guide for Members and Leaders* (Thousand Oaks, CA: Sage, 1999); Kim Ribbink, "Seven Ways to Better Communicate in Today's Diverse Workplace," *Harvard Management Communication Letter,* November 2002: 3–5.

8. "Diversity," Nissan Global website, retrieved April 25, 2011, from www.nissan-global.com/EN/COMPANY/DIVERSITY/.

9. Peter W. Cardon and Bryan Marshall, "International Opportunities for Business Students," *National Business Education Yearbook* 48 (2010): 223–235.

10. Adam Bryant, "Get a Diploma, but Then Get a Passport," *Corner Office* (blog), *The New York Times*, July 31, 2010, www.nytimes.com/2010/08/01/business/01corner.html.

11. Peter W. Cardon, Bryan A. Marshall, Nipul Patel, Natalya Goreva, and Renée J. Fontenot, "A Comparison of Study Abroad and Globalization Attitudes among Information Systems, Computer Science, and Business Students: Recommendations for IS Curriculum Design," *Issues in Information Systems* 10, no. 1 (2009): 28–39.

12. Millikin and Fu, "The Global Leadership of Carlos Ghosn at Nissan": 121.

13. Ghosn and Riés, *Shift: Inside Nissan's Historic Revival:* 8.

14. Ibid.

15. Iris Varner and Linda Beamer, *Intercultural Communication in the Global Workplace,* 3rd ed. (Boston: McGraw-Hill, 2005).

16. Carol Briam, "Outsourced: Using a Comedy Film to Teach Intercultural Communication," *Business Communication Quarterly* 73, no. 4 (2010): 383–398; Peter W. Cardon, "Using Films to Learn about the Nature of Cross-Cultural Stereotypes in Intercultural Business Communication Courses," *Business Communication Quarterly* 73, no. 2 (2010): 150–165.

17. Ghosn and Riés, *Shift: Inside Nissan's Historic Revival:* 88.

18. S. P. Verluyten, *Cultures: From Observation to Understanding* (Leuven, Belgium: ACCO, 2007); S. P. Verluyten, *The Use of Video Excerpts in Intercultural Training,* paper presented at the 73rd Annual Convention of the Association for Business Communication, April 15, 2008.

19. Varner and Beamer, *Intercultural Communication in the Global Workplace*; J. W. Neuliep, *Intercultural Communication: A Contextual Approach* (Thousand Oaks, CA: Sage, 2009): 168–169; Cardon, "Using Films to Learn about the Nature of Cross-Cultural Stereotypes in Intercultural Business Communication Courses"; T. Dimnik and S. Felton, "Accountant Stereotypes in Movies Distributed in North America in the Twentieth Century," *Accounting, Organizations and Society* 31: 130.

20. C. R. Berg, *Latino Images in Film: Stereotypes, Subversion, Resistance* (Austin: University of Texas, 2002); M. Wingfield and B. Karaman, "Arab Stereotypes and American Educators," *Social Studies and the Young Learner* 7, no. 4 (March/April 1995): 7–10; D. E. Mastro, "A Social Identity Approach to Understanding the Impact of Television Messages," *Communication Monographs* 70, no. 2 (2003): 98–113.

21. Andrew Kohut, Richard Wike, Juliana Menasce Horowitz, Erin Carriere-Kretschemer, Jacob Poushter, Mattie Ressler, and Bruce Stokes, *Obama More Popular Abroad Than at Home, Global Image of U.S. Continues to Benefit* (Washington, DC: Pew Research Center, 2010).

22. Juan Antonio Fernandez and Laurie Underwood, *China CEO: Voices of Experience from 20 International Business Leaders* (Singapore: John Wiley & Sons, 2006): 265.

23. Robert V. Levine and Ara Norenzayan, "The Pace of Life in 31 Countries," *Journal of Cross-Cultural Psychology*, no. 2 (March 20, 1999): 178–205.

24. Ghosn and Riés, *Shift: Inside Nissan's Historic Revival:* 79.

25. Ribbink, "Seven Ways to Better Communicate in Today's Diverse Workplace."

26. Victoria Emerson, "An Interview with Carlos Ghosn, President of Nissan Motors, Ltd. and Industry Leader of the Year," *Journal of World Business* 36, no. 1 (Spring 2001).

27. R. J. House, P. J. Hanges, M. Javidan, P. W. Dorfman, and V. Gupta, eds., *Culture, Leadership, and Organizations: The GLOBE Study of 62 Societies* (Thousand Oaks, CA: Sage, 2004).

28. The scores in these rankings have been converted to a scale from 0 to 100 from the 7-point Likert scales provided in the GLOBE study. These conversions are similar in approach to how Geert Hofstede classified cultures to allow easier comprehension for readers.

29. M. J. Gelfand, D. P. S. Bhawuk, L. H. Nishii, and D. J. Bechtold, "Individualism and Collectivism," in R. J. House, P. J. Hanges, M. Javidan, P. W. Dorfman, and V. Gupta, eds., *Culture, Leadership, and Organizations: The GLOBE Study of 62 Societies* (Thousand Oaks, CA: Sage, 2004): 437–512; Geert Hofstede, *Culture's Consequences: Comparing Values, Behaviors, Institutions, and Organizations across Nations,* 2nd ed. (Thousand Oaks, CA: Sage, 2001); Neuliep, *Intercultural Communication: A Contextual Approach,* 4th ed.

30. Ibid.

31. Keith Jackson and Miyuki Tomioka, *The Changing Face of Japanese Management* (New York: Routledge, 2004).

32. Ghosn and Riés, *Shift: Inside Nissan's Historic Revival.*

33. Fernandez and Underwood, *China CEO: Voices of Experience from 20 International Business Leaders:* 268.

34. Joseph A. Vandello and Dov Cohen, "Patterns of Individualism and Collectivism across the United States," *Journal of Personality and Social Psychology* 77, no. 2: 279–292.

35. Hofstede, *Culture's Consequences: Comparing Values, Behaviors, Institutions and Organizations across Nations.*

36. M. Javidan, "Performance Orientation," in R. J. House, P. J. Hanges, M. Javidan, P. W. Dorfman, and V. Gupta, eds., *Culture, Leadership, and Organizations: The GLOBE Study of 62 Societies* (Thousand Oaks, CA: Sage, 2004): 239.

37. Javidan, "Performance Orientation": 239–281.

38. Ghosn and Riés, *Shift: Inside Nissan's Historic Revival:* 7.

39. N. Ashikanasy, V. Gupta, M. S. Mayfield, and E. Trevor-Roberts, "Future Orientation," in R. J. House, P. J. Hanges, M. Javidan, P. W. Dorfman, and V. Gupta, eds., *Culture, Leadership, and Organizations: The GLOBE Study of 62 Societies* (Thousand Oaks, CA: Sage, 2004): 282–342.

40. Ibid.

41. D. N. den Hartog, "Assertiveness," in R. J. House, P. J. Hanges, M. Javidan, P. W. Dorfman, and V. Gupta, eds., *Culture, Leadership, and Organizations: The GLOBE Study of 62 Societies* (Thousand Oaks, CA: Sage, 2004): 395.

42. Ibid., 395–436.

43. Fernandez and Underwood, *China CEO: Voices of Experience from 20 International Business Leaders:* 275.

44. H. Kabasakal and M. Bodurm, "Humane Orientation in Societies, Organizations, and Leader Attributes," in R. J. House, P. J. Hanges, M. Javidan, P. W. Dorfman, and V. Gupta, eds., *Culture, Leadership, and Organizations: The GLOBE Study of 62 Societies* (Thousand Oaks, CA: Sage, 2004): 569.

45. Ibid.

46. Ghosn and Riés, *Shift: Inside Nissan's Historic Revival:* 44.

47. Ibid., 83.

48. M. S. De Luque and M. Javidan, "Uncertainty Avoidance," in R. J. House, P. J. Hanges, M. Javidan, P. W. Dorfman, and V. Gupta, eds., *Culture, Leadership, and Organizations: The GLOBE Study of 62 Societies* (Thousand Oaks, CA: Sage, 2004): 602–653; Hofstede, *Culture's Consequences.*

49. Ibid.

50. C. G. Emrich, F. L. Denmark, and D. N. den Hartog, "Cross-Cultural Differences in Gender Egalitarianism," in R. J. House, P. J. Hanges, M. Javidan, P. W. Dorfman, and V. Gupta, eds., *Culture, Leadership, and Organizations: The GLOBE Study of 62 Societies* (Thousand Oaks, CA: Sage, 2004): 343–394.

51. "The Transcultural Leader: Carlos Ghosn, CEO of Renault, Nissan," retrieved April 30, 2011, from INSEAD, http://knowledge.insead.edu/ILSTransculturalLeaderGhosn080501.cfm?vid=45.

52. Calculations from the *World Values Survey* data set. Data available for download at worldvaluessurvey.org.

53. "The Transcultural Leader: Carlos Ghosn, CEO of Renault, Nissan."

54. Ghosn and Riés, *Shift: Inside Nissan's Historic Revival:* 82.

55. Ibid., 81.

56. Neuliep, *Intercultural Communication: A Contextual Approach:* 29.

57. Emerson, "An Interview with Carlos Ghosn, President of Nissan Motors, Ltd. and Industry Leader of the Year."

58. Fernandez and Underwood, *China CEO: Voices of Experience from 20 International Business Leaders:* 265.

59. Millikin and Fu, "The Global Leadership of Carlos Ghosn at Nissan": 121–137.

60. Ghosn, "Saving the Business without Losing the Company."

61. Ghosn and Riés, *Shift: Inside Nissan's Historic Revival:* 167–168.

62. Chryscia Cunha, Mariana Barros, and Kelly Franca, "Brazil," retrieved April 30, 2011, from Executive Planet (www.executiveplanet.com/index.php?title=Brazil); Sergei Ivanchuk, "Russia," retrieved April 30, 2011, from Executive Planet (www.executiveplanet.com/index.php?title=Russia); Madhukar Shukla, "India," retrieved April 30, 2011, from Executive Planet (www.executiveplanet.com/index.php?title=India); "China," retrieved April 30, 2011, from Executive Planet (www.executiveplanet.com/index.php?title=China); Terri Morrison and Wayne A. Conaway, *Kiss, Bow, or Shake Hands,* 2nd ed. (Avon, MA: Adams Media, 2006).

63. Sarah Moore, Leon Grunberg, and Alan J. Krause, "Generational Differences in Workplace Expectations: A Comparison of Production and Professional Workers," *Current Psychology* 34 (2015): 346–362.

64. Alec Levenson and Jennifer J. Deal, *Generational Conflict at Work: Separating Fact from Fiction* (Alexandria, VA: SHRM Foundation, 2015); Jennifer J. Deal, *Retiring the Generation Gap: How Employees Young & Old Can Find Common Ground* (San Francisco, CA: Jossey-Bass, 2007).

65. Anick Tolbize, *Generational Differences in the Workplace* (Minneapolis, MN: Research and Training Center on Community Living, University of Minnesota, 2008); Jean M. Twenge, Stacy M. Campbell, Brian J. Hoffman, and Charles E. Lance, "Generational Differences in Work Values: Leisure and Extrinsic Values Increasing, Social and Intrinsic Values Decreasing," *Journal of Management* 36, no. 5 (2010): 117–114; EY, "Survey Shows Younger Managers Rise in the Ranks," 2013, *EY* website, available at http://www.ey.com/Publication/vwLUAssets/EY-Survey_shows_younger_managers_rising_in_the_ranks/$FILE/Executive-Summary-Generations-Research.pdf; Nancy M. Schullery, "Workplace Engagement and Generational Differences in Values," *Business Communication Quarterly* 76, no. 2 (2013): 252–265; A. J. Nicholas and Salve Regina, "Generational Perceptions: Works and Consumers," *Journal of Business and Economics Research* 7, no. 10 (2009): 47–52.

66. Ibid.

67. Ibid.

68. Ibid.

69. EY, "Survey Shows Younger Managers Rise in the Ranks."

70. Dennis Finn and Anne Donovan, "PwC's NextGen: A Global Generational Study," 2013, PwC website, available at http://www.pwc.com/gx/en/hr-management-services/publications/assets/pwc-nextgen.pdf.

71. Knoll Workplace Research, "What Comes after Y? Generation Z: Arriving in the Office Soon," Knoll website, 2014, available at https://www.knoll.com/media/938/1006/What-Comes-After-Y.pdf.

72. Dan Schawbel, "Gen Y and Gen Z Global Workplace Expectations Study," Millennial Branding website, September 2, 2014, available at http://millennialbranding.com/2014/geny-genz-global-workplace-expectations-study/.

73. "Winning the Generation Game," September 28, 2013, The *Economist*, available at http://www.economist.com/news/business/21586831-businesses-are-worrying-about-how-manage-different-age-groups-widely-different; Rebecca R. Hastings, "Generational Differences Exist, But Beware of Stereotypes," October 18, 2012, SHRM website, available at https://www.shrm.org/hrdisciplines/diversity/articles/pages/generational-differences-stereotypes.aspx.

74. Tolbize, *Generational Differences in the Workplace*.

75. "10 Principles for Working across Generations," Center for Creative Leadership website, available at http://insights.ccl.org/multimedia/podcast/10-principles-for-working-across-generations/.

76. Alison Griswold, "Millennials Are the Most Financially Conservative Generation Since the Great Depression," *Business Insider*, January 30, 2014, available at http://www.businessinsider.com/millennials-financially-conservative-generation-2014-1.

77. Deborah Tannen, "The Power of Talk: Who Gets Heard and Why," *Harvard Business Review*, September–October 1995: 138–148; Deborah Tannen, *You Just Don't Understand: Women and Men in Conversation* (New York: William Morrow Paperbacks, 2007).

78. Barbara Annis and John Gray, *Work with Me: The 8 Blind Spots between Men and Women in Business* (New York: St. Martin's Press, 2013).

79. Annis and Gray, *Work with Me: The 8 Blind Spots between Men and Women in Business*.

80. Sloane Crosley, "Why Women Apologize and Should Stop," *The New York Times* online, June 23, 2015, available at http://www.nytimes.com/2015/06/23/opinion/when-an-apology-is-anything-but.html?_r=2.

81. Ketchum, *Ketchum Leadership Communication Monitor,* May 2014, available at https://www.ketchum.com/sites/default/files/2014_klcm_report.pdf.

82. Adi Ignatius, "Now Is Our Time," *Harvard Business Review*, April 2013: 84–88; Sheryl Sandberg, *Lean In: Women, Work, and the Will to Lead* (New York, Knopf, 2013); Sheryl Sandberg and Adam Grant, "Speaking while Female," *The New York Times* online, January 12, 2015, available at http://www.nytimes.com/2015/01/11/opinion/sunday/speaking-while-female.html; Tannen, "The Power of Talk: Who Gets Heard and Why"; Tannen, *You Just Don't Understand: Women and Men in Conversation*.

83. Ignatius, "Now Is Our Time": 87.

84. Sandberg, *Lean In: Women, Work, and the Will to Lead*.

85. Daphne Jameson, "Reconceptualizing Cultural Identity and Its Role in Intercultural Business Communication," *Journal of Business Communication* 44, no. 3 (2007): 199–235.

86. Adam Bryant, "The X Factor When Hiring? Call It 'Presence,'" *Corner Office* (blog), *The New York Times*, June 26, 2010, www.nytimes.com/2010/06/27/business/27corner.html.

87. K. Ohmae, *The Next Global Stage: Challenges and Opportunities in Our Borderless World* (Upper Saddle River, NJ: Wharton School, 2005); Thomas L. Friedman, *The World Is Flat: A Brief History of the Twenty-First Century* (New York: Farrar, Straus and Giroux, 2005); Peter W. Cardon, "The Importance of Teaching about Globalization in Business Education," *Journal for Global Business Education* 7 (2007): 1–20.

# Principles for Business Messages

PART

THREE

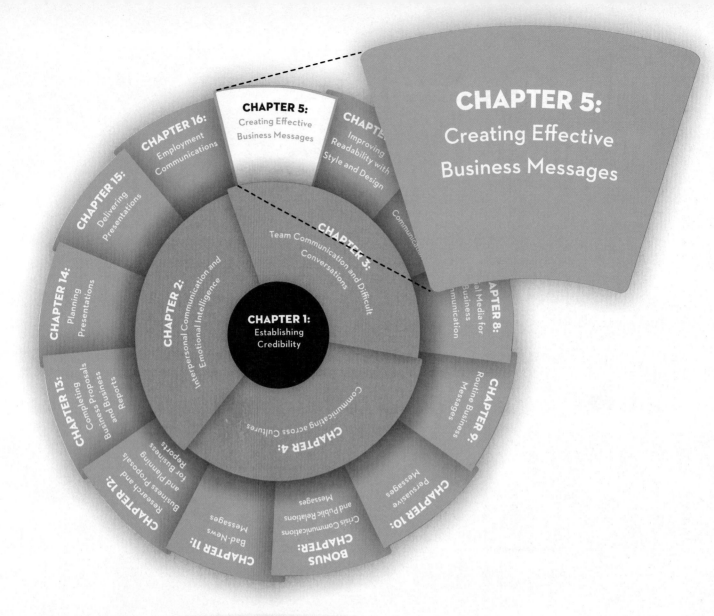

CHAPTER 5:
Creating Effective
Business Messages

CHAPTER 5:
Creating Effective
Business Messages

 ESTABLISHING
CREDIBILITY

 PRINCIPLES OF INTERPERSONAL
COMMUNICATION

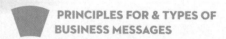 PRINCIPLES FOR & TYPES OF
BUSINESS MESSAGES

 Learning Objectives

After studying this chapter, you should be able to do the following:

**LO5.1** Explain the goals of effective business messages and the process for creating them.

**LO5.2** Identify the needs of your audience in the AIM planning process.

**LO5.3** Gather the right information and refine business ideas in the AIM planning process.

**LO5.4** Develop your primary message and key points in the AIM planning process.

**LO5.5** Explain and apply positive and other-oriented tone in business messages.

You will have countless opportunities over your career to communicate important messages. Every situation will be unique and involve an array of business problems and recipients. In all your communications, however, this principle will remain constant: Effective messages emerge from a consistent planning process and a positive and other-oriented tone.

This chapter first explains the process of developing business messages. Then, we focus on the most critical stage—planning—followed by a discussion of tone. Although the chapter is concerned particularly with writing, the principles transfer effectively to any type of communication.

Throughout, we will provide examples from the chapter case about a challenging communication task. Not all communication tasks demand such rigorous planning and preparation. In fact, the majority will be fairly routine, meaning they will require less time and encounter little resistance from your readers. However, even routine messages require a strategic focus on planning and tone. As you apply these principles to your communications, you will find that you are far more effective and influential.

**Hear Pete Cardon explain why this matters.**

**bit.ly/cardon5**

---

**CHAPTER CASE:** JUSTIFYING A WELLNESS PROGRAM AT EASTMOND NETWORKING

**WHO'S INVOLVED**

*Latisha Jackson, HR intern*

- Working as a summer intern in the human resource department
- Assigned to research options for a wellness program

*Jeff Brody, HR director*

- Has held current position for five years
- Trying to develop initiatives that improve employee well-being and morale amid steep budget cuts

*Lisa Johnson, finance manager*

- Has held current position for three years
- Specializes in developing budgets and financial forecasts

**THE SITUATION**

Jeff recently asked Latisha to spend around ten hours per week to develop a wellness program as an effort to improve employee morale and productivity. However, because the company is facing major budget constraints, executives are skeptical of resource-intensive initiatives. Jeff wants Latisha to focus her attention on the financial implications of a wellness program first. He wants her to present her preliminary findings within one month.

Latisha was excited about the opportunity to keep working on the wellness program initiative, even on this limited basis. She was also slightly nervous—one month was a short time to analyze how a wellness center would affect the financial well-being of the company, and she wanted to prove she was up to the task.

Each week, she gathered information. She talked to HR directors at several local businesses of roughly the same size that had implemented wellness programs in the past few years and also met with several wellness program vendors.

One of the trickiest parts of the project was estimating the financial impact of a wellness program. Latisha had taken a few classes in finance but had no real experience. So, she met with the finance manager, Lisa Johnson, and showed her the information she had collected. Lisa agreed to spend some time estimating the potential return on investment from a wellness program. After Lisa provided an estimate, Latisha was ready to draft her initial findings and recommendations for Jeff.

**TASK**

**1**
How can Latisha address Jeff's and other key decision makers' needs and concerns? (See the "The AIM Planning Process for Effective Business Messages" section.)

**2**
How should Latisha organize the information she has found? (See the "The AIM Planning Process for Effective Business Messages" section.)

**3**
How should Latisha organize her message? (See the "The AIM Planning Process for Effective Business Messages" section.)

**4**
How can Latisha strike the right tone? (See the "Setting the Tone of the Message" section.)

## The Process for Creating Business Messages

**LO5.1** Explain the goals of effective business messages and the process for creating them.

Writing effective business messages involves a process—one that involves examining, developing, and refining business ideas in a way that provides business value to your audience. The very process that we explain in this section drives excellence in business thinking. Furthermore, it drives collaboration and productivity in your work relationships.

The process of developing business messages is fairly straightforward: *plan*, *write*, and *review*. You've likely been trained and coached in a similar process many times during your education. Nearly all business professionals have been trained in this process. Yet few business professionals excel at it and, consequently, few business professionals produce excellent written communication. Making this process a habit requires discipline and scheduling.

Notice Figure 5.1, which depicts the stages and goals for creating effective messages. We will focus on each of the three stages (planning, writing, and reviewing) in this chapter and the following one. It's worth noting that these stages are not necessarily linear and often overlap one another. Business writers frequently move back and forth between the stages.

Expert writers, however, more carefully and consciously break these stages apart. For example, they are more likely to analyze the needs of the audience, identify and collect the right information to tackle a problem, and identify the primary message and key points before starting a formal draft of a business message. On the other hand, poor and average writers are more likely to begin drafting or writing right away. They often address planning issues—audience analysis, information gathering, and message development—as they go. Consequently, they tend to write in a less organized, perhaps even haphazard, manner. They generally produce less strategic and influential messages.

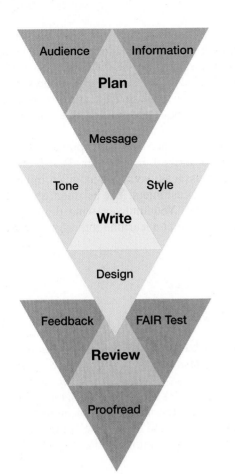

**PLAN: Get the content right.**

- Understand your *audience*.
- Gather the right *information*.
- Develop your *message*.

**WRITE: Get the delivery right.**

- Set the right *tone*.
- Apply a clear and concise *style*.
- Focus on navigational *design*.

**REVIEW: Double-check everything.**

- Get *feedback*.
- Ensure your message is *fair*.
- Make sure to *proofread*.

**FIGURE 5.1**

The Stages and Goals of Effective Message Creation

Developing expertise in this process makes you more effective, plus it makes you more efficient. In Figure 5.2, you'll see a chart that contrasts the time that poor, average, and expert business writers commit to planning, writing, and reviewing. Not surprisingly, poor writers spend less overall time than average and expert writers. They are aimless and sloppy. They generally spend little or no time planning and usually do not review their messages before sending them.[1]

The contrast between average business writers and expert business writers is most intriguing. Expert business writers not only produce more effective written

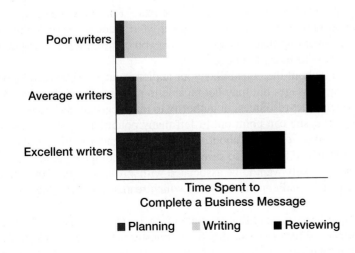

Time Spent to
Complete a Business Message

■ Planning   ■ Writing   ■ Reviewing

**FIGURE 5.2**

Time Spent by Poor, Average, and Expert Writers Developing a Complete Business Message

*Source:* Time estimates based on author's observation of thousands of business students and consistent with decades of research about expertise as described in Michael Pressley and Christine B. McCormick, *Advanced Educational Psychology for Educators, Researchers, and Policymakers* (New York: HarperCollins, 1995).

communications, but they also do so more quickly than average writers. Their secret is to devote a much higher percentage of their time to the planning and reviewing stages. In particular, they spend far more time planning than average or poor writers. They take the time to understand the business issues well, piece together great ideas, make sure the ideas meet the needs of their audiences, and structure their messages for greatest clarity and impact. Once they start drafting, the content is essentially in place.

As you craft business messages, maintain a listener-centered approach (as opposed to a message-centered approach as described in Chapter 3). In the listener-centered approach to writing business messages, you seek as much input as reasonably possible from colleagues, clients, and customers. You ask them about their opinions, preferences, and areas of expertise. You find out what those to whom you are writing really want and expect. You adopt a learning, other-oriented approach to writing.

# The AIM Planning Process for Effective Business Messages

**LO5.2** Identify the needs of your audience in the AIM planning process.

**connect**

Visit http://connect.
mheducation.com for an
exercise on this topic.

The most important stage of creating effective business messages is planning. Throughout the remainder of the book, we will refer to the three-component AIM planning process for developing influential messages. It focuses on three areas: (1) **A**udience analysis; (2) **I**nformation gathering; and (3) **M**essage development. In short, the planning process should include analyzing the needs of your audience, gathering the right information to meet those needs, and then developing your message. The AIM planning process unleashes your best thinking and allows you to deliver influential messages.

## Audience Analysis

Effective business communicators possess an uncanny ability to step into the shoes of their audience members. They think about their audience's needs, priorities, and values. They envision how their readers will respond when getting the message—in thought, feeling, and action. They also consider how the message will affect their working relationships. Effective business communicators regularly take the following actions to tailor their messages to others: identify reader benefits and constraints, consider reader values and priorities, estimate personal credibility, anticipate reactions, and consider secondary audiences.

**Identifying Reader Benefits and Constraints**   For many messages, this is the single most important planning step. Simply put, your readers respond when you provide them with something that they value. When you communicate no apparent benefits, your readers are unlikely to engage.

Similarly, think about the constraints your audience faces. Your readers will often see value in your messages but may not be able to respond as you hope because they don't have enough time, resources, or authority to make certain decisions.

In Latisha's case, she can point out to Jeff many potential benefits of the wellness program. Presumably, Jeff cares about the employees and would like them to have better health. Jeff would also like to save money for the company. And, like most employees, Jeff would likely want to be associated with any successful work initiative. In this regard, Latisha's challenge is choosing which reader benefits appeal most to Jeff in this situation.

Latisha should keep in mind that no matter how much Jeff views the wellness program as beneficial, he likely faces a number of constraints. He would certainly need to get agreement for a project of this size from other members of the leadership team. So, he would need to persuade others and risk his own credibility. In addition, since the company faces a financial crisis, any initiative may be viewed with higher-than-usual scrutiny and even skepticism. Latisha should anticipate these constraints and develop her message accordingly.

**Considering Reader Values and Priorities**   Being an effective business communicator requires that you learn about other people—what they value, prioritize, and prefer. **Values** refer to enduring beliefs and ideals that individuals hold. Because values are at the core of belief systems, appeals to an individual's values can have strong influence. Generally, people hold workplace values—beliefs and ideals about the appropriate way to approach business problems, resolve issues, and choose goals. **Priorities** involve ranking or assigning importance to things, such as projects, goals, and tasks. Priorities tend to shift more often than values.

Latisha has not known Jeff for long, but she can attempt to understand some of his values and priorities. She believes that he is fundamentally invested in the wellness program initiative because of his strong commitment to employees. He seems to value detailed analysis and careful decision making. Based on his comments, he seems to prioritize efficiency and cost-cutting. This may be due to the current financial situation or it may be due to deeper, long-held values. He also refers frequently to the "company president," which suggests a respect for the chain of command. Jeff's frequent mention of the company president may mean that Jeff is under a great deal of pressure to perform according to the president's expectations.

**Estimating Your Credibility**   As discussed in Chapter 1, your readers will inevitably judge your recommendations, requests, and other messages based on their view of your credibility. If your credibility is low, consider how to strengthen your message in ways that overcome your lack of credibility.

Many entry-level professionals face this situation; they have relatively low professional credibility because they are viewed as the newcomers. Establishing a professional reputation takes time. It takes less time, however, if you stay aware of your strengths, weaknesses, and goals. Most important, your reputation depends on adding value in the workplace. Yet, overcoming a reputation as a newcomer isn't easy. Changing your reputation will likely take at least six months. To break out of a reputation as an inexperienced newcomer, consider the following options:[2]

- Set up a time to talk with your boss. Explain your growth in various areas and ask for his/her ideas about improving your professional reputation.
- Ask your boss if you can take on any higher-responsibility projects.
- Make sure you fit in with the corporate culture in terms of professional dress and communication style.
- Attend a lot of meetings to get to know as many colleagues as possible. Participate appropriately.
- Create a professional blog about a niche area.

As a newcomer, Latisha recognizes that Jeff has many reasons to doubt her credibility. She is an undergraduate business student without a degree or significant business experience. She has worked for Jeff for only a short time, so he can't make a good judgment about her ability to get things done. But he obviously saw promise in her or he wouldn't have hired her to develop a work initiative that was so important to him. Latisha felt that her credibility would be enhanced by including a trusted, competent voice in her memo. As a result, she sought the opinion of Lisa Johnson. By highlighting Lisa's estimate and opinions, Latisha elevates her own credibility. Lisa is competent in her area (finance) and reliable (she has a track record at Eastmond). Jeff will likely give more credence to Latisha's message because it references Lisa's cash flow estimate.

> **Audience Analysis Components**
>
> - Identify reader benefits and constraints.
> - Consider reader values and priorities.
> - Estimate your credibility.
> - Anticipate reactions.
> - Consider secondary audiences.

**Anticipating Reactions**   In the planning stage, envision how others will respond to your message. Imagine how your readers will think, feel, and act as they read it. Always think about what you want to achieve in terms of workplace relationships. Most business activities cannot be separated from the web of working relationships involved. Sometimes your positions or ideas may displease others. In these instances, consider how you can articulate your views most constructively.

Latisha believes that Jeff will respond sensibly to a clearly articulated, logical justification of the wellness center. Based on the strength of the cash flow estimates, Latisha thinks he will respond favorably. Even if he disagrees, she assumes he will respect her hard work and reward her with challenging assignments.

**Keeping Secondary Audiences in Mind**   In most situations, you should anticipate that individuals other than your primary recipient will view your messages. In some cases, you will distribute your message to additional individuals whom it will affect. For example, you might copy team members on a correspondence between you and a client so that they are aware of project progress. In other cases, your primary recipient will forward your message or otherwise share the information with others. You should consider which secondary audiences will view your messages and, if necessary, modify them accordingly.

Latisha recognizes that her proposal for developing a wellness program would impact everyone in the organization and would require significant resources. If Jeff finds merit in the proposal, he will undoubtedly share the message with a variety of individuals involved in the decision-making process.

## Information Gathering

Developing great business ideas involves sorting out the business issues and objectives, collecting as many relevant facts as possible, and making sound judgments about what the facts mean and imply. You are making sense out of often complex and confusing pieces of business information.

Excellent business thinkers possess a number of characteristics. First, they clearly and precisely identify and articulate key questions and problems. Second, they gather information from a variety of sources. Third, they make well-reasoned conclusions and solutions. Fourth, they remain open to alternatives to approaching and reasoning about the business problem—that is, they are mentally flexible. They can hold opposing views, avoid either/or thinking, avoid one-way linear thinking, and are open to nonconventional solutions. Finally, they are skilled at communicating with others to figure out and solve complex problems.[3]

Business professionals use many methods of bringing out their best thinking. Some write notes, some draw diagrams, some brainstorm with colleagues, some write ideas in outline form, and some just examine the ideas in their minds. Generally, for complex problems, such as the opening case, writing ideas down in some form is an important part of developing sound ideas from the information gathered. In this section, we focus on three broad areas: (1) identifying the business problem(s); (2) analyzing the business problem(s); and (3) clarifying objectives.

**Identifying the Business Problem(s)**   To remain competitive and profitable, businesses constantly need to identify and overcome problems. One of the best reputations you can gain as a business professional is that of a problem solver. The first step in problem solving is identifying business problems. This involves understanding an organization's business objectives and related challenges. It involves asking many questions from a lot of angles. Once you're asking the right questions, you can gather the right information.

In Latisha's case, she has been given a charge: Find out how a wellness program would affect Eastmond. This is a classic business problem. Latisha can break the problem down by asking a variety of questions: How do wellness programs affect

---

**Information Gathering Components**

- Identify the business problems.
- Analyze the business problems.
- Clarify objectives.

**LO5.3**   Gather the right information and refine business ideas in the AIM planning process.

**connect**

Visit http://connect. mheducation.com for an exercise on this topic.

health care costs? What benefits do health care programs deliver to employees? How do other businesses measure return on investment for wellness programs? How do wellness programs impact productivity, absenteeism, morale, retention, and recruiting?

**Analyzing the Business Problem(s)**    After gathering information to your questions, you can focus on analysis. Analyzing the business problem typically involves uncovering relevant facts, making conclusions, and taking positions. **Facts** are statements that can be relied on with a fair amount of certainty (most things are not absolutely certain in the business world) and can be observed objectively. **Conclusions** are statements that are reasoned or deduced based on facts. **Positions** are stances that you take based on a set of conclusions. In the workplace, you will often make recommendations, which are a type of position.

Latisha analyzed the business problem by collecting a variety of facts and making five or six broad conclusions about corporate wellness programs based on those facts (see Figure 5.3). For example, she concluded that the return on investment for wellness programs is substantial (her second-to-last conclusion) based on findings from several academic and corporate studies, listed with bullet points. This form of outlining facts and conclusions can be particularly helpful once Latisha begins writing.

Latisha also relied on insiders for information. She asked Lisa Johnson, the company's finance manager, to estimate the financial impact a wellness program would have on health care costs and revenues (see details in the opening chapter case). In many cases, you conduct data gathering and analysis within your networks of colleagues and other business partners.

**Clarifying Objectives**    As you're gathering information and analyzing it, also clearly identify your goals. You are essentially asking yourself, "Now that I understand the problem, what exactly do I want to accomplish?" Knowing how committed you are to various work outcomes will help you decide how hard to push certain positions. It will also help you balance your preferred work outcomes with your work relationships.

Latisha has carefully thought about her attitudes toward developing a wellness program. She is certain she wants the chance to work on the initiative. She is passionate about this issue and wants to gain experience combining her interests in management and health. Latisha has thought about whether her self-interests are too strong. But, she feels confident that this initiative is good for the company: It will benefit the employees and it will save the company money. She is committed to taking a strong position.

## Message Development

Once you have analyzed the needs of your audience and gathered the right information, you develop your basic message. This includes identifying and framing the primary message and setting up the logic with supporting points and a call to action. The questions you will address include the following:

1. *Framing the primary message.*
   a. What is the primary message?
   b. What simple, vivid statement (15 words or fewer) captures the essence of your message?

2. *Setting up the logic of your message.*
   a. What are your supporting points?
   b. What do you want to explicitly ask your readers to do (call to action)?
   c. How will you order the logic of your message?

**LO5.4** Develop your primary message and key points in the AIM planning process.

 **connect**

Visit **http://connect. mheducation.com** for an exercise on this topic.

**FIGURE 5.3**

Analysis of Facts and Conclusions during Information Gathering[4]

---

| **Analysis of Wellness Programs** |
|---|

*Most Americans suffer poor health due to lifestyle-related issues.*

- The U.S. surgeon general has stated that about 75 percent of all illnesses are due to lifestyle. (American Institute for Preventive Medicine)

- 68 percent of Americans are overweight (BMI of 25 or greater); 34 percent of American adults are obese (a body mass index [BMI] of 30 or greater). (American Institute for Preventive Medicine)

- Overweight and obesity raise the risk for type 2 diabetes, high blood pressure, high cholesterol, coronary heart disease, stroke, asthma, cancers, and many other illnesses. (American Institute for Preventive Medicine)

*Employees with poor health raise health care costs to employers.*

- For example, compared to employees with low health risks, employees with the following conditions are associated with costs to the employer that are significantly higher: depression (70.2 percent higher cost); stress (46.3 percent); glucose (34.8 percent); weight (21.4 percent); tobacco (19.7 percent); blood pressure (11.7 percent); exercise (10.4 percent). (American Institute for Preventive Medicine)

*Most employers make wellness programs available to their employees.*

- Most companies have created wellness programs. About 73 percent of large companies, 56 percent of medium-sized companies, and 44 percent of small companies currently have wellness programs available to their employees. (American Institute for Preventive Medicine)

- Companies implement wellness programs for a variety of reasons. In a survey of businesses, the top reasons were to (1) increase employee morale, (2) improve employee health, (3) reduce health care costs, (4) reduce accidents on the job, (5) reduce absenteeism, and (6) increase productivity (8 percent). (American Institute for Preventive Medicine)

- Mid- to large-sized companies spend on average about 2 percent of their health care claim costs on wellness programs. (National Business Group on Health)

*Employers benefit significantly from providing wellness programs to their employees, including lower health care costs, lower absenteeism, higher productivity, and higher morale.*

- A review of 56 scientific studies about the impact of corporate wellness programs found the following average benefits:
  - Percent change in sick leave absenteeism: average: −26.8 percent
  - Percent change in health costs: −26.1 percent
  - Percent change in workers' compensation/disability management costs: −32.0 percent
- Reduced presenteeism losses. (Chapman)
- Increased productivity by 2 percent to 52 percent. (Chapman)
- A recent study of 200 people at three major corporations revealed that an employee's quality of life, mental performance, and time management were 15 percent better on days when they exercised. (Chapman)
- A Johnson & Johnson study showed that employees who participated in a corporate wellness program reported more positive attitudes in organizational commitment, supervision, working conditions, job competence/security, and pay/benefits. (Chapman)

*The return on investment (ROI) for corporate wellness programs is substantial.*

- Studies generally indicate a $4 to $6 ROI for every dollar spent on wellness programs. In terms of just medical costs: $3.93 (28 studies); absenteeism: $5.07 (18 studies); medical costs, absenteeism, and workers' comp: $5.93 (42 studies); and medical costs and absenteeism: $5.81 (56 studies). (George)

- Many companies and organizations have reported the impact of their wellness programs. For example, the following companies reported the following ROIs: Northeast Utilities: 6:1; Motorola: 3.93:1; Wisconsin Education Insurance Group: 4.75:1.; DuPont: 1.42:1 due to reduced absenteeism; Citibank: 4.56:1; Bank of America: 5.96:1; General Mills: 3.50:1; Washoe County School District: 15.6:1; Pfizer: 4.29:1 for fitness centers. (George)

- For employees who participate in wellness programs, significant savings occur. Just by enrolling in fitness programs, companies can save hundreds of dollars. Coca-Cola reported saving $500 per person who enrolled in a corporate fitness program. Pacific Bell reported $300 in savings. Prudential Insurance reported $262. (George)

- Savings reach optimal point in years 3 or 4. (George)

- Reduced health care costs by 20 percent to 55 percent. (George)

**FIGURE 5.3**

(*Continued*)

---

*Companies have many decisions to make when implementing wellness programs.*

- Corporate wellness programs are diverse. Hundreds of national and local companies specialize in providing corporate wellness programs. Many companies, especially large companies, develop in-house wellness programs. The range of services offered is immense. Among mid- to large-sized companies, the average number of wellness programs offered is 21.
- For companies with wellness programs, the most common incentives are premium reductions (34 percent), cash/bonuses (20 percent), merchandise (19 percent), gift cards (17 percent), other incentives (17 percent), and health account contributions (13 percent). (Capps)
- For wellness programs, about 45 percent of corporate expenses are devoted to prevention and lifestyle wellness and about 43 percent to disease/illness management (after onset of illness). The most common prevention and lifestyle programs include employee assistance programs (92 percent), on-site flu shots (90 percent), stress management (68 percent), preventive-care reminders related to screenings or annual exams (68 percent), and smoking cessation (66 percent). The most common condition-management programs include nurse hotlines, diabetes disease management, coronary artery disease management, congestive heart failure management, and asthma disease management. (American Institute for Preventive Medicine)

---

**Framing the Primary Message**   Framing involves showcasing a message from an overarching theme. It focuses a reader or listener on a certain key idea or argument and highlights the premises and support for this key idea or argument. As one management communication expert said, "No communication skill . . . is more critical to the manager than the ability to frame an issue effectively."[5] Your job in framing the message is to help your reader see the issue from a strategic perspective. Just as a frame draws out particular aspects of a painting, the frame you apply to your message can create a unique prism through which your audience will read.

Strategic communicators consider alternative frames before they settle on the one that will be most compelling. Ideally, it should be a vivid statement with rational and emotional appeal. One standard you'll encounter frequently in this book is whether a reader would remember the frame later. Regarding your frame, ask questions such as the following: Will readers remember my primary message two hours from now? What about in two days or two weeks? Will this frame make readers more likely to support my call to action?[6]

The art of creating effective frames involves capturing your primary message in a short, memorable statement of 15 words or fewer. Eduardo Castro-Wright, former president and CEO of Wal-Mart Stores USA, discussed this strategy in the context of organizational communication: "We have a very clear view of what we do for consumers around the world. And we can describe our complete strategy in 10 words. And that makes it very easy to get everybody energized and aligned."[7]

As Latisha was thinking about how to justify the wellness program, she came up with three options for framing the message:

Frame A—Creating a wellness program is the right thing to do. We are responsible for our employees.

Frame B—Creating a wellness program will cut costs and improve morale at the same time.

Frame C—Wellness programs will increase our profitability.

She thinks each frame is powerful. She personally relates to Frame A with her passion for physical fitness and personal health. However, she thinks this case is weakest in the current financial situation and with Jeff's apparent budgetary limitations. She believes that Frame B is strong. The company needs to cut costs, and Jeff has explicitly noted the company president's interest in improving morale. She also believes that Frame C is strong. The emphasis on profitability is a broader concept; it is the ultimate

**Message Development Components**

- Frame the primary message.
- Set up the structure and logic of the message.

measure of strong financial performance and encompasses not just lower expenses but also increased revenues.

The choice between Frame B and Frame C is difficult. Ultimately, Latisha selects Frame C for several reasons. First, Frame C has stronger external (from other companies) and internal evidence (from Lisa's cash flow estimate). With Jeff's preference for brief, to-the-point, result-oriented, and well-reasoned positions, she believes this frame is best suited for this communication approach. Second, she believes the concept of profitability emphasizes the return on investment for this project more so than any other frame. She wants to emphasize that a wellness program is an asset—not a liability of any sort.

**Setting Up the Message Framework**  Most business arguments employ a **direct** or **deductive** approach. In other words, they begin by stating the primary message, which is typically a position or recommendation. Then they lay out the supporting reasons. Most business messages conclude with a call to action. The call to action in many cases is a more detailed and elaborate version of the initial position or recommendation.

Figure 5.4 illustrates the framework of most deductive business arguments. Generally, a reader could get the gist of your message—the primary message, rationale, and

**FIGURE 5.4**

Typical Deductive Framework for a Business Argument and Related Paragraph Structure

| Typical Paragraph Organization in a Deductive Business Message | Deductive Business Message Components |
|---|---|
| **Primary message** as topic sentence. xx xxxxxxxxxxxxxxxxxxxxxxxxxxxxxxxxxxxx xxxxxxxxxxxxxxxxxxxxxxxxxxxxxxxx. *Preview sentence.*<br><br>*Key Point 1* as topic sentence. xxxxxxxxx xxxxxxxxxxxxxxxxxxxxxxxxxxxxxxxxxxxxxx xxxxxxxxxxxxxxxxxxxxxxxxxxxxxxxxxxxxxxxx xxxxx.<br><br>*Key Point 2* as topic sentence. xxxxxxxxxxx xxxxxxxxxxxxxxxxxxxxxxxxxxxxxxxxxxxxxxxx xxxxxxxxxx.<br>*Key Point 3* as topic sentence. xxxxxxxxxx xxxxxxxxxxxxxxxxxxxxxxxxxxxxxxxxxxxxxxxx xxxxxxxxxx.<br>*Call to action* as topic sentence. xxxxxxxxx xxxxxxxxxxxxxxxxxxxxxxxxxxxxxxxxxxxxxxxx xxxxxxxxxxxxxxxxxxxxxxxxxxxxxxxxxxxxxxxx. | **Opening Paragraph**<br>• *Primary message* as topic sentence.<br>• *Preview sentence* as concluding sentence: We should do [position] because of Key Point 1, Key Point 2, and Key Point 3.<br>**Body**<br>• *Supporting paragraphs* for each key point.<br>• *Key points* as topic sentences.<br>• Most paragraphs are three to five sentences and 40 to 100 words.<br>**Concluding Paragraph**<br>• *Restates* primary message.<br>• Contains a *call to action*— specific steps to be taken. |

call to action—simply by reading the opening paragraph, the first sentence of each supporting paragraph, and the final paragraph. In fact, many of your readers, who are generally busy, will do exactly that. They will skim the communication to understand the main ideas and implications. If they see merit in your ideas, they will go back and read the entire message more carefully.

In upcoming chapters, we will focus on many types of messages for common business situations. The framework for these various messages may differ slightly from the one illustrated in Figure 5.4. For some messages, such as when delivering bad news (see Chapter 10), you may adopt a more **indirect** or **inductive** approach, in which you will provide supporting reasons first followed by the primary message. In all messages, however, the importance of framing and arranging supporting ideas to accentuate the main idea remains the same.

One option for setting up the structure and appearance of various documents is to use templates. For ideas on enhancing the structure and appearance of various types of business messages, see the Technology Tips feature.

When you are setting up the logic of your message, you may find that sketching out or diagramming it is helpful. Latisha's logic for Frame C involves the claim that a wellness program will increase profitability. It will do so directly through reducing health care costs and indirectly through increasing revenues. To support this frame, she is making the case that a wellness program will directly decrease absenteeism and increase productivity, which will then increase revenues. By diagramming her logic, she tightens her thinking about the problem and transfers her ideas more effectively into written form (Figure 5.5).

As you set up the structure of the message, carefully test its logic. Business decisions are consequential. Seasoned businesspeople expect solid business logic to support important decisions, and they dismiss ideas that are based on flimsy reasoning. If you ensure that your messages are built on strong reasoning, you will be far more influential because your company will benefit and you will gain credibility.[8] To build

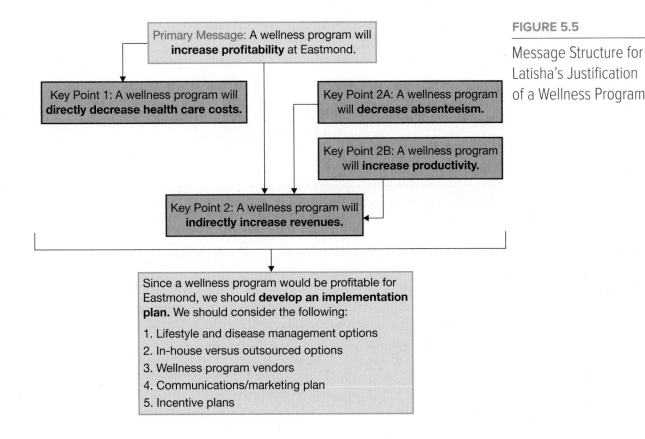

**FIGURE 5.5**

Message Structure for Latisha's Justification of a Wellness Program

# TECHNOLOGY TIPS

## USING BRAINSTORMING AND MIND-MAPPING SOFTWARE

You will set up many types of business messages. Many excellent communicators use brainstorming and mind-mapping software to help tie their ideas together and prioritize their main points. These platforms are particularly helpful when collaborating with a team on important projects. You can find dozens of free software platforms for download or on the cloud.

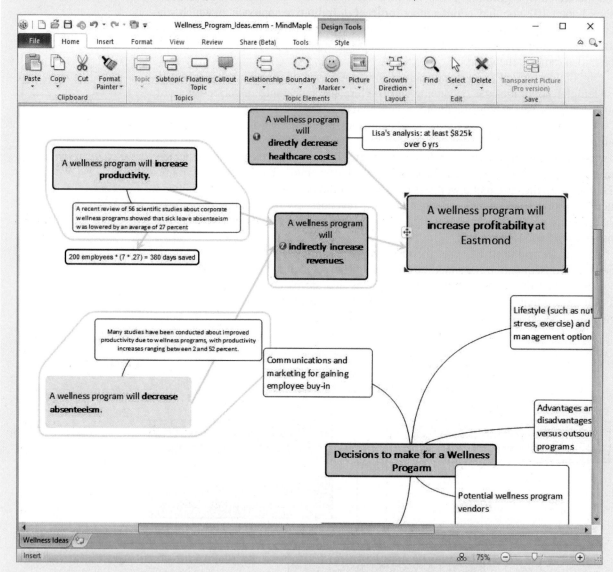

As you experiment with these software platforms, consider trying out the following strategies:

- Use a variety of tools to help you organize and tie your ideas together, including cause/effect relationships, groups, and subtopics.

- If you don't know how your ideas tie together, feel comfortable leaving them as stand-alone topics. Not everything fits together nicely—avoid feeling the pressure to make your ideas too tidy.

- Use tools that help prioritize the value of ideas (numbers or other forms of highlighting).

- For groups, you can use these platforms much like whiteboards to generate and tie ideas together.

Play with the platforms to find what works best for you. Remember, you might realize paper and pen help you structure your ideas best. In any case, commit to laying out the structure of your ideas carefully.

**TABLE 5.1**

Avoiding Unsupported Generalizations

| Less Effective | More Effective |
|---|---|
| A wellness program would reduce absenteeism because our employees would be sick less and feel more energetic. | We can expect that a wellness program will reduce absenteeism. A recent review of 56 scientific studies of corporate wellness programs showed that once the program was in place, sick leave absenteeism was an average of 27 percent lower. In our case, the average employee takes seven sick leave days per year. Assuming a similar reduction in sick leave absenteeism for our 200 full-time employees, we could gain approximately 380 additional workdays per year from our employees. |
| Without any supporting facts, this broad generalization will be viewed skeptically by many readers. | This statement confidently states an expectation based on research and shows how findings from the research could apply to this situation. |

well-reasoned business positions, avoid the following types of logical inconsistencies: unsupported generalizations, faulty cause/effect claims, weak analogies, either/or logic, slanting the facts, and exaggeration.

**Avoiding Unsupported Generalizations** This issue boils down to providing supporting facts for your claims. As you look at the examples in Table 5.1, notice that the less effective example is a blanket claim without support. The more effective example provides a variety of supporting facts.

**Avoiding Faulty Cause/Effect Claims** As you analyze business issues, you are often trying to identify causes and effects. For example, when proposing new initiatives, you will generally claim that your actions will *cause* a certain result. The ability to precisely predict effects is always tricky, so choose your language and reasoning carefully. If readers are troubled by one of your cause/effect claims, they will become increasingly picky about your reasoning throughout the message (see Table 5.2).

**Avoiding Weak Analogies** As you make sense of business issues, you will often try to identify analogies with other organizations, people, or things. Strong analogies serve to bolster your arguments. However, weak analogies may lead to inaccurate conclusions and recommendations. Be sure that the analogies you make are based on close and relevant similarities (see Table 5.3).

**Avoiding Either/Or Logic** One of the main characteristics of critical thinking is to remain flexible and open to alternative explanations and options. In business, you will always want to stay aware of alternative ways of solving the same problem. Furthermore, most of your readers will respond better to you when they view you as flexible and open to other ideas (including their own). In the less effective example in Table 5.4, the claim is that wellness programs are the only way to increase employee morale—that is, *either we provide a wellness program and improve employee morale, or we don't provide a wellness program and continue to have low morale*. In the more effective claim, providing a wellness program is still identified as a way of increasing employee morale. However, this claim does not eliminate other options for improving employee morale.

**TABLE 5.2**

Avoiding Faulty Cause/Effect Claims

| Less Effective | More Effective |
|---|---|
| Lisa Johnson's calculations show that Eastmond will definitely save at least $820,000 over the next six years by implementing a wellness program. | Lisa Johnson's initial estimates show that Eastmond could achieve net savings of about $820,000 over the next six years by implementing a wellness program. She emphasized that her estimates are "safe" and "modest." In other words, she used assumptions that projected low-end savings and high-end expenses. She estimated that Eastmond would save approximately $1.6 million in health care costs over six years. It would cost approximately $780,000 to run and manage the wellness program over this time period (see Lisa's attached estimate for assumptions and other details). |
| This statement assumes that a wellness program will result in a definite result: at least $820,000 in savings. The certainty of this claim would raise skepticism among many readers. | This statement provides facts, assumptions, and calculations to make a confident estimate. The statements are carefully crafted to avoid stating absolute outcomes. |
| Last year we turned down two major contracts worth nearly $100,000 due to a lack of personnel. This was in large part due to low employee productivity on other projects, which occurs because our employees do not have access to a wellness program. | Last year we turned down two major contracts worth nearly $100,000 due to a lack of personnel. Were we to have our employees working at their highest levels of performance, perhaps we would be able to accept profitable projects such as those. Implementing a wellness program is one approach to improving productivity and potentially gaining more contracts. |
| This statement casually states several causes that are nearly impossible to demonstrate convincingly. The most unconvincing claim—without strong evidence—is that the lack of a wellness program caused the company to turn down two contracts. | This statement does not attribute low productivity in the past as the single cause of turned-down projects. Rather, it focuses on wellness programs as a possible contributor to increased productivity, which could result in more business opportunities for the company. The language is measured and objective. |

**TABLE 5.3**

Avoiding Weak Analogies

| Less Effective | More Effective |
|---|---|
| Since many companies such as Coca-Cola and Prudential have lowered health care costs by up to 55 percent after implementing wellness programs, we can assume similar savings when we start our program. | In studies of wellness programs, small companies such as ours typically achieve savings of 20 to 35 percent within three years. Therefore, in her estimate, Lisa assumed that Eastmond will achieve 20 percent savings by the fourth year of implementation. |
| This statement is a weaker analogy because it compares a smaller organization, Eastmond, with large organizations that can take a different approach in terms of personnel, resources, and program options. Readers in smaller organizations would consider this a weak analogy. | This statement is a stronger analogy because it makes an analogy to similar-sized organizations with similar resources and constraints. Readers are far more likely to consider this a credible analogy. |

**TABLE 5.4**

Avoiding Either/Or Logic

| Less Effective | More Effective |
|---|---|
| Without providing a wellness program, employees will continue to suffer from low morale. | Providing a wellness program is one option for improving employee morale. |
| This logic is either/or: without a wellness program, employees will have low morale; with a wellness program, they will have high morale. | This statement does not imply that a wellness program is the only option for improving employee morale. Readers will perceive this statement as confident but grounded and measured. |

**TABLE 5.5**

Avoiding Slanting the Facts

| Less Effective | More Effective |
|---|---|
| Many studies have been conducted about improved productivity due to wellness programs, with productivity increases of up to 52 percent. | Many studies have been conducted about improved productivity due to wellness programs, with productivity increases ranging between 2 and 52 percent. |
| This statement leaves out the bottom of the range to imply higher productivity increases. | This statement provides the bottom of the range and thus provides complete information. |

**TABLE 5.6**

Avoiding Exaggeration

| Less Effective | More Effective |
|---|---|
| A wellness program would completely change our work environment for the better, allowing us to reach levels of performance previously unimagined. | A wellness program could significantly improve morale, an issue that our company president is particularly interested in. |
| Many readers would view this statement with skepticism since the language seems exaggerated and unbelievable. This would lead some readers to call into question the credibility of the writer and the entire message. | This statement projects confidence but does not contain exaggerated, unrealistic, or overly ambitious language. |

**Avoiding Slanting the Facts** Slanting means presenting only those facts that are favorable to your position. To maintain your credibility, avoid slanting in all cases. While slanting may provide short-term benefits, many executives and managers have lost a lifetime of credibility when their gross misrepresentation was exposed. At a minimum, when readers notice that you have slanted the facts, they will be skeptical of the logic and reasoning of your entire message (see Table 5.5).

**Avoiding Exaggeration** As with slanting, exaggeration impacts readers' perceptions of your overall credibility as well as the credibility of the message. Be careful not to make exaggerated claims, as illustrated in Table 5.6.

# Setting the Tone of the Message

**Principles for Setting the Right Tone**

- Demonstrate positivity.
- Show concern for others.

**LO5.5** Explain and apply positive and other-oriented tone in business messages.

**connect**

Visit http://connect. mheducation.com for an exercise on this topic.

How many times have you heard phrases such as these? "It's not what he said, but how he said it," or "She said one thing but meant another." People often build resistance not to the content of a message but to the way it is delivered. One of your primary goals as a communicator is to express your messages in ways that respect and inspire others. Readers judge a message partially by its **tone**—the overall evaluation the reader perceives the writer to have toward the reader and the message content. Readers will judge your message based on how positive and concerned they think you are.

Business communicators generally aim to project positivity and concern for others in all business messages. By following the suggestions in this section, you will more effectively project messages with these tones. Many of the examples provided focus on the sentence level (primarily due to space constraints). However, tone is generally perceived across an entire message. Applying these principles across an entire message will dramatically alter the overall tone of the message.

## Positivity

A positive attitude in the workplace improves work performance, allows more creativity, provides more motivation to excel, facilitates more helpfulness between co-workers, and gains more influence on clients and customers.[9] Bottom line, your ability to remain positive and exude optimism in your communications can strongly influence others. You can adopt a number of techniques to make your messages more positive.

**Display a Can-Do, Confident Attitude**  Focus on actions you can accomplish, and demonstrate a realistic optimism, as illustrated in Table 5.7. At the same time, be careful not to exaggerate or set unrealistic expectations.

**Focus on the Positive Rather Than Negative Traits of Products and Services**  Emphasize what products and services are rather than what they are not (see Table 5.8).

**TABLE 5.7**

Displaying a Can-Do, Confident Attitude

| Less Effective | More Effective |
| --- | --- |
| Let me know if you want me to keep working on the implementation plan. | I look forward to putting together a detailed implementation plan. |
| This statement is weak—it expresses little enthusiasm or passion for pursuing this project. | This statement is strong. It expresses an enthusiasm for putting together a successful plan. |
| Based on the information I have access to, and if everything goes according to Lisa's analysis, I think that a wellness program might increase profitability at Eastmond. | Based on a cash flow estimate from Lisa Johnson in finance and other studies about corporate wellness programs, we can be confident that a wellness program here at Eastmond would increase profitability. |
| This statement is qualified with too many weak words—*based on . . .*, *if, think, might.* Collectively, these words display a lack of confidence in the program. | This statement expresses confidence that the program will be profitable based on well-developed estimates. It does not seem exaggerated. |

**TABLE 5.8**

Focusing on Positive Traits

| Less Effective | More Effective |
|---|---|
| A wellness program is not just an exercise program. | A wellness program is a comprehensive approach to preventive health care. |
| Without any additional elaboration, this sentence does not provide any positive information about a wellness program. | This sentence effectively frames the positive and total impacts of a wellness program. It is a strategic statement. |
| A wellness program is not a perk. | A wellness program would be an asset to our company, bringing in a strong return on investment. |
| Without any follow-up sentences, this statement falls short of what it could accomplish with positive phrasing. | This positive statement effectively frames the wellness program as an asset. |

**TABLE 5.9**

Using Diplomatic, Constructive Terms

| Less Effective | More Effective |
|---|---|
| I would like to present my argument for why we should continue with the wellness program initiative. | Thank you for giving me a few weeks to provide you with some additional information about how wellness programs could benefit Eastmond. |
| The term *argument* unnecessarily implies contention and difference of opinion. | This statement prefaces the goal of the communication with a compliment, which is a show of solidarity. |
| Your characterization of the wellness program as a perk is inaccurate since the wellness program would actually save the company money. | The wellness program would feel like a perk to employees, which could boost morale. Yet, unlike most perks, it would actually save us money. |
| The phrase your *characterization* immediately creates a me-versus-you tone. | By stating the perception of the wellness program being a perk in neutral terms, the statement would not be perceived as confrontational or divisive. |

**Use Diplomatic, Constructive Terms Related to Your Relationships and Interactions**   Find ways to avoid terms that unnecessarily focus on differences and may imply opposing or even adversarial relationships or positions (see Table 5.9).

## Concern for Others

In every facet of business communication, focusing on others is important. It is a basic component of your credibility (caring). In content and form, your message should show that you have the interests of your audience in mind. Therefore, avoid any sense of self-centeredness. Also aim for a tone that is inviting—that implies your interest in your readers' opinions, feelings, needs, and wants. The following

**TABLE 5.10**

Using You-Voice, We-Voice, Impersonal Voice, and I-Voice Appropriately

| | Appropriate Situations | Examples |
|---|---|---|
| **You-Voice** | *Use when focus is solely on the reader.* It is particularly well suited to describing how products and services benefit customers, clients, and colleagues.<br><br>*Avoid* when pointing out the mistakes of others or when the statement may be presumptuous. | **Effective:** You will receive regular updates about preventive health care workshops and other opportunities after you enroll in the wellness program.<br><br>**Effective:** You may be interested in Lisa's cash flow analysis. She found that a wellness center would save approximately $825,000 over six years. |
| **We-Voice** | *Use when focus is on shared efforts, interests, and problems.* It is particularly well suited to messages within a company (i.e., work team). | **Effective:** Were we to have our employees available more often and working at their highest levels of performance, we might not be forced to turn down lucrative projects such as those.<br><br>**Effective:** We could further discuss the estimates for how a wellness program could impact Eastmond. |
| **Impersonal Voice** | *Use when rational and neutral analysis is expected.* It is well suited for explaining business ideas, plans, and reports. | **Effective:** A wellness program would directly reduce health care costs and indirectly increase revenue through lower absenteeism and higher productivity.<br><br>**Effective:** The implementation plan would include five components. |
| **I-Voice** | *Use with nonthreatening verbs (i.e., think, feel) when there is bad news, difference of opinion, or even blame involved.* It is well suited for situations that could result in personal disappointments. Used most often in oral communication. | **Effective:** I think right now is not the right time to focus on a wellness program.<br><br>**Effective:** I think your ideas about the wellness program make a lot of sense, but the company is not in a position to make the initial investments to get it started. |

guidelines will help you demonstrate concern for others (also referred to as *other-oriented language* in some parts of the book).

**Avoid Relying Too Heavily on the I-Voice**   The subject of a sentence almost always becomes the focus or emphasis. Generally, place the focus on your reader (you-voice), your shared interests with the reader (we-voice), or simply the business issue at hand (impersonal voice). Table 5.10 provides guidelines for selecting appropriate subjects for sentences.

Typically, readers sense tone over an entire message. The guidelines for choosing appropriate subjects for your sentences influence tone—for good or bad—over the entirety of a paragraph or message. Notice in Table 5.11 how the repeated use of the I-voice amplifies the self-centered tone, whereas the repeated use of we-voice and you-voice amplifies a tone that reflects other-orientation.

**Respect the Time and Autonomy of Your Readers**   The business world can be a hectic, deadline-filled environment. In many situations you will want fast responses. If you show consideration for others' time as well as for their sense of autonomy, you will often achieve your intended results more effectively than if your words sound bossy and demanding (see Table 5.12). Keep in mind that statements you can say with a nonpushy tone may be decoded as pushy when in written form.

TABLE 5.11

## Ineffective Use of I-Voice

| Less Effective | More Effective |
|---|---|
| I would like to know as soon as possible when you could meet. I want to go over the estimates with you to show you how strong the case is for pursuing this option. Also, I have developed a timeline for writing the implementation plan that I want to show you right away. | Please let me know when there is a convenient time to meet. We could further discuss the estimates for how a wellness program could impact Eastmond. Also, if you think we should pursue the wellness program initiative, we could discuss the timeline for developing an implementation plan. |
| The repeated use of I-voice may be perceived as self-centered, inconsiderate, or pushy. | The repeated use of we-voice will likely be perceived as team-oriented and flexible. |
| I've set up the wellness program so that you will have access to exercise programs, health workshops, immunization shots, preventive care checkups, and disease management options. I'm especially proud of the exercise programs that I have set up. In my experience, I always work better when I've gotten exercise. I'm more productive and worry-free. I also want you to know that there are incentives to participate in the wellness program. For example, I've made sure that you will get $200 taken off your annual deductible if you enroll in the wellness program. | The wellness program will provide you with many options for managing your personal health, including exercise programs, health workshops, immunization shots, preventive care checkups, and disease management options. Ideally, participation in the various exercise programs will take away some of your stress and worries. You will have a variety of incentives available for enrolling in the program. For example, you will get $200 taken off of your annual deductible as soon as you enroll. |
| The repeated use of I-voice may come off as self-absorbed or insincere. | The repeated use of you-voice frames everything in terms of reader benefits. |

TABLE 5.12

## Showing Respect for Time and Autonomy

| Less Effective | More Effective |
|---|---|
| Call me as soon as you get out of your meeting. | Please give me a call when it's convenient. |
| This abrupt and demanding sentence would sound bossy to some people. | Using the courteous term *please* and focusing on the message recipient's convenience (rather than your own) shows respect. |
| We need to meet before Monday to go over the proposal. Have your administrative assistant set up a time for us and get back to me as soon as you know a time. | I think discussing the proposal with you before Monday would give us a chance to include your ideas in the proposal before we submit it on Wednesday. I'm available anytime before noon on Thursday or Friday. Is there a time that works for you? We could meet at your office or talk by phone. |
| These sentences will be interpreted as overly demanding to some readers. In written form, these statements can easily be misinterpreted. | These statements focus on achieving results together by a deadline while still respecting the time of the message recipient. |

**TABLE 5.13**

Giving Credit to Others

| Less Effective | More Effective |
|---|---|
| The wellness program could also impact revenues at Eastmond. | Lisa also helped me understand how a wellness program could impact revenues at Eastmond. |
| This statement implies that the writer is responsible for this analysis. | This statement implies that Lisa was instrumental in the analysis. |
| I gave Lisa information about wellness programs so she could plug the numbers in and see what it meant for Eastmond. As I anticipated, the estimate showed that Eastmond would save about $825,000 over six years. | Lisa Johnson's initial estimates of potential savings due to a wellness program show that Eastmond could save about $825,000 over the next six years by implementing a wellness program. |
| These statements give credit to Lisa yet imply that the *real* analysis was conducted by the writer. | This sentence gives full credit to Lisa for her time-consuming, thorough, and insightful work. |

**Give Credit to Others**   *What comes around goes around* is a maxim that holds true in many situations in the business world. Show your genuine appreciation and sincere recognition for the efforts of others (see Table 5.13), and it will pay off in many ways, including through improved camaraderie and willingness of others to give you ample and deserved credit in other situations. In short, make sure not to take credit for the work of others.

## Sending the Right Meta Messages

A related notion to tone is that of meta messages. Whereas tone relates to the overall attitudes or feelings that writers convey toward a message and its recipients, **meta messages** are the overall but often underlying messages people take away from a communication or group of communications. Meta messages are encoded and decoded as a combination of content, tone, and other signals.

In your written and oral communications, think about the lasting meta messages you send. Over the course of many communications—conversations, email exchanges, content on user profiles, comments on social networking websites, discussions during meetings—you send meta messages that become the basis for your reputation. These meta messages form others' impressions of your credibility: your competence, caring, and character. Some positive meta messages that business professionals might hope to send include "I'm skilled in my area" (competence), "I want you to succeed on this project" (caring), and "I will follow our corporate code of conduct" (character).

Mixed signals occur when the content of a message conflicts with the tone, nonverbal communication, or other signals. Sending mixed signals is not only confusing, but it also frequently results in negative meta messages. Even if a business message is well reasoned and justified, if readers perceive a selfish or manipulative tone, they may decode meta messages such as "I'm not being straight with you" or "I'm opportunistic." In a job interview, an applicant may say the right things but because of unprofessional dress send meta messages such as "I'm not serious about this job" or "I don't understand the culture of this company."

**FIGURE 5.6**

## Latisha's Message to Justify a Wellness Program

Underlining is added to distinguish between facts, conclusions, and positions. Refer to Figure 5.5 to see how the planned message structure matches the final document.

| | |
|---|---|
| To: | Jeff Brody, Personnel Director |
| Cc: | Lisa Johnson, Finance Manager |
| From: | Latisha Jackson, Intern |
| Date: | June 14, 2017 |
| Subject: | Increasing Profitability with a Corporate Wellness Program |

> Primary message as subject line and topic sentence.

Thank you for giving me a few weeks to provide you with some additional information about how wellness programs could benefit Eastmond.

Based on a cash flow estimate from Lisa Johnson in Finance and other studies about corporate wellness programs, we can be confident that a wellness program here at Eastmond would increase profitability. A wellness program would directly reduce healthcare costs and indirectly increase revenue through lower absenteeism and higher productivity.

### Reduced Expenses Due to Wellness Program

> Key Point 1. Most important key point placed first for emphasis.

Lisa Johnson's initial estimates show that Eastmond could *achieve net savings of about $825,000 over the next six years by implementing a wellness program*. She emphasized that her estimates are "safe" and "modest." In other words, she used assumptions that projected low-end savings and high-end expenses. She estimated that Eastmond would save approximately $1.6 million in healthcare costs over six years. It would cost approximately $780,000 to run and manage the wellness program over this time period (see Lisa's attached estimate for assumptions and other details).

**Table of Cash Flow Estimates** (in thousands of dollars)

| Savings in | Year 1 | Year 2 | Year 3 | Year 4 | Year 5 | Year 6 | Total |
|---|---|---|---|---|---|---|---|
| Healthcare Costs | $0 | $107 | $214 | $428 | $428 | $428 | $1,605 |
| Wellness Center Expenditures | $130 | $130 | $130 | $130 | $130 | $130 | $780 |
| Net Cash Flow | ($130) | ($23) | $84 | $298 | $298 | $298 | $825 |

**Assumptions:** 1. Per-employee savings are 0% of healthcare costs ($10,700 annually) at Year 1; 5% at Year 2; 10% at Year 3; 20% at Year 4 and after; 2. Per-employee costs to run a wellness program are $650 per year.

### Increased Revenue Due to Wellness Program

> Key Point 2A.

We can expect that a wellness program will reduce absenteeism. A recent review of 56 scientific studies about corporate wellness programs showed that sick leave absenteeism was lowered by an average of 27 percent. In our case, the average employee takes seven sick leave days per year. Assuming a similar reduction in sick leave absenteeism for our 380 full-time employees, we would gain approximately 380 work days per year from our employees.

Notice Latisha's final memo in Figure 5.6. It is well analyzed, positive, and other-oriented. She intends the memo to appeal logically and emotionally to Jeff and others who read it. Ideally, it will send meta messages such as "I can be trusted with important projects" or "A wellness program makes financial sense for this company, and I'm the right person to continue working on it."

In addition to reviewing the final memo for its tone and meta messages, take a few moments to notice its logic and structure. It contains color-coded underlining to distinguish between facts, conclusions, and positions. Immediately following the final memo, you'll find the Communication Q&A, which offers additional insights as it provides one business professional's ideas and approaches to crafting effective messages.

**FIGURE 5.6**

*(Continued)*

---

Jeff Brody                          Page 2                          June 14, 2017

**Key Point 2B.**

We can also expect that a wellness program will increase productivity.  Many studies have been conducted about improved productivity due to wellness programs, with productivity increases ranging between 2 and 52 percent. Regarding exercise, one recent study found that on days that employees exercised, their mental performance and time management were 15 percent better.

**Key Point 2.**

By reducing absenteeism and increasing productivity, a wellness program would indirectly increase revenue. Lisa explained that precisely estimating the exact value of lower absenteeism and higher productivity is difficult but that we would most likely increase revenue. As an example, she said that last year we turned down two major contracts worth nearly $100,000 due to a lack of personnel. Were we to have our employees working at their highest levels of performance, perhaps we would be able to accept lucrative projects such as those.

**Call to Action.**

### Recommendation for Developing an Implementation Plan

Please let me know when you would be able to meet. We could further discuss the estimates for how a wellness program could impact Eastmond. Also, if you think we should pursue the wellness program initiative, we could discuss an implementation plan. This plan would address some of the following issues:

1. Lifestyle (such as nutrition, stress, exercise) and disease management options
2. Advantages and disadvantages of in-house versus outsourced wellness programs
3. Potential wellness program vendors
4. Communications and marketing for gaining employee buy-in
5. Incentives for maximizing employee participation

Enc.:   5-Year Financial Impact Estimates of Wellness Program

cc:     L. Johnson

---

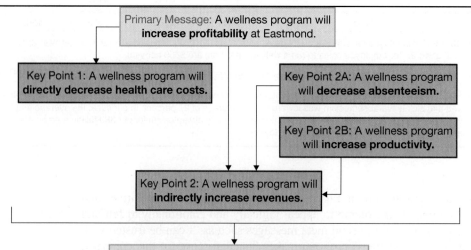

# COMMUNICATION Q&A

## CONVERSATIONS WITH CURRENT BUSINESS PROFESSIONALS

**Pete Cardon: For important written business messages, what process do you go through?**

**Kim Asbill:** First, I listen. I also ask a lot of questions. The more, the better! Sometimes I brainstorm and come to a meeting prepared with a list of questions. Some clients communicate better verbally, and they tell you their business message. That's when you take really good notes and try to repeat and rephrase what they are saying to demonstrate understanding. Other clients respond best to written information. In that case, I often craft a message on my own based on my knowledge of the situation and use the written document to communicate back and forth until the message is correct.

**PC: What strategies do you use to get the right tone in your writing?**

**KA:** You have to know your audience to get the right tone. When I worked at an ad agency, one of our clients was Nickelodeon cable TV network. We worked on a campaign called "The Big Help" designed to encourage kids to volunteer in their communities. For that client, the tone was very informal and fun. You weren't allowed to use the word *child*. You had to use *kid*. You can imagine, writing for a bank or an electric utility would be much more formal. You have to know what your goal is too. Are you trying to get more customers to eat at a local restaurant? Maybe you are using a persuasive tone. Are you informing young mothers about how to install a car seat properly? Maybe your tone is focused on a step-by-step process.

**PC: How do you think business writing is changing?**

**KA:** I think the digital media age has changed business writing profoundly. Email was the first thing to change the way people communicate in business. The need for good writers in the workplace is more important than ever. The ability for these writers to communicate correctly for different audiences in a variety of mediums, traditional and digital, is what will set them apart in this new age of technology.

**PC: What advice would you give young professionals about writing effective messages in the business world?**

**KA:** Write. Write all the time! Think before you write. Use outlines. Remember your audience. Less is more. Read good writing. Attend workshops on writing; even webinars are great. Volunteer your writing skills to organizations you care about. Don't be shy about asking someone to proof your work. And never stop learning!

***Kim Asbill*** *is the owner of Asbill Public Relations and a public relations manager at SCANA. She has worked in public relations for various businesses and organizations for over two decades.*

Courtesy of Kim Asbill

# Chapter Takeaway for *Creating Effective Business Messages*

**LO5.1 Explain the goals of effective business messages and the process for creating them. (pp. 140–142)**

**The Stages and Goals of Effective Message Creation**

**PLAN: Get the content right.**

- Understand your *audience*.
- Gather the right *information*.
- Develop your *message*.

**WRITE: Get the delivery right.**

- Set the right *tone*.
- Apply a clear and concise *style*.
- Focus on navigational *design*.

**REVIEW: Double-check everything.**

- Get *feedback*.
- Ensure your message is *fair*.
- Make sure to *proofread*.

---

**LO5.2 Identify the needs of your audience in the AIM planning process. (pp. 142–144)**

| Audience Analysis | | |
|---|---|---|
| • Identify reader benefits and constraints. <br> • Consider reader values and priorities. | • Estimate your credibility. <br> • Anticipate reactions. | • Consider secondary audiences. |

---

**LO5.3 Gather the right information and refine business ideas in the AIM planning process. (pp. 144–145)**

| Information Gathering | | |
|---|---|---|
| • Identify the business problems. | • Analyze the business problems. | • Clarify objectives. |

See an *example of information gathering* in Figure 5.3.

---

**LO5.4 Develop your primary message and key points in the AIM planning process. (pp. 145–154)**

| Message Development | Testing Logic | |
|---|---|---|
| • Frame the main point. <br> • Set up the structure/logic of the message. | **Avoid** the following: <br> • Unsupported generalizations <br> • Faulty cause/effect claims <br> • Weak analogies | • Either/or logic <br> • Slanting of facts <br> • Exaggeration |

See an *example of a deductive framework* in Figure 5.4.
See *typical paragraph structure* in a deductive business message in Figure 5.5.

---

**LO5.5 Explain and apply positive and other-oriented tone in business messages. (pp. 154–161)**

| Setting the Right Tone | |
|---|---|
| **Demonstrate positivity.** | **Show concern for others.** |
| • Display a can-do, confident attitude. <br> • Focus on positive rather than negative traits. <br> • Use diplomatic, constructive terms. | • Avoid relying too heavily on I-voice. <br> • Respect the time and autonomy of your readers. <br> • Give credit to others. |

# Key Terms

conclusions, 145

deductive, 148

direct, 148

facts, 145

indirect, 149

inductive, 149

meta messages, 158

positions, 145

priorities, 143

tone, 154

values, 143

# Discussion Exercises

**5.1 Chapter Review Questions** (LO5.1, LO5.2, LO5.3, LO5.4, LO5.5)

A. Describe each of the three components in the AIM planning process for business messages: audience analysis, idea development, and message structuring.

B. Explain the general nature of excellence in business thinking and how it applies to the idea development stage of planning messages.

C. Discuss basic considerations in the audience analysis stage of planning messages.

D. Describe the nature of framing for business messages.

E. Explain common types of logical inconsistencies in business messages.

F. Discuss the importance of achieving positive and other-oriented tone in business messages.

**5.2 Communication Q&A Discussion Questions** (LO5.1, LO5.2, LO5.3, LO5.4, LO5.5)

Read the comments and advice of Kim Asbill in the Communication Q&A section. Respond to the following questions:

A. What does Asbill say about the process of writing messages? What two strategies will you better incorporate into your approach to writing?

B. She also mentions tone several times. According to her, what is the importance of tone? What type of tone does she try to project?

C. In what ways does she say that business writing is changing? How will you adapt to some of these changes?

D. What pieces of advice that she gives are most relevant for your writing? Explain.

**5.3 Worst Words to Use at Work? Displaying Confidence with Words** (LO5.5)

In a *Forbes* magazine article called "Worst Words to Say at Work," business consultant and psychotherapist Linnda Durre listed nine words or phrases that show someone is not confident.[10] These phrases, according to Durre, cause others to perceive you as undependable and untrustworthy. To read the article, go to www.forbes.com/2010/04/26/words-work-communication-forbes-woman-leadership-career.html. Then respond to each of the following, which are excerpted from her article, with four to five sentences about whether you agree or disagree with her point of view:

A. *Try* is a weasel word. "Well, I'll try," some people say. It's a cop-out. They're just giving you lip service when they probably have no real intention of doing what you ask.

B. *Whatever*—This word is a trusted favorite of people who want to dismiss you, diminish what you say, or get rid of you quickly. . . . It's an insult and a verbal slap in the face. It's a way to respond to a person without actually responding.

C. *Maybe* and *I don't know*—People will sometimes avoid making a decision and hide behind these words. Sometimes during a confrontation people will claim not to know something or offer the noncommittal response "maybe," just to avoid being put on the spot.

D. *I'll get back to you*—When people need to buy time or avoid revealing a project's status, they will say, "I'll get back to you," and they usually never do.

E. *If*—Projects depend on everyone doing his or her part. People who use *if* are usually playing the blame game and betting against themselves. They like to set conditions rather than assuming a successful outcome.

F. *Yes, but . . .*—This is another excuse. You might give your team members suggestions or solutions and they come back to you with "Yes, but . . ." as a response. They don't really want answers, help, or solutions.

G. *I guess . . .*—This is usually said in a weak, soft-spoken, shoulder-shrugging manner. It's another attempt to shirk responsibility—a phrase is muttered only when people half agree with you, but want to leave enough leeway to say, "Well, I didn't really know. . . . I was only guessing."

H. *We'll see . . .*—How many times did we hear our parents say this? We knew they were buying time, avoiding a fight or confrontation, or really saying no.

# Evaluation Exercises

**5.4 Evaluating Latisha's Proposal for an Implementation Plan of a Wellness Program** (LO5.2, LO5.3, LO5.4, LO5.5)

Based on the completed message from Latisha in Figure 5.6, answer the following questions:

A. How effectively is this message framed? Would you suggest any changes?

B. How effective is the business logic? Would you suggest any changes?

C. How effective is the tone? Would you suggest any changes?

**5.5 Evaluating a Business Message** (LO5.2, LO5.3, LO5.4, LO5.5)

Choose a business message to evaluate. You could find a recent letter you have received from a business, go to a website and choose a message for customers or stockholders, or use a message specified by your instructor. Select a message that contains at least three or four paragraphs. Evaluate the message in the following ways:

A. How effectively are facts and conclusions written?

B. How effectively is the message targeted to its audience? Do you have any suggestions for how it could have been better adapted for the audience?

C. Does it have any logical inconsistencies? Explain.

D. Does the message portray a tone of positivity? Other-orientation? Describe your viewpoint with examples.

**5.6 Self-Assessment of Approach to Writing** (LO5.2, LO5.3, LO5.4, LO5.5)

Evaluate yourself with regard to each of the practices listed in the table below. Circle the appropriate number for each.

| Before sending important written messages, I . . . | 1 (Rarely/Never) | 2 (Sometimes) | 3 (Usually) | 4 (Always) |
|---|---|---|---|---|
| Make sure I gather all the facts. | 1 | 2 | 3 | 4 |
| Think carefully about what the facts mean. | 1 | 2 | 3 | 4 |
| Take time to think about what my audience wants and needs. | 1 | 2 | 3 | 4 |
| Spend time envisioning how my audience will respond. | 1 | 2 | 3 | 4 |
| Think about how the gist of my message could be captured in one short statement. | 1 | 2 | 3 | 4 |
| Map out the main supporting ideas for my primary message. | 1 | 2 | 3 | 4 |
| Check the message for logical consistency. | 1 | 2 | 3 | 4 |
| Make certain the tone is positive (as appropriate). | 1 | 2 | 3 | 4 |
| Ensure that the tone is other-oriented. | 1 | 2 | 3 | 4 |
| Reread the message to make sure everything is correct. | 1 | 2 | 3 | 4 |

Add up your score and consider the following advice:

35–40: You are a strategic writer. You nearly always think carefully about the strength of your message and its intended influence on your audience. Keep up the great work.

30–34: You are a careful writer. You have many good habits in writing preparation. Identify the areas where you need to improve. By preparing slightly more in these areas, you will become a powerful, strategic writer in the workplace.

25–29: You are a somewhat careful writer. Sometimes and in some ways you are careful about your writing. You occasionally ask the right questions about getting your message right for your audience. You are inconsistent, however. Focus on preparing carefully for all important messages.

Under 25: You are a casual writer. You rarely take enough time to think carefully about your written messages. Even if you are a gifted and savvy writer, at some point your lack of preparation will harm your work achievements. Make a habit of spending more time in the preparation stage asking questions about how to construct your message to appropriately influence your audience.

Once you've completed the short assessment, write about three areas of writing preparation in which you intend to improve. Describe specific steps you will take to improve and benchmarks for checking your progress.

# Application Exercises

**5.7 Avoiding Logical Errors** (LO5.4)

For each of the following sentences, identify what you consider to be logical inconsistencies. Explain whether these inconsistencies relate to unsupported generalizations, faulty cause/effect claims, either/or logic, slanting the facts, or exaggeration. Then revise the sentences to eliminate the logical inconsistencies.

A. Jim's Old Fashioned Burgers provides the best management training program in the industry.

B. The training consists of five stages: manager-in-training, second assistant manager, first assistant manager, restaurant manager, and regional director. The training places you on the fast track to success; advancing from one stage to the next takes from as few as three months up to just two years.

C. Many trainees eventually become upper-level executives, showing that hands-on training is better than getting a business degree.

D. Eventually, approximately 10 percent of trainees become regional directors. Employees from this elite group are those who show perseverance and determination to reach their professional goals.

E. Because just 5 percent of Jim's employees are selected for the training program, your acceptance in the program shows that you have great leadership potential.

F. We encourage you to apply for the training program so that you avoid staying in the same position without making career progress.

G. Restaurant managers make approximately $35,000 to $40,000 per year. The annual salary has grown at approximately 5 percent per year during the past three years, far outpacing income growth for restaurant managers at McDonald's or Burger King. So reaching the restaurant manager stage places you in a better economic position than you would be in at competing restaurants.

### 5.8 Displaying a Can-Do, Confident Tone (LO5.5)

For each of the following items, rewrite the sentences to achieve a better can-do, confident tone.

A. Even though I do not have any supervisory experience, I think I have excellent leadership skills.

B. I have excellent leadership skills and will certainly increase profitability as I am promoted through the ranks of the training program.

C. I might be a good candidate for the training program since I work so hard.

D. We feel that next year's annual profits could increase if the economy picks up and if we are able to fill all of our management positions.

E. We believe that improving customer service is one way of driving increased revenues.

### 5.9 Focusing on Positive Traits (LO5.5)

For each of the following items, rewrite the sentences to achieve a more positive tone.

A. All employees who show commitment and strong leadership skills are eligible for the management training program, even if they lack any higher education.

B. None of the training requires you to go through a traditional, businesslike educational program.

C. You will begin as a manager-in-training and will do far more than flip burgers.

D. Those employees who do not show exceptional leadership skills at the manager-in-training stage do not advance to the next stage of training.

E. We are seeking individuals who do not settle for average customer service.

F. You will lose your opportunity to be considered for the program unless we receive your application by July 1.

G. Employees who have not done poorly on their performance reviews are eligible to apply for the program.

### 5.10 Using Diplomatic, Constructive Terms (LO5.5)

For each of the following items, rewrite the sentences to achieve a more positive, constructive tone.

A. You probably won't be accepted into the management training program because you haven't worked here long enough to show any commitment.

B. Your contention that you have enough supervisory experience to make you qualified is questionable.

C. I think you must reconsider your views on the management training program if you expect it to succeed. You're just not in touch with reality if you expect to get quality managers without paying them higher salaries sooner in the program.

### 5.11 Using Appropriate Voice (LO5.5)

For each of the following items, rewrite the sentences in you-voice, we-voice, or I-voice to achieve a more effective tone.

A. I'm happy to offer you a spot in the manager-in-training program.

B. I'm positive that this opportunity will help your career.

C. You must turn in the application before July 1.

D. I will lead the first orientation session for the program, and then I'll turn the remainder of the afternoon meetings over to my colleague.

E. I've come up with some ideas for the training program, and I'd like to meet as soon as possible to get some discussion going. I want us to focus on a conversation about the salaries and benefits that would motivate more employees to apply for the program.

### 5.12 Respecting the Time and Autonomy of Others (LO5.5)

Rewrite each of the following items twice. Rewrite the first time assuming that you are writing to a peer. Rewrite the second time assuming that you are writing to a subordinate.

A. Get back to me before Friday afternoon about your availability for an interview.

B. I think we should review the manager-in-training applicants. Please come to my office on Tuesday at 9:30 a.m.

C. I have chosen the five applicants who are most strongly suited for the training program. Could you send me an email confirming that you agree with my selections?

D. I'm swamped with other projects, and we need to make the selections for the training program. Please take care of it yourself before this Friday at noon. You can count on me agreeing with your selections.

### Case for Problems 5.13 through 5.15: Learning about Stress Management Programs for Eastmond Networking

When Jeff arrived back at the office, he spent 15 minutes reading Latisha's proposal to work on a wellness program. He found the work impressive and insightful. If only more of his employees had the same drive, initiative, and analytical skills as Latisha, thought Jeff, Eastmond would be far more successful. If Latisha kept up this level of analysis in her work, Jeff would definitely find a way to employ her full-time at Eastmond. Her thorough and thoughtful approach to this business problem showed she could excel in many of the entry-level management positions at the company.[11]

However, Jeff wasn't quite ready to move forward on implementing her plan. He was concerned about the expense. Although he trusted the estimates on returns, he was worried about the cash investments needed in the first few years before Eastmond would see returns. Before Latisha worked on a plan, he wanted her to do some more background work and investigate a more modest investment. He was especially interested in learning more about how a disease management program could impact the company.

Jeff approached Latisha and explained what he wanted, and he asked her to write a brief report similar to the one she had already done.

He said, "I'd like you to focus on just the biggest problems. You know, programs to help with diabetes or heart health. Maybe we could help employees lower their cholesterol levels and their blood pressure. I'm thinking that we should learn how we can get the biggest bang for our buck—focus on say four or five of the costliest health problems and go from there. Also, I'd like to get a sense of the best way to prioritize our limited dollars to invest in disease management."

"If you're looking for some specific interventions that can make the biggest difference," Latisha answered, "we should start with stress. Stress costs us more in terms of health care costs and lower productivity than any other health care risk covered in a wellness or disease management program. Stress management programs are fairly inexpensive and deliver results pretty quickly."

"Really?" he said. "Stress costs more than heart disease or diabetes? OK, then how about you focus on stress management programs for the next week or two and write up what you find out. We'll go forward from there."

Latisha spent the next week learning about corporate stress management programs. She learned the following:

- Health care costs of people suffering chronic, extreme stress are 46 percent higher than for those who are not.
- According to the American Medical Association, stress is as bad for your heart as smoking and high cholesterol.
- Forty percent of job turnover is due to stress.
- Stress reduction programs can have major impacts. In one company, 42 percent of 5,900 employees suffered moderate to severe stress. In fact, 80 percent of doctor visits for these employees were related to stress. After a stress reduction program, employee physician services dropped from $7.4 million annually to $5.3 million annually.
- Employees with various health risks directly increase health care costs to employers. For example, compared to employees with low health risks, employees with the following conditions significantly increase costs to the employer: depression (70.2 percent higher cost); stress (46.3 percent); glucose (34.8 percent); weight (21.4 percent); tobacco (19.7 percent); blood pressure (11.7 percent); exercise (10.4 percent).
- According to the Department of Health and Human Services, employees suffer the following risk factors: stress, 44 percent; overweight, 38 percent; use alcohol excessively, 31 percent; high cholesterol, 30 percent; have cardiovascular disease, 25 percent; don't exercise, 24 percent; smoke, 21 percent; don't wear seat belts, 20 percent; are asthmatic, 12 percent; are diabetic, 6 percent.
- One study showed the annual per-employee absenteeism costs for the following conditions as follows: stress, $136; weight issues, $70; tobacco use, $44; glucose problems, $29.
- The Canadian Institute of Stress showed the following results for corporate stress management programs: work stress: 32 percent improvement; work satisfaction: 38 percent improvement; absenteeism: 18 percent reduction; disability days: 52 percent reduction; grievances: 32 percent reduction; productivity: 7 percent improvement; quality measures: 13 percent improvement; work engagement: 62 percent improvement.
- Stress management programs are most effective when offered in conjunction with broad wellness programs.
- Setting up stress management programs is challenging. Other disease management programs are more easily defined in terms of who has conditions and how to treat them (i.e., diabetes, heart disease).
- Most employees do not enroll in stress management programs unless there are incentives.
- Stress management can be achieved through workplace policies that alleviate work and personal stress. Some companies have tried flextime, allowing work at home, child care initiatives, sick child care, and other incentives to help employees reduce stress and be more productive.
- Stress management can also involve training through workshops and professional coaching.
- Lisa estimates that hiring a full-time professional coach for the workplace would cost approximately $60,000 per year (salary plus benefits and other related costs). The coach would run workshops, distribute educational materials, and also offer one-to-one coaching in stress relief. The coach would be qualified to work on other wellness areas such as weight loss, exercise, and dietary improvements. Assuming that Eastmond offered $150 reductions on health care premiums per year, Lisa estimates the company could achieve 90 percent participation (about 175 employees) in a basic stress management program. She thinks it's reasonable to assume that Eastmond could save about $500 per enrolled employee between health care and absenteeism costs.

### 5.13 Idea Development by Organizing Facts into Conclusions and Recommendations (LO5.2)

Assume you are Latisha and you will write a proposal to Jeff asking that Eastmond develop a stress management program. You can use any of the facts she has discovered and even search for some online (there's lots of information about stress management), but your task is to make sense of the facts you've gathered. Organize them into groups that support three or four major conclusions (in a format similar to Figure 5.4). Then write three or four recommendations you would make based on your conclusions.

### 5.14 Writing a Proposal in Support of Developing a Stress Management Program (LO5.2, LO5.3, LO5.4, LO5.5)

Assume the role of Latisha. Write a proposal to develop a stress management program. Use well-justified logic to support your conclusions and recommendations.

### 5.15 Writing a Proposal to Broaden the Focus of a Wellness Program (LO5.2, LO5.3, LO5.4, LO5.5)

Assume the role of Latisha. You have concluded that although a stress management program would be beneficial, focusing on stress management without a comprehensive wellness program is shortsighted and less cost-effective. Use well-justified logic to support your conclusions and recommendations.

# Language Mechanics Check

**5.16 Review the semicolon and colon rules in Appendix A. Then rewrite each sentence to add semicolons and colons where needed (you may need to replace other forms of punctuation in some instances).**

A. IBM's two most important business units are Global Technology Services and Global Business Services.

B. IBM primarily focuses on B2B business, on the other hand, Microsoft primarily focuses on B2C business.

C. IBM has U.S. offices in Armonk, New York, New York City, New York and Santa Clara, California.

D. Even though IBM is a well-recognized brand, most people don't know much about its products or services for many reasons, including that it focuses mostly on B2B products and services, that its products and services are highly technical, and that it doesn't explain its well-known products, such as Watson, to the public.

E. IBM's two most important business units are the following Global Technology Services and Global Business Services.

F. IBM was forced to lay off roughly 15 percent of its North American employees, however, that does not indicate a decline in revenues.

G. IBM's top executive team includes the following individuals; Virginia M. Rometty, CEO, Steven A. Mills, Senior VP and Group Executive of Software & Systems, Robert C. Weber, Senior VP of Legal & Regulatory Affairs and General Counsel, and John E. Kelly III, Senior VP and Director of Research.

H. IBM faces several major challenges; it's so large that it's difficult to lead and manage, it faces stiff challenges from cloud providers, and it's not well equipped to deal with growing demand for rented software and computer systems.

I. The top vendors for enterprise social networking platforms are IBM, Jive, Microsoft, Cisco, and Salesforce.

J. I originally wanted to apply for a job at IBM: however, I ended up deciding to apply at Cisco.

# Endnotes

1. These time estimates are based on observing thousands of business students and are consistent with decades of research about expertise as described in Michael Pressley and Christine B. McCormick, *Advanced Educational Psychology for Educators, Researchers, and Policymakers* (New York: HarperCollins, 1995).

2. Elizabeth Garone, "How to Escape a Reputation as a Novice," *The Wall Street Journal,* October 8, 2008.

3. Roger Martin, "How Successful Leaders Think," *Harvard Business Review,* June 2007: 72–83; Richard Paul and Linda Elder, *The Miniature Guide to Critical Thinking Concepts and Tools* (Dillon Park, CA: Foundation for Critical Thinking Press, 2008); David Carrithers and John C. Bean, "Using a Client Memo to Assess Critical Thinking of Finance Majors," *Business Communication Quarterly* 71, no. 1 (2008): 10–26.

4. Statistics and other information came from a variety of sources, including the following: American Institute for Preventive Medicine, *The Health & Economic Implications of Worksite Wellness Programs* (Farmington Hills, MI: Author, 2008); Elizabeth Mendes, "Americans Exercise Less in 2009 Than in 2008; Having a Safe Place to Exercise Contributes to Exercise Frequency," *Gallup Poll Briefing,* January 15, 2010; Katherine Capps, *Employee Health & Productivity Management Programs: The Use of Incentives* (Lyndhurst, NJ: IncentOne, 2007); Pamela Kufahl, "America's Obesity Rate at a 10-Year Plateau, Study Finds," *Club Industry* 26, no. 2 (2010); Larry Chapman, "Meta-Evaluation of Worksite Health Promotion Economic Return Studies: 2005 Update," *The Art of Health Promotion,* July/August 2005: 1–15; Michael George, *Corporate Fitness and the Bottom Line* (Petaluma, CA: Inspired Fitness, 2008); U.S. Department of Health and Human Services, *Prevention Makes Common "Cents"* (Washington, DC: U.S. Department of Health and Human Services, September 2003); American College of Sports Medicine, *ACSM's Worksite Health Promotion Manual* (Champaign, IL: American College of Sports Medicine, 2003); Buck Consultants, *Working Well: A Global Survey of Health Promotion and Workplace Wellness Strategies* (San Francisco: Buck Consultants, 2008); National Business Group on Health, "New Study Finds Most Employers Spend Nearly 2% of Health Care Claims Budget on Wellness Programs," January 25, 2010, retrieved April 21, 2010, from www.businessgrouphealth.org/pressrelease.cfm?ID=149.

5. Melissa Raffoni, "Framing for Leadership," *Harvard Management Communication Letter* 5, no. 12 (2002): 3–4.

6. Lyle Sussman, "How to Frame a Message: The Art of Persuasion and Negotiation," *Business Horizons* 42, no. 4 (1999): 2–6; Raffoni, "Framing for Leadership."

7. Adam Bryant, "In a Word, He Wants Simplicity," *Corner Office* (blog), *The New York Times,* May 23, 2009, www.nytimes.com/2009/05/24/business/24corner.html.

8. Jane Thomas, *Guide to Managerial Persuasion and Influence* (Upper Saddle River, NJ: Pearson Education, 2004).

9. Timothy A. Judge and Remus Ilies, "Is Positiveness in Organizations Always Desirable?" *Academy of Management Executive* 18, no. 4 (2004): 151–155.

10. Linnda Durre, "Worst Words to Say at Work," *Forbes,* April 26, 2010, retrieved August 5, 2010, from www.forbes.com/2010/04/26/words-work-communication-forbes-woman-leadership-career.html.

11. This case problem uses information from several additional resources, including the following: American Institute for Preventive Medicine, *A Worksite Wellness White Paper* (Farmington Hills, MI: American Institute for Preventive Medicine, 2009), retrieved August 5, 2010, from www.healthylife.com/template.asp?pageID=75; Catherine Calarco and Bruce Cryer, *Return on Investment Paper* (Boulder Creek, CA: HeartMath, 2009); HealthAdvocate, *Setting Up a Stress Management Program: A Checklist for Success* (Plymouth Meeting, PA: HealthAdvocate, 2010).

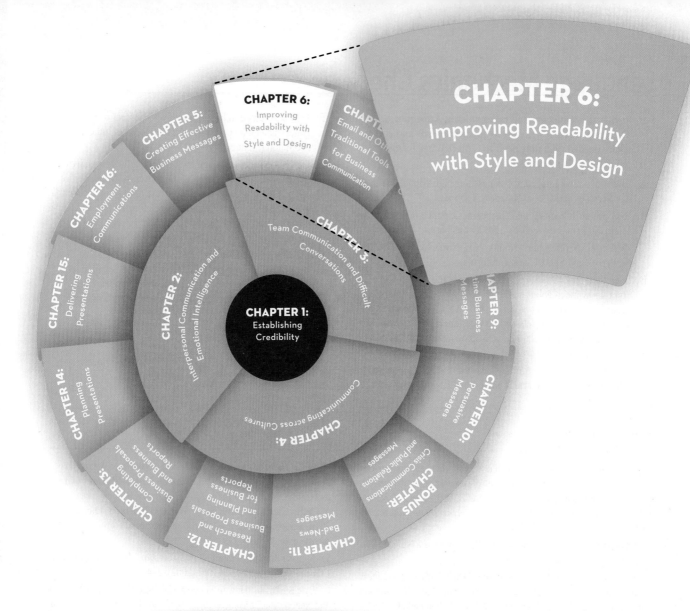

# CHAPTER 6:
## Improving Readability with Style and Design

CHAPTER 6:
Improving Readability with Style and Design

**ESTABLISHING CREDIBILITY**

**PRINCIPLES OF INTERPERSONAL COMMUNICATION**

**PRINCIPLES FOR & TYPES OF BUSINESS MESSAGES**

 **Learning Objectives**

After studying this chapter, you should be able to do the following:

**LO6.1** Describe and apply the following principles of writing style that improve ease of reading: completeness, conciseness, and natural processing.

**LO6.2** Explain and use navigational design to improve ease of reading.

**LO6.3** Describe and apply the components of the reviewing stage, including a FAIR test, proofreading, and feedback.

In Chapter 5, we focused on getting your message right with the AIM planning process. Then we introduced the importance of tone as you begin formally drafting your message. In this chapter, we focus on style and design—the next considerations as you draft your message. At this point, *your entire focus should be making your message easy to read.*

In short, your audience members—whether executives, managers, other professionals, or clients and customers—are typically preoccupied with many projects and overwhelmed with messages and information. When you make your messages easy to read, your audience is more likely to read them carefully and understand them as you intended.[1]

Many of the principles in this chapter focus on simplifying your words and sentences. This should not be confused with oversimplifying and minimizing your message. Your messages should contain the best of ideas with strong support. If your message is difficult to read, however, your ideas may not even be considered.

In this chapter, we discuss four broad goals. The first three goals relate to writing style and include being complete, concise, and natural. The final goal is to design your document for rapid navigation. Throughout the chapter, you will find less effective and more effective examples of each of these style and design elements. These examples come directly from the chapter case. Make sure to skim Stephanie's original difficult-to-read brochure draft (see Figure 6.1) so you understand the context for the chapter examples. By the end of the chapter, you will see the revisions that result in the final version of the brochure (see Figure 6.3).

**Hear Pete Cardon explain why this matters.**

bit.ly/cardon6

**CHAPTER CASE:** PROMOTING FRANCHISES AT SUNRISE GREETING CARDS AND FLOWERS

Stephanie Jorgenson, owner and founder

**WHO'S INVOLVED**

- Started her greeting card business 20 years ago
- Has expanded to 32 stores
- Wants to set up franchises

**THE SITUATION**

Over the past 20 years, Sunrise Greeting Cards and Flowers has succeeded far beyond Stephanie Jorgenson's original expectations. Her model of high-end greeting cards, flower arrangements, and other special-occasion gifts appealed to a growing customer base. In fact, even with increasing accessibility to low-end greeting cards at department stores and free e-cards, she found that her customers had grown more loyal and purchased more than ever.

In recent years, Stephanie has received many requests from people to open franchises. Because she was not in a position to expand as quickly as the market seemed to dictate, she thought franchising would be a good option.

© Ariel Skelley/Blend Images LLC

Six months ago, she hired a franchising consultant, who provided her with a basic strategy and action plan to make franchising possible. With her top management team, she set up the basic terms for franchises.

One of Stephanie's immediate goals was to produce a brochure to explain opportunities for franchisee opportunities. Stephanie had thought carefully about the audience for the brochure. She wanted financially strong and ambitious individuals. She also wanted people with a strong sense of optimism and customer orientation. She felt that success in her business was strongly related to genuine delight in helping others celebrate their special moments.

In terms of message structure, she had seen a number of brochures that she felt could be good models. Generally, they included an introductory message from the company president. Then, they typically contained information about financial qualifications and application procedures. She wanted a brochure that would be upbeat but also clear about the strong financial position needed to qualify for a franchise.

Her plan was to distribute the brochure personally to contacts at industry expos she attended throughout the year. She also envisioned mailing it, placing it on the company website, and sending it by email.

Stephanie drafted a document (see Figure 6.1) for the brochure. She asked several of her colleagues for input on the content. They all told her the same thing: "This is hard to read."

**TASK**  **1**  **2**

| | |
|---|---|
| How can Stephanie improve the writing style of the document so that potential franchisees will easily read it? (See the "Improving Ease of Reading with Completeness," "Improving Ease of Reading with Conciseness," and "Improving Ease of Reading with Natural Style" sections.) | How can Stephanie improve her document's navigational design so that potential franchisees can find important pieces of information rapidly? (See the "Improving Ease of Reading with Navigational Design" section.) |

## Improving Ease of Reading with Completeness

**LO6.1** Describe and apply the following principles of writing style that improve ease of reading: completeness, conciseness, and natural processing.

Visit http://connect. mheducation.com for an exercise on this topic.

Most of your messages in the workplace have a clear goal: to update your team members, to promote a service to a client, to give an assignment, and so on. Your goal of completeness means that your message provides all the information necessary to meet that purpose. Your colleagues, clients, and other contacts expect complete information so they can act on your message immediately. Otherwise, they will need to contact you to get additional information or, worse yet, ignore your message altogether. You can achieve completeness with three basic strategies: (1) providing all relevant information; (2) being accurate; and (3) being specific.

### Provide All Relevant Information

One challenge is to judge which information is relevant for your message. After all, providing too much information can distract your readers and weigh down your document. On the other hand, not providing enough information can leave your reader wondering how to respond. The key to providing *all but only* relevant information is to plan, write, and review your message strategically. Repeatedly asking yourself what information is necessary for the purpose of your message will help you accomplish this.

**FIGURE 6.1**

## Stephanie's Original, Difficult-to-Read Brochure

> This document is difficult to read. It contains long paragraphs and long sentences. It flows poorly. It is not designed to help a reader navigate it for information. Most readers would get frustrated as they attempt to learn how to purchase a franchise.

Hello Potential *Sunrise Greeting Cards and Flowers* Shop Owner! Would you like to be part of one of the most exciting businesses—providing those special somethings for those special someones on those special occasions and do you want to make your wildest dreams come true? There are many reasons for owning a Sunrise store, and it is wonderful to see happy customers day in and day out and be in a line of business where there are such great loyal customers. They are refined and appreciative of excellent craftsmanship and expect creative, original, and upscale greeting cards and flower arrangements. Our brand is one of the most strongly recognized among our customers and is associated with positive characteristics such as quality and reliability, and our customers associate these qualities with the special occasions in their lives. By owning a Sunrise store, you automatically tap into a brand that will provide profitability and join the Sunrise family. To help you reach your goals, we provide you with the products and resources to succeed. We also create a tight-knit group of store owners and managers who share tricks of the trade with one another, and to this end, we organize an annual retreat for store owners and managers that provides synergistic solutions and proactive approaches to managing our stores.

We have made an estimate that you will need an initial investment of between $290,000 and $605,000. The initial investment costs include the following: fixtures ($60,000–$90,000); inventory ($80,000–$190,000); store improvements ($20,000–$130,000); retail equipment ($20,000–$35,000); miscellaneous expenses ($10,000–$30,000); and an initial franchise fee ($50,000). Fixtures include product displays, stock room components, and signing. Inventory includes greeting cards, gifts, flowers, and non-Sunrise items. Store Improvements include carpeting, electrical, plumbing, lighting, etc. Retail Equipment includes point-of-sale cash registers and software, pricing machines, accounting software, etc. Miscellaneous Expenses include various deposits, license fees, promotional costs, etc. You can pick possible locations for your new store.

Sunrise will make the final approval about your proposed sites and may suggest alternate locations based on our marketing formula, which has worked successfully in the past. As far as financial requirements, you must have a minimum net worth of $350,000, and you also will need minimum unencumbered assets of between $120,000 and $265,000. You may not finance more than two-thirds of the initial investment to open the store. You must also have access to financing in the range of $170,000 to $340,000 (assuming that you finance two thirds of the initial investment costs). Confirmation of loan, terms, and collateral is required. You will need to show that you can maintain an outside income of at least 80 percent of your present income for a period of at least two years to show that you have adequate financial stability as you get your business started. You will need to show that your liquid assets are available for investment and operations of your new Sunrise Gift Cards and Flowers shop, and the capital must be from your personal assets; capital in a current business will not be recognized as available to a new store. Sunrise does not provide loans.

Sunrise will assist in the business planning, such as helping in the development of a marketing plan, budgeting plan, and a break-even analysis consultation will be provided with your active participation. The budgeting plan that will be provided includes initial investments (building, fixtures, products, etc.), marketing costs, personnel expenditures, insurance and other potential expenses needed to run a Sunrise store, and an analysis of your chosen location will also be provided that includes demographics, traffic patterns, competitors, and a related analysis will be given to you that contains estimates of retail sales and revenue.

Stephanie Jorgenson, President and Owner
Sunrise Greeting Cards and Flowers, LLC
Stephanie@Sunrisegiftcards.com, 1-800-SUN-SET9

Typically, paragraphs should contain 40 to 80 words. For routine messages, paragraphs as short as 20 to 30 words are common and appropriate. As the level of information and analysis grows deeper, some paragraphs will be longer. Rarely should paragraphs exceed 150 words. In a matter of seconds, you can easily check how many words are in your paragraphs with nearly all word processing software.

One primary cause of overly lengthy paragraphs is placing more than one main idea or topic in the paragraph. Your readers can process the information in your message far more easily if you create unified paragraphs in which each paragraph focuses on one idea or topic. Paragraphs with more than one idea often confuse readers. Even worse, readers may miss some ideas altogether. The process of unifying helps you control paragraph length and even tighten your business reasoning (see Table 6.3).

## TABLE 6.3

### Controlling Paragraph Length

| Less Effective | More Effective |
|---|---|
| As far as financial requirements, you must have a minimum net worth of $350,000. Also, you will need minimum unencumbered assets of between $120,000 and $265,000. You may not finance more than two-thirds of the initial investment to open the store. You must also have access to financing in the range of $170,000 to $340,000 (assuming that you finance two-thirds of the initial investment costs). Confirmation of loan, terms, and collateral is required. You will need to show that you can maintain an outside income of at least 80 percent of your present income for a period of at least two years. This allows you to have adequate financial stability as you get your business started. You will need to show that your liquid assets are available for investment and operations of your new Sunrise Greeting Cards and Flowers shop. Capital must be from your personal assets; capital in a current business will not be recognized as available to a new store. Sunrise does not provide loans. | Minimum financial requirements include a net worth of $350,000 with unencumbered liquid assets of between $120,000 and $265,000 (these financial requirements must be from personal assets, not from capital in a current business). You will need to show that these liquid assets are available for investment in your Sunrise store. You will also need to show that you can maintain an outside income of at least 80 percent of your present income for a period of at least two years.<br><br>You are required to finance less than two-thirds of the initial investment costs. Assuming that you can, you will need access to financing in the range of $170,000 to $340,000. Confirmation of loan, terms, and collateral is required. Sunrise does not provide loans. |
| This paragraph contains 168 words. It also contains excessive numerical figures. | This paragraph contains the same information but has been edited for conciseness and divided into two paragraphs. It contains one paragraph of 80 words and one paragraph of 44 words. Altogether, the information has been presented in 30 fewer words. |
| The right to open a new Sunrise store will be awarded based on the business plan, market potential in your chosen area, personal interviews, and financial criteria. Running a Sunrise store can be extremely profitable. Once approved, new Sunrise stores can typically be opened in 3 to 12 months. The minimum store size is based on location. In shopping malls, the minimum size should be approximately 2,500 square feet. In strip shopping centers, the minimum size should be approximately 3,400 square feet. Currently, average annual profit per Sunrise store is $153,000, with ranges between $49,000 and $215,000. Profit level depends on many factors, including choosing the right location, market demand, square footage, and managing the store effectively. Typically, profits become relatively stable after the first three years of operation. | The right to open a new Sunrise store will be awarded based on the business plan, market potential in your chosen area, personal interviews, and financial criteria. Once approved, new Sunrise stores can typically be opened in 3 to 12 months.<br><br>Currently, average annual profit per Sunrise store is $153,000, with ranges between $49,000 and $215,000. Profit level depends on many factors, including location, market demand, square footage, and management. Typically, profits become relatively stable after the first three years of operation. |
| This paragraph has two ideas or topics: (a) awarding the right to open a store and (b) average annual profit per store. This paragraph contains 130 words. | The revised paragraph is broken into two separate, unified paragraphs with 42 and 41 words, respectively. |

Try to keep most sentences under 20 words.

**FIGURE 6.2**

Comprehension Rate and Sentence Length

*Source:* Figure adapted from Ann Wylie, "How to Make Your Copy More Readable: Make Sentences Shorter," *Comprehension*, January 14, 2009, retrieved March 3, 2012, from http://comprehension.prsa.org/?p=217.

## Use Short Sentences in Most Cases

Like relatively short paragraphs, short sentences allow your readers to comprehend your ideas more easily. Consider Figure 6.2, which depicts the data from a study conducted by the American Press Institute.[4] Readers were tested on their overall comprehension based on the length of sentences. When sentences had 10 words or fewer, readers had nearly 100 percent comprehension. Once sentence lengths reached around 20 words, comprehension dropped to about 80 percent. Thereafter, comprehension dropped rapidly. Sentence lengths of 28 words resulted in just 30 percent comprehension.

As a rule of thumb, then, for routine messages, aim for average sentence length of 15 or fewer words. For more analytical and complex business messages, you may have an average sentence length of 20 or fewer words. Of course, you will often deal with complex ideas and need to go above 20 words in some of your sentences. Use your judgment to minimize sentence length (see Table 6.4).

## Avoid Redundancy

One way to reduce word count and make your messages easier to read is to avoid redundancies, which are words or phrases that repeat the same meaning. For example, consider the phrase *past history*; history can only be past, so there's no need to use both words. By eliminating redundancies, you can reduce overall word count (see Table 6.5).

## Avoid Empty Phrases

Many phrases simply fill space without adding additional meaning. Many of these phrases are common in conversations but are not needed for written messages (see Table 6.6).

## Avoid Wordy Prepositional Phrases

Eliminating extra words allows you to get your ideas across as efficiently as possible. You will often find that you can reduce word count by 30 to 40 percent simply by converting many of your prepositional phrases into single-word verbs. Like other elements of style we have discussed already, prepositional phrases are not bad in themselves. In many cases, they are perfectly appropriate. Rather, their overuse leads to wordiness and less clarity (see Table 6.7).

**TABLE 6.4**

Using Short Sentences

| Less Effective | More Effective |
|---|---|
| Our brand is strongly recognized among our customers and is associated with positive characteristics such as quality and reliability, and our customers associate these qualities with the special occasions in their lives. | To our customers, our brand represents quality products that help them celebrate special occasions. |
| This sentence contains 32 words. | This sentence contains the same ideas in just 14 words. |
| Our team of experienced managers will apply our well-developed formula for analyzing the demographics, traffic patterns, local competitors, and other factors of your chosen location to provide you with estimates of retail sales and revenue. | Our team of experienced managers will apply our well-developed formula for analyzing the demographics, traffic patterns, local competitors, and other factors of your chosen location. From this analysis, we will provide you with estimates of retail sales and revenue. |
| This sentence contains 35 words. | The less effective sentence has been split into one 25-word sentence and one 14-word sentence. |
| Sunrise has aggressively advertised in print and radio in regional markets in recent years, and Sunrise has developed excellent brand recognition with its various advertising and promotional materials that will directly benefit your store, which, of course, depends and varies on your chosen store location. | In recent years, Sunrise has aggressively advertised in print and radio in regional markets. As a result, Sunrise brand recognition is strong. Your store will benefit from Sunrise regional advertising and promotional campaigns. |
| This sentence contains 45 words. | The less effective sentence has been split into three sentences with 14, 8, and 11 words, respectively. |

**TABLE 6.5**

Avoiding Redundancy

| Less Effective | More Effective |
|---|---|
| To help you reach your goals, we provide you with the products and resources to succeed. | We provide you with the products and resources to succeed. |
| This sentence has 16 words. *To help you reach your goals* and *to succeed* are redundant phrases. | This sentence has 10 words. It removes redundancy. |
| We organize a fun-filled annual retreat each year for store owners and managers to share and discuss problems, solutions, and opportunities with one another. | We organize a fun-filled annual retreat for store owners and managers to share and discuss problems, solutions, and opportunities. |
| This sentence has 24 words. *Annual* and *each year* are redundant. *Share and discuss* implies *with one another*, making *with one another* redundant. | This sentence has 19 words. It removes redundancies. |

**TABLE 6.6**

Avoiding Empty Phrases

| Less Effective | More Effective |
|---|---|
| Needless to say, the profitability of a store depends on many factors. | The profitability of a store depends on many factors. |
| This sentence contains 12 words. | This revision contains 9 words. |
| With all due respect, Sunrise suggests other locations for your store based on our marketing formula. | Sunrise suggests other locations for your store based on our marketing formula. |
| This sentence contains 16 words. | This revision contains 12 words. |

**TABLE 6.7**

Avoiding Wordy Prepositional Phrases

| Less Effective | More Effective |
|---|---|
| In an effort to maximize your profitability as a Sunrise owner, you should be in attendance at each annual retreat. | Attending the annual Sunrise retreats helps you maximize profitability. |
| This sentence contains 20 words. | This revision of the less effective sentence contains 9 words. |
| In the business planning process, please keep in mind that at Sunrise, we are here for you. | Please remember that we will help you with business planning. |
| This sentence contains 17 words. | This revision of the less effective sentence contains 10 words. |

## Improving Ease of Reading with Natural Style

The closer you match your writing style to the way your readers think and talk, the easier it is for them to process the information you present. Ease of processing means your readers need less mental effort to understand your message, which is especially important for readers who are busy and preoccupied with other work challenges.

Several broad principles support the strategies in this section. First, people can generally process information more quickly when writers use action verbs. Second, people tend to think in a doer-action-object pattern, so using this pattern in your writing enhances comprehension. Furthermore, when the subject or doer is missing from the sentence, readers may become confused. Third, people generally process simple, short words more quickly than long, complex ones.

### Use Action Verbs When Possible

As a business writer, you want to project a positive, can-do, action-oriented tone whenever possible. Indeed, fostering action is the basic purpose of most workplace communication. Using action verbs focuses on the goal of coordinating action in the workplace and livens up your writing. Also, it usually reduces word count.

**TABLE 6.8**

Using Action Verbs

| Less Effective | More Effective |
|---|---|
| We <u>have made an estimate</u> that you will <u>need an initial investment</u> of between $290,000 and $605,000. | We <u>estimate</u> that you will <u>initially invest</u> between $290,000 and $605,000. |
| This sentence contains 17 words. | This revision contains 11 words. |
| Sunrise <u>is</u> a company with excellent customer service. | Sunrise <u>provides</u> excellent customer service. |
| This sentence contains 8 words. | This revision contains 5 words. |

Typically, then, you can focus on two types of revisions to achieve more effective action verbs. First, find nouns that you can convert to action verbs. For example, *have a meeting* becomes *meet* or *have a discussion* becomes *discuss*. Second, find forms of the verb *to be* (e.g., be verbs such as *is, are, am*) and convert them to action verbs (see Table 6.8). For example, *Sunrise is a great place to open a franchise with* becomes *Sunrise provides great opportunities for franchises.*

### Use Active Voice

One way to immediately improve your writing is to use active rather than passive voice in most sentences. Active voice and passive voice contain the following grammatical patterns:

**Active voice:** Doer as Subject + Verb + Object
**Passive voice:** Object as Subject + Be Verb + Verb + Doer (Optional)

Consider the following examples:

**Active voice:** Sunrise provides free training for up to three people for each new store.
**Passive voice:** Free training is provided for up to three people for each new store.

In active voice, this sentence immediately identifies the doer (Sunrise). It then uses a strong verb (provides) and proceeds to the object (free training). In passive voice, this sentence begins with the object of the action (free training), proceeds to a weak verb (is), then employs a strong verb (provided), and leaves out the doer, thus lacking the clarity of active voice.

Using active voice in writing includes many benefits. The doer-action-object allows for faster processing because most people's natural thinking occurs in this way. It also emphasizes the business orientation of action. Perhaps most important, it specifies the doer. Because business activities depend on accountability and coordination, knowing the identity of the doer of an action is usually important. Furthermore, writing in the active voice usually results in fewer words (see Table 6.9).

While active voice is the preferred writing style for most business writing, passive voice is sometimes better when attempting to avoid blaming others or sounding bossy. Some research reports also use passive voice to emphasize neutrality (see Table 6.10).

### Use Short and Familiar Words and Phrases

Whenever possible, choose short, conversational, and familiar words. Using longer, less common words to "sound smart" rarely pays off. They slow processing and distract

**TABLE 6.9**

Using Active Voice Appropriately

| Less Effective (Passive Voice) | More Effective (Active Voice) |
|---|---|
| A marketing plan, budgeting plan, and break-even analysis <u>will be provided</u> to you with your active participation. | Sunrise will work directly with you to create a marketing plan, budgeting plan, and break-even analysis. |
| This passive sentence de-emphasizes who will create the plan and lacks an action-oriented tone. | The active verb construction in this sentence helps achieve a more engaging, action-oriented tone. |
| An analysis of your chosen location <u>will also be provided</u> that includes demographics, traffic patterns, competitors, and a related analysis <u>will be given</u> to you that contains estimates of retail sales and revenue. | Sunrise will use its well-developed formula for analyzing the demographics, traffic patterns, local competitors, and other factors of your chosen location. Sunrise will also provide you with estimates of retail sales and revenue. |
| This sentence contains two sets of passive verbs. Again, it de-emphasizes who will create the plan and lacks an action-oriented tone. It is also wordy. It contains 33 words. | These sentences clearly identifies that Sunrise will conduct the analyses. It is action-oriented. It is also easier to read. It breaks the thoughts into two sentences of 21 and 12 words, respectively. |

**TABLE 6.10**

Using Active Voice Appropriately

| Less Effective (Active Voice) | More Effective (Passive Voice) |
|---|---|
| <u>Since you did not meet the financial criteria,</u> we have denied your application for a Sunrise franchise. | <u>Since financial criteria were not met,</u> your application for a Sunrise franchise was not accepted at this time. |
| This active verb construction emphasizes the reader's failures. | This passive verb construction provides the bad news without assigning blame or directly pointing out failure. |
| <u>You need to complete the application forms carefully</u> for us to seriously consider your application. | <u>Application forms that are completed carefully</u> allow us to better determine the merit of your application. |
| This active verb construction might be perceived as bossy (sounds like an order) or demeaning (implies the reader is not smart enough to understand basic procedures). | This passive verb construction emphasizes the importance of carefully completing the forms without directly implying the reader is likely to make elementary mistakes. |

from your message. They may even inadvertently send the signal that you are out of touch, quirky, or even arrogant (see Table 6.11).

## Use Parallel Language

Using parallel language means that you apply a consistent grammatical pattern across a sentence or paragraph. Parallelism is most important when you use series or lists. For example, when you describe a product with three characteristics, use the same grammatical pattern for each—that is, for example, choose adjectives or nouns or verbs for all of them. When you use consistent grammatical patterns for items in lists and series, readers can process the information far more naturally and quickly (see Table 6.12).

**TABLE 6.11**

## Using Short, Familiar Words and Phrases

| Less Effective | More Effective |
|---|---|
| Sunrise <u>advocates</u> that you seek <u>consultation</u> with us during the application process. | Sunrise <u>suggests</u> that you seek our <u>advice</u> during the application process. |
| *Advocates* is a word that is less familiar to many readers. Furthermore, *advocates* and *consultation* are words that may suggest the need for legal counsel to some readers. | This sentence contains short, familiar words that allow for ease of reading. |
| Sunrise <u>bestows</u> you with many <u>opulent</u> greeting cards and <u>singular</u> flower arrangements that can only be found in Sunrise stores. | Sunrise <u>provides</u> you with many <u>upscale</u> greeting cards and <u>unique</u> flower arrangements that can only be found in Sunrise stores. |
| This sentence contains infrequently used adjectives (*opulent, singular*). These terms sound overblown and will confuse many readers. | This sentence contains shorter, more familiar terms that capture the intended meaning. |
| To <u>facilitate this course of action</u>, we organize a <u>convivial</u> annual retreat for store owners and managers where we <u>collectively</u> discuss our <u>mutual</u> challenges, solutions, and opportunities. | To help <u>make this happen</u>, we organize a <u>fun-filled</u> annual retreat where store owners and managers can discuss our <u>shared</u> problems, solutions, and opportunities. |
| This sentence contains rarely used or stuffy words (*course of action, convivial, collectively, mutual*) that will frustrate many readers. | This sentence avoids stuffy, formal-business-sounding words (*course of action, collectively, mutual*) and replaces them with shorter, more conversational words. |

**TABLE 6.12**

## Using Parallel Language

| Less Effective | More Effective |
|---|---|
| Our customers are <u>refined</u> and <u>purchase high-end products.</u> | Our customers are <u>refined</u> and <u>upscale.</u> |
| The two characteristics of customers are not parallel. They are in the following pattern: adjective and verb–object. | The two characteristics of customers are parallel. They are both adjectives. |
| | OR |
| | Our customers <u>appreciate refined craftsmanship</u> and <u>purchase high-end products.</u> |
| | The two characteristics of customers are parallel. They both follow verb–object patterns. |
| Sunrise will work directly with you to <u>create a marketing plan, develop a budgeting plan, and break-even analysis.</u> | Sunrise will work directly with you to create a <u>marketing plan, budgeting plan, and break-even analysis.</u> |
| The three items in the list are not parallel. They are in the following pattern: verb–object, verb–object, noun. | The three items in the list are parallel. They are each nouns (each are objects of the verb *create*). |
| | OR |
| | Sunrise will work directly with you to <u>create a marketing plan, develop a budgeting plan, and set up a break-even analysis.</u> |
| | The three items in the list are parallel. They each follow verb–object patterns. |

**TABLE 6.12**

*(Continued)*

| Less Effective | More Effective |
|---|---|
| Profit level depends on many factors, including <u>choosing the right location</u>, <u>market demand</u>, <u>square footage</u>, and <u>managing the store effectively</u>. | Profit level depends on many factors, including <u>location</u>, <u>market demand</u>, <u>square footage</u>, and <u>management</u>. |
| The four factors do not have matching grammatical patterns. They are in the following pattern: verb–object, noun, noun, verb–object. | The four factors are parallel. They are each nouns. |
| | OR |
| | Profit level depends on many factors, including <u>choosing the right location</u>, <u>meeting market demands</u>, <u>leasing adequate store space</u>, and <u>managing the store effectively</u>. |
| | The four factors are parallel. They each follow a verb–object pattern. |

## Avoid Buzzwords and Figures of Speech

To keep your writing natural and engaging, make sure you don't distract your readers with overused or out-of-place words or phrases. Buzzwords, which are workplace terms that become trite because of overuse, can stir negative feelings among some readers. In Table 6.13, you can see one list of annoying buzzwords cited in a recent survey of executives.[5] (Dozens of such lists exist because business professionals become so agitated by these overused words.)

Figures of speech, such as idioms and metaphors, which contain nonliteral meanings, are generally out of place or inappropriate in business writing. Because they are nonliteral, they lack the precise meanings needed in business. Also, some idioms and metaphors have become so clichéd that they have lost almost all meaning (see Table 6.14).

## Avoid *It Is/There Are*

Readers naturally want to know precisely *who* or *what* the subject of a sentence is, particularly in business writing, where specificity is so important. Most sentences that

**TABLE 6.13**

The Most Annoying Buzzwords

| | |
|---|---|
| Leverage | At the end of the day |
| Reach out | Synergy |
| It is what it is | Solution |
| Viral | Think outside the box |
| Game changer | On the same page |
| Disconnect | Customer-centric |
| Value-add | Do more with less |
| Circle back | Downsizing |
| Cutting edge | Overworked |

*Source:* "WHAT'S THE BUZZ? Survey Reveals Most Overused Workplace Terms," online article retrieved July 2014.

**TABLE 6.16**

Using Headings

| Less Effective | More Effective |
|---|---|
| Sunrise will make the final approval about your proposed sites and may suggest alternate locations based on our marketing formula, which has worked successfully in the past. As far as financial requirements, you must have a minimum net worth of $350,000, and you also will need minimum unencumbered assets of between $120,000 and $265,000. You may not finance more than two-thirds of the initial investment to open the store. You must also have access to financing in the range of $170,000 to $340,000 (assuming that you finance two-thirds of the initial investment costs). Confirmation of loan, terms, and collateral is required. You will need to show that you can maintain an outside income of at least 80 percent of your present income for a period of at least two years to show that you have adequate financial stability as you get your business started. You will need to show that your liquid assets are available for investment and operations of your new Sunrise Greeting Cards and Flowers shop, and the capital must be from your personal assets; capital in a current business will not be recognized as available to a new store. Sunrise does not provide loans. | **Financial Requirements & Financing**<br>Owning a Sunrise shop requires a strong financial position and evidence of the ability to finance a new business.<br><br>**Financial Requirements.** Sunrise seeks franchise owners who are in a financially sound position. The minimum requirements include a total net worth of $350,000, with unencumbered liquid assets of between $120,000 and $265,000. You will need to show that these liquid assets are personal rather than capital in a current business and available for investment in your Sunrise store. You will also need to show that you can maintain an outside income of at least 80 percent of your present income for at least two years.<br><br>**Financing.** You are required to finance less than two-thirds of the initial investment costs. Assuming that you finance up to two-thirds of the initial investment costs, you will need access to financing in the range of $170,000 to $340,000. Confirmation of loan, terms, and collateral is required. Sunrise does not provide loans. |
| This paragraph is 198 words with far too many numbers. Many readers would have a hard time locating the key information. | Visually, these paragraphs are far more appealing and inviting. The headings immediately orient the reader to the content. |

**TABLE 6.17**

Applying Formatting to Key Words and Phrases

| Less Effective | More Effective |
|---|---|
| *Sunrise will work directly with you to create a marketing plan, budgeting plan, and break-even analysis.* | *Sunrise will work directly with you* to create a marketing plan, budgeting plan, and break-even analysis. |
| By italicizing everything, nothing is highlighted. | By italicizing one short phrase, you emphasize it. |
| Sunrise will provide **free training** for up to three people for each new store. | Sunrise will provide **free training** for up to three people for each new store. |
| Applying two formatting features (bold and underlining) may appear overbearing. | Applying one formatting feature (bold) is sufficient to highlight the phrase. |

## Use Bulleted and Numbered Lists

You will often use lists in business writing. When you set these items apart with bullets or numbers, your readers notice and remember the items more easily (see Table 6.18).

## Use White Space Generously

Your readers will form an immediate impression about your document based on how much white space (areas without text) it has. Documents with too much text and not

**TABLE 6.18**

Using Bulleted and Numbered Lists

| Less Effective | More Effective |
|---|---|
| The brochure for prospective franchisees should first and foremost show how committed we are to the success of the franchisee. We can do this by providing a warm and inviting message from Stephanie on the front of the brochure. Then we should provide basic information that all prospective franchisees would be interested in, such as information about initial investment costs and profit potential, financial requirements and financing, our involvement in opening a new franchise store, and the application process. We should also have a section about our commitment to their success after they open a store. | The brochure for prospective franchisees should accomplish two main goals: (1) show our commitment to the success of franchisees and (2) provide basic information about becoming a franchisee. The brochure should contain the following sections:<br><br>• Opening letter from Stephanie.<br>• Initial investment costs and profit potential.<br>• Financial requirements and financing.<br>• Sunrise involvement in opening a new franchise store.<br>• Sunrise support after opening a store.<br>• Application process. |
| Without bullets, this paragraph contains a lot of items that are difficult for the reader to remember. Furthermore, it takes longer for the reader to visualize the components of the brochure. | With bullets, this paragraph allows the reader to rapidly process the information and visualize the components of the brochure. Furthermore, the use of enumeration and bullets more clearly distinguishes the overarching goals of the brochure and the components of the brochure. |

enough white look daunting or cluttered. On the other hand, documents with too much white space may look insufficient. Many students are trained in the university setting to double-space documents. In the workplace, double-spaced documents are rare, however.

### Keep It Simple

Visual appeal is not the first consideration for most written business communications. Rather, the goal is to get your message across in an easy-to-read manner. As you design your document, focus first on easy navigation for your reader. Avoid formatting features that distract from the main message. See Figure 6.3 for effective use of navigational features and white space.

## Reviewing Your Message

You will recall from Chapter 5 that expert business writers use their time differently than do average business writers (see Figure 5.2 in Chapter 5). They devote more time to planning and reviewing and proportionately less time to drafting. They spend most of their time—before and after drafting—carefully thinking about how the message will influence and affect others.

Many business professionals get anxious to send their messages as soon as they finish drafting them. It is human nature to want to move on to the next task. Resist the urge to move on without carefully reviewing your messages. During the reviewing stage, you will improve your message, making it far more successful. You will also minimize the possibility of embarrassing and damaging mistakes.

The reviewing process includes three interrelated components: conducting the FAIR test, proofreading, and getting feedback (not generally needed for routine messages). These reviewing components ensure that you show fairness, get the message right, avoid errors, and get perspectives from trusted colleagues. For short, routine messages (one to four paragraphs), expert business writers can

**LO6.3** Describe and apply the components of the reviewing stage, including a FAIR test, proofreading, and feedback.

# TECHNOLOGY TIPS

## USING SPELLING AND GRAMMAR CHECKS

Most word processing software programs contain spelling and grammar checks to help you avoid misspellings and grammatical mistakes. Many of these programs, such as Microsoft Word, also have tools to evaluate writing style and ease of reading. Typically, these tools are not set by default. You will need to manually select them. (In Microsoft Word, you can access these additional tools by changing settings in the *Proofing* area of *Word Options*.)

When you run spelling and grammar checks, you can review your document sentence by sentence for passive voice, noun clusters, and other elements. Once you finish the check, you will see a final calculation of readability statistics. Keep in mind that the software is not perfect. Generally, however, it will help you improve your writing style.

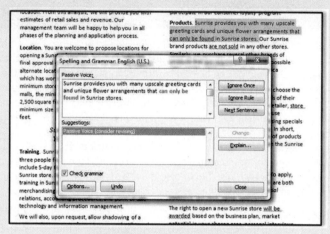

*Source:* Microsoft Office Word 2007

*Source:* Microsoft Office Word 2007

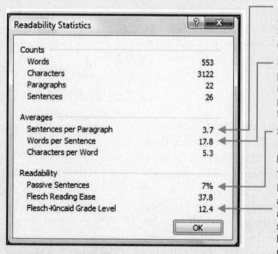

*Source:* Microsoft Office Word 2007

Should aim for 3 to 5 sentences in analytical business messages; 1 to 3 sentences in routine emails and digital communications.

Should aim for fewer than 20 words per sentence in analytical business messages and fewer than 15 words per sentence in routine, straightforward business messages.

Should generally aim for less than 15 percent of all sentences to be passive sentences.

The Flesch Reading Ease and Flesch-Kincaid Grade Level scores are calculated based on word length and sentence length. Typically, you should aim for Flesch-Kincaid Grade Level scores of 10 or less for routine messages and 12 or less for more analytical business messages.

**FIGURE 6.3**

Stephanie's Final, Easier-to-Read Brochure (compare to original version in Figure 6.1)

| Statistical Comparison of Original and Final Versions of Brochure | | |
|---|---|---|
| | Original Version | Revised Version |
| Paragraphs (#) | 8 | 21 |
| Longest Paragraph | 216 words | 95 words |
| Average Paragraph Length | 143 words | 55 words |
| Average Sentence Length | 23 words | 15 words |

## Owning a Franchise

*Sunrise Greeting Cards and Flowers*

Hello Potential *Sunrise* Shop Owner!

Would you like to own and run one of the most exciting businesses—providing happy customers with cards and flowers for those special occasions?

As a Sunrise store owner, you would be in a business with loyal customers who appreciate refined and excellent craftsmanship. They expect creative, original, and upscale greeting cards and flower arrangements, and Sunrise delivers. To our customers, our brand represents quality products that help them celebrate special occasions.

When you own a Sunrise store, you tap into a brand that provides profitability, and you also become part of the Sunrise family. We provide you with the products and resources to succeed. We create a tight-knit group of store owners and managers who share ideas about improving our brand and sales performance. To help make this happen, we organize a fun-filled annual retreat where store owners and managers can discuss our shared problems, solutions, and opportunities. We build success together.

In this brochure, you'll find basic answers to your questions about investment costs and profit potential; financial requirements and financing; Sunrise involvement in opening your store; Sunrise commitment to your success after you open your store; and the application process.

I will always be willing to personally answer your questions and explain the wonderful benefits of running a Sunrise business. Please call me or email me anytime to chat about your future with Sunrise!

*Stephanie*
Stephanie Jorgenson, President and Owner
Sunrise Greeting Cards and Flowers, LLC
Stephanie@sunrisegiftcards.com
1-800-SUN-SET9

### *Initial Investment Costs & Profit Potential*

Initial investment costs for Sunrise shops are comparable to other franchises in the industry, yet average profits from our shops exceed industry averages by 20 to 50 percent.

**Initial Investment Costs.\*** The initial investment typically ranges from $290,000 to $605,000. The table below shows ranges for the initial investment costs.

| | Low | High |
|---|---|---|
| Fixtures | $ 60,000 | $ 90,000 |
| Inventory | 80,000 | 190,000 |
| Store Improvements | 20,000 | 130,000 |
| Retail Equipment | 20,000 | 35,000 |
| Miscellaneous | 10,000 | 30,000 |
| Initial Franchise Fee | 50,000 | 50,000 |
| **Total Initial Costs** | **$240,000** | **$525,000** |
| Plus Working Capital | $ 50,000 | $ 80,000 |
| **Total Required Capital** | **$290,000** | **$605,000** |

*\*See our website, sunrisegiftcards.com/franchisees, for detailed information about these expenses.*

**Profit Potential.** Currently, average annual profit per Sunrise store is $153,000, with ranges between $49,000 and $215,000. Profit level depends on many factors, including location, market demand, square footage, and management. Typically, profits become relatively stable after the first three years of operation.

### *Financial Requirements & Financing*

Owning a Sunrise shop requires a strong financial position and evidence of the ability to finance a new business.

**Financial Requirements.** Sunrise seeks franchise owners who are in a financially sound position. The minimum requirements include a total net worth of $350,000, with unencumbered liquid assets of between $120,000 and $265,000. You will need to show that these liquid assets are personal rather than capital in a current business and available for investment in your Sunrise store. You will also need to show that you can maintain an outside income of at least 80 percent of your present income for at least two years.

often check for fairness and proofread in just a few minutes. For long, important messages, such as business proposals or business plans, the reviewing stage may take weeks or months.

## Conduct a FAIR Test

In Chapter 1, we introduced the FAIR test as a way of ensuring ethical business communication. Of course, you will consider such issues during the planning and writing stages. Also, during the review process you can also take the time to think about the degree to which your entire message conforms to standards for facts, access, impacts, and respect. For important messages—particularly those that involve complicated business issues—apply the FAIR test:

- *Facts:* Are you confident in your facts? Are your assumptions clear? Have you avoided slanting the facts or made other logical errors?
- *Access:* Have you granted enough access to message recipients about decision making and information? Have you granted enough access to the message recipients to provide input? Are you open about your motives, or do you have a hidden agenda?
- *Impacts:* Have you thought about how the message will impact various stakeholders? Have you evaluated impacts on others from ethical, corporate, and legal perspectives?
- *Respect:* Have you demonstrated respect for the inherent worth of others: their aspirations, thoughts, feelings, and well-being? Have you shown that you value others?

## Proofread

Proofreading involves rereading your entire document to make sure it is influential and accurate. You might consider rereading each sentence several times, each time with a different focus. On your first pass, place yourself in the position of your audience members. Imagine how they will respond. On your second pass, check for problems with writing style and language mechanics.

## Get Feedback

As one business writing expert stated, one of the best ways to ensure that your communication is effective and fair is to get feedback from others:

> Ask some people whose judgment you respect to give it a test read and get their reaction. Do they think it's too energetic or hyperbolic for the audience and the occasion? Or is it too frosty? Similarly, do they think the writing is too distant or too familiar? What are the offending words or phrases? How can they be changed to do the job at hand? Using test readers is hardly rocket science, but those willing to go through this trouble invariably produce more effective writing.[6]

This advice reveals an important point: Your trusted colleagues are giving your message a trial run—trying to simulate how the intended message recipient will respond. As they review your message, they can provide insights about making it better. Before they begin to read, ask them to consider whether you have framed the idea correctly, whether the business logic holds up, whether the message has the intended effects, whether the tone is appropriate, and so on. Effective business communicators make a habit of getting this advance feedback for important messages. In the Communication Q&A with Ronald Scott, you can learn more about the importance of clarity, tone, and accuracy in business writing.

# COMMUNICATION Q&A

### CONVERSATIONS WITH CURRENT BUSINESS PROFESSIONALS

**Pete Cardon: How important are writing skills in the workplace?**

**Ronald Scott:** They are vital. Members of my staff are regularly required to take complex and technical ordinance language and explain it in plain terms to citizens or customers. This requires the ability to capture the essence and translate it into simple language that the customer can understand and act on. In today's workplace, having good writing skills is an asset that will distinguish an employee from his or her peers. One of the first opportunities an employer has to assess writing skills is when he or she reviews an application for employment or a résumé. A basic review of these two documents can either thoroughly impress or completely horrify a potential employer.

**PC: How much time do you spend writing? What types of writing?**

**RS:** I spend approximately half my time writing. Examples include writing emails; drafting letters to customers, citizens, and businesses; drafting letters to local, state, and federal officials; reviewing and correcting written documents and reports prepared by staff; creating policy and procedure manuals; creating form letters; creating grant application and grant documents; and creating budget documents and periodic budget reports.

**PC: How formal is business writing?**

**RS:** Typically, business writing is a formal means of communication. Recently, one of my employees wrote a letter to a customer he knew quite well. After his salutation he wrote, "How are you doing today? I hope you are doing well and that you are feeling better." While this language may have been acceptable for an in-person exchange, it seemed too casual and inappropriate for a business letter.

**PC: What kinds of writing mistakes do you see most often in the workplace? How damaging are these mistakes? Could you give a recent example?**

**RS:** In my profession we often communicate with large businesses about the cost of development permits for large projects. Some permit fees can be in excess of $50,000. A missing zero in a letter estimating permit fees can make a big difference when a business is preparing its budget. Recently, an employee addressed a letter to a customer about a code violation. He wrote, "You will not need a building permit to complete this work." He intended to write, "You will need a building permit to complete this work." What a difference one word made. Some delicate negotiations were necessary to make the situation right with that customer.

**PC: How is writing in the workplace different from writing for school projects?**

**RS:** Business writing requires you to maintain business relationships (even when giving bad news), build and maintain company loyalty and morale, retain customers/clients, and portray a positive image for yourself and your company. Academic writing focuses more on its subject than on the reader's reactions or on the goal of cultivating a long relationship with the reader. When writing for business purposes, we need to make sure we do not hamper business transactions and workflow due to misuse of language, inappropriate expressions and emotions, or lack of empathy.

***Ronald Scott*** *has been the chief development officer at Eau Claire Cooperative Health Centers and the director of community development for Lexington County in South Carolina. He is currently a juris doctor candidate at the University of South Carolina.*

Courtesy of Ronald Scott

# Chapter Takeaway for *Improving Readability with Style and Design*

**LO6.1 Describe and apply the following principles of writing style that improve ease of reading: completeness, conciseness, and natural processing. (pp. 170–182)**

| Improving Ease of Reading with Writing Style | | |
|---|---|---|
| **Completeness** | **Conciseness** | **Natural Style** |
| • Provide all relevant information.<br>• Be accurate.<br>• Be specific. | • Control paragraph length.<br>• Use short sentences.<br>• Avoid redundancy.<br>• Avoid empty phrases.<br>• Avoid wordy prepositional phrases. | • Use action verbs when possible.<br>• Use active voice.<br>• Use short and familiar words and phrases.<br>• Use parallel language.<br>• Avoid buzzwords and figures of speech.<br>• Avoid *it is/there are*. |

See *examples of writing style improvements* in Tables 6.1 through 6.15.

**LO6.2 Explain and use navigational design to improve ease of reading. (pp. 182–185)**

| Improving Ease of Reading with Navigational Design | | |
|---|---|---|
| • Headings<br>• Highlighting | • Lists<br>• White space | • Simplicity |

See *examples of navigational design* in Tables 6.16 through 6.18.

**LO6.3 Describe and apply the components of the reviewing stage, including a FAIR test, proofreading, and feedback. (pp. 185–189)**

**FAIR Test:** Evaluate your message in terms of facts, access, impacts, and respect.
**Proofreading:** Ask trusted colleagues to review your message for effectiveness and accuracy.
**Feedback:** For important messages, ask trusted colleagues to give input about effectiveness and fairness.

# Discussion Exercises

**6.1 Chapter Review Questions** (LO6.1, LO6.2, LO6.3)

Answer the following questions:

A. How does complete writing improve ease of reading?

B. How does concise writing improve ease of reading?

C. How does natural writing improve ease of reading?

D. How does document design improve ease of reading?

E. Do you think that complete and concise writing are competing goals? Explain.

**6.2 Communication Q&A Discussion Questions** (LO6.1)

Answer the following questions based on the comments from Ronald Scott in the Communication Q&A:

A. What does Scott say about the importance of writing? What are several examples he provides to illustrate his points?

B. Based on his statements, what are a few guidelines for determining if your writing is formal enough but not too formal?

C. What does he say about the importance of accuracy in writing?

D. What are some distinctions he makes between academic and business writing?

E. Scott advises young professionals to take writing seriously. What are a few ways you can do that?

# Evaluation Exercises

**6.3 Analyzing a Corporate Message** (LO6.1, LO6.2)

In July 2015, Stephen Elop announced major changes at Microsoft. Read the message at http://news.microsoft.com/2014/07/17/stephen-elops-email-to-employees/.

Analyze this message for ease of reading in the following ways:

A. Identify and revise five sentences that are not complete.

B. Identify and revise five sentences that are not concise.

C. Identify and revise five sentences that are not natural.

D. Explain three strategies for designing the document for faster navigation.

E. Revise the document. Attempt to cut the length in half. Use headings and other design features to improve navigation.

**6.4 Identifying Areas for Personal Improvement** (LO6.1, LO6.2)

Identify three writing principles from this chapter that you most need to work on. For each principle, write a paragraph about why you want to improve in this area and how you will go about doing it. Choose from the following writing principles: be specific; be accurate; control paragraph length; use short sentences in most cases; avoid redundancy; avoid empty phrases; avoid wordy phrases; use action verbs when possible; use active voice; use short and familiar words and phrases; use parallel language; avoid buzzwords and figures of speech; avoid *it is* and *there are*; use headings; apply formatting to key words and phrases; use bulleted and numbered lists; use white space generously.

# Application Exercises

**Case for Exercises 6.5 through 6.18: Promoting the Supply Chain Management Club**

Your roommate is the president of the Supply Chain Management Club. She wants you to help her revise a flyer that she has drafted to attract more members. Here is her draft.

Joining a Student Club

Have you thought about joining a student club? If so, we are organizing an information session to orient you to our club.

The purpose of the Supply Chain Management Club (SCMC) that we have here on campus is to support Supply Chain and Operations Management (SCOM) majors as well as other interested majors if they choose to gain a broader and balanced understanding of the opportunities, career paths, trends, and current burning issues in global supply chain management. Each and every semester, SCMC has facility tours, discussion panels, faculty interactions, and résumé workshops in order for our members to gain a glimpse into the real world of global supply chain management and the nature of this constantly evolving and developing business field.

There are many, many reasons for being an SCMC member. It goes without saying that many of you want financial aid, and SCMC has received boatloads of generous donations to offer scholarships for qualifying SCMC students. All SCMC club members learn to market themselves more effectively by joining the club. There is an SCMC Placement Coordinator specifically directed to search for every possible job that you could apply for, and these jobs are placed on the SCMC website where you can view them anytime and anywhere. These jobs are in a plethora of industries, like Business Services, Consumer Products and Services, Food and Beverage, Health, Industrial, Public Sector, and Technology and Communications. Also, through SCMC and by also gaining a membership in ISM, certification opportunities will be at your fingertips. The sky's the limit in this club. SCMC board members are currently looking for new opportunities and are researching the potential of funding future group workshops and certification programs that we haven't had access to in the past.

The most popular part of the club that students like the most are the abundant events that are scheduled. Plant tours and speeches by supply chain professionals are constantly being scheduled for SCMC club members to attend. These events create a big impact on your future career by giving you the opportunities to gain exposure to real-world professionals. One of the great opportunities you have as a member in the club is the opportunity to be in touch with the SCMC alumni group, which gives you a networking chance with people already working in supply chain management.

There are many opportunities to learn special skills since there are special-interest groups within the club. For example, there is a special-interest group devoted to learning about various software tools for global supply chain management. In the software group, you can learn statistical software programs such as POM for Windows, Excel Solver, ProcessModel, and SPSS as well as learning mapping software such as MapPoint. Skills acquired in these special-interest groups can be placed on your résumé in conjunction with other skills developed in your studies from the SCOM major. It can't be stated enough how much these extra skills can enhance your qualifications to be a supply chain manager.

The Supply Chain Management Club (SCMC) is designed to help club members understand the critical and essential organizational function of global supply chain and operations management that creates and distributes products and services; measures their quality and instigates the processes whereby quality improvement occurs; and simultaneously creates nimble, streamlined, and efficient business processes and supply chains. This critical business function is responsible for short-term survival and long-term profitability and growth of the organization in all types of businesses, such as large or small, manufacturing or service, or even for-profit or nonprofit. In today's globally interconnected economy, prowess in global supply chain and operations management is the benchmark of the great manufacturers, retailers, and major companies, such as Dell, Walmart, Southwest Airlines, Toyota, and Bank of America. Supply chain management is the fundamental competency that determines success in today's business world, and by joining the SCMC club, you literally have success in your hands since so many major businesses will need your services.

The Supply Chain Management Club (SCMC) is extremely practical with many career options in global manufacturing firms in production, purchasing, quality control, distribution and supply chain management; in service firms as general operations management and logistics/supply chain management; and in consulting firms as business process and quality improvement consultants. In fact, even if you are pursuing other professions as primary careers, SCOM skills and competencies make one a better accountant, better at financial analysis, better as marketing manager, or even better at managing human resources or managing information technology for a company.

The club is affiliated with the Institute for Supply Chain Management (ISM), which was founded in the year 1915 and is the biggest supply chain management association in the world and is recognized by supply chain professionals far and wide as the repository of best practices in the field. The ISM website can be visited at the following website: www.ism.ws/.

A pizza party will be held in the business building on January 29 to introduce you to the club. This meeting will provide a lot of information about reasons for joining the club.

All of our regular meetings are at the Marriott next to the business school. A speech is always *given by an important industry professional. Dinner is served at just $10.*

Rewrite each of the following sentences from her draft to be complete, concise, and natural. The sentences are organized by principles from the chapter; however, note that many sentences contain additional style issues for you to correct. Make reasonable embellishments as necessary.

**6.5  Be Specific** (LO6.1)

A. Have you thought about joining a student club? If so, we are organizing an information session to orient you to our club.

B. A pizza party will be held in the business building on January 29 to introduce you to the club.

C. This meeting will provide a lot of information about reasons for joining the club.

D. All of our regular meetings are at the Marriott next to the business school.

**6.6  Be Accurate** (LO6.1)

A. Supply chain management is the fundamental competency that determines success in today's business world, and by joining the SCMC club, you literally have success in your hands since so many major businesses will need your services.

B. All SCMC club members learn to market themselves more effectively by joining the club.

**6.7  Use Short Sentences in Most Cases** (LO6.1)

Cut these sentences by more than 50 percent. Use more than one sentence if necessary.

A. The purpose of the Supply Chain Management Club (SCMC) that we have here on campus is to support Supply Chain and Operations Management (SCOM) majors as well as other interested majors if they choose to gain a broader and balanced understanding of the opportunities, career paths, trends, and current burning issues in global supply chain management.

B. The Supply Chain Management Club (SCMC) is designed to help club members understand the critical and essential organizational function of global supply chain and operations management that creates and distributes products and services; measures their quality and instigates the processes whereby quality improvement occurs; and simultaneously creates nimble, streamlined, and efficient business processes and supply chains.

C. This critical business function is responsible for short-term survival and long-term profitability and growth of the organization in all types of businesses, such as large or small, manufacturing or service, or even for-profit or nonprofit.

**6.8  Avoid Redundancy** (LO6.1)

Remove redundancies and shorten these sentences.

A. Each and every semester, SCMC has facility tours, discussion panels, faculty interactions, and résumé workshops in order for our members to gain a glimpse into the real world of global supply chain management and the nature of this constantly evolving and developing business field.

B. There is an SCMC Placement Coordinator specifically directed to search for every possible job that you could apply for, and these jobs are placed on the SCMC website where you can view them anytime and anywhere.

C. The most popular part of the club that students like the most are the abundant events that are scheduled.

**6.9  Avoid Empty Phrases** (LO6.1)

Remove empty phrases and shorten these sentences.

A. It goes without saying that many of you want financial aid.

B. It can't be stated enough how much these extra skills can enhance your qualifications to be a supply chain manager.

**6.10  Avoid Wordy Prepositional Phrases** (LO6.1)

Rewrite these sentences to reduce wordy prepositional phrases.

A. Skills acquired in these special-interest groups can be placed on your résumé in conjunction with other skills developed in your studies from the SCOM major.

B. One of the great opportunities you have as a member in the club is the opportunity to be in touch with the SCMC alumni group, which gives you a networking chance with people already working in supply chain management.

**6.11  Use Action Verbs When Possible** (LO6.1)

Rewrite these sentences to include action verbs.

A. The Supply Chain Management Club (SCMC) is extremely practical with many career options.

B. These events create a big impact on your future career by giving you the opportunities to gain exposure to real-world professionals.

**6.12  Use Active Voice** (LO6.1)

Rewrite these sentences to use active voice instead of passive.

A. Plant tours and speeches by supply chain professionals are constantly being scheduled for SCMC club members to attend.

B. A speech is always given by an important industry professional.

**6.13  Use Short and Familiar Words and Phrases** (LO6.1)

Replace uncommon words with familiar words and phrases.

A. These jobs are in a plethora of industries.

B. In today's globally interconnected economy, prowess in global supply chain and operations management is the benchmark of the great manufacturers, retailers, and major companies, such as Dell, Walmart, Southwest Airlines, Toyota, and Bank of America.

**6.14  Use Parallel Language** (LO6.1)

Rewrite these sentences so the language is parallel.

A. SCOM skills and competencies make one a better accountant, better at financial analysis, better as marketing manager, or even better at managing human resources or managing information technology for a company.

B. In the software group, you can learn statistical software programs such as POM for Windows, Excel Solver, ProcessModel, and SPSS as well as learning mapping software such as MapPoint.

**6.15 Avoid Buzzwords and Figures of Speech** (LO6.1)

Rewrite these sentences to eliminate buzzwords and figures of speech.

A. Also, through SCMC and by also gaining a membership in ISM, certification opportunities will be at your fingertips.

B. The sky's the limit in this club.

C. SCMC has received boatloads of generous donations to offer scholarships for qualifying SCMC students.

**6.16 Avoid *It Is* and *There Is/Are*** (LO6.1)

Rewrite these sentences to improve clarity.

A. There are many opportunities to learn special skills since there are special-interest groups within the club.

B. There is a special-interest group devoted to learning about various software tools for global supply chain management.

**6.17 Setting Up Effective Navigational Design** (LO6.2)

A. If you were going to use headings in this document, how would you group sections? What headings would you use?

B. Which parts of the document would you consider converting to bulleted or numbered lists?

C. What other strategies would you consider for making the document easy to navigate?

**6.18 Revising the Supply Chain Management Club Flyer** (LO6.1, LO6.2)

Revise the entire student club flyer. Create an effective flyer to help promote the Supply Chain Management Club. Make sure the document is as easy to read as possible while retaining all relevant information.

**6.19 Converting the Sunrise Brochure into a Frequently Asked Questions Document** (LO6.1, LO6.2)

Convert the Sunrise brochure into a Frequently Asked Questions document. Assume that you will place it on the Sunrise website.

**Case for Problems 6.20 and 6.21: Expressing Interest as a Prospective Sunrise Franchise Owner**

Stephanie recently gave Jenny Li one of the franchise brochures while at an industry exhibition. Jenny Li was eager to learn more about franchise opportunities with Sunrise. She wrote the following letter to introduce herself and describe her qualifications.

---

Dear Stephanie,

It was an honor to meet you at the Flower Exhibition. It is with great interest that I write this letter to describe my genuine hopes to be a franchisee. There are many reasons why I am interested in this opportunity, and there are many reasons why I am qualified to be a franchisee for you. I have been in the flower industry for over twelve years in various capacities such as starting as a flower deliverer, then I acted as a flower arranger, and finally for the last eight years I was the shop manager for a flower shop in the mall. In my time as a shop manager, I was told by the shop owner and dozens of employees that I was the right person to lead the shop and that sales were higher at my location than any other shop in that chain (which has 18 shops at malls in my state and the three surrounding states). In fact, sales at my shop have increased every quarter that I have been the shop manager with the exception of just two quarters in the eight years of my stewardship. I am very proactive in my approach to sales and think that my approach of keeping repeat customers happy is the key to success at my shop and which I seek to continue as a franchisee. I have used so many marketing techniques to gain our customers' attention. Such as, I have created a Facebook group and I send specials to the people in that group. Not to mention I send targeted coupons by mail and email that are sent to the customers with specific types of interests. There is no substitute for knowing your customers. I also do many great special events at seasonal periods and have won prizes for flower arrangements many times that bring the shop good press. My flower arrangements were even featured in some TV commercials for the flower shops across our region. There are not any Sunrise stores near here and I believe from the bottom of my heart that this is the right time to invest in this area. I know without any doubt that you will be impressed with my work ethic and my focus on the customer. Needless to say, the customer is king, and we need to treat them that way. I am capable of meeting all of the financial obligations. Thank you and hope to hear from you soon. Most of all, is I love people, and if you are caring for your customers, you will achieve your goals and reach the pinnacle of success.

Regards,

Jenny

---

**6.20 Revising a Message for Readability** (LO6.1, LO6.2)

Analyze this message for ease of reading in the following ways:

A. Identify and revise five sentences that are not complete.

B. Identify and revise five sentences that are not concise.

C. Identify and revise five sentences that are not natural.

D. Explain three strategies for designing the document for faster navigation.

**6.21 Rewriting a Message for Readability and Effectiveness** (LO6.1, LO6.2, LO6.3)

Rewrite the entire document. Ensure that the message is easy to read and effectively highlights Jenny's potential for owning and running a Sunrise franchise.

Use the following table with statistics about the cereal industry[7] for Problems 6.22 through 6.33. In some cases, you will need to carefully review the information in the table to get the correct answers.

## Comparisons between Kellogg Company and General Mills

| | Kellogg Company (K) | General Mills (GM) |
|---|---|---|
| **Top-Selling Cereal** | Special K | Cheerios |
| **Market Share in Cereal Industry** | 34 percent | 31 percent |
| **Number of Employees** | 30,900 | 33,000 |
| **Headquarters** | Battle Creek, Michigan | Minneapolis, Minnesota |
| **CEO Annual Salary** | $11.5 million | $11.1 million |
| **Main Products** | Ready-to-eat cereals, cookies, toaster pastries, cereal bars, frozen waffles, and meat alternatives | Ready-to-eat cereals, yogurt, ready-to-serve soup, dry dinners, frozen vegetables, dough products, baking mixes, frozen pizza, snacks |
| **Newly Introduced Products** | Special K crackers, fruit crisps, and chocolate pretzel bars. New Special K flavors such as cinnamon pecan, fruit and nut clusters, and blueberry | Chocolate Cheerios, Yoplait Delights yogurt parfaits, Wanchai Ferry frozen foods, Betty Crocker gluten-free dessert mixes, new Häagen-Dazs ice cream flavors |
| **North American Revenues** | 67.7 percent of total revenues | 81.6 percent of total revenues |
| **Worldwide Revenues** | $12.5 billion | $14.8 billion |
| **Worldwide Advertising Expenses** | $1.1 billion | $908 million |
| **Net Sales Percentage to Walmart** | 44 percent | 30 percent |
| **Negative Media Attention** | Product recalls due to potential salmonella contamination | Ammonia leaks at its manufacturing facilities |
| **Least Nutritious Children's Cereals (NPI is a nutritional ranking for cereals ranging from 34 [worst] to 72 [best] and issued by the Rudd Center.)** | Corn Pops (NPI: 35.8); Froot Loops (NPI: 38.0); Apple Jacks (NPI: 40.0) | Reese's Puffs (34.0); Golden Grahams (36.0); Lucky Charms (36.0); Cinnamon Toast Crunch (36.6); Trix (38.0); Count Chocula (38.0) |
| **Yogurt Sales** | N/A | General Mills yogurt brands include Yoplait, Trix, Yoplait Kids, Go-GURT, Fiber One, YoPlus, and Whips! Approximately $1.5 billion in yogurt sales |

Other statistics about the breakfast cereal industry:

- Approximately two-thirds of all cereals are sold with a deal (discounts, coupons).
- The total cereal market in the United States is approximately $9 billion.
- Gross profit margins in the breakfast cereal industry average between 40 percent and 45 percent.
- The global cereal market is approximately $28.7 billion.
- The ten cereals most marketed on TV to children are the following (company and percentage of sugar content displayed in parentheses): 1. Cinnamon Toast Crunch (GM; 33 percent); 2. Honey Nut Cheerios (GM; 32 percent); 3. Lucky Charms (GM; 41 percent); 4. Cocoa Puffs (GM; 44 percent); 5. Trix (GM; 38 percent); 6. Frosted Flakes (K; 37 percent); 7. Fruity and Cocoa Pebbles (Post; 37 percent); 8. Reese's Puffs (GM; 41 percent); 9. Corn Pops (K; 41 percent); 10. Froot Loops (K; 41 percent).

**6.22 Being Accurate** (LO6.1)

Use the preceding table to proofread the following items and correct them as needed.

A. Please address correspondence to the following address: General Mills, PO Box 1493, Minneapolis, MI.

B. The annually salary for General Mills' CEO is higher than that of Kellogg Company's CEO by approximately $400 thousand.

C. With nearly half of their net sales to Walmart, General Mills and Kellogg Company are extremely dependent on a single retailer.

D. General Mills has six children's cereals with NPI rankings below 40, whereas Kellogg's has just three.

E. General Mills spends approximately 8.1 percent of its total revenues on advertising, whereas Kellogg Company spends roughly 8.8 percent of its total revenues on advertising.

F. Kellogg's children's cereals are the least nutritious cereals in the industry.

G. Since only about one in four boxes of cereal is sold without deals of some kind, cereal producers must constantly market new and exciting discounts and coupons.

H. General Mills reached $1.5 million in yogurt sales last year.

I. One of Kellogg Company's worst negative publicity resulted from ammonia leaks at some its manufacturing facilities.

J. The United States cereal market accounts for approximately 35.1 percent of the world market.

**6.23 Being Specific** (LO6.1)

Use information from the preceding table to revise the following sentences and make them more specific.

A. General Mills markets through television to children far more than other cereal makers.

B. Gross profit margins in the breakfast cereal industry are quite high.

C. Kellogg's Company and General Mills have each experienced negative media attention recently.

D. General Mills is more dependent on the North American market than Kellogg Company.

E. While General Mills and Kellogg Company have similar product mixes, they each market several products not offered by the other.

F. Kellogg Company and General Mills are the top two cereal makers.

G. Kellogg Company and General Mills have each introduced new flavors for their products in recent years.

H. General Mills offers the least nutritious children's cereal on the market.

I. Kellogg's cereals include three children's cereals with NPI scores at 40 or below: Corn Pops, Froot Loops, and Apple Jack's.

**6.24 Using Short Sentences in Most Cases** (LO6.1)

Revise each of the following items to make the sentences shorter and more readable.

A. General Mills is a dominant player in the American yogurt industry with $1.5 billion in sales, and it sells yogurts under a variety of brands, including Yoplait, Trix, Yoplait Kids, Go-GURT, Fiber One, Whips!, and YoPlus.

B. The two cereal giants, Kellogg Company and General Mills, do not remain complacent with their existing products lines but rather routinely develop and market new products—after all, Kellogg Company has recently introduced new products such as Special K crackers, fruit crisps, and chocolate pretzel bars, and General Mills has recently added new products such as Chocolate Cheerios, Yoplait Delights yogurt parfaits, Wanchai Ferry frozen foods, and Betty Crocker gluten-free dessert mixes.

C. The total cereal market in the United States is $9 billion, which is just a small and decreasing portion—31.4 percent—of the worldwide market, which is seeing robust growth in the BRIC countries of Brazil, Russia, India, and China.

**6.25 Avoid Redundancy** (LO6.1)

Revise each of the following sentences to eliminate redundancy.

A. Discount coupons for select Kellogg's cereals contain rebates of between 10 and 20 percent that can save you money.

B. Kellogg Company definitely needs to view crisis communications for the salmonella outbreak as absolutely necessary.

C. Please make advance reservations for the bloggers conference hosted at General Mills to see how you can connect and cooperate together with other corporate bloggers.

**6.26 Avoid Empty Phrases** (LO6.1)

Revise each of the following items to eliminate empty phrases.

A. Needless to say, General Mills is by all accounts among the worst offenders of marketing less healthy cereals to children.

B. In my personal opinion, Kellogg's children's cereals are in a very real sense superior to General Mills in terms of nutritional value.

C. The point I am trying to make is that parents, for all intents and purposes, are usually unaware of how unhealthy most children's cereals are.

**6.27 Avoid Wordy Prepositional Phrases** (LO6.1)

Revise each of the following items to eliminate wordy prepositional phrases.

A. In view of the recent rankings about nutritional values for cereals, I think we should focus for the next product development cycle on a reduction in sugar content and an increase in fiber content.

B. For companies in the food industry, a heavy proportion of sales to Walmart provides advantages in terms of higher revenues and a boost in name recognition but disadvantages in terms of lower margins on sales and reduction in customer perceptions of quality.

C. In light of the product recalls in recent times, Kellogg Company is in no position to tout a reputation for food safety.

### 6.28 Use Action Verbs When Possible (LO6.1)

Improve each of the following sentences by using action verbs.

A. Kellogg Company has new product developments and marketing efforts as part of its rebranding strategy that demonstrates a healthy-food focus.

B. General Mills is a company with strong yogurt brand, and it is in a position of leverage in this regard to achieve higher visibility for healthy foods.

C. The CEO of Kellogg will provide an announcement about new corporate strategy, give his explanation for how the company will reach its goals, and do a presentation about the current financial situation.

### 6.29 Use Active Voice (LO6.1)

Revise each of the following sentences to switch them from passive to active voice.

A. The NPI rankings were widely publicized in media outlets and were a cause for concern among many cereal executives.

B. The new Special K flavors—cinnamon pecan, fruit and nut clusters, and blueberry—were introduced last year, and Kellogg reports that they have been a huge success.

C. Market strategies to promote healthier cereals were the focus of discussions among industry insiders.

D. Your inaction in confronting the potential salmonella contamination lost us millions of dollars in revenues.

E. Quick crisis communications were the key to General Mills quickly eliminating negative press about the ammonia leaks.

### 6.30 Use Short and Familiar Words and Phrases (LO6.1)

Revise the following sentences to eliminate unnecessarily long and/or unfamiliar words and phrases.

A. General Mills has abated the public's denouncements of its high-sugar children's cereals by curtailing sugar content by 8 percent on average.

B. The preeminent cereal brands for the dominant duo of cereal makers, Kellogg Company and General Mills, are Special K and Cheerios, respectively.

C. By incentivizing discount programs with multi-purchase point allocations and associated rewards, cereal makers could develop enhanced affinity to brands.

### 6.31 Use Parallel Language (LO6.1)

Revise the following sentences for parallelism.

A. Kellogg Company and General Mills produce ready-to-eat cereals and also are selling cereal bars.

B. At the bloggers conference hosted by General Mills, the sessions will include the following: (a) reaching a business audience, (b) best practices in tagging, and (c) how to partner with companies.

C. Special K is Kellogg's leading cereal and is continuing to match sales targets.

D. Wanchai Ferry frozen foods are named after the famous tourist spot in Hong Kong, which is known for excitement, attracting boisterous crowds, and creates an exotic atmosphere.

E. Make sure to sign up for RSS feeds from the General Mills Investor Relations page to stay updated with stock prices and for gaining the latest news about the company.

### 6.32 Avoid Buzzwords and Figures of Speech (LO6.1)

Revise the following sentences to eliminate buzzwords and clichéd figures of speech.

A. The latest hot news for the industry is that Kellogg's and General Mills will develop synergistic working relationships with international partners to get a piece of the pie in the BRIC countries.

B. General Mills' latest strategy is nothing more than a swing for the fence.

C. Just as an FYI, I want everyone to come ready to our next meeting to think outside of the box.

### 6.33 Avoid *It Is/There Are* (LO6.1)

Revise the following sentences to eliminate the phrases *it is* and *there are*.

A. It is gratifying that General Mills has reduced sugar content in its children's cereals so that there are fewer children who face obesity.

B. There are several new product lines for Kellogg Company that it hopes will show that there is still plenty of innovation and creativity at the company.

C. It is critical for Kellogg Company to tell the public that there is a risk of salmonella contamination in some of its products and that there will be full rebates for products purchased with peanuts as ingredients.

### Case for Problems 6.34 and 6.35: Creating a Database of Prospects

Kip recently hired Tia for a marketing internship. Kip arranged to meet her next Tuesday and explain the major project that she would complete during her internship. The project involves creating a database of meeting planners (people who organize large conventions and off-site meetings). Unfortunately, Kip had to leave on a sudden business trip and would miss the meeting. He wanted to make sure Tia could start working on the project right away. So, he emailed her from the airport to give her the information she needed. His email message, however, was rushed and somewhat confusing.

---

SUBJECT: Work Schedule

Hi Tia,

I was just asked to make a quick business trip to a trade show that will have me gone from the office for the next four days during next week. We had scheduled to meet on Tuesday, at which time I was going to walk you through the process of developing a full, complete, and comprehensive database of meeting planners at state and federal agencies nearby. Since I will be unable to attend our meeting and give you direction, I thought I would give you some ideas so you can get started. I'm currently waiting for a flight at the airport, so I apologize for any typos.

As you know, one of your responsibilities this summer will be to help us develop a database of prospects. What we are looking for, in particular, are meeting planners at state and federal agencies located within 500 miles. We feel that this could be an opportunity if we choose to start developing our capacity to hold green meetings and to include green meetings as part of our core strategic initiatives moving forward. One reason for this is that we think government agencies are more likely to seek out green meetings, and another reason is that, in our past experience, government agencies that hold meetings here are more likely to give us repeat business, thus allowing us to gain more reliable and loyal business.

In order to allow us to act swiftly if we start to market green meetings to government agencies, we want you to create a database that includes information of designated meeting planners in these state and federal agencies located within 500 miles of us that will allow us to send out periodic marketing messages via email, mail, and phone. On top of this contact information, we would like to gather information such as how often they hold meetings, for how many people, etc. We also want to find out the extent to which they have prioritized green (or eco-friendly) meetings in the past. Some of the information is already assembled and organized in our current database that contains all federal and state agencies (this file is located on the intranet). For some of these state and federal governmental agencies, we have some information in the database already that states who the meeting planners are and whether we've met with them in the past; however, this information is mostly incomplete (probably less than 5 to 10 percent complete). We want you to contact all of the agencies to find out as much information as you can. For each meeting planner you talk to, you should ask them what their key criteria are in making their venue selection. Also, please include a field with a rating for how promising the lead is that contains your estimation (or whoever is updating the database) of how likely you think this particular client could be.

As far as the process for making contact with meeting planners, we've generally found that it's best to phone first so that you get in direct contact with a meeting planner and get more accurate and reliable information. You should make a call to find out which person is in charge of meetings. Once you get the contact information for this person (or office), try calling them directly. If your call is not returned within three business days, then make one more direct call. If they do not return the call, then use email to try to arrange information. Of course, it goes without saying, make sure that you are polite as possible so that these meeting planners will want to do business with us in the future.

In the event that you have questions, please give me a call on my mobile phone.

Thanks, Tia, for working on this. Kip

Sent from iPad. Please excuse brevity and typos.

---

### 6.34 Identify and Rewrite Non-concise Sentences (LO6.1)

For each of the following issues, identify three sentences from the email message that are problematic and rewrite to make them more concise: (a) unnecessarily long sentences, (b) redundancy, (c) empty phrases, and (d) wordy prepositional phrases.

### 6.35 Rewrite the Email Message (LO6.1)

Ensure that the message is more concise. In addition to making sentence-level changes, also ensure that paragraph length is appropriate and eliminate unneeded information. As you rewrite the message, focus on making the message as clear as possible.

# Language Mechanics Check

**6.36 Review the dashes and hyphens rules in Appendix A. Then, rewrite each sentence to add dashes and hyphens where needed.**

A. My supervisor is well known for her expertise in predictive analytics.

B. Training that is the key to keeping skills up to date.

C. One well known approach to maintaining up to date skills is to enroll in two analytics courses per year.

D. Her consulting role with demanding clients is high stress.

E. She has had a high stress consulting role for a long time.

F. She applies a statistics based approach to developing solutions.

G. Her long time philosophy has been to break even on new initiatives.

H. Let's take an easy does it approach to implementing this changes.

I. Her calm and collected temperament helps her in high pressure situations.

J. I would definitely describe her as solutions oriented.

# Endnotes

1. Granville N. Toogood, *The Articulate Executive: Learn to Look, Act, and Sound Like a Leader* (New York: McGraw-Hill, 1996).

2. The National Commission on Writing for America's Families, Schools, and Colleges, *Writing: A Ticket to Work . . . Or a Ticket Out: A Survey of Business Leaders* (New York: CollegeBoard, September 2004).

3. Adam Bryant, "Ensemble Acting, in Business," *Corner Office (blog), The New York Times*, June 6, 2009, www.nytimes.com/2009/06/07/business/07corner.html.

4. Figure adapted from Ann Wylie, "How to Make Your Copy More Readable: Make Sentences Shorter," *Comprehension*, January 14, 2009, retrieved March 3, 2012, from http://comprehension.prsa.org/?p=217.

5. Accountemps, "What's the Buzz? Survey Reveals Most Overused Workplace Terms," retrieved March 3, 2012, from http://accountemps.rhi.mediaroom.com/Buzzwords.

6. Richard Bierck, "Find the Right Tone for Your Business Writing," *Harvard Management Communication Letter* 4, no. 9 (2001): 10–11.

7. Cereal nutrition facts are based on 2009 figures from the Rudd Center: www.cerealfacts.org/media/Marketing_Rankings/Brand_Nutrition.pdf.

**ESTABLISHING CREDIBILITY**

 **PRINCIPLES OF INTERPERSONAL COMMUNICATION**

 **PRINCIPLES FOR & TYPES OF BUSINESS MESSAGES**

 **Learning Objectives**

After studying this chapter, you should be able to do the following:

**LO7.1** Explain the trade-offs associated with richness, control, and constraints when choosing a communication channel.

**LO7.2** Apply principles for writing effective emails.

**LO7.3** Explain how to handle emotion effectively in online communications.

**LO7.4** Describe strategies for effective instant messaging in the workplace.

**LO7.5** Describe strategies for managing digital message overload.

**LO7.6** Explain principles for effective phone conversations and videoconferences.

For nearly two decades, email has been the primary written business communication tool.[1] Even with so many emerging communication tools, *email remains the channel of choice for most professionals.*

Writing emails will likely consume much of your time early in your career. One study showed that corporate employees spend 25 percent of their days on email-related tasks. By comparison, they spend 14 percent of their time in personal meetings and 9 percent of their time in phone conversations.[2] The average business professional receives 76 emails per day and sends 33 emails per day.[3]

In this chapter, we first focus on principles for adopting the right communication channel. Then, we focus on the most common form of written business communication: emails. We also discuss other important communication channels such as texts, phone calls, and group voice and video calls.

> **Hear Pete Cardon explain why this matters.**
>
> bit.ly/cardon7

**CHAPTER CASE:** COMMUNICATING WITH EMAILS, TEXTS, AND CALLS AT THE PRESTIGIO HOTEL

**WHO'S INVOLVED**

Haniz Zogby, marketing assistant

Jaclyn Peha, technology intern

### Haniz Uses Emails with Clients to Establish Terms

Haniz is helping Better Horizons Credit Union run an annual financial literacy fair. One of her responsibilities is to develop sponsorship agreements with local businesses. One of her clients, Stephanie Jorgenson from Sunrise Greeting Cards, called Haniz this morning and discussed making some changes to the sponsorship agreement. Stephanie negotiated a 10 percent reduction in the sponsorship fee. She also wanted clarification about issues such as logo displays and booth size. Haniz wants to immediately update the agreement and send an email to Stephanie with a summary of changes.

**SITUATION 1**

### Haniz and Jaclyn Handle a Delicate Situation by Email

Haniz and Jaclyn recently met about making changes to the website. Haniz thought the conversation went well and they reached some agreements about how to proceed. Jaclyn, on the other hand, thought she wasn't given a fair chance to express some of her ideas. She wrote a late-night email to Haniz with her complaints. Now Haniz wants to resolve an uncomfortable situation with Jaclyn and also make progress on improving the website.

**SITUATION 2**

SITUATION 3    **Jaclyn Works with Colleagues and Customers via Texting and Calls**
Jaclyn is supporting several colleagues and clients with tech support. She uses texts
and calls to help coordinate and arrange meetings.

**TASK**

**1** How can Haniz use email effectively with clients?

**2** How can Haniz handle an emotionally charged email?

**3** How can Jaclyn use texts and calls to collaborate with her colleagues?

# Strategically Selecting Channels for Communication

**LO7.1** Explain the trade-offs associated with richness, control, and constraints when choosing a communication channel.

**connect**

Visit http://connect.
mheducation.com for an
exercise on this topic.

You have so many useful communication tools and technologies for getting in touch with your colleagues, your customers, and other contacts. Having so many options, however, also presents dilemmas about selecting an appropriate **communication channel**—the medium through which a message is transmitted. Examples of communication channels include emails, phone conversations, and face-to-face dialogue. Each communication channel has strengths and drawbacks, the topic we explore in this section.

Strategically selecting a communication channel means that you choose the one that is best able to meet your work objectives. Sometimes a quick phone call or text message is the most efficient way to figure out a meeting time. Other times you will need a face-to-face meeting to clarify misunderstandings about projects. In many of your working relationships, you'll use many communication channels—email, social media, calls, face-to-face conversations—on a daily or weekly basis. Strategically choosing a communication channel involves three basic considerations related to their limitations: richness, control, and constraints.

**Richness** involves two considerations: the level of immediacy and the number of cues available. **Immediacy** relates to how quickly someone is able to respond and give feedback. In high-immediacy communication, people have immediate access to a variety of **cues**, including social cues (turn-taking), verbal cues (tone of voice), and nonverbal cues (gestures, facial expressions). Generally, face-to-face communication is considered the richest, since each person involved can get immediate verbal and nonverbal feedback. Richer communication typically leads to more trust-building, rapport, and commitment. It is generally the most efficient way to accomplish communication objectives quickly and is less likely to lead to misunderstandings.[4]

**Control** refers to the degree to which communications can be planned and recorded, thus allowing strategic message development. **Planning** implies that the communication can be tightly drafted, edited and revised, rehearsed, and otherwise strategically developed before delivery. **Permanence** refers to the extent to which the message can be stored, retrieved, and distributed to others. Control may be your primary concern for many important communications.

**Constraints** refer to the practical limitations of coordination and resources. **Coordination** deals with the effort and timing needed to allow all relevant people to participate in a communication. **Resources** include the financial, space, time, and other investments necessary to employ particular channels of communication. A meeting of ten corporate employees who fly in from different cities is a high-constraint communication that requires extensive coordination and resources.

At the most basic level, communication channels can be divided between the spoken and the written. Spoken messages in the workplace are generally high in richness but low in control. In other words, when people speak to one another face-to-face, they get immediate verbal and nonverbal feedback and respond accordingly. This leads to rapid understanding and bonding. However, they cannot prepare a set message (low planning) or keep a permanent record that can be reviewed and distributed to others (low permanence).

In terms of constraints, spoken communication can range from low to high depending on a number of factors. For example, speaking to a colleague in the next office might require little scheduling (coordination) and few additional monetary and time resources. However, if colleagues are dispersed in various offices separated by time zones, scheduling could be challenging, and the company and the employees might invest a great deal of money and time on travel and related expenses to facilitate rich face-to-face conversation.

By contrast, written messages in the workplace are generally low in richness since they typically do not allow immediate feedback and lack a variety of social, verbal, and nonverbal cues. Yet, they present a number of benefits. Individuals can carefully craft messages at their own pace and on their schedule (high in planning and low in coordination). Moreover, many business professionals consider writing to be conducive to deep thinking on business matters. Furthermore, writing creates a permanent record. Because written records are text-based, it is far easier to search and retrieve relevant information. Generally, the constraints (resources and coordination) of writing are quite low.

Broadly speaking, the benefits of spoken versus written messages reflect an important point: Choosing between communication channels is generally a matter of trade-offs. There is no such thing as a perfect communication channel. Written business communication complements the weaknesses of spoken business communication and vice versa.

The distinctions between spoken and written business messages mirror the relative benefits and weaknesses of synchronous and asynchronous communications. **Synchronous communication** occurs in real time; the individuals involved give immediate responses to one another and engage in turn-taking. **Asynchronous communication** does not occur in real time. Individuals involved in such communication can pay attention to and respond to communications at a time of their choosing. Most successful working relationships depend on both synchronous and asynchronous communication. Scholars Arvind Malhotra, Ann Majchrzak, and Benson Rosen have studied hundreds of virtual teams over nearly a decade and concluded the following about successful communication between teams:[5]

> Most successful virtual team leaders establish a synchronous as well as an asynchronous collaboration rhythm. . . . Successful virtual teams use the time between meetings to asynchronously (through use of electronic discussion threads and annotation of documents in the repository) generate and evaluate ideas. By working asynchronously virtual team members can pick and choose when they can make their contributions. This allows team members with diverse backgrounds to have a different rhythm and pace of generating their own ideas and digesting others' ideas. Leaders also use asynchronous discussion threads to identify areas of disagreements because the discussion threads give members with different language capabilities time to share their thoughts in their non-native languages in ways that they find difficult in synchronous (fast-paced audio-conference) sessions.[6]

Table 7.1 summarizes the features of several communication channels in terms of richness, control, and constraints. Of course, the evolving nature of communication technologies impacts the richness, control, and constraints. For example, many messaging platforms now allow video chat, which make them richer than in the past.

**TABLE 7.1**

## Richness, Control, and Constraints of Various Communication Channels

Red indicates a major limitation. Green indicates a major strength.

| Communication Channel | Richness Immediacy + Cues | Control Planning + Permanence | Constraints Coordination + Resources | When to Use |
|---|---|---|---|---|
| Written messages | ✗ Low | ✓ High | ✓ Low | Ideal for asynchronous communication, matters that require documentation, and messages that need to be crafted with a lot of thought and precision. |
| Spoken communication | ✓ High | ✗ Low | ✓ Low to ✗ High | Ideal for matters that require rapport-building, discussion, brainstorming, clarification, and immediate feedback. Preferred for sensitive and emotion-packed situations. |
| **Asynchronous Communication Channels** | | | | |
| Email | ✗ Low | ✓ High | ✓ Low | For one-to-one or one-to-many business messages. Email is the dominant communication tool for private, written business messages. |
| Messaging (including texting)* | ✗ Low to ✓ High | Medium | ✓ Low | For short, one-to-one, one-to-many, and many-to-many messages. Ideal for quick announcements and scheduling. Not well suited for important or complex business messages. |
| Social media | ✗ Low to ✓ High | Medium to ✓ High | ✓ Low to Medium | For team and networked communication. Facilitates a one-stop work space containing project and meeting information, shared files, and communication platforms (see Chapter 8). |
| **Synchronous or Real-Time Communication Channels** | | | | |
| Phone conversations | Medium to ✓ High | ✗ Low to Medium | ✓ Low to Medium | For one-to-one conversations between parties in different locations. A fairly rich communication channel to quickly discuss and clarify workplace issues. |
| Conference calls | Medium to ✓ High | ✗ Low to Medium | Medium to ✗ High | For team conversations. Typically less rich than one-to-one phone conversations because many participants do not provide cues continuously during the conversation. |
| Web conferences/ webinars | Medium to ✓ High | Medium to ✓ High | Medium to ✗ High | For team meetings/sales presentations. A richer form of interacting than conference calls but typically requires more coordination due to technology requirements. |
| Videoconferences | ✓ High | ✗ Low to Medium | Medium to ✗ High | For team meetings. A richer form of interacting than conference calls but typically requires more expensive equipment and careful scheduling and planning. |

*Note:* Table is modified and adapted from Pearn Kandola's *The Psychology of Effective Business Communications in Geographically Dispersed Teams.*

*As a communication channel, messaging (including texting) isn't simple to classify. You can see in this table that messaging may be considered asynchronous. In the workplace, many professionals are not able to respond immediately because they are in meetings or events that make it difficult to respond immediately. Yet, in many situations, professionals use messaging in a synchronous manner. See the section later in the chapter about instant messaging.

As ambiguity and sensitivity in your communications increase, you will generally seek richer forms of communication, such as face-to-face conversations, meetings, phone calls, and videoconferences. For less ambiguous, highly detailed, and highly analytical messages, you will likely turn to higher-control channels. Thus, communicating with letters, emails, blogs, wikis, podcasts, and other asynchronous communication channels may be particularly helpful.

Many work factors affect the communication channels you choose. In some cases, companies develop protocols for communicating. The stage of a project may be important, for instance. Generally, projects begin with face-to-face meetings because rich communication is particularly important to develop trust, establish work roles, and brainstorm in the early stages of a project. Later in the project, more control and fewer constraints may allow business professionals to work on their own schedules with less face-to-face meeting time. As a result, more of the communication may become mediated by communication technologies (i.e., email, wikis, phone calls, videoconferences).

Furthermore, some types of communication are considered more formal and appropriate for certain types of business activities. Typically, written communication is considered more formal. Proposals, agreements, contracts, and similar documents are written because that implies that the content is in certain and unambiguous terms.[7] In the remainder of this chapter, we'll explore a variety of essential business communication tools, including emails, instant messaging, phone calls, and group voice and video calls.

## Creating Effective Emails

Email communication is the primary form of written business communication. Most business professionals spend between 20 and 50 percent of their time reading and writing email (see Figure 7.1).[8] Most analysts expect email to be the primary tool for at least the next five years in most companies.[9] Some forward-thinking companies are increasingly adopting social networking platforms (SNPs) for employee communication (discussed in Chapter 8); however, even in companies that adopt these SNPs, employees will continue to use private electronic messages within these platforms, which function nearly identically to emails. Furthermore, many of your colleagues, clients, and other contacts will likely prefer to use email systems for many years to come.

Writing effective emails involves applying the principles of writing style that we discussed in Chapters 5 and 6. It also involves adapting to the unique characteristics of email. In this section, we explain basic principles for using emails effectively, including the basic components that ensure ease of reading. Then, we focus on managing emotion and maintaining civility in electronic communications.

### Use Email for the Right Purposes

Email is easy and convenient. Before quickly sending out an email, however, consider whether it is the best communication channel for your work purposes.

Because emails are not rich—meaning lacking in virtually all verbal and nonverbal cues associated with face-to-face communication and lacking immediate feedback—they are best suited for routine, task-oriented, fact-based, and nonsensitive messages.[10] Emails may be used to praise others but should rarely be used to criticize others.[11]

Email communication has few constraints (low cost, little coordination) and high control (the writer can think them out carefully, and they provide a permanent record). Yet because it is not a rich form of communication, it is rarely appropriate for sensitive or emotional communication tasks. It is also less efficient than real-time conversations for making joint decisions.

**LO7.2** Apply principles for writing effective emails.

**connect**

Visit http://connect.mheducation.com for an exercise on this topic.

## Principles of Effective Emails

- Use for the right purposes.
- Ensure ease of reading.
- Show respect for time.
- Protect privacy and confidentiality.
- Respond promptly.
- Maintain professionalism and appropriate formality.
- Manage emotion effectively.
- Avoid distractions.

**FIGURE 7.1**

## Time Devoted to Email by Business Professionals

*Source:* Based on December 2015 survey of 1,004 marketing, R&D, and IT managers in the following industries: Finance, Banking, and Insurance; Health Care and Social Assistance; Manufacturing; and Retail and Wholesale Trade. Findings of this survey first presented at the following academic conference: Peter W. Cardon, "The Role of Leadership Communication and Emotional Capital in Driving Internal Social Media Use," presentation at the Association for Business Communication Southeast/Midwest Regional Conference, St. Louis, MO, April 23, 2016.

**Time Spent Reading and Writing Email per Week**

- < 2 hours: 16.4
- 2–5 hours: 31.3
- 6–10 hours: 23.8
- 11–15 hours: 10.2
- 16–20 hours: 7.2
- > 20 hours: 11.2

Percentage of Managers

### Ensure Ease of Reading

In all written communication, ensuring ease of reading is critical. It is even more critical in emails and other digital messages. Simply put, your readers are unlikely to read your message unless you make it easy for them. Compare the ease of reading in the less effective and more effective examples of emails in Figures 7.2 and 7.3. Think about how quickly a reader can process the information. Also, use the following tips to ensure ease of reading in your emails.

**FIGURE 7.2**

## Less Effective Email

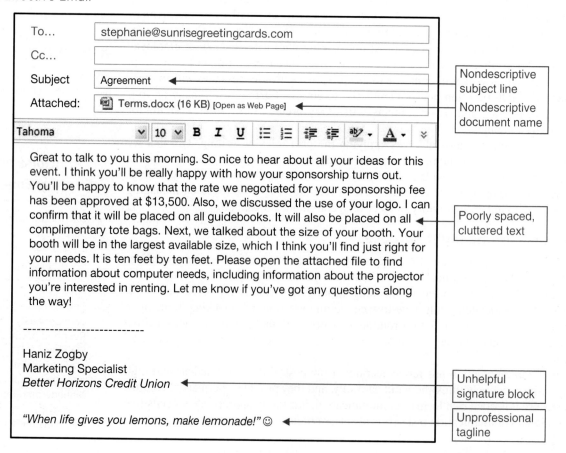

To... stephanie@sunrisegreetingcards.com

Cc...

Subject: Agreement — Nondescriptive subject line

Attached: Terms.docx (16 KB) [Open as Web Page] — Nondescriptive document name

Tahoma | 10 | **B** *I* <u>U</u>

Great to talk to you this morning. So nice to hear about all your ideas for this event. I think you'll be really happy with how your sponsorship turns out. You'll be happy to know that the rate we negotiated for your sponsorship fee has been approved at $13,500. Also, we discussed the use of your logo. I can confirm that it will be placed on all guidebooks. It will also be placed on all complimentary tote bags. Next, we talked about the size of your booth. Your booth will be in the largest available size, which I think you'll find just right for your needs. It is ten feet by ten feet. Please open the attached file to find information about computer needs, including information about the projector you're interested in renting. Let me know if you've got any questions along the way!

— Poorly spaced, cluttered text

----------------------------

Haniz Zogby
Marketing Specialist
*Better Horizons Credit Union* — Unhelpful signature block

*"When life gives you lemons, make lemonade!"* ☺ — Unprofessional tagline

**FIGURE 7.3**

More Effective Email

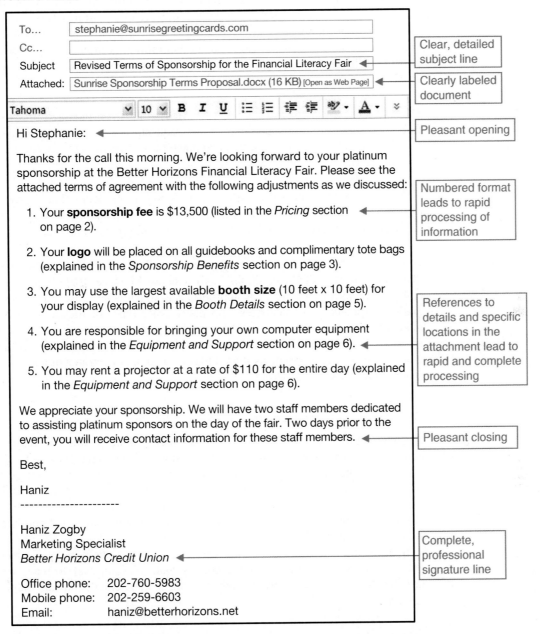

**Provide a Short, Descriptive Subject Line**  Message recipients make immediate judgments about the importance of a message based on the subject line. If it is not clear and compelling, recipients may not open the message right away. Furthermore, when business professionals search for prior email messages, they often scan the subject lines in their in-boxes. Without a descriptive subject line, they may miss the message. Good subject lines are generally five to ten words long. By contrast, poor subjects are either too short (1 or 2 words) and thus nondescriptive or too long (12 words or longer) and thus difficult to process. Fundamentally, subject lines frame your entire message; they serve the same role that headlines do in newspapers and magazines.

**Components of Effective Emails**

- Subject line
- Greeting*
- Message
- Closing*
- Signature block*
- Attachments*

*optional

**Keep Your Message Brief Yet Complete**   Get to the point within three or four sentences, and keep your paragraphs about half the size of those in business documents—ideally 30 to 50 words long. Consider placing the most critical information at the beginning so readers gather the most relevant information immediately. This is an important strategy because most people are so inundated with messages that they often pay more attention to the beginning, skimming or skipping latter portions. This is especially important as business professionals increasingly use mobile devices.

**Clearly Identify Expected Actions**   Most emails are intended to spur action. Effective emails contain specific and clear requests so that recipients know exactly how to respond. In many cases, you can place these directions in the subject line for greatest clarity.

**Provide a Descriptive Signature Block**   Signature blocks should provide clear contact information. This allows recipients to easily contact you through richer communication channels if needed. It also enhances your professional image.

**Use Attachments Wisely**   Attachments allow business professionals to share files that do not display effectively in an email window. Messages that are more than several paragraphs long are typically appropriate as attachments. Also, pictures and other graphics, spreadsheets, databases, and many other types of files are nearly always more appropriate as attachments. However, be careful about sending attachments that are too large, since they may fill others' email boxes. Also, consider whether these documents are more appropriate as shared files on a company intranet or another location (such as Google Drive or Dropbox).

## Show Respect for Others' Time

Because email communication is so convenient, some people overuse and even abuse it. With business professionals sending and receiving hundreds of emails each week, they often experience information overload and email fatigue. Every time you write an email, you might want to envision your colleagues and clients who are receiving them. Imagine their time pressures and the line of emails awaiting their response. Assume they will likely have low tolerance for poorly written, sloppy, unclear emails.

In the business world, where time pressures can be overwhelming, you can engender goodwill by writing emails that are professional, relevant, easy to read, and other-oriented. To show your respect for others when sending email, consider the following advice.

**Select Message Recipients Carefully**   Before sending an email, think about the workload you are creating for your colleagues or other message recipients. Not only do they commit time to reading your email, but they also often interrupt another work task to do so. If you are requesting information or action, your colleagues are further committed in terms of time. So, make sure the email is necessary and relevant for each of your message recipients.

**Provide Timelines and Options**   If you use email to coordinate tasks with deadlines, provide detailed information about time frames and your availability. If you are setting up appointments, make sure you have provided several options. By clearly providing timelines and schedules, you minimize the number of emails needed to coordinate your efforts, thus saving time. By providing options, you show respect for your colleagues' schedules.

**Be Careful about Using the Priority Flag**    You will routinely make requests of others that are time-sensitive. If you too often set the priority flag on such emails, your colleagues may become annoyed, perceiving you as pushy. In fact, some business professionals are more likely to ignore emails when the priority flag is set. If you need something urgently, mention it politely in the subject line or use a rich communication channel such as a phone call to gain buy-in.

**Let Others Know When You Will Take Longer Than Anticipated to Respond or Take Action**    If you can't respond to a request made in an email, reply immediately and explain how soon you can respond in full. You might use phrases such as "I will respond to your email by next Tuesday," or "I can take care of this by the end of next week."

**Avoid Contributing to Confusing and Repetitive Email Chains**    Email chains are groups of emails that are sent back and forth among a group of people. As the number of messages and people involved in an email chain increases, confusion can build. Consider the following complaint of a business professional:

> One of my biggest pet peeves has to do with forwards. My company will often send out a corporate email to the all-hands list, then a program manager will forward that email to the same all-hands list "in case you didn't get this," then the department head will forward the same email back to the same all-hands list "in case you didn't get this." Often another layer or two of management feels compelled to forward the same email down to their organizational levels for the same reason. I'm not exaggerating when I say that I often have to delete the same email five or six times! Please, if you're in the habit of forwarding announcements for "FYI" reasons, pay attention to which lists you're forwarding to and which people are already on those lists.[12]

Three features contribute to email chains: *forward*, *copy*, and *reply to all.* The forward feature allows you to send any message you receive to others with the click of the mouse. As always, make sure that those you are forwarding the message to *need* to see the email. Also, consider whether the original sender would consider it appropriate for you to forward the email to others; after all, he or she did not place those people on the original email. Similarly, many business professionals consider use of the *blind carbon copy* feature a breach of privacy. Furthermore, the ease of forwarding and copying can create other problems. Once you send an email, you have no control over whether others will forward it, and to whom, which leads to a good standard articulated by Tony DiRomualdo, strategy and IT researcher: "Don't say anything you would not want the entire planet to read at some point."[13]

Many business professionals use the *copy* feature liberally to let everyone in a department or work unit in on the conversation. Of course, one of your goals is transparency, allowing others in your relevant work group to know how decisions are being made. But copying too many people can lead to information overload. Furthermore, copying too many people on an email can dilute responsibility. When five or six people receive an email about accomplishing a specific task, uncertainty may arise about exactly who is supposed to do what. The more people you copy, the less likely you will get a response. Also, some people perceive copying a direct supervisor or boss on emails between peers as a subtle power play.[14]

The *reply to all* feature can contribute to confusing email chains in many of the same ways as the *forward* and *copy* features. In an email conversation of more than four or five people, various message recipients can lose track of the sequence of messages or miss some messages altogether. Reply email chains become especially confusing when some colleagues are using just the *reply* feature whereas others are using the *reply to all* feature. One advantage of team blogs and wikis in the workplaces is that they remove some of the inefficiencies and confusion of email chains by placing messages and shared content in a central location rather than in various, separate email boxes.

## Protect Privacy and Confidentiality

Be careful about not spreading—purposely or inadvertently—sensitive or confidential information. Because emails are so convenient to send, even the rare mistake in an address line can result in damaging professional consequences. Consider, for example, that eight out of ten marketing and advertising executives say they have made mistakes via email, such as sending job offers to the wrong people or revealing confidential salary information to the entire company.[15] Double-checking that you have placed the correct people in the address line before you hit the send button is a worthwhile habit that requires just a few extra moments.

## Respond Promptly

Most business professionals expect fast responses to emails. Of course, what seems like a quick response to one person seems like a delayed response to another. One recent study of business professionals found that nearly all business professionals expect an email response within one day.[16] Younger professionals are more likely to expect a response immediately. The majority of business professionals in all age groups expect a response within one to two hours. If you choose not to check your email more than a four to five times a day (a strategy recommended later in the chapter), let others know how soon to expect replies.

## Maintain Professionalism and Appropriate Formality

Email communication is typically considered fairly formal. Many business professionals are particularly sensitive to "sloppy" email. Management consultant Beverly Langford reported what thousands of business leaders have observed about an overly casual attitude toward email use:

> Many people seem to forget that email is, in fact, written communication, and, consequently, treat it much less carefully. Workplace email messages often contain terse and offhand remarks and project a flippant attitude that is sometimes excessive, even bordering on the unprofessional. Those who write the emails often seem to be overlooking how their message is coming across to the receiver. Further, when composing emails, many people don't seem to be nearly as concerned with structure and correctness as they would be when putting something on paper. This . . . is ironic because often many more people see an email than would ever see a hard copy of a memo or letter because it's so easy for the recipient to forward an email to anyone he or she chooses.[17]

Unfortunately, because so many more people can potentially see an email than would ever see a hard copy of a message, having high standards is even more important. In the past few years, a preference has emerged for less formal, stuffy writing. Still, you'll want to achieve a balance between formality and the friendliness associated with casual writing. Generally, you are better off erring on the side of too much formality as opposed to too much casualness. Consider the following recommendations.

**Avoid Indications That You View Email as Casual Communication**   Certain casual ways of writing and formatting appear unprofessional—for example, using all lowercase letters or nonstandard spelling (i.e., *hey barbara, how r u*), using excessive formatting (i.e., flashy background colors, unusual fonts), providing extraneous information in the signature line (i.e., favorite quotations), and typing in all caps (IMPLIES ANGER). Humor and sarcasm, too, can be misinterpreted in digital communications, even among close colleagues. Furthermore, even when considered funny, it can draw attention away from your central message.

**Apply the Same Standards of Spelling, Punctuation, and Formatting You Would for Other Written Documents**   Carefully review your message for typos, spelling, punctuation, or grammatical problems before sending it. For important messages, consider first composing with word processing software. This will help you apply a higher level of seriousness. In addition, you'll be able to use spell-check and grammar-check features that are more reliable than those within email systems. Finally, you can ensure that you do not inadvertently send the message without making sure it is polished and complete.

**Use Greetings and Names**   Although not technically required, consider using short greetings and the names of your message recipients. As one of Dale Carnegie's most famous pieces of networking advice goes, "A person's name is to that person the sweetest most important sound in any language."[18] This advice applies to most communication situations, including emails. People leave out names in emails for several reasons. Some professionals view the use of greetings and names as excessively formal, resembling letters. Other professionals view emails as the equivalent of memos. In fact, the layout of most emails—with a recipient line, sender line, and subject line—resembles memos. Traditionally, the format for memos calls for omitting a personal greeting and name.

In a recent study, a communication researcher was given access to the emails in two organizations. One was a low-morale organization and one was a high-morale organization. She found that the presence or absence of greetings and names at the beginning of emails was a strong indicator of company climate (see Figure 7.4).[19] In the low-morale organization, just 20 percent of the emails contained greetings, and just 36 percent contained names. By contrast, in the high-morale organization, 58 percent contained greetings, and 78 percent contained names. The same trend was shown in closings. In the low-morale organization, just 23 percent of the emails contained a polite closing and a name compared to 73 percent in the high-morale organization.

The conventions of using greetings and names are sometimes dropped as an email chain emerges and functions much like a conversation. Typically, professionals with blue and hub MVSs (see Chapter 2) (those with the strongest people-orientation) show a stronger preference for greetings and names. If you're having an ongoing email exchange with a blue or a hub and you notice that he or she is using a formal greeting in each email, consider reciprocating. On the other hand, if you're a blue or a hub and like to see greetings and names in every email but your colleagues are not doing so, avoid getting hung up on it. Assume that they view emails much like memos or that they view excessive use of greetings and names in back-and-forth email chains as repetitive and unnecessary.

**FIGURE 7.4**

Use of Email Greetings and Names in a Low-Morale and a High-Morale Organization

*Source:* Data from Joan Waldvogel, "Greetings and Closings in Workplace Email," *Journal of Computer-Mediated Communication* 12, no. 2 (2007).

## Manage Emotion and Maintain Civility

**LO7.3** Explain how to handle emotion effectively in online communications.

■ **connect**

Visit http://connect. mheducation.com for an exercise on this topic.

Many managers cite the lack of emotion in emails as positive. They see email as a channel that allows the exchange of messages in minimal form—objective, task-based, and straightforward. As one manager explained, "With email I find myself answering without all the kindness necessary to keep people happy with their job."[20]

Yet, avoiding emotion entirely, even for task-based messages, is nearly impossible. Business professionals often want to invoke some emotion—perhaps enthusiasm or a sense of urgency. Even when senders intend to convey a relatively nonemotional message, recipients may experience an emotional reaction.

In the absence of face-to-face communications, emails tend to elicit either the neutrality effect or the negativity effect. The **neutrality effect** means that recipients are more likely to perceive messages with an intended positive emotion as neutral. That is, the sender may wish to express enthusiasm about an event, but the receiver decodes the information without "hearing" the enthusiasm.[21] The **negativity effect** means that recipients are more likely to perceive messages that are intended as neutral as negative.[22] The effects of emotional inaccuracy due to the neutrality and negativity effects can lead to conflict escalation, confusion, and anxiety.[23] Expert business communicators remain aware of these tendencies.

Two characteristics of asynchronous electronic communications can lead to feelings of anger and frustration more so than in face-to-face communications. First, people often feel comfortable writing things they would not say in person. In some cases, this sense of online freedom leads to **flames**, which are emails or other digital communications with "hostile intentions characterized by words of profanity, obscenity, and insults that inflict harm to a person or an organization."[24]

The second aspect of asynchronous electronic communications that can lead to anger and frustration is **cyber silence**, which is nonresponse to emails and other communications. During the nonresponse stage, message senders often misattribute explanations for the silence. They sometimes wonder if message recipients are purposely avoiding or even ignoring them.[25] As the length of time between messages increases, they often experience more frustration and anger.[26]

As a message sender, grant the benefit of the doubt to your recipients when responses take longer than you expected. Instead of getting frustrated, consider giving them a phone call. Keep in mind that they may have different expectations about a reasonable time frame to respond to your email. If they routinely take longer than you expect, politely mention that you would appreciate quicker responses.

In Chapter 2, we discussed the importance of civility. Civility is likewise important in electronic communication. **Cyber incivility** is the violation of respect and consideration in an online environment based on workplace norms. Research has shown that "fast-paced, high-tech interactions may add to incivility, as people believe that they do not have time to be 'nice' and that impersonal contacts [such as electronic communications] do not require courteous interaction."[27]

Shockingly, recent research shows that 91 percent of employees reported experiencing either active or passive cyber incivility from supervisors in the workplace.[28] **Active incivility** involves direct forms of disrespect (i.e., being condescending, demeaning, saying something hurtful). **Passive incivility** involves indirect forms of disrespect (i.e., using emails for time-sensitive messages, not acknowledging receipt of emails, not replying to emails). Cyber incivility has been shown to lead to lower job satisfaction and organizational commitment. Active incivility was the most damaging. In Figure 7.5, you can see a summary of this research. One interesting finding was that male and female supervisors engaged in different types of incivility. Male supervisors were far more likely to engage in active incivility, whereas female supervisors were far more likely to engage in passive incivility.

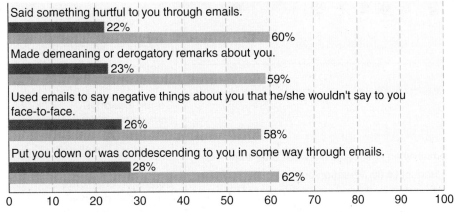

**Active and Passive Incivility through Emails of Supervisors**
*(Percentage of Employees Who Stated Their Current Supervisor Had Engaged in Email Incivility)*

**Active Email Incivility**

Said something hurtful to you through emails.
22%
60%

Made demeaning or derogatory remarks about you.
23%
59%

Used emails to say negative things about you that he/she wouldn't say to you face-to-face.
26%
58%

Put you down or was condescending to you in some way through emails.
28%
62%

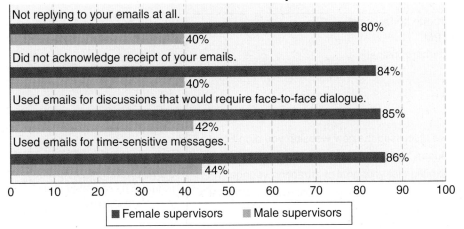

**Passive Email Incivility**

Not replying to your emails at all.
80%
40%

Did not acknowledge receipt of your emails.
84%
40%

Used emails for discussions that would require face-to-face dialogue.
85%
42%

Used emails for time-sensitive messages.
86%
44%

■ Female supervisors   ■ Male supervisors

**FIGURE 7.5**

Active and Passive Incivility from Supervisors

*Source:* Based on information from Vivien K.G. Lim and Thompson S.H. Teo, "Mind Your E-manners: Impact of Cyber Incivility on Employees' Work Attitude and Behavior," *Information & Management* 46 (2009): 419–425. Copyright © 2009.

Inevitably, you will be the target of what you consider uncivil electronic communications. In nearly all situations, your goal should be to avoid escalation. You can take several steps to constructively address uncivil emails: reinterpretation, relaxation, and defusing. **Reinterpretation** involves adjusting your initial perceptions by making more objective, more fact-based, and less personal judgments and evaluations. When people are distressed, they often make extreme, subjective, and overly personal judgments. By reinterpreting the event, you allow yourself to take the communication less personally. This is easier said than done. Many people engage in relaxation techniques to help constructively reinterpret the event. **Relaxation** involves releasing and overcoming anger and frustration so that you can make a more rational and less emotional response. People use a variety of methods to alleviate the physiological impact of anger, including counting to ten, taking time-outs, engaging in deep breathing, and looking for the humor in the situation.[29]

In the opening case, Jaclyn expressed frustration with a conversation she had with Haniz. Jaclyn, perhaps unwisely, fired off an angry email (see the bottom message in Figure 7.6), and Haniz responded (the top message in Figure 7.6). Regardless of whether Jaclyn was correct about Haniz's approach to developing the website, email is rarely an effective communication channel to air complaints or to

**FIGURE 7.6**

Less Effective Response to an Angry Email

Reply  Reply All  Forward

Re: Issues

**Zogby, Haniz**

**To:**  Jaclyn Peha

**Cc:**  Christine Russo

We need to talk about this email when I get back in a week after the holiday. I thought we had a productive conversation but you obviously were not candid or professional. Also, please empty your voice mail. I tried reaching you several times only to get your full voice mail box.

**From:** Jaclyn Peha [jaclyn@betterhorizons.net]
**Sent:** Saturday, July 1 9:54 PM
**To:** Haniz Zogby[haniz@betterhorizons.net]

**Subject:** Issues

Haniz, the other day when we discussed the new website, you didn't give me a chance to explain my ideas, and i don't think you made the conversation fair. I tried to explain that your goal of attracting younger customers is good, but we need to create a more interactive website that's plugged into social media if we're going to make this happen. You seem to just want the easiest, quickest solution. Before we start developing the site any more, let's meet and change things up a bit. Jaclyn

**Impersonal.** Leaves out greeting and name.

**Confrontational.** Immediately creates a *me-versus-you* approach with the phrase "We need to talk."

**Defensive/attacking.** Focuses on defending rather than understanding Jaclyn's point of view.

**Accusatory.** Jaclyn lays blame on Haniz in every regard. The repeated use of *you-voice* increases the accusatory tone.

discuss emotionally charged issues. Figure 7.7 presents a more effective response from Haniz to this exchange.

**Defusing** involves avoiding escalation and removing tension to focus on work objectives. You can take several steps to defuse the situation when you receive an uncivil email. First, focus on task-related facts and issues in your reply. Second, focus on shared objectives and agreements. Third, express interest in arranging a time to meet in person. If this is not possible, attempt a richer channel of communication such as a phone call or web meeting with video. Defusing the situation with an immediate email is only part of the process in restoring or perhaps even strengthening a working relationship. A follow-up meeting is nearly always essential to renew cooperation on shared work efforts.

You often will need to respond to electronic messages that you feel are unfair or inappropriate. Notice how Haniz escalates the problem in the less effective response by writing in an impersonal, defensive, and confrontational manner. By contrast, notice how she defuses the situation in the more effective response by avoiding defensiveness, focusing on shared interests, and arranging for a time to meet face-to-face. Your ability to defuse uncivil electronic communications during your career will pay off in many ways: It will help your colleagues and teams stay on task and perform better; it will

**FIGURE 7.7**

More Effective Response to Defuse an Angry Email

Reply   Reply All   Forward   ▾ ▪   ▪▪ ▾   🖻   🖨   🖃   ✕   🖻 ▾   ⬆ ⬇        ❓

Meeting to Improve the Website

**Zogby, Haniz**

**To:**      Jaclyn Peha

Hello Jaclyn,

I'm sorry to hear that you did not think our conversation was fair. I'm glad you're thinking about how we can use the website to better attract younger customers.

When we're both back in the office, let's set up a time to discuss plans for the website. Would you be willing to come up with your three major ideas to make the website more interactive and connected to our social media platforms?

When we meet, I'd like to get a sense of the resources we would need to commit to your ideas. We need to make sure these ambitious plans make business sense.

Would you like to include anyone else in our meeting? Do you think the entire marketing team should participate in this discussion?

Enjoy your holiday weekend!

Haniz

> **Cordial and personal.** Uses Jaclyn's name and extends warm wishes.

> **Validating.** Compliments Jaclyn on her desire to improve the website.

> **Inviting.** Asks for Jaclyn's input in terms of ideas and people who should be included in the decision-making process.

> **Nondefensive.** Haniz makes it clear that making "business sense" is an important part of the discussion. Yet, she does so without sounding defensive or intimidating (she is in the position of a superior).

> **Focus on rich communication.** Haniz temporarily defuses the situation by email but realizes these issues require rich communication. So, she identifies a meeting as the next step in the process.

help you develop a reputation for constructively resolving differences; and it will lead to more satisfying work experiences. The ability to defuse such situations requires high emotional intelligence, especially in self-awareness and self-management.

## Instant Messaging in the Workplace

Instant messaging (IM) or texting are among the most popular features on mobile phones. American adults IM on their phones more frequently than they access the Internet, send or receive email, or participate in video chats.[30] Instant messaging is ideal for short and simple business messages that contain announcements, questions, confirmations of plans, quick tips, support, and congratulations. Most business professionals consider IM a less formal communication channel than email.

Instant messaging is a relatively new and undeveloped form of communication in the workplace, and attitudes toward it vary significantly. Many professionals consider IM impersonal, uninteresting, rude, intrusive, or inadequate. On the other hand, many professionals associate IM in the workplace with exactly the opposite qualities: warm and personal, nice, less intrusive than calls, fun, inviting, and helpful. As you message with colleagues and other contacts, consider the following tips.

**LO7.4** Describe strategies for effective instant messaging in the workplace.

FIGURE 7.8

Instant Messages to Show Support

## Evaluate the Meta Message of Instant Messaging

In Chapter 5, you read about *meta messages*, the overall but often underlying messages that others decode from your communications. Because professionals hold so many attitudes toward instant messaging, think about how they'd interpret your use of IM. One colleague might decode your instant message as saying, "You're not important enough for a phone call." Another colleague might decode the *same* instant message as saying, "I want to keep you in the loop, so I'm messaging you."

## Use IM for Simple and Brief Conversations, Not for Important Decisions

IMs are best used for short, uncomplicated messages and conversations. If there's any level of complexity or ambiguity, you're better off speaking to others directly or sending an email where you have more space for detailed information. Generally, if the exchange requires more than three or four instant messages, you should probably use an email or make a call.

## Make Sure Your Tone Is Positive, Supportive, and Appropriately Fun

You should reserve most messaging for straightforward, positive messages. IM can be a particularly effective way to send quick notes of support, congratulations, and appreciation to close colleagues (see Figure 7.8). Messaging is also a chance to use a light and fun tone when you're sure that's a style that message recipients will appreciate. One risk of IM is that with a focus on conciseness, IM messages may come across as commanding, abrupt, or unfeeling. Similarly, an excessively casual tone may diminish the perceived importance of your message. In nearly all cases, avoid using IM for bad or unpleasant news.

## Don't Ask Questions You Can Get Answers to Yourself

Many tools such as instant messaging allow professionals to get questions answered quickly by their colleagues. Be careful about overusing this approach to getting information, especially when you can get the information yourself without much effort. When professionals ask questions and offload their own work via instant messages or emails too often, they get reputations as *takers* rather than *givers*.

FIGURE 7.9

Mismatched Messaging Styles

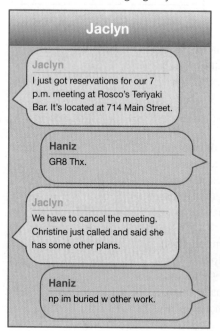

## Be Careful about Abbreviated Language, Emoticons, Acronyms, and Emoji

Abbreviated language, acronyms, emoticons, and emoji are some of the fun features of instant messaging. Until you know the IM style of others in the workplace, you should err on the side of complete sentences and standard language conventions. In Figure 7.9, you will notice how Jaclyn uses a short message to tell Haniz the location of a business meal. Jaclyn uses complete sentences and standard language conventions, while Haniz uses abbreviated language and acronyms. Haniz should consider adopting more standard language conventions to match Jaclyn's style. On the other hand, Jaclyn should notice that Haniz enjoys using some abbreviated language. Jaclyn might consider using some nonstandard language conventions when instant messaging with Haniz.

## Avoid Sarcasm and Jokes in Most Cases

While most people use IM playfully and with humor in their personal lives, trying to use sarcasm and jokes in the workplace is often misunderstood or misinterpreted. Even colleagues who know one another well often misinterpret attempts at humor and sarcasm in instant messages.

## Avoid Rescheduling Meeting Times or Places

Instant messaging is often a convenient way of confirming meeting plans, especially those that involve offsite locations. It's also a convenient way of saying you're running a few minutes late. While slightly changing meeting plans via IM is handy in rare cases, avoid doing so unless absolutely necessary. Many professionals have gained reputations as not being reliable because they frequently adjust meeting times and locations at the last minute via IM. In situations where you must change plans, consider placing a call as a show of courtesy and as a way of efficiently and clearly adjusting plans.

## Consider Turning Off Sound Alerts for Incoming Messages/Emails

This can be especially distracting when you work in shared workspaces. It's also a matter of productivity (as we'll discuss in the next section).

## Identify Yourself

Other than for people you text or IM often, you can't be certain whether you're part of your message recipients' address lists. Simply stating your name ("Hi. This is Jaclyn . . .") will help avoid confusion in many cases.

## Clearly End the IM Exchange

Some IM exchanges become awkward as they drag on. Send signals that the exchange is complete ("Thanks for the update. Talk to you tomorrow.").

## Avoid Personal IM during Work Hours

Increasingly, professionals bring their home lives into the workplace. This isn't surprising given the convenience of so many communication tools. Most workplaces have some policies about avoiding personal communications (including IM), although these policies are generally loosely enforced. You'll notice that exercising discipline and avoiding personal digital messages will help you gain the respect of your colleagues and establish your professionalism.

## Avoid Sending Instant Messages after Work Hours

Many new communication tools lead to professionals blurring the line between personal time and work time. IM, compared to emails and other communication tools, may be considered even more intrusive when sent after hours because of the expectation of immediate responses.

## Establish Rules with Your Colleagues for Instant Messaging in Meetings

Instant messaging is increasingly common during meetings in *some* organizations. Texting can be used to prompt team members about topics to cover, give quick updates as needed to team leaders, ask for information from colleagues or clients outside of the meeting, and assist teammates in a variety of ways (see Figure 7.10). Some organizations' cultures encourage this, whereas others strictly discourage it. So, pay attention to the culture of texting at your company. Of course, even where texting is encouraged in meetings, it can also be abused (see Figure 7.11). In any case, discuss with your teammates what you consider appropriate in meetings. Similarly, use the messaging app or platform that is recommended and supported by your organization.

**FIGURE 7.10**

A Potentially Effective Instant Message in a Meeting

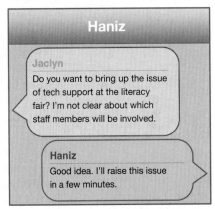

**FIGURE 7.11**

An Ineffective Instant Message in a Meeting

# Managing Your Digital Communication Efficiently

**LO7.5** Describe strategies for managing digital message overload.

Constantly checking incoming messages—emails, texts, IMs, and other digital messages—or simply hearing message alerts distracts business professionals from concentrating on the tasks at hand. As you are bombarded with incoming messages, your productivity decreases for two reasons: You are distracted from your immediate tasks, and you try to multitask.

Interruptions from digital messages, or *e-interruptions,* are extremely costly to your performance. One recent study found that the average worker loses 2.1 hours per day due to interruptions. Many of these distractions are email and other incoming messages. Many business professionals check their email every five minutes, which amounts to 96 e-interruptions in an eight-hour day. Distractions affect your performance for much longer than the few moments you take to acknowledge and respond to incoming messages. A Microsoft study found that it takes 15 minutes on average to refocus after an interruption. Furthermore, these disruptions have been shown to reduce attention spans, increase stress, and even reduce creativity. The cost to companies is enormous. Intel estimates that large companies lose about $1 billion per year because of email overload. [31]

Many business professionals erroneously assume they can respond immediately to all incoming messages *and* focus sufficiently on work tasks. This is simply not the case. A University of Michigan study found that productivity drops by up to 40 percent when people try to do two or more things at once. A variety of research about the brain shows that it is not hardwired to multitask effectively.[32]

In most business positions, however, you need to respond to others as soon as possible. This places you in a delicate balancing act; how can you stay responsive to others yet focus enough to achieve peak performance in your work tasks? Consider the following guidelines:[33]

- *Check digital messages just four to five times each day at designated times.* Unless your job calls for it (or your boss demands it!), try not to check your messages more than every 45 minutes. Consider taking some interruption-free periods during the day exclusively devoted to email so you can concentrate on communicating with others. For example, you might schedule 30 minutes to an hour at 8 a.m., 11 a.m., 1 p.m., and 4 p.m. each day to communicate via email and other online tools.

- *Wean yourself off checking your mobile devices constantly.* Most professionals get anxious if they don't check their phones every 15 minutes or even more frequently. A variety of anxieties, such as FOMO (fear of missing out) and FOBO (fear of being offline), drastically cut many professionals' productivity. Consciously extending the periods between when you glance or check your devices can dramatically improve your effectiveness.

- *Develop strategies to manage your inbox.* Experiment with various ways of staying current with your email. Common strategies include LIFO (last in, first out), reverse chronological, and inbox zero. *LIFO* is most common and involves top-down reading of your email list. This helps you deal with your most current emails. Some of the older email messages sometimes involve issues that have been worked out already. The risk is you may read and respond to a more current message without the context needed from prior messages. The *reverse chronological* solves this problem by ensuring you see the original messages first. It also rewards people in the order they sent messages to you. Yet, you may also expend time reading and responding to issues that have already been addressed or solved. *Inbox zero* is a strategy of immediately taking action on every email and keeping your inbox empty by the end of each session. You can use a variety of email tools such as filters and rules to efficiently read and respond to your most important email.

- *Turn off message alerts.* Over the course of a day, these alerts can distract you and reduce your focus.

- *Use rich channels such as face-to-face and phone conversations to accomplish a task completely.* Back-and-forth email chains and other sets of asynchronous digital

## (⏻) TECHNOLOGY TIPS

### GENDER MATTERS WHEN IT COMES TO EMAILS, TEXTS, AND CALLS

Not surprisingly, there's a big difference in how professionals of various generations use texts, emails, and calls. There's also a big difference between how women and men use these technologies. Overall, women tend to focus more on active listening and building rapport. In Figure 7.5, you can see some of the differences in how male and female supervisors use emails. In texts, women tend to send longer and more complex messages, use more greetings and closings, use more emoticons, and provide more relational and emotional content. By contrast, men tend to send far more one-sentence or one-thought texts that are primarily task-oriented.[34] Similarly, at informal meetings such as business lunches, women are about twice as likely as men to think various mobile phone actions are rude or unacceptable, whether it's taking calls, sending or receiving texts, or simply glancing at a phone to see the time.[35]

© Beyond Fotomedia GmbH/Alamy

messages may repeatedly draw attention away from tasks at hand. As appropriate, use rich, synchronous communication to take care of the matter immediately so that distractions do not compound themselves.

- *Reply immediately only to urgent messages.* When you reply immediately to nonurgent messages, you set a precedent. Others form an expectation that you can be interrupted at any time for any matter.

- *Avoid unnecessarily lengthening an email chain.* You can shorten email chains by placing statements such as "no reply necessary" in the subject line. You can also shorten email chains by not sending messages such as "got it" or "thanks." At the same time, make sure you don't abruptly end an email chain when others would appreciate a reply. For example, some business professionals appreciate short notes of gratitude and confirmation.

- *Use automatic messages to help people know when you're unavailable.* Set up automatic messages to let people know when you are out of the office for more than one day.

## Building Connections with Phone Conversations

Compared to less rich channels such as email, phone calls generally allow business professionals to connect more deeply, resolve problems more quickly, make important decisions better, and manage conflict more effectively.[36] In the past decade, mobile phones have transformed business communication. Most business professionals carry at least one phone at all times for calls, texting, Internet use, scheduling, and much more. In many ways, mobile phones increasingly serve as a communication center for many managers and executives.

Ironically, the increased use of mobile phones in people's personal lives has actually led to a downward trend in calls. In fact, making calls is just the fifth most used function of smartphone users on their phones.[37] However, business professionals continue to use landline and mobile calls extensively (see Figure 7.12).[38] For most business professionals, less calling translates into lost opportunities. Refining the art and skills of phone calls can help you become a more dynamic and savvy communicator. Keep in mind the following guidelines for one-to-one calls in the workplace.

**LO7.6** Explain principles for effective phone conversations and videoconferences.

© Hongqil Zhang/123RF

**FIGURE 7.12**

Time Devoted to
Calling among
Business Professionals

*Source:* Based on December 2015
survey of 1,004 marketing, R&D,
and IT managers in the following
industries: Finance, Banking, and
Insurance; Health Care and Social
Assistance; Manufacturing; and Retail and Wholesale Trade. Findings of
this survey first presented in the following academic conference: Peter
W. Cardon, "The Role of Leadership
Communication and Emotional Capital in Driving Internal Social Media
Use," presentation at the Association
for Business Communication South-
east/Midwest Regional Conference,
St. Louis, MO, April 23, 2016.

**Time Spent Speaking on the Phone per Week**

Percent of Managers

## Schedule and Plan for Your Phone Calls

Like other forms of business communication, think ahead about your key discussion topics and points. Many phone conversations are much like meetings, so consider sending an invitation with an agenda to your conversation partner (see Figure 7.13 for an example). For less formal conversations, at least plan your purpose and major points to cover. Out of respect for your conversation partners' time, let them know roughly how long the call will take.

## Ensure Quality Audio

Especially for important calls, you should test your audio quality before the call. Although mobile phones provide reliable audio quality in most locations, they're still less predictable than landline connections. You might consider using landline calls whenever possible to enhance audio quality.

**FIGURE 7.13**

Sample Meeting
Request and Agenda
for a Phone Call

**Website Development Meeting**

| July | | |
|------|---|---|
| **14** | | |
| Tue | | |

| When | Tue July 14, 2017, 1:30 to 3:00 p.m. |
|------|--------------------------------------|
| Where | Call 888-742-8812 |
| Who | Zogby, Haniz |

| Yes | Maybe | No |
|-----|-------|-----|

**Agenda**
Tue July 14, 2017

1. Discuss goals of the website.
   - Which components will serve existing customers?
   - Which components will serve to attract new members?
   - What messaging will we aim for with each group?
   - How will social media be integrated with the website?
2. Identify examples/models of interactive websites in our industry.
3. Create a timeline for completing the mock website.
4. Determine roles for members of the marketing team.

### Open with a Warm Greeting and Use Your Caller's Name

You've read this advice several times in this book, and you'll hear it several more times: Calling others by name personalizes and elevates your communications with them.

### After Brief Small Chat, Direct the Conversation to the Issues at Hand

Most callers appreciate a few light comments to start a conversation, but be careful not to let this initial small talk drag on. Most effective business calls get to the issues at hand within one to two minutes.

### Speak with a Pleasant, Enthusiastic Voice

Although others cannot see you, your nonverbal behaviors are often reflected in your voice. Consider sitting up straight or standing up, breathing deeply, intonating clearly, gesturing, and even smiling as you would if you were in person. These nonverbal actions will often carry through in a pleasant, professional voice and help you avoid a monotone. From time to time, consider listening to your recorded voice to pick up on ways in which you can speak more professionally and energetically.

### Share Conversation Time Equally

Phone calls are a great opportunity to deepen relationships and get work done when each person shares conversation time equally. Make sure you're not dominating a conversation by taking up more than your fair share of speaking time. Similarly, if your conversation partner is taking too much of the time, politely interject now and then to balance the speaking time.

### Apply the Rules of Active Listening and Avoid Multitasking

Enter a phone call eager to learn about the ideas of your conversation partner and ready to express your views as well. Amazingly, roughly six in ten professionals admit to multitasking during phone calls.[39] Make sure the call is your entire focus. Also, make sure you don't sound rushed—this often sends a signal that you're more interested in other people or matters.

### Take Notes on Important Points and Summarize Next Steps at the End of the Call

As you're speaking, take some notes so you can recall the most important points of agreement. At the end of the call, take a few minutes to wrap up and summarize next steps.

### Close with Appreciation

In nearly all calls, you should find a way to express appreciation to your conversation partner. Simple phrases such as "thanks for taking the time to . . ." or "it has been great to get your ideas about . . ." can end the call on a warm note and pave the way for easier follow-up.

### Follow Up on Agreements

Many professionals often don't follow through on commitments they make to each other on calls. This happens most often when neither person documents the content and agreements of their conversation. Consider sending a message within a few hours of your call while the conversation is still fresh in your minds (see Figure 7.14 as an example). This dramatically improves the likelihood that you will accomplish your shared objectives.

**FIGURE 7.14**

Sample Follow-up
Message with Action
Items

### Follow-up to Our Phone Call about the Website

**Peha, Jaclyn**

**To:** Haniz Zogby

**Cc:** Raj Naykodi

Hello Haniz,

Thanks for the opportunity to talk about ideas for the new website. I've attached a document with detailed notes. I believe we agreed to finish the final proposal for new features on the website by August 5. We agreed to the following roles:

- **Haniz:** marketing strategy, integration of social media into website, budgeting, project timeline
- **Jaclyn and Raj:** analysis of competitors' websites, mock-ups of new features intended to attract new members (with a focus on younger members), analytics options

Let me know if my notes and these roles match your recollections of our conversation.

Best,
Jaclyn

## Participating in and Leading Group Voice and Video Calls

Increasingly, you'll participate in video conferences, web conferences, and conference calls to meet with groups of colleagues and other professional contacts. Most business professionals spend at least five hours each week on video and web conferences.[40] Sometimes you'll have video and other times you may only have audio. You'll sometimes use high-end videoconferencing platforms and other times use web conferencing tools such as Google Hangouts or Skype. Many of the tips that we discussed for one-to-one calls apply, as do the guidelines for effective virtual meetings discussed in Chapter 3. In addition, consider the following tips.

### Practice Using the Technology before the Group Call

There are many options for group voice and video calls. Even if you often participate in or even lead these calls, you may not be up to date with various platforms or new tools. If you're leading the call, send out information about the technology to participants so they can be prepared. When the first five to ten minutes of group calls are consumed by participants trying to figure out the technology, the meetings rarely turn out productive or engaging.

### Use Your Webcam Effectively

The power of group video calls is the ability to have rich conversations full of nonverbal cues. You lose this advantage unless you carefully position your webcam so you are speaking directly to your listeners. Make sure that you've got good lighting and a clean background. Also, maintain direct eye contact with your webcam as much as possible so that other meeting participants can see your interest level and understand your nonverbal cues.

© Blend Images/Alamy

## COMMUNICATION Q&A

### CONVERSATIONS WITH CURRENT BUSINESS PROFESSIONALS

**Pete Cardon: What's an example of a project you have worked on recently that involves extensive collaboration and coordination? What are the communication challenges you faced on this project?**

**Catherine Norris:** One of the major challenges of the project I am coordinating is communicating the need for change and how that change can improve performance in cost and quality. If the stakeholders are convinced that they need to make changes, then they are more likely to achieve quality and cost goals. Simply put, if I do not effectively communicate why change is needed, then the project fails.

*Catherine Norris*, director of physician network services at Lexington Medical Center, has worked in the health care industry for 25 years in a variety of capacities, including management and nursing.

Courtesy of Catherine Norris

**PC: How do you use communication technologies?**

**CN:** The persons I work with on a daily basis have a broad range of familiarity with communication technologies such as social networking, blogs, and wikis. Some people are very comfortable with these methods, and others have never used them. Therefore, I use the technology communication tool that best fits the situation and is easiest. After all, if the project team and stakeholders do not use a given technology, then there is no point in forcing it.

The project team relies heavily on the use of email, the corporate intranet, and the Internet to communicate. For example, we use email to send routine messages and document attachments back and forth for review and approval. The advantage of using email is that the messages can be tracked. Furthermore, email communication is precise and efficient. You can access your email when you have the time as opposed to waiting to schedule a live face-to-face meeting. Many people today carry smartphones and have email access anywhere. Work gets done efficiently without wasting time.

The project team uses the corporate intranet to schedule meetings and access intranet links to our progress documents for projects. This is a place where internal users can review shared documents, update project assignments, and view project news and webcast links online. Conference phone calls and webcasts for product training and remote meetings have been a very effective means of communicating too.

**PC: How do you choose when to use various communication technologies?**

**CN:** Although I find email very effective for routine messages, face-to-face communication is crucial when the message needs emphasis. That is why our project team has conducted one-on-one, face-to-face meetings to communicate quality and cost performance data to our stakeholders. By doing so, we emphasize why we should focus on these goals now. In addition, it allows for a two-way dialogue with a personal touch. If we used an impersonal communication method like email or a written report delivered to a mailbox, we would miss a valuable opportunity to develop a personal relationship and dialogue around performance improvement.

## Use Interactive Tools Wisely

Most videoconference platforms have many options to make meetings interactive, including screen sharing, polling, online chat, and other features. These tools are excellent when used with purpose. Be careful, however, not to use the tools simply for the sake of being interactive.

## Start the Call with Purpose and Take Charge

Many professionals make a judgment within the first few minutes about the importance of the call. Unless you get people interested and engaged quickly, many participants will tune out and start multitasking.

## Follow the Guidelines of Effective Virtual Meetings

The tried-and-true practices of using an agenda, getting each participant involved, and following up with minutes and action items are essential.

# Chapter Takeaway for *Email and Other Traditional Tools for Business Communication*

**LO7.1 Explain the trade-offs associated with richness, control, and constraints when choosing a communication channel. (pp. 202–205)**

See *summaries of trade-offs* of communication channels in Table 7.1.

**LO7.2 Apply principles for writing effective emails. (pp. 205–211)**

| Principles of Effective Emails | | Components of Effective Emails | |
|---|---|---|---|
| • Use for the right purposes. | • Respond promptly. | • Subject line | • Closing* |
| • Ensure ease of reading. | • Maintain professionalism and appropriate formality. | • Greeting* | • Signature block* |
| • Show respect for time. | • Manage emotion effectively. | • Message | • Attachments* |
| • Protect privacy confidentiality. | • Avoid distractions. | *optional | |

See *examples of ineffective and effective emails* in Figures 7.1 and 7.2.

**LO7.3 Explain how to handle emotion effectively in online communications. (pp. 212–215)**

| Responding to Uncivil Communications | | |
|---|---|---|
| • Reinterpret | • Relax | • Defuse |

See *examples of ineffective and effective responses to uncivil emails* in Figures 7.6 and 7.7.

**LO7.4 Describe strategies for effective instant messaging in the workplace. (pp. 215–217)**

| Guidelines for Texting in the Workplace | |
|---|---|
| • Evaluate the meta message of an instant message or text. | • Avoid sarcasm and jokes in most cases. |
| • Use IMs or texts for simple and brief messages, not for conversations. | • Avoid rescheduling meeting times or places. |
| • Make sure your tone is positive, supportive, and appropriately fun. | • Consider turning off sound alerts for incoming IMs/emails. |
| • Don't ask questions you can get answers to yourself. | • Identify yourself. |
| • Be careful about abbreviated language, emoticons, acronyms, and emojis. | • Clearly end the instant messaging exchange. |
| | • Avoid personal IMs during work hours. |
| | • Avoid sending IMs after work hours. |
| | • Establish rules with your colleagues for instant messaging in meetings. |

See *examples of instant messaging* in Figures 7.8 through 7.11.

**LO7.5 Describe strategies for managing digital message overload. (pp. 218–219)**

| Principles for Managing Emails to Avoid Distractions | |
|---|---|
| • Check digital messages just two to four times each day at designated times. | • Reply immediately only to urgent messages. |
| • Turn off message alerts. | • Avoid unnecessarily lengthening an email chain. |
| • Use rich channels such as face-to-face and phone conversations to accomplish a task completely. | • Use automatic messages to help people know when you're unavailable. |

**LO7.6 Explain principles for effective phone conversations and videoconferences. (pp. 219–223)**

| Guidelines for Phone Calls and Videoconferences | |
|---|---|
| • Schedule and plan for your phone calls. | • Take notes on important points and summarize next steps at the end of the call. |
| • Ensure quality audio. Open with a warm greeting and use your caller's name. After brief small chat, direct the conversation to the issues at hand. | • Close with appreciation. |
| | • Follow up on agreements. |
| | • Practice using the technology before the group call. |
| • Speak with a pleasant, enthusiastic voice. Share conversation time equally. | • Use your webcam effectively. |
| | • Use interactive tools wisely. |
| • Apply the rules of active listening and avoid multitasking. | • Start the call with purpose and take charge. |
| | • Follow the guidelines of effective virtual meetings (see Chapter 3). |

See an *example of a meeting request and agenda for a phone call* in Figure 7.13 and an *example of a follow-up email after a call* in Figure 7.14.

# Key Terms

active incivility, 212
asynchronous communication, 203
communication channel, 202
constraints, 202
control, 202
coordination, 202
cues, 202
cyber incivility, 212

cyber silence, 212
defusing, 214
flames, 212
immediacy, 202
negativity effect, 212
neutrality effect, 212
passive incivility, 212
permanence, 202

planning, 202
reinterpretation, 213
relaxation, 213
resources, 202
richness, 202
synchronous communication, 203

# Discussion Exercises

**7.1 Chapter Review Questions** (LO7.1, LO7.2, LO7.3, LO7.4, LO7.5, LO7.6)

A. Compare and contrast spoken versus written communication in terms of richness, control, and constraints.

B. Describe three communication channels not listed in Table 7.1 and their strengths and weaknesses in terms of richness, control, and constraints.

C. What strategies can you use to ensure ease of reading in your emails and other digital communications?

D. What strategies can you use to show respect for the time of others?

E. Explain the neutrality effect and negativity effect in digital communications. What do they imply for how you write digital messages?

F. What strategies can you use to avoid email overload and, as a result, increase your productivity?

G. Explain the following components of constructively responding to uncivil digital messages: reinterpretation, relaxation, and defusing.

H. What strategies do you think are most important for effective texting in the workplace?

I. What are some strategies you can use to make better phone calls in the workplace?

**7.2 Questions about Communication Q&A with Catherine Norris** (LO7.1, LO7.2, LO7.3)

Read the Communication Q&A featuring Catherine Norris. Answer the following questions:

A. What principles does Norris use when deciding which communication technologies to use? In what ways do you agree and/or disagree?

B. In her view, how is the corporate intranet useful?

C. According to her, what are the main benefits and drawbacks of email? What future role does it have in business communications? In what ways do you agree and/or disagree?

D. According to her, what are the benefits and drawbacks of face-to-face communication? In what ways do you agree and/or disagree?

E. What was the most valuable information from this interview for you?

**7.3 Information Overload Due to Digital Messages** (LO7.5)

Go to the Information Overload Research Group's website (iorgforum.org). Read a research article, blog entry, or other content about a topic of interest. In three to five paragraphs, explain the following: (a) main points in the article, (b) your views of the main points, and (c) three strategies you will adopt to avoid information overload in the workplace.

**7.4 Internet Communication Taking Over** (LO7.1, LO7.4, LO7.5, LO7.6)

As researchers Simon Wright and Juraj Zdinak stated, "Internet communication is slowly taking over traditional phone-based voice communication and face-to-face communication. Restrictions to local or regional communities no longer apply: The Internet has enabled easy global communication."[41] Think about your future career and answer the following questions:

A. Is the prospect of communicating primarily via the Internet liberating? Explain.

B. Do you view the possibility of less face-to-face communication as disappointing? Explain.

C. What personal characteristics and skills are particularly well suited to success for predominantly Internet-based communication?

# Evaluation Exercises

**7.5 Evaluating Email Messages** (LO7.2)

Compare the less effective and more effective emails in Figures 7.1 and 7.2 in the following ways:

A. Analyze the writing for each email based on tone, style, or design.

B. Evaluate them based on three of the principles for effective emails from this chapter.

C. Make two recommendations for improving the more effective email.

**7.6  Description of Past Work or School-Related Emails** (LO7.2)

Think of recent emails you have received related to work and school. Describe three effective email practices and three ineffective email practices you have observed. Describe each of these practices in detail (a paragraph each) and provide specific examples from emails you have received. You don't need to reveal who sent the emails.

**7.7  Self-Assessment for Email Practices** (LO7.2)

Evaluate your typical practices with regard to email for school or work by circling the appropriate number for each of the following items.

|  | 1 (Disagree) | 2 (Somewhat Disagree) | 3 (Somewhat Agree) | 4 (Agree) |
|---|---|---|---|---|
| I almost always reread my email message in its entirety before sending it. | 1 | 2 | 3 | 4 |
| I write emails in a professional and sufficiently formal manner. | 1 | 2 | 3 | 4 |
| I think carefully about what to write in the subject line. | 1 | 2 | 3 | 4 |
| I use a spell-checker for important email messages. | 1 | 2 | 3 | 4 |
| I envision how the recipient of my email message will respond when she/he receives it. | 1 | 2 | 3 | 4 |
| I think about the preferred communication channel of my message recipient before writing an email. | 1 | 2 | 3 | 4 |
| I read emails from others carefully and in their entirety before responding. | 1 | 2 | 3 | 4 |
| Before sending a reply email, I make one last check to see that I have responded to everything requested. | 1 | 2 | 3 | 4 |
| I regularly schedule uninterrupted time to focus on reading and responding to emails. | 1 | 2 | 3 | 4 |
| I set up an automatic email response or in other ways let others know when I will not be responsive to emails for an extended period (e.g., during vacation time). | 1 | 2 | 3 | 4 |

Add up your score and consider the following advice:

35–40:   You are a *strategic* communicator by email. You carefully plan your emails and make sure that you send a professional communication. Notice the items you did not place a 4 next to and focus on improving in these areas.

30–34:   You are a *careful* communicator by email. You generally plan your emails well. However, you sometimes send them without enough thought or without reviewing them sufficiently. Focus on spending slightly more time in the planning stage.

25–29:   You are an *above average* communicator by email. Sometimes you plan your emails well. Make sure to spend more time before sending an email. Always make sure your content is completely professional before sending it.

Under 25:   You *need to improve* your approach to writing emails. You are too casual. Consider altering your orientation so that you view email as an important, formal business communication tool in which slight mistakes can damage your career.

Write three goals you have for becoming a more effective communicator by email. Go through the items in the survey one by one to help you think of areas where you most need to improve.

**7.8  Assessment of Prior Email or Other Electronic Communication** (LO7.2, LO7.3)

Think of an important email or other electronic communication you have sent in which others misunderstood your emotions and/or intent. How did the other person respond? Did you think the response was fair? Why did this person misunderstand? Did the lack of richness of the communication channel have an impact? How could you have written or approached your message differently to avoid misunderstandings?

### 7.9 Responding to Cyber Incivility (LO7.3)

Respond to the following questions:

A. What types of cyber incivility have you observed or heard about?

B. Based on your own experiences or those of your friends or colleagues, describe a situation in which someone was the target of cyber incivility. Describe the cyber incivility. How well did the target respond? How well did the target reinterpret, relax, and/or defuse the situation?

C. Compare the less effective and more effective responses to an angry email depicted in Figures 7.6 and 7.7. Explain three specific ways in which the more effective response defuses the situation. Also, suggest two improvements you would make to the more effective response in Figure 7.7.

### 7.10 Responding to Digital Messages and Managing Your Time (LO7.5)

Answer the following questions about appropriately responding to digital messages:

A. What do you think is an appropriate response time to the following types of digital messages: texts, microblog messages (such as tweets), and emails?

B. Have others ever found your response time surprisingly fast? Have others ever found your response time to be slow enough to be considered impolite or uncivil? How can you influence the expectations of others regarding how quickly you respond to their digital messages?

C. Explain cyber silence. Provide three examples that you have observed.

D. What is the best way to respond to cyber silence when you need a response from someone else?

E. What three strategies do you or will you use in the upcoming five years to avoid e-interruptions in the workplace?

## Application Exercises

### 7.11 Choose the Right Communication Channel (LO7.1)

Assume the role of Jaclyn (from the chapter case prior to writing an angry email). She has just had a conversation with Haniz about developing a new website. Jaclyn feels that Haniz dominated the conversation and didn't allow her to express her ideas. She thinks the plan to develop the website is incomplete because it doesn't involve the integration of social media. She wants to approach Haniz and discuss the web development plan in more detail. However, she doesn't know how to start the conversation. She is just an intern. Haniz technically isn't Jaclyn's boss, but she is the lead person on the web development project. What would be the best communication channel for this discussion under each of the following circumstances? You may select more than one communication channel or even a combination of

communication channels. Defend each answer with a discussion of richness, control, and constraints.

A. Haniz is in her office with the door open.

B. Haniz is in her office with the door closed, and she is not taking calls.

C. Haniz is out of town for two weeks.

D. Jaclyn is out of town for two weeks.

E. Jaclyn is nervous and uncomfortable about approaching Haniz.

F. Jaclyn thinks Haniz doesn't want to complicate the project by focusing on social media.

G. Haniz has a green MVS (see Chapter 2 for a description of MVSs) and Jaclyn has a blue MVS.

H. Jaclyn has a red MVS and Haniz has a hub MVS.

## Language Mechanics Check

**Review the quotation marks, italics, and parentheses rules in Appendix A. Then, rewrite each sentence to add quotation marks, italics, and parentheses where needed.**

A. The term big data gets misused and overused at marketing conferences.

B. Geraldine gave the speech Making Big Data Work for You.

C. A Wall Street Journal reporter interviewed her after the speech.

D. She has received the Marketer of the Year Award twice 2007, 2011.

E. I think her key catchphrase was big data is a big mess without planning.

F. Big data refers to the exponential growth in data volume, data velocity, and data variety.

G. Geraldine cited a study called Managing Big Data in the Journal of Marketing Science.

H. She sent us the slide deck an attachment in a May 15 email with all the findings from her study.

I. After finishing her presentation, she told our employees, I'm happy to help your marketing team make a plan to use big data in your business.

J. She told us that we could find a lot of useful information in the Harvard Business Review and MIT Sloan Management Review.

# Endnotes

1. "Corporate Intranets 'Useless' to Business," Concentra website, March 2, 2010, retrieved July 6, 2010, from http://live.lewispr.com/concentra/2010/03/02/corporate-intranets-%E2%80%98useless%E2%80%99-to-business-598.

2. Sara Radicati, ed., and Masha Khmartseva, *Email Statistics Report, 2009–2013* (Palo Alto, CA: Radicati Group, April 2009).

3. Radicati Group, "Email Statistics Report, 2015–2019," Radicati Group website, 2015, available at http://www.radicati.com/wp/wp-content/uploads/2015/02/Email-Statistics-Report-2015-2019-Executive-Summary.pdf.

4. Pearn Kandola, *The Psychology of Effective Business Communications in Geographically Dispersed Teams* (San Jose, CA: Cisco, 2006); Likoebe M. Maruping and Ritu Agarwal, "Managing Team Interpersonal Processes through Technology: A Task-Technology Fit Perspective," *Journal of Applied Psychology* 89, no. 6 (2004): 975–990.

5. Arvind Malhotra, Ann Majchrzak, and Benson Rosen, "Leading Virtual Teams," *Academy of Management Perspectives* 21 (2007): 64.

6. Malhotra et al., "Leading Virtual Teams": 60–70.

7. Roy A. Cook and Gwen O. Cook, *Guide to Business Etiquette*, 2nd ed. (Upper Saddle River, NJ: Prentice Hall, 2011); Susan Bixler and Lisa Scherrer Dugan, *How to Project Confidence, Competence, and Credibility at Work: 5 Steps to Professional Presence* (Avon, MA: Adams Media, 2001); Beverly Langford, *The Etiquette Edge: The Unspoken Rules for Business Success* (New York: American Management Association, 2005); Dale Carnegie Training, *The 5 Essential People Skills: How to Assert Yourself, Listen to Others, and Resolve Conflicts* (New York: Simon & Schuster, 2009).

8. Based on December 2015 survey of 1,004 marketing, R&D, and IT managers in the following industries: Finance, Banking, and Insurance; Health Care and Social Assistance; Manufacturing; and Retail and Wholesale Trade. Findings of this survey first presented at the following academic conference: Peter W. Cardon, "The Role of Leadership Communication and Emotional Capital in Driving Internal Social Media Use," presentation at the Association for Business Communication Southeast/Midwest Regional Conference, St. Louis, MO, April 23, 2016.

9. Jeanne C. Meister and Karie Willyerd, *The 2020 Workplace: How Innovative Companies Attract, Develop, and Keep Tomorrow's Employees Today* (New York: HarperCollins, 2010).

10. Langford, *The Etiquette Advantage: The Unspoken Rules for Business Success.*

11. Alan Murray, "Should I Use Email?" *The Wall Street Journal* website, retrieved July 15, 2010, from http://guides.wsj.com/management/managing-your-people/should-i-use-email/.

12. Michael Hyatt, "Email Etiquette 101," retrieved July 15, 2010, from http://michaelhyatt.com/2007/07/email-etiquette-101.html.

13. Nick Morgan, "Don't Push that Send Button!" *Harvard Management Communication Letter*, August 2002: 4.

14. Bixler and Dugan, *How to Project Confidence, Competence, and Credibility at Work: 5 Steps to Professional Presence*: 116.

15. Greg Wright, "Twitter with Care: Web 2.0 Usage Offers Few Second Chances," Society for Human Resource Management website, July 30, 2009, retrieved June 28, 2010, from www.shrm.org/hrdisciplines/technology/Articles/Pages/TwitterCarefully.aspx.

16. Peter W. Cardon, Melvin Washington, Ephraim A. Okoro, Bryan Marshall, and Nipul Patel, "Emotional Intelligence and Norms of Civility for Mobile Phone Use in Meetings," presentation at the Association of Business Communication 75th Annual Convention, Chicago, October 28, 2010.

17. Beverly Langford, *The Etiquette Advantage: The Unspoken Rules for Business Success.*

18. Dale Carnegie, *How to Win Friends and Influence People* (New York: Simon & Schuster, 1981): 83.

19. Joan Waldvogel, "Greetings and Closings in Workplace Email," *Journal of Computer-Mediated Communication* online 12, no. 2 (2007), retrieved from http://jcmc.indiana.edu/vol12/issue2/waldvogel.html.

20. Kristin Byron, "Carry Too Heavy a Load? The Communication and Miscommunication of Emotion by Email," *Academy of Management Review* 33, no. 2 (2008): 313.

21. Ibid.

22. Ibid.

23. Ibid.

24. Mei Alonzo and Milam Aiken, "Flaming in Electronic Communication," *Decision Support Systems* 36 (2004): 205.

25. Kandola, *The Psychology of Effective Business Communications in Geographically Dispersed Teams*: 5.

26. Norman A. Johnson, Randolph B. Cooper, and Wynne W. Chin, "Anger and Flaming in Computer-Mediated Negotiation among Strangers," *Decision Support Systems* 46 (2009): 663.

27. Vivien K. G. Lim and Thompson S. H. Teo, "Mind Your E-manners: Impact of Cyber Incivility on Employees' Work Attitude and Behavior," *Information & Management* 46 (2009): 419.

28. Lim and Teo, "Mind Your E-manners: Impact of Cyber Incivility on Employees' Work Attitude and Behavior": 419–425.

29. Johnson et al., "Anger and Flaming in Computer-Mediated Negotiation among Strangers": 660–672.

30. Pew Research Internet Project, "Mobile Technology Fact Sheet," January 2014, *Pew Research Internet Project website*, retrieved from www.pewinternet.org/fact-sheets/mobile-technology-fact-sheet/.

31. Joe Robinson, "Email Is Making You Stupid," *Entrepreneur*, March 2010: 61–63.

32. Ibid.

33. Ibid.; Sally McGhee, "4 Ways to Take Control of Your Email Inbox," Microsoft At Work website, retrieved July 15, 2010, from www.microsoft.com/atwork/productivity/email.aspx; Alex Cavoulacos, "4 Strategies for Keeping Your Inbox Empty: Which One Is Right for You?" (2016), The Muse website, available at www.themuse.com/advice/4-strategies-for-keeping-your-inbox-empty-which-one-is-right-for-you; Larry Rosen and Alexandra Samuel, "Conquering Digital Distraction," *Harvard Business Review*, June 2015: 110–113.

34. Richard Ling, "The Socio-Linguistics of SMS: An Analysis of SMS Use by a Random Sample of Norwegians," in Richard Ling and Per Pedersen, eds., *Mobile Communications: Re-negotiation of the Social Sphere* (London: Springer, 2005).

35.   Melvin Washington, Ephraim A. Okoro, and Peter W. Cardon, "Perceptions of Civility for Mobile Phone Use in Formal and Informal Meetings," *Business and Professional Communication Quarterly* 77: 52–64; Lindsay Gellman, "Taking Your Phone into a Meeting? Read This First," *The Wall Street Journal* online, October 24, 2013, retrieved from http://blogs.wsj.com/atwork/2013/10/24/taking-your-phone-into-a-meeting-read-this-first/.

36.   Anthony K. Tjan, "Don't Send That Email. Pick up the Phone!" *HBR Blog Network,* November 1, 2011, retrieved from http://blogs.hbr.org/2011/11/dont-send-that-email-pick-up-t/.

37.   Jeffrey Kluger, "We Never Talk Any More: The Problem with Text Messaging," *CNN*, retrieved from www.cnn.com/2012/08/31/tech/mobile/problem-text-messaging-oms/; Pamela Paul, "Don't Call Me, I Won't Call You," *The New York Times,* March 18, 2011, retrieved from www.nytimes.com/2011/03/20/fashion/20Cultural.html; O², "Making Calls Has Become Fifth Most Frequent Use for a Smartphone for Newly-Networked Generation of Users," *The Blue* blog, retrieved from http://news.o2.co.uk/?press-release=Making-calls-has-become-fifth-most-frequent-use-for-a-Smartphone-for-newly-networked-generation-of-users.

38.   Based on Cardon, "The Role of Leadership Communication and Emotional Capital in Driving Internal Social Media Use."

39.   Kevin Young, "The High Cost of Multitasking," *The Fuze* blog, January 21, 2014, retrieved from http://blog.fuze.com/the-high-cost-of-multitasking-infographic/.

40.   Based on Cardon, "The Role of Leadership Communication and Emotional Capital in Driving Internal Social Media Use."

41.   Simon Wright and Juraj Zdinak, *New Communication Behaviors in a Web 2.0 World—Changes, Challenges, and Opportunities in the Era of the Information Revolution* (Paris: Alcatel-Lucent, 2008): 6.

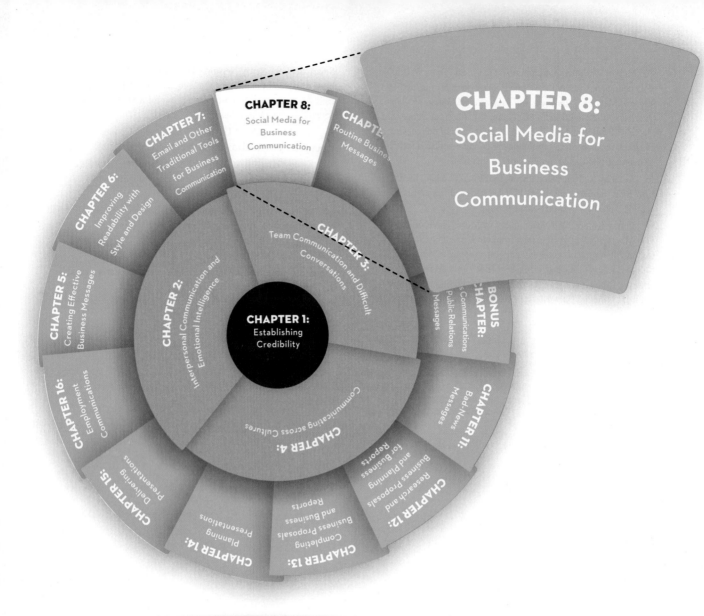

CHAPTER 8:
Social Media for
Business
Communication

ESTABLISHING
CREDIBILITY

PRINCIPLES OF INTERPERSONAL
COMMUNICATION

PRINCIPLES FOR & TYPES OF
BUSINESS MESSAGES

## Learning Objectives

After studying this chapter, you should be able to do the following:

**LO8.1** Explain characteristics of the emerging Social Age.

**LO8.2** Use blogs, wikis, forums, and other social tools for effective communication within organizations.

**LO8.3** Create blogs for effective external communications.

**LO8.4** Build a credible online reputation.

**LO8.5** Describe the ethical use of social media for work.

With all the social media tools available to collaborate and communicate with others, you're entering the workplace at an exciting time! These social tools include shared files and work-spaces, blogs, microblogs (such as Twitter), wikis, and other collaboration tools. Compared to email and other nonsocial technologies, these social tools can dramatically improve productivity. The average knowledge worker in the United States spends about 28 hours per week reading and sending emails, searching for information, and collaborating internally. By transitioning to social tools, the average knowledge worker can save roughly six to eight hours per week and produce better work.[1]

Even for professionals familiar with using social media in their personal lives, using social tools for work isn't always natural or simple. It takes some hard work to figure out how to use these tools well and establish your professional voice. While these social tools can help you gain professional opportunities more quickly than ever, these same tools can magnify and broadcast mistakes as well. So, it's worth carefully thinking about how to use these tools well in your career. This chapter provides a variety of strategies for you to use social tools to connect and collaborate with colleagues, customers, and other contacts.

> **Hear Pete Cardon explain why this matters.**
>
>
>
> **bit.ly/cardon8**

**CHAPTER CASE:** COMMUNICATING WITH SOCIAL MEDIA AT THE PRESTIGIO HOTEL

**WHO'S INVOLVED**

Andrea Garcia, general manager

Nancy Jeffreys, director of marketing

Barbara Brookshire, director of conventions

Jeff Anderton, marketing assistant

Kip Yamada, marketing associate

The Prestigio Marketing Team

### The Marketing Team Uses Blogs, Status Updates, and Shared Files for Team Communication

The marketing team has recently started using enterprise social software, which functions in many ways like Facebook but is customized for use within an organization. The team is using blogs, status updates, shared files, and other tools to follow up with one another related to action items agreed on in meetings; discuss ongoing projects and campaigns; and update one another about their accomplishments.

**SITUATION 1**

**The Marketing Team Discusses Policies for Handling Customer Complaints**

Nancy, the director of marketing and advertising, and Kip, a marketing associate, recently disagreed about how to handle authorization for refunds. Kip thought that front-desk employees should be able to make refunds for up to $500 without authorization from managers. He thought this policy showed trust in the front-desk employees and also showed goodwill toward hotel guests. Nancy was concerned that this would place front-desk employees in awkward situations when guests made unreasonable claims. She thought that front-desk employees should not be authorized to make refunds for more than $50 without authorization from managers. Nancy and Kip agreed to open up a forum to the marketing team to see what their views are on this issue.

**The Marketing Team Uses Blogs for External Communications**

The marketing team has started using blog posts on its website and social media platforms to give customers, prospects, and other stakeholders an inside view of the company. They hope to better promote the organization to their stakeholders.

**TASK**

**1**

How will the marketing team use social tools to work more efficiently together?

**2**

How can the marketing team discuss the issue of authorization for refunds on a discussion forum?

**3**

How can the marketing team use blogs to improve the Prestigio's brand?

## Communicating in the Workplace in the Social Age

**LO8.1** Explain characteristics of the emerging Social Age.

**Visit** http://connect. mheducation.com for an exercise on this topic.

Many online communication tools used in business—social networking, blogs, messaging, discussion forums, and others—are driving profound changes in how people connect and collaborate in the workplace. These changes are so profound that workplace culture is moving into a new era: from the Information Age to the Social Age (see Figure 8.1). The **Social Age** is an era in which people engage in networked communication, collaborate across boundaries, and solve problems communally.[2] However, even though the communication technologies that have paved the way for the Social Age are changing rapidly (in months and years), workplace culture is relatively slow to change (in years and decades). So, as you read this section, keep in mind that cultural norms and values more significantly influence the impact of social media in the workplace than do its technical capabilities.

The evolution of the Internet during the past 15 years from Web 1.0 to Web 2.0 platforms is the primary driver of the Social Age. In the original Internet, referred to as **Web 1.0**, most web pages were read-only and static. As the Internet evolved, referred to as **Web 2.0**, what emerged was the read-write web, where users interact extensively with web pages—authoring content, expressing opinions, and customizing and editing web content among other things. Web 2.0 communication tools, often referred to as **social media**, include social networks, blogs, wikis,

FIGURE 8.1

The Evolving
Workplace

| Industrial Age | Information Age | Social Age |
|---|---|---|
| Command-and-control (Little communication between teams and units) | Mass two-way communication (Extensive communication between teams and units) | Networked communication (Extensive communication between individuals with shared interests) |
| Respect for position | Respect for expertise and position | Respect for expertise and contributions to the network |
| Holding authority is power | Holding knowledge is power | Sharing knowledge is power |
| Efficiency, competitiveness, and authority are key values | Autonomy, innovation, and achievement are key values | Transparency, honesty, and camaraderie are key values |

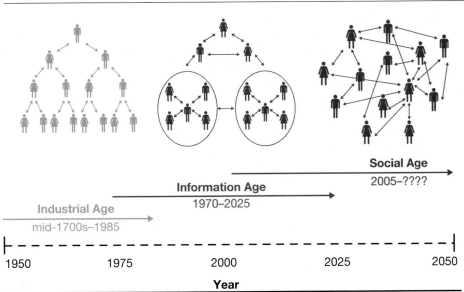

gaming, podcasts, and information tagging. In simple terms, Web 1.0 communication tools are primarily passive and static. By contrast, Web 2.0 communication tools are interactive, customizable, and *social*.[3] **User 1.0** refers to an individual who primarily uses and prefers Web 1.0 tools, whereas **User 2.0** refers to an individual who primarily uses and prefers Web 2.0 tools (see Table 8.1).[4] The emerging Social Age involves adopting many workplace norms and values from users of Web 2.0 tools.

TABLE 8.1

Comparisons between User 1.0 and User 2.0

| User 1.0 | User 2.0 |
|---|---|
| Passively reads and searches for content. | Actively creates and shares content online. |
| Depends on content creator; does not express own opinion. | Can express opinions and even change the content presented. |
| Gets the web as is. | Customizes web pages and content. |
| Email is the main communication tool. | Peer-to-peer programs are the main communication tools. |
| The computer is the main access point. | Connects from mobile devices. |
| Connected online for time-limited sessions. | Connected online all the time. |

### Major Components of Social Networking Platforms

- User profiles*
- Blogs/microblogs*
- Wikis
- Private messaging systems**
- Discussion forums*
- RSS feeds
- Social bookmarking
- Rating and tagging
- Video sharing
- Podcasts
- Mashups

*Given more attention in this section because they are writing-intensive
**Nearly identical to email in function and form

Increasingly, companies are adopting social networking platforms that contain Web 2.0 communication tools (also called *enterprise social software* and *Enterprise 2.0*) in the workplace. These platforms contain many of the features available on social networking websites: user profiles, microblogs, blogs, wikis, and file uploading. They often include a variety of other communication and collaboration tools as well, including online audio and video calls, shared work spaces, calendars, and private messaging (or email) systems. Thus, most companies—especially medium- to large-sized businesses—are increasingly moving toward corporate intranets that contain both Web 1.0 and Web 2.0 tools.

The emerging work culture associated with the Social Age presents many benefits to companies and business professionals in the context of team and networked communication (see Table 8.2).[5] When social media are used for professional purposes, teams can communicate more efficiently; companies can interface more responsively with customers, clients, and suppliers; customers and other interested individuals can be directly involved in the development of products and services; and anyone with shared professional interests can communicate easily, not needing to travel to see one another.

Social media also present many challenges and risks. The primary challenges are cultural. Some of them are age-based: older employees are more accustomed to the communication tools they have used for years and decades. Typically, the Web 1.0 tools reinforce many older employees' work values, such as privacy and autonomy. The use of social media creates a free flow of information that, in many cases, runs counter to traditional business approaches to decision making, lines of authority, team formation, performance incentives, and so on.

One basic challenge of using social media internally is getting employees to participate. In most companies, participation in blogs and wikis is fairly low.

**TABLE 8.2**

Benefits and Challenges of Social Media in the Workplace

| Benefits of Social Media | Challenges and Risks of Social Media |
|---|---|
| *To companies:*<br>• Team communication and collaboration<br>• Succession planning<br>• Recruitment and on-boarding<br>• Idea sharing/knowledge management<br>• Skills development and training<br>• Interfacing with customers, suppliers, and partners<br>• Decreased time to market for new products and services<br>• More innovative, creative, effective, and profitable approaches to work problems<br>• Less time and fewer resources needed for business travel | *To companies:*<br>• Lack of adoption and penetration<br>• Lack of permanence<br>• Confusion over which communication channels to use<br>• Distraction from work, too much socializing<br>• Lack of control of information provided externally and internally<br>• Lack of systems for rewarding networked and team communication and collaboration |
| *To business professionals:*<br>• Build professional networks internally and externally<br>• Access business expertise and knowledge more rapidly<br>• Enhance camaraderie with peers | *To business professionals:*<br>• Lack of boundaries between professional and private lives<br>• Lower productivity due to multitasking<br>• Excessive opportunism and self-promotion<br>• Mistakes and incompetence broadcast to larger audiences |

The case of Wikipedia is instructive. Although millions of Internet users consider Wikipedia to be a reliable source of information, only a small fraction of users are also Wikipedia authors and contributors. Wikipedia is consistently among the ten most visited websites. Yet, less than 1 percent of users ever contribute to its entries.[6]

Social media use also presents a variety of risks. For companies, social media can lead to lower productivity when employees use them for social and entertainment purposes, release confidential and proprietary information, post inappropriate comments that lead to reputation loss for companies, and go around lines of authority. On an individual level, social media can lead to major credibility loss (discussed further in "Managing Your Online Reputation").

## Using Social Media Tools for Communication within Organizations

Using social tools for everyday communication has dramatic impacts in the workplace. Various research suggests that productivity can grow by between 10 and 25 percent.[7] In this section, we briefly touch on several of the social software tools you can expect to use in the workplace: dashboards, user profiles, blogs and status updates, and discussion forums (usually simply called *forums*). We focus on these tools for a few reasons. They are among the most widely used and most effective social tools, and they involve significant written communication.

**LO8.2** Use blogs, wikis, forums, and other social tools for effective communication within organizations.

### Organize Your Dashboard to Control Your Communication and Information Flow

Nearly all social software systems contain a *dashboard*, your front page when you log in, which operates as your communication and information hub.Your  dashboard gives you many opportunities to learn and connect with others. By setting up your dashboard strategically, you can learn more about the people in your organization and develop business expertise each day. You can also allow  others to learn more about you and enhance your credibility within your  organization.

In most cases, you can customize the dashboard to display the features that most interest you. For most teams, displaying status updates and other project notifications should be most prominent. You can also display your mail, your schedule, the communities you belong to, people you follow in the organization, and even use plug-ins for external social readers to learn more about your industry and your field (the "Guidelines for Using Social Media in the Workplace" section contains information about using social readers).

### Create a Complete and Professional Profile

In your profile, you provide information about yourself, such as your position, contact information, professional interests, and current projects. You can usually provide a picture and list personal interests outside of work. Profiles are an excellent way of finding people within an organization with needed expertise or shared professional interests. Profiles as part of enterprise social software systems appear much like those in Facebook and LinkedIn.

In your profiles, make sure you provide complete information. This is a chance for colleagues and clients who do not know you well to learn about your professional background, abilities, and interests. Colleagues in your organization who do not know you well may be more likely to contact you for projects and other opportunities based

**FIGURE 8.5**

## Appropriate Reactions to Shared Files

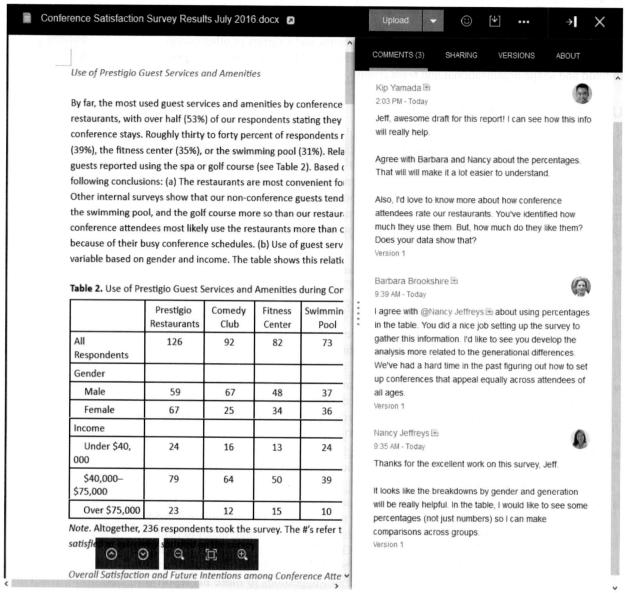

© John A Rizzo/Pixtal/SuperStock; © image100/PunchStock; © Photodisc/Getty Images

- *Avoid leading posts.* Just as leading questions hinder listening in face-to-face communication, leading posts harm online discussions. Figure 8.6 displays an abbreviated discussion forum that is not effective. Take a few minutes to read it. One of the first things you'll notice is the leading subject line, which is nothing more than Kip's strong opinion. This immediately places the forum on the wrong trajectory.

- *Avoid ignoring competing points of views.* Many ineffective forums are the result of professionals sharing their own views but not acknowledging the views of others. You'll notice a variety of posts in the ineffective forum (Figure 8.6) where Kip and Nancy state their views but don't directly acknowledge one

**FIGURE 8.6**

## An Ineffective Example of a Forum Conversation

 Kip Yamada
3 Posts

### Creating a Policy for Front Desk Employees Giving Refunds That Makes for Happy Employees and Satisfied Guests

😊 Like

Today 6:30 PM  |  Tags: employee, policy, refund, satisfaction

Our current policy about asking managers to authorize refunds is problematic in a variety of ways. First, it's ridiculous we don't trust our front desk employees to make good judgments about whether employees deserve refunds. Second, it creates extra wait times for many of our guests with legitimate complaints. Our employees spend five minutes talking to a manager behind the scenes while our guests wait in line getting more and more impatient. Raising the amount front desk employees can refund without managers' authorization to $500 is a no brainer.

Reply

*Updated on Today at 6:54 PM by Kip Yamada*

---

 Nancy Jeffreys
2 Posts

**Re: Creating a Policy for Front Desk Employees Giving Refunds That Makes for Happy Employees and Satisfied Guests**

😊 Like

Today 6:33 PM

We need to be careful about changing policies based on HUNCHES. We developed the current policy after years of experience and recognizing that most guests with large refund requests are unfounded. Our front desk employees actually prefer the current policy and have preferred it for years.

Reply  |  Response Permalink

*Updated on Today at 6:41 PM by Nancy Jeffreys*

---

 Barbara Bro...
1 Post

**Re: Creating a Policy for Front Desk Employees Giving Refunds That Makes for Happy Employees and Satisfied Guests**

😊 Like

Today 6:45 PM

What is the current policy and how was it developed?

Reply  |  Edit  |  Delete  |  Response Permalink

---

 Kip Yamada
3 Posts

**Re: Creating a Policy for Front Desk Employees Giving Refunds That Makes for Happy Employees and Satisfied Guests**

😊 Like

Today 6:54 PM

I've talked to several of the front desk employees who don't like the current policy and want more freedom to make decisions about refunds. Recently, one of our long-time guests, Janis Friedman, was so aggravated with the refund process that she moved some of her business meetings to a competing hotel. If the front desk employee would have gone with her initial instincts in the case of Janis, she wouldn't have taken her business elsewhere

Reply  |  Response Permalink

---

 Nancy Jeffreys
2 Posts

**Re: Creating a Policy for Front Desk Employees Giving Refunds That Makes for Happy Employees and Satisfied Guests**

😊 Like

Today 6:56 PM

Trust me - the front desk employees do not want a policy that gives them more freedom to give larger refunds. That basically gives guests the green light to make outlandish claims, and then these employees are stuck in a situation where they have to reject these guests, who are often angry. 😠

Reply  |  Response Permalink

---

 Kip Yamada
3 Posts

**Re: Creating a Policy for Front Desk Employees Giving Refunds That Makes for Happy Employees and Satisfied Guests**

😊 Like

Today 7:05 PM

See this is just the problem. The current policy assumes that our guests are not telling the truth or that they make absurd claims. In my experience we can generally trust our guests. If they are upset, it's often for a good reason. I guess nothing will really change around here unless we can trust our guests.

Reply  |  Response Permalink

another's points. Professionals, even in forums, often "talk over" one another. This doesn't help Kip or Nancy influence others. It also discourages teammates from participating in the forum.

- *Avoid strong, rigid language.* Rarely are forums the right outlet to persuade others from the outset. Rather, the goal of forums is to explore one another's ideas and build solutions together. Strong and rigid language signals that people are not open to the ideas of the team. This language can come in the form of *either-or options* (i.e., "the only way to . . ."), *finality*—implying the issue is not open to debate (i.e., "we already decided to . . ."), *exaggeration* (i.e., "the best way to . . ."), and otherwise *judgmental terms* (i.e., "ridiculous"). As a rule of thumb, if you sense that you or others are trying to "win the argument," you should stop and reflect whether the direction of the discussion is helpful for your team and its goals.

- *Avoid complaining.* Complaining can drag down any conversation, including an online discussion. The major problem with complaining is dwelling on the inability to avoid negative outcomes. You'll notice that Kip's comments in the ineffective forum often contain this sense of exasperation and certainty of poor outcomes. Many professional forums contain rants. These rants on enterprise social networking platforms remain as permanent records and sometimes serve as the first impressions colleagues have of one another.

- *Avoid blaming.* Blaming is similar to complaining in that it often places responsibility entirely on others. It is more serious, however, because it often serves as an attack on others. In the ineffective forum, Kip and Nancy indirectly blame one another throughout the forum. Kip blames Nancy for not understanding the needs of front desk employees and guests. Nancy blames Kip for forming his conclusions based on hunches rather than careful research.

- *Avoid off-topic points.* The major value of forums is holding targeted, specific conversations. When professionals start discussing unrelated issues, the forum loses its value for several reasons: (a) the discussion is unlikely to produce results for the original purpose; (b) some participants discontinue participating; and (c) the discussion loses its appeal as a reference in later conversations.

- *Avoid excessively short or lengthy posts.* Typically, posts that are too short show that participants aren't engaging the forum sufficiently. On the other hand, excessively lengthy posts often go unread. They also may signal that the writer is disinterested in a back-and-forth discussion with teammates.

- *Avoid sarcasm.* Sarcasm is usually misinterpreted on forums. One reason sarcasm doesn't work on forums is that it generally applies to a context at a shared moment. Since forums often run over days and weeks, this shared context at a point in time is missing.

You can use a variety of strategies to make forums effective ways for your teams to produce better work. Consider the following strategies:

- *Read your peers' comments completely and carefully.* You'll save time by making sure you read every comment carefully. By doing so, you provide better comments and show that you care about your teammates. In fact, you'll often realize your influence grows as others see your efforts to learn from them.

- *State the purpose of the forum clearly.* The subject line for the forum should clearly lay out the question or purpose of the forum. In the effective forum in Figure 8.7, you can see that the forum subject is posed as a clear, specific question. Also, make sure the first few posts clearly describe why the issue is important and provide some background. This motivates other team members to participate.

- *Use flexible, open, and inviting language.* You can express your views with confidence while also signaling that you want to hear from others. Using phrases such as *I think, I suggest,* or *perhaps we should* allows you to voice your opinions while staying open to others.

**FIGURE 8.7**

## An Effective Example of a Forum Conversation

 Kip Yamada
5 Posts

**What Should Our Policy Be for Front Desk Employees Providing Refunds?**

☺ 1 Like

Today 11:21 AM | Tags: customer, desk, front, policy, refund, satisfaction, service

> ⬆ This question has not been answered yet.

Our current policy is that front desk employees must get managers' authorizations for any refund requests over $50.

I think we should raise this amount to $500. Several front desk employees have told me they want this latitude. I also know of several cases where guests with legitimate refund requests became so upset with the lengthy refund process that they moved some of their business to other hotels.

Nancy thinks the current policy is working well. She'll share her reasoning in a post to this forum. Nancy and I would like your input about this policy.

Reply

 Nancy Jeffreys
3 Posts

**Re: What Should Our Policy Be for Front Desk Employees Providing Refunds?**
Today 11:23 AM

☺ 3 You like this  -  Unlike

I agree with Kip that we can't afford to lose valued guests who make reasonable requests. I think it's worth revisiting our current policy. As a matter of background, we created the policy for the following reasons:

- Several years ago we concluded that roughly 70 percent of refund requests over $50 are not justified. Generally, managers are trained to handle these rejections.
- When we talked to all front desk employees several years ago, the majority preferred the policy of deferring to managers. They thought some guests accepted rejections more easily from managers.

As I mentioned, I think it's worth revisiting the policy, so please share your views and experiences.

Reply | Response Permalink

 Barbara Bro...
2 Posts

**Re: What Should Our Policy Be for Front Desk Employees Providing Refunds?**
Today 11:26 AM

☺ 2 Like

Thank you, Kip and Nancy, for sharing this information about the policy. I think we're trying to find a balance between accommodating guests who have reasonable complaints and politely rejecting guests who do not have reasonable complaints.

As far as front desk employees, I think there's been several changes since a few years ago. Many of the front desk employees now aspire to manager positions, so they tend to hold longer-term views of the importance of the guests to Prestigio's brand and LT business.

Reply | Edit | Delete | Response Permalink

 Kip Yamada
5 Posts

**Re: What Should Our Policy Be for Front Desk Employees Providing Refunds?**
Today 11:36 AM

☺ 3 You like this  -  Unlike

Thank you to each of you for offering your input. I suggest we spend about 15 to 20 minutes at our next marketing meeting to finalize our ideas about this policy. Based on our discussion, here are the major points of agreement:

- We should consider raising the amount front desk employees can refund without authorization to between $150 and $200.
- We should consider providing more training to front desk employees about handling disgruntled guests.
- We should informally survey front desk employees about our ideas.

Reply | Response Permalink

- *Build on the ideas of others and pose questions.* The best forums result from team members referencing and connecting each other's ideas. Posing questions will often help draw out the ideas of teammates.
- *Show appreciation for your teammates and their ideas.* You don't have to agree with everything your colleagues suggest to show appreciation. Find ways to see merit in their ideas. Use their names to show your interest in them individually. Assume that they are acting in the interest of the team and the organization.

- *Participate often.* Forums work well when all team members visit the forum regularly. One major threat to productive discussions is inconsistency. First comers sometimes state their views and then never return to the forum. Late-comers may disrupt the process by not entering the discussion until after other team members have developed a consensus. If these latecomers go against the hard-earned consensus of the team, they cost the whole team time and morale. Consistent participation by each team member makes the process smooth and productive.

- *Meet in real time for touchy points.* Forums are excellent for fairly routine conversations. If the online discussion gets contentious or raises sensitive issues, schedule a time for the team to discuss the issues in real time. You'll accomplish much more in a real time conversation and reduce the likelihood of misunderstandings.

- *Summarize and, as appropriate, identify next steps.* The purpose of most forums is to help a team discuss an issue and arrive at solutions. By the end of the forum, summarize the discussion and identify actions your team will take.

- *Talk with your team about ways to make forums help your decision making and coordination.* Much like we discussed in Chapter 3 about team communication, your team should evaluate its performance. As part of this process, your team should periodically discuss how well forums work and how you can improve them.

### Other Social Media Tools

Many other communication tools exist on social networking platforms. Further-more, Enterprise 2.0 platforms are constantly evolving and adding communication tools. You would be wise to experiment with all the communication tools available on these platforms so you can identify and use the channels best suited for your audiences.

## Writing Blogs for External Audiences

**LO8.3** Create blogs for effective external communications.

**connect**

Visit http://connect.mheducation.com for an exercise on this topic.

Increasingly, stakeholders expect an insider view of organizations. One effective way of *telling the story* of your organization is through blog posts. Usually, these posts originate on a corporate website. Then, these posts are generally linked to a variety of public social networking platforms, such as Facebook, Google+, LinkedIn, Instagram, and Pinterest. Also, many professionals now write blogs about their professional interests. These blogs are a powerful way of personal branding. In this section, we'll discuss these two forms of writing blogs for external audiences.

### Write Posts for Your Organization

The primary goal of blogs for organizations is effective public relations (PR). Tra-ditionally, PR was viewed as media relations, and the primary vehicles for PR mes-sages were press releases. Over the past several decades, during the Information Age, the scope of PR broadened and it became a key component of the market-ing mix.[10] PR has been defined as "the management function that establishes and maintains mutually beneficial relationships between an organization and the var-ious publics on whom its success depends."[11] In other words, PR is fundamentally about *building relationships* with employees, customers, communities, the media, and other stakeholders.

A primary goal of building these relationships is to improve corporate reputation or credibility. Elliot Schreiber, one of the foremost authorities on public relations, recently defined **corporate reputation** on the Institute for Public Relations website:

> From the perspective of the organization, reputation is an intangible asset that allows the company to better manage the expectations and needs of its various stakeholders, creating differentiation and barriers vis-à-vis its competitors. From the perspective of stakeholders, reputation is the intellectual, emotional and behavioral response as to whether or not the communications and actions of an organization resonate with their needs and interests.[12]

This definition reveals several key aspects of reputation. First, it is an asset; it has value. Studies suggest that reputation directly contributes to between 3 and 7.5 percent of annual revenues. For some companies, reputation can increase revenue even more. Second, having a positive reputation is not enough. A company's reputation must differentiate it from its competitors. Third, a primary goal of public relations is managing the expectations of stakeholders. And most important, through public relations, a company develops a reputation that delivers value to stakeholders based on their own needs and interests.[13]

**Idea Development for Public Relations Messages**    Because a primary goal of PR is to create distinctive brand value for a company, any individual message should be considered a piece in this larger effort. So, the first step is to clarify your company's brand and, through discussion, gain a shared sense of the brand message. Without this agreement among colleagues, a company may produce nonunified, perhaps even confusing, messages.

Many PR messages center on drawing positive attention to products and services, especially those that are newly launched, recently improved, or recently awarded or otherwise recognized. Developing your ideas for PR messages involves understanding these products and services completely and accurately. Furthermore, it involves identifying which products and services the company intends to highlight. Thus, it requires discussions of the company's strategy for promoting various products and services. Once you have done all this, you are ready to act much like a news reporter. You gather accurate and reliable information that tells a compelling story of what the company has done.

> **Components of Press-Release Style Blog Posts**
> - Headline
> - Dateline
> - PR story
> - Boilerplate
> - Contact information
> - Call to action

**Message Structure for Public Relations Messages**    In the press-release style, which still accounts for most written PR messages, the main components include a headline, dateline, the story, a boilerplate, and contact information. The *headline* immediately captures the attention of stakeholders. Next, the *dateline* allows readers to identify when the story occurred. Then, the *PR story*—whether it's announcing a product launch, an act of charity, an event, or some other type of notable corporate activity—is written in third person in what is often referred to as *inverted pyramid style*.

The *story* should answer the basic questions of *who*, *what*, *when*, *where*, and *why* quickly within the first paragraph. The story then provides supporting details—the second tier of the inverted pyramid. At the end of the PR story, a *boilerplate* or *positioning statement* briefly explains background about the company: the nature of its business, its products and services, its customers, and its *unique selling position,* meaning what distinguishes it from competitors. Typically, minor PR announcements are just 100 to 300 words, and major announcements are generally 500 to 800 words.[14] You can see an example of this type of blog post in Figure 8.8.

Another common approach to PR messages is the op-ed style. Traditionally, a corporate leader would write an opinion piece in first person about a challenge or issue shared by the company and the public. As with press releases, the scope of the op-ed approach for PR has grown. Just a decade ago, op-eds were written for newspapers and

**FIGURE 8.8**

A Press-Release Style Blog Post

| MENU | *The Prestigio* | Find & Reserve | Meetings & Events | Reservations |

Blog>

**The *Prestigio Market Restaurant* Adds Spice to the Menu**

July 18, 2016
Posted by Kip Yamada

The award-winning Prestigio Market Restaurant just turned up the heat! Head Chef Fiona Nickerson unveiled three new menu items last week, each featuring a new combination of spices.

Chef Fiona spent the past six months working on these new menu items. The dishes include Coconut Curry Chicken, Szechuan Tofu, and Jamaican Jerk Wild Wings.

I asked Chef Fiona about trends in spicy foods. She explained, "We've seen an explosion of interest in spicy foods in the past few years. Not just jalapeños and red chile peppers but also anchos, Szechuan peppers, turmeric, coriander, and cumin."

Chef Fiona explained that each new dish is a fusion of ethnic dishes with local tastes. Coconut Curry Chicken combines Bengali-style curry with our area's famous love of coconuts. Szechuan Tofu is inspired by a Chinese-style bean curd dish with a mix of locally grown green beans and peppers.

The restaurant has always been famous for its wings. Chef Fiona beamed as she talked about the new Jamaican Jerk Wild Wings. "I think our wing lovers are going to love this dish. We marinate these wings overnight with a combination of jalapeños, thyme, black pepper, nutmeg, and a few other spices. It literally took us six months of daily trials to get this one just right!"

Last night I joined Louise and Jim Adams. Louise offered this assessment of the Coconut Curry Chicken: "The flavors are delicious. I loved it. Just the right kick!" Jim exclaimed his verdict on the Jamaican Jerk Wild Wings: "I try the wings wherever I go. I have never tasted anything quite like these wings. Just awesome!"

These new menu items are July Special Items, so they'll remain at 20 percent off for the rest of the month. To get a sneak peak, watch Chef Fiona work her magic on these dishes in this YouTube clip.

- - - - - - - - - - - - - - - - - - - - - - - - - - - - - - - - - - - - - - - - - - - - - - - - - - - - - - - - -

The Prestigio Market Restaurant is open from 11 a.m. to 9 p.m. daily and serves a variety of delicious and healthy menu items. All fruits and vegetables are organic and sourced within 50 miles of the restaurant. You can contact Kip Yamada to arrange business events at the restaurant or contact the reservation desk for small group reservations.

other periodicals on an irregular basis. Now, however, the op-ed style is common on corporate blogs, where business leaders can regularly share their opinions and experiences. You can see an example of this type of op-ed in Figure 8.9.

## Write Posts for a Professional Blog

Increasingly, business professionals have opportunities to build personal brands with social media tools. One of the best ways of establishing thought leadership is to create blog posts that focus on areas of expertise or interests. Many professionals create

**FIGURE 8.9**

An Op-Ed Style Blog Post

| MENU | *The Prestigio* | Find & Reserve | Meetings & Events | Reservations |

Blog>

**Green Meetings Make Us Leaner and Improve the Bottom Line**

July 25, 2016
Posted by Andrea Garcia and Jeff Anderton

Meeting planners often ask us, "Do green meetings really make a difference?" One planner even commented to us, "I wonder if green meetings are like so-called 'low-fat' foods. They sound great but I'm still overweight."

We started implementing green meetings at the Prestigio a few years ago, and we can say definitively, *"Yes, green meetings make a difference."* As far as environmental impacts, we're leaner than ever. We're also passing major savings on to conference organizers.

With just a few simple measures, here's what we accomplished last year with green meetings:

- *We served water in pitchers rather than bottles.* We estimate we saved nearly 40,000 gallons of water as a result.

- *We helped meeting planners, at their request, use apps and e-reader formatted programs rather than printed conference schedules.* We estimate we saved roughly 800 trees.

- *We ensured that over 90 percent of produce in our restaurants was grown within 50 miles.* We estimate we significantly reduced our carbon footprint associated with food deliveries.

We've already started additional steps to make more dramatic impacts. Within the next year, we will replace all our vans with hybrid versions and require our vendors to meet green standards. Within two to three years, our hotel will be LEED certified. We anticipate overall drops in carbon emissions by almost 30 percent.

Some of these measures save money and others cost more. Overall, these measures drop conference costs significantly. Last year we priced green conferences seven percent lower than non-green conferences. In fact, we estimate that the average green conference saved organizers more than $18,000.

Yes, green meetings make a difference. They're better for the environment and better for the pocketbook.

- - - - - - - - - - - - - - - - - - - - - - - - - - - - - - - - - - - - - - - - - - - - - - - - - - - - - - - - - - - - - - - - - - - - - - -

The Prestigio Hotel & Resort is a high-end resort committed to excellence in conferences, events, and other special occasions in an environmentally friendly, responsible way. You can learn more about conferences and events by contacting Barbara Brookshire.

their own blogs (many free platforms exist such as WordPress and Google's Blogger). Other professionals post their entries on well-known social networking platforms such as LinkedIn. While you can distinguish yourself on these external platforms, you can also write blog posts on enterprise social networking platforms that help give you a reputation of expertise within your organization.

Typically, you can employ several strategies on your own professional blogs. First, develop a theme that readers easily recognize and that captures your areas of expertise or interests. Second, make sure your blog posts maintain a professional, fun, and helpful tone. Third, make sure your content is accurate. You can quickly gain a reputation as an expert with strong posts yet gain a reputation as a novice if there are obvious mistakes in your content. Most blog writers enhance their credibility by providing hyperlinks to their source or reference material. This helps readers make judgments about the quality of your posts. Also, make sure your content is interesting and front-loaded. You've got only 5 to 15 seconds to draw your readers in, so make sure you capture their interest immediately. Finally, stay responsive to your readers' comments. You can often learn what your readers are looking for by sifting through comments. Because so many styles exist for professional blogs, you should read the blogs of popular business and management bloggers to figure out some options that might work for you. You can see one example of a professional blog in Figure 8.10. Jeff Anderton, a marketing assistant at the Prestigio, has his own blog about digital marketing and customer loyalty. This blog can serve as a way for Jeff to continue to develop professional knowledge and develop a personal brand that will provide professional opportunities.

# Guidelines for Using Social Media in the Workplace

Many communication tools fall under the social media platform. Generally, you can apply the following advice to any of them.

## Principles for Professional Social Media Use

- Be an active contributor.
- Read, listen, and learn.
- Focus on content.
- Make your content accessible.
- Make your messages authentic and friendly.
- Be responsive and help others.
- Respect boundaries.
- Participate in communities.

## Be an Active Contributor and Join Communities

If your company or professional group has committed to using social networking platforms, make sure you contribute regularly and respond to the comments and work of others. As an example, for individual blogs, those employees who gain the largest followings (and thus a reputation for thought leadership) make blog entries and other posts two to three times per week.

Online communities are excellent places to network and participate with professionals in your organization and those with shared professional interests outside your organization. Your company's digital platform will likely offer many ways to join online communities. Some communities are built around committees, task forces, and teams with specific charges or tasks. Other communities are built around shared professional interests, such as finance or project management. These communities are often called *communities of practice* and allow you to share and learn from other professionals in your area. Yet other communities are focused on personal interests and hobbies. Generally, actively participating in these communities will open up many professional and learning opportunities.

## Read, Listen, and Learn

Social media offer an ideal means of continuously learning about your company, your industry, and your discipline. In Chapter 3, we focused on the importance of having a listening-centered approach to communication. Used wisely, social media give you many ways to read, listen, and learn.

With the wealth of online information, you can take steps on a weekly basis to learn more about your areas of expertise, your industry, and other topics of interest. Using social reading platforms (such as LinkedIn Pulse, Digg Reader, or Flipboard), you can weed out less relevant information and efficiently access information to develop your knowledge and skills. Ideally, you will set apart at least several hours per week to read and learn with a social reader. To make the best use of these platforms, consider the following strategies:

- *Identify the 20 to 50 sources of information that are most helpful to you.* This is the most time consuming part about setting up a social reader. You'll likely need to experiment over time to identify the best mix of information for you. Consider

**FIGURE 8.10**

An Example of a Personal Professional Blog

## The Digital Strategies and Customer Loyalty Blog

**Home**          **About**          **Past Blog Posts**

### How Much Service and Content Should You Give Away for Free?

August 1, 2016
Posted by Jeff Anderton

**About Jeff**

I'm a marketing assistant at the Prestigio Hotel. I write about trends in digital marketing and customer loyalty. All views are my own.

Many software and consulting companies rely on a business model of giving away content and services. To make money, of course, these companies need paying customers. This business model is called *freemium* (combines the words *free* and *premium*). A well-known freemium company is LinkedIn. Most customers pay nothing for free profiles with a small proportion of customers paying for premium services.

In the recent *Harvard Business Review* article "Making 'Freemium' Work," Vineet Kumar provides an overview of the freemium business model. He presents the cases of LinkedIn, NYTimes.com, Spotify, and Dropbox. Kumar explains that freemium companies must figure out how to offer some features for free to attract new users, yet retain other features that are reserved for premium users. So, how do you do that? Kumar gives some hints but not any specific answers.

Over the past few weeks, I've read articles by many of the experts on freemium business models. They generally recommend the following strategies to find the "sweet spot" between offering too much or too little free content:

1. *Use the RIGHT MODEL.* Freemium expert Lincoln Murphy has examined this business model for nearly a decade and identified seven distinct freemium business models. Some companies even use more than one business model for various products and services. To know which model to use, freemium companies should know answers to the following questions: (a) Will the content or services remain free forever? (b) Will users or organizations purchase the content or services? (c) Is the primary purpose to get customers to upgrade or to get them to purchase other products or services (a cross-sell strategy)? (d) Is the base product intended to create an ecosystem? Without answering these questions carefully, companies may choose the wrong model and get the free/premium mix wrong.

2. *Keep track of the RIGHT METRICS.* One company that's mastered the mix between free and premium content is Breaking Into Wall Street, an educational service about landing a finance position. Its founder and president, Brian DeChesare, recently sat down for an interview with *Forbes* and mentioned all freemium companies must measure the following: (a) What is the cost of content creation? (b) How long will free content attract new customers? (c) What are the costs of updating free content? (d) What is the expected ROI on free content?

3. *Hire the RIGHT PEOPLE to oversee the process.* Among the most successful creators of a freemium company was David Sacks, founder and CEO of Yammer. He recently guest authored the article "When Freemium Beats Premium" for the *WSJ*. Sacks says that "a lot of effort, experimentation, and fine-tuning" are needed to succeed with freemium. So, yes, it's important to capture the right metrics. You need people who understand data. But, it's also important to hire people who embrace uncertainty and use a trial-and-error process to figure out what to give away for free and what to reserve for paid customers.

**FIGURE 8.11**

A Social Reader to Build Your Expertise

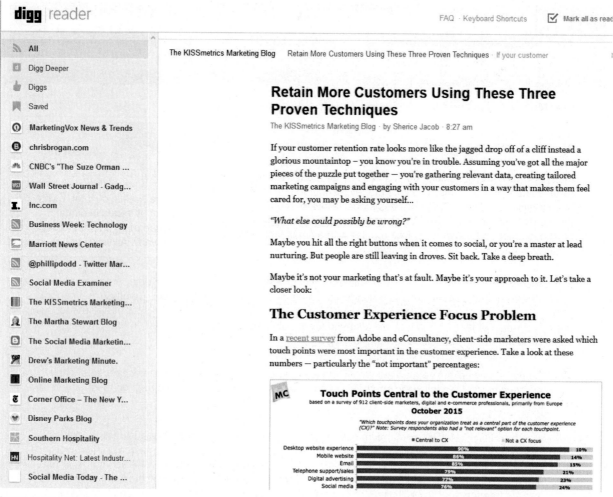

Source: Digg.com/reader

following professionals you admire (inside and outside your company), companies of interest (including competitors), and news sources related to your professional interests and expertise (set up as RSS feeds to important periodicals and thought leaders). For example, notice how Kip sets up a social reader on DiggReader.com in Figure 8.11. Digg Reader allows him to rapidly access information about social media marketing and the hospitality industry.

- *Use hashtag and other topical searches to track important information to you.* In addition to following sources of information, wisely using automated searches allows you to get relevant information for your professional interests. You can use a variety of platforms to automate this process. Notice in Figure 8.12 how Kip uses Tweetdeck to create a news feed based on various automated searches (with hashtags such as #hotelmarketing and #eventprofs). With several weeks or months of experimentation, you can generally set up search-based newsfeeds that help you find the best of your company's digital platform and the Internet with little effort on your part.

- *Take time to read important articles and posts.* Most online readers are skimmers. Skimming is important to quickly extract key ideas. You will learn more deeply and notice you are more informed than many of your peers by setting

**FIGURE 8.12**

A Customized Newsfeed on Tweetdeck

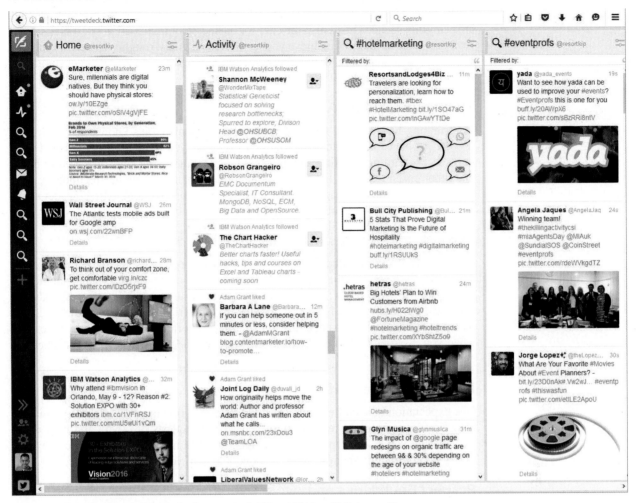

John A Rizzo/Pixtal/SuperStock; Tweetdeck.twitter.com; (reel): © Donald Erickson/Getty Images RF

aside at least a few hours per week for dedicated, comprehensive reading of key articles and posts in your area. Commit to taking enough time to process this information well.

● *Recognize and praise the contributions of others.* Make sure to like and compliment the well-developed content of others. Many of your colleagues and other contacts will greatly appreciate your well crafted, specific praise. They'll also likely return that appreciation when you post your own content.

## Focus on Content

Blogs, wikis, forums, and even newsfeeds are collaborative tools. In other words, they are intended to help you work more effectively with your team members, other colleagues, and clients. The primary goal is not to entertain; it is to provide value to others and increase your professional, not social, credibility (as discussed in "Managing Your Online Reputation").[15] The content of your posts should focus on your work projects, meetings, shared goals, experiences, and expertise and knowledge.

Of course, social media are called *social* for a reason. They provide professionals with rich and exciting communication tools. Including social content is good to a point. In high-performing teams, 60 to 70 percent of all comments are directly related to work, about 15 to 20 percent of comments are supportive, and about 10 to 15 percent are primarily social. This is also the case for business communication via social media. As a good rule of thumb to achieve your professional goals, roughly 70 percent of your social media content should be directly related to work, roughly 20 percent should be supportive, and roughly 10 percent should be social.

### Make Your Content Accessible

Contributing to blogs and wikis increases your organization's knowledge. However, if other people can't find and use your contributions, you have not accomplished your purpose. By naming, labeling, indexing, and tagging (applying keywords to your blogs and other posts) well, you help others find your information (see the Technology Tips about tagging in the "Managing Your Online Reputation" section). Also consider using links to your files to help others open them immediately.

### Make Your Messages Authentic and Friendly

Authenticity is key to effective social media messages. Social media readers expect sincerity and the raw truth. Your messages should not come off as spin and should not contradict who you really are. Be clear about your intentions. Your messages should also have a friendly tone. However, authenticity and friendliness do not mean sloppy writing or rudeness. When engaging in collaborative writing, keep a friendly tone even when you disagree with others. Avoid any urges to delete the comments of others or engage in edit wars.[16]

### Be Responsive and Help Others

One expectation of social networks is that you are a good member of the community. As a good member, you respond positively to the requests of others and help when possible. As you gain a reputation for responding and helping others, you can expect that other community members will respond and help you.

### Respect Boundaries and Avoid Oversharing

The many communication tools available in the emerging Social Age allow people to communicate with nearly anyone at nearly anytime from nearly any location about nearly anything. In other words, the division between professional and private lives is becoming increasingly blurred. Stay observant about where your colleagues draw lines to preserve their lives away from work.

Similarly, notice the frequency with which your colleagues and other contacts appreciate new posts and other social media content. Some employees gain a reputation for oversharing in overall content. They may also overshare when they post so much more than their colleagues that they appear domineering or self-centered.

## Managing Your Online Reputation

**LO8.4** Build a credible online reputation.

**connect**

Visit http://connect.
mheducation.com for an
exercise on this topic.

Although nearly all business professionals are aware of social networking and the importance of strong online reputations, most are still learning to manage their online presences strategically. And although younger people are often expert at developing an online social persona, they are less skilled at developing an online professional presence.[17] As you read this section, think about the opportunities and risks for you as you develop your online reputation.

First, think carefully about developing a **personal brand** in a professional sense—a unique set of professional skills and attributes that others associate with you.[18] In the

**TECHNOLOGY TIPS**

## USING TAGGING FOR KNOWLEDGE MANAGEMENT

One of the strongest benefits of enterprise social software is the ability to tag and index documents and other content so you and your colleagues can find information rapidly. In some organizations, the intranet may contain millions of web pages and files with the collective knowledge of the organization. By providing tags and other information in your posts and files, you make it possible for any colleague in your organization to find your messages. Similarly, if you are writing online business messages for external audiences, your tags can lead customers, clients, and other contacts to your messages with simple Internet searches.

In the image at right, you can see an example of how information can be labeled and tagged for a discussion forum. You can take similar actions for any type of business message in enterprise social software platforms to allow others to quickly find your content.

final chapter of this book, when we turn to job applications, we discuss the notion of promoting your personal brand in more detail. Here, we introduce the idea of building your personal brand and using it as an asset in your career progression. Increasingly, you will express your personal brand through social media tools. One major goal, then, for your online activities is to build a reputation that showcases your credibility and personal brand.

Whether or not you have intentionally created an online presence, potential and current employers, colleagues, and clients will judge your credibility based on online information about you. Thus, you need to take as much control as you can of your online reputation. As portrayed in Table 8.3, one helpful approach is to consider the meta messages, or overall and underlying messages that others decode from your online communications.[19] These meta messages become one basis for your online reputation.

For example, consider two students, Jenny and Regina, who create blogs about their study-abroad experiences in Spain. Jenny's blog describes her observations of her homestay family, the people in the community, and her efforts to learn Spanish. She frequently talks about the generosity they extend to her. She posts pictures of cultural and historical sites as well as many of the people she meets. Her blog sends a meta message, "I'm grateful to the people in Spain for providing me with such a rich learning experience." This meta message feeds into a reputation for open-mindedness, flexibility, curiosity, and appreciation of others.

Regina, on the other hand, mostly posts pictures of herself at pubs. She describes the many friends she has made who are also American study-abroad students. Her longest entry explains how glad she was to go to the Hard Rock Café and get a hamburger "just like back at home." To many readers, the meta message Regina sends is, "I'm having a great time with my American friends in Spain." This meta message may feed into a reputation for complacency and closed-mindedness.

Take a few minutes to think about Table 8.3. You will notice a variety of positive meta messages and related reputations. You can see that these meta messages and reputations are grouped into four areas: personal and private; professional and private; personal and public; and professional and public. In each domain of your online communications, you should think about the meta messages you would like

**TABLE 8.3**

Developing a Credible Online Reputation

| | Positive Meta Messages | Sought-After Reputations |
|---|---|---|
| **Personal and Private** (for family and friends) Example: a family blog | *I'm a good listener* (competence) *I can take care of you* (competence) *I hope the best for you* (caring) *You can always count on me* (caring) *You can trust me* (character) *I'm a fun person* (character) | Communicative, interpersonal skills Dependable, reliable, capable Considerate, caring, concerned Loyal, committed Honest, trustworthy Fun-loving, exciting |
| **Professional and Private** (for work colleagues) Examples: a corporate blog or wiki | *I will get the job done* (competence) *I am a good team member* (competence) *I want you to succeed* (caring) *I want to work with you* (caring) *I will do what I say* (character) *I abide by the rules* (character) | Competent, skilled, dependable Bring out the best in others Supportive, caring Team-oriented, collaborative Sincere, genuine, integrity Moral, ethical, fair |
| **Personal and Public** (for society) Example: social networking website such as Facebook | *I have certain abilities* (competence) *I have certain interests* (competence) *I want to share my experiences and ideas* (caring) *I want to learn about you* (caring) *I have certain social values and priorities* (character) *I live my life according to certain beliefs* (character) | Talented, skilled, capable Determined, focused, driven Open, networked, independent Inquisitive, curious, considerate Activist, cause-driven, passionate Moral, understanding |
| **Professional and Public** (for professional peers) Example: professional social networking website such as LinkedIn | *I am an expert* (competent) *I want to lead a professional discussion* (competent) *I want to share my ideas with you* (caring) *I want to understand your experiences* (caring) *I am committed to my industry* (character) *I think my profession should maintain high standards* (character) | Thought leader, forward-thinking Initiative, leadership, open-minded Generous, giving, collaborative Learning, inquisitive, curious Professional, passionate, committed Ethical, disciplined, consistent |

to send so that you build a credible reputation. Also, because many of your online communications are accessible to personal friends as well as professional contacts, you need to consider whether you are prioritizing your professional or your social reputation.

Social media tools make developing a personal brand easier than ever. You can broadcast your expertise and business interests to an ever-growing network of business professionals. However, social media tools also make it easier than ever to damage your personal brand and online reputation. When you make inaccurate or unprofessional posts, your incompetency, unprofessionalism, and other mistakes are broadcast to a much larger network. In fact, one mistake can undermine your reputation.[20]

Some business professionals damage their reputations because their social media use sends meta messages that they are self-promoters and careerists. Other employees view their online communications as opportunistic and self-centered, believing the self-promoters place their personal career interests ahead of the organization's interests.[21] Generally, the reputation as a self-promoter comes from excessively drawing attention to one's own professional skills and interests. As you adopt other-oriented,

**Nonstrategic.** Does not draw attention to professional interests.

**Nonflattering.** Some people who do not know Kip will form their first impressions of him based on his interest in vulgar and violent movies and games.

**Nonpersonal.** Most business professionals are eager to see a picture in profiles.

**FIGURE 8.13**

Less Effective Personal Social Networking Profile

© Digital Vision/Getty Images;
© Philippe Widling/Design Pics;
© Royalty-Free/Corbis;
© Royalty-Free/Corbis; © Brand X Pictures; © Brand X Pictures;
© John Dowland/Getty Images;
© ximagination/123RF; © Jamie Grill/Blend Images LLC

listening-centered approaches to social media use, you can highlight your own professional skills and interests without reaching what others consider excessive self-promotion.

Compare Kip's online profiles for Facebook, LinkedIn, and Twitter (in Figures 8.13, 8.14, and 8.15). In particular, compare his less effective and more effective Facebook profiles. The evaluations of the examples are based on professional standards, not social standards. Think about the meta messages these profiles may send. At the same time, think about your own online profiles and social networking activity. What meta messages are you sending? What type of reputation are you building?

Social media use is particularly well suited for networked communication. As we have discussed, working in networks is an increasingly important skill and integral to success in the emerging Social Age. As part of large professional networks, seek a reputation as a giver, not a taker. Similarly, always honor your commitments. In networked communication, word gets around quickly about which members are considered givers, which honor commitments, and which do not.

## Using Social Media Ethically

LO8.5 Describe the ethical use of social media for work.

The use of social media—even private use—complicates your relationship with your employer. Consider the following cases:[22]

> An employee who works in research and development updates his Facebook status, bemoaning the fact that he has to cancel his weekend golf plans due to yet another project delay. Other Facebook users connect this with a highly anticipated product launch, and the company's stock price declines.

**FIGURE 8.14**

## More Effective Personal Social Networking Profile

© Royalty-Free/Corbis; © John A Rizzo/Pixtal/SuperStock; © Photodisc/Getty Images; © Don Hammond/Design Pics; © John A Rizzo/Pixtal/SuperStock; © Don Hammond/Design Pics; © Dimitri Vervits/ImageState; © Pixtal/AGE Fotostock; © Andersen Ross/Blend Images LLC; © C. Borland/Photo-Link/Getty Images; © John A Rizzo/Pixtal/SuperStock; © John A Rizzo/Pixtal/SuperStock; © Tim Robberts/Getty Images

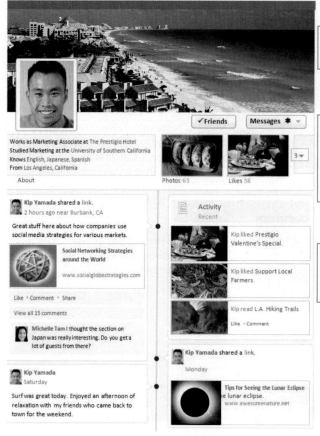

**Strategic.** Draws attention to professional interests in a variety of locations.

**Nondistracting.** Kip provides personal information that does not distract attention away from his professional interests.

**Warm and personal.** The profile picture displays Kip as a professional, friendly person.

**FIGURE 8.15**

## Using Social Media for Work Purposes

© John A Rizzo/Pixtal/SuperStock

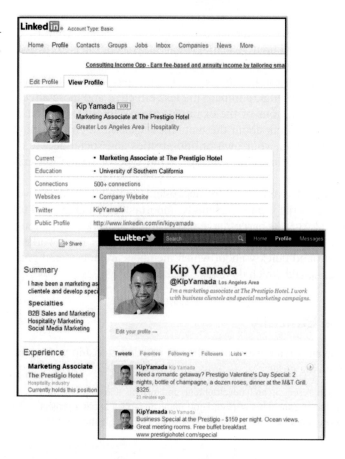

A salesperson posts a derogatory comment on Twitter about a prospective client's headquarters city as he lands there the day before a critical presentation. Someone forwards the tweet to the CEO, who cancels the meeting.

An employee is terminated for cause. A few weeks later, she asks a former colleague to recommend her on LinkedIn. The former colleague writes a glowing recommendation. The terminated employee later uses this recommendation as evidence in a discrimination suit, claiming she was terminated unfairly.

As these various examples illustrate, much more than your online reputation is at stake with social media use; the reputation and performance of your company is at stake as well. The line between what you believe is private use of social media and your role as an employee can be murky because your private actions can damage your employer and hurt your career.

In short, constantly try to understand evolving norms for social media use in a professional context. For your own protection and that of your company, become familiar with your company's acceptable-use policies for social networking websites.[23] Coca-Cola recently compiled a set of social media guidelines for its employees (see the guidelines at this link: www.coca-colacompany.com/stories/online-social-media-principles). The guidelines include statements such as the following: "You are responsible for your actions. We encourage you to get online and have fun, but use sound judgment and common sense." "You are an important ambassador for our Company's brands, and you're encouraged to promote them as long as you <u>make sure you disclose that you are affiliated with the Company.</u>" "When you see posts or commentary on topics that require subject matter expertise, such as ingredients, obesity, the Company's environmental impacts, or the Company's financial performance, avoid the temptation to respond to these directly."[24] In addition to understanding your organization's external social media policies, seek advice about using social media tools within the organization. Read the Communication Q&A with Simon Vaughan for his thoughts about working in new ways with social media tools.

# 💬 COMMUNICATION Q&A

**Peter Cardon: What kind of work do you do with organizations?**

**Simon Vaughan:** My aim is to enable organizations to work in new ways, assisting them in deriving the maximum benefit from their investment in social software. Although I specialize in helping organizations who are implementing IBM Connections (I have used IBM Connections since it was launched in 2007 and have helped influence the development of the product) and implement new collaborative ways of working, the methodology and adoption techniques that I have developed can be applied to any implementation and any business sector. I have helped organizations in the United States, Europe, and Africa move forward on their journey to becoming open, *social* organizations. I am always looking for further opportunities to assist any organization move forward on its *social* journey!

**PC: Why is it important for professionals to use social tools in the workplace? Are these important for all employees?**

**SV:** What I feel is very important is for individuals to derive benefit from the use of social tools in any business-related activity that they perform in their role. Without employees really knowing it, it is now becoming the norm for people to work in a social way. By working "out loud" and in an open manner (maybe by just sharing documents, taking part in open discussions, sharing their expertise, or co-editing a document), this style of work is now becoming common practice without people having to realize (or think!) that they are in fact working in an "open" or "social" way.

**PC: What are the benefits of an organization adopting these new ways of working?**

**SV:** In my view, by adopting an open way of working in the organization, the organization develops a culture of trust, innovation, and transparency. Quite often the organization just needs to see some use cases and benefits from working in new ways to realize that the use of social within the organization can have a profound effect on their bottom line! Use cases and examples of working in new ways are therefore very important, but the most critical aspect to encourage new ways of working is to appoint champions who can help other people and embed the change into the organization. These champions are often subject-matter experts (HR specialists, finance specialists, etc.) in the organization and often prove to be a key focal point in fostering new ways of work.

**PC: In your experience working with organizations, what are some of the key challenges to adopting social tools?**

**SV:** The key challenge is to focus on the benefits from working in new ways, changing behavior, and not just getting hung up on chasing the ROI that most organizations want to see for any "social" investment. It is important to demonstrate measurable, positive benefits and a positive ROI from the use of social, but in my experience, it is important to emphasize that the real goal is to deliver cultural change and change the way people work! My view is that there is often no right way to use a blog, a wiki, or a forum (or other social tool)—the right way is to understand what you are trying to achieve and use the tool that you feel will get the work done (i.e., ask a question and get an answer—use a forum; develop a way of expressing yourself—use a blog; work collaboratively on a document—use a wiki). Education and enablement is also key and the organization needs to have leadership that is supportive of working in new ways and wants to drive change within the organization. In my experience, no one is ever going to question how you use social if the use case has a measurable, positive impact on getting work done!

**PC: For young professionals, what concluding advice would you give about developing skills to use social tools effectively during their careers?**

**SV:** Do not be afraid to take the lead in working in new ways. Practice being open and share everything as in the future you will be judged on what you share, not on what you know!

**Simon Vaughan** *is co-founder of SocialStudent. com. He has helped organizations around the world use social tools to transform the way they work. Simon can be contacted on Twitter at @SimplyS1mon or via email at Simon@ Svaughan.com.*

Courtesy of Simon Vaughan

# Chapter Takeaway for *Social Media for Business Communication*

## LO8.1 Explain characteristics of the emerging Social Age. (pp. 232–235)

### Characteristics of the Social Age

- Networked communication.
- Respect for expertise and contributions to the network.
- Knowledge sharing.
- Transparency, honesty, and camaraderie.

## LO8.2 Use blogs, wikis, forums, and other social tools for effective communication within organizations. (pp. 235–244)

### Principles for Using Internal Communication Tools in the Social Age

- Organize your dashboard to control your communication and information flow.
- Create a complete and professional profile.
- Use blogs and status updates for team communication.
- Use shared files to collaborate.
- Solve problems with discussion forums.

### Principles for Using Forums

- Read your peers' comments completely and carefully.
- State the purpose of the forum clearly.
- Use flexible, open, and inviting language.
- Build on the ideas of others and pose questions.
- Show appreciation for your teammates and their ideas.
- Participate often.
- Meet in real time for touchy points.
- Summarize and, as appropriate, identify next steps.
- Talk with your team about ways to make forums help your decision making and coordination.

### General Principles for Using Social Media

- Be an active contributor and join communities.
- Read, listen, and learn.
- Focus on content.
- Make your content accessible.
- Make your messages authentic and friendly.
- Be responsive and help others.
- Respect boundaries and avoid oversharing.

See *examples of a profile* in Figure 8.2, a *blog used for announcements* in Figure 8.3, *status updates for team coordination* in Figure 8.4, and *appropriate reactions to shared files* in Figure 8.5.

See an *ineffective example of a forum* in Figure 8.6 and an *effective example of a forum* in Figure 8.7.

## LO8.3 Create blogs for effective external communications. (pp. 244–252)

See a *press-release style corporate blog post* in Figure 8.8, an *op-ed style blog post* in Figure 8.9, and an *example of a professional blog post* in Figure 8.10.

## LO8.4 Build a credible online reputation. (pp. 252–255)

See Table 8.3 for *types of positive meta messages you seek to establish your online reputation*.

See *examples of ineffective and effective social networking profiles* in Figures 8.13 through 8.15.

## LO8.5 Describe the ethical use of social media for work. (pp. 255–258)

# Key Terms

# Discussion Exercises

**8.1 Chapter Review Questions** (LO8.1, LO8.2, LO8.3, LO8.4, LO8.5)

A. What are some characteristics of the Social Age?

B. What are some strategies for organizing a dashboard to help you work more efficiently with your teams?

C. What do you think are some of the most important pieces of information for a professional profile on an enterprise social networking platform?

D. When do you think you should use blogs and wikis in teams? How should you decide which to use?

E. What do you think are the primary challenges to running an effective forum?

F. Which strategies do you consider most important when leading a forum? Explain.

G. What elements of tone are most important for social media messages?

H. What strategies can you use to build a credible online reputation?

I. How can you use social media ethically from the perspective of your employer?

**8.2 Communication Q&A Questions** (LO8.1, LO8.2)

A. What does Simon Vaughan say about the new ways of working? What do you think would be his definition of the Social Age? Explain.

B. When Vaughan says that many employees are now starting to use social tools without even knowing it, what does he mean? What does this suggest about persuading others to use social media for business communication?

C. Vaughan says that social tools help organizations develop a "culture of trust, innovation, and transparency." How important do you think this type of culture is? Explain your views.

D. Vaughan suggests that companies should show that social tools help get work done, but also suggests that companies shouldn't get hung up on ROI. What do you think he means? Do you think you can demonstrate the benefits of using social tools without demonstrating ROI?

E. Vaughan says that "in the future you will be judged on what you share, not on what you know." Explain ways that you agree or disagree with this statement. Provide a few concrete examples.

**8.3 Social Media, Online Expression, and Collaboration** (LO8.1, LO8.2, LO8.4)

Vineet Nayar, CEO of HCL Technologies, recently commented about the use of new communication channels. He specifically mentioned the use of social networking and the growing importance of Web 2.0 tools:

> As my kids became teenagers, I started looking at Facebook a little more closely. It was a significant amount of collaboration. There was open understanding. They didn't have a problem sharing their status. Nothing seemed to be secret, and they were living their lives very openly, and friends were commenting on each other and it was working. Here is my generation, which is very security-conscious and privacy-conscious, and I thought, what are the differences? This is the generation coming to work for us. It's not my generation. So we started having people make their presentations and record them for our internal website. We open that for review to a 360-degree workshop, which means your subordinates will review it. Your managers will read it. Your peers will read it, and everybody will comment on it. I will be, or your manager will be, one of the many who read it. So, every presentation was reviewed by 300, 400 people. What happened? There were two very interesting lessons that I learned. One, because your subordinates are going to see the plan, you cannot lie. You have to be honest. Two, because your peers are going to see it, you are going to put your best work into it. Third, you didn't learn from me. You learned by reviewing somebody else's presentation. You learned from the comments somebody else gave you. For the 8,000 people who participated, there was a massive collaborative learning that took place.[25]

Based on Nayar's comments and your own experiences, answer the following questions:

A. What are the potential personal and group benefits from using Web 2.0 communication channels?

B. What are some of the differing attitudes between generations about online expression? What impact might these differences have on workplace communication?

C. In what ways do online communications lead to more honesty and higher-quality work?

D. In what ways might online communications lead to less honesty and lower-quality work?

### 8.4 Challenges to Adopting Social Media for Professional Use (LO8.1, LO8.2, LO8.5)

Andrew McAfee, one of the premier experts on Enterprise 2.0 systems, commented about the challenges of adopting such systems and the shift in orientation needed by management to unleash a culture of User 2.0.

> I thought these technologies [such as Facebook, Wikipedia, Flickr, and YouTube] were essentially so cool that when you dropped them in an organization, people flocked to them. That was the assumption I carried around in my research. I very quickly had that overturned. This is not an overnight phenomenon at all. And while there are pockets of energy, getting mass adoption remains a pretty serious challenge for a lot of organizations.
>
> If you're a middle manager who essentially views your job as one of gatekeeping or refereeing information flows, you should be pretty frightened by these technologies, because they're going to greatly reduce your ability to do that. If you're someone who sees your job as managing people and fundamentally getting the human elements right that will lead your part of the organization to succeed, these technologies are not at all harmful to you. One of the things that we've learned is that there's no technology—even these great new social technologies—that's a substitute for face time. If you have another view of yourself, which is that you're someone who's responsible for output, these tools should be your best friend. Because all the evidence we have suggests that Enterprise 2.0 helps you turn out more and better products and actually is not a vehicle for time wasting or for chipping away at what you're supposed to be doing throughout the day.[26]

Based on McAfee's comments, contents of the chapter, and your own experiences, respond to the following questions:

A. What are the major obstacles to adopting Web 2.0 communication tools in the workplace?

B. McAfee distinguishes between information gatekeepers and managers of people. Explain what you think he means by this distinction and its relevance to the adoption of social software.

C. When are Web 2.0 communication tools more efficient than Web 1.0 communication tools such as email?

D. When are Web 1.0 communication tools such as email better choices than Web 2.0 communication tools?

E. Place yourself in the position of a middle or upper manager. Describe two ways in which the use of social media tools by your subordinates would benefit you and two ways in which they would threaten you.

### 8.5 Social Media Use and Interpersonal Skills (LO8.1, LO8.2, LO8.4)

Jeffrey Zaslow, in a November 5, 2009, article called "The Greatest Generation (of Networkers)" in *The Wall Street Journal*, examined attitudes about Millennials in the workplace. Consider a few of the comments:

> Because so many people in their teens and early 20s are in this constant whir of socializing—accessible to each other every minute of the day via cell phone, instant messaging and social-networking websites—there are a host of new questions that need to be addressed in schools, in the workplace, and at home. Chief among them: How much work can "hyper-socializing" students or employees really accomplish if they are holding multiple conversations with friends via text messaging, or are obsessively checking Facebook?
>
> Some argue they can accomplish a great deal: This generation has a gift for multitasking, and because they've integrated technology into their lives, their ability to remain connected to each other will serve them and their employers well. Others contend that these hyper-socializers are serial time-wasters, that the bonds between them are shallow, and that their face-to-face interpersonal skills are poor.
>
> Does text messaging prepare one to interact in the workplace? "The unspoken attitude is, 'I don't need you. I have the Internet,'" says P.M. Forni, the 58-year-old director of the Civility Initiative at Johns Hopkins University, which studies politeness and manners. "The Net provides an opportunity to play hide-and-seek, to say and not say, to be truthful and to pretend. There is a lot of communication going on that is futile and trivial."
>
> That's far too harsh an assessment, says Ben Bajarin, 32, a technology analyst at Creative Strategies, a consulting firm in Campbell, California. He argues that because young people are so adept at multimedia socializing, their social skills are actually strengthened. They're good at "managing conversations" and getting to the pithy essence of an issue, he says, which will help them in the workplace.
>
> While their older colleagues waste time holding meetings or engaging in long phone conversations, young people have an ability to sum things up in one-sentence text messages, Bajarin says. "They know how to optimize and prioritize. They will call or set up a meeting if it's needed. If not, they text." And given their vast network of online acquaintances, they discover people who can become true friends or valued business colleagues—people they wouldn't have been able to find in the pre-Internet era.[27]

Answer the following questions related to this passage from Zaslow:

A. In what ways do communication tools enhance the effective development of interpersonal skills needed in the workplace?

B. In what ways do communication tools hamper the effective development of interpersonal skills needed in the workplace?

C. What are some of the most valuable communication skills that Millennials bring to the workplace?

D. What are communication skills that you think Millennials most need to develop?

E. It's safe to assume that some non-Millennial workers hold a viewpoint similar to that of P. M. Forni in the preceding passage. What does this imply for you as you enter the workplace?

### 8.6 Blogs on Communication Technology (LO8.1, LO8.2, LO8.3, LO8.4, LO8.5)

Select a blog entry about the impact of communication technologies on corporate culture from a well-known thinker. Search for a blog that interests you or choose from the following:

- Andrew McAfee's blog: http://andrewmcafee.org/blog/
- Jonathan Zittrain's blog: http://futureoftheinternet.org/

Based on the blog entry, respond to the following items:

A. Briefly summarize the topic of the blog entry.

B. According to the entry, what is the impact of communication technology on corporate culture?

C. Describe your feelings and attitudes regarding the entry. Do you agree or disagree with certain points? Are you enthusiastic or pessimistic about various parts of the entry?

D. Explain how the topic will affect you in the workplace.

**8.7 Internet Communication Taking Over** (LO8.1, LO8.2, LO8.4)

As researchers Simon Wright and Juraj Zdinak recently stated, "Internet communication is slowly taking over traditional phone-based voice communication and face-to-face communication. Restrictions to local or regional communities no longer apply: The Internet has enabled easy global communication."[28] Think about your future career and answer the following questions:

A. Is the prospect of communicating primarily via the Internet liberating? Explain.

B. Do you view the possibility of less face-to-face communication as disappointing? Explain.

C. What personal characteristics and skills are particularly well suited to success for predominantly Internet-based communication?

**8.8 Setting Boundaries** (LO8.4, LO8.5)

In a recent survey of corporate employees, 76 percent thought it was OK to friend another employee who was a peer. Only 35 percent thought it was OK to friend a supervisor, and only 30 percent thought it was OK to friend a supervisee.[29] Answer the following related questions:

A. Do you think it is appropriate to friend a supervisor or supervisee on Facebook or another social networking website? What problems could arise by doing so? What work benefits might you achieve? What social boundaries should exist between supervisors and supervisees?

B. Do you think the boundaries between private life and work life are blurred by communication technologies such as social networking? What standards or principles do you want to use to keep parts of your private life separate from your colleagues?

C. Have you ever talked to your colleagues or classmates about your communication preferences? For example, have you discussed preferences for certain communication channels or expected response times? Describe your experiences.

**8.9 Ethical Use of Social Media** (LO8.5)

Reread the three examples of personal social media use that hurt employers (see the beginning of the "Using Social Media Ethically" section). For each item, do the following:

A. Explain why the social media use was unethical.

B. Describe a similar behavior you have observed.

C. Recommend how employees can avoid such problems.

**8.10 Corporate Social Media Guidelines** (LO8.5)

Read Coca-Cola's social media guidelines at the following link: http://www.coca-colacompany.com/stories/online-social-media-principles. Respond to the following items:

A. Generally, what is the difference between speaking "on behalf of the Company" and speaking "about" the company?

B. The policy states that employees are responsible for following the Code of Business Conduct in all public settings. Do you think your online activities on public social networking websites constitute a public setting? Explain.

C. The policy tells employees they should be "conscientious when mixing your business and personal lives." Give five examples of posts that many people might consider private or personal *and* that could damage a company's image.

D. The policy encourages employees to post items that "inspire moments of optimism and happiness." Give five options for employees to make these types of posts. What value do these types of posts provide to Coca-Cola? How might posting as a Coca-Cola employee create opportunities for employees?

E. What types of online conversations about the company are appropriate? Inappropriate?

# Evaluation Exercises

**8.11 Choosing the Right Type of Digital Message** (LO8.1, LO8.2)

For each of the following communication tasks, identify which communication channel you think would work best: email, blogs, or wikis. Write several sentences explaining why you would choose that communication channel. Assume you are a manager sending these messages to your subordinates:

A. Giving updates about an ongoing project.

B. Providing feedback on individual performance.

C. Sending a note of appreciation to one of your subordinates for excellent work.

D. Providing meeting minutes.

E. Setting up a working document about ground rules for participation in meetings.

F. Extending birthday wishes.

G. Sharing ideas with a few but not all of your subordinates.

H. Announcing a meeting for the whole team.

I. Announcing a meeting with two of the team members.

J. Working on a joint marketing proposal.

**8.12 Evaluation of a Professional Blog** (LO8.3, LO8.4)

Choose a professional blog of interest to you. Read a minimum of ten posts. Then, in one to two pages, respond to the following questions:

A. What is the name and web address of the blog?

B. What is the target audience for this blog?

C. How does the content meet the needs of readers?

D. Why would the target audience choose this blog over other similar blogs?

E. How does the blog author(s) establish credibility?

F. What type of online reputation does the blog author(s) create?

G. What design features make the blog effective?

H. What three aspects of this blog will you apply most to your blog?

### 8.13 Evaluation of the Tweets of Business Leaders (LO8.3, LO8.4, LO8.5).

View the recent tweets of two or three business leaders (you might consider looking for accounts of business leaders you're interested in; or, you could find lists of business leaders' accounts such as the following: www.huffingtonpost.com/vala-afshar/the-top-50-social-chief-e_b_3380055.html). Then, write a short report about your observations of these business leaders' tweets. Include the following in your short report:

A. Comparisons between the tweets of your chosen business leaders in terms of the following: (1) style and content of tweets, (2) frequency of tweets, and (3) goals of tweets.

B. Three tips for business leaders when they create tweets.

### 8.14 Evaluating Meta Messages (LO8.4)

Based on the less effective and more effective social networking profiles depicted in Figures 8.13 and 8.14, respond to the following items:

A. What meta messages does each profile send to professionals who do not know Kip? Choose two primary meta messages for each profile.

B. What meta messages does each profile send to colleagues who do know Kip? Choose two primary meta messages for each profile.

C. What meta messages does each profile send to family members and friends? Choose two primary meta messages for each profile.

D. What three recommendations would you make to Kip to improve his Facebook profile (Figure 8.13) and his LinkedIn profile (Figure 8.15) to enhance his professional credibility?

### 8.15 Evaluating Your Online Reputation (LO8.4)

A. Currently, what type of online reputation do you have in a professional sense?

B. In four or five sentences, explain the personal brand you would like to develop over the next five years.

C. Explain three strategies you will employ to develop your personal brand in your online communications. Devote at least one paragraph to each strategy.

### 8.16 Sending the Right Meta Messages with Your Online Communications (LO8.4)

Using Table 8.3 as a guide, do the following for each domain of your online reputation: personal and private; professional and private; personal and public; and professional and public:

A. What are the online communication channels you will use for each domain?

B. Will you use the same channels for more than one domain? If you share any of the communication channels for more than one domain, how will you prioritize which audiences to choose content for?

C. What are the primary meta messages you want to send? Choose two meta messages for each domain and explain how you intend to send these meta messages.

# Application Exercises

### 8.17 Digital Sabbatical (LO8.1, LO8.5)

For 24 hours, avoid using your mobile device or a computer for any communication or accessing online information. (You might consider notifying your friends and family that you will be unavailable during this period.) Write a one- to two-page account of your experience. Consider including discussion about the following:

A. How you felt going without communication (anxiety, relief, stress, peace, etc.).

B. How you felt going without access to digital information (empowered, helpless, out of the loop, etc.).

C. How you think going without digital communications impacts your quality of life, productivity, and/or routines.

D. Based on your experience, give two or three recommendations for how professionals should go about handling digital communication and information.

### 8.18 Social News Reader (LO8.2, LO8.4)

Using a social reading platform (such as LinkedIn Pulse, Flipboard, or Digg Reader), set up a feed of articles and posts that match your professional interests. At a minimum, take the following actions:

A. Follow at least five feeds in your business discipline (e.g., marketing, finance).

B. Follow at least five feeds from an industry of interest.

C. Follow at least five feeds from organizations of interest.

D. Follow at least five feeds of professionals you admire.

Experiment with your social reader for at least one week. Then, report the following:

1. What are the professional interests that you cater to with your social reader?

2. What platform did you use? How easy was it to set up feeds for information of interest?

3. What content is most useful and interesting?

4. What adjustments have you made to make your social reader more useful?

5. What strategies will you use in the future to use social readers for professional purposes?

**8.19 Twitter News Feed** (LO8.2, LO8.4)

Using Tweetdeck or another similar platform, set up a news feed based on searches. Use a minimum of ten hashtags for your searches. Experiment with your search-based news feed for at least one week. Then, report the following:

A. What are the professional interests that you cater to with your search-based news feed?

B. What platform did you use? How easy was it to set up feeds for information of interest?

C. What content is most useful and interesting?

D. What adjustments have you made to make your searches more effective at providing interesting content?

E. What strategies will you use in the future to use search-based news feeds for professional purposes?

**8.20 LinkedIn Profile** (LO8.4)

Based on your LinkedIn profile, respond to the following items:

A. What is your LinkedIn profile address?

B. What are the main traits that stand out about you on your LinkedIn page?

C. What are the main abilities that stand out about you on your LinkedIn page?

D. Which parts of your LinkedIn profile best promote who you are as a professional?

E. Which parts of your LinkedIn profile least promote who you are as a professional?

F. What are three changes you intend to make to improve your LinkedIn profile?

G. What three groups would you like to join and participate in?

H. Which three organizations should you follow? Why?

I. Which three professionals should you follow? Why?

**8.21 Professional Blog** (LO8.3, LO8.4)

Write a blog about a business issue or topic of interest to you and that provides content that is valuable to others. You should develop the blog with a specific audience in mind and provide original, insightful entries. Also, you should develop your blog with your own career interests and desired online reputation in mind. You will write five entries. Each entry should be roughly 700 to 1,000 words. The five entries should combine to meet the needs of your target audience and develop your personal brand. For each blog post, consider applying the following formula: (a) one or two takeaway messages; (b) a catchy title and opening; (c) a winning tone for blogs—helpful, personalized, positive, informative, fun, and interesting; (d) hyperlinks to interesting articles, videos, etc.; (e) images if you'd like (not required); and (f) concise writing with fairly short paragraphs.

# Language Mechanics Check

**8.22 Review the numbers, dates, and currency rules in Appendix A. Then, rewrite each sentence to correct the numbers, dates, and currency where needed.**

A. We should focus on these 2 markets for now.

B. We should focus on seven of the fifteen geographic regions.

C. 15 regions will have new supervisors as of June 20th, 2016.

D. Each purchase above 500 dollars must be approved by June 31st, 2015 to get reimbursed.

E. Employees can contribute up to 7.5% of their salaries to the retirement plan.

F. Nearly 1/3 of our employees contribute the maximum amount to retirement plans.

G. Employees may have up to 4 2MB websites.

H. Employees make an average of 23 dollars per hour.

I. Our revenue for the year topped $2,500,000,000.

J. We gave employee recognition awards to nearly 2/3 (65.3 %) of our employees last quarter.

# Endnotes

1. Michael Chui, James Manyika, Jacques Bughin, Richard Dobbs, Charles Roxburgh, Hugo Sarrazin, Geoffrey Sands, and Magdalena Westergren, *The Social Economy: Unlocking Value and Productivity through Social Technologies* (McKinsey Global Institute, July 2012).

2. Maria Azua, *The Social Factor: Innovate, Ignite, and Win through Mass Collaboration and Social Networking* (Upper Saddle River, NJ: IBM Press, 2010).

3. Michael Chui, Andy Miller, and Roger P. Roberts, "Six Ways to Make Web 2.0 Work," *McKinsey Quarterly* [online version] no. 1 (2010).

4. Simon Wright and Juraj Zdinak, *New Communication Behaviors in a Web 2.0 World—Changes, Challenges and Opportunities in the Era of the Information Revolution* (Paris: Alcatel-Lucent, 2008): 10.

5. Wright and Zdinak, *New Communication Behaviors in a Web 2.0 World*; Andreas M. Kaplan and Michael Haenlein, "Users of the World, Unite! The Challenges and Opportunities of Social Media," *Business Horizons* 53, no. 1 (2010): 59–68; AON Consulting, *Web 2.0 and Employee Communications: Summary of Survey Findings* (Chicago: AON Consulting, March 2009); Jacques Bughin, Michael Chui, and Andy Miller, "How Companies Are Benefiting from Web 2.0," *McKinsey Quarterly* 17, no. 9 (2009); Andrew McAfee, *Enterprise 2.0:*

*New Collaborative Tools for Your Organization's Toughest Challenges* (Boston: Harvard Business Press, 2009); Avanade, *CRM and Social Media: Maximizing Deeper Customer Relationships* (Seattle, WA: Avanade, 2008); Jennifer Taylor Arnold, "Twittering and Facebooking While They Work," *HR Magazine* 54, no. 12 (December 1, 2009); Soumitra Dutta, "What's Your Personal Social Media Strategy?" *Harvard Business Review,* November 2010: 127–130.

6. McAfee, *Enterprise 2.0: New Collaborative Tools for Your Organization's Toughest Challenges.*

7. Chui et al., *The Social Economy: Unlocking Value and Productivity through Social Technologies*; Azua, *The Social Factor: Innovate, Ignite, and Win through Mass Collaboration and Social Networking.*

8. Wright and Zdinak, *New Communication Behaviors in a Web 2.0 World.*

9. Andy Beal and Judy Straus, *Radically Transparent: Monitoring and Managing Reputations Online* (Indianapolis, IN: Wiley Publishing, 2008).

10. Lucy Harr and Dick Radtke, *PR for CUs* (Credit Union Executives Society, 2004): 1; Elliot S. Schreiber, "Reputation," Institute for Public Relations website, December 2, 2008, retrieved from www. instituteforpr.org/topics/reputation/.

11. Schreiber, "Reputation."

12. Andy Green, *Effective Personal Communication Skills for Public Relations* (Philadelphia: Kogan Page, 2006).

13. Patty Deutsche, *Elements of a PR Plan* (San Francisco: e-agency, 2011).

14. Daniel Nations, "The Business Wiki," retrieved November 20, 2010, from http://webtrends.about.com/od/wiki/a/business-wiki.htm.

15. Goetz Boue, *Don't Say Web 2.0, Say Intranet 2.0* (London: Concentra, 2009); Dutta, "What's Your Personal Social Media Strategy?"; Beal and Straus, *Radically Transparent: Monitoring and Managing Reputations Online.*

16. Dutta, "What's Your Personal Social Media Strategy?"

17. Josh Hyatt, "Building Your Brand and Keeping Your Job," *Fortune,* August 16, 2010: 74.

18. Adapted from Dutta, "What's Your Personal Social Media Strategy?": 129.

19. Greg Wright, "Twitter with Care: Web 2.0 Usage Offers Few Second Chances," Society for Human Resource Management online.

20. Hyatt, "Building Your Brand and Keeping Your Job."

21. Jennifer Taylor Arnold, "Twittering and Facebooking While They Work," *HR Magazine* 54, no. 12 (December 1, 2009).

22. Arnold, "Twittering and Facebooking While They Work."

23. Coca-Cola, "Social Media Principles," available at http://www.coca-colacompany.com/stories/online-social-media-principles.

24. Adam Bryant, "He's Not Bill Gates, or Fred Astaire," *Corner Office* (blog), *The New York Times,* February 13, 2010, retrieved from www.nytimes.com/2010/02/14/business/14cornerweb.html.

25. Roger P. Roberts, "An Interview with MIT's Andrew McAfee," *McKinsey Quarterly,* no. 1 (2010).

26. Jeffrey Zaslow, "The Greatest Generation (of Networkers)," *The Wall Street Journal,* November 5, 2009, retrieved from http://online.wsj.com/news/articles/SB10001424052748704746304574505643153518708.

27. Wright and Zdinak, *New Communication Behaviors in a Web 2.0 World*: 6.

28. "Online Etiquette & the Workplace," Liberty Mutual The Responsibility Project website, retrieved July 6, 2010, from www.responsibilityproject.com/infographics/rp-survey-online-etiquette-the-workplace#fbid=67LBedVyvn7.

29. Edelman Trust Barometer 2007 as presented in Andy Beal and Judy Straus, *Radically Transparent: Monitoring and Managing Reputations Online* (Indianapolis, IN: Wiley Publishing, 2008).

# Types of
# Business Messages

# PART

# FOUR

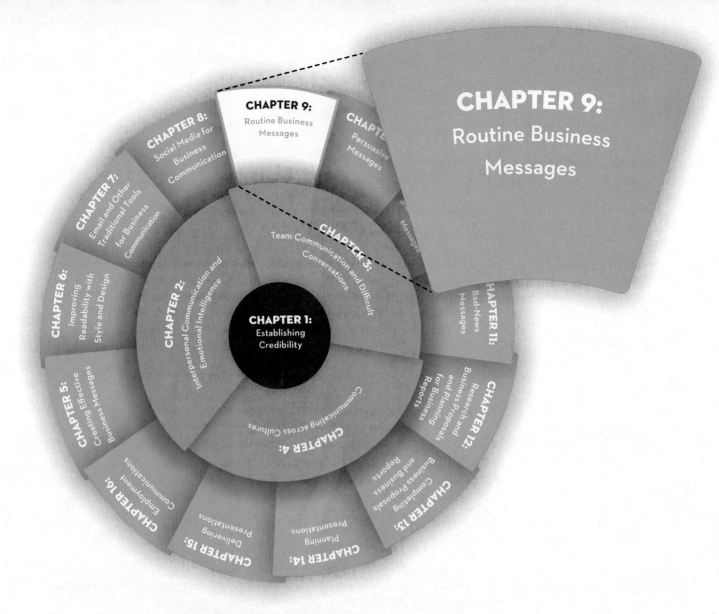

**CHAPTER 9:**
Routine Business Messages

ESTABLISHING CREDIBILITY

PRINCIPLES OF INTERPERSONAL COMMUNICATION

PRINCIPLES FOR & TYPES OF BUSINESS MESSAGES

## Learning Objectives

After studying this chapter, you should be able to do the following:

**LO9.1** Describe how delivering routine messages impacts credibility.

**LO9.2** Describe the process for developing routine business messages.

**LO9.3** Construct task-oriented routine messages, including requests,

expectations, directions, responses to inquiries, announcements, and claims.

**LO9.4** Construct relationship-oriented routine messages, including appreciation, apologies, and expressions of sympathy.

The vast majority of business messages are routine. In routine messages, you are dealing with straightforward information that does not require in-depth analysis, so you generally expect your readers to react positively, and you do not anticipate resistance.

Most routine messages are simple. Yet, routine messages should not be treated as unimportant or inconsequential. They are the glue that holds together most coordinated business actions. In this chapter, we discuss common types of routine messages. Many of them primarily focus on work tasks, such as making requests, setting expectations, providing directions, making inquiries, providing announcements, and making claims. Other routine messages focus on maintaining and improving workplace relationships, such as showing appreciation, offering apologies, and expressing sympathy. The final two types of messages, apologies and expressions of sympathy, are unlike other messages in this chapter in that they occur far less frequently. However, like other messages in this chapter, they are fairly straightforward and require you to compose them fairly quickly.

The day-in-and-day-out routine messages you send may be among the most important for establishing your credibility in the workplace, especially early in your business career. Your approach to routine business messages strongly influences how others evaluate your responsiveness, reliability, attention to detail, commitment, and professionalism.

Read the chapter case about a typical morning at work for Bryan Atkins, an account executive at an advertising firm. Throughout the chapter, you'll see the routine messages Bryan completes before 11 a.m. While Bryan can answer most routine messages with emails of less than one paragraph, we focus on those examples that require slightly more effort. As a result, the examples are generally three to five paragraphs long.

**Hear Pete Cardon explain why this matters.**

**bit.ly/cardon9**

**LO9.1** Describe how delivering routine messages impacts credibility.

## CHAPTER CASE: ROUTINE EMAILS AT SMITH & SMITH ADVERTISING

Bryan Atkins

**WHO'S INVOLVED**

**Account executive at Smith & Smith Advertising**

- Works extensively with clients to ensure they are satisfied with various advertising campaigns
- Leads and coordinates work with the creative teams working on these campaigns

**Bryan Requests Software Licenses for Several Marketing Analysts**

Bryan and several marketing analysts had spent the past few weeks discussing the purchase of statistical software. The software would help the analysts better target customers with online ads and predict online campaign performance.

© Hongqi Zhang/123RF

**SITUATION 1 (8 A.M.)**

Bryan needs approval from one of the partners, Andrea Johansen, to purchase the software licenses. He thought this was a straightforward request but knew Andrea expected him to provide a rationale for and details about the software purchases.

**SITUATION 2**
**(9 A.M.)**

### Bryan Responds to Messages in His Inbox from Employees and Prospects

After the meeting, Bryan sat down at his computer to find 37 new messages from colleagues, clients, and prospects. Bryan thought all of the messages were important enough that he needed to respond to them within two to three hours. Several were most urgent:

- A member of the creative team, Barry Evermore, said he and his partner, John Anderson, had just finished an account and were waiting for new assignments.
- A new member of the creative team, John Anderson (Barry Evermore's partner), was scheduled to take a company trip, but he was unfamiliar with travel procedures at Smith & Smith. He was asking Bryan how to set up his trip.
- A potential client emailed Bryan about services offered by Smith & Smith.

**SITUATION 3**
**(9:30 A.M.)**

### Bryan Makes an Announcement

Bryan works on a committee of account executives and IT specialists to create policies for the firm. The committee just created new bring your own device (BYOD) policies. He will finish drafting a memo to let all employees know about the new policies.

**SITUATION 4**
**(9:40 A.M.)**

### Bryan Takes Care of Overcharges from a Vendor

This morning, Bryan noticed that a hotel had overcharged Smith & Smith by not applying a negotiated rate to several hotel stays for members of his creative team. He wanted to resolve the matter immediately.

**SITUATION 5**
**(10:05 A.M.)**

### Bryan Shows Appreciation to His Creative Team

During the morning, Bryan took a call from a recent client, Ana Galleraga, director of the local zoo. "Hey, Bryan," she said. "Just wanted to let you know what a great success we're having with the ad campaign you developed. Since we started putting up billboard ads and running the radio spots last month, we've increased participation in all of our community educational programs. We're also getting lots of comments about how beautiful the billboards are. Please let everyone over there know what a great job they've done. And, we'd like to figure out how to use the campaign concept in our online marketing." Of course, Bryan told her that the agency could help her out in that regard.

**SITUATION 6**
**(10:30 A.M.)**

### Bryan Issues a Brief Apology

Over the weekend, Bryan worried about insensitive comments he made in last Friday's leadership team meeting. Bryan had accused his colleagues of caring more about one of their clients than about their own employees. This particular client frequently made unreasonable requests, but Bryan and other members of the executive management team never pushed back because the client accounted for nearly one-quarter of Smith & Smith's total revenues. Bryan will apologize quickly at the beginning of the team's 10:30 meeting.

**SITUATION 7**
**(11:30 A.M.)**

### Bryan Expresses Sympathy to a Longtime Client

Bryan wanted to write a sympathy card to his close client Felipe Bravo. Over the weekend, Felipe's wife, Rosa, passed away after a long battle with cancer. Bryan and Felipe have worked together for nearly a decade, and Bryan wanted to express his genuine sympathy to Felipe.

**TASK**

**1** How will Bryan write a routine request for the purchase of new software? (See the "Making Requests" section.)

**2**
- How can Bryan best set expectations for Barry and John's upcoming work schedule? (See "Setting Expectations."
- How can Bryan most efficiently help John make travel plans? (See "Providing Directions.")
- How can Bryan respond in a way that best answers the potential client's questions and maximizes the likelihood that he will become a client? (See "Responding to Inquiries.")

**3** How should Bryan announce the firm's new BYOD policy so that his colleagues will get all the key information rapidly? (See the "Creating Announcements" section.)

**4** How should Bryan make sure the excessive charges are refunded or credited? (See "Making Claims.")

**5** How should Bryan go about congratulating his creative team on its excellent work? (See "Showing Appreciation.")

**6** How can Bryan make amends for his inappropriate comments? (See the "Making Apologies" section.)

**7** How should Bryan express condolences to his client? (See "Expressing Sympathy.")

# Developing Routine Messages

Since you will send and receive so many routine messages in any given business day, one of your primary goals is efficiency: You need to produce credible messages quickly. Excellent business communicators can develop routine written messages—even those that require several paragraphs—in a matter of minutes. The examples in this chapter should generally take 5 to 15 minutes to complete.

Typically, routine messages require less time to complete than other types of business messages. Also, compared to other types of business messages, routine messages require proportionately less time for planning and reviewing. *Developing routine messages quickly, however, does not mean abandoning the writing process of planning, drafting, and reviewing.*

For most routine messages, you can accomplish the AIM planning process fairly quickly (see Figure 9.1). Because you generally are working with straightforward matters and your audience is likely to respond positively, you don't need much time for *audience analysis* or *information gathering*. Still, make sure to identify and gather relevant, accurate, and up-to-date information. Ask yourself questions such as the following: *How would my audience want to receive this information? How much detail do my audience members expect?*

The most important planning step is *message development*. Since routine messages are so common and your readers are likely overloaded with so many other messages and tasks, your primary challenge is to make sure your readers pay attention. Therefore, your message should be direct and front-loaded. The primary message should have ten words or fewer, and you should typically place it in the subject line of your email to

**LO9.2** Describe the process for developing routine business messages.

**connect**

Visit http://connect. mheducation.com for an exercise on this topic.

## Components of Routine Messages

- State the *primary message* (ten words or fewer).
- Provide *details* in paragraphs of 20 to 80 words.
- *Restate* the request or key message in more specific terms.
- State *goodwill*.

FIGURE 9.1

The Writing
Process for Routine
Messages

## PLAN: Get the content right.

- Identify the exact needs of your *audience*.
- Gather relevant, accurate, and up-to-date *information*.
- Create a front-loaded, direct, complete, and detail-oriented *message*.

## WRITE: Get the delivery right.

- Aim for a helpful, professional, reader-centered *tone*. Show respect for your readers' time.
- Apply a concise, easy-to-read, action-oriented *style*.
- Use subject lines and formatting to create a simple navigational *design*.

## REVIEW: Double-check everything.

- Get *feedback* when writing on behalf of a team or unit.
- Ensure your message is *FAIR*.
- Make sure to *proofread*.

immediately capture attention. Furthermore, the primary message should appear in the first sentence or two of the message and again in the closing if your message is several paragraphs long.

In the body of the routine message, you should provide short paragraphs with related details. To make sure your message receiver will comply, include all needed information. Not only are readers less likely to comply when you don't provide enough information, but you also lose credibility. Once you establish a reputation for providing incomplete, overly general messages, your readers are less likely to pay close attention to your future messages.

As you *write* the message, aim for a helpful, professional, and reader-centered tone. Focus on making the message easy to read. Readers expect to understand your primary message in under 10 to 15 seconds, so use short sentences and paragraphs. Design your message so readers can find information in just moments. Use bullets, numbering, special formatting, and external links to relevant information to highlight key ideas.

Your proofreading in the *reviewing* stage should take a minute or two. Since business professionals send so many routine messages each day and their content can be repetitive, they often do not take time to reread them. Avoid this impulse to hit "send" without rereading your messages. By rereading, you will make sure the content is complete and without errors. Even minor typos can distract your readers from complying with your messages.

Since routine messages are straightforward and rarely sensitive, you generally do not need to ask for feedback from trusted colleagues. However, when you speak on behalf of your team, you might check with other team members to ensure they agree about the content. The most important aspect of the FAIR test is checking for accuracy—that is, making certain your information is accurate and reliable.

# Making Requests

You will make thousands of requests of others during your career, and others will make thousands of requests of you. Requests are the essence of people coordinating work efforts, buying and selling products and services, and maintaining work relationships.

Routine requests involve cases where you expect little or no resistance from message recipients. Like all routine messages, routine requests should contain clear and specific subject lines, often stating the entire *request*. As you reread the message before sending it, one question you'll ask yourself is whether the message recipient will understand exactly what to do.

For most requests, you will use a portion of the message to provide the *rationale* for the request. Since you expect a favorable response, you typically do not need to be particularly persuasive. However, justifying the request shows your professionalism and attention to detail. It also helps a company maintain transparency by keeping written records of why certain decisions were made.

One primary goal for routine requests is to retain *goodwill* with the recipient. No one wants to feel bossed around, so make sure you achieve a positive, other-oriented tone. Also, when working with superiors, be careful about setting deadlines. Even in today's flatter organizations, being bossy to the boss can be counterproductive. Finally, when making requests, showing respect for the recipient's time goes a long way in maintaining goodwill.

In Bryan's request memo to Andrea for new software (see Figures 9.2 and 9.3), the request is routine because Andrea will likely approve his request. The primary

**LO9.3**  Construct task-oriented routine messages, including requests, expectations, directions, responses to inquiries, announcements, and claims.

**connect**

Visit **http://connect. mheducation.com** for an exercise on this topic.

---

**FIGURE 9.2**

Less Effective Routine Request

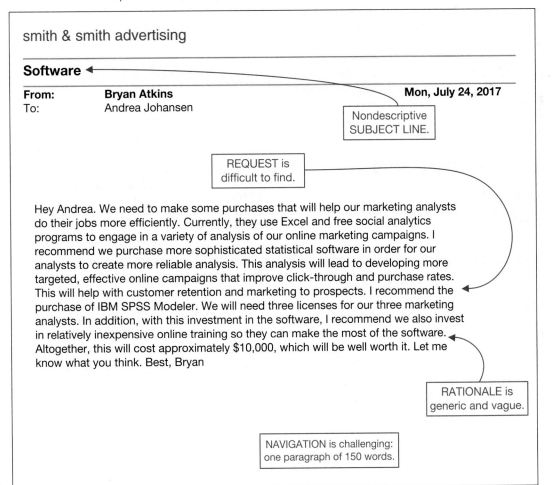

smith & smith advertising

**Software** ◄ — Nondescriptive SUBJECT LINE.

From: **Bryan Atkins**          **Mon, July 24, 2017**
To:      Andrea Johansen

REQUEST is difficult to find.

Hey Andrea. We need to make some purchases that will help our marketing analysts do their jobs more efficiently. Currently, they use Excel and free social analytics programs to engage in a variety of analysis of our online marketing campaigns. I recommend we purchase more sophisticated statistical software in order for our analysts to create more reliable analysis. This analysis will lead to developing more targeted, effective online campaigns that improve click-through and purchase rates. This will help with customer retention and marketing to prospects. I recommend the purchase of IBM SPSS Modeler. We will need three licenses for our three marketing analysts. In addition, with this investment in the software, I recommend we also invest in relatively inexpensive online training so they can make the most of the software. Altogether, this will cost approximately $10,000, which will be well worth it. Let me know what you think. Best, Bryan

RATIONALE is generic and vague.

NAVIGATION is challenging: one paragraph of 150 words.

**FIGURE 9.3**

More Effective Routine Request

---

smith & smith advertising

SUBJECT LINE short
(9 words) but effective.

---

**Purchase of IBM SPSS Modeler for Our Marketing Analysts**

---

**From:** **Bryan Atkins** **Mon, July 24, 2017**

To: Andrea Johansen

REQUEST stated
clearly and upfront.

Dear Andrea:

Can you provide a purchase authorization for statistical software for our three marketing analysts?

During the past month, our marketing analysts (Moku Singh, Elissa Morales, and Josh Liebowitz) and I have explored ways to improve the prediction and tracking of online ad campaigns. Over the past few years, the analyst team members have relied primarily on spreadsheets and other basic statistical software. With more complex data than ever, they now need more sophisticated tools.

RATIONALE is
specific and clear.

Moku and Josh attended several workshops this past month about using various statistical software packages. They also talked to marketing analysts at other firms about the tools they use. One of their contacts showed them how she improved click-through rates and purchases on several online ad campaigns by more than 40 percent by using predictive modeling and other techniques.

After comparing several software packages and learning about training options, Moku and Josh recommend purchasing the following items

| Item | Number | Cost | Note |
|---|---|---|---|
| SPSS Modeler License | 3 | $9,399 | Negotiated discounted rate of $3,133 per license |
| SPSS Modeler Online Training | 3 | $2,250 | 2-day online training at $750 per student |
| Estimated Tax | 1 | $816 | Based on 7.5% sales tax |
| **Total** | | **$12,465** | |

Andrea, we're eager to make these purchases and allow the analyst team to begin using these tools. Please let me know if you can authorize these purchases.

Thanks,

Bryan

NAVIGATION is easy:
Paragraphs are 14, 60, 59,
58, and 27 words long.

goal is to convey the information in an easy-to-read, complete format. In the more effective message (see Figure 9.3), Bryan justifies the request with sufficient rationale and detail. He is direct but not bossy or domineering, which is important since he is writing to his boss.

## Setting Expectations

Working with others involves setting expectations, especially when you are in management and supervisory roles. Many young business professionals—especially first-time managers—are not comfortable with telling others what to do. They are nervous about overstepping their authority and disrupting a friendly feeling with subordinates. Yet, setting expectations is directly tied to your credibility and ability to foster interpersonal trust in the workplace. Dennis S. Reina and Michelle L. Reina have examined the nature of trust in hundreds of companies over the past few decades and say this about setting clear expectations:

> A lack of clarity regarding expectations causes misperceptions and misconstrued intentions. When people's expectations are not met, they may feel a range of emotions. They may feel disappointed, discounted, taken advantage of, angry, or hurt. The result may be distrust and feelings of betrayal. . . . When people don't find out what is expected of them until they run into a wall, go down the wrong road, or fail to get a promotion or pay raise, it's too late. In these kinds of situations, people may experience a range of emotions from disappointment to betrayal.[1]

So, although setting expectations is often a routine matter, failure to do it can lead to lasting professional disappointments and breakdowns in working relationships.

Three components are central in setting expectations for those you manage: describing responsibilities, providing deadlines, and discussing coordination. Describing *responsibilities* means designating tasks and work outcomes to certain employees, providing *deadlines* means setting out the timeline by which the work should be accomplished satisfactorily, and discussing *coordination* involves providing guidelines for how employees should communicate and cooperate with one another. From time to time, you should also describe your own role and responsibilities to supervisees. When you do so, they see they are accountable to you and you are also accountable to them. This means you may need to occasionally own up to your own mistakes and accept responsibility when everything has not gone as expected.

Notice the differences between the less effective and more effective expectation-setting messages in Figures 9.4 and 9.5, in which Bryan makes a new assignment and sets out the deadlines for Barry and John, two of his supervisees. The less effective example violates the basic requirements of routine messages because it does not provide the key message clearly at the beginning. It is also difficult to read. In the more effective message, Barry and John can grasp the key messages within seconds. They can process all of the information rapidly and understand the responsibilities, deadlines, and coordination associated with these new accounts.

## Providing Directions

Another common type of routine message provides directions for others. Messages that provide directions share many similarities with those that set expectations. The primary distinction is that directions typically include specific—often step-by-step—guidelines for accomplishing particular tasks.

Since describing step-by-step procedures is so specific, insufficient detail can frustrate your readers. For routine matters, you are generally safe reviewing your own work and making sure it is complete. For more technical and complicated procedures, make sure you have several people test the procedures to find where you can better clarify the steps involved.

---

**Components of Requests**

- Make request.
- Provide rationale.
- Call to action.*
- State goodwill.

*Optional—appropriate at the end of lengthy messages

---

**Components of Expectations**

- Explain overall expectation.
- Describe responsibilities.
- Provide deadlines.
- Discuss coordination.
- State goodwill.

---

**Components of Directions**

- State goal.
- Give step-by-step directions.
- State goodwill.

**FIGURE 9.4**

Less Effective Example of Setting Expectations

smith & smith advertising

> SUBJECT LINE reveals little about the expectations.

**Deadlines**

| From: | Bryan Atkins | **Mon, July 24, 2017** |
|-------|--------------|------------------------|
| To: | Barry Evermore, John Anderson | |

Hey Barry and John. You two will be our lead team for the following two projects: Jansen Slippers and Forrester Eyeglasses. Tentatively (depending on our discussions with each client over the next week or so and a few other factors), I expect the following deadlines over the next two months. For Jansen, we will present the preliminary concepts to the client on Friday, July 10. Then, we'll present initial layout/copy on Wednesday, August 5. We'll wrap up by completing the final layout/copy by August 21. With Forrester, we are going to present preliminary concepts on Friday, July 17. We'll do the initial layout and copy on Friday, August 14. We'll finish the final layout/copy on Wednesday, September 2. We really value these new clients and want to make sure we get repeat business from them, so you two need to step it up and really be on your game. Stop by my office this afternoon at 3 and we'll talk this over some more. Bryan

> TONE is demanding and bossy.

> NAVIGATION is challenging: Deadlines are buried.

**FIGURE 9.5**

More Effective Example of Setting Expectations

smith & smith advertising

**Tentative Deadlines for Jansen Slippers and Forrester Eyeglasses; Can You Meet This Afternoon?**

| From: | Bryan Atkins | **Mon, July 24, 2017** |
|-------|--------------|------------------------|
| To: | Barry Evermore, John Anderson | |

Hi Barry and John,

> EXPECTATIONS stated clearly and immediately.

We have just secured two new accounts: Forrester Eyeglasses and Jansen Slippers. You two will form our lead creative team on these promising accounts. I recommended you for these accounts to the executive management team due to your excellent past work on fashion and clothing accounts.

> RESPONSIBILITIES and DEADLINES are displayed.

Tentatively, I expect the following deadlines over the next two months:

| Action | Deadline |
|--------|----------|
| Preliminary Concepts Presented to Jansen | (F) July 10 |
| Preliminary Concepts Presented to Forrester | (F) July 17 |
| Initial Layout/Copy Presented to Jansen | (W) August 5 |
| Initial Layout/Copy Presented to Forrester | (F) August 14 |
| Final Layout/Copy Completed for Jansen | (F) August 21 |
| Final Layout/Copy Completed for Forrester | (W) September 2 |

> COORDINATION to be addressed.

I would like to stop by your offices later this afternoon to discuss priorities for these clients. Can we meet in Barry's office at 3 p.m.? If that doesn't work, how about 4 p.m. today? Let me know which time works best for you.

> TONE is positive and upbeat.

Bryan

**FIGURE 9.6**

Less Effective Directions

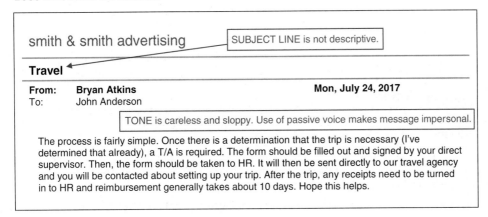

In messages with procedures and directions, make the steps stand out clearly by enumerating each one. This helps your reader keep track of progress completing the tasks. Steps that are written in narrative form within a paragraph are typically difficult to follow.

Notice the differences between the less effective and more effective messages in Figures 9.6 and 9.7, where Bryan gives directions to John on how to make company travel arrangements. The less effective example in Figure 9.6 has an unhelpful and careless tone, written almost entirely in passive voice. The message is abrupt and insufficiently detailed. Many readers will decode a meta message of "I don't have time for you." In the more effective example in Figure 9.7, Bryan provides clear directions by pasting the human resources policies into the message and inserting his own comments as additional guidelines and tips. He also tells John where to go for more information. In reality, Bryan could have simply emailed "check the HR intranet portal." Yet, this more effective message, written in just three to four minutes, is a strong sign of Bryan's willingness to help John. Many readers will decode a meta message of "I want to help you out as much as possible."

## Responding to Inquiries

The very nature of working with others involves asking and responding to questions. One of the most important strategies for responding to inquiries is to set off each question so your readers can quickly identify responses to particular questions. You generally can do this using bullets or numbered lists and/or special formatting (i.e., bold or italics). When choosing between bullets or numbered lists, consider whether the order of the items is important. If the order is important, use numbered lists. Otherwise, use bullets. Also, consider telling your readers where to get additional and more specific information by providing links to FAQ web pages or other relevant web pages.

Notice the difference between Bryan's less effective and more effective responses to an inquiry from a prospect in Figures 9.8 and 9.9. In the less effective response in Figure 9.8, Bryan mixes responses in a single paragraph. (The original inquiry is located at the bottom of Figure 9.8; it is a poorly written inquiry with all the questions embedded in one paragraph.) In the more effective response in Figure 9.9, Bryan gives each question its own section and highlights each in bold. By structuring the email this way, he helps the reader easily navigate the various answers. He also uses links to web pages with further information and attempts to schedule a face-to-face meeting where he can answer questions in a richer medium.

**Components of Inquiry Responses**

- Provide responses.
- State goodwill.

FIGURE 9.7

## More Effective Directions

---

smith & smith advertising | DIRECTIONS are specific and clear.

### Procedures for Setting Up Travel

**From:** **Bryan Atkins**  **Mon, July 24, 2017**
To: John Anderson

John,

For complete details, go to the *Travel* section of the **Human Resources intranet portal**. You will immediately find all policies and forms that you need.

Here are the basic steps pasted directly from the HR intranet portal with several *comments from me inserted in italics*.

1. Complete a "Travel Authorization" (T/A) form with approval signature from your immediate supervisor.

   *(I'm the supervisor. You can get the latest T/A form off the HR intranet portal at the following link:* T/A Form.*)*

2. Submit the T/A to Human Resources (HR). HR will forward it directly to our designated travel agency.

   *(Our current designated travel agency is Dawson Travel.)*

3. An agent from the travel agency will contact you directly and develop your trip itinerary with you. The travel agency will bill Smith & Smith directly for your airfare, accommodations, and car rentals.

   *(You should do this right away. You may be able to choose an airline that you have frequent flier miles with if you can book far enough in advance. If you book within two weeks of the travel, you are required to use discount airlines.)*

4. After completing your trip, turn in receipts for incidental expenses to HR. You will be reimbursed for these expenses and receive a daily stipend to cover meals.

   *(Make sure to review the company policies so you know which incidental expenses are covered and how much your daily stipend will be.)*

This should get you started. For questions about filling out the T/A, you'll get more help from HR. As soon as you get the T/A form filled in, just let me know and I'll sign it right away.

Bryan

TONE is professional and helpful.

---

## Creating Announcements

**Components of Announcements**

- Gain attention.
- Give announcement.
- Provide details.
- Call to action.*
- State goodwill.

*For some announcements

Business executives and managers routinely make announcements. Announcements are updates to policies and procedures, notices of events, and other correspondences that apply to a group of employees and/or customers. Announcements are one form of one-to-many communications.

Since announcements are generally broadcast to a large number of receivers (often as emails or corporate intranet posts), many employees and customers gloss over them. To prevent employees and customers from ignoring announcements, the subject line must be specific and must create interest. Furthermore, announcements, especially for events, should be designed to let readers gather all relevant information in 10 to 15 seconds. Thus, formatting is especially important.

**FIGURE 9.8**

Less Effective Response to an Inquiry

To...  Joel Yang [joel.yang@doityourselfsports.com]

Subject:  RE: Questions about Advertising

---

Hello Joel:

Thanks for getting in touch with us here at Smith & Smith. Answers to all of your questions can be found on our website (**Smith & Smith website**). Generally, you'll find that our rates are extremely competitive with other agencies. More important, we have a great record of return on investment and help you track this figure. Also, our agency has been at the forefront of all forms of online advertising and marketing for the past fifteen years. We have been instrumental in helping small companies rapidly grow their revenues and expand. See the following web page about our online advertising with examples of our work: **Smith & Smith online advertising and social media**. We can meet at a time and place convenient for you. This week I'm available from 2 to 4 on Tuesday, 9 to 11:30 on Wednesday, and in the morning or afternoon on Thursday. Please let me know a time that is best for you.

Bryan

> *Nonunified Response:* A single paragraph contains answers to all of the questions.

---

**From:** Joel Yang [joel.yang@doityourselfsports.com]
**Sent:** Mon, July 24, 2017 at 8:34 AM
**To:** Bryan Atkins [bryanatkins@smith+smith.com]
**Subject:** Questions about Advertising

Hi Bryan, I contacted Andrea Johansen about developing some ads. She recommended that I contact you directly. Basically, I'm interested in pricing for various advertising options. You've probably seen our used sports equipment stores around town. We've decided to change our business model and devote half of our retail space to new sports equipment. Anyway, we want to get the word out. We've always developed in-house advertising which I think has been amateurish. Of course, we don't have a big budget. So, we want quality advertising but we're concerned about pricing. How do your rates compare to other advertising agencies? Do you have any specialists in online advertising? What about with social media? When could we meet and talk about what you might provide us? Thanks a lot. Joel

---

In the less effective announcement from Bryan about new computing policies (see Figure 9.10), he provides most of the necessary information about the new policies but buries most of it in long paragraphs. He leaves out some important information, such as dates. Missing dates are among the most common mistakes on announcements. While most announcements of this type (for new policies) are tempered in tone, they should still carry some enthusiasm when the announcements include good news. This announcement has quite positive news for most employees. Bryan's more effective announcement (see Figure 9.11) contains complete information in concise form. The formatting allows

**FIGURE 9.9**

More Effective Response to an Inquiry

| To... | Joel Yang [joel.yang@doityourselfsports.com] |
| --- | --- |
| Subject: | Responses to Your Questions; Setting Up a Time to Meet |

| Arial | 10 | **B** *I* <u>U</u> |

Hello Joel:

Thanks for getting in touch with us here at Smith & Smith. I suggest that we meet in person so we can learn more about your marketing and advertising needs. After we talk for 15 to 30 minutes, I could give you a good idea of what your options are and whether our agency is a good fit for you.

Our website (Smith & Smith website) has answers to each of your questions. I've responded briefly below with links to our website for more information:

**How do your rates compare to other advertising agencies?**

Our rates are extremely competitive with other agencies. More important, we have a great record of return on investment and help you track this figure. We also specialize in building brands, which is particularly important in your case since you are adjusting your business model to include new sports equipment. See the following web page with ten case studies of our clients and the returns they received on their advertising: Smith & Smith case studies.

**Do you have any specialists in online advertising? What about in social media?**

Yes. Our agency has been at the forefront of all forms of online advertising and marketing for the past 15 years. We have been instrumental in helping small companies rapidly grow their revenues and expand. See the following web page about our online advertising with examples of our work: Smith & Smith online advertising and social media.

**When could we meet and talk about what you might provide us?**

At a time and place convenient for you. I would be more than happy to visit your office. I am available during the following times this week:

| | |
| --- | --- |
| Tuesday: | 2 p.m.–4 p.m. |
| Wednesday: | 9 a.m.–11:30 a.m. |
| Thursday: | 9 a.m.–11:30 a.m., 2 p.m.–4 p.m. |

Please let me know a time that is best for you. You can call directly anytime.

Bryan

--------------------------

Bryan Atkins
Account Executive
Smith & Smith Advertising
803-777-1848

> SPECIFIC responses
> to all questions.

> NAVIGATION is easy with
> questions as headings.

**FIGURE 9.10**

Less Effective Announcement

---

## MEMORANDUM

**TO:**      Smith & Smith Advertising Employees

**FROM:**      Bryan Atkins

**DATE:**      Mon, July 24, 2017

**SUBJECT**      New Policies

> INFORMATION is incomplete (missing key dates) and difficult to read. The TONE lacks enough enthusiasm.

On behalf of the Committee for Technology, I'm sharing several new policies that impact employees at S&S. We deliberated carefully about these new policies to meet our stated objectives of making computing more accessible and convenient for employees while also safeguarding information systems security for our advertising firm. These policies will go into effect in the next week. All these policies relate to using your own devices for work.

The first set of BYOD policies makes mobile computing easier for employees. Employees who use their own mobile phones for work can receive reimbursement for up to $75 per month for voice and data plans (previously this was capped at $30 per month). We felt that this amount more accurately reflected the costs many employees incur for voice and data on behalf of the firm. Also, several policies directly address the major expenses of owning your own computers that you use for work. S&S will reimburse employees for up to $1,200 per year for desktop computers, laptops, tablets, or other mobile computer devices used primarily for work purposes. The great news is that any unused money will roll over for use in the following year. Finally, S&S must use a new ticketing system through the HelpDesk for all requests.

There will also be new security measures. We've learned that many of our S&S resources and information are vulnerable to attacks. These new policies will be minimally inconvenient for employees yet make substantial improvements to our security. All devices—including mobile phones—are now required to have a log-in. Also, employees will need to update their log-in passwords to the S&S intranet every six months. Your supervisors will continue updating you about the new policies, and you can read all BYOD and computing policies on the intranet.

---

employees to grasp all essential information in about 15 seconds. It also contains more positive, inviting language. One reason that the more effective announcement is better than the less effective announcement is the grouping and arrangement of information. By taking an extra five to ten minutes to organize the information carefully, Bryan ensures that employees have a far better understanding of the new policies.

## Making Claims

Claims are requests for other companies to compensate for or correct the wrongs of mistakes they have made. As with other requests, you should immediately state what the *claim* is and what you expect the company to do for you. You also will provide a *rationale* for your claim in the body of the message and close with a call to *action*—a specific request.

    As you write claims, keep in mind that your goal is to have your claim honored. Focus on facts first and emotions second, if at all. Lay out a logical, reasonable, and professional explanation for your claim. Emotional claims are far more likely to be rejected. Also, remember that you will often work with the same people again and again. So, be polite and focus on the long-term working relationship.

> **Components of Claims**
>
> ---
>
> - Make claim.
> - Provide rationale.
> - Call to action.
> - State goodwill.

**FIGURE 9.11**

More Effective Announcement

---

## MEMORANDUM

| | |
|---|---|
| **TO:** | Smith & Smith Advertising Employees |
| **FROM:** | Bryan Atkins |
| **DATE:** | Mon, July 24, 2017 |
| **SUBJECT** | New Bring Your Own Device (BYOD) Policies |

> **INFORMATION** is complete and easy to process. Most readers will recognize all essential information within 15 seconds. **RATIONALE** is clear and concise. **TONE** is positive and helpful

Beginning on July 1, 2017, several new BYOD policies will go into effect to provide employees with more mobile and home computing options and ensure better security for Smith & Smith.

These new policies were developed by a committee comprised of IT managers and account executives. The policies were approved by the executive team on June 19, 2017.

### New Policies to Support Mobile and Home Computing

- *Reimbursement for voice/data plans:* Employees who use their own mobile phones for work can receive reimbursement for up to $75 per month for voice and data plans (previously this was capped at $30 per month).

- *Reimbursement for mobile and home computers:* S&S will reimburse employees for up to $1,200 per year for desktop computers, laptops, tablets, or other mobile computer devices used primarily for work purposes. Any unused money will roll over for use in the following year.

- *IT Support:* S&S employees must use a new ticketing system through the HelpDesk for all requests. IT support will now be available Monday through Saturday, 8 a.m. to 7 p.m.

### New Security Policies

- *Log-in on all devices:* All devices—including mobile phones—are now required to have a log-in.

- *S&S intranet password updates:* Employees will need to update their log-in passwords to the S&S intranet every six months. Passwords must contain at least eight characters and must include at least one letter, one number, and one special character.

Your supervisors will continue updating you about the new policies. Also, *you can read all BYOD and computing policies in the "Computing" section located on your S&S dashboard.*

---

In Bryan's less effective claim to the Prestigio Hotel about a billing error (see Figure 9.12), phrases such as "you have not honored" and "you overcharged" unnecessarily and perhaps unfairly question Jeff's intent. The message focuses first on frustration and second on the merits of the claim. Abrupt phrases such as "please take care of this matter immediately" can easily be misinterpreted as rude. Notice how the more effective claim (see Figure 9.13) balances directness with politeness. Bryan justifies the claim with an objective description of the overbilling and provides an attachment with the agreement. He politely asks for an adjustment to the account while also complimenting Jeff on the excellent service the hotel provides. Note that in writing claims messages as well as any other kinds of messages, you may be able to save time by using voice recognition software (VRS), as discussed in the Technology Tips box.

**FIGURE 9.12**

Less Effective Claim

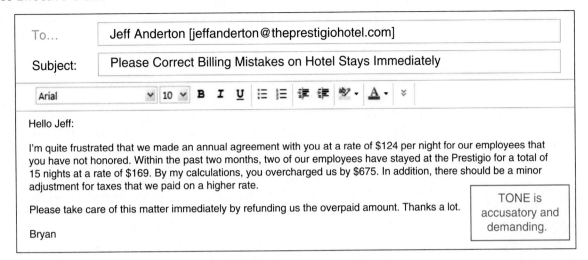

To... Jeff Anderton [jeffanderton@theprestigiohotel.com]

Subject: Please Correct Billing Mistakes on Hotel Stays Immediately

Arial | 10 | **B** *I* U

Hello Jeff:

I'm quite frustrated that we made an annual agreement with you at a rate of $124 per night for our employees that you have not honored. Within the past two months, two of our employees have stayed at the Prestigio for a total of 15 nights at a rate of $169. By my calculations, you overcharged us by $675. In addition, there should be a minor adjustment for taxes that we paid on a higher rate.

Please take care of this matter immediately by refunding us the overpaid amount. Thanks a lot.

Bryan

> TONE is accusatory and demanding.

**FIGURE 9.13**

More Effective Claim

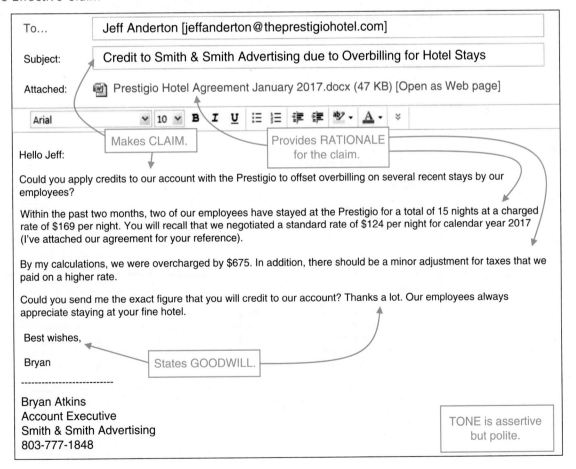

To... Jeff Anderton [jeffanderton@theprestigiohotel.com]

Subject: Credit to Smith & Smith Advertising due to Overbilling for Hotel Stays

Attached: Prestigio Hotel Agreement January 2017.docx (47 KB) [Open as Web page]

Arial | 10 | **B** *I* U

> Makes CLAIM.

> Provides RATIONALE for the claim.

Hello Jeff:

Could you apply credits to our account with the Prestigio to offset overbilling on several recent stays by our employees?

Within the past two months, two of our employees have stayed at the Prestigio for a total of 15 nights at a charged rate of $169 per night. You will recall that we negotiated a standard rate of $124 per night for calendar year 2017 (I've attached our agreement for your reference).

By my calculations, we were overcharged by $675. In addition, there should be a minor adjustment for taxes that we paid on a higher rate.

Could you send me the exact figure that you will credit to our account? Thanks a lot. Our employees always appreciate staying at your fine hotel.

Best wishes,

Bryan

> States GOODWILL.

-------------------------

Bryan Atkins
Account Executive
Smith & Smith Advertising
803-777-1848

> TONE is assertive but polite.

# Showing Appreciation

**LO9.4** Construct relationship-oriented routine messages, including appreciation, apologies, and expressions of sympathy.

Employees at all levels of an organization desire to feel appreciated. Sadly, polls show that employees express thanks to one another less now than ever since polling on this issue began. Just 10 percent of employees say supervisors thank them daily. More than half (55 percent) of employees say they are thanked never, seldom, or only occasionally.[2]

A sincere expression of thanks also helps achieve business goals and strengthens work relationships. Joseph Ungoco of a popular public relations agency in New York is a staunch believer that thank-you notes help his agency maintain effective working relationships and strongly impact repeat business. He sends handwritten thank-you notes within 48 hours to partners and clients.[3]

Appreciation messages vary significantly in terms of formality. Thank-you notes for customers and clients or for special occasions demand more formality. Thank-you messages for colleagues and others you see each day should be less formal and should not feel over the top. In any case, several components are standard for appreciation messages. They should begin with an expression of *thanks*, provide a quick *rationale* for the thanks, and end with a statement of *goodwill*.

Appreciation messages should be genuine, simple, warm, and personal. To show your sincerity, focus exclusively on the recipient. Appreciation messages should not appear self-serving in any way; state any reference to yourself carefully to avoid drawing attention away from those you are thanking.

In the workplace, showing your appreciation will help build connections. Be careful, however, about excessive or exaggerated displays of gratitude. First, readers may view them as insincere. Second, they may cross boundaries of what is considered professional.

Notice the differences between Bryan's less effective and more effective appreciation messages to his team in Figures 9.14 and 9.15. In the less effective example, the exaggerated and excessive phrases of gratitude (i.e., "a fabulous job," "feel

## Components of Appreciation Messages

- Give thanks.
- Provide rationale.
- State goodwill.

**connect**

Visit http://connect.mheducation.com for an exercise on this topic.

---

**FIGURE 9.14**

Less Effective Appreciation Message

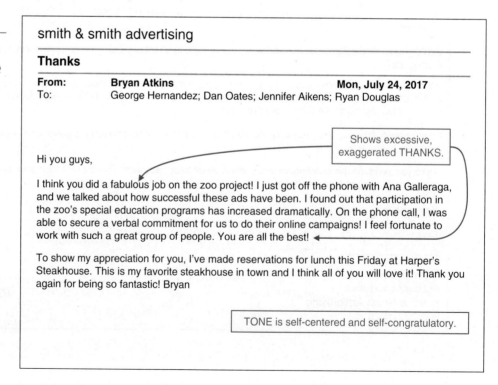

smith & smith advertising

**Thanks**

From: **Bryan Atkins**      **Mon, July 24, 2017**
To:      George Hernandez; Dan Oates; Jennifer Aikens; Ryan Douglas

Shows excessive, exaggerated THANKS.

Hi you guys,

I think you did a fabulous job on the zoo project! I just got off the phone with Ana Galleraga, and we talked about how successful these ads have been. I found out that participation in the zoo's special education programs has increased dramatically. On the phone call, I was able to secure a verbal commitment for us to do their online campaigns! I feel fortunate to work with such a great group of people. You are all the best!

To show my appreciation for you, I've made reservations for lunch this Friday at Harper's Steakhouse. This is my favorite steakhouse in town and I think all of you will love it! Thank you again for being so fantastic! Bryan

TONE is self-centered and self-congratulatory.

**FIGURE 9.15**

More Effective Appreciation Message

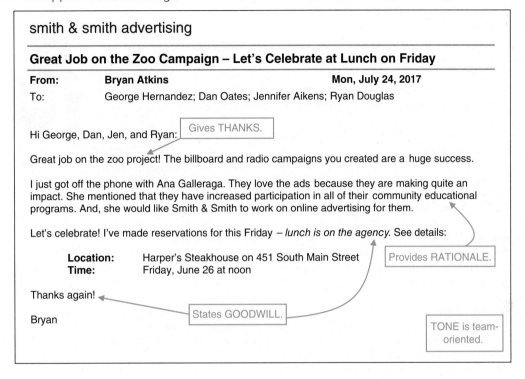

fortunate," "you are all the best!") appear unprofessional or insincere. Also, the message contains far too much focus on Bryan and implies he now deserves thanks for his own actions (securing a new deal, providing lunch). In the more effective example, Bryan focuses entirely on the group. He shows enthusiasm within professional boundaries.

## Making Apologies

Even with the best of intentions, colleagues sometimes let one another down. Differences in communication style, personality clashes, and careless comments are sometimes factors in personal offenses. Business professionals who are high in emotional intelligence notice how their actions impact others. When they intentionally or unintentionally do harm, they seek to improve the workplace relationships right away. In some cases, making apologies is the appropriate response.

However, all apologies are not necessarily good apologies. As stated by management communication specialist Holly Weeks, "Offering the right apology, particularly in the corporate world, is not as simple as saying, 'I'm sorry.' Done right, an apology can enhance both reputations and relationships. Done wrong, an apology can compound the original mistake, sometimes to disastrous consequences."[4]

Effective apologies achieve several important results. First, they help repair working relationships so that you can refocus on solving problems together. Second, they can rebuild your reputation. When you've made offenses or mistakes that harm others, your credibility is weakened. Your reputation for competence, caring, and/or character may be questioned.[5]

Typically, an apology includes the following elements: *acknowledgment* of a mistake or an offense, an expression of *regret* for the harm caused, acceptance of *responsibility*,

**Components of Apologies**

- Make acknowledgment.
- Express regret.
- Take responsibility.
- Offer commitment.
- State goodwill.

# TECHNOLOGY TIPS

## VOICE RECOGNITION SOFTWARE

During the past decade, the accuracy and ease of using voice recognition software (VRS) have increased dramatically. You can use this software to rapidly put your thoughts in text format, allowing you to write routine and complex messages much more efficiently. You can use stand-alone VRS platforms (e.g., Dragon NaturallySpeaking, ViaVoice) or embed the software in your operating system (e.g., Microsoft Windows).

© Tom Wang/123RF

Keep in mind the following tips as you use voice recognition software for written business messages:

*Take time to learn the software and increase its accuracy.* You generally need some initial training sessions with the software so it recognizes your words accurately. You can train the software to recognize your voice with high accuracy within 15 to 30 minutes. Over time, you can add specialized terminology that you use frequently in your profession.

*Use voice recognition software for planning and drafting your document.* Most people are unable to write down thoughts as quickly as they can think of them. This is particularly the case during the brainstorming stage when you are grappling with many ideas. By using voice recognition software, you're more likely to get all those thoughts recorded as text.

*Use VRS for routine messages.* Since most routine messages are fairly straightforward and can be pieced together rapidly, you can often save time by using VRS. Even if you save just a few minutes per routine message, this may add up to several hours over the course of any given week due to the high volume of messages.

*Review your messages carefully before sending.* VRS is not perfect. It will inevitably make mistakes, so you need to carefully edit for accuracy. You should also check the message to make sure you have the right formality and tone for written communication. Many business professionals find that when using VRS, the act of speaking causes them to use less-formal language and phrases that require nonverbal cues.

and a *commitment* that the offense will not be repeated. Effective apologies should be timely and sincere.

Apologies are ineffective when they are vague and clichéd. For the apology to be effective, others must sense that the apologizer is sincere, genuine, and acting without an agenda. Effective apologies must focus on others, not you. During an apology, if the recipient decodes any behavior as defensive, it casts doubt on the apologizer's sincerity.[6]

Before apologizing, consider the business implications. If you are dealing with customers and clients, an apology may imply legal responsibility. For serious matters, you might seek the company's legal counsel. Internally, an apology may become a permanent record in a performance review or other files (in rare situations). So, you might consider the potential costs of an apology to your company and your career. Generally, however, apologies for routine mistakes and offenses pose little risk to either your company or your career. They are likely to restore and perhaps even enhance your company's and your personal credibility.

Notice Bryan's apology in Figure 9.16 for unfair statements he made at a meeting. The apology contains the basic elements: acknowledgment, regret, responsibility, and commitment. It is short, simple, sincere, and forward-looking. Colleagues who have known Bryan for years will likely accept the apology quickly and redirect their efforts to working together effectively.

**FIGURE 9.16**

An Apology

"Good morning, everyone. I want to take just a few moments to apologize. Last Friday in our executive management meeting, I made several unfair comments."

"I complained that several of you care more about our clients than you do about our employees. I also said that you ask our employees to work excessive hours on weekends and evenings because you are never willing to say 'no' to our clients, even when they make unreasonable demands."

ACKNOWLEDGMENT of mistake.

"These statements were inaccurate and unfair. I have known each of you for many years, and I am certain that all of you care deeply about our employees."

Statement of REGRET.

"Over the weekend, I thought about my comments a lot. I am frustrated that we—myself included—give in to unreasonable demands from a few of our clients. I think we end up putting too much stress on our employees as a result. I am sorry that I misdirected my frustration with the demands of our clients at all of you."

Statement of RESPONSIBILITY.

"At some point, I hope we can discuss how to negotiate with our clients when we view their demands as unreasonable. For my part, I will avoid any blaming. I would certainly like to hear your experiences, perspectives, and suggestions."

COMMITMENT to avoid such behavior in the future and approach frustrations constructively.

## Expressing Sympathy

When your colleagues and other close professional contacts encounter personal losses—such as the sickness or even the passing away of loved ones—it is appropriate for you to extend your sincere sympathies. Although you may have maintained strictly professional relations with others, expressing condolences, concern, and support can help them cope with personal grief and pain.

The foremost requirement of any expression of sympathy is that it be sincere. These difficult moments are challenging and awkward. You may feel uncertain about what to say, which words to use. Your genuine concern will compensate for any deficiencies in the words you use. Typically, keep your expressions of sympathy brief. For deaths, state your support and concern to the person who has experienced the loss. Make the note personal by mentioning the deceased person by name and your positive impressions and memories. When possible, handwrite your expression of sympathy on a nice card (see Figure 9.17 for an example of a sympathy message). And read the Communication Q&A for one businessperson's thoughts on delivering routine messages of all kinds.

**Components of Sympathy Messages**

- Express sympathy.
- Offer support.
- State goodwill.

**FIGURE 9.17**

An Expression of Sympathy

© Burke/Triolo Productions/Getty Images; © Mark Steinmetz

WITH DEEPEST SYMPATHY

Dear Felipe

I was so sorry to hear of Rosa's passing this past week. Please accept my deepest sympathies to you at this time of personal loss for you and your children.

Felipe, please let me know if there is anything I can do to help out during this difficult time. You are in my thoughts.

Bryan

Bryan Atkins
1713 Patterson Dr.
Delmont, TX 90321

Felipe Bravo
733 Fremont Blv., Apt. 14
Houston, TX 91832

# COMMUNICATION Q&A

## CONVERSATIONS WITH CURRENT BUSINESS PROFESSIONALS

**Peter Cardon: How do most of your customers contact you? What kinds of matters do they contact you about?**

**Aubrey Marshall:** All of our major contact with our customers is through an online messaging system similar to email. Most customers are interested in routine things like price, quantity, availability, product consistency, product quality, shipping time, and basic quilting inquiries. Some just want to thank us for the products. Others tell us that the prices are too high, or question our shipping costs and so forth. I have found that customers expect to hear back right away. My employees are trained to respond with detail-oriented messages. They also treat all people with courtesy, even if the customers have made unjustified requests or comments.

**PC: Can you tell me more about your philosophy of responding to customers' messages?**

**AM:** We respond to hundreds of customers per day. Our employees who respond to customers are absolutely critical. They must write messages that are clear, concise, and friendly. We try to stay very professional. We always use a salutation and a "sincerely" at the end. For mistakes, we try to express how sorry we are at the beginning of the message and give several alternatives to rectify the problem. We also understand that no matter what we say or do, the customer is free to be upset. We just have to have thick skin and work harder on helping the next customer.

**PC: How do you express appreciation in your messages? How much difference does it make?**

**AM:** After a purchase we send a personalized message to every single customer. We thank our customers for their purchases and give them tracking information for their packages. We also ask for feedback and give them our phone number to contact us if there are any problems.

**PC: How important are social media platforms for your business?**

**AM:** We depend on gaining the trust of our customers, and we can do that with Facebook, Pinterest, Instagram, Twitter, Google+, and the YouTube channel. We even write a blog to give our customers ideas about how to use our materials. We find that social networking has been the primary driver for the business. We follow all of our suppliers and the designers who work with them. We do a lot of giveaways and have thousands of followers. One thing we have learned is social media takes a lot of effort. We have to post frequently and create interesting content for our customers.

**PC: For young professionals, what concluding advice would you give for creating effective daily communications?**

**AM:** Always stay on top of your messages, whether they be through email or from a supplier's messaging system. Set aside time every day to respond. And never take shortcuts. Respond to every message carefully. You never know how much business you might lose if customers feel that you have not provided a careful, in-depth response to their questions and concerns. I also think that you need to train your employees to respond in a way that will drive repeat business. It's not as simple as you might think. You need to take time with your employees to talk about how best to respond to all types of daily messages.

***Aubrey Marshall*** *started an online retail business, SouthernFabric.com in 2004 selling fabrics and notions to quilters. About 70 percent of her sales are in the United States. The remaining sales are primarily in Canada and Australia.*

Courtesy of Aubrey Marshall

# Chapter Takeaway for *Routine Business Messages*

---

**LO9.1 Describe how delivering routine messages impacts credibility. (pp. 269–271)**

Delivering effective routine messages improves your **reputation for personal credibility.**

| | | |
|---|---|---|
| It shows **competence** when you know how to manage and resolve routine business tasks. | It shows **caring** when you are responsive to others and show respect for their time. | It shows **character** when you live up to your promises and your company's commitments. |

---

**LO9.2 Describe the process for developing routine business messages. (pp. 271–272)**

| Components of Routine Messages | |
|---|---|
| • State primary message (ten words or fewer). | • Restate request or key message in more specific terms. |
| • Provide details in paragraphs of 20 to 80 words. | • State goodwill. |

---

**LO9.3 Construct task-oriented routine messages, including requests, expectations, directions, responses to inquiries, announcements, and claims. (pp. 273–283)**

**Construct routine business requests.**

| Components of Requests | | See *examples of business requests* in Figures 9.2 and 9.3. |
|---|---|---|
| • Make request. | • Call to action (for some). | |
| • Provide rationale. | • State goodwill. | |

**Compose routine sets of expectations.**

| Components of Expectations | | | See *examples of expectation-setting messages* in Figures 9.4 and 9.5. |
|---|---|---|---|
| • Explain overall expectation. | • Provide deadlines. | • State goodwill. | |
| • Describe responsibilities. | • Discuss coordination. | | |

**Construct routine sets of directions.**

| Components of Directions | | | See *examples of directions* in Figures 9.6 and 9.7. |
|---|---|---|---|
| • State goal. | • Give step-by-step directions. | • State goodwill. | |

**Compose routine responses to inquiries.**

| Components of Inquiry Responses | | See *examples of responses to inquiries* in Figures 9.8 and 9.9. |
|---|---|---|
| • Provide responses. | • State goodwill. | |

**Construct routine announcements.**

| Components of Announcements | | | See *examples of announcements* in Figures 9.10 and 9.11. |
|---|---|---|---|
| • Gain attention. | • Provide details. | • State goodwill. | |
| • Give announcement. | • Call to action (for some). | | |

**Compose routine claims.**

| Components of Claims | | See *examples of claims* in Figures 9.12 and 9.13. |
|---|---|---|
| • Make claim. | • Call to action. | |
| • Provide rationale. | • State goodwill. | |

---

**LO9.4 Construct relationship-oriented messages, including appreciation, apologies, and expressions of sympathy. (pp. 284–288)**

| Components of Appreciation Messages | | | See *examples of appreciation messages* in Figures 9.14 and 9.15. |
|---|---|---|---|
| • Give thanks. | • Provide rationale. | • State goodwill. | |

**Compose apologies.**

| Components of Apologies | | | See an *example of an apology* in Figure 9.16. |
|---|---|---|---|
| • Make acknowledgment. | • Take responsibility. | • State goodwill. | |
| • Express regret. | • Offer commitment. | | |

**Construct routine expressions of sympathy.**

| Components of Sympathy Messages | | | See an *example of a sympathy message* in Figure 9.17. |
|---|---|---|---|
| • Express sympathy. | • Offer support. | • State goodwill. | |

# Discussion Exercises

**9.1 Chapter Review Questions** (LO9.1, LO9.2)

A. Describe the AIM planning process for routine messages.

B. Explain the importance of reviewing for routine messages. What considerations should you make? What are your primary goals?

C. Identify the preferable message structures for various types of routine messages.

**9.2 Communication Q&A Discussion Questions** (LO9.1, LO9.2)

A. How does Aubrey Marshall approach routine communications?

B. What benefits and drawbacks does she see in electronic communication?

C. What piece of information or advice do you think is most useful?

# Evaluation Exercises

**9.3 Evaluating Routine Requests** (LO9.3)

A. Compare Bryan's less effective and more effective requests for a new server in Figures 9.2 and 9.3. Identify three ways in which Bryan improved the message.

B. How do you think the more effective message will impact work outcomes?

C. How do you think the more effective message will impact workplace relationships?

D. What two changes could you make to improve the more effective example?

**9.4 Evaluating Routine Expectations Messages** (LO9.3)

A. Compare Bryan's less effective and more effective messages regarding his expectations for Barry and John in their new assignment (see Figures 9.4 and 9.5). Identify three ways in which Bryan improved the message.

B. How do you think the more effective message will impact work outcomes?

C. How do you think the more effective message will impact workplace relationships?

D. What two changes could you make to improve the more effective example?

**9.5 Evaluating Routine Directions Messages** (LO9.3)

A. Compare Bryan's less effective and more effective messages giving directions for how to arrange company travel (see Figures 9.6 and 9.7). Identify the ways in which he improved the message.

B. How do you think the more effective message will impact work outcomes?

C. How do you think the more effective message will impact workplace relationships?

D. What two changes could you make to improve the more effective example?

**9.6 Evaluating Routine Inquiries** (LO9.3)

A. Compare Bryan's less effective and more effective responses to an inquiry from a client (see Figures 9.8 and 9.9). Identify three ways that he improved the message.

B. How do you think the more effective message will impact work outcomes?

C. How do you think the more effective message will impact workplace relationships?

D. What two changes could you make to improve the more effective example?

**9.7 Evaluating Routine Announcements** (LO9.3)

A. Compare Bryan's less effective and more effective announcements about the firm's new computing policies (see Figures 9.10 and 9.11). Identify three ways that he improved the message.

B. How do you think the more effective message will impact work outcomes?

C. How do you think the more effective message will impact workplace relationships?

D. What two changes could you make to improve the more effective example?

**9.8 Evaluating Routine Claims** (LO9.3)

A. Compare Bryan's less effective and more effective claims to the Prestigio Hotel about its rate (see Figures 9.12 and 9.13). Identify three ways that he improved the message.

B. How do you think the more effective message will impact work outcomes?

C. How do you think the more effective message will impact workplace relationships?

D. What two changes could you make to improve the more effective example?

**9.9 Evaluating Routine Appreciation Messages** (LO9.4)

A. Compare Bryan's less effective and more effective messages of appreciation to his staff (see Figures 9.14 and 9.15). Identify three ways that he improved the message.

B. How do you think the more effective message will impact work outcomes?

C. How do you think the more effective message will impact workplace relationships?

D. What two changes could you make to improve the more effective example?

**9.10 Evaluating Routine Apologies** (LO9.4)

A. Examine Bryan's apology in Figure 9.16. How do you think this apology will impact work outcomes?

B. How do you think this apology will impact workplace relationships?

C. What two changes could you make to improve the apology?

**9.11 Evaluating Sympathy Messages** (LO9.4)

A. Examine Bryan's sympathy message in Figure 9.17. How do you think this sympathy message will impact work outcomes?

B. How do you think this sympathy message will impact workplace relationships?

C. What two changes could you make to improve the sympathy message?

**9.12 Evaluating Your Approach to Writing** (LO9.1, LO9.2)

Evaluate yourself with regard to each of the writing practices listed in the table below. Circle the appropriate number for each.

| | 1 – Rarely/Never | 2 – Sometimes | 3 – Usually | 4 – Always |
|---|---|---|---|---|
| Before I write routine messages, I make sure I've gathered all of the relevant information. | 1 | 2 | 3 | 4 |
| Before I write routine messages, I spend a significant amount of time analyzing and piecing together the information. | 1 | 2 | 3 | 4 |
| Before I write routine messages, I learn as much as I reasonably can about the needs of the message receiver(s). | 1 | 2 | 3 | 4 |
| As I write routine messages, I think about how the message receiver(s) will feel while reading the message. | 1 | 2 | 3 | 4 |
| As I write routine messages, I think about how the message receiver(s) will respond. | 1 | 2 | 3 | 4 |
| As I write routine messages, I think about how quickly and easily the message receiver(s) will be able to read the message. | 1 | 2 | 3 | 4 |
| Before sending a routine message, I place myself in the position of the message receiver(s) and reread the message imagining how the message will be interpreted. | 1 | 2 | 3 | 4 |
| Before sending a routine message, I carefully double-check the entire message to make sure it is appropriate and accurate. | 1 | 2 | 3 | 4 |
| Before sending a routine message, I frequently ask people I trust to read the message or ask them how they would handle the communication. | 1 | 2 | 3 | 4 |
| Before sending a routine message, I use a spell-checker. | 1 | 2 | 3 | 4 |

Add up your score and consider the following advice:

**35–40:** You are a *strategic, other-oriented* writer. You think about how to send a well-thought-out message that meets the needs of others. Continue with such awareness of the impact of your written messages.

**30–34:** You are a *careful, considerate* writer. You spend time thinking about the content of your message and the needs of your message receiver(s). Consider taking more time in the planning process to think your message through even more carefully, and pay close attention to the needs and potential responses to your written messages by message receivers.

**25–29:** You are an *inconsistent but self-aware* writer. Sometimes you are careful about developing your message and considerate of the needs and reactions of others. Other times you are not. Always engage in excellent analysis when you craft your message and think carefully about your message receiver(s).

Under 25: You *need to improve* your approach to writing. You likely send most messages without spending enough time to think through the problems and impacts on others. Often this approach is harmless. Sometimes, however, you will not be influential in the way you want. Change your orientation to writing to spend most of your time preparing and reviewing.

After going through the self-assessment exercises, identify three specific goals you have for improving your approach to writing. Write four or five sentences about each goal.

# Application Exercises

## 9.13 Request for a Letter of Recommendation (LO9.1, LO9.2, LO9.3)

Find a specific job, internship, or graduate study listing that you would be interested in pursuing. Make sure it requires a letter of recommendation. Your task is to request a letter of recommendation from one of your instructors. Assume that you will write an email making the request.

Answer the questions listed below to help you plan your request. Then write the request.

A. Why would your instructor want to write a letter of recommendation for you? What would increase your instructor's willingness and delight in writing a letter for you?

B. What tone will you try to project in your email?

C. What information about you would your instructor need to write an effective letter of recommendation?

D. How can you make it easier for your instructor to write a letter of recommendation?

E. How can you show courtesy to your instructor since she/he is using her/his own time to do a favor for you?

F. How will you order your message? What will be the subject line?

G. Write the email request for a letter of recommendation.

## 9.14 Writing a Memo with Group Goals and Expectations (LO9.3)

Think about a group project you've worked on in school or at work. Ideally, you will choose a currently active group project. Assume the role of group leader (you can make up facts as necessary). Write a document that includes the following:

- Group member names.
- Group goals and ultimate outcomes.
- Group member roles.
- Timeline for completing various activities and coordinating with one another.

## 9.15 Writing Procedures for Getting into Graduate School (LO9.3)

Go to the website of a graduate school you are interested in or to the graduate school website for your current university. Rewrite the directions for applying to a graduate program of interest to you. Make them clearer and simpler to read.

## 9.16 Responding to Inquiries (LO9.3)

Assume you are an advisor for students in your program or major. A prospective student sends you the following message: "Hi, I'm interested in your major. Can you give me some information about it? What is the placement rate of your students in the workplace upon graduation? How much money do they usually get? What are the professors like? Do I have to have a minimum GPA to get in the program? Any information would be helpful. Thanks, Jack." Respond to this message with sufficient detail. Remember your goal is to make a favorable impression on this prospective student.

## 9.17 Making Announcements (LO9.3)

Place yourself in the position of an advisor in your program. The upcoming semester will begin soon. Send an announcement to all current students with items they should be aware of for the upcoming semester. Include deadlines and make sure students will pay attention to the announcement.

## 9.18 Changing the Vacation Policy at APECT Consulting (LO9.3)

Ruth Weinstein had worked at APECT Consulting for the past 18 years. Shortly after becoming president several years ago, she recognized that turnover was quite high. The average consultant at the firm left after five to six years of employment. In exit interviews, departing consultants consistently talked about "being burned out" or "needing an extended break." Most of these departing employees still had months of unused paid vacation leave, which consistently prompted Ruth to ask, "Why didn't you use your vacation time?" Consultants often said they felt a pressure to avoid vacation, especially if they were early-career professionals trying to prove themselves. Some consultants said they thought they'd lose certain client accounts if they took time off.

After several years of concerns about employees overworking, Ruth decided to learn more about how vacation time might affect the business. She started examining research about vacation time. She read a 2013 study jointly conducted by the Society for Human Resource Management and the U.S. Travel Association.[7] The study showed that human resources (HR) professionals overwhelmingly thought vacation affected job performance (94%), morale (92%), wellness (92%), a positive culture (90%), productivity (90%), and retention (88%). Strong majorities of human resources professionals also thought vacation time impacted creativity (70%), employee engagement (68%), staying with the organization longer (60%), and taking fewer sick days (58%).

The current policy allows APECT employees to take paid time off (PTO) based on years of employment: 5 vacation days for employees with fewer than 3 years of employment; 10 vacation days for employees with between 3 and 5 years of employment; 15 days for employees with between 5 and 10 years of employment; and 20 days for employees with more than 10 years of employment.

As Ruth talked to her human resources team, she was told how the current roll-over policy did not provide an incentive to take vacation days during any given year. Since employees could simply roll over their vacation days at the year's end, they could accumulate large numbers of vacation days. The human resources team told Ruth that the average consultant had accumulated 23 days of PTO. Furthermore, when consultants left the firm, they received cash payouts for unused PTO. With an average payout at approximately $330 per accumulated PTO day, most consultants did not feel motivated to use all their vacation time.

After talking to the human resources team for roughly three months, examining vacation plan policies at competing firms, and informally talking to about a dozen consultants at the firm, Ruth and the HR team developed a new vacation policy. Beginning on January 1, 2018, employees with fewer than 10 years of employment at the firm will receive 15 days of vacation per year, and employees with more than 10 years of employment will receive 20 days of vacation per year. The amount of roll-over and cash payouts will be dramatically reduced. Employees can only roll over a maximum of 5 days per year and cannot accumulate more than 25 total days of vacation. Employees will no longer gain cash pay-outs from unused PTO days after January 1, 2018. On January 1, 2018, the firm will give employees cash pay-outs for all accumulated PTO vacation days. Ruth drafted the following announcement to employees:

---

SUBJECT: Mandatory Vacation Policy Effective January 1

As I hold exit interviews with departing consultants, I've been troubled by how many of our employees have failed to take all of their vacation time. Our average consultant has 33 days of accumulated PTO. While I understand many of the pressures many of you feel to stay working and keep commitments to our clients, this amount of unused vacation time is unacceptable. Research convincingly shows that employees who use more vacation time are happier and more productive at work.

I have been reviewing this matter with the HR team for months. I have come to the firm conclusion that our firm needs a change in policy that incentivizes you employees to take time off so that you are more productive when you're here in the workplace.

Beginning on January 1, 2018, employees with fewer than 10 years of employment at the firm will receive 15 days of vacation per year, and employees with more than 10 years of employment will receive 20 days of vacation per year. The amount of roll-over and cash payouts will be dramatically reduced. Employees can only roll over a maximum of 5 days per year and cannot accumulate more than 30 total days of vacation. Employees will no longer gain cash pay-outs from unused PTO days after January 1, 2018. On January 1, 2018, the firm will give employees cash pay-outs for all accumulated PTO vacation days.

I will hold town hall meetings on November 2 and November 11 to tell you about the changes in more detail and explain how they help you out.

Best, Ruth

---

Your task: Rewrite the message to improve its tone and more adequately announce the changes. Make sure to briefly mention the rationale for the changes and explain the impacts on employees.

### 9.19 Building a Culture of Safety: Providing Directions at Fordham Springs Manufacturing (LO9.3)

About three months ago, an assembly worker at Fordham Spring Manufacturing (FSM) narrowly avoided a fatal assembly-line accident. While the company had avoided an accident with an injury for nearly 950 days, the company's president, Jackie Bentworth, was extremely concerned. The narrowly avoided accident was one of at least three such incidents in the past year. As a result, she formed the Safety Guidelines Committee to develop new procedures to improve the safety culture.

Jackie assigned Roy Bang, an engineer, to lead this seven-person committee.

The committee developed a 65-page, comprehensive guidebook called the Fordham Spring Manufacturing Safety Guidelines. Roy placed the guidelines on the company's intranet where all employees could see them. He also broke the guidelines into separate webpages so that employees could easily find sought-after information quickly. He also planned to lead employee town hall meetings about the new safety guidelines on June 3, June 8, and June 10. He hoped all managers would attend these town hall meetings.

Roy wanted to share the new responsibilities and guidelines with employees throughout the organization. He decided to personally contact each of the managers to provide an overview of their responsibilities. First, he decided to contact mid-level managers because they played a major role in promoting safety among supervisors and assembly-line employees. FSM currently had eight mid-level managers. Each of these managers oversaw production of one of FSM's core products. The current managers included Steve Easton, Jeffrey Thompson, Deshawn Miles, Angie Zambroni, Brad Wilhemson, Parker Jones, Sandra Argesion, and Daniel King. Roy drafted the following message to send to the mid-level managers:

---

SUBJECT: New Procedures

Hi everyone,

Congratulations! We have now gone nearly 950 days without any major accidents or injuries! A new set of safety guidelines will be of assistance in continuing this excellent record of safety and concern for the well-being of all employees. After all, we have had at least three close calls that could have been devastating accidents for employees and the company. So, we can never be complacent.

During the past nine months, our Safety Guidelines Committee has undertaken the responsibility to develop definitions of various duties and responsibilities of managers at various levels of the organization. The duties and guidelines were developed after extensive review of industry standards and ten meetings were undertaken in the pursuit of the development of clear-cut, concrete, and unambiguous roles and responsibilities for employees at every level or the organization, from the shop floor to the C-suite.

Since you are a mid-level manager, I wanted to take this opportunity to share with you the pertinent responsibilities and guidelines that apply to you. All mid-level managers are expected to adhere to the following responsibilities: all mid-level managers should understand, implement, and monitor safety guidelines (the new guidelines are attached to this message); all mid-level managers are in charge of the quarterly evaluation of supervisors' adherence to relevant safety guidelines; all mid-level managers are responsible for making sure that all employees conduct Work Activity Safety Planning before the beginning of all new projects; all mid-level managers are responsible for the provision of safety training and certification of all supervisors and assembly workers; all mid-level managers have the responsibility of the placement of safety performance expectations in the job position descriptions of all supervisors and all assembly workers; all mid-level managers are responsible for the conducting of weekly inspections of all assembly line areas with the accompaniment of relevant supervisors; responsibility of the coaching and mentoring of supervisors and assembly line workers in new safety procedures; responsible for participation in accident review procedures in order to communicate "lessons learned" to all relevant supervisors and assembly-line workers.

If by chance there is a serious injury in your assigned work area, please be advised that the committee has identified the followed procedures: ensuring immediate medical treatment for the injured employee; securing the accident area; contacting of the Director of Personnel as soon as the employee is under appropriate medical treatment and the accident area is secured; creation of an official accident report with all information completed as directed to the Director of Personnel within 24 hours.

Thank you for all you do for the safety of your designated employees. You truly make a difference.

Best wishes, Roy Bang

---

Your task: Rewrite this message to mid-level managers. Rewrite with a focus on the following goals: (1) make the responsibilities and directions more clear, (2) improve the writing style to make the message easier to read, (3) make the message more personable, and (4) briefly provide the background and rationale for the new safety responsibilities and guidelines.

### 9.20 Making Claims (LO9.3)

Think about a product or service you have purchased in the past that did not work properly. Write a claim to the company about it. Explain why your claim is justified and suggest action. Focus on achieving an assertive but friendly tone.

### 9.21 Expressing Appreciation (LO9.4)

Assume that you just received and accepted an offer for a job you've wanted. You believe one of your references may have been instrumental in helping you get the job. Write a note of appreciation.

### 9.22 Making Apologies (LO9.4)

Assume you lost your temper when discussing a group project with one of your classmates. You left the meeting early because you were frustrated that your classmate insisted on doing everything his way. You still feel that he is dominating the project, but your behavior was inappropriate. Write an apology to your classmate in a way that repairs some of the damage between the two of you and allows the group to work more effectively together.

### 9.23 Expressing Sympathy (LO9.4)

Assume your boss's mother has just passed away. Write a note that you could include in a card.

# Language Mechanics Check

**9.24 Review the grammar rules in Appendix A. Then, rewrite each sentence to correct grammatical mistakes where needed.**

A. Each customer should provide their complete purchase information for all refund requests.

B. Either Jake or Jen will give you their laptop when it's your turn to present.

C. Jen gave her presentation about giving back to your communities at the board meeting.

D. I serve our clients in the Western region, she serves our clients in the Southeastern region.

E. Jim's organization and the Chinese delegation is creating a Sino-American think tank.

F. The training manual for managers are online.

G. She thinks that we should keep a 6-week supply of inventory, he thinks we should keep a 2-week supply of inventory.

H. Getting 90 percentile, the GMAT score should help him get into a top MBA program.

I. The benefits at this company is one of the key attractions for new employees.

J. Jen's company provides their employees with many benefits.

# Endnotes

1. Dennis S. Reina and Michelle L. Reina, *Trust and Betrayal in the Workplace* (San Francisco: Berrett-Koehler Publishers, 2006): 19–20.

2. Joanna L. Krotz, "The Power of Saying Thank You," Microsoft Business, retrieved July 7, 2010, from www.microsoft.com/business/en-us/resources/marketing/customer-service-acquisition/the-power-of-saying-thank-you.aspx#Thepowerofsayingthankyou.

3. Ibid.

4. Holly Weeks, "The Art of the Apology," *Harvard Management Update,* May 19, 2003.

5. Barbara Kellerman, "When Should a Leader Apologize—and When Not?" *Harvard Business Review,* April 2006: 72–81; Weeks, "The Art of the Apology."

6. Ibid.

7. Society for Human Resource Management, "Vacation Time Is Time Well Spent, HR Professionals Say in New SHRM Survey," November 12, 2013, available at https://www.shrm.org/about-shrm/press-room/press-releases/pages/vacationbenefits.aspx.

CHAPTER 10:
Persuasive Messages

 **ESTABLISHING CREDIBILITY**

 **PRINCIPLES OF INTERPERSONAL COMMUNICATION**

 **PRINCIPLES FOR & TYPES OF BUSINESS MESSAGES**

## Learning Objectives

After studying this chapter, you should be able to do the following:

**LO10.1** Describe the relationship between credibility and persuasion.

**LO10.2** Explain the AIM planning process for persuasive messages and the basic components of most persuasive messages.

**LO10.3** Explain how the tone and style of persuasive messages impact their influence.

**LO10.4** Create compelling internal persuasive messages.

**LO10.5** Compose influential external persuasive messages.

**LO10.6** Construct effective mass sales messages.

**LO10.7** Evaluate persuasive messages for effectiveness and fairness.

In many business situations, you hope to persuade others. In internal business communications, you may want your boss, peers, or colleagues to consider or adopt your ideas when their perspectives differ from yours. In external business communications, you will want to persuade your clients, customers, and prospects to use your products and services. Persuasion involves influencing others to see the merits of your ideas and act on your requests, even when they initially resist. In this chapter, we explore strategies for persuading others through writing.

In some ways, all business messages contain an element of persuasion—that is, you are hoping to influence the way others think, feel, or behave. Many of the concepts in this chapter will enhance your ability to make any kind of request. However, the approaches in this chapter are most applicable to situations in which your audience will initially resist your requests.

Throughout this chapter, you will see examples of persuasive messages at Better Horizons Credit Union. The chapter case provides the background.

Hear Pete Cardon explain why this matters.

bit.ly/cardon10

## CHAPTER CASE: SHIFTING COURSE AT BETTER HORIZONS CREDIT UNION

**WHO'S INVOLVED**

Haniz Zogby

**Marketing specialist and loan officer**

- Started working at Better Horizons nearly five years ago. She has worked 20 to 30 hours per week while attending college with a major in finance and a minor in event management.
- Started as a teller. Within a few years, she was promoted to positions of teller supervisor, loan officer, and marketing specialist.
- Currently working on marketing initiatives under the direction of Christine Russo.

Christine Russo

**President and CEO**

- Has worked at Better Horizons for approximately ten years.
- Currently interested in increasing the number of young members. With declining numbers of young members, she is concerned that the credit union does not have good long-term prospects.

**SITUATION 1**

### Christine Wants to Build Support for New Banking Services That Meet the Needs of Younger Members

Christine recognized that people under the age of 30 were not joining the credit union. Christine wanted to write a message to board members about adopting marketing strategies and services that appeal to younger members. She planned to follow up by presenting her ideas in person at an upcoming meeting. The board is composed of longtime members who favor what they consider a "personal," "friendly," and "homey" credit union environment. They view moves to online

As you consider the needs of others in the workplace, you should always keep in mind the deep and underlying hopes of others. Your colleagues will generally want to help when they share the same purposes and values. Similarly, your colleagues nearly always want to feel appreciated and needed. For colleagues and customers, you can consider a variety of psychological principles of influence. Also, you should consider whether you are making a logical appeal or an emotional one in your persuasive messages.

**Persuade through Shared Purpose and Shared Values**  In today's networked and more open work environment, professionals increasingly work in teams and communities (within organizations) tied together by a shared purpose and shared values. As a result, many professionals are highly motivated by appeals to support their organizations, their teams, and their colleagues because colleagues genuinely want to help.

When you make appeals to shared purpose and shared values, your credibility is typically the most important factor in gaining your colleagues' support. You can influence others best when they believe you are sincerely acting on behalf of the organization and them (caring), you are candid about the reasons behind your requests (character), and others are confident that your ideas will really make a positive difference (competence). While these types of appeals are often effective, use them sparingly. When overused, appeals to purpose and values may be interpreted as self-serving or insincere. You'll notice a persuasive message later in the chapter (Figure 10.5) that is primarily based on an appeal to shared purpose.

**Show People They Are Sincerely Needed and Appreciated**  You can influence colleagues and partners far more easily when they know you appreciate them for their hard work, their abilities, and their good intentions. By complimenting them and expressing appreciation to them, they often will want to return that goodwill to you (discussed further in a few paragraphs in relation to the principle of *reciprocity*). Similarly, most of your colleagues want to feel needed. They want to feel that they are essential to getting work done. Your ability to persuade colleagues is often closely tied to how needed and appreciated you make them feel. Of course, your colleagues must trust your sincerity when you show them they are needed and appreciated.

**Understand Methods of Influence**  Dr. Robert Cialdini, a marketing psychologist, has spent his career studying how people are influenced in business and marketing environments. He has examined research in this area for four decades, plus he spent three years taking undercover jobs in car dealerships, telemarketing firms, fund-raising organizations, and other buyer-seller environments to learn the most influential ways of getting people to say yes. Based on his work, he has identified six principles of persuasion (aside from the price and quality of products and services). These principles include reciprocation, consistency, social proof, liking, authority, and scarcity.[3] Haniz's message to recruit credit union members for the Hope Walkathon offers an interesting example for applying these various principles (see Figure 10.7 for her completed message).

**Reciprocation** is a principle of influence based on returning favors. As defined by Cialdini, "We should try to repay, in kind, what another person has provided us."[4] Cialdini cited an interesting study in which a professor sent Christmas cards to a random sample of strangers to see what would happen. Many of the card recipients reciprocated, sending cards to the professor without attempting to find out who he was. The study showed that even card receivers who did not know the card sender and who might not interact with the card sender in the future felt compelled to return the favor of sending a card. People tend to feel obligated to pay back others when they've received something of value.[5]

Haniz uses the principle of reciprocation in her message in several ways. For example, she focuses on a lengthy reciprocal relationship that the credit union has with the local breast cancer center, and the walkathon serves as the mechanism that draws the two organizations together. The credit union helps the center by generating walkathon donations, and the center helps the credit union and the larger community through more effective breast cancer treatment and education. Furthermore, the message implies a reciprocal relationship between the credit union and its members by offering various free items, such as a T-shirt, a water bottle, and a cancer guide, to members who are willing to participate in the walkathon.

**Consistency** is based on the idea that once people make an explicit commitment, they tend to follow through or honor that commitment. In other words, they want to stay consistent with their original commitment. Cialdini cited several studies to make this point. In one, psychologists found that horse racing fans become more confident that their horses would win after placing a bet. Once they made a final commitment, they were further convinced of the correctness of their choice.[6]

Haniz appeals to commitment and consistency in several ways. Foremost, she appeals to the credit union's long commitment to the fight against breast cancer. Some credit union members will want to continue to honor this long-standing collective commitment and will appreciate that their credit union is doing so. She also provides links in the message for people to immediately act on their interest in the walkathon. A link to register right now serves as an immediate commitment to participate.

**Social proof** is a principle of influence whereby people determine what is right, correct, or desirable by seeing what others do. Haniz employs several appeals to social proof in her letter. She describes the level of participation and contribution among members in last year's walkathon, implying that the popularity and financial impact of this event make it a good cause. Also, the walkathon itself is a type of social proof; the gathering of thousands of people wearing team T-shirts and marching in unison for a cause is powerful imagery.[7]

**Liking** is a principle of influence whereby people are more likely to be persuaded by people they like.[8] Haniz appeals directly to this principle by describing Betty Williams, who is a breast cancer survivor, the benefactor of the breast center, a credit union member, and a participant in the walkathon. Betty Williams is presumably a person most people in the community know and like, a woman many of the credit union members may know from running into her at the credit union or other community events, and a woman who is passionate about an important cause (a reason for liking). Haniz emphasizes in the message that walkathon participants will join this likable and respected community member at the walkathon.

**Authority** is a principle of influence whereby people follow authority figures. The number of celebrity endorsements in advertising is evidence of how authority can impact persuasion.[9] Although Haniz does not appeal to a national celebrity, she does appeal to a prominent local community member—again Betty Williams. With Betty's level of influence and personal experience combating cancer, she is likely seen as an authority. Furthermore, Haniz also appeals to members to support the Betty Williams Breast Center, a group of expert professionals who collectively are authorities on breast cancer.

**Scarcity** is a principle of influence whereby people think there is limited availability of something they want or need, so they must act quickly.[10] Haniz employs this principle in terms of time. She explains that the walkathon occurs only once each year (limited time period to participate) and that participants must sign up by a given deadline (limited time period to sign up).

You will apply these principles most often in external persuasive messages, and you should always apply them fairly. Cialdini describes them as "weapons of influence."[11] The very term *weapons* implies that they are powerful and can do harm. In the "Apply the FAIR Test" section near the end of the chapter, we further discuss the appropriate use of these principles.

**Persuade through Emotion and Reason**    Most people justify their business decisions based on the soundness of ideas, not feelings. Savvy business communicators, however, understand the importance of injecting emotion into their persuasive messages. While they appreciate the place of reason in business and consumer decisions, they understand that resistance to ideas, products, and services is often emotional. Conversely, they are aware that their target audiences often possess strong emotional attachment to competing ideas, products, and services. Thus, effective communicators find ways to appeal to the core emotional benefits of products, services, and ideas.[12]

Even in internal persuasive messages, emotional appeals are critical, as indicated by Craig Conway, president and CEO of PeopleSoft:

> Good communicators have an enormous advantage over poor communicators because so much of running a company is inspirational. . . . You just have to be able to persuade people that they are a part of something bigger. If you have a creative vision and you can communicate it in a compelling way to get people excited, you will recruit better people as a result. Then, it is easy to convince the world that you have a more dynamic company.[13]

Part of understanding your audience is identifying the needs and values that resonate emotionally for them.

Typically, internal persuasive messages focus mostly on logical appeals. External persuasive messages, with the exception of those that emphasize price, generally include strong emotional appeals. As you develop persuasive messages, think about how to get the right mix of logical and emotional appeals. Generally, you will supply both but emphasize one or the other. Keep in mind that even when you choose to make strong emotional appeals in written messages, you should generally avoid the tone of mass advertising, where exaggeration, sarcasm, and over-the-top appeals are acceptable and even effective. Later in the chapter, you will notice several messages created by Haniz and Christine—two based more strongly on logical appeals (Figures 10.5 and 10.8) and two on emotional appeals (Figures 10.7 and 10.9).

## Gather the Right Information

Gathering the right information and developing your ideas for persuasive messages is critical. Since your audience is resistant to the message, one of your key tasks is to establish credibility. Developing strong ideas in the interest of your audience helps you demonstrate your voice of competence. It involves gaining a deep understanding of the benefits and drawbacks of your ideas, products, and services. In addition, it involves gaining a thorough understanding of competing ideas, products, and services.

Thus, before attempting to persuade others, expert business communicators seek to understand products, services, and ideas in great depth so that they can speak from an authoritative and *competent* perspective. To address the issue of attracting younger credit union members, Christine and Haniz spend months learning about the strategies that other credit unions use. When Haniz works on a message that promotes her credit union over local banks, she carefully analyzes and compares the major products and services offered by her credit union and those of competing banks. When Haniz works on a message to persuade credit union members to join the Hope Walkathon, she learns all she can about participation in this event and how it helps in the fight against breast cancer.

## Set Up the Message

Most business writing is **direct** and **explicit**. It is direct in that you begin with a main idea or argument and then provide the supporting reasons. It is explicit in that nothing is implied; statements contain full and unambiguous meaning. When you write directly and explicitly, you help your readers understand your message and you show respect for their time.

---

### Components of Persuasive Messages

- Gain attention.
- Raise a need.
- Deliver a solution.
- Provide a rationale.
- Validate the views, preferences, and concerns of others.
- Give counterpoints (optional).
- Call to action.

**TABLE 10.1**

Effective Attention-Getters

| Type of Attention-Getter | Example |
|---|---|
| Rhetorical question | Did you know that average credit union members save $400 per year compared to bank customers? |
| Intriguing statistic | In the past five years, we've lost over 200 members—over 10 percent of our membership. |
| Compelling and unusual fact(s) | You've probably heard car dealers boast about their near-zero percent interest rates—but there's a catch! By financing with car dealers, you give up your opportunity to receive manufacturer rebates and your power to negotiate on price. |
| Challenge | Please join our team in this year's Hope Walkathon in the fight against breast cancer. |
| Testimonial | "I never knew I could have so much negotiating power with a preapproved loan. By getting my car loan through Better Horizons, I negotiated a great deal with the car dealer. This is the way to buy cars!" |

Compared to other business messages, persuasive messages are somewhat more **indirect** and **implicit**. They are sometimes indirect in that they provide the rationale for a request before making the specific request. They are sometimes implicit in that the request or some of the rationale for the request may be implied. In other words, sometimes the reader needs to read between the lines to grasp the entire meaning. Implicit statements politely ask people to do or think differently. Also, explicitly stating some types of benefits is considered poor form—for example, matters of financial or career gain in internal persuasive requests.[14]

**Attention** The first task of most persuasive messages is to gain the attention of your readers. You can do this in a variety of ways, including asking a rhetorical question, providing a compelling or interesting fact, revealing a compelling statistic, issuing a challenge, or posting a testimonial.[15] For internal persuasive messages, the primary means of gaining attention is demonstrating a business need—a gap between what is and what could be.[16] You generally have more flexibility in external persuasive messages as you choose your attention-getters. See Table 10.1 for examples of attention-getters Haniz might use for some of her communication tasks.

**Need, Solution, and Rationale** In the body of your message, your first task is to tie your product, service, or idea to the *needs* of your readers. The best way to reduce the resistance your reader may have is to show that your message meets your readers' needs. Once you've stated the need, you may describe your *solution,* which is a recommended product, service, or idea. Many readers will remain skeptical unless you provide convincing support. So, you will need to provide a strong *rationale*, meaning solid reasons why your product, service, or idea really benefits them. After all, you are more than likely attempting to influence skeptics.[17]

As you structure your message, consider how *direct* you should be. If your audience members are strongly and emotionally resistant to your solution, consider a more indirect approach so they warm up to your ideas before you suggest a solution. To make your message less direct, provide the rationale before the solution.

**Validation** At some point in the body of the message, you should validate your readers by showing appreciation for their views, preferences, and concerns. **Validation** implies that you recognize and appreciate others' needs, wants, ideas, and preferences as legitimate and reasonable, "especially when they are different than your own." By validating your readers, you show respect for them and demonstrate a balanced perspective.[18]

**Counterpoints**   Traditionally, communicators overcame objections by providing counterpoints to any of the audience members' objections. In other words, they showed how their own ideas, products, or services were superior to the competing ideas, products, or services the audience favored.

Overcoming objections with counterpoints, however, is risky in the post-trust era. This approach may unnecessarily carry a *me-versus-you* tone and delegitimize the readers' concerns. Michael Maslansky, in his research about emerging trends in sales messages in the PTE, states that validation is "using words to let people know that their concerns are valid," and that it is the "polar opposite of overcoming objections."[19] He says the "new sales mantra [is to] agree with objections."[20] This perhaps ironic approach shows respect and balance because you validate the potential customer's feelings and ideas. When you validate your readers, they are more likely to accept the merits of your persuasive message.

Thus, consider carefully whether to include counterpoints to your readers' objections. When you know people well and believe that you will not create a *me-versus-you* adversarial stance, tactfully state how your ideas, products, and services outperform those of your readers.

Skilled business communicators understand that building support for their ideas takes time. Especially for persuasion within companies, you will generally use a mix of communication channels. Rarely will your ideas be accepted and enacted with one written message. However, one written message can make a powerful statement and open avenues of communication that lead to acceptance and adoption of your ideas.

**Action**   You conclude persuasive messages with a call to action, which asks your readers to take a specific step toward the purchase of a product or service or acceptance of an idea. However, a call to action should not be a hard sell; pressuring others is increasingly ineffective in the PTE.[21] In external persuasive messages, the call to action is typically a specific and explicit step. In internal persuasive messages, the call to action is sometimes explicit and sometimes implicit. It is more likely to be implicit for controversial change ideas and when corresponding with superiors who have ultimate decision-making authority.

## Getting the Tone and Style Right for Persuasive Messages

**LO10.3**  Explain how the tone and style of persuasive messages impact their influence.

**connect**

Visit http://connect. mheducation.com for an exercise on this topic.

The tone for persuasive messages should be confident and positive, yet at the same time avoid exaggeration or hype. This is tricky! You will no doubt need to make some trade-offs. The more confident and positive you make your message, the more you risk being perceived as pushy or exaggerated. As you reduce confidence and positivity, you risk your product, service, or idea being perceived as weak or unexciting. One benefit of asking colleagues to read your persuasive message before you send it is they can help you decide if you have achieved the right level of confidence and positivity without sacrificing believability.

The writing style of your message should be action-oriented and lively. But again, you risk being perceived as unbelievable or overly enthusiastic if you overdo the language. However, you risk being perceived as dull or unexceptional if you don't use engaging, lively language. Proofreading by yourself and with the help of colleagues will help you get the right writing style to set your message apart.

### Apply the Personal Touch

Recently, a number of competing developers delivered presentations to a property owner, each hoping to persuade him to sell them 4,000 acres of much-sought-after property. The presentations were nearly identical, so the property owner was unsure how to choose the best developer. A few days later, the property owner received a handwritten thank-you note from one candidate. The property owner immediately awarded the deal to that developer because he had taken the time to write a message of appreciation.[22]

Often, your competitors are nearly identical to you. Your colleagues and customers will be more easily persuaded when you show interest in them personally, speak to them in personal terms, understand their specific needs, and demonstrate that you are seeking benefits for them. Personalizing your messages is not easy, though, as Michael Maslansky points out:

> For all of us, selling ideas or products or ourselves begins with a need to talk about something that we have and the audience should need, want, or agree with. The problem is that too often, we focus on the first part—what we want to sell, and too little on the second—why they want to buy . . . and yet, our audience demands increasingly that messages, products, and services speak directly to them.[23]

Creating messages that *speak directly* to customers and colleagues requires that you use language that helps your customers and colleagues feel the product, service, or idea is just for them.[24]

One of the primary strategies you can use to personalize persuasive messages is your selection of voice—either you-voice, we-voice, I-voice, or impersonal voice (as introduced in Chapter 2). Table 10.2 offers guidance on choosing the appropriate

> ### Guidelines for Tone for Persuasive Messages
>
> - Apply the personal touch.
> - Use action-oriented, lively language.
> - Write with confidence.
> - Offer choice.
> - Show positivity.

### TABLE 10.2

## Voice in Persuasive Messages

| Voice | Appropriate Cases | Cautions | Examples |
|---|---|---|---|
| You-voice | Use in external persuasive messages to emphasize reader benefits. | Presumptuousness—assuming you know what is good for someone else | When you take out an auto loan, you get a variety of resources to help you in your car shopping, including a free copy of a *Kelley Blue Book*, access to free Carfax reports, Mechanical Breakdown Insurance (MBI), and Guaranteed Auto Protection (GAP). <br><br> In this example, you-voice helps show direct benefits to the customers. Overuse across an entire message, however, may come across as presumptuous, overbearing, or exaggerated. |
| We-voice | Use in internal persuasive messages to emphasize shared work goals. | Presumptuousness—assuming you share common beliefs, ideas, or understanding with your colleagues | At Better Horizons, we've instilled a personal touch into every aspect of our business. We've reinforced this culture with face-to-face services. Our tellers welcome members by name. When members come into the credit union, they know we care about them as people, not just as customers. The warm, friendly, genuine, and personal approach we take to serving our members is why I'm so proud to work here. <br><br> In this passage, we-voice instills a sense of shared values, priorities, and goals. We-voice can instill a strong sense of teamwork. When audience members have different perspectives, however, they may resent that you are stating agreement where it does not exist. |
| I-voice | Use in all persuasive messages sparingly. | Overuse implies self-centeredness | After examining the results of other credit unions, I am convinced that these tools can build emotional connections and loyalty with our members. <br><br> In this example, I-voice is used to show a personal opinion and shows respect for audience members who are not yet fully persuaded. Frequent use of I-voice across an entire message, however, may come across as emphasizing your interests rather than those of the audience. |
| Impersonal voice | Use in persuasive messages to emphasize objectivity and neutrality. | Overuse may depersonalize the message | The basic difference between credit unions and banks is that credit union members own and control their credit unions whereas bank account holders have no stake or control in their financial institutions. <br><br> In this example, impersonal voice helps show objectivity. An entire persuasive message in impersonal voice, however, may fail to connect on a personal level with the audience. |

voice. Generally, you-voice is more effective in external persuasive messages to customers and clients because it emphasizes the benefits they receive from your products and services. From the customer's perspective, the you-voice shows them that they are the center of attention.

Writing in the you-voice to customers is more than just a stylistic choice. It forces you to consciously consider the readers' needs and wants. It forces you to personalize the message for them. By contrast, the we-voice in external messages can focus too much attention on your company and de-emphasize benefits to the customer. Notice the difference in overall tone in the two messages in Figures 10.4 and 10.5. In the less effective example, the you-voice is hardly used at all compared to the dominating we-voice. In the more effective example, the you-voice takes center stage over the we-voice. The extensive use of you-voice in the more effective message sends a strong meta message: *This message is about you.*

Another method of personalizing a message is to make your statements tangible. By definition, *tangible* means something can be touched; it is material or substantial. In a business communications context, making the statement **tangible** implies that the readers can discern something in terms that are meaningful to them. This allows the reader to sense the impact on a personal level.[25] You often can achieve a tangible feel by combining you-voice with specificity. Consider the examples in Table 10.3, from messages that Haniz is working on for the credit union.

As you reread your message, keep in mind the following advice from sales specialist Ralph Allora: "Read the letter aloud. If it doesn't sound like you're having a conversation with the client over the phone, then you're not using the right tone."[26] This in part is a test of whether you have personalized your message enough.

### TABLE 10.3

Making Tangible Statements

| Less Effective | More Effective |
|---|---|
| Credit unions save members about $8 billion a year thanks to better interest rates and reduced fees. | On average, credit union members save $400 each year compared to bank customers thanks to lower loan rates and fees. |
| The benefit is not tangible. Customers are not sure what the benefit would be for them personally. | This benefit is tangible; the customers know how much they will save on an individual level. |
| In recent years, many credit unions have lost membership because younger individuals are not attracted to them. | In the past five years, we've lost over 200 members—over 10 percent of our membership. And we simply aren't attracting younger members. |
| This statement focuses on a general trend for credit unions but does not indicate an impact on a particular credit union. | This statement invokes a sense of what is happening right here at our credit union. Identifying the amount (as well as a percentage) helps the reader discern the impact. |
| We provide lower rates on car loans. Our car loan rates are between 1.5 and 1.75 percentage points lower than at any of the banks in town. | **You pay lower rates on car loans.** You can get car loan rates at Better Horizons that are 1.5–1.75 percentage points lower than at any other bank in town. Consider the savings:<br>• On a 4-year $15,000 new car loan: You save about $680.<br>• On a 4-year $5,000 used car loan: You save about $200. |
| This statement doesn't help the customers understand how much in dollars they would save on a car loan at Better Horizons. | This statement allows customers to easily think about how much savings they would receive by getting a car loan with Better Horizons. |

**TABLE 10.4**

Using Action-Oriented and Lively Language

| Less Effective | More Effective |
|---|---|
| The Betty Williams Breast Center has a nationally accredited program for treatment of breast cancer. | The Betty Williams Breast Center runs a nationally accredited program for treatment of breast cancer. |
| The weak verb *has* implies little action on the part of the Betty Williams Breast Center. | The action verb *runs* implies a full-fledged and active effort on the part of the Betty Williams Breast Center. |
| Better Horizons has always been known for its personal approach to our members. Our transactions have always occurred through face-to-face services. Our tellers are friendly to all members. | At Better Horizons, we've instilled a personal touch into every aspect of our business. We've reinforced this culture with face-to-face services. Our tellers welcome members by name. When members come into the credit union, they know we care about them as people, not just as customers. |
| Uses unexciting, weak verbs: *has been known, have occurred, are* (notice how passive verbs detract from a sense of action and engagement). The central theme of personalized service does not come through. For example, consider the contrast between *our tellers are friendly* versus *our tellers welcome members by name*. | Uses a positive, diverse set of action verbs: *instilled, reinforced, welcome, care*. Uses adjectives and nouns to further emphasize a central theme of personalized service: *personal touch, face-to-face services, name*. |

## Use Action-Oriented and Lively Language

In persuasive messages, you have somewhat more license to write creatively. Focus on using action-oriented and lively words to achieve a sense of excitement, optimism, or other positive emotions. Use strong nouns and verbs to add to the excitement of the message. Some sales messages sound dull because of overuse of and reliance on words such as *provide* and *offer*.[27] Across the entire message or thought, the action-oriented and lively language should emphasize a central theme. See Table 10.4 for examples from documents Haniz is working on for two of her projects.

## Write with Confidence

As you display more confidence in your idea, your product, or your service, you can more effectively influence your audience. Effective persuaders provide compelling and simple reasons for action. They should show confidence in these ideas, as illustrated in Table 10.5, again with examples from two of Haniz's projects. Emotionally, the writer's confidence allows the audience to gain confidence in the message. In internal persuasive messages, expressing confidence in key players, who can make the change occur, is crucial. These key players include upper-level executives who will actively endorse and authorize resources as well as those managers and employees who will put the ideas into motion.[28]

## Offer Choice

Michael Maslansky and his research team have examined the reactions of tens of thousands of customers and clients to many types of written messages. In this section, we illustrate a few findings from the financial industry. For example, in Figure 10.1, you see four statements that were sent to respondents. In the hypothetical scenario that was presented to them, a company is attempting to do a good thing—give its employees an opportunity to put money in a retirement account.

The four statements state essentially the same thing but are phrased differently. Each is written fairly well and appeals to some individuals. The statement that appeals to the

**TABLE 10.5**

Writing with Confidence

| Less Effective | More Effective |
|---|---|
| At our upcoming board meeting, I would like to discuss possible ways of appealing to younger members. We can talk about how various strategies might appeal to this group. | At our upcoming board meeting, I will present a vision of how we can build marketing strategies and product offerings to appeal to younger members. These strategies will not only attract younger members to our credit union but also increase our business across other age groups. |
| These statements are an attempt to achieve an other-orientation; they show sensitivity to involving others in the decision making. However, they show no confidence in the ideas or policies that the audience resists. | These statements imply confidence in the change message: These are ideas and policies that will make a difference. Furthermore, the writer can make them happen. The argument is logic-based but also contains an excitement about possibilities. |
| Please think about how Better Horizons can help you in your banking. | We encourage you to stop by Better Horizons and make direct comparisons with your current bank. You'll find that banking with Better Horizons saves you money, provides convenience when you travel, and offers services to meet nearly any banking need. |
| This nonspecific request sounds weak and unconfident. It gives the reader an excuse to easily dismiss the message. | This request lays down a challenge to make direct comparisons, confidently implying that Better Horizons can outperform competitors. It then directly states specific benefits to the potential member. |

**FIGURE 10.1**

Most Effective Statements to Persuade Skeptical Employees *(Creating Salary Deduction for 401[k] Scenario)*

*Note:* The survey involved a hypothetical situation where employers would automatically deduct 7 percent of an employee's salary and place it into a 401(k). This process would help employees save money for the future. The employees would have the option to opt-out.

*Source:* Adapted from *The Language of Trust: Selling Ideas in a World of Skeptics* by Michael Maslansky, Scott West, Gary DeMoss, and David Saylor, Copyright © 2010 by Van Kampen Investor Services, Inc.

*Statement #1:* This process is automatic, but not required. It's voluntary. If you don't want to be enrolled or you don't like any of the choices we made, you can always opt-down to a lower level or opt-out.

**40%**

*Statement #2:* We have established the investment rate and default option based on general retirement guidelines, but you may change your investment rate or stop participating in the plan at any time.

**23%**

*Statement #3:* We do not want to tell you what to do with the money, but we do want to help you understand your options and make the most of the money that you do save for retirement.

**22%**

*Statement #4:* We believe we have a responsibility to provide you with information and guidance about the most effective strategies for saving and investing to achieve your retirement goals.

**15%**

**Percentage of Employees Who Preferred Statement**

**TABLE 10.6**

Emphasizing Choice

| Less Effective | More Effective |
|---|---|
| You owe it to the women in your lives to make a difference. | You can help make a difference for women here in our community. |
| This appeal focuses on obligation and pressure. Most readers will not respond positively. | This appeal focuses on volunteerism and contribution to the community without telling the reader what to do. |
| The walkathon will be held on Saturday, October 6 at 9:00 a.m. at Central Park. Do your part to improve the lives of women in our community! | The walkathon will be held on Saturday, October 6 at 9:00 a.m. at Central Park. Please join Betty and the rest of the Better Horizons team for a day of fun, excitement, and hope! |
| This request is a guilt trip; it emphasizes the readers' duty. | This request recognizes the readers' choice to participate in a fun and exciting approach to a good cause. |

most people (40 percent) emphasizes choice rather than intent. It uses the you-voice rather than the we-voice, which is preferable for many messages written to consumers (this is most similar to a consumer situation). It contains three short sentences with 7, 2, and 29 words. The emphasis on choice (other-orientation), use of you-voice (other-orientation), and simple language combine to make this the most influential statement. By contrast, the other options each contain one long sentence (30, 36, and 27 words).

In the PTE, customers and clients consider choice an indicator of credibility. They view simple language (not implying lack of sophisticated knowledge) as a display of transparency and respect. In contrast, they view overly complex language as potentially deceptive.[29] Similarly, effective persuasive messages avoid statements that may be perceived as pressure tactics. Hard sells are increasingly ineffective in a PTE, especially in written format.[30] Compare Haniz's less effective and more effective persuasive statements in Table 10.6, all of which you will see again in her messages located later in the chapter.

In persuasive messages, always be careful about being perceived as presumptuous—unfairly assuming that you know or even share the thoughts, feelings, and intentions of others. Many people are easily offended when you presume to know or even dictate how they will think, feel, or react to your messages.[31]

## Show Positivity

Positivity in persuasive messages helps your audience focus on the benefits rather than the drawbacks of what you are trying to promote. Maslansky and his team's research helps demonstrate that subtle changes to more positive wording are generally more persuasive. For example, they asked consumers to identify which of three pairs of phrases were more persuasive in promotional material about investment options.

In the first pair of statements, 90 percent of consumers thought the statement *making sure you have enough money as long as you live* was more effective than the statement *managing longevity risk*. Overwhelmingly, the consumers thought the benefit (having long-term financial security) was more influential than the possible drawback (avoiding financial loss).

For the second pair of statements, 81 percent of consumers thought the statement *making sure you can afford to maintain your lifestyle* was more persuasive than the statement *managing inflation risk*. Similarly, the vast majority of consumers in the case thought that the benefit (maintaining your lifestyle) was more compelling than the drawback (possibly losing your current buying power).

**TABLE 10.7**

Statements to Avoid in the Post-Trust Era

| Type | Examples That Don't Work |
|------|--------------------------|
| Trust me | "Trust me" or "We speak your language" |
| Unbelievable | "Your call is important to us" or "We care about our customers" |
| Too good to be true | "This is the right product for you" or "We give you guaranteed results" |
| Excuses | "What you need to understand is . . ." or "Our hands are tied" |
| Explanations | "This was taken out of context" or "I can explain" |
| Fear tactics | "Are you concerned about the security of your family?" or "Act now or you'll miss this opportunity" |

*Sources:* Adapted from *The Language of Trust: Selling Ideas in a World of Skeptics* by Michael Maslansky, Scott West, Gary DeMoss, and David Saylor, Copyright © 2010 by Van Kampen Investor Services, Inc.

For the third pair of statements, 63 percent of consumers thought the statement *making sure you can participate in the gains while reducing your downside risk* was more persuasive than *managing market risk*. In this case, consumers were more positively influenced by the statement about risk (a drawback) when it was preceded by a phrase about gains (the benefit).[32]

In addition to being positive, avoiding superlatives gives you the best chance of persuading your audience. Phrases such as *best product on the market, state-of-the-art technology,* or *best-in-class service* sound increasingly hollow. Maslansky's research with consumers shows that terms such as *comfortable retirement* rather than *dream retirement; protection* rather than *guarantee; financial security* rather than *financial freedom; effective* rather than *best of breed* are more persuasive.

Consumers perceive too-good-to-be-true statements as attempts to convince them of "the merits without making a rational argument. And they [too-good-to-be-true statements] fail because they suggest an inherent bias that ruins the integrity of the communicator."[33] Table 10.7 highlights the kinds of phrases that are increasingly ineffective with today's skeptical consumers. Table 10.8 contrasts messages from Haniz's projects that persuade with and without exaggeration.

**TABLE 10.8**

Avoiding Exaggeration and Superlatives

| Less Effective | More Effective |
|----------------|----------------|
| You can trust us at Better Horizons to make your financial dreams come true. | As a nonprofit, member-controlled financial institution, Better Horizons can provide you with higher rates on savings accounts, better terms on loans, and lower fees. |
| This statement uses phrases that seem unbelievable *(you can trust us)* and exaggerated *(make your financial dreams come true).* It is positive but not plausible. | This statement focuses on specific benefits and uses words that nearly all people view positively *(nonprofit, member-controlled, savings, better, lower fees).* It is both positive and plausible. |
| Pay attention to these facts or risk losing money to banks. | Consider some of the following reasons to join Better Horizons and start saving today. |
| This statement focuses on fear and applies pressure. Most customers would consider the writer not credible. | This statement is inviting and nonthreatening. It uses pressure-free *(consider)* and positive *(join, start saving)* words. |

# Creating Internal Persuasive Messages

Internal and external persuasive messages contain many common elements: They gain *attention*, raise a *need*, deliver a *solution*, provide a *rationale*, show *appreciation* for differences of opinion, give *counterpoints*, and call readers to *action*. Nevertheless, internal and external persuasive messages differ in some ways (see Table 10.9). Internal messages more often focus on promoting ideas, whereas external messages more often focus on promoting products and services. Also, internal persuasive messages tend to be slightly more direct and explicit, and they tend to be based on logical appeals. In contrast, external persuasive messages tend to be slightly more indirect and implicit, and they tend to be based on emotional appeals.

Christine, with the help of Haniz, constructed a letter to warm board members to the idea of adding new financial products and using more online and social networking tools to better reach younger members. Most board members are resistant to this message because they fear depersonalizing Better Horizons, which is known for its warm, community-oriented business model. In the less effective message (see Figure 10.2), Christine is generally positive. However, she shows little confidence in the new ideas. The message generally contains short, dull, and nontangible comments.

In the more effective message (see Figure 10.3), Christine personalizes the letter, addressing each board member individually, and begins with a tangible business problem. Then, she tactfully discusses her ideas and concludes with calls to action. The message contains conviction and vision without sounding too pushy. It uses a variety of implicit approaches to persuade board members that online services and social networking do not undermine personalized service. This message will open avenues for more constructive conversations when Christine meets with the board members in person.

**LO10.4** Create compelling internal persuasive messages.

## TABLE 10.9

Components of Internal and External Persuasive Messages

|  | **Internal Messages (Typically for Ideas)** | **External Messages (Typically for Products and Services)** |
|---|---|---|
| Attention | Overview of a business problem | Catchy statement |
| Need | Description of a business problem | Description of unmet *needs* or *wants* of your customers |
| Solution | Description of *how* your idea or policy addresses the business problem | Description of *how* your product or service benefits customers |
| Rationale | Elaboration about *why* your idea or policy is the best option | Elaboration about *why* your product or service will benefit the customer |
| Appreciation | Appreciation for decision makers' perspectives and resistance to your ideas | Recognition of customers' resistance to your product or service |
| Counterpoints | Explanation of why your ideas are better than competing ideas (typically those of decision makers who comprise your target audience) | Explanation of why your product/service is better than competing products/services (typically those favored by the target audience) |
| Action | Recommendations for a course of action or further discussion about an idea or policy | Description of a specific step for the customer to take toward purchase of a product or service |

**FIGURE 10.2**

Less Effective Internal Persuasive Message

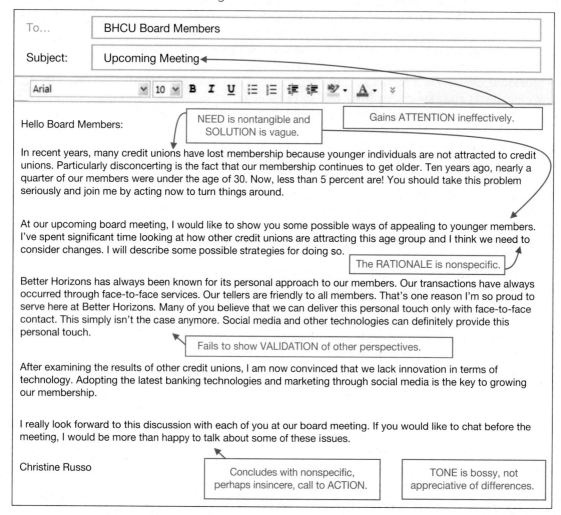

To... BHCU Board Members

Subject: Upcoming Meeting

Arial | 10 | **B** *I* U

Hello Board Members:

> NEED is nontangible and SOLUTION is vague.

> Gains ATTENTION ineffectively.

In recent years, many credit unions have lost membership because younger individuals are not attracted to credit unions. Particularly disconcerting is the fact that our membership continues to get older. Ten years ago, nearly a quarter of our members were under the age of 30. Now, less than 5 percent are! You should take this problem seriously and join me by acting now to turn things around.

At our upcoming board meeting, I would like to show you some possible ways of appealing to younger members. I've spent significant time looking at how other credit unions are attracting this age group and I think we need to consider changes. I will describe some possible strategies for doing so.

> The RATIONALE is nonspecific.

Better Horizons has always been known for its personal approach to our members. Our transactions have always occurred through face-to-face services. Our tellers are friendly to all members. That's one reason I'm so proud to serve here at Better Horizons. Many of you believe that we can deliver this personal touch only with face-to-face contact. This simply isn't the case anymore. Social media and other technologies can definitely provide this personal touch.

> Fails to show VALIDATION of other perspectives.

After examining the results of other credit unions, I am now convinced that we lack innovation in terms of technology. Adopting the latest banking technologies and marketing through social media is the key to growing our membership.

I really look forward to this discussion with each of you at our board meeting. If you would like to chat before the meeting, I would be more than happy to talk about some of these issues.

Christine Russo

> Concludes with nonspecific, perhaps insincere, call to ACTION.

> TONE is bossy, not appreciative of differences.

In the more effective message, Christine chooses to send the message in two forms. She sends it as a letter first (depicted in Figure 10.3) and as a follow-up email a few days later. In letter format, the message feels more personalized and shows the importance of the message. Likewise, it allows Christine to provide a printed-out enclosure as a courtesy.

In Figures 10.4 and 10.5, you can see a less effective and a more effective example of Christine asking employees to volunteer as mentors to new employees. In the less effective example, Christine comes across as bossy and demanding. Leaders rarely capture the hearts and minds of their employees when they fail to offer choice, portray problems in excessively negative terms, and don't validate legitimate concerns. You'll notice that Christine makes all these mistakes in the less effective example. In the more effective example, Christine offers choice throughout the message, appeals to shared purpose throughout the message, offers a positive vision, and validates the employees' real concerns about time commitments. Although this is a relatively simple message, Christine is likely to inspire many employees to volunteer as mentors as long as employees view her as credible and sincere.

## FIGURE 10.3

More Effective Internal Persuasive Message

# BETTER HORIZONS CREDIT UNION
### Est. 1937

June 9, 2017

Matthew L. Poon, Ph.D.
19 Foxworthy Dr.
Pescaloosa, FL 91214

RE: Discussion at Our Upcoming Board Meeting about Gaining Younger Members

Dear Dr. Poon:

In the past five years, we've lost over 200 members—over 10 percent of our membership. This is largely because we are not attracting younger members. Ten years ago, nearly a quarter of our members were under the age of 30. Now, less than 5 percent are! Unless we can attract younger members, we risk a steady decline in membership over at least the next decade.

At our upcoming board meeting, I will present a vision of marketing strategies and product offerings to appeal to younger members. Not only will these strategies help attract younger members, they will also increase our business across other age groups. With several of our best employees, I've spent months examining how other credit unions attract members in this age group. I look forward to your feedback about implementing the following strategies to attract younger members:

- Increasing our social networking presence on Facebook, Twitter, and blogs
- Promoting regular contests and events that cater to younger members (see for example a recent American Idol–like contest to create videos for credit unions at the following website: www.youngfreehq.com/contest/)
- Creating additional online account and lending services, including enhanced bill pay options
- Providing additional products geared to children of current members, including reloadable prepaid debit cards, teen checking and saving, mobile and online banking, and loan options for younger members (i.e., student loans, more car loan options)

At Better Horizons, we've instilled a personal touch into every aspect of our business. We've reinforced this culture with face-to-face services. Our tellers welcome members by name. When members come into the credit union, they know we care about them as people, not just as customers. The warm, friendly, genuine, and personal approach we take to serving our members is why I'm so proud to work here.

At first, I was concerned that online services and social networking might depersonalize the Better Horizons experience. I've often wondered over the past few months, *Would these new services and technologies hurt our brand that is built on personal touch?* After examining the results of other credit unions, I am convinced that these tools can build emotional connections and loyalty with our members. They can strengthen personal conversations with our members. And, they may be the key to growing our membership.

I really look forward to this discussion with each of you at our board meeting. If you would like to chat before the meeting, please call me anytime; I'd love to hear what you think.

You'll find an enclosed research report written by a leading credit union consultancy group that includes findings and recommendations about gaining younger members in credit unions. Can you take about 15 to 30 minutes to read through this report before the board meeting? The report has really influenced my ideas for moving the credit union forward. Thanks again for your support and ideas.

Best wishes,

*Christine Russo*

Christine Russo
President and CEO
Better Horizons Credit Union

Enc.: Best Practices of Credit Unions Research Report

2737 Better Horizons Loop, Pescaloosa, FL 91214 • Phone: 803-784-7300 • Email: info@bhcu.org • Web: www.bhcu.org

*Gains ATTENTION effectively.*

*Provides compelling NEED and introduces SOLUTION.*

*Provides RATIONALE.*

*Shows VALIDATION of other perspectives and subtly offers COUNTERPOINTS.*

*Concludes with call to ACTION.*

**FIGURE 10.4**

Less Effective Message to Employees

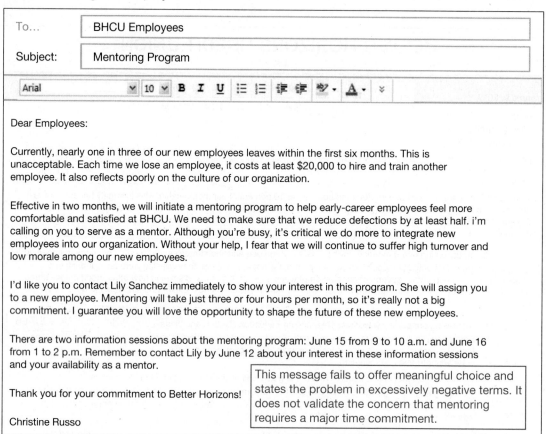

To... BHCU Employees

Subject: Mentoring Program

Dear Employees:

Currently, nearly one in three of our new employees leaves within the first six months. This is unacceptable. Each time we lose an employee, it costs at least $20,000 to hire and train another employee. It also reflects poorly on the culture of our organization.

Effective in two months, we will initiate a mentoring program to help early-career employees feel more comfortable and satisfied at BHCU. We need to make sure that we reduce defections by at least half. i'm calling on you to serve as a mentor. Although you're busy, it's critical we do more to integrate new employees into our organization. Without your help, I fear that we will continue to suffer high turnover and low morale among our new employees.

I'd like you to contact Lily Sanchez immediately to show your interest in this program. She will assign you to a new employee. Mentoring will take just three or four hours per month, so it's really not a big commitment. I guarantee you will love the opportunity to shape the future of these new employees.

There are two information sessions about the mentoring program: June 15 from 9 to 10 a.m. and June 16 from 1 to 2 p.m. Remember to contact Lily by June 12 about your interest in these information sessions and your availability as a mentor.

> This message fails to offer meaningful choice and states the problem in excessively negative terms. It does not validate the concern that mentoring requires a major time commitment.

Thank you for your commitment to Better Horizons!

Christine Russo

## Constructing External Persuasive Messages

**LO10.5** Compose influential external persuasive messages.

Haniz writes two external persuasive messages. The first is a flyer for community members who are participating in free financial planning and tax assistance workshops sponsored and led by Better Horizons. The second is an email encouraging Better Horizons members to join the Hope Walkathon. The first message uses more logical appeals. It deals with reasons Better Horizons is a better option than local banks. The second message uses more emotional appeals. It focuses on pride in team and community, a sense of contribution to an important cause, and an exciting and hope-filled activity. It contains many facts but relies most heavily on garnering feelings of dedication and enthusiasm.

Notice the differences between the less effective and more effective examples in Figures 10.6 and 10.7. In the less effective message (Figure 10.6), most components of persuasive messages are present except for a show of appreciation and a call to action. However, it employs we-voice when the potential customer should be the entire focus of the message, and it does not provide tangible benefits.

By contrast, in the more effective flyer (Figure 10.7), Haniz wrote a message that employs you-voice and describes tangible benefits to focus the entire message on the customer. The formatting makes each benefit stand out. The

**FIGURE 10.5**

## More Effective Message to Employees

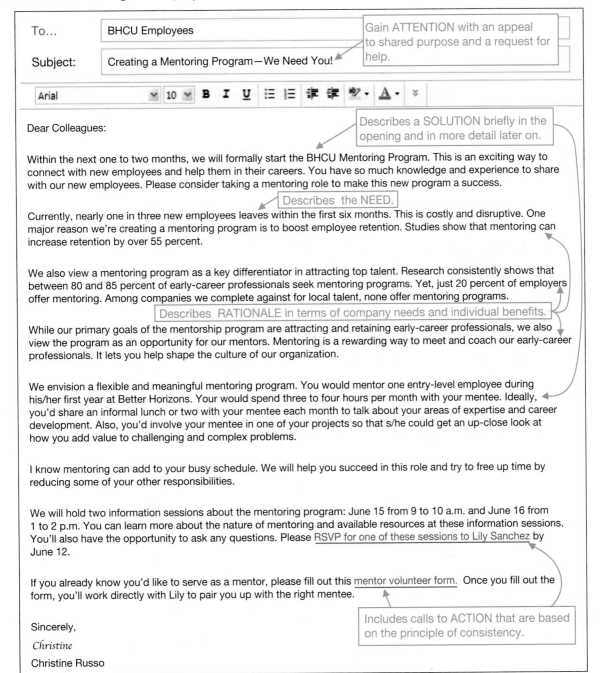

To... BHCU Employees

Subject: Creating a Mentoring Program—We Need You!

> Gain ATTENTION with an appeal to shared purpose and a request for help.

Arial ⌄ 10 ⌄ **B** *I* U ☰ ☰ ☷ ☷ ✎ ⌄ **A** ⌄ ⌄

Dear Colleagues:

> Describes a SOLUTION briefly in the opening and in more detail later on.

Within the next one to two months, we will formally start the BHCU Mentoring Program. This is an exciting way to connect with new employees and help them in their careers. You have so much knowledge and experience to share with our new employees. Please consider taking a mentoring role to make this new program a success.

> Describes the NEED.

Currently, nearly one in three new employees leaves within the first six months. This is costly and disruptive. One major reason we're creating a mentoring program is to boost employee retention. Studies show that mentoring can increase retention by over 55 percent.

We also view a mentoring program as a key differentiator in attracting top talent. Research consistently shows that between 80 and 85 percent of early-career professionals seek mentoring programs. Yet, just 20 percent of employers offer mentoring. Among companies we complete against for local talent, none offer mentoring programs.

> Describes RATIONALE in terms of company needs and individual benefits.

While our primary goals of the mentorship program are attracting and retaining early-career professionals, we also view the program as an opportunity for our mentors. Mentoring is a rewarding way to meet and coach our early-career professionals. It lets you help shape the culture of our organization.

We envision a flexible and meaningful mentoring program. You would mentor one entry-level employee during his/her first year at Better Horizons. Your would spend three to four hours per month with your mentee. Ideally, you'd share an informal lunch or two with your mentee each month to talk about your areas of expertise and career development. Also, you'd involve your mentee in one of your projects so that s/he could get an up-close look at how you add value to challenging and complex problems.

I know mentoring can add to your busy schedule. We will help you succeed in this role and try to free up time by reducing some of your other responsibilities.

We will hold two information sessions about the mentoring program: June 15 from 9 to 10 a.m. and June 16 from 1 to 2 p.m. You can learn more about the nature of mentoring and available resources at these information sessions. You'll also have the opportunity to ask any questions. Please RSVP for one of these sessions to Lily Sanchez by June 12.

If you already know you'd like to serve as a mentor, please fill out this mentor volunteer form. Once you fill out the form, you'll work directly with Lily to pair you up with the right mentee.

> Includes calls to ACTION that are based on the principle of consistency.

Sincerely,

*Christine*

Christine Russo

---

tangible statements help the customer quickly identify with the worth of the benefits; for example, saving $680 on a car loan (more effective message) is a far clearer benefit than paying 1.5 to 1.75 percentage points less (as in the less effective message).

The more effective example also provides an influential appreciation statement (the less effective example provides no appreciation statement) that anticipates

**FIGURE 10.6**

Less Effective External Persuasive Message Based on Logical Appeals

| This message does not highlight key ideas. | **BETTER HORIZONS CREDIT UNION**<br>Est. 1937 | This message is not personalized or tangible. |

### 8 Reasons to Join Better Horizons Credit Union

Credit unions save members about $8 billion a year thanks to better interest rates and reduced fees. So, you can trust us to make your financial dreams come true. Pay attention to these facts or risk losing money to banks:

1. We are a member-based organization. That means our members can have a voice. They can serve on committees and even be elected to the Board of Directors.
2. We provide lower rates on car loans. We offer car loan rates at between 1.5 and 1.75 percentage points lower than any of the banks in town.
3. We provide lower rates on unsecured loans. We offer unsecured loans at a full 2 percentage points lower than any bank.
4. We provide mortgages more conveniently and at lower costs to our members. For example, a 30-year mortgage is as low as 5.31 percent compared to rates of 5.35 to 5.42 percent at competitor banks in town. The average closing costs are $1,900 compared to between $2,800 and $3,000 at competitor banks.
5. We provide higher interest on checking and savings accounts. Currently, we offer between .3 and .5 percentage points more interest than any bank in town.
6. We charge less in fees. For example, overdraft fees at Better Horizons are $19 compared to $35 to $50 at other local banks.
7. We provide a free retirement and financial planning advisor. Better Horizons has always employed a full-time financial planning advisor to help members with any of their financial planning questions.
8. Credit unions are safer than banks. In the recent economic downturn, banks were five times more likely to fail than credit unions. Better Horizons has always been in excellent financial condition, even during economic downturns.

Please think about how Better Horizons can help you in your banking. Please stop by anytime and meet with Ms. Norah Stevens or another membership specialist to learn more. Or, fill out the online membership application. We look forward to seeing you!

2737 Better Horizons Loop, Pescaloosa, FL 91214 • Phone: 803-784-7300 • Email: info@bhcu.org • Web: www.bhcu.org

the thoughts of skeptical consumers. In italics, it asks, *With all these benefits, why wouldn't everyone choose credit unions?* This validates the thinking of customers who might otherwise dismiss all these benefits as too good to be true. The paragraph explains why some people prefer banks and encourages customers to make direct comparisons themselves. Finally, the message concludes with a call to action—a cash reward to new members who join before September 1. Most effective sales messages provide incentives to motivate purchase of products or services.

**FIGURE 10.7**

More Effective External Persuasive Message Based on Logical Appeals

# BETTER HORIZONS CREDIT UNION
### Est. 1937

**When You Join Better Horizons Credit Union, You're Not a Customer—You're an Owner**

*Eight Reasons to Join Better Horizons Credit Union*   Gains ATTENTION.

*Did you know that average credit union members save $400 per year compared to bank customers?* The basic difference between credit unions and banks is that credit union members own and control their credit unions whereas bank account holders have no stake or control in their financial institutions. As a nonprofit, member-controlled financial institution, Better Horizons can provide you with higher rates on savings accounts, better terms on loans, and lower fees. Consider some of the following reasons to join Better Horizons and start saving today:

1.  **You come first.** You are not just a customer; you are an owner and member. That means you have a voice in how the credit union is run. You can serve on committees and even be elected to the Board of Directors.

2.  **You pay lower rates on car loans.** You can get car loan rates that are between 1.5 and 1.75 percentage points lower than at any of the banks in town. Consider the savings:
    - On a 4-year $15,000 new car loan: You save about $680.
    - On a 4-year $5,000 used car loan: You save about $200.

    Provides a NEED and SOLUTION.

3.  **You pay lower rates on unsecured loans.** You can get unsecured loans for unforeseen expenses at much lower rates at credit unions than banks. On average, unsecured loans are a full 2 percentage points lower than any bank. Consider the savings:
    - On a 3-year $15,000 unsecured loan: You save about $640.
    - On a 3-year $5,000 unsecured loan: You save about $215.

    Provides RATIONALE.

4.  **You can get mortgages more conveniently and at lower costs.**
    - You can get mortgages approved within one business day at Better Horizons.
    - On a 30-year mortgage, you can get a rate as low as 5.31 percent compared to rates of 5.35 to 5.42 percent at competitor banks in town. For a $200,000 mortgage, that amounts to a savings of between $1,800 and $4,900 over the course of the loan.
    - You can get closing costs that average $1,900 compared to between $2,800 and $3,000 at competitor banks.

5.  **You earn higher interest on your checking and savings accounts.** Currently, you earn between .3 and .5 percentage points more interest than at any bank in town. That can add up fast. For an account with an average of $5,000, that will bring you an extra $15 to $25 per year.

6.  **You pay less in fees.** If banking fees bother you, credit unions are the place for you. Overdraft fees, late payment fees on credit cards, and many other fees are lower at Better Horizons than at any local bank. For example, overdraft fees at Better Horizons are $19 compared to $35 to $50 at other local banks.

7.  **You will have a free retirement and financial planning advisor.** Better Horizons has always employed a full-time financial planning advisor who can help you with your financial planning questions.

8.  **Your savings are safest at credit unions.** In the recent economic downturn, banks were five times more likely to fail than credit unions. Better Horizons has always been in excellent financial condition, even during economic downturns.

    Shows VALIDATION of other perspectives.

*With all these benefits, why wouldn't everyone choose credit unions?* That's a good question. Some people prefer banks because they often have branches and ATMs throughout the country, which is convenient for travel. Also, some people say that banks offer more services. And, many people don't know much about credit unions at all. We encourage you to stop by Better Horizons and make direct comparisons with your current bank. You'll find that banking with Better Horizons saves you money, provides convenience when you travel, and offers services to meet nearly any banking need.

Please stop by anytime and meet with Ms. Norah Stevens or another membership specialist to learn more. Or, fill out the online membership application. New members who complete an application before September 1 will receive $50 cash in their new checking account.

Concludes with call to ACTION.

2737 Better Horizons Loop, Pescaloosa, FL 91214 • Phone: 803-784-7300 • Email: info@bhcu.org • Web: www.bhcu.org

**FIGURE 10.8**

Less Effective External Persuasive Message Based on Emotional Appeals

| To... | Anderson, Jamal; Anderson, Jennifer; Baker, William; Belk, Crystal; Belk, Jonathan; Belk, Ralph; Belk, Sally; Bi, Hu; Cardwell, Stephanie; Carter, Branson; Carter, Elizabeth; Casey, Stephen; Casey, Rick; Cedar, Brian; Cedar, Rebeka; |
|---|---|
| Subject: | Your Duty to the Women in Your Lives |

Arial   10   **B** *I* U

Dear Credit Union Member:

> This message is not personalized, shames the readers, and employs excessive negative language.

Please join Better Horizons in our fight against breast cancer, one of the deadliest cancers for women. You owe it to the women in your lives to make a difference. Think about the following facts:

- About 182,460 women will develop breast cancer this year in our country.
- Breast cancer ranks second among cancer deaths in women.

Breast cancer affects all of us deeply–a mother, a wife, a daughter, a friend. If you really care, you'll join us in this fight.

All proceeds of the Hope Walkathon are for the Betty Williams Breast Center and are used for community education, research, and support for low-income patients and families. The Betty Williams Breast Center has a nationally accredited program for treatment of breast cancer. It helps do research in a national network of breast centers that are at the forefront of research for improving treatments. The breast center is active in educating our community about detecting breast cancer early. It spreads the word about breast self-exams and mammograms. The Betty Williams Breast Center began with an initial donation by Betty Williams, a breast cancer survivor and longtime Best Horizons member. Betty would certainly want to see you out there trying to help the victims of this horrible disease.

Registration is just $50 per person. If you are not able to participate in the walkathon, you are still welcome to register and make your donation to the Betty Williams Breast Center. Each Better Horizons participating member will receive a Hope Walkathon T-shirt, a Better Horizons water bottle, and a copy of *Lifestyle Choices to Help Avoid Cancer*. Best of all, you are part of the Better Horizons effort to stop breast cancer.

To join the Better Horizons Credit Union team, complete an online application or send your application by mail. Just complete the application by September 21 to secure your spot and Better Horizons T-shirt. Your T-shirt will be mailed to you so that you can wear it for the walkathon and represent Better Horizons with pride! The walkathon will be held on Saturday, October 6 at 9:00 a.m. at Central Park. Do your part to improve the lives of women in our community!

Now notice the differences between the less effective and more effective external persuasive messages in Figures 10.8 and 10.9, both of which use emotional appeals to rally people to sign up for the Hope Walkathon. In the less effective example (Figure 10.8), Haniz includes several statements that readers could perceive as guilt trips. It uses a series of extremely negative terms within the first few sentences (i.e., *deadliest, cancer deaths*) without providing hopeful words, an approach that could lead readers to think participating in the walkathon would make little difference. Furthermore, the message is not personalized. Rather than focusing on the local and credit union communities, it exclusively examines the problem in a national context.

In the more effective example (Figure 10.9), the message is far more personalized, upbeat, positive, and pressure-free. Instead of citing national statistics, it provides statistics about the local community and the credit union. It places more emphasis on Betty Williams, who is tied to the community and credit union. It describes the fun and excitement the reader will feel being part of a team. It does not avoid some of the negative terms (i.e., *deadliest, diagnosed*) associated with breast cancer; however, it uses far more positive and constructive words and phrases (i.e., *hope, prevention, treatment, survival, you can make a difference, 95 percent*) to create an overall hopeful and inspiring message. While both messages contain a call to action, the call to action in the more effective example includes a direct link to sign up online. The more effective example provides other links as well so readers can learn more about the walkathon and the Betty Williams Breast Center.

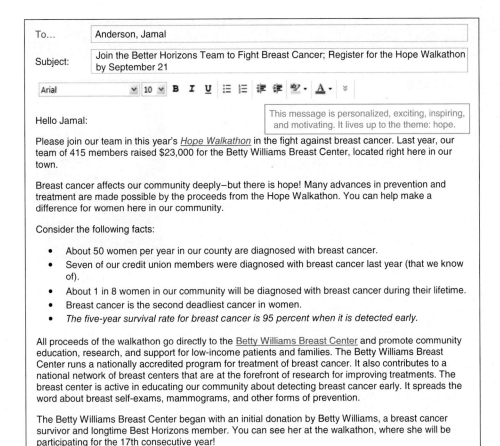

**FIGURE 10.9**

More Effective External
Persuasive Message
Based on Emotional
Appeal

Advances in technology offer businesspeople many innovative options for delivering persuasive messages. The Technology Tips box focuses on the use of video messages for internal messages, but video can also be a powerful tool for delivering external messages, persuasive and otherwise.

## Composing Mass Sales Messages

Even if you are not in a marketing position, you may participate in developing **mass sales messages**—messages sent to a large group of consumers and intended to market a particular product or service. Often in the form of mass emails, online ads, or sales letters, these messages generally have low success rates (ratio of number of purchases to number of message recipients). For example, a company sending out 7,000 sales letters may achieve only a 2 percent success rate (140 sales directly attributable to the mailings)—enough to make the effort profitable. Since mass emails and online ads are much less expensive than hard-copy sales letters (costs generally involve purchasing

**LO10.6** Construct effective mass sales messages.

## ⏻ TECHNOLOGY TIPS

### VIDEO SHARING IN THE WORKPLACE

Video sharing sites such as YouTube allow anyone to create and share video clips. The widespread popularity of YouTube reflects a deep desire by most people to be seen and heard. It also demonstrates the power that visual imagery can play in developing messages. Most companies have used YouTube, other social networking websites, and their own websites to distribute video marketing messages for many years. They have also realized the power of online videos for training and internal announcements.

© Tom Grill/Corbis RF

Recently, however, companies have started giving employees the option of developing video podcasts. One of the first known such efforts was that of Microsoft, which in 2007 launched Academy Mobile, a YouTube-like website just for Microsoft employees and only for internal use. Employees can exercise their creativity to develop videos that increase camaraderie and share organizational knowledge. They can also gain strong name recognition within their companies.

Developing videos and podcasts in the workplace offers opportunities to persuade others and demonstrate thought leadership. When given the chance to share videos and podcasts in the workplace, keep these tips in mind:

*Focus on the message.* Plan your video message the same way as any other message: Analyze the needs of your colleagues (audience analysis), gather and analyze the most relevant information (idea development), and piece together the video message in a compelling and influential manner (message structuring).

*Learn the software.* Developing well-produced, professional videos takes more than a camera. Learn about video-editing software (such as Camtasia). Also, watch video podcasts created by popular colleagues (those colleagues who have a lot of followers).

*Use the tools strategically.* Develop video messages that benefit your company and your career. While entertainment value is important, your primary goal should be to educate your colleagues about a shared workplace challenge. Remember the online reputation that you seek. What skills and knowledge do you want to be known for? What personal traits do you hope to accentuate? How can you present yourself as a thought leader?

---

### Structure of Mass Sales Messages

- Gain attention.
- Generate interest.
- Build desire.
- Call to action.

consumer email lists and online ads but no paper or postage), expected success rates may be much lower.

A secondary benefit of mass sales messages is that even when consumers do not respond with immediate purchases, these messages can raise a company's brand awareness. Consumers may keep the company in mind when making a purchase one, two, or more years in the future. On the other hand, many consumers resent mass sales messages. Excessive sales letters and spam emails may lower brand value in some cases.

While most of the principles from this chapter apply to sales messages, the structure of mass sales messages is adjusted to increase the success rate. Even modest improvements in the success rate—for example, from 2 percent to 3 percent—can make tens of thousands of dollars' difference in revenue. The model used most successfully for mass sales messages is the AIDA approach: *a*ttention, *i*nterest, *d*esire, and *a*ction. This approach begins and ends like other persuasive messages; it must first gain *attention* and it should end with a specific call to *action*.

Typically, the attention-getter needs to be livelier and even more provocative than with internal persuasive messages. After gaining attention, the next step is to build interest and curiosity. Then, the sales message should focus on building *desire*. That is, you want potential customers thinking, "I want this product or service." You conclude with a specific call to action that the potential customer can take to begin the purchase process.

Most effective sales messages contain a **central sales theme**. Like other messages, sales messages are strongest when they contain a coherent, unified theme that consumers can recognize quickly. However, whereas your colleagues and clients who know you will grant you a window of 30 seconds or so to provide your main point, recipients of mass sales messages may give you only a few seconds. Thus, your sales message should stick to a single, recognizable theme that resonates within seconds.

One of the most common sales themes is price. Sales messages that focus on price tend to emphasize it immediately, generally in the attention-getter. Sales messages that emphasize other attributes typically de-emphasize price by making a brief mention of it near the end of the message. Some sales messages omit any references to price. This is a risky strategy for mass sales messages since most consumers expect at least some information about price right away.

In Figures 10.10 and 10.11, you can see two mass sales messages that Haniz and her colleagues created to promote the credit union's auto loans. In the first message (Figure 10.10), the central selling theme is price: Better Horizons Credit Union's auto loans cost less than dealer financing. So, the attention-getter focuses on this theme in the subject line and opening paragraph. The first paragraph arouses interest

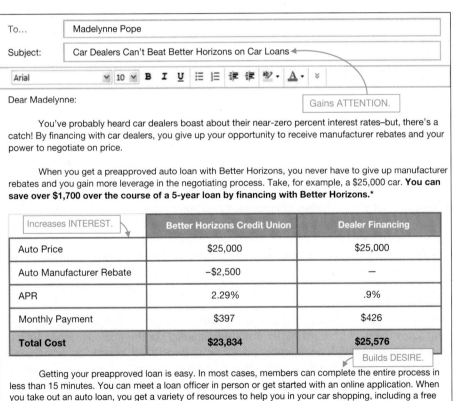

**FIGURE 10.10**

A Mass Sales Message with a Strong Logical Appeal

**FIGURE 10.11**

## A Mass Sales Message with a Strong Emotional Appeal

Photo: © Eric Audras/Getty Images RF

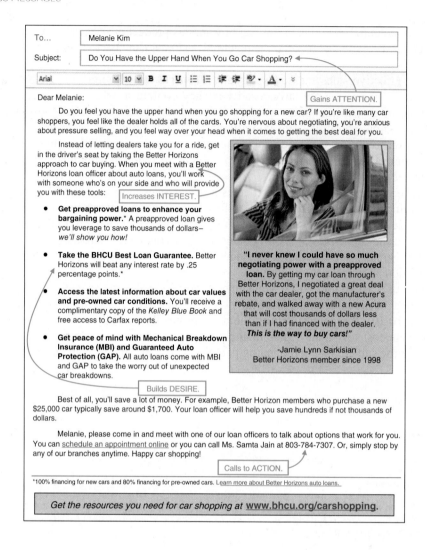

by pointing out the perhaps underappreciated fact that accepting low-rate dealer financing generally involves sacrificing rebates and negotiating power. The prominent and well-designed table likewise increases interest with its easy-to-process comparison between getting an auto loan versus dealer financing. The final paragraphs build desire by showing the ease and perks of getting an auto loan and providing information about how to apply right away. This sales message primarily makes a logical appeal.

In the next sales message (Figure 10.11), Haniz and her colleagues highlight a different sales theme with a primarily emotional appeal. In this message, they focus on going car shopping with confidence and strength, directly addressing an anxiety many car shoppers have of getting taken advantage of when making a car purchase. The emotional appeal involves several influence strategies, including social proof (with the testimonial of a satisfied member who has saved money by taking out an auto loan) and reciprocation (with the warm offer to get help from a loan officer and an invitation to "work as a team" against the car dealers). You typically have much more freedom of creative expression in mass sales messages than you do with other types of persuasive messages. Haniz uses this creative license with metaphorical language tied to playing cards ("upper hand," "dealer holds the cards") and driving ("take you for a ride," "get in the driver's seat").

**FIGURE 10.12**

Less Effective Mass Email

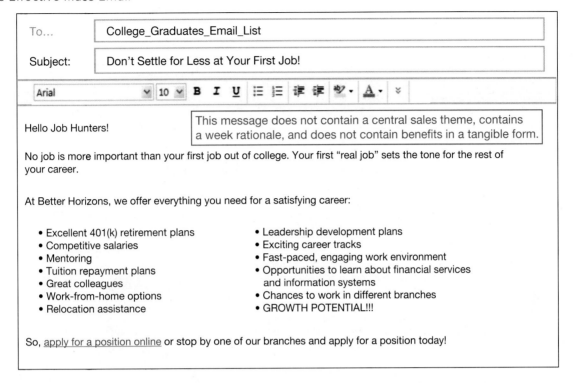

The examples you've observed so far focus on consumers. You can also apply the AIDA approach to other types of mass promotions. For example, Better Horizons seeks to attract the best college graduates to apply for open positions. It has access to an email list of current college students who have attended job fairs nearby. In Figures 10.12 and 10.13, you can see a less effective example and a more effective example of Haniz encouraging college students to apply for open positions. In the less effective example, you'll notice that Haniz tries a strategy of stating all the benefits of working at Better Horizons. This generic strategy fails because it ends up emphasizing nothing. In other words, it lacks a central sales theme. This message also fails to explain benefits in tangible terms. In the more effective example, Haniz focuses on a central sales theme (employer programs that create career advantages for early-career professionals). She focuses on just three programs, allowing her to provide specific and concrete statements of benefits to potential employees. Also, by formatting with italics, bold fonts, and other features, she ensures potential employees get the gist of the message rapidly.

## Reviewing Persuasive Messages

Always carefully review your persuasive messages, especially since nearly all of them are high-stakes communications. They can potentially provide you with more professional opportunities and enhanced credibility, or they can close off future opportunities and diminish your credibility. Likewise, because you are a representative of your organization, your persuasive messages may raise or decrease customer loyalty, revenues, and brand value.

**LO10.7** Evaluate persuasive messages for effectiveness and fairness.

**FIGURE 10.13**

More Effective Mass Email

| To... | Emily Smith |
|---|---|
| Subject: | Get Your Career on the Right Track at Better Horizons Credit Union |

| Arial | 10 | **B** *I* <u>U</u> |

> Gains ATTENTION with a central sales theme: employer programs that help early-career professionals the most.

Dear Emily:

No job is more important than your first job out of college. Your first "real job" sets the tone for the rest of your career.

> Builds INTEREST with evidence-based conclusions.

Finding an employer that invests in you will make a dramatic impact on your career opportunities. Check out how much difference various employer programs make for early-career professionals:

- *Employees who received early-career mentoring earn between $5,500 and $22,500 more per year* compared to employees who did not receive mentoring. Read more...

- *Employees who partcipate in leadership development programs are twice as likely to gain managerial or supervisory positions within their first two years after college.* Read more...

- *Employees with employer-based student loan repayment plans purchase homes three years sooner* than employees without these repayment plans. Read more...

At Better Horizons, we're committed to your career success. That's why all new employees have access to mentoring programs, leadership development programs, and student loan payback plans:

- **Better Horizons Mentoring Program**. All new employees are assigned a seasoned mentor who has worked in financial services or information services. Mentors generally take mentees out for lunch once or twice per month, spend several hours coaching mentees each month, involve mentees in important projects, and share ideas about career development.

- **Better Horizons Leadership Development Program**. All employees are eligible to participate in our various leadership programs catered to specialties in mortgages, investment services, and information technology.

> Increases DESIRE with a list of tangible benefits at Better Horizons.

- **Better Horizons Student Loan Repayment Program**. Once employees have been with us for six months, we reimburse them for student loans up to $300 per month.

So, please check out our open positions for tellers, financial specialists, IT specialists, loan officers, and more. Also, my team and I would enjoy meeting you in person at the upcoming PCC Job Fair.

> Calls to ACTION with a link to open positions and an invitation to a job fair.

Best wishes,

*Haniz*

Haniz Zogby

> The entire message sticks to a tight, unified CENTRAL SALES THEME.

Photo: © laflor/Getty Images RF

### Get Feedback and Reread

Persuasive messages are directed to others who *resist* your ideas, products, or services. Read your message carefully. Imagine yourself in your audience members' position and consider how they would respond. Make sure you ask trusted colleagues to read your messages. Ask them how they would respond and how they think you can better construct the message to get your intended results. You may be best served to seek out trusted colleagues who may be resistant in the same way as your audience. These colleagues may provide the most insight to you about crafting your message carefully.

### Apply the FAIR Test

Persuasive messages can be intentionally designed to manipulate colleagues and customers. In a business communications context, **manipulation** involves attempting to influence others by some level of deception so you can achieve your own interests. You may face many strong temptations to manipulate others through persuasive messages—to elevate your career, get a commission on that extra sale, get that bonus for exceptional performance, or pad your ego for being right.

By applying the FAIR test, you can avoid sending persuasive messages that manipulate others. This is especially the case for sales messages because any misrepresentation of your product or service is unethical. Use Figure 10.14 as a guide as you discuss with your colleagues whether your persuasive messages are fair. And by considering the experience of a business professional (see the Communication Q&A), you can learn to be more thoughtful and skillful when crafting persuasive messages.

**FIGURE 10.14**

## Are Your Persuasive Messages FAIR?

**Facts** (How *factual* is your persuasive message?)

- Have you presented *all* the facts correctly?
- Have you presented information that allows colleagues, customers, and consumers to make informed decisions that are in their best interests?
- Have you carefully considered various interpretations of your data? Have you assessed the quality of your information?

**Access** (How *accessible* or *transparent* are your motives, reasoning, and information?)

- Are your motives clear or will others perceive that you have a hidden agenda? Have you made yourself accessible to others so that they can learn more about your viewpoints?
- Have you fully disclosed information that colleagues, customers, or consumers should expect to receive?
- Are you hiding any information that casts your recommendations in a better light? Are you hiding real reasons for making certain claims or recommendations?
- Have you given stakeholders the opportunity to provide input in the decision-making process?

**Impacts** (How does your communication *impact* stakeholders?)

- Have you carefully considered how your ideas, products, and services will impact colleagues, customers, and consumers?
- Have you made recommendations to colleagues, customers, and consumers that are in their best interests?

**Respect** (How *respectful* is your communication?)

- If you were the customer or the colleague, would you feel that the tone of the message was appropriate?
- Does the message offend or pressure? Does it show that your colleagues' and customers' needs are important?
- Would a neutral observer consider your communication respectful?

# COMMUNICATION Q&A

**Peter Cardon: Can you describe when you had to persuade a candidate about a job opportunity s/he was hesitant to pursue? How did you approach persuading the candidate to consider the role?**

**Lea Adams:** I recently spoke with a candidate who was relatively happy in his current role and wasn't particularly energized to relocate his family for another career opportunity. After reassuring him that I understood his position, I asked him what types of roles he was interested in so we could stay in touch. After a few minutes of chatting, I asked a more direct question, "Has your current company outlined a development or succession plan for you?" He thought about it and somewhat embarrassingly answered, "Well, no and that sort of bothers me." That simple question broke ground in our conversation, and I was able to discuss how my client has a strong track record of developing internal talent pipelines and aggressively promoting from within. After spending time getting to know the candidate, I understood that he was looking for upward mobility and that he didn't immediately see it in the opportunity I was presenting. After a brief dialogue, I was able to better piece together a bigger picture that was appealing to his long-term goals. His tone shifted and he was eager to explore the opportunity, despite a potential relocation.

**PC: When you work with clients, in what ways do you try to influence them? How do you prepare to make effective pitches and proposals?**

**LA:** When presenting a slate of candidates to a client, my primary objective is to entice them enough to invite the candidates for an in-person interview. In preparing for pitches, it's important to succinctly hit the highlights. Crafting a brief but poignant message often is more time intensive than a "data dump," so I'm disciplined about preparation. Additionally, I make a point to address the pros and the cons of a candidate. Addressing concerns demonstrates an ability to partner, which instills trust. Last, I make a recommendation for the next steps but deliberately make a point to ensure the client concurs. This tactic establishes credibility as an advisor and reassures clients you are acting in their best interests.

**PC: In your experience, what are some of the most common mistakes professionals make when trying to persuade colleagues and clients?**

**LA:** Talking too much is the biggest mistake professionals make when they try to persuade colleagues and clients. Colleagues and clients want to feel heard, but more important, they want to be understood. If you listen with the intent of understanding your clients and colleagues, it's amazing the profound impact you can have by saying very little.

**PC: What concluding advice would you give about persuading others in the workplace?**

**LA:** In my line of work, the best candidates are the ones who are gainfully employed and making great strides in their respective organizations. It's my job to persuade them to lift their head and consider an opportunity outside of their company. When approaching candidates, I make a point to acknowledge that they are busy. Once I have candidates on the phone, I pay close attention to their pace and cadence and then mimic their style, of course without being disingenuous. This combination makes people feel respected and understood and therefore they are more willing to sacrifice a highly valuable resource—time. Oftentimes in closing, I'll say something to the effect of, "Thanks for your time . . . I'll let you get back to what you're paid to do." Humor goes a long way and people tend to find it disarming and pleasantly memorable. However, know your audience, as misplaced humor can come across as cheesy, or worse, offensive.

**Lea Adams** *Lea Adams is an executive recruiter at Spencer Stuart, a global executive search and leadership advisory firm. She is a member of the firm's consumer practice and works with colleagues to execute C-Suite search assignments primarily for private-equity backed consumer services and packaged goods companies. She previously held a variety of roles at a boutique executive recruiting firm.*

Courtesy of Lea Adams. Photo by John Shyrock.

# Chapter Takeaway for *Persuasive Messages*

**LO10.1 Describe the relationship between credibility and persuasion. (p. 299)**

Delivering effective persuasive messages improves your **reputation for personal credibility.**

| It shows **competence** when you know everything about your product, service, or idea. | It shows **caring** when you explain how your product, service, or idea benefits others. | It shows **character** when you provide completely reliable and honest information. |
|---|---|---|

**LO10.2 Explain the AIM planning process for persuasive messages and the basic components of most persuasive messages. (pp. 299–304)**

**Audience Analysis:** Identify the needs of your audience and learn how it is influenced.

**Information Gathering:** Gather extensive information about products, services, and ideas that you are writing about.

**Message Development:** Gain attention, tie needs to benefits, provide rationale, show appreciation, and call your audience to action.

| Components of Persuasive Messages | | |
|---|---|---|
| • Gain attention.<br>• Raise a need.<br>• Deliver a solution. | • Provide a rationale.<br>• Validate the views, preferences, and concerns of others.<br>• Give counterpoints (optional). | • Call to action. |

| Types of Attention-Getters | | |
|---|---|---|
| • Rhetorical question<br>• Intriguing statistic | • Compelling and unusual facts<br>• Challenge | • Testimonial |

See *examples of attention-getters* in Table 10.1.

**LO10.3 Explain how the tone and style of persuasive messages impact their influence. (pp. 304–310)**

| Guidelines for Tone and Style for Persuasive Messages |
|---|
| • Apply the personal touch.<br>• Use action-oriented, lively language.<br>• Write with confidence.<br>• Offer choice.<br>• Show positivity. |

See *examples of tone and style choices* in Tables 10.2 through 10.8.

**LO10.4 Create compelling internal persuasive messages. (pp. 311–314)**

| Components of Internal Persuasive Messages | |
|---|---|
| • Gain attention: overview of a business problem.<br>• Raise a need: description of a business problem.<br>• Deliver a solution: description of *how* your idea or policy addresses the business problem.<br>• Provide a rationale: elaboration about *why* your idea or policy is the best option.<br>• Validate: appreciation for decision makers' perspectives and resistance to your ideas. | • Give counterpoints (optional): explanation of why your ideas are better than competing ideas (typically those of decision makers who comprise your target audience).<br>• Call to action: recommendations for a course of action or further discussion about an idea or policy. |

See *examples of internal persuasive messages* in Figures 10.2 through 10.5.

**LO10.5 Compose influential external persuasive messages. (pp. 314–319)**

| Components of External Persuasive Messages | |
|---|---|
| • Gain attention: catchy statement.<br>• Raise a need: description of unmet *needs* or *wants* of your customers.<br>• Deliver a solution: description of *how* your product or service benefits customers.<br>• Provide a rationale: elaboration about *why* your product or service will benefit the customer. | • Validate: recognition of customers' resistance to your product or service.<br>• Give counterpoints (optional): explanation of why your product/service is better than competing products/services (typically those favored by the target audience).<br>• Call to action: description of a specific step for the customer to take toward purchase of a product or service. |

See *examples of external persuasive messages* in Figures 10.6 through 10.9.

**LO10.6 Construct effective mass sales messages. (pp. 319–323)**

| Structure of Mass Sales Messages | | | |
|---|---|---|---|
| • Gain attention. | • Generate interest. | • Build desire. | • Call to action. |

See *examples of mass sales messages* in Figures 10.10 through 10.13.

**LO10.7 Evaluate persuasive messages for effectiveness and fairness. (pp. 323–326)**

**Feedback:** Have trusted colleagues check for accuracy, honesty, and influence.

**FAIR Test:** Make sure your claims are factual and nondeceptive.

**Proofreading:** Carefully reread the message several times. Envision the response of the audience.

# Key Terms

authority, 301

central sales theme, 321

consistency, 301

direct, 302

explicit, 302

implicit, 303

indirect, 303

liking, 301

manipulation, 325

mass sales messages, 319

reciprocation, 300

scarcity, 301

social proof, 301

tangible, 306

validation, 303

# Discussion Exercises

**10.1 Chapter Review Questions** (LO10.1, LO10.2, LO10.3)

A. Describe how credibility forms a basis for persuasion.

B. Explain how the tone and style of persuasive messages impact their persuasiveness. Specifically, address how personal touch, action-oriented language, confidence, choice, and positivity affect how message recipients respond.

C. Explain the AIM planning process for persuasive messages and the basic components of most persuasive messages.

**10.2 Applying Key Terms** (LO10.1, LO10.2, LO10.3)

Explain each key term above and provide a concrete example of how it impacts persuasive messages.

**10.3 Communication Q&A Discussion Questions** (LO10.1, LO10.2, LO10.3)

Read Lea Adams's comments in the Communication Q&A section. Respond to the following questions:

A. What does Adams say about finding out the needs of others in the persuasion process? How does she go about listening to her clients? How much effort does this process take?

B. She says preparing a short pitch often takes more time than a longer pitch. Why do you think this is the case? What does this mean for some projects you're working on right now?

C. What does she say about establishing credibility with clients? Elaborate on points she makes across several responses.

D. What is the most interesting piece of advice she gives about persuasion? Explain.

**10.4 Should You Use Persuasion Sparingly?** (LO10.1, LO10.3)

Some people suggest that all business communication is a form of persuasion—that is, you are attempting to motivate others to think and/or do as you suggest. Others suggest that you should use persuasion only in rare circumstances. For example, in the recent Dale Carnegie Training book called *The 5 Essential People Skills*, the authors write the following:

> It has been said that persuasion is like a savings account: The less you use it, the more you've got. Learn how to use your powers of persuasion well and at the appropriate moments. With time and practice, you'll be able to have positive influence on people's decisions in any number of areas.[34]

Write three or four paragraphs describing your perspectives on how often and when you should use persuasion in the workplace.

**10.5 Character and Persuasion** (LO10.1, LO10.7)

As Aristotle famously stated, "Character may almost be called the most effective means of persuasion." Do you think this is true in today's business world? Explain your viewpoints with three or four supporting points and examples.

# Evaluation Exercises

**10.6 Analyzing a Sales Message** (LO10.6)

Find an interesting sales message that you have received recently in the mail or through email. If you can't find one readily, go to the website of a company that sells products or services that interest you. Find a sales message of sufficient length to analyze. Analyze it in the following ways:

A. Which psychological tools of influence (consistency, reciprocation, social proof, authority, liking, scarcity) does it use? Provide examples.

B. What emotional appeals are used? What about logical appeals? Would you consider this sales message to be catering more to emotion or logic? Explain.

C. Do you consider this sales message warm and inviting?

D. Do you consider this sales message plausible?

E. Do you consider this sales message respectful?

F. Do you trust the sales message?

G. What are two changes you think could be made to improve its effectiveness?

**10.7 Analyzing the Better Horizons Promotional Message** (LO10.5)

Analyze the Better Horizons flyer (Figure 10.7) in the following ways:

A. Which psychological tools of influence (consistency, reciprocation, social proof, authority, liking, scarcity) does it use? Provide examples.

B. What emotional appeals are used? What about logical appeals? Would you consider this message as catering more to emotion or logic? Explain.

C. Do you consider this message warm and inviting?

D. Do you consider this sales message plausible?

E. Do you consider this sales message respectful?

F. Do you trust this message?

G. What are two changes you think could be made to improve its effectiveness?

**10.8 Persuasion Self-Assessment** (LO10.1, LO10.2, LO10.3, LO10.7)

Evaluate yourself with regard to each of the persuasive practices listed in the table below. Circle the appropriate number for each.

| | 1 – Rarely/Never | 2 – Sometimes | 3 – Usually | 4 – Always |
|---|---|---|---|---|
| I can persuade others to see merit in my ideas even when they initially disagree. | 1 | 2 | 3 | 4 |
| Before trying to persuade others, I think about what their needs are. | 1 | 2 | 3 | 4 |
| Before trying to persuade others, I think about the best ways to influence them. | 1 | 2 | 3 | 4 |
| I feel comfortable expressing my viewpoints even when I know others disagree. | 1 | 2 | 3 | 4 |
| I can persuade others without offending them. | 1 | 2 | 3 | 4 |
| Even when others disagree with me, I offer my perspective without putting down their opinions. | 1 | 2 | 3 | 4 |
| I can write strong persuasive messages. | 1 | 2 | 3 | 4 |
| When I persuade others, I try to open up avenues for future discussion. | 1 | 2 | 3 | 4 |
| I realize that most people are not persuaded immediately. I communicate with others realizing that the process will likely involve many steps. | 1 | 2 | 3 | 4 |
| I show respect for others with whom I disagree. | 1 | 2 | 3 | 4 |

Total your score and consider the following advice:

35–40: You are an *effective persuader*. You likely influence others as intended in most cases. Continue honing your persuasive skills and ensure that you always act with the interests of others in mind.

30–34: You are a *conscientious persuader*. You are aware of the needs of others, you are confident of presenting your perspectives, and you feel that you can show respect to others who think differently. Continue working on developing your persuasive abilities.

25–29: You are an *average persuader*. You are persuasive in many cases, but you will be far more effective if you consistently apply principles of effective persuasion. Identify those areas where you most need to improve and you will see rapid improvement.

Under 25: You are a *less effective persuader*. Think carefully about the areas in which you can most improve. You can dramatically change your influence on others by mastering just a few principles of persuasion.

Based on the self-assessment, identify three areas in which to improve your approach to persuasion. Write three goals and elaborate on each with a supporting paragraph.

# Application Exercises

**Case for Problems 10.9 through 10.11:** Promoting New Services at Better Horizons Credit Union

Christine Russo works at Better Horizons and is developing several new services the credit union could offer. One idea is for credit union members to take a five-day cruise to the Bahamas. Two afternoons of the cruise will be devoted to financial planning workshops, including choices such as retirement planning, trusts and estates, insurance, charitable giving, taxes, and college savings. Also, a finance boot camp for teenagers will provide basic information about savings and checking accounts, loans, and budgeting.

In another initiative, Christine wants to set up a new rewards program for credit union members who use their Better Horizons debit or credit cards. Each purchase with the debit or credit card will contribute to their total reward points, which customers can redeem for brand-name merchandise, hotel accommodations, airline tickets, cruises, and other travel options (detailed in an online and paper merchandise and travel catalog). Members get one point for each dollar spent on their credit cards and one point for every two dollars spent on their debit cards. One advantage of the program is that points can be combined across accounts. So, family members or friends who are members of the credit union can transfer their points to one another's accounts and more quickly gain rewards. The program involves no fee, and members with the cards are automatically enrolled in the program.

### 10.9 Selling an Idea to the Better Horizons Board (LO10.4)

Assume the role of Christine and write a letter to the board describing your ideas for the financial planning cruise and the new rewards program.

### 10.10 Promoting the Financial Planning Cruise to Better Horizons Credit Union Members (LO10.5)

Write a sales message to Better Horizons members to promote the financial planning cruise. Feel free to add additional details (i.e., price and dates for the cruise).

### 10.11 Writing a Sales Letter for the New Better Horizons Special Rewards Card (LO10.5, LO10.6)

Write a sales message to Better Horizons members to promote the new rewards programs. Feel free to add additional details (i.e., types of rewards).

### 10.12 Creating a Message to Promote Joining a Student Club (LO10.4, LO10.5, LO10.6)

A. Select a student club of interest to you. You may already be a member or you may know little about the club. In any case, write a message to encourage other students to join. Describe benefits that membership brings and specific steps for joining the club or learning more about it.

B. In a separate message, describe the students you are targeting; reasons for resistance among these students, how your message appeals to this group, and the mix of communication channels you'll use to distribute the message. Address the message to the president of the club.

### 10.13 Writing a Sales Letter for Your Computer Store (LO10.6)

Assume you own a computer retail store located near your campus (give the store any name you want). You have sold fewer PCs in recent years due to the strong demand for Macs among university students. You will write a sales letter to reach all student housing units. Your goal is to encourage students to purchase PCs at your store. You can do online research to help you contrast PCs with Macs and identify pricing levels. In the sales letter, attempt to show students the advantages of PCs compared to Macs and get them to take specific steps to learn more about or even purchase a PC at your store.

### 10.14 Writing a Sales Letter for a Credit Union That Targets University Students (LO10.6)

Write a sales letter that targets university students and promotes joining a local credit union. In addition to using materials from this chapter, go online and find comparisons of benefits between credit unions and banks. It's easy to find plenty of information in just 20 to 30 minutes.

### 10.15 Writing a Sales Letter for a Bank That Targets University Students (LO10.6)

Write a sales letter that targets university students and promotes joining a local bank. Find information online about local credit unions and banks, select the financial institution that interests you the most, and then promote it with an effective sales letter.

### 10.16 Persuading University Students to Start a Retirement Account (LO10.5, LO10.6)

Write a message that targets university students and persuades them to start a retirement account. You'll find lots of information online about the benefits of starting a retirement account early. Spend a few hours learning about options before writing your letter.

### 10.17 Developing a Promotional Message at the EdFirst Foundation (LO10.5, LO10.6)

Angela Nguyen, director of donor relations, sighed. She glanced at the statistics for the last quarter. Donations to the EdFirst were down 6 percent. Even worse, donations were down nearly 23 percent from two years ago. The foundation received about 5 percent of its revenue from program participants, about 35 percent from federal and state grants, and roughly 60 percent from individual donations. The foundation would need to drop critical services if donations didn't pick up soon.

The EdFirst Foundation provided mentoring, after-school programs, and other resources for K–12 children from low-income families in inner cities. Any child in any of the ten cities EdFirst operated in qualified for the program. Children from families that fell below the federal poverty line received all services for free. Children from families above the poverty line received the services at highly discounted rates of between $25 and $75 per year. Approximately 92 percent of children participating in EdFirst programs came from families that fell under the federal poverty line.

The foundation employed some full-time center directors and part-time staff members. However, most of the work was done by volunteers. For example, all mentors were volunteers. The average mentor had served for nearly 7 years and volunteered an average of 2.3 hours per week to help struggling students. Volunteers also helped with after-school programs held in EdFirst facilities, developed educational materials, and recruited children to join the programs.

Recently, Angela commissioned several third parties to evaluate the performance of the foundation. In the first evaluation, an independent evaluator identified the following impacts for children participating in EdFirst programs:

- Reading levels improved by 1.4 grade levels after 6 months of active participation.
- Reading levels improved by 2.3 grade levels after 12 months of active participation.
- Math scores improved by 1.9 grade levels after 6 months of active participation.
- Math scores improved by 2.6 grade levels after 12 months of active participation.
- High school graduation rates in areas served by EdFirst stood at 43 percent. In these same areas, the high school graduation rate for individuals who had participated for at least one year between the ages of 12 and 18 years old was 72 percent. The high school graduation rate for individuals who had participated for at least three years between the ages of 12 and 18 years old was 96 percent.

In the second evaluation, a separate independent accreditor found the following about the foundation:

- 92 percent of all donations were used directly for the educational programs. In other comparable non-profit organizations, an average of 78 percent of all donations were used directly for educational programs.

- 89 percent of EdFirst volunteers had undergraduate degrees, and 38 percent had graduate degrees.
- 97 percent of parents of EdFirst program participants were "extremely satisfied" with EdFirst services.

While EdFirst aimed to keep expenses as low as possible, it incurred significant costs to rent and own various education centers, supply textbooks and other curricular materials, provide transportation to and from its centers for program participants and volunteers, and run various after-school activities.

Angela was extremely frustrated. With all the good news about the positive impacts on inner-city kids and operational efficiency, she realized the foundation would have to cut back services for some kids or even close some centers if donations didn't pick up. Based on her calculations, the average cost to support a child in the program for an entire year was just $236.

She decided that she would send a message to prior donors who had not donated in over a year. She would ask these prior donors to enroll in the "EdFirst Support a Kid" program. Enrolling in this program involved a $20 monthly donation.

**Your Task:** Assume you are in charge of sending a message to past donors. Write a message to past donors asking them to join the "EdFirst Support a Kid" program.

### 10.18 A Message Do-Over for a Persuasive Message to a Colleague (LO10.4)

Samantha Parkinson works as a marketing intern for a start-up software company. She is working on an account for a new social networking platform for professionals. The platform, called *LinkedB2B*, allows professionals to connect in many ways similar to LinkedIn. However, it also sets up in-person networking events in several major cities and focuses on geographic proximity to connect professionals. The platform also emphasizes business-to-business (B2B) relationships rather than recruiting and consulting.

Currently, LinkedB2B charges a rate of $19 per month to all professionals on the network. It charges businesses $149 to have up to ten users on the network. So far, the network has nearly 9,000 members, most of which are in three major cities: Houston, Dallas, and Los Angeles. Typically, LinkedB2B hosts networking events three times per year in these cities. To attend the events, attendees must be LinkedB2B members. Generally, admission prices for the networking events are around $30.

Samantha believes the network should offer free accounts, like LinkedIn, so that LinkedB2B can grow its membership base. She thinks that members should pay for only premium services. Samantha decided to share her conclusions with her boss, Bianca Genova. Bianca originally created LinkedB2B and considers it her greatest professional achievement. Samantha sent the following message:

*SUBJECT: Changing our Pricing Model*

*Hey Bianca,*

*Unfortunately, our current pricing model simply doesn't bring in enough members for us to be lucrative. 9,000 members really is next to nothing in our business. To survive, we will need to get far more paying members. Ironically, we can get more paying members only by offering our membership for free. LinkedIn is the model we must follow in order to do this. It makes so much money because it*

*gets professionals hooked to free memberships, then professionals see the added value of premium services and can't resist paying. If we changed to a free model up front, we could get hundreds of thousands or even millions of members. I estimate that within one year, we could get at least 500,000 members if we opened up LinkedB2B for free. If we could get just 10 percent of these members to purchase premium services, we would have roughly 50,000 paying members, which is a fivefold increase over where we are now. The way to make this happen involves focusing on the following cities: Houston, Dallas, Los Angeles, San Francisco, Portland, and Seattle. We will offer free memberships to all professionals. At the free membership level, professionals can display their profiles. Our pricing for premium services would remain the same at the individual and organization levels. At the premium level, members would be able to do the following: attend networking events at discounted rates (generally 30 to 50 percent less), send ten free messages per month to non-contacts, use the blogging platform, and organize groups. I know you want this platform to succeed, so let's plan on meeting this Friday and I can give a more specific plan for making this happen.*

*Samantha*

Complete the following tasks:

A. Evaluate the effectiveness of Samantha's message.
B. Rewrite the message to improve it. Feel free to reasonably embellish the message as directed by your instructor.

### 10.19 A Message Do-Over for a Sales Message (LO10.6)

Bianca Genova is the VP of sales for a social networking platform called LinkedB2B (see assignment 10.17 for more background). One of her goals is to increase attendance at in-person networking events for LinkedB2B members. She is currently using Los Angeles as a test market to explore new ways of attracting members to the events. The Los Angeles market now has approximately 2,500 members. On average, just 40 members attend in-person networking events. This is enough to cover costs of the events but does little to generate profits. Bianca believes that by increasing attendance at these events to between 150 and 200 people, the events will help her company in the following ways: they will make the events more profitable; they will make LinkedB2B membership more valuable; and they will increase LinkedB2B's brand value of growing business-to-business relationships. Bianca created a message to attract more members to these events.

*SUBJECT: Come Network to Find New Business Partners!!!*

*Dear LinkedB2B Members of Southern California!*

*We are so happy to bring you more and better networking events to help you build your professional networks and build your careers. As a LinkedB2B member, you know how important it is to cultivate your networks and find the next great business partner. But, did you know how much difference it makes to not only meet people online but also in person? Our internal surveys show that members who attended LinkedB2B events in the last year say they found three new business partners at these events. Ninety-three percent of these members also say they gained new business insights. We're now going to take our networking events to the next level by making more opportunities for you to find business partners and more opportunities for you to get cutting-edge business knowledge to transform your organizations' performance. Beginning on May 3, we will begin holding networking events every two months that involve a speaker series. On May 3 the speaker will be Jeff Sedgewick, an expert in B2B social media. On July 7 the speaker will be Janna Chen, an expert in B2B ecosystems. Then, on September 4, we're fortunate to have world-renowned author and expert of deal-making and conflict resolution Madison Avery talk about how to get a deal done. Now, all events will include two complimentary drinks and light refreshments. Also, we're adding a new e-introduction feature that will allow you to see who is attending the event ahead of time. This same tool will help you follow up with people you meet at the event.*

*Sincerely,*

*Bianca*

Complete the following tasks:

A. Evaluate the effectiveness of Bianca's message.

B. Rewrite the message to improve it. Feel free to reasonably embellish the message as directed by your instructor.

# Language Mechanics Check

**10.20 Review the "Commonly Misspelled and Confused Words" section in Appendix A. Then, rewrite each sentence to make any needed corrections.**

A. We want your advise on the affects of this monetary policy.

B. She said the team lacked complimentary skills, which was one reason for such moral.

C. Your order is already, so please pick it up sooner then 6 p.m.

D. His key incite was that the new policy had no effects at all.

E. This initiative will insure that all employees will not loose their retirement options.

F. It's okay to accept credit cards.

G. The principal behind this guideline is that we trust our employees.

H. Since she's already accepted the offer, let's precede as if she's a current employee.

I. We provided complimentary items to all attendees accept for employees.

J. Please apprise her performance and then send her advice.

# Endnotes

1. Michael Maslansky, *The Language of Trust* (New York: Prentice Hall, 2010): 6.

2. Liz Simpson, "Get Around Resistance and Win Over the Other Side," *Harvard Management Communication Letter*, 2003: 3.

3. Robert B. Cialdini, *Influence: The Psychology of Persuasion* (New York: HarperCollins, 2007).

4. Ibid., 17.

5. Ibid.

6. Ibid.

7. Ibid.

8. Ibid.

9. Ibid.

10. Ibid.

11. Ibid.

12. Ralph Allora, *Winning Sales Letters—from Prospect to Close* (New York: McGraw-Hill, 2009).

13. Meredith D. Ashby and Stephen A. Miles, *Leaders Talk Leadership: Top Executives Speak Their Minds* (New York: Oxford University Press, 2002): 160–161.

14. Matthew J. Mazzei, Christopher L. Shook, and David J. Ketchen Jr., "Selling Strategic Issues: Crafting the Content of the Sales Pitch," *Business Horizons* 52: 539–543.

15. Beverly Ballaro, "Six Ways to Grab Your Audience Right from the Start," *Harvard Management Communication Letter*, 2003: 3–5.

16. Mazzei et al., "Selling Strategic Issues: Crafting the Content of the Sales Pitch."

17. Tom Sant, *Persuasive Business Proposals: Writing to Win More Customers, Clients, and Contracts*, 2nd ed. (New York: AMACOM, 2004); Allora, *Winning Sales Letters—from Prospect to Close*.

18. Simpson, "Get Around Resistance and Win Over the Other Side."

19. Maslansky, *The Language of Trust*: 35.

20. Ibid., 37.

21. Allora, *Winning Sales Letters—from Prospect to Close*; Sant, *Persuasive Business Proposals: Writing to Win More Customers, Clients, and Contracts*.

22. Stephen M. R. Covey, *The Speed of Trust* (New York: Free Press, 2006).

23. Maslansky, *The Language of Trust*: 39.

24. Allora, *Winning Sales Letters—from Prospect to Close*.

25. Maslansky, *The Language of Trust*.

26. Allora, *Winning Sales Letters—from Prospect to Close*.

27. Ibid.

28. Mazzei et al., "Selling Strategic Issues: Crafting the Content of the Sales Pitch."

29. Maslansky, *The Language of Trust*.

30. Ibid.

31. Allora, *Winning Sales Letters—from Prospect to Close*.

32. Maslansky, *The Language of Trust*: 232–242.

33. Ibid., 116.

34. Dale Carnegie Training, *The 5 Essential People Skills: How to Assert Yourself, Listen to Others, and Resolve Conflicts* (New York: Simon & Schuster, 2009): 137.

CHAPTER 11:
Bad-News
Messages

 **ESTABLISHING CREDIBILITY**

 **PRINCIPLES OF INTERPERSONAL COMMUNICATION**

 **PRINCIPLES FOR & TYPES OF BUSINESS MESSAGES**

 **Learning Objectives**

After studying this chapter, you should be able to do the following:

**LO11.1** Describe how delivering bad news impacts your credibility.

**LO11.2** Explain considerations for deciding which channels to use when delivering bad-news messages.

**LO11.3** Summarize principles for effectively delivering bad-news messages.

**LO11.4** Compose effective bad-news messages in person and in writing for various audiences, including colleagues, external partners, and customers.

**LO11.5** Deliver and receive negative performance reviews constructively.

**LO11.6** Review bad-news messages for effectiveness and fairness.

Business inevitably involves giving bad or disappointing news to people. Perhaps you need to turn down a proposal, reject the business of a supplier, deny the claim of a customer, give a negative performance review to a subordinate, reject the idea of a colleague, explain that you do not like a product or service, notify your boss of mistakes you've made, or even tell employees that they will be laid off. Not all communications in business are pleasant. Because business is competitive by nature, turning others down is common.

Delivering really bad news is extremely stressful to most business professionals. In the Great Recession that began in 2008, 37 percent of human resource workers considered changing profession due to the frequency with which they were forced to deliver the news to employees that they were being laid off.[1] Management consultant Mark Blackham explained this uncomfortable predicament: "Bad news is bad news no matter how you spin it. It changes people's futures. This is one part of life that is not much fun, and you cannot make it better with words."[2]

In this chapter, we focus on several principles for delivering bad news in person and in writing. In the majority of workplace situations, you and your organization will continue to hold a working relationship with the recipients of bad news—whether they are colleagues, external partners, or customers. Therefore, your overarching goal is to create a path forward that is in the long-run interests of each person involved in the situation. Moreover, one of your goals is to help bad-news recipients maintain a positive image of your organization. Read the following short case, which will be the basis for five examples of delivering bad news shown throughout this chapter.

**Hear Pete Cardon explain why this matters.**

**bit.ly/cardon11**

## CHAPTER CASE: BAD NEWS AT MARBLE HOME MAKEOVERS

*Juan Hernandez*

*Cindy Cooper*

*Jake Adelman*

**WHO'S INVOLVED**

**Business manager at Marble Home Makeovers (The business fabricates marble countertops, tiles, vanities, and bathtubs. It also installs and remodels home bathrooms and kitchens.)**
- Overseeing fast growth as the company transitions from a small, regional company to a large, nationwide supplier

**Loan officer at Wilson Citizen Bank**
- Has acted as a small-business loan specialist for the prior four years

**Shift supervisor at Marble Home Makeovers**
- Promoted to shift supervisor two years ago largely due to his ability to improve employee morale

**Cindy Cooper Informs Juan That Marble Home Makeovers's Credit Line Will Be Reduced Substantially**

Cindy is in charge of small-business loans. Bank officials just decided that the bank was holding excessively risky credit lines with the majority of its small-business clients. Cindy was told to rein in dozens of these credit lines by reducing them by

**SITUATION 1 (TUESDAY AFTERNOON)**

(Juan Hernandez character): © Purestock/Getty Images RF; (Cindy Cooper character): © Mike Powell/Getty Images RF; (Jake Adelman character): © David Sacks/Digital Vision/Getty Images RF

50 to 75 percent. She called and met with several of these clients over the past week, many of whom stated they did not know how to meet the bank's sudden demands.

Next, Cindy needed to contact Juan and inform him that the bank would be cutting the credit line from $100,000 to between $30,000 and $50,000. She knew this would be difficult news for Juan because Marble Home Makeovers faced some challenging cash constraints.

SITUATION 2
(WEDNESDAY
MORNING)

**Juan Needs to Break the News to All Employees That Work Hours Will Be Reduced**
Juan Hernandez sighed in frustration. He'd slept poorly last night because of anxiety. Today was going to be a long day. He had lots of bad news to pass around—to employees, suppliers, and customers. Juan had delivered bad news many times before, but it never got easy.

Juan gathered most of the employees for a 15-minute meeting. He broke the news that the company was temporarily suspending any overtime work and cutting back on shifts. Juan knew some of the workers lived from month to month and that these new changes would hurt them. The meeting, however, was cut short by a surprise safety inspection by an Occupational Safety and Health Administration (OSHA) officer. Thus, Juan needed to send out an email to clarify the news he had delivered in the meeting. He had not had a chance to answer all the questions, and some employees were not at work that day. He definitely wanted to get out more complete information right away.

SITUATION 3
(WEDNESDAY
AFTERNOON)

**Juan Needs to Turn Down the Request of a Supervisor**
One of the supervisors, Jake Adelman, requested that two production workers get to retain all their shifts. Jake is sympathetic to these two workers' personal financial situations. Jake's well-intentioned request is not fair to other employees. Juan needs to tactfully turn down this request.

SITUATION 4
(WEDNESDAY
AFTERNOON)

**Juan Needs to Inform an Unhappy Customer That He Is Rejecting Her Claim**
Juan needs to respond to an email complaint from a customer who complained that a marble countertop the company had installed in her home had a crack. She requested that Marble Home Makeovers replace the countertop or pay her $495 (the original price). The countertop had been manufactured and installed five years previously, well beyond the two-year warranty.

SITUATION 5
(WEDNESDAY
AFTERNOON)

**Juan Delivers Negative Feedback to an Employee**
Juan conducts quarterly performance reviews for each of his shift supervisors. Today, he is meeting with Jake Adelman, who is one of the most popular employees in the company. Jake is outgoing, friendly, and inspiring to his workers. Juan has become close friends with Jake, and they regularly go out for lunch together.

One of Jake's primary responsibilities is to ensure that each outgoing shipment to construction wholesalers is complete and that all items are free of defects. In the past few months, however, several wholesalers have complained that Jake's shipments did not contain the correct items. In two cases, nearly every item in the shipments contained defects. Juan deemed Jake's quarterly performance as poor and knew he needed to confront Jake about these problems.

**TASK**

**1**

How can Cindy inform Juan of changes to his credit line and also preserve business with Marble Home Makeovers? (See the section on delivering bad news in person to customers.)

**2**

How can Juan write a message to employees informing them that they will have reduced work hours without excessively reducing employee morale and commitment? (See the section on delivering bad news in writing to colleagues.)

③ How can Juan turn down a supervisor's request and still maintain goodwill? (See the section on turning down requests and ideas.)

④ How can Juan reject this customer's claim but retain her loyalty? (See the section on delivering bad news in writing to customers.)

⑤ How can Juan tell one of the most popular employees that he is not performing well? (See the section on delivering bad news in person for performance reviews.)

## Maintaining Credibility When Delivering Bad News

*How* you deliver bad news strongly impacts your credibility. Any perceived dishonesty or deception can damage your credibility.[3] Communication specialist Dave Zielinski described how failing to effectively deliver bad news during tough times can damage credibility over the long term:

LO11.1 Describe how delivering bad news impacts your credibility.

> Employees, who have long memories, tend to remember how they were treated, not what marching orders they received, in times of corporate turmoil. When it comes to how they perceive the organization in the aftermath of such troubles, those who communicated openly, honestly and frequently will lay the foundation for future loyalty and overall organizational health.[4]

Zielinski's point is clear: Honesty and openness are key. Although people do not like to get bad news, they expect the truth.

Research shows that honesty and openness can lead to more trust in the bad-news bearer. The consulting firm Siegel+Gale conducted research about delivering bad news during the Great Recession. Through the research involving hundreds of customers of financial service companies, the consultants concluded the following:

> During this time of economic crisis, many organizations struggle to communicate unfavorable news—from lower earnings and shrinking market share, to cuts in service and increases in prices. While many assume that communicating bad news to customers shakes relationships and breeds mistrust, Siegel+Gale's latest . . . survey reveals that delivering bad news the right way can actually strengthen customer relationships and lay the foundation for increased trust when conditions improve.[5]

Although one should never view the delivery of bad news opportunistically, those who deliver bad news appropriately enhance their credibility. It shows character on your part to tell people the truth, even when it's hard for all parties involved. In particular, bearing responsibility for your own role in causing the bad news shows your commitment to transparency and honesty, further bolstering character. It shows caring when you do all you can to lessen the impact of bad news on others and exhibit forward thinking that considers their needs. It shows competence when you have a track record of success in tough situations and demonstrate a good plan for overcoming the challenges you face.

## Applying the AIM Planning Process for Bad-News Messages

Planning is critical to delivering bad news in a way that best serves all parties involved and leaves the door open for productive cooperation in the future. Yet, since bad news should be delivered in a timely manner, planning must be tackled as soon as possible. Many times, bad-news recipients are hurt less by the bad news than by how long it took to receive it. Your challenge, then, is to start planning efficiently as soon as you discover the unpleasant news.

### Guidelines for Bad-News Messages

- Deliver the bad news in a timely manner.
- Choose the right mix of channels.
- Sympathize with the bad-news recipients and soften the blow.
- Provide a simple, clear rationale.
- Explain immediate impacts.
- Focus on solutions and long-term benefits.
- Show goodwill.

# Understand How the Bad News Will Affect Your Audience

Delivering bad news often creates stress, anxiety, and other strong emotions. You may feel eager to relieve yourself of these feelings. More than with other types of messages, you may need to work hard to focus your message on serving others. You can make the situation better for the recipients by understanding the nature of the bad news and its impacts on them, delivering the news in a timely manner, and choosing the right mix of communication channels.

**Deliver the Bad News in a Timely Manner**   The adage *no news is bad news* applies when colleagues, clients, or customers know you are in the process of making decisions that can impact them. In the absence of information, they often assume the worst. Sometimes, as people are wondering what the bad news may be, they may even pass their speculations on as part of the rumor mill. In these cases, you lose control of the message and can lose credibility if others think you have wrongfully withheld information. Never wait too long to deliver bad news.[6]

On the other hand, don't deliver bad news when you don't know the details because this can cause unnecessary anxiety. For example, announcing that there *might* be budget cuts or layoffs or pay cuts without any specifics could cause more alarm than is warranted. You will be the judge of this.[7]

**LO11.2** Explain considerations for deciding which channels to use when delivering bad-news messages.

**connect**

Visit http://connect. mheducation.com for an exercise on this topic.

**Choose the Right Mix of Channels**   Generally, bad news is best delivered in person. This allows rich communication, where you can use verbal and nonverbal cues to show your concern and sensitivity. You get immediate feedback from those receiving bad news and can respond to their discomforts right away. In many unpleasant situations, you can immediately come up with options and solutions.

However, delivering bad news in writing also has advantages. By placing the bad news in writing, you can control the message more carefully and ensure that you state the bad news precisely and accurately. However, you do not have the ability to respond immediately if the message recipients misinterpret the bad news. Moreover, many people view bad news in written form as callous and impersonal. See Table 11.1 for a summary of advantages and disadvantages of delivering bad news in person and in writing.

As you consider which communication channels to use, analyze the nature of the bad news. In research from medical and social psychology literature, researchers have identified three aspects of the bad news that impact how you approach delivering it: severity, controllability, and likelihood. **Severity** is how serious or detrimental the bad news is. **Controllability** is the degree to which the bad-news message receiver can alter the outcome. **Likelihood** relates to the probability of the bad event occurring.[8]

As controllability decreases and likelihood and/or severity increase, richer channels of communication are most appropriate. For example, laying someone off should certainly be done in person. There is no controllability (the employee cannot undo being laid off), there is complete likelihood, and there is high severity (the employee will be unemployed and potentially without income and other benefits such as health insurance). When bad news becomes more controllable, less likely, and/or less severe, less-rich channels are more often justified. In Table 11.2, you can see appropriate responses in terms of richness for various combinations of severity and controllability.

Of course, your preferred communication channel is not always available. For example, if you work in a virtual team, you may not have the option of delivering bad news in person. Or if you hold a high-level leadership position, you simply cannot take time to speak to each person affected by your decisions. Where possible and appropriate, choose richer communication channels.

**TABLE 11.1**

Advantages and Disadvantages of Bad News in Verbal and Written Forms

| **Verbal Delivery** | **Written Delivery** |
|---|---|
| *Advantages* | *Advantages* |
| • Can use and observe nonverbal cues<br>• Can more easily demonstrate intentions<br>• Can more effectively clarify and explain the bad news<br>• Can respond to concerns immediately | • Can craft message more carefully<br>• Can document the message more easily<br>• Can provide a message that serves as a reference (provide directions, suggestions, and options for future actions)<br>• Can deliver message to more people more efficiently |
| *Disadvantages* | *Disadvantages* |
| • May hinder effective delivery, interpretation, and discussion of bad news due to strong emotions<br>• Requires more time<br>• Less able to document the bad news<br>• Less able to provide directions that bad-news recipients can reference later | • Unable to demonstrate concern through nonverbal cues<br>• Unable to immediately respond to concerns<br>• Unable to work out mutual solutions<br>• Less able to control long-term impacts on working relationships |

**TABLE 11.2**

Types of Bad News and Richness of Communication Channels

| Type of Bad News | Example | Written Only (Example: Email) | Verbal Not in Person (Example: Phone) | Verbal + Nonverbal Not in Person (Example: Video Call) | Verbal + Nonverbal in Person (Example: Meeting) | In Person + Written (Example: Meeting + Follow-up Memo) |
|---|---|---|---|---|---|---|
| Low Severity + High Controllability | Colleague's idea is rejected | * | * | * | * | * |
| Low Severity + Low Controllability | Customer claim is rejected (Figure 11.8) | * | * | * | * | * |
| Medium Severity + High Controllability | Vendor chooses another supplier (Figure 11.6) | * | ✔ | ✔ | ✔ | ✔ |
| Medium Severity + Low Controllability | Employees given fewer work hours (Figure 11.4) | ✗ | ✗ | ✔ | ✔ | ✔ |
| High Severity + High Controllability | Employee receives poor performance rating (Figure 11.10) | ✗ | ✗ | ✗ | ✔ | ✔ |
| High Severity + Low Controllability | Employee laid off | ✗ | ✗ | ✗ | ✗ | ✔ |

* = depends on communication channel in use or preferred by bad-news recipient; ✗ = rarely acceptable; ✔ = preferred.

**LO11.3** Summarize principles for effectively delivering bad-news messages.

## Gather Information from a Variety of Sources

Gathering the facts from a variety of sources is critical for bad-news messages. Often, you are dealing with emotionally charged issues, situations that are open to multiple interpretations, and/or situations where the potential consequences are severe. If you gather as much information as you can from a variety of sources, you're more likely to make objective judgments and propose fair solutions. Make sure you are aware of your own emotions and how they impact your thinking. You might ask yourself whether your reaction to the situation involves any defensiveness, rashness, or favoritism.

## Develop Your Message

One choice you'll make when delivering bad news is whether to make your message more or less direct. For most bad-news messages, you'll ease into the bad news and allow the affected person to prepare for the potential shock. In less direct messages, you'll describe the rationale for the bad news first, whereas in more direct messages, you'll give the bad news and then provide the rationale.

Generally, you will deliver less-direct bad news when you work with customers, clients, and contacts you don't know very well. When working with colleagues, you can typically be more direct than you are with customers and clients. In particular, you should generally be most direct when delivering bad news to superiors, who have limited time and need the key pieces of information up front. Still, in most of your relationships with colleagues, some indirectness helps prepare your colleagues to accept the bad news or negative feedback constructively.

You also can make judgments based on the motivational values of others (as you learned about in Chapter 2). Professionals with assertive-directing motivational values (reds) prefer more directness in all situations, including those involving bad news. Professionals with analytic-autonomizing motivational values (greens) prefer less-direct bad news that is characterized by the most attention to the rationale. Professionals with hub motivational value systems (roughly equal focus on assertiveness, analysis, and altruism) also prefer less-direct bad news that is characterized by a focus on the future and a desire for harmony. Professionals with altruistic-nurturing motivational values (blues) prefer the least-direct bad news with heavy attention paid to displays of concern and shows of goodwill.

**Sympathize with the Bad-News Recipient and Soften the Blow** When bad-news message recipients know you are concerned about them, they generally respond without antagonism and even appreciate your honesty. In person, most people make a judgment about your genuine concern for them based on many factors, including your past treatment of them and your nonverbal behavior. In writing, you are less able to use nonverbal behavior to show your sincere concern and appreciation.

For written messages, several techniques help the bad-news recipient prepare emotionally. First, using a neutral subject line often helps the reader recognize that the news will likely not be positive. However, since it is not direct (does not state the bad news), it allows the reader to momentarily adjust psychologically to accept the bad news.

Also, in some communications, you may use a one- or two-sentence buffer to start the bad-news message, which softens the blow. A **buffer** is a statement to establish common ground, show appreciation, state your sympathy, or otherwise express goodwill. Table 11.3 provides several examples, each of which is intended to draw connections between the message sender and message recipient and reduce the sudden emotional impact for the recipient.

When you show sympathy to your readers, you let them know you share their sorrow or trouble in some part. However, limit such expressions to one or two sentences, and make them sincere and professional. Avoid taking responsibility if you are not at fault. For example, the statement "We're sorry to hear about the crack in your countertop" does not imply responsibility, whereas the statement "We're sorry that the countertop we installed has malfunctioned" may.

### Components of *Indirect* Bad-News Messages

- Ease in with a buffer.
- **Provide a rationale.**
- **Deliver the bad news.**
- Explain impacts.
- Focus on the future (as appropriate).
- Show goodwill.

Visit http://connect.mheducation.com for an exercise on this topic.

### Components of *Direct* Bad-News Messages

- Ease in with a buffer.
- **Deliver the bad news.**
- **Provide a rationale.**
- Explain impacts.
- Focus on the future (as appropriate).
- Show goodwill.

**TABLE 11.3**

Buffers for Bad-News Messages

| Type of Buffer | Example |
|---|---|
| Neutral statement | SUBJECT: Decision on Bid for Annual Contract with Marble Home Makeovers |
| Appreciation | Thank you for submitting your competitive bid to supply and deliver plastic resins for the upcoming year. |
| Sympathy | We're sorry to hear about the crack in your countertop. |
| Common ground | Reducing work hours creates unwanted financial challenges for our employees. |
| Compliment | Thank you for your excellent work, especially during this temporary period of cash flow challenges. |

When delivering bad news, you may choose to use a form of buffer referred to as a **teaser message.** These messages, often written, signal to recipients that an upcoming conversation or other communication may involve unpleasant news. The teaser message prepares recipients emotionally yet does not reveal specific information. Neutral statements such as "I have some feedback to give you this afternoon" or "I'll share with you what our clients thought of your ideas" help employees prepare for news that may be partially negative.[9]

**Deliver the Bad News**   Throughout the delivery of bad news, find ways to express concern for recipients. By showing that you care, you may help them bear the news better and respond constructively. Generally, make the expression of concern brief, and stay attentive to the receiver's response. Be aware that excessive displays of concern may sound like a pity trip.

Get to the point fairly quickly—that is, express the bad news and explain the reasons for it clearly. Recipients of bad news generally expect an explanation for why a decision was made. Stick to the facts so recipients will not try to fill in the blanks and come to the wrong conclusions. If you skirt around the bad news, your audience often views your efforts as evasive, thus weakening your credibility.[10]

In written bad-news messages, the neutral subject line and short buffer can soften the blow and show sympathy. However, make the buffer statement short, and, again, get to the bad news fairly quickly. You don't want readers to feel you are purposely downplaying or hiding the bad news by burying it within the message. You also don't want readers to get their hopes up only to have them dashed later in the message. In these instances, bad-news recipients may even feel misled. If you find yourself writing an extremely indirect bad-news message, ask yourself whether you should instead meet in person or pick up the phone.

**Provide a Clear Rationale and Specific Feedback**   Recently, research about delivering bad news to customers in the financial industry has shown that when banks clearly explained the reasons for the bad-news decision, customers felt more trust toward the bank. In response to letters that offered little (i.e., "market conditions and maintaining profitability on your account") or no explanation, customers made comments such as the following: "This makes me feel like the bank wants to squeeze me for all they can. They're not interested in me as a loyal customer; I'm just a number to them." By contrast, customers who received full explanations in the letters were twice as likely to consider the organizations credible. They used statements such as the following: "They seemed honest and up front. They were forthcoming and direct with their information, which is always good." Furthermore, the researchers showed that clear, specific, and simple language built trust, whereas vague, general, and legal language created suspicion and anger.[11]

The most obvious and primary benefit of using simple and specific language is that recipients are more likely to interpret the information as honest and up front. An additional reason to use simple and specific language is that bad-news recipients struggle to process information in bad-news situations. Since many recipients may experience strong emotions and begin thinking ahead about what the bad news means for them, they are less capable of processing complex information.

**Explain Immediate Impacts**   Once you've explained the bad news and the reasons for it, discuss the immediate impacts on recipients. In most situations, avoid moving directly to a discussion of what the bad news means for the company. Your focus should now be on the bad-news recipients, who will naturally be wondering, "What does this mean for me right now?"[12]

Resist the impulse to minimize the negative impact. By honestly describing the negative impacts, you address the foremost concern in the recipients' minds—themselves. If you skip this step, which many people prefer to do since it is not pleasant, you may lose the attention of the bad-news recipients for two reasons. First, they can't process other topics. They are fixated only on the potential impacts on themselves. Second, they may be annoyed if you move immediately to what you consider the silver lining, showing you are detached from their immediate needs.

**Focus on Solutions and Long-Term Benefits**   Most bad news is not permanent. In other words, it usually involves a temporary setback. So once you've described the immediate impacts on the recipients, move to a constructive, forward-looking approach. Where possible, describe realistic solutions, steps to overcoming the current problems, and/or the benefits that current sacrifices make possible. Ideally, you can describe solutions and benefits that the bad-news recipient can control.[13]

Recent research has shown that when managers take a solution-oriented approach to negative situations, employees receiving the bad news respond much more positively and productively. In fact, one study showed that when bad-news recipients are offered options to solve problems, they are 20 percent more effective at solving subsequent tasks and 19 percent less agitated.[14]

Focusing on solutions and long-term benefits should take a positive tone. However, be careful about the good news/bad news approach. The recipients of bad news may react negatively if they perceive that you are downplaying the impact of the bad news on them.[15]

**Show Goodwill**   Keeping the door open to working together constructively in the future should be one of your top priorities in nearly all cases. You may be demoting an employee from a current position today but promoting that same employee two or three years down the road. You may be denying the claim of a customer today but hoping for that customer's repeat business far into the future, and you're definitely trying to ensure that customer tells others that you are credible. You may say no to a supplier today but expect good terms on contracts from that same supplier in the future. It's not even uncommon for companies to ask laid-off employees to return to the company. In the process of delivering bad news, try not to burn bridges.

## Getting the Tone, Style, and Design Right

When you discuss bad news with others, use your tone and nonverbal behaviors to show your interest and concern. Notice the recipient's nonverbal behavior as you deliver the news. Your ability to manage emotions—yours and others'—during a bad-news discussion strongly influences your future working relationship. Research about providing feedback in performance reviews has shown that providing negative feedback with a positive tone actually makes employees feel more positive than when they receive positive feedback with a negative tone. In other words, the power of delivery often outweighs the content of your message in feedback situations.[16]

When you write your bad-news messages, carefully consider tone, style, and design. Aim for a *tone* of genuine concern in a professional manner. Also inject some positive direction to the message, but don't provide false hope or seem out of touch with the impacts on message recipients. Use a writing *style* that is simple, accurate, and jargon-free. Doing so helps people process information quickly and accurately. Since bad-news recipients may be experiencing strong emotions and allowing their thoughts to wander, they are less able to process information accurately. Therefore, use clear language that they will not misinterpret. Finally, maintain a simple *design*. If your message looks too slick, bad-news recipients may believe the message is designed more to impress than to meet their needs.

## Delivering Bad News to Clients

In any business, you develop close working relationships with clients over time. You become aware of their needs and hopes. In many cases, you've had to struggle to gain their business and you're constantly working to keep them satisfied with your products and services. Providing bad news to these clients is stressful, since you do not want to let them down, and you know that your success depends on their business.

In the first situation from the chapter case, Cindy Cooper needs to inform Juan Hernandez that the bank will reduce the credit line to his business by between 50 and 75 percent within a few months. Since Marble Home Makeovers is currently in a poor cash position, this new policy is serious and could be viewed as medium severity. Since the bank has some flexibility in establishing the new credit line terms (reduction of between 50 and 75 percent within 60 to 90 days), Juan may be able to negotiate the best possible terms. Therefore, he does have some control. In Cindy's less effective approach (see Figure 11.1), she writes an email message, which is not as rich and personal as required based on the severity of this situation. In the more effective delivery (see Figure 11.2), Cindy calls Juan, meets with him, and follows principles for delivering bad news effectively.

**LO11.4** Compose effective bad-news messages in person and in writing for various audiences, including colleagues, external partners, and customers.

**connect**

Visit **http://connect. mheducation.com** for an exercise on this topic.

**FIGURE 11.1**

Less Effective Delivery of Bad News to a Client

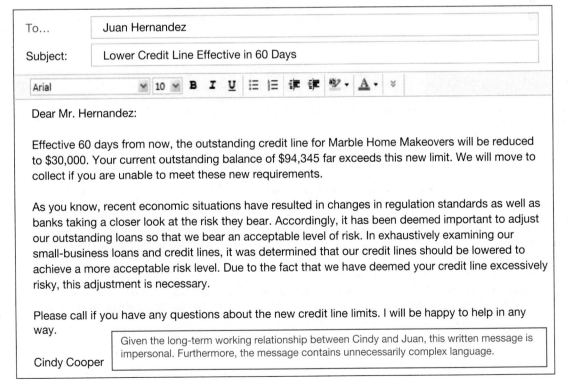

To...  Juan Hernandez

Subject:  Lower Credit Line Effective in 60 Days

Arial  10  **B**  *I*  U

Dear Mr. Hernandez:

Effective 60 days from now, the outstanding credit line for Marble Home Makeovers will be reduced to $30,000. Your current outstanding balance of $94,345 far exceeds this new limit. We will move to collect if you are unable to meet these new requirements.

As you know, recent economic situations have resulted in changes in regulation standards as well as banks taking a closer look at the risk they bear. Accordingly, it has been deemed important to adjust our outstanding loans so that we bear an acceptable level of risk. In exhaustively examining our small-business loans and credit lines, it was determined that our credit lines should be lowered to achieve a more acceptable risk level. Due to the fact that we have deemed your credit line excessively risky, this adjustment is necessary.

Please call if you have any questions about the new credit line limits. I will be happy to help in any way.

Given the long-term working relationship between Cindy and Juan, this written message is impersonal. Furthermore, the message contains unnecessarily complex language.

Cindy Cooper

## FIGURE 11.2

### More Effective Delivery of Bad News to a Client

Cindy was tired of telling her small-business clients the disappointing news that their credit lines would soon be severely reduced. She sighed and called the next person on her list: "Juan, the bank is making some adjustments to small-business credit lines. I'd like to meet in person as soon as possible to explain what this means for your business." Juan replied, "I can stop by this afternoon since I'm in town today." Having worked with Juan for over five years, she knew meeting the bank's demands would be challenging for his business.

> Phone call with a somewhat urgent but neutral tone serves as a BUFFER and allows Juan to prepare emotionally.

[Later at the bank]

**Cindy:** Juan, thanks for stopping by on such short notice. The bank is making some major changes to the terms of our small-business credit lines, and I wanted to let you know about these changes right away. Because of so many recent bank failures around the country, we requested an audit to help us evaluate our situation. The audit results showed that we hold far too much debt, and we're implementing several policies to place the bank in a safer financial position. These policies will impact your business, so I wanted to explain the new terms and discuss how we can work together in meeting them.

> Provides RATIONALE for changes in credit line terms.

**Juan:** This sounds serious. What are the changes?

**Cindy:** For most small-business credit lines, including yours, we're reducing the credit line by between 50 and 75 percent. We expect to make the policy effective in 60 to 90 days, and the bank will move to collect on outstanding credit above the new limits. Today, I'd like to discuss ways to lower your outstanding credit so that you'll remain on good terms once the new policy goes into place.

> Delivers the BAD NEWS.

**Juan:** Well, Cindy, this comes as quite a surprise. This will put tremendous strain on our business. Exactly how much do we need to pay back and in what time frame?

**Cindy:** In your case, you're currently using nearly $94,000 of your $100,000 credit line. We will cut the credit line to between $30,000 and $50,000 in 60 to 90 days. Based on our conversation today, including your ideas for reducing your outstanding balance, I'll make a determination this afternoon. What are your projections for cash flow over the next three to six months? What can you do to improve your cash situation rapidly?

> Explains IMMEDIATE IMPACTS.

**Juan:** We are facing some challenging cash constraints, but the long-term position looks strong. We've expanded during the past two years from a regional market to a national one. Our revenue has grown by 400 percent in just one year, and we've increased the number of employees from 15 to 50 in a year and a half. With all this growth, we've moved into a new building and invested heavily in new equipment and facility improvements.

We currently have five bids on several large projects. I expect us to get at least two of these. If we receive any of the five bids, we could immediately pay back the credit line.

**Cindy:** What if you do not receive any of the bids?

> Adopts a listening orientation.

**Juan:** In that case, our only option would be to lay off employees or reduce work hours. We do currently hold some excess inventory. We could temporarily reduce work hours and thus lower payroll expenses by relying on this inventory . . .

> Focuses on the FUTURE and shows GOODWILL.

[After continued discussion, Cindy decides to cut the credit line to $50,000 in 90 days since Juan has agreed to temporarily reduce payroll expenses. The employees will not be happy about this change.]

Photos: Cindy: © Mike Powell/Getty Images RF; Juan: © Purestock/Getty Images RF

## Delivering Bad-News Announcements

One characteristic of high-performing organizations is that employees volunteer information with one another, even when it is bad news. In many organizations, however, employees are reluctant to share bad news. They do not want to disappoint others, and they do not want to be blamed. When many employees in an organization avoid sharing bad news, the result is the mum effect. The **mum effect** occurs when the chain of messages within an organization is filtered at each level to leave out or inaccurately state the bad news. The message that top executives often hear ends up being unrealistically rosy.

One tragic example of the mum effect is the 1986 space shuttle explosion. During the investigation, Nobel laureate Richard Feynman found that engineers had predicted the probability of a main engine failure at between 1 in 200 and 1 in 300. Top decision makers at the National Aeronautics and Space Administration (NASA), however, had been informed by reports that had progressively gotten more positive through several layers of bureaucracy, and they had thus believed the probability of main engine failure was closer to 1 in 100,000. While the shuttle disaster is an extreme example, businesses repeatedly underperform and even fail on projects due to the mum effect.[17]

When most employees deliver bad news and negative feedback to one another in open, honest, caring, and rich environments, organizations tend to exhibit higher morale. On the other hand, when most employees do not share bad news or do so impersonally, organizations tend to exhibit lower morale. In practice, many companies have cultures of delivering bad news impersonally. In a survey of 292 employees, only 37 percent stated that the primary means of delivering bad news in their companies was face-to-face meetings. The other primary means of bad-news delivery were emails (29 percent), letters and memos (12 percent), internal employee websites (8 percent), teleconferences or videoconferences (6 percent), and company newsletters (3.5 percent).[18]

McGraw Wentworth, a consulting firm, recently issued a report about delivering bad news during the Great Recession. The report explained, "Using an impersonal e-mail format to deliver bad news is very poor business form. Your employees will feel your organization has no respect for them. They will not forget the callous way they received bad news and when the economy turns around, they may be the first people looking for new opportunities."[19]

In all management positions, you will need to give bad news to your boss, your peers, or those you supervise from time to time. Your ability to deliver bad-news messages constructively will foster a transparent and open work culture. As appropriate, internal bad-news messages should show appreciation for the efforts of employees and look to the future.

In Juan's case, he is delivering a bad-news announcement to the production workers that the company needs to reduce their hours for three months. He broke the news first in a rich environment—a meeting. Next, he is writing a follow-up to provide complete details and serve as a reference to employees. In the less effective example (see Figure 11.3), Juan leaves out a buffer and focuses primarily on the needs of the company. This approach will anger many employees and reduce company loyalty. In the more effective example (see Figure 11.4), Juan focuses on the employees—their needs and concerns. He does not sugarcoat the news. He clearly describes the reasons for reducing work hours. He also clearly explains the likely negative impacts (specific ranges of loss in income). Many employees will likely respect him for his openness and honesty. Juan concludes the message with forward-looking and positive thoughts about opportunities for the employees. This is appropriate as long as Juan can deliver on these promises.

**FIGURE 11.3**

Less Effective Bad-News Message to Employees

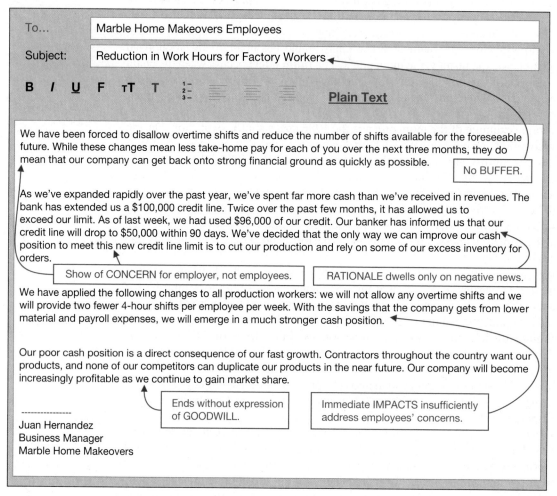

**To...** Marble Home Makeovers Employees

**Subject:** Reduction in Work Hours for Factory Workers

**B** *I* **U** F ᴛT T   Plain Text

We have been forced to disallow overtime shifts and reduce the number of shifts available for the foreseeable future. While these changes mean less take-home pay for each of you over the next three months, they do mean that our company can get back onto strong financial ground as quickly as possible.

No BUFFER.

As we've expanded rapidly over the past year, we've spent far more cash than we've received in revenues. The bank has extended us a $100,000 credit line. Twice over the past few months, it has allowed us to exceed our limit. As of last week, we had used $96,000 of our credit. Our banker has informed us that our credit line will drop to $50,000 within 90 days. We've decided that the only way we can improve our cash position to meet this new credit line limit is to cut our production and rely on some of our excess inventory for orders.

Show of CONCERN for employer, not employees.

RATIONALE dwells only on negative news.

We have applied the following changes to all production workers: we will not allow any overtime shifts and we will provide two fewer 4-hour shifts per employee per week. With the savings that the company gets from lower material and payroll expenses, we will emerge in a much stronger cash position.

Our poor cash position is a direct consequence of our fast growth. Contractors throughout the country want our products, and none of our competitors can duplicate our products in the near future. Our company will become increasingly profitable as we continue to gain market share.

Ends without expression of GOODWILL.

Immediate IMPACTS insufficiently address employees' concerns.

----------------
Juan Hernandez
Business Manager
Marble Home Makeovers

## Turning Down Requests and Ideas

Your colleagues will often approach you with requests and ideas. Turning down colleagues is challenging because you want to preserve productive and comfortable working relationships. Most often, you should use richer communication channels if possible—that is, in person or by phone. Writing makes sense, however, when the bad news is not severe, when your audience prefers corresponding in written form, or when you're responding to a written request. When you break bad news in writing, you should generally follow up with a phone call or visit.

When turning down requests or ideas with close colleagues, one of the most common mistakes is to offer **token appreciation**. Token appreciation is an expression of thanks or gratitude for a request or idea while immediately dismissing the request or idea as implausible or even inappropriate. While token appreciation is often given with the intent of not hurting feelings, it is often perceived as insincere or manipulative. One of the most common forms of token appreciation is the *yes-but* statement. Statements such as "I like your idea, but. . ." or "You make a good point, however. . ." are often stated in a way that dismisses the requests or ideas of others without any intention of taking the ideas or requests seriously.

When turning down requests and ideas, appealing to values and principles is often appropriate. Yet, savvy communicators do so without coming across as morally superior. Bad-news recipients often become defensive when they feel their requests are denied *and* their requests are viewed as invalid or illegitimate.

**FIGURE 11.4**

More Effective Delivery of Bad News to Employees

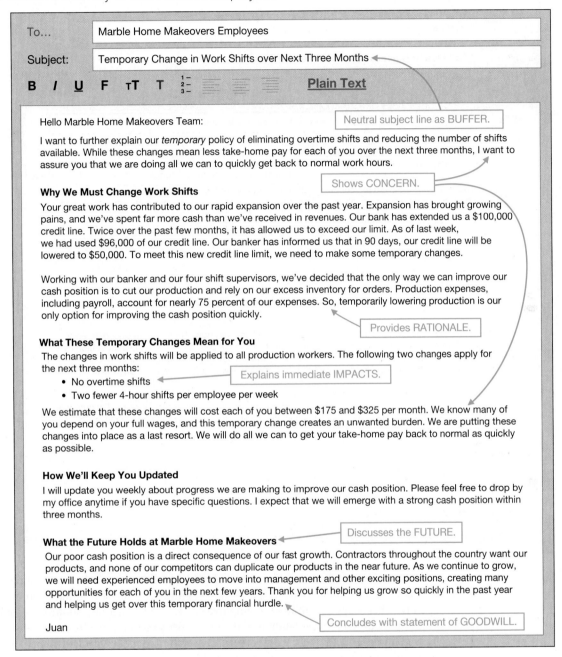

To... | Marble Home Makeovers Employees

Subject: | Temporary Change in Work Shifts over Next Three Months

B  *I*  U  F  ᴛT  T  1—2—3—  Plain Text

Hello Marble Home Makeovers Team:

Neutral subject line as BUFFER.

I want to further explain our *temporary* policy of eliminating overtime shifts and reducing the number of shifts available. While these changes mean less take-home pay for each of you over the next three months, I want to assure you that we are doing all we can to quickly get back to normal work hours.

Shows CONCERN.

**Why We Must Change Work Shifts**

Your great work has contributed to our rapid expansion over the past year. Expansion has brought growing pains, and we've spent far more cash than we've received in revenues. Our bank has extended us a $100,000 credit line. Twice over the past few months, it has allowed us to exceed our limit. As of last week, we had used $96,000 of our credit line. Our banker has informed us that in 90 days, our credit line will be lowered to $50,000. To meet this new credit line limit, we need to make some temporary changes.

Working with our banker and our four shift supervisors, we've decided that the only way we can improve our cash position is to cut our production and rely on our excess inventory for orders. Production expenses, including payroll, account for nearly 75 percent of our expenses. So, temporarily lowering production is our only option for improving the cash position quickly.

Provides RATIONALE.

**What These Temporary Changes Mean for You**

The changes in work shifts will be applied to all production workers. The following two changes apply for the next three months:

Explains immediate IMPACTS.

- No overtime shifts
- Two fewer 4-hour shifts per employee per week

We estimate that these changes will cost each of you between $175 and $325 per month. We know many of you depend on your full wages, and this temporary change creates an unwanted burden. We are putting these changes into place as a last resort. We will do all we can to get your take-home pay back to normal as quickly as possible.

**How We'll Keep You Updated**

I will update you weekly about progress we are making to improve our cash position. Please feel free to drop by my office anytime if you have specific questions. I expect that we will emerge with a strong cash position within three months.

Discusses the FUTURE.

**What the Future Holds at Marble Home Makeovers**

Our poor cash position is a direct consequence of our fast growth. Contractors throughout the country want our products, and none of our competitors can duplicate our products in the near future. As we continue to grow, we will need experienced employees to move into management and other exciting positions, creating many opportunities for each of you in the next few years. Thank you for helping us grow so quickly in the past year and helping us get over this temporary financial hurdle.

Juan

Concludes with statement of GOODWILL.

Also, excellent communicators avoid turning down requests and ideas in a way that closes the conversation. While they may say "no" to the particular request or idea, they remain open to related solutions. They also take time to hear people out and strengthen the working relationship.

After Juan sent out the bad-news announcement to temporarily reduce work hours for production workers, one of the supervisors requested that Juan continue to allow full shifts for two of the workers. In the less effective response (see Figure 11.5; Jake's original message is in the bottom of this figure), Juan is dismissive of Jake's idea, which is amplified by *yes-but* statements. Unnecessarily using negative words such as *unfortunately* also accentuates the dead-end nature of this idea and request.

**FIGURE 11.5**

Less Effective Example of Turning Down a Request.

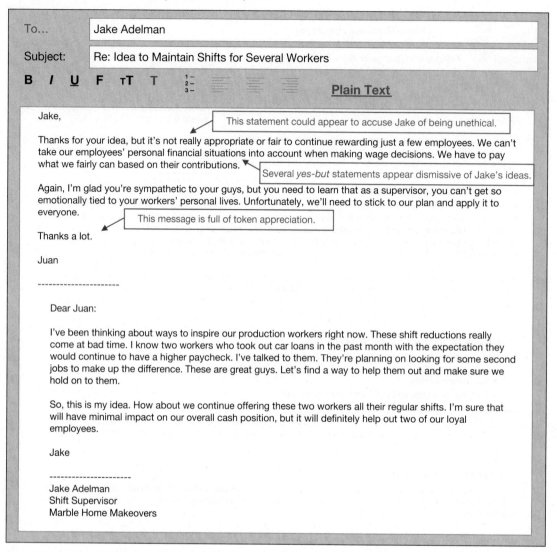

In the more effective response (see Figure 11.6), Juan shows genuine appreciation for Jake's request. Juan tactfully states that meeting the request is unlikely but remains open to other ways of helping the employees. He's clear that any solutions should be available to all employees without indicating Jake's original idea is potentially *unfair* by benefiting just a few of the employees. By seeking to meet with Jake in person, Juan shows his sincere interest in hearing Jake's ideas.

## Delivering Bad News to Customers

In many positions, you will have direct contact with customers. You have probably already worked in jobs where you interacted extensively with customers and likely had to deliver bad news. You certainly have been an angry customer who has received bad news, so you can relate! Bad-news messages to customers contain the same essential components as other bad-news messages. However, when writing this kind of bad-news message, you want to emphasize the options available—solutions the customer has control over. In most bad-news situations, customers are interested only in solutions. They do not want long descriptions of why you can't meet their demands.

**FIGURE 11.6**

More Effective Example of Turning Down a Request.

To...  Jake Adelman

Subject:  Let's Talk about Options for Employees

**B** *I* <u>U</u> F ᴛT T  1– 2– 3–  ☰ ☰ ☰  **Plain Text**

Dear Jake:

*Neutral subject line and appreciation as BUFFERS.*

Thanks for sharing your ideas about supporting several of our production workers. I'm glad you're worried about the financial burden our temporary policy places on them.

*Provides RATIONALE and mentions IMPACTS.*

Several other managers and I wrestled with setting up the temporary reductions in work shifts. We think this solution is the best way to get our business back into a safe cash position and avoid any lay-offs. It does make life more difficult for our production workers for the next three months.

*Shows CONCERN.*

I'm interested in learning more about what employees are telling you. I'm sure hearing their challenges makes your job tougher too.

*Discusses the FUTURE.*

Perhaps we could meet in the next day or two. We could discuss options for helping our employees during the next three months. We can't offer additional pay during this period, but we may have options to reward or support the employees in other ways. I'm eager to hear some of your ideas. Whatever options we discuss, I'd like to ensure that we make these options open to all employees.

I'm available between 1 and 3 p.m. tomorrow or between 9 a.m. and noon on Friday. Do you have a convenient time to talk for about 30 minutes? Happy to meet at your office or mine.

Best,

*Concludes with Statement of GOODWILL.*

Juan

Also, they do not want to be blamed for anything. Even when customers are at fault, use neutral language (avoid you-voice and use passive verbs) to point out mistakes.

Juan is in a situation with a customer who has made an unreasonable claim, so he is not going to replace the product or provide a refund. You will often encounter similar situations. In the less effective example (see Figure 11.7), Juan unnecessarily

**FIGURE 11.7**

Less Effective Bad-News Message to a Customer

To...  Naomi Gregory

Subject:  Denial of Claim #615A

**B** *I* <u>U</u> F ᴛT T  1– 2– 3–  ☰ ☰ ☰  **Plain Text**

Naomi:

*No BUFFER.*

We're sorry that there is a crack in the countertop we manufactured and installed. Unfortunately, since you did not purchase the countertop with a warranty, you will not receive a refund.

We have two options for you. First, you could repair it yourself. This process is simple if you are handy at fixing things around the house. Just go to various online websites and see how to repair the crack. The other option is to have one of our experts come out and fix it. We would charge a minimum fee for a service visit and probably would not charge for materials. We make no money on these visits. The charge basically covers our expenses. But, we are dedicated to your satisfaction and will provide this service to make your countertop just like new.

Good luck,

*Show of CONCERN emphasizes company's reputation rather than customer's problem.*

*Nondetailed advice shows poor attention to immediate IMPACTS and solutions for the FUTURE.*

Juan

blames the customer. Because he uses you-voice ("since you did not purchase the countertop with a warranty, you will not receive a refund"), the tone is accusatory and even confrontational. Furthermore, the message is not helpful enough. It offers some hastily written, vague advice. The customer will likely decode this response as uncaring.

In the more effective message (see Figure 11.8), Juan provides both a buffer and an expression of sympathy in the first sentence. Although Juan denies the claim, he

**FIGURE 11.8**

More Effective Bad-News Message to a Customer

To...    Naomi Gregory

Subject:    Repairing Your Countertop

**B** *I* <u>U</u> F ᴛT T    1–2–3–    Plain Text

Dear Ms. Gregory:

> Positive subject line as BUFFER and show of CONCERN cushion the claim denial.

We're sorry to hear about the crack in your countertop. Fortunately, the countertop can be repaired, and it will appear as new as the day it was installed.

Since the countertop in your home was not purchased with a warranty, we are unable to provide a refund or fix the countertop without charge.

> RATIONALE is accurate and brief.

You have two options for inexpensively returning your countertop to its original, beautiful appearance. The first option is for you to repair the crack yourself. The second option is for us to send one of our repair technicians to your home on a service visit ($75).

> The majority of the message focuses on the FUTURE– solving the customer's problem.

Option #1: Repairing the Crack Yourself

To repair the crack yourself, purchase a cultured marble repair kit (typically $30 to $40). You will likely need to purchase the kit online since none of the local stores carry them. If you are willing to drive 20 miles, Jack's Hardware Shop carries the kits at a price of $44.95.

When you purchase the cultured marble repair kit, make sure to carefully match the colors to your countertop. You may need to purchase some tints to modify the color slightly.

If you choose to repair the crack yourself, I suggest that you watch a video tutorial of this process. You can find video tutorials on the websites of companies that sell these repair kits. You can also find dozens of video tutorials on YouTube.

Option #2: Scheduling a Service Visit ($75)

We would be more than happy to send someone out for a service visit. Our service technicians can repair the crack in less than an hour. As long as the crack is routine (which it is, based on your description), our repair technician would charge no additional amount for materials.

This option is a good choice if you're worried about repairing the crack yourself. Our repair technicians can repair cracks and other routine problems quickly. Your countertop would look just like the day we installed it.

I recommend the service visit option for one additional reason. The most difficult part of repairing cracks is getting an exact color match, and our service experts can do this reliably.

Please let us know if you would like a service visit. I could have someone there within one day of your request.

Best wishes,

Juan Hernandez

> Level of detail and expression of GOODWILL show CONCERN for the customer.

provides thorough, detailed options for helping this customer. Most customers would be delighted with this level of responsiveness. This message expresses goodwill. In every part of the letter, the attention to detail and expressed hope to get the countertop fixed show goodwill.

In jobs where you interact often with customers, you are unlikely to have enough time to write an original bad-news message like Juan's to each customer. However, you probably face three or four broad types of complaints. By using templates with common explanations and solutions, you can quickly tailor a message to individual situations. For example, Juan could create a template that contained two options—one for customers who might fix the products themselves and the other for customers who might want a service visit. Then he could rapidly modify various details for the individual situation.

## Delivering and Receiving Negative Performance Reviews

Nearly all professionals engage in regular performance appraisals; sometimes they are appraising others, and sometimes they are themselves being appraised. Face-to-face reviews are often among the most stressful experiences for employees and sometimes for managers. These situations are particularly stressful when the manager must deliver negative performance reviews.[20] In this section, we will first consider the appraisal from the manager's point of view and then turn to the employee who is being appraised.

**LO11.5** Deliver and receive negative performance reviews constructively.

Visit **http://connect. mheducation.com** for an exercise on this topic.

### Deliver Negative Feedback

In most performance appraisals, you are evaluating excellent or good performers. In these cases, you should focus on an overall positive message. When evaluating poor performers, however, you should be clear about the need for improvement. You can generally apply the principles we have discussed earlier in the chapter regarding delivering bad news. In addition, keep the following in mind:[21]

- *Adopt a team-centered orientation.* Even when you are evaluating a poor performer, maintain a mentality that you are working together as a team. Maintain a constructive, forward-looking tone.

- *Avoid sugarcoating the bad news.* Make sure the poor performer realizes she/he must improve (the next few sections will give tips for doing this tactfully and constructively).

- *Explain the impacts of the individual's poor performance on organizational performance.* One major goal of performance appraisals is to help poor performers understand how they are hurting organizational performance.

- *Link to consequences.* Another major goal of performance appraisals is to help employees understand how poor performance impacts their employment opportunities at the organization as well as their ability to meet their career goals.

- *Probe for reasons performance is not higher.* Ask employees to discuss their perspectives on their poor performance. Often, you will identify root causes of poor performance that will help the employee improve rapidly. You may even uncover issues that impact the organization more broadly.

- *Emphasize problem solving rather than blaming.* As much as possible, adopt a positive, forward-looking tone. You are seeking solutions that help the poor performer improve. This is good for the poor performer's career, work relationships, and morale.

- *Be firm.* Many managers want to shrink from delivering negative feedback, especially when poor performers are defensive. Remain firm that the employee must improve.

You will undoubtedly need to deliver negative performance reviews from time to time. Your overall approach to these conversations and your choice of words are important in determining how useful the reviews are. Thus, use statements that offer clear and targeted feedback, focus on actions and results rather than attitudes and intentions, and establish measurable and realistic expectations.

In the final situation from the opening case, Juan needs to give a negative performance evaluation to Jake, one of the shift supervisors. Juan does not want to harm his working relationship with Jake, and he's nervous about how Jake will react. In the next few pages, you'll find Juan's less effective and more effective approaches to talking to Jake. You'll also find abbreviated versions of the performance appraisal in Figures 11.9 and 11.10.

**FIGURE 11.9**

## Less Effective Delivery of Bad News during a Performance Review

| Conversation | Encoding/Decoding |
|---|---|
| **Juan:** Jake, did you watch last night's game?<br>**Jake:** Yeah, that was awesome . . . [talk about sports for several minutes]. | **Juan encodes:** I value you as an employee. |
| | **Jake decodes:** Juan values my positive impact here. |
| **Juan:** Well, let's get down to business. I'd like to thank you for how supportive you are of the employees. You really boost morale around here more so than anyone else . . . [continues talking about accomplishments and strengths for ten minutes]. | **Juan encodes:** You have performed poorly with shipments. I want you to improve. |
| **Juan:** One issue I want to raise for the review is that our customers have complained about several of your shipments. I think we should talk about how to avoid shipments that contain any items with defects. | **Jake decodes:** Juan is making a blanket judgment by calling me *careless*. He is overlooking all the good work I do. |
| **Jake:** I'll try to make sure that we don't have any mistakes on future orders. The other shift supervisors and I have talked about some ways of avoiding any future problems. | **Jake encodes:** You need to hold everyone responsible. |
| **Juan:** Jake, none of the other shift supervisors have had these problems—only you. I think this shows that you've been careless, and you're not really looking out for our customers. | **Juan decodes:** Jake is making excuses and blaming others. |
| **Jake:** Look, I'm sorry that there were some mistakes. But I'm not the one who packs the shipments. Those who are careless are the employees packing the shipments. | **Juan encodes:** You are the supervisor; you are responsible. |
| **Juan:** But, Jake, you're the one responsible for inspecting and approving the shipments, not the employees on your shift. Remember, every time our shipments have mistakes, it comes back on me. I have to take the fall for it with our owner. And I'm the one who has to hear the complaints from our customers. | **Jake decodes:** Juan wants me to spend my time micromanaging my employees. And, he just cares about making himself look good. |
| **Jake:** OK, well, I'll make sure the employees on my shift are more careful. | **Jake encodes:** OK, I'll watch out for problems. |
| **Juan:** We need to really focus on getting everything right from now on. I'm counting on you. Well, again, thank you for your efforts for the company and all your great work. See you later on for lunch. | **Juan decodes:** Good, Jake's gotten the message he needs to improve. |
| | **Juan encodes:** Now that you know my position, let's go to lunch. |
| The sandwich approach to delivering bad news dilutes the message and gives Jake a false sense that his performance is acceptable. Feedback and expectations are vague. | **Jake decodes:** Great. Juan is generally happy with me and my performance. |

Photos: Juan: © Purestock/Getty Images RF; Jake: © David Sacks/Digital Vision/Getty Images RF

**FIGURE 11.10**

## More Effective Delivery of Bad News during a Performance Review

**Juan:** Jake, for today's performance review, I want to focus most of our attention on one issue: making sure all your shipments contain the correct items and that they are all defect-free. We have received four complaints about your shipments in the past month. In the most serious complaint, your shipment to Carnegie Homebuilders contained 14 sinks of the wrong size. Four of those sinks were cracked or chipped. What do you think are some of the reasons for the incorrect shipments and the defective items?

**Jake:** I rely on my crew to produce defect-free items and pack the shipments. As a result, I don't actually see every shipment that goes out. Since I don't micromanage, I believe that my approach shows trust in the employees. Even though we have made a few mistakes, overall I think the working climate results in higher overall productivity.

**Juan:** I appreciate your focus on the employees, and I do think morale is high in your production crew. Ultimately, you bear responsibility for their performance, so I would like to discuss how to avoid costly shipment mistakes. The problems with the shipment to Carnegie Homebuilders cost us approximately $5,000 due to material and labor costs. I'm also concerned that they'll be less likely to choose us in the future. What are some ways you can manage your crew to avoid shipment mistakes in the future?

[Jake and Juan discuss approaches to managing the crew and improving quality for 30 minutes.]

**Juan:** Jake, for this quarter, I've given you an overall performance rating of 2, which indicates poor performance. This means that in the short term you're unlikely to receive a promotion or bonus. However, I'm confident in your ability and that of your crew to get all shipments correct . . . [Jake and Juan continue discussing the rating].

**Juan:** In our next quarterly performance review, we'll discuss how well you've done with your shipments. The standard will be to receive no complaints from customers for incorrect orders or deficient products. Also, we'll discuss your progress on the goals you've outlined for managing your production crew. Thanks, Jake, for your ideas today, and I look forward to discussing your progress during the next few weeks and months.

> Jake realizes the severity of his poor performance. Juan's open, clear, specific, and problem-solving approach is not threatening and shows his commitment to supporting Jake's improvement efforts.

**Juan encodes:** I want to focus on your ability to get shipments correct.

**Jake decodes:** Juan is serious that I need to improve my shipments.

**Jake encodes:** My management style may cause some problems, but it also results in higher morale and productivity.

**Juan decodes:** Jake is not taking responsibility for the mistakes.

**Juan encodes:** Your management style has many benefits. It's still your responsibility to make sure shipments are correct. Incorrect shipments harm the company. Let's discuss ways to manage employees and avoid mistakes.

**Jake decodes:** Juan is looking out for the best interests of the organization.

**Juan encodes:** Your overall performance was poor for this quarter. I want you and your crew to succeed.

**Jake decodes:** I need to avoid any mistakes on shipments if I'm going to get promoted. Jake will support me if I show positive results.

**Juan encodes:** This is exactly how we will evaluate your performance.

**Jake decodes:** I know what Juan wants me to do.

Photos: Juan: © Purestock/Getty Images RF; Jake: © David Sacks/Digital Vision/Getty Images RF

**Give Clear and Targeted Feedback** When providing feedback for poor performance, many managers want to soften the bad reviews so they employ the sandwich approach of good news–bad news–good news (compliment–negative feedback–niceties). However, the sandwich approach may inadvertently encourage

**TABLE 11.4**

Giving Clear and Targeted Feedback

| Less Effective | More Effective |
|---|---|
| *Juan:* Jake, as usual, I'd like to thank you for how supportive you are of the employees. You really boost morale around here more than anyone else. . . . One thing I want to raise for the review is that on several of your shipments, our customers have complained. I think we should talk about how to avoid shipments that contain any items with defects. . . . Well, again, thank you for your efforts for the company and all your great work. See you later on for lunch. | *Juan:* Jake, for today's performance review, I want to focus on one issue: making sure all your shipments contain the correct items and that they are all defect-free . . . [spends most of time discussing how to improve in this area]. |
| This sandwich approach to bad news (compliment–bad news–niceties) combined with Juan's roundabout language dilute the primary message that Jake needs to improve his performance. Juan may inadvertently send the signal that Jake's performance is not poor or that his mistakes are relatively insignificant. | This approach is clear and targeted. Jake will recognize the importance of improving in this area. |

poor performers. Instead, the review should emphasize the bad news so employees know how important it is for them to improve (see Table 11.4 for less effective and more effective examples of giving clear and targeted feedback).

**Focus on Actions and Results, Not Attitudes and Intentions**   Provide feedback only on that which is observable. You can accurately observe actions and results; however, you can never know the thoughts and feelings of others with certainty. Furthermore, if you focus on attitudes and intentions, you are far more likely to be perceived as judgmental and provoke defensiveness (see the less effective and more effective examples in Table 11.5).

**Establish Measurable and Realistic Expectations**   Negative performance reviews without measurable and realistic goals may demoralize employees. Employees who receive negative reviews generally want a clear path to regaining positive ratings; they want to be on good terms with their supervisors, and they usually take pride in doing well. Make sure to discuss how they can improve performance in specific ways. You might even set up a development plan that includes action steps, timelines, specific goals, training, and resources needed. By setting clear expectations for improvement,

**TABLE 11.5**

Focusing on Actions and Results, Not Attitudes and Intentions

| Less Effective | More Effective |
|---|---|
| *Juan:* Jake, we've gotten a number of complaints from wholesalers that your shipments are not correct. I think this shows that you've been careless, and you're not really looking out for our customers. None of the other shift supervisors have had these problems—only you. | *Juan:* Jake, we have received four complaints about your shipments in the past month. In the most serious complaint, your shipment to Carnegie Homebuilders contained 14 sinks of the wrong size. The invoice you placed in the shipment did show the correct order, however. In addition, four of the sinks you shipped were cracked or chipped. |
| This critique focuses exclusively on characteristics of Jake—carelessness and inattentiveness. | This critique focuses on Jake's actions and the results of those actions. These comments are less likely to provoke defensiveness or a counterproductive response from Jake. |

**TABLE 11.6**

Establishing Measurable Expectations

| Less Effective | More Effective |
|---|---|
| *Juan:* Jake, we need to really focus on getting everything right from now on. I know you and your crew will do great and turn things around for our next performance review. | *Juan:* Jake, in our next quarterly performance review, we'll discuss how well you've done with your shipments. The standard will be to receive no complaints from customers for incorrect orders or for deficient products. Also, we'll discuss your progress on the goals you've outlined for managing your production crew. Thanks, Jake, for your ideas today, and I look forward to discussing your progress during the next few weeks and months. |
| This closing statement is vague. Jake does not know the standard by which Juan will evaluate him for the next performance review. | This closing statement is specific and measurable. Jake knows the standards by which Juan will evaluate him for the next performance review. |

you lay the groundwork for accountability later on (see Table 11.6 for less effective and more effective examples).

Increasingly, companies provide options for all or part of performance reviews to be conducted online. Typically, these online reviews allow you to give more frequent feedback to your employees. Read the Technology Tips box later in this section for guidelines on delivering feedback with these systems.

## Receive Negative Feedback

In nearly all business positions, from entry-level to executive, you will have many opportunities to get feedback about your performance and potential. Seeking and receiving feedback, even when it's negative, will help you develop the skills you need to make an impact in the workplace and move into new positions. To accept negative feedback and respond to it well requires high emotional intelligence, since you may feel many emotions, including fear, anxiety, and perhaps even anger. To avoid counterproductive responses to negative emotions, learn to recognize and name these emotions. Then develop a reframing statement to respond more effectively. See Table 11.7 for ideas about reframing statements.[22]

**TABLE 11.7**

Reframing Your Thoughts to Initiate Feedback Conversations

| Possible Negative Emotion | Counterproductive Response | Reframing Statement |
|---|---|---|
| Anger (*I'm mad at my boss because she doesn't pay attention to my work.*) | Acting out (complaining, showing irritability) | It's my responsibility to get feedback and guidance from my boss. |
| Anxiety (*I don't know what to expect.*) | Avoiding (*I'm too busy to get feedback.*) | Getting feedback can provide me with opportunities. |
| Defensiveness (*My boss doesn't know what he's talking about.*) | Not supporting the boss (*I'm not going to make him look good.*) | Being defensive prevents me from knowing what he thinks. |
| Fear of Reprisal (*I don't want to do this.*) | Denial (*I'm doing fine so I don't need feedback.*) | Getting an honest assessment of my work will help me. |
| Fear of Personal Rejection (*I'm worried she doesn't like me.*) | Withdrawal (being quieter than usual, feeling demotivated) | My performance on the job isn't related to whether she likes me. |

# TECHNOLOGY TIPS

## PROVIDING PERFORMANCE FEEDBACK WITH APPRAISAL SOFTWARE

Most companies require performance reviews—some monthly, some quarterly, some annually—for all employees. Some innovative companies are now doing real-time performance reviews with social software. The social software allows supervisors and their employees to more regularly and interactively review employee performance. When you are in a supervisory position, you will be responsible for providing both positive and negative feedback to employees. Increasingly, you will provide this feedback with the use of appraisal software of some form.

As you provide feedback in online appraisal systems, keep in mind the following tips:

*Provide regular and frequent feedback.* One major benefit of appraisal software, particularly platforms that include social software, is that you can efficiently give your employees more feedback so they can increase performance. Establishing a regular pattern of feedback can increase your employees' motivation and performance.

*Prepare your feedback carefully.* Most appraisal software allows you to directly enter your comments into fields in a database. Once you enter the information, it is available to the employees and other managers. So, prepare your comments carefully. Consider drafting your comments in a word processing program first. If you're delivering negative feedback, you may first want to draft the feedback, wait a few hours or a few days, and then review your comments to ensure they are accurate and productive. Also, if you are giving negative feedback, first notify your employee in person. Use the moment to establish goals for improvement. Avoid blindsiding your employees by entering negative feedback in the performance database without first talking to them about it.

*Keep your feedback objective and personal.* Some employees feel that receiving feedback via appraisal software is too automated and impersonal. This is especially likely when the software is mostly composed of quantifiable and standard metrics that are used for all employees. These metrics do help provide consistency in feedback across the organization, but they lead some employees to "feel like a number." However your company's evaluation software is set up, find ways to provide more nuanced and open-ended feedback to recognize your employees' unique achievements. Make sure to include a shared, open-ended, goal-oriented, and positive discussion that keeps your employees motivated and productive.

*Set up a face-to-face meeting as soon as possible if you detect hard feelings.* Even in a social software environment that allows more interaction than do Web 1.0 communication tools, some employees may become discouraged with negative feedback or feel that feedback is not fair. Stay alert to such situations. When you notice this, set up a time to meet in person so that you can use a richer communication channel to reestablish rapport and reenergize your employees to focus on work goals.

# Reviewing Bad-News Messages

**LO11.6** Review bad-news messages for effectiveness and fairness.

The reviewing stage of bad-news messages is extremely important. Bad news involves unpleasant impacts on others, so you should carefully consider whether you are handling the situation appropriately. Also, since recipients can easily take bad news the wrong way and feel disappointed or angry, make sure to review your written and oral messages carefully so you can deliver the news respectfully.

## Get Feedback and Reread

When writing bad-news messages, always reread them several times. Place yourself in the position of the recipients so you can try to imagine how they may feel and react. An extra 10 to 30 minutes of proofreading can lead to constructive work together in the future and avoid time lost resolving an unnecessarily escalated difference. Also, if the message does not need to be delivered immediately, consider writing it, waiting a few hours or days, and then rereading it. Often, you will find that your strong emotions, such as anxiety and nervousness, affected the tone of the original message. When you deliver a bad-news message in person, you have less control. Yet, you can still prepare your intended message (mentally or in note form) and review it as you would a written bad-news message.

In some situations, consider asking trusted colleagues to review your message and give feedback. They may be able to give you a neutral and objective view of the situation. Generally, it is appropriate to talk to colleagues about bad-news messages that

**FIGURE 11.11**

## Are Your Bad-News Messages FAIR?

**Facts** (How *factual* is your communication?)
- Have I gathered all the relevant facts? Have I examined various accounts of the same events?
- Is my perspective of the facts influenced by defensiveness, favoritism, or some other bias?
- Is the rationale for this bad news based on sound facts and conclusions?

**Access** (How *accessible* or *transparent* are your motives, reasoning, and information?)
- Are my motives clear, or will others perceive that I have a hidden agenda?
- Is it clear how the decision was made?
- Am I giving enough information to bad-news recipients for them to respond well?
- Am I hiding any information that casts me in a better light or concealing the real reasons for the bad news?

**Impacts** (How does your communication *impact* stakeholders?)
- Have I considered all the ways in which this message will impact others in the near term and long term?
- What have I done to lessen the negative impacts on recipients?
- Am I doing what I can to provide opportunities—as appropriate—to the bad-news recipients?

**Respect** (How *respectful* is your communication?)
- Would recipients consider my communication respectful?
- Have I stated the message in a way that recognizes the inherent worth of others?

you plan to deliver to groups of customers or employees. However, it is not appropriate to ask others to read messages that include confidential matters. For example, negative feedback for an individual employee should typically be private.

## Apply the FAIR Test

For all bad news, spend time reflecting on each component of the FAIR test before delivering the message. Since bad-news messages impact others in undesirable ways, take the time to make sure you have been as fair as possible. Read through some of the questions you might ask yourself in Figure 11.11. Also, consider the thoughts of James Sloan, the business professional featured in the Communication Q&A.

 **COMMUNICATION Q&A**

**CONVERSATIONS WITH CURRENT BUSINESS PROFESSIONALS**

**Pete Cardon: How often do you have to give bad news to others? What types of bad news?**

**James Sloan:** Unfortunately, as the CFO, I often have to give bad news. The bad news I typically have to share is that certain business processes are not functioning as expected or are out of compliance with company policies or outside regulations. Occasionally, the news may include information related to an investigation of fraud or a violation with our company code of conduct. Furthermore, as a manager, I need to help my staff improve, and that includes being honest about poor performance or identifying areas of improvement.

**PC: Can you describe a situation when you delivered bad news in person? How did you go about it?**

**JS:** I think it is always best to deliver bad news in person. It allows for better interaction, a more thorough discussion, and information gleaned from body language. The receiver has less opportunity to read more into the underlying issue or to take things too personally, as we often tend to do.

Probably, the most difficult experiences I have had were related to terminating employees. On one occasion, I had to fly into Chicago and lay off several of my data-center managers and staff. Some had worked for the company for their entire careers. It was difficult and emotional. I made sure I was calm and honest but not overly emotional even though I could feel how devastating it was for some of them. I tried to be prepared to answer any question I thought they would ask, but there were a few I could not answer. So, I committed to get back to them. I tried to be positive and help them see beyond the moment. It did not always work, but I tried.

**PC: Can you describe a situation when you delivered bad news in writing? How did you go about it?**

**JS:** I had a manager who worked for me, based in Europe. He was a solid performer but did not like administrative tasks. This individual aspired to replace me, but the higher you move up within an organization, the more administrative your tasks tend to be. After several informal discussions related to certain administrative tasks, and after I allowed a period of time for change, I saw little improvement. I finally resorted to email that I intentionally sent on a Friday so he would have the entire weekend to digest what I had to say. The email addressed the topics we had discussed previously, with specific examples of dates when something was requested and when it was delivered or not. I made sure my facts were accurate and specific. I detailed the reasons for the tasks and further explained that while I fully supported him moving up in the organization, I could not honestly recommend him until he improved in this area. The email was honest and straightforward, and it upset him. However, over the weekend, he calmed down, and we had a good conversation on Monday. His performance improved; but, it is an area in which he will always struggle.

**PC: What are some guidelines for choosing which communication channels to use?**

**JS:** Dole is a worldwide organization that operates in 90 countries. Face-to-face communication is not always feasible, nor is speaking on the phone always convenient given all the time zones. My preferred order of communicating bad news is face-to-face, phone, and then email. However, I always follow up an email with a face-to-face meeting or a phone call.

**PC: Why would you prefer email over a videoconference or webcast?**

**JS:** Timeliness of communicating bad news is often critical. Setting up a video conference often takes a lot of coordination and would result in a delay. Sometimes an email is the best way to initially communicate bad news. It is fast and provides the receiver an opportunity to read the information, digest it, and many times calm down enough to have a rational conversation about it. An email should always be followed up with a face-to-face meeting or a phone call. I feel a web conference is better for training or conducting online meetings than for communicating bad news.

**PC: What happens in the workplace when people delay giving bad news?**

**JS:** No one wants to be surprised with bad news. I find it best to communicate information as soon as I have it. Sometimes people hide the bad news, hoping it will go away, or they delay communicating it in the hopes it will get resolved. I have never seen any good that comes from delaying giving bad news.

**PC: Can delivering bad news strengthen your work relationships or enhance your credibility? Do you have any examples?**

**JS:** Absolutely! In order to have credibility, your colleagues need to know they can trust you. Part of acquiring trust is being honest. Honesty requires communicating the good and the bad equally. It is our human nature to want to be more positive and complimentary. We will give others a false sense of security and we will fail them by not helping them know areas where they can improve. We are doing a disservice to our colleagues by not helping them to be better.

**PC: For young professionals, what concluding advice would you give for delivering bad news?**

**JS:** Be positive, but be honest. Both qualities will take you far in any career. Whenever delivering bad news, make sure you are open about what the issue is and provide advice or guidance on how to improve the situation. Then, people will see that your goals are truly in their best interest and you are not simply one who points out faults just to bring others down. None of us is perfect, and if we are honest with ourselves and others, we can all improve together.

*James Sloan is the chief financial officer (CFO) at Swire Coca-Cola, USA and is president of Monkey Mountaineering USA, Inc. He is a CPA and has held various financial and IT related roles over the course of his career, including CFO positions at Dole Fresh Vegetables and Modere Inc. His career has included key roles at AT&T, Worthington Industries, Inc., and Dole Food Company, Inc. He also serves on the board of directors for CONA Services LLC and is on the Advisory Council for Humanitarian Experience for Youth.*

Courtesy of James Sloan

# Chapter Takeaway for *Bad-News Messages*

**LO11.1 Describe how delivering bad news impacts your credibility. (pp. 337–338)**

Delivering effective bad-news messages improves your **reputation for personal credibility.**

| | | |
|---|---|---|
| It shows **competence** when you generate a forward-looking plan to overcome challenges. | It shows **caring** when you lessen the negative impacts on others and focus on their needs. | It shows **character** when you are completely transparent and honest. |

**LO11.2 Explain considerations for deciding which channels to use when delivering bad-news messages. (pp. 338–339)**

| Guidelines for Choosing the Right Communication Channel for Bad-News Messages | | |
|---|---|---|
| • **Advantages of oral communication:** can use and observe nonverbal cues; can more easily demonstrate intentions; can more effectively clarify and explain the bad news; can respond to concerns immediately. | • **Advantages of written communication:** can craft message more carefully; can document the message more easily; can provide a message that serves as a reference (provide directions, suggestions, and options for future actions); can deliver message to more people more efficiently. | • When a bad-news message is more severe, more likely, and/or less controllable, **choose richer communication channels when possible.** |

**LO11.3 Summarize principles for effectively delivering bad-news messages. (pp. 340–343)**

**Audience Analysis:** Understand how the bad news will impact others and think carefully about how best to convey it.

**Information Gathering:** Get your facts straight and understand competing versions of events before delivering the bad news.

**Message Development:** Deliver the bad news in a productive manner. Ease into the bad news but avoid sugarcoating it.

| Guidelines for Bad-News Messages | | |
|---|---|---|
| • Deliver the bad news in a timely manner.<br>• Choose the right mix of channels. | • Sympathize with the bad-news recipients and soften the blow.<br>• Provide a simple, clear rationale. | • Explain immediate impacts.<br>• Focus on solutions and long-term benefits.<br>• Show goodwill. |

**LO11.4 Compose effective bad-news messages in person and in writing for various audiences, including colleagues, external partners, and customers. (pp. 343–351)**

| Components of *Indirect* Bad-News Messages | | Components of *Direct* Bad-News Messages | |
|---|---|---|---|
| Show CONCERN. | | Show CONCERN. | |
| • Ease in with a buffer.<br>• **Provide a rationale.**<br>• **Deliver the bad news.** | • Explain impacts.<br>• Focus on the future (as appropriate).<br>• Show goodwill. | • Ease in with a buffer.<br>• **Deliver the bad news.**<br>• **Provide a rationale.** | • Explain impacts.<br>• Focus on the future (as appropriate).<br>• Show goodwill. |

See *examples of bad-news messages* in Figures 11.1 through 11.8.

**LO11.5 Deliver and receive negative performance reviews constructively. (pp. 351–356)**

| **Principles for Delivering Negative Performance Reviews** | | **Style for Delivering Negative Performance Reviews** |
|---|---|---|
| • Adopt a team-centered orientation.<br>• Avoid sugarcoating the bad news.<br>• Explain the impacts of the individual's poor performance on organizational performance. | • Link to consequences.<br>• Probe for reasons performance is not higher.<br>• Emphasize problem solving rather than blaming.<br>• Be firm. | • Give clear and targeted feedback.<br>• Focus on actions and results, not attitudes and intentions.<br>• Establish measurable and realistic expectations. |

See *examples of delivering negative performance reviews* in Figures 11.9 and 11.10.

**LO11.6 Review bad-news messages for effectiveness and fairness. (pp. 356–358)**

**Feedback**: Ask several trusted colleagues who can empathize with the bad-news recipients to review your message.

**FAIR Test**: Pay particular attention to the *Impacts* of the bad news on others and how to express it with *respect*.

**Proofreading**: Reread your message several times slowly, imagining how your message recipients will feel and respond.

# Key Terms

# Discussion Exercises

**11.1 Chapter Review Questions** (LO11.1, LO11.2, LO11.3, LO11.6)

A. Describe reasons for hesitancy in delivering bad news and the impact of the mum effect.

B. Explain how delivering bad-news messages impacts credibility.

C. Describe the criteria for evaluating bad-news messages in terms of controllability, likelihood, and severity.

D. Explain considerations for deciding which channels to use when delivering bad-news messages.

E. Summarize principles for effectively delivering bad-news messages.

**11.2 Key Terms** (LO11.1, LO11.2, LO11.3, LO11.6)

Explain each key term and how it would impact a specific business communication situation.

**11.3 Communication Q&A Discussion Questions** (LO11.1, LO11.2, LO11.3, LO11.6)

Read James Sloan's thoughts about delivering bad news. Respond to the following questions.

A. According to Sloan, what are some principles for choosing an appropriate communication channel when delivering bad news?

B. How does he explain the relationship between delivering bad news and credibility?

C. He describes an experience when he had to deliver bad news in person. What approach did he take? Do you think this is an appropriate way to deliver bad news? Explain.

D. Sloan describes an experience when he had to deliver bad news in writing. What approach did he take? Do you think this is an appropriate way to deliver bad news? Explain.

E. What does he say about the timeliness of delivering bad news?

F. He mentions several times that one should be positive when delivering bad news. Explain how you think people can deliver bad news and be positive at the same time.

# Evaluation Exercises

**11.4 Analyzing a Bad-News Message from Microsoft executive vice president Stephen Elop to Employees** (LO11.3, LO11.6)

In 2014, Stephen Elop of Microsoft announced layoffs of 12,500 employees. Read his email to employees: https://news.microsoft.com/2014/07/17/stephen-elops-email-to-employees/. Then, answer the following questions:

A. Is the bad news delivered immediately? Do you think it is delivered too directly? Too indirectly? Explain.

B. Is there a buffer? Is there an attempt to soften the blow? Explain.

C. How effective is the opening paragraph?

D. How effectively does the message explain immediate impacts?

E. Is the tone appropriate?

F. Conduct a FAIR test of the message.

G. Overall, what three changes would you suggest to make the bad-news message more effective?

**11.5 Analyzing a Bad-News Message Delivered to You** (LO11.3, LO11.6)

Describe a bad-news message you received in the workplace or at school. Evaluate the message in the following ways:

A. Was the bad news delivered in a timely manner? Do you think it was delivered too directly? Too indirectly? Explain.

B. Was there a buffer? Was there an attempt to soften the blow? Explain.

C. Were you told of or did you discuss immediate impacts?

D. Was the tone appropriate?

E. Was the delivery of bad news to you FAIR?

F. Overall, what three changes would have made the delivery of the bad news more effective?

**11.6 Assess Your Ability to Deliver Bad News** (LO11.1, LO11.2, LO11.3, LO11.6)

Evaluate yourself with regard to each of the practices listed in the table below. Circle the appropriate number for each.

| | 1 – Rarely/Never | 2 – Sometimes | 3 – Usually | 4 – Always |
|---|---|---|---|---|
| When I need to pass on bad news, I avoid it as long as possible. | 1 | 2 | 3 | 4 |
| I have a hard time breaking bad news. | 1 | 2 | 3 | 4 |
| When I break bad news, I understate how bad it really is. | 1 | 2 | 3 | 4 |
| When I pass on bad news, I use texts, emails, or other non-face-to-face messages to avoid conflict or uncomfortable situations. | 1 | 2 | 3 | 4 |
| When I share unpleasant news, I say as little as possible and expect others to read between the lines. | 1 | 2 | 3 | 4 |

Add up your score and consider the following advice:

16–20: You are *conflict avoidant.* You usually avoid delivering bad news because you feel uncomfortable doing so. When you break bad news, you understate it. You generally have good intentions, but sometimes you make matters worse by not confronting uncomfortable situations. Try thinking about the benefits to you and the bad-news recipients when delivering bad news right away.

12–15: You are *somewhat conflict avoidant.* You often avoid unpleasant conversations and communications. Sometimes, you prefer to leave issues unresolved rather than risk the uncomfortable interactions to address these issues.

10–11:   You *sometimes confront bad news in a timely manner*. In many situations, you confront uncomfortable situations right away, yet you shy away from doing so in other cases.

Under 10:   You *usually confront bad news in a timely manner*. You confront bad news and difficult situations immediately and with sensitivity.

Write three goals you have for constructively delivering bad news in the workplace.

### 11.7 Assess Your Prior Experiences Delivering Bad News (LO11.1, LO11.2, LO11.3)

Briefly describe your own experiences delivering bad news in the following ways:

A. Delivering it too late and negatively affecting the bad-news recipient more than you intended.

B. Delivering it right away and creating the best possible outcomes for all involved.

C. Delivering it using a communication channel that wasn't appropriate.

D. Delivering it using a communication channel that was appropriate.

E. Not telling the whole truth.

Based on these experiences, write three principles for delivering bad news that you will live by in the workplace. Elaborate on each with one paragraph.

### 11.8 Assess Token Appreciation (LO11.4)

Over the course of one week, keep a journal about token appreciation. Focus on situations where people may hold differences of opinion. Think about various ways in which people use *yes-but* statements. As you write, feel free to use pseudonyms or non-identifying information. Each day, describe the following:

A. What's an example of token appreciation you heard someone else say? Why do you think it was token appreciation? How might this person have addressed this situation more honestly and constructively?

B. What's an example of token appreciation that you engaged in? What were your intentions? Could you have approached this situation more honestly and constructively? How?

At the end of the journal, describe what you learned by assessing token appreciation over the course of a week. List three principles that you think would help people avoid token appreciation and more meaningfully manage differences of opinion.

# Application Exercises

### Case for Problems 11.9 through 11.11: Bad News at Jensen Chemicals and Hardware Depot

Juan Hernandez for many years had worked with Jensen Chemicals to supply plastic resins. However, Juan had recently accepted a bid from another supplier. Juan sent the following message to Nick Jensen:

*Hi Nick:*

*Thank you for submitting your competitive bid to supply and deliver plastic resins for the upcoming year.*

*We reviewed the bids with three chief criteria in mind: price, delivery schedule, and inventory management.*

*We have accepted Hunter Chemical's bid to supply and deliver plastic resins for the upcoming year. Hunter Chemicals offered us slightly better pricing. Also, we were impressed with Hunter Chemical's ability to deliver product on shorter notice and link their online order system directly to our online inventory system.*

*Nick, we have always appreciated the dependable service your company has provided. We will continue purchasing lumber supplies from you, and I will notify you next year when we are ready to accept bids again for chemical supplies.*

*Best wishes, Juan*

Nick Jensen shook his head in frustration as he read Juan Hernandez's email notifying him that his company had lost the bid to supply chemicals to Marble Home Makeovers for the upcoming year. He'd had a hunch that his uncle's store, Jensen Chemicals and Hardware Depot, would not get the bid. However, it was still disappointing, and he was worried that unless the store changed its business model, it would be out of business within five years. The store had lost nearly 30 percent of its business in supplying chemicals in the past two years. It simply couldn't compete with larger regional companies.

Nick knew he needed to talk to his uncle, Mike Jensen, the owner. Mike owned five businesses but no longer got involved much in managing them. He spent about half of his time on vacations. Nick thought he should email Uncle Mike and tell him what he considered ominous signs for his company. He might recommend that they sell this portion of the business to a larger chemical manufacturer and supplier, and get out of chemicals altogether. They would probably take a loss to do so, but selling now could also help them cut their losses. Nick knew his uncle loved having a stake in chemicals. He was also embarrassed that while Mike had entrusted him with a management position, the chemical portion of the business was performing so poorly. The good news, however, was that business-to-business hardware sales were in great shape.

Nick dreaded several other pieces of bad news he needed to deliver right away. Over a decade ago, during their most profitable years, management at Jensen Chemicals and Hardware Depot had implemented many benefits. One program allowed employees to be reimbursed for their tuition for up to two classes per semester if they received grades of a B or higher. Currently, 20 employees consistently took advantage of the program. Nick needed to inform all employees that the program would be discontinued immediately, as it cost the company too much. Employees currently enrolled could be reimbursed for courses during the present semester. Employees who had fewer than four courses left to receive an undergraduate degree would continue receiving reimbursement until they graduated. This included just three employees.

Finally, Nick needed to inform customers that the Jensen Chemicals and Hardware Depot Elite Customers program would be discontinued after the current rewards cycle. Under the program, customers who spent more than $1,000 in a calendar year automatically qualified for a 10 percent discount on all purchases in the following year. The program had been quite popular, and Nick knew that many customers would be upset. However, he had done the math and felt it was a money loser for the company. To soften the disappointment to customers, in letters to all previous Elite Customers, he was including a 20 percent discount coupon on any single purchase. In addition, customers could still reach Elite Customer status for this year and qualify for discounts next year.

### 11.9 Writing a Bad-News Message about Jensen Chemicals and Hardware Depot (LO11.4)

Assume the role of Nick and write an email to your uncle explaining why you think the company needs to get out of chemicals. You think the chemicals division could be sold for around half a million dollars. You currently have about $740,000 in debt related to the chemicals division. You would need to lay off ten employees, all of whom have been loyal to the company for many years. However, you think it's necessary because the chemical division lost nearly $200,000 last year, and you expect things to get worse.

### 11.10 Writing a Bad-News Message about Elimination of Tuition-Reimbursement Program (LO11.4)

Assume the role of Nick and write a bad-news announcement to all employees explaining the elimination of the tuition-reimbursement program. Explain that the company has lost money in three of the four prior years and that you need to take actions to make the company profitable again.

### 11.11 Writing a Bad-News Message about Elimination of Elite Customer Program (LO11.4)

Assume the role of Nick and write a bad-news announcement to all former Elite Customers explaining the elimination of the program.

### 11.12 Rewriting a Corporate Bad-News Message (LO11.4)

In 2014, Stephen Elop of Microsoft announced layoffs of 12,500 employees. Read his email to employees—https://news.microsoft.com/2014/07/17/stephen-elops-email-to-employees/—and then rewrite it to make it more effective.

### 11.13 Message Do-Over for a Bad-News Message to a Colleague (LO11.4)

Recently, Samantha Parkinson, a marketing intern, sent a message to Bianca Genova, her boss, about changing the pricing model for a social networking platform (see Exercise 10.17 for background). Bianca was upset when she read Samantha's message. She thought Samantha's ideas were poorly developed. She also thought the message was disrespectful and unappreciative. She sent the message below:

*SUBJECT: Re: Changing our Pricing Model*

*Samantha,*

*LinkedB2B is not LinkedIn. Period.*

*We are a premier social networking service for professionals. We focus on B2B networking. Our competitive advantage is that we are not LinkedIn. We are far more valuable to our members than*

*LinkedIn. THAT IS WHY WE CHARGE FOR ALL MEMBERS. As soon as we reduce our service to a free service, we lose our advantage. Furthermore, we send the message that anyone can join. Quite frankly, we only want professionals who are serious about networking to join. As soon as we open the service up to anyone willing to create a username and a password, then our loyal members will recognize that most of the members are no longer as valuable as contacts.*

*Please avoid spending any time developing your own ideas. We've set up a variety of activities for you to work on—identifying prospects to contact directly about our service, developing content to help in B2B relationship-building, and contacting professionals who have failed to renew their memberships. This is all we want you to do. You've done a fine job at this so far, and we want you to DEVOTE ALL OF YOUR ENERGIES TO YOUR JOB DESCRIPTION.*

*Best,*

*Bianca*

Complete the following tasks:

A. Evaluate the effectiveness of Bianca's message.
B. Rewrite the message to improve it. Feel free to reasonably embellish the message as directed by your instructor.

### 11.14 Message Do-Over for a Bad-News Message to a Professional Contact (LO11.4)

Bianca Genova has worked hard to make networking events for LinkedB2B more attractive to members (see Exercises 10.17, 10.18, and 11.13 for background). She developed a speaker series as one strategy to attract members to attend the events. Several months ago, she invited a prominent author and speaker, Madison Avery, to an event on September 4. On August 21, Madison sent the following note:

*SUBJECT: Speaking Cancellation*

*Dear Bianca,*

*I regret to inform you that I cannot speak at your September 4 networking event. I will return the $2,000 advance that you sent me.*

*In the past month, I have suffered some health issues. I anticipated recovering more quickly. My doctor has advised that I avoid all travel for several months to avoid some of these problems. On top of that, my father-in-law died two weeks ago. As a result, I've spent most of my time attempting to help my husband deal with this tragic time. I appreciate your understanding.*

*Madison*

At this time, 179 professionals have signed up for the event. Bianca needs to write a message to all professionals who have RSVP'd and paid for the event. She will explain that she will find a fill-in speaker on the same topic and she will offer refunds to any person who no longer wants to attend the event.

Complete the following tasks:

A. Evaluate how well Madison delivers bad news.
B. Rewrite Madison's note to more effectively deliver bad news.
C. Assume the role of Samantha and write a message to members that delivers the bad news and also helps promote the networking event even in the absence of Madison as a speaker.

### 11.15 Notifying Guests That the Rewards Program Will Be Downgraded (LO11.4)

Nancy Jeffreys, director of marketing, just met with Andrea Garcia, the general manager. Nancy showed Andrea how several of the Prestigio's marketing programs and campaigns did not seem to be paying off. Regarding the rewards program she commented, "I think we should lower rewards for several reasons. During the past two years since introducing the program, we've tracked the behavior of our guests. I compared guests who've been coming here for at least the past four years. After starting the rewards program, these guests did stay more days each year, probably because they could use their rewards points. However, altogether they paid for fewer nights. I estimate that we lose nearly $14,000 per year giving these guests perks that don't justify the expense. Also, our rewards program is currently far more generous than any of our local or national competitors. We should fall in line with their rewards programs to ensure we're maximizing revenue."

Andrea considered Nancy's reasoning fairly compelling and thorough. She asked, "What do you recommend?" Nancy responded, "I definitely think we need to increase the number of rewards points (or Prestigio Points) needed to get a free night from 9,000 to 15,000 for most hotel rooms. Generally, that means a guest would need to pay for five nights at the hotel to get a free night. In the past, it would have required about three nights. Also, the current policy is that rewards points never expire. I think we should change the policy so that rewards points expire in two years in the absence of purchase activity at the Prestigio."

Andrea responded, "Well, those seem like reasonable changes. What about our affiliation with the Galaxy Hotel Alliance?" Nancy answered, "I think we should get out of this alliance. It was a good idea originally, since guests could choose to have their points redeemed at roughly 100 hotels nationwide that were part of this alliance. But, it costs us a lot to be part of this alliance, and I don't think we're seeing any returns."

Andrea agreed that these changes made sense. She asked Nancy whether guests in the rewards program should be notified of all these changes and how they should be notified.

Nancy stated, "I think we should be open about this and tell all our guests about these changes. Every major hotel chain has made similar changes recently, so we're in line with industry changes. It's true that most major hotel chains have not gone out of their way to tell guests that reward points are no longer as valuable, but I think we're more likely to garner dissatisfaction from guests when they find out we tried to sneak these changes through without telling them."

Andrea said, "Okay, let's move forward with these changes. One more question. We've got regular members and Elite status members. We've traditionally given Elite status members free Wi-Fi access, free access to the Prestige Lounge (a club on the second floor with free snacks, drinks, and other amenities), and free in-room snacks. Do you think this makes sense?"

Nancy replied, "I'm glad you brought this up. We've done some analysis on this and paid attention to what some other hotel chains are doing. We recommend now providing these services and amenities at 50 percent discounts."

"Great," said Andrea. "By the way, do you think there's anything positive we can include in the message?"

"Definitely," said Nancy. "We could point out many of the improvements in our business lounge, which has new computer terminals, free Wi-Fi, a mini-bar, and other services. Also, we could mention many of our August specials, including weekend getaways for rooms at just $119 per night."

"Thanks for all your analysis of the rewards programs and the changes we need to make," said Andrea. "Go ahead and contact our rewards members as soon as you're ready."

YOUR TASK: Assume the role of Nancy. Write a message to Elite status members notifying them of changes to the rewards program. You can assume that the changes will take place three months from now.

# Language Mechanics Check

### 11.16 Review all rules in Appendix A about punctuation, number usage, and grammar. Then, rewrite each sentence to make all needed corrections.

A. If you go to just about any companies website you'll find many references to corporate social responsibility, or CSR for short.

B. In fact many companies have dedicate entire sections on they're websites to CSR. They even publish CSR reports under names such as Giving Back, Sharing the Wealth, and Citizenship Report.

C. The reality however, is corporate giving to charity are far less than it was twenty years ago.

D. In 1986 the average company donated 2.1% of it's profits to charity.

E. Now the average company donates around .8% of it's profits to charity.

F. Some of the most profitable and most well known companies in the technology sector gives less than .5% of its profits.

G. Some companies are extremely generous yet do not give much to local, communities.

H. For example Google gives roughly 8% of its profits to charity.

I. Yet almost none of this money goes to communities in cities near their corporate headquarters.

J. Unless companies can increase charitable giving to these local communities their efforts to promote their CSR activities will come across as insincere.

# Endnotes

1. Ed Frauenheim, "Over HR: Is It Time to Get Out?" *Workforce Management,* January 22, 2009: 22.

2. "Comment on Breaking Bad News," *New Zealand Management* 55, no. 9 (2008): 16.

3. McGraw Wentworth, "Tips on Delivering Bad News," *The ViewsLetter* 12, no. 2 (2009): 1–4.

4. Dave Zielinski, "Crisis Presenting: How to Deliver Bad News," *Presentations,* February 1, 2001.

5. Siegel+Gale, *Turning Bad News into Good Vibes* (New York: Author, 2009): 1.

6. Lauren Dixon, "Good Practices for Delivering Bad News," April 13, 2010, retrieved July 20, 2010 from http://webatsimon.com/ good-practices-for-delivering-bad-news/; "Comment on Breaking Bad News."

7. McGraw Wentworth, "Tips on Delivering Bad News."

8. Kate Sweeny and James A. Shepperd, "Being the Best Bearer of Bad Tidings," *Review of General Psychology* 11, no. 3 (2007): 235–257.

9. "Does It Matter How Your Boss Delivers Bad News to Employees?" retrieved July 25, 2010, from www.a2ethics.org/ node/246.

10. Dixon, Lauren, "Good Practices for Delivering Bad News," *Women Entrepreneurs Blog* (April 13, 2010), available at http:// webatsimon.com/good-practices-for-delivering-bad-news/.

11. Siegel+Gale, *Turning Bad News into Good Vibes*: 4.

12. Dixon, "Good Practices for Delivering Bad News."

13. Michael Maslansky, *The Language of Trust* (New York: Prentice Hall, 2010).

14. Michelle Gielan, "You Can Deliver Bad News to Your Team Without Crushing Them," *Harvard Business Review* blog, March 21, 2016, available at https://hbr.org/2016/03/ you-can-deliver-bad-news-to-your-team-without-crushing-them.

15. McGraw Wentworth, "Tips on Delivering Bad News"; Sherry Law, "How to Soften Blow When You Have to Give Bad News," *Denver Business Journal,* August 18, 2006.

16. Daniel Goleman, Richard Boyatzis, and Annie McKee, "Realizing the Power of Emotional Intelligence: Primal Leadership," *Harvard Business Review,* December 2001: 42–51.

17. ChongWoo Park, Ghiyoung Im, and Mark Keil, "Overcoming the Mum Effect in IT Project Reporting: Impacts of Fault Responsibility and Time Urgency," *Journal of the Association for Information Systems* 9, no. 7 (2008): Article 17; A. Tesser and S. Rosen, "The Reluctance to Transmit Bad News," *Advances in Experimental Social Psychology* 8 (1975): 193–232.

18. PRWeb, "Only One-Third of Companies Give Employees Bad News Face-to-Face—IABC Study," January 20, 2006, retrieved July 20, 2010, from www.jobbankusa.com/news/business_human_ resources/companies_give_employees_bad_news.html.

19. McGraw Wentworth, "Tips on Delivering Bad News."

20. Rebecca Knight, "Delivering an Effective Performance Review," *Harvard Business Review blog,* November 3, 2011.

21. Knight, "Delivering an Effective Performance Review"; Kathleen Jordan, *Performance Appraisal: The Basics* (Boston: Harvard Business Press, 2009); Brian Cole Miller, *Keeping Employees Accountable for Results* (New York: American Management Association, 2006).

22. Adapted from table in Jay M. Jackman and Myra H. Strober, "Fear of Feedback," *Harvard Business Review,* April 2003: 101–107.

# Reports and Presentations

# PART

# FIVE

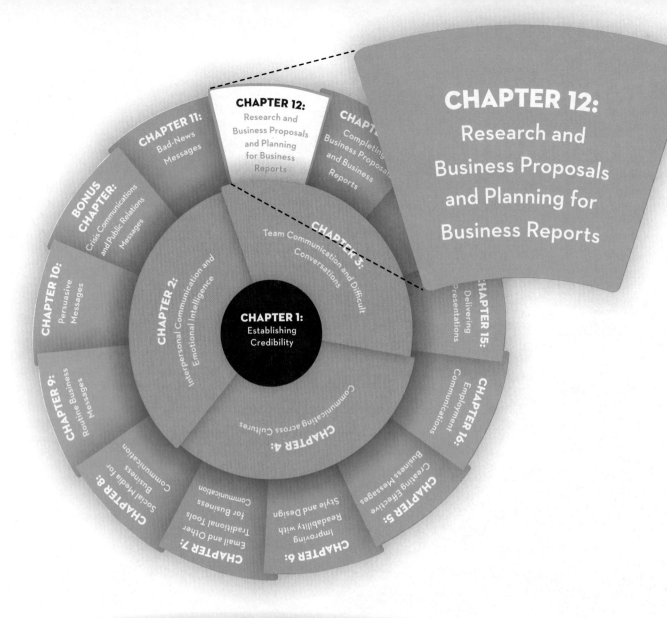

# CHAPTER 12:
## Research and Business Proposals and Planning for Business Reports

 **ESTABLISHING CREDIBILITY**

 **PRINCIPLES OF INTERPERSONAL COMMUNICATION**

 **PRINCIPLES FOR & TYPES OF BUSINESS MESSAGES**

---

## Learning Objectives

After studying this chapter, you should be able to do the following:

**LO12.1** Explain how planning and conducting business research for reports impacts your credibility.

**LO12.2** Create research objectives that are specific and achievable.

**LO12.3** Explain principles of effective design for survey questions and choices.

**LO12.4** Develop charts and tables to concisely display data and accentuate key messages.

**LO12.5** Evaluate the usefulness of data sources for business research.

**LO12.6** Conduct secondary research to address a business problem.

**LO12.7** Evaluate research data, charts, and tables for fairness and effectiveness.

In your career, you'll be responsible for reading and preparing an amazing variety of business reports. Common types include business plans, project reports, status or progress reports, financial plans, marketing plans, strategic plans, and technical reports. Reports can range from a single page to thousands of pages. One characteristic is common to all types: the purpose is to provide sound information, analysis, and advice to decision makers.

Compared to most daily business correspondence, reports are considered more reliable, authoritative, thorough, and final. As decision-making tools, they are typically commissioned by and written for middle-level or upper-level managers or external stakeholders (i.e., loan officers, stockholders). Because of their role in decision making, most reports take much more time to create than daily business correspondence. Furthermore, many reports are written collaboratively since they contain complex information that requires the talents and resources of many professionals.

Many reports rely on business research. A person who can conduct business research will have many opportunities for success and advancement. Research is the process of searching for knowledge. In business, you may want to know how consumers think and feel; understand employees' attitudes about a new policy; forecast sales based on past performance and carefully selected assumptions; use internal data to identify consumer behavioral patterns; or examine data to address a variety of business problems.

Conducting and reporting research can enhance your credibility in a variety of ways. You demonstrate an often-rare competency in the workplace when you can zero in on core business problems and collect and analyze data that relates to these problems. You show caring by involving key decision makers in the process and conducting research that meets their needs. Also, your character is significantly enhanced when decision makers recognize that they can count on you to deliver results in an objective and unbiased fashion.

In this chapter, we consider several approaches to planning and conducting research for reports. Overall, the purpose is to gather and analyze data that will drive excellent decision making and high organizational performance. First, we focus on setting research objectives, a process that ensures you identify the most relevant data for your business goals. Then, we examine the processes of primary and secondary research to ensure that you will gather reliable data. We also discuss how to effectively present numerical and other information in charts, graphs, and tables so that your complex data is easy to understand and supports your key messages. Read the following case, which serves as the basis for examples provided in Chapters 12 and 13.

**Hear Pete Cardon explain why this matters.**

bit.ly/cardon12

**LO12.1** Explain how planning and conducting business research for reports impacts your credibility.

---

## CHAPTER CASE: ANALYZING CUSTOMER SATISFACTION AT THE PRESTIGIO HOTEL

**WHO'S INVOLVED**

**Jeff Anderton, marketing assistant**

- Has worked at the Prestigio for three months
- Roles include marketing of meetings and conventions to professional groups and tracking customer satisfaction
- Graduated a year ago with a marketing major and statistics minor

**Andrea Garcia, general manager**

- Has worked as general manager for one year
- Started at the Prestigio nearly nine years ago in a position similar to Jeff's marketing assistant position
- Expects thorough data and analysis before making decisions

**THE SITUATION**

The Prestigio is a four-star hotel that gains much of its business from conventions and meetings. In recent years, it has lost revenue in nearly all areas. In particular, for each of the past two years, the Prestigio has lost between 5 and 10 percent in revenues for conferences. Thus, Andrea wonders if they need to reevaluate their strategy on meetings. She is concerned about the drop in business and wants good research to understand how to move forward.

Andrea recently asked Jeff to work on two marketing research projects. She expects him to complete them in roughly three months.

For the first project, she wants Jeff to analyze guest satisfaction at the Prestigio compared with its three chief competitors: the Grand Swan, Great Falls, and Wyatt. She wants Jeff to use an online hotel rating system to conduct the analysis. Andrea also wants to know if satisfaction ratings have improved in relation to two recent initiatives: increasing the guest-to-staff ratio and increasing the amount of customer service training. Jeff determines that he can best gather the data with primary research, through a survey he will develop.

For the second project, Andrea wants Jeff to gather information about eco-friendly or green meetings. Traditionally, the Prestigio has not focused on green meetings. However, in the past year, Andrea has noticed that meeting planners and other guests frequently inquire about green meetings. She wants to know if the Prestigio should invest more resources in such options. Jeff will use a combination of primary and secondary research to address the research objectives for this project.

**TASK**

**1** Gather and analyze guest satisfaction ratings for the Prestigio and its competitors.

**2** Gather information about best practices in green meetings.

## Analyzing Your Audience for Business Reports

The planning stage for many types of business reports—especially those based on research—often takes months, even years. Like other communications, you can apply the AIM planning process to develop your message based on good ideas that meet the needs of decision makers.

The first step in developing research-based business reports is identifying what decision makers want to accomplish. In many cases, they will commission the reports and have clear goals in mind. In other cases, they do not have clear goals. In all cases, you should spend time with your target audience of decision makers to carefully consider their primary business goals, research objectives, and expectations.[1]

During the research and report writing process, consider updating decision makers and involving them in the process. This increases the likelihood that you will develop a report that is useful to them.

## Gathering Information through Primary Research

With a clear understanding of what decision makers want from reports, you are ready to begin research. For important business decisions, gathering data can take weeks, months, and even years. Since many reports are intended to aid high-stakes decision making, getting the right information, analyzing it correctly, and making related recommendations needs to be done carefully and completely.

Business research can be broadly categorized as primary and secondary. **Primary research** refers to the analysis of data that you, people from your organization, or others under your direction (i.e., consultants) have collected. **Secondary research** refers to the analysis of data collected by others with no direction from you or members of your organization.

Primary research is generally most reliable and useful for your business reports because you can focus it to meet your specific research objectives and get feedback directly related to your organization and its needs. However, conducting primary research is often time-consuming, intrusive, and expensive. In some cases, primary research might suffer from a bias toward preexisting opinions and beliefs. For example, a marketing director who is convinced that a new product will be successful when it hits the market may misinterpret consumer research to fit his/her preexisting opinions. Common types of primary research include analysis of internal data, survey research, focus groups, interviews, and case studies.

In this chapter, we focus on one of the most common types of primary research: surveys. Survey research is increasingly common because of the ease with which online surveys can be administered (see Technology Tips). Generally, survey research involves administering written questionnaires. Most survey questions are **closed questions**, which restrict respondents to certain answers (rating scales, multiple choice, etc.). Some survey questions are **open-ended questions**, allowing respondents to answer in any way they choose. Closed questions can be more easily quantified and analyzed. However, open-ended questions allow you to understand an issue in more depth.

## Develop Research Objectives

Once you have identified what your audience of decision makers needs, you will carefully define your research problems. Defining research problems involves stating your research objectives in specific, targeted, and achievable statements. Notice in Table 12.1 how Jeff develops research objectives for two of his research projects.

## Create Surveys

With online survey technology readily available and easy to use, you will likely have many opportunities to use it in the workplace. Surveys are particularly useful because you can quickly get the responses of dozens if not hundreds of colleagues, current or

**LO12.2** Create research objectives that are specific and achievable.

**LO12.3** Explain principles of effective design for survey questions and choices.

**TABLE 12.1**

Creating Research Objectives

| Less Effective | More Effective |
|---|---|
| Determine how satisfied our conference guests are. | Determine guest satisfaction among conference attendees for key conference amenities and services. |
| This objective is not specific enough. The statement does not lead to a focused approach to research. | This objective is specific. The statement leads to a focused approach to research. |
| Understand green meetings. | Identify key trends impacting the market demand for green meetings held at hotels. |
| This objective is not specific. It is too broad and lacks context. | This objective is specific. It focuses on a context that is relevant to the Prestigio. |

**■ connect**

Visit http://connect.
mheducation.com for an
exercise on this topic.

potential customers, or members of other groups of interest. Online surveys are a nice tool because you can automatically dump all the data you collect into a spreadsheet. Of course, online surveys are not always convenient or possible, so you will sometimes use traditional paper-and-pencil questionnaires.

Ideally, you will have opportunities to learn about effective survey design, data collection, and analysis in some of your university courses. If you don't have this opportunity, many excellent books can help you develop your survey research skills. However, to develop your survey skills, you will need more than how-to knowledge. You also need to practice several times; there's no substitute for conducting several surveys and using the data to solve business problems in the workplace.

Generally, surveys should be short. Rarely can you get accurate data from surveys that take longer than five minutes to complete. Most consumer research questionnaires contain fewer than five or six questions. If the survey takes too long, respondents may become impatient and provide less-than-accurate responses or skip questions. The exception is when you pay respondents to take a survey. The obvious drawback is the high cost.

Another key to getting reliable data is designing the survey questions effectively. Survey questions should be (1) simple to answer, (2) non-leading, (3) exhaustive and unambiguous, and (4) limited to a single idea.

> **Principles for Survey Questions**
>
> - Simple to answer
> - Non-leading
> - Exhaustive and unambiguous
> - Single idea

**Survey Questions Should Be Simple to Answer**   As you design most surveys, envision respondents who are eager to complete the items quickly and who will spend minimal time thinking about any given item. Survey questions should contain short questions and short response options. Thus, respondents should be able to read the entire question in 10 to 20 seconds and select a response that matches their true opinions and feelings within just a few seconds. In Table 12.2, you will notice how Jeff is developing survey questions for his research about guest satisfaction.

**Survey Questions Should Be Non-Leading**   Be sure the questions in your survey are **non-leading**. A leading question is one that suggests an answer. Often, the leading question is designed to gain a preferred response from the survey designer's perspective. Sometimes, leading questions are phrased to imply how a respondent

**TABLE 12.2**

Creating Simple Survey Questions

| Less Effective | More Effective |
|---|---|
| On a scale from 1, not satisfied, to 4, extremely satisfied, how satisfied were you in the following areas related to your conference experience (if you have no opinion or did not use the following services, simply mark N/A)? | How satisfied were you with the following aspects of your conference experience? |

**Less Effective**

| | 1 | 2 | 3 | 4 | N/A |
|---|---|---|---|---|---|
| Conference Meals | ○ | ○ | ○ | ○ | ○ |
| Internet Pricing | ○ | ○ | ○ | ○ | ○ |
| Internet Speed in Rooms | ○ | ○ | ○ | ○ | ○ |

**More Effective**

| | 1– Not Satisfied | 2– Somewhat Satisfied | 3– Satisfied | 4– Extremely Satisfied | N/A– Not Applicable |
|---|---|---|---|---|---|
| Conference Meals | ○ | ○ | ○ | ○ | ○ |
| Internet Pricing | ○ | ○ | ○ | ○ | ○ |
| Internet Speed in Rooms | ○ | ○ | ○ | ○ | ○ |

The question is 39 words long. Many respondents will be confused about how to answer the questions without labels for the numerical values.

The question contains just 12 words. Formatting and labels allow respondents to quickly and precisely process the information.

**TABLE 12.2**

(*Continued*)

| Less Effective | More Effective |
|---|---|
| Rank-order each of the following guest services and amenities in providing value to you during your conference stay. (Rank-order each item. Place a 1 next to your favorite item, a 2 next to your second-favorite item, and so on. Do not place a number next to an amenity or service that you did not use during your stay.)<br><br>_____ Spa<br>_____ Fitness center<br>_____ Outdoor swimming pool<br>_____ Prestigio golf course<br>_____ Prestigio comedy club<br>_____ One of the Prestigio restaurants | Which of the following GUEST SERVICES AND AMENITIES did you use during your conference stay? **Check ALL that apply.**<br><br>☐ Spa      ☐ Prestigio golf course<br>☐ Fitness center      ☐ Prestigio comedy club<br>☐ Outdoor swimming pool      ☐ One of the Prestigio restaurants |
| This question is complicated to answer. Many respondents will not spend time to carefully rank each item. Other responses may be inaccurate or unreliable. | This question is easy to answer. Respondents are given just one choice and can make this judgment within a few seconds. |

should answer. For example, the following leading question would likely lead many respondents to provide insincere answers: *As a citizen in the country with the most per capita carbon emissions in the world, how interested are you in learning about green meeting options?* Leading questions often do not allow respondents to provide their genuine thoughts or impressions. So, leading questions in surveys can produce unreliable and unusable information (see Table 12.3).

**Survey Choices Should Be Exhaustive and Unambiguous** Survey choices should be complete. Being **exhaustive** means that all possibilities are available, and being **unambiguous** means that only one choice is appropriate (see Table 12.4).

**Survey Questions Should Contain One Idea** Survey questions that contain more than one idea are difficult for respondents to answer (see Table 12.5).

**TABLE 12.3**

Creating Non-Leading Survey Questions

| Less Effective | More Effective |
|---|---|
| To show my support for the green meeting movement, I would recommend the Prestigio as a good site for a business conference.<br><br>1. Strongly disagree<br>2. Disagree<br>3. Neutral<br>4. Agree<br>5. Strongly agree | I would recommend the Prestigio as a good site for a business conference.<br><br>1. Strongly disagree<br>2. Disagree<br>3. Neutral<br>4. Agree<br>5. Strongly agree |
| This survey question is leading. It suggests to respondents a correct or right answer. It would not provide reliable or useful results. | This survey question is non-leading. It does not suggest or manipulate a response. It would likely provide useful data. |

**TABLE 12.4**

Creating Exhaustive and Unambiguous Survey Choices

| Less Effective | More Effective |
|---|---|
| Age:<br>A. Under 30<br>B. 31 to 40<br>C. 41 to 50<br>D. 50 to 64 | Age:<br>A. 30 and under<br>B. 31 to 40<br>C. 41 to 50<br>D. 51 to 65<br>E. Over 65 |
| These choices are neither exhaustive nor unambiguous. They are not exhaustive because respondents who are 65 and over would not have a choice to select. They are not unambiguous because two of the choices overlap (C and D); in other words, a person who is 50 could select either option. | These choices are both exhaustive and unambiguous. Any respondent of any age would find just one correct response. |

**TABLE 12.5**

Creating Survey Questions with a Single Idea

| Less Effective | More Effective |
|---|---|
| How much do you know about green meetings and possible savings on these meetings?<br>A. Nothing at all<br>B. A little<br>C. Some<br>D. A lot | How much do you know about green meeting options for your business?<br>A. Nothing at all<br>B. A little<br>C. Some<br>D. A lot |
| This question contains two ideas: (1) what the respondent knows about green meetings and (2) what the respondent knows about possible savings on green meetings. This is confusing to the respondent and impossible for the researcher to interpret. | This question contains one idea. As a result, the question is easy for the respondent to answer and easy for the researcher to analyze. |

Furthermore, they are impossible to correctly analyze. Notice Jeff's completed survey in Figure 12.1.

### Analyze Your Data

Once you've conducted your surveys, your next step is to analyze the data. This job may feel exhilarating. Or it may feel overwhelming and even daunting. Even small sets of data from relatively few survey questions can be analyzed and configured in nearly limitless ways. As you develop your primary research skills, consider the following advice:

1. *Learn as much as you can about forecasting and other forms of statistical and quantitative analysis.* Unless you apply good principles of analysis, you can easily get flawed results. Furthermore, unless you are careful you can, without any intention of doing so, allow your preconceived ideas and biases to affect how you interpret the data.

2. *Learn as much as you can about spreadsheet, database, and statistical software.* You likely will have a course in spreadsheet software (i.e., Excel). Make the most

**FIGURE 12.1**

Example of Simple, Easy-to-Complete Online Survey

| Feedback on Your Conference Stay at *The Prestigio* | Exit This Survey |
|---|---|

Thanks for your participation in this survey. When you complete this survey by clicking the "Done" button, you will be given a printable coupon worth $10 at any Target store.

**1. Gender:**

○ Male
○ Female

**2. Age:**

○ Under 30    ○ 51 to 65
○ 31 to 40    ○ Over 65
○ 41 to 50

**3. Income Level:**

○ Under $30,000      ○ $50,000–$74,999
○ $30,000–$39,999    ○ $75,000–$100,000
○ $40,000–$49,999    ○ Over $100,000

**4. How many days of Internet service did you purchase during your conference visit?**

○ 0    ○ 2
○ 1    ○ 3

**5. How satisfied were you with the following aspects of your conference experience?**

|  | 1–<br>Not Satisfied | 2–<br>Somewhat Satisfied | 3–<br>Satisfied | 4–<br>Extremely Satisfied | N/A–<br>Not Applicable |
|---|---|---|---|---|---|
| Conference Meals | ○ | ○ | ○ | ○ | ○ |
| Internet Pricing | ○ | ○ | ○ | ○ | ○ |
| Internet Speed in Rooms | ○ | ○ | ○ | ○ | ○ |
| Business Center | ○ | ○ | ○ | ○ | ○ |
| Staff & Service | ○ | ○ | ○ | ○ | ○ |
| Meeting Rooms | ○ | ○ | ○ | ○ | ○ |

**6. Please respond to the following statements based on your experiences during your recent conference at the Prestigio.**

|  | 1–<br>Strongly Disagree | 2–<br>Disagree | 3–<br>Neutral | 4–<br>Agree | 5–<br>Strongly Agree |
|---|---|---|---|---|---|
| Overall, I was satisfied with the conference experience. | ○ | ○ | ○ | ○ | ○ |
| I would like to attend another business conference held at the Prestigio. | ○ | ○ | ○ | ○ | ○ |
| I would recommend the Prestigio as a good site for a business conference. | ○ | ○ | ○ | ○ | ○ |

**Which of the following GUEST SERVICES AND AMENITIES did you use during your conference stay? Check ALL that apply.**

☐ Spa              ☐ Outdoor swimming pool    ☐ Prestigio comedy club
☐ Fitness center   ☐ Prestigio golf course    ☐ One of the Prestigio restaurants

**Done**

of this training and continue experimenting with the software to feel comfortable analyzing data. Also, develop a basic understanding of databases. All companies store tremendous amounts of information in databases. If you understand basic database design, you will know what types of information you can extract to answer your research questions. Finally, statistical software (i.e., SPSS, SAS, SYSTAT) can help you conduct analyses far more rapidly and efficiently than can spreadsheet software.

3. *Rely on others in your analysis.* You will likely work with colleagues who have quantitative analysis skills in certain disciplines and for certain types of business problems, and you can turn to them for technical help. Also, you can turn to others for analytical help, because when you analyze data in a group, you are less likely to inadvertently misinterpret the data.

4. *Stay focused on your business problem and look for the big picture.* Often, company databases or survey data contain so much information that you can easily be overwhelmed by the many ways to use it. As you discipline yourself to focus on your key research problems, you are less likely to get bogged down looking at tangential issues.

## Communicate with Charts and Tables

Nearly all business activities and goals are measured and quantified: profit and loss, operating expenses, marketing expenditures, employee turnover, performance evaluations, market share, budgets, customer behavior, quality, and so on. Simply put, business executives and managers communicate with numbers. Some management experts even describe the ability to communicate numbers as a core managerial competency. Thus, in this section, we'll focus on using charts and tables to communicate numerical information.

After conducting survey research or other forms of business research, you typically have many statistics and figures that you could include in reports to decision makers. However, presenting this information effectively is challenging. In fact, most managers communicate numerical information poorly. Also, while business managers tend to like numbers, few listeners and readers can absorb a lot of them at one sitting. As one communication expert mentioned to managers, "The chances are good that you love numbers a lot more than most of your audience members do. . . . Overloading your audience members with data is a sure way to guarantee they'll forget almost everything you say."[2] Although most managers communicate with numbers with the intention of persuading and inspiring, they most often end up confusing or boring their audience.

The most fundamental mistake that executives and managers make when communicating with numbers is failing to focus on the main message, which tends to be nonnumerical. Phrases such as, "I'm going to spend a few minutes going through the numbers," or "Let me give you some background by running through the numbers" can cause your audience to tune out.[3] As you will learn in more detail in the next sections, your presentation's takeaway message should be your first and primary consideration when communicating with charts and tables. As you read through the next few pages, notice how Jeff designs charts and tables for his research at the Prestigio Hotel. In particular, pay attention to how these charts and tables are useful for Andrea, who is the general manager and primary decision maker.

**LO12.4** Develop charts and tables to concisely display data and accentuate key messages.

**Designing Effective Charts**   Charts can effectively convey complex numerical information in a simple, appealing format. A well-designed chart can express a strong message and leave a lasting visual impression on viewers and readers. Since many viewers and readers immediately gravitate to them, charts have the potential to draw readers into a document or presentation almost instantaneously.

Overall, the message of the chart is central. As Dona Wong, graphics director of *The Wall Street Journal* from 2001 to 2010, explained, "It is the content that makes graphics interesting. When a chart is presented properly, information just flows to the viewer in the clearest and most efficient way. There are no extra layers of colors, no enhancements to distract us from the clarity of the information."[4] As with other business messages, planning is the key component of developing charts.

Effective business communicators carefully select the few data relationships that most support their business messages. Top graphic designer Nigel Holmes, who is credited with coining the term *explanation graphics*, notes that charts must do more than describe or inform. They should explain important business ideas or relationships that support the key messages of a communication. Furthermore, charts should not require much mental effort for the reader. As Holmes points out, "Charts that don't explain themselves are worse than no charts."[5]

Throughout this chapter you'll find charts and tables that illustrate the strategic use of data to address the concerns of Andrea from the chapter case. While dozens of chart options are available, this section focuses on the three types used primarily within the workplace: line charts, pie charts, and bar charts. Several other chart and figure types are illustrated with less detail. Mastering the design principles of these most common and relevant charts will enable you to create other, less common types if you choose to do so.

Generally, **line charts** are useful for depicting events and trends over time. For example, stock prices over time would make the most sense when presented in the form of a line chart. **Pie charts** are useful for illustrating the pieces within a whole. Market share would be best illustrated with a pie chart. **Bar charts** are useful to compare amounts or quantities. The bar chart, with its many forms, is the most versatile of these charts since it can be used to compare many types of data.

## Create Effective Charts

As you create charts, focus on the following criteria: (1) title descriptiveness, (2) focal points, (3) information sufficiency, (4) ease of processing, and, most important, (5) takeaway message. In the following pages, you will find a discussion of each of these criteria. Also, you will find less effective and more effective examples for each major type of chart. Each of the examples is supplemented with explanations about these five criteria.

**Title Descriptiveness**  Most readers look first at the chart's title to grasp its message. Thus, the title should explain the primary point of the chart. However, it must be short enough for the reader to process quickly (generally less than ten words). In some cases you may add a subtitle if the short title is not sufficient.

Consider Figure 12.2, which illustrates identical information with a less effective and more effective line chart. In the less effective chart on the left, the chart title is a short and relatively unhelpful phrase, "Staff & Service Ratings." By contrast, the chart title in the more effective chart on the right uses a title and a subtitle. The main title, "Improvement in Staff & Service Ratings," uses the first word to immediately point out the main theme of the chart. The subtitle, in just seven words, accentuates the idea that the improvement was intentional or goal-based ("Raising Our Performance") and that the improvement far exceeded that of primary competitors.

**Focal Points**  A chart should draw the reader's attention to the most-critical relationships and ideas. Much like unified paragraphs (Chapter 6), in which all sentences focus on one main idea, each of the chart's focal points should support one main idea. The focal points can be visually generated in many interesting ways—for example, font choices (**bold,** *italics*), color, size, and callout boxes.

In the more effective line chart in Figure 12.2, a variety of focal points highlight the improvement in staff and service ratings at the Prestigio. The callout box centered in the chart directs the reader to the point in time when the Prestigio launched its staff and service initiative, allowing the reader to trace the improvement in ratings since that

■ connect

Visit http://connect.
mheducation.com for an
exercise on this topic.

**FIGURE 12.8**

## Finding Valuable Information with Library Resources

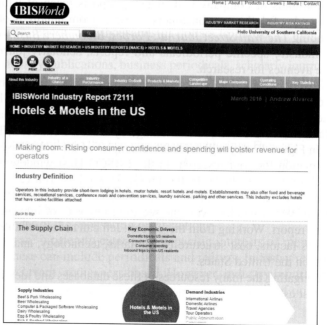

*Sources:* (top) Ebsco.com; (bottom left) ProQuest.com; (bottom right) IBISWorld.com

**TABLE 12.10**

Strategies for Using Search Terms Effectively

| Strategy | Example | Number of Hits in ProQuest |
|---|---|---|
| Use Boolean operators. | "Green Meetings"<br>Green *and* Meetings<br>Green *or* Meetings | 140<br>14,607<br>5,959,688 |
| Use alternative keywords. | Eco-Friendly *and* Conventions<br>Eco-Friendly *and* Meetings<br>Green *and* Conventions | 13<br>98<br>1,477 |
| Use closely related ideas. | Green *and* Hotels<br>Eco-Friendly *and* Hotels<br>Eco-Friendly *and* Convention Centers | 10,443<br>422<br>5 |

these various databases simply to become familiar with what's available. You should also seek a business librarian to help you identify those databases that best match your interests and needs.

Each of the databases contains search features, and several basic strategies will help you make the most of them. When you manually search, you can use Boolean operators *(and, or)* to widen your search. For example, when Jeff wants to find more information about "green meetings," his initial search of this phrase yields 140 results by searching the abstracts of potential sources. By looking for both words separately (using *and*), his search yields more than 14,000 results. By looking for either phrase (using *or*), he finds nearly 6 million results (see Table 12.10). Also, consider using alternative keywords and closely related ideas. Finding the right sources requires persistence. You might spend hours looking for useful information and then rapidly find dozens of relevant and useful sources.

Once you enter your term, most online business databases provide a list of suggested topics based on commonly indexed terms. These can be very helpful. Notice, for example, Figure 12.9. You will see the many combinations of indexed terms (with the thesaurus tool) that result from a manual search for green meetings in Ebsco Host. By clicking on these various suggested searches, you can rapidly find which combinations of search terms yield the best results.

## Document Your Research

As you collect secondary research, keeping track of the information sources is critical. Decision makers expect excellent documentation of your information because this helps them evaluate the credibility of your report. Since they often make high-stakes decisions based on reports, they expect to know *exactly* what the basis is for facts, conclusions, and recommendations you present.

When you keep track of your sources during the research stage, you can efficiently and accurately document your report. Many novice report writers waste time during the drafting stage trying to retrace their steps and find the sources for certain pieces of information. Worse, they may make errors in documentation by providing an incorrect source, casting doubt on the credibility of the report.

To avoid these problems, experienced writers have a system for recording all sources during the research stage. Not all report writers use the same system; some use word processing software, while others use spreadsheets or databases. The key is to create a system that allows you to accurately and efficiently record sources

**FIGURE 12.9**

Using Suggested
Terms in Online
Business Databases

*Source:* Ebsco.com

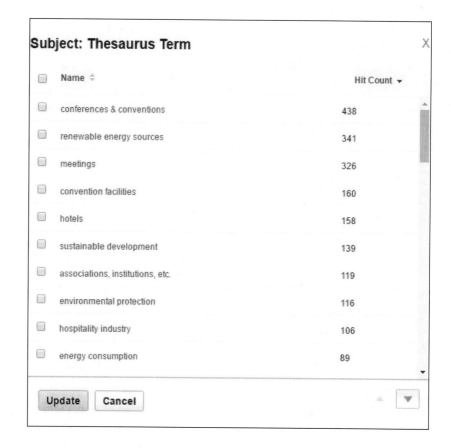

for your information. In Figure 12.10, you can see how Jeff combines taking notes with keeping track of his sources. This approach helps him organize his information and allows him to rapidly provide documentation once he begins drafting his report.

## Use Online Information for Business Research

For most business research, the information you can access through business databases and other sources at your library is generally the most reliable. However, you will also likely use Internet searches outside your library system to find relevant information on your topic. As you do so, keep in mind the following strategies:

- *Always evaluate data quality.* The range in quality on the web is immense. Make sure you're not using sources that are uninformed or inaccurate.

- *Do more than just "Google it."* You can employ many strategies for online research, including the following:

  - *Go to reputable business and industry websites and conduct searches.* For example, Jeff may go directly to general periodical or business news sites such as *Bloomberg Businessweek* or CNBC.com to do searches. Or he may go to industry sites. When he goes to the Convention Industry Council website, he finds a variety of sources that are not available at his library and that are more current than the information in business databases (see Figure 12.11).

  - *Find online discussions and forums about your selected topic.* You can learn what current professionals are saying about a topic by visiting online discussions and forums. For example, on LinkedIn, you can view the conversations of

**FIGURE 12.10**

## System for Recording Secondary Research Sources during Note Taking

Torrence, S. (2010, November). Change the world one meeting at a time: APEX/ASTM sustainability standards nearly set. *Corporate Meetings & Incentives, 29* (11), 18–21.

- According to MeetGreen, a 3-day conference with 300 attendees creates waste equivalent to 33 small vehicles; water resources that would fill half of an Olympic-sized swimming pool; greenhouse gases to fill 25 million basketballs.
- Convention Industry Council Accepted Practices Exchange (APEX) is collaborating to work on APEX/ASTM Sustainable Meetings Standards. These evolving standards can be found at the following website: Meetingsnet.com/green/apex-astm-sustainability-standards.
- 9 areas of APEX/ASTM standards: (a) accommodation; (b) audiovisual and production; (c) communications and marketing; (d) destinations; (e) exhibits; (f) food and beverage; (g) meeting venues; (h) onsite offices; (i) transportation.
- The EPA initiated green meetings standards with the formation of the Green Meeting Industry Council.
- Government planners often required to comply with standards.

Richard K. Miller & Associates. (2010). *2010 Travel & Tourism Market Research Handbook* (Loganville, GA: Author).

- Green Meeting Industry Council envisions a green meeting industry with zero net environmental impact by 2020.
- MeetingNews 2010 survey of meeting planners:
  - 93 percent report they at least occasionally use green meetings.
  - Most common green meeting practices are the following: reduce paper by using digital alternatives (79%); on-site recycling programs (61%); host cities that requires less travel (48%).
  - 10 percent measure carbon footprint.
  - 40 percent say there are not enough green meeting venues.
  - 46 percent believe green meetings are too expensive.
- Websites that measure carbon footprint of events: carboncounter.org; carbonfootprint.com; carbonfund.org; myfootprint.org; zerofootprint.net.

Lowe, M. C. (2010, October). The greening of hotels: A look at what major chains are doing to support eco-friendly meetings. *Meetings & Conventions, 45*(10), 45–56.

- *Kimpton:* In 2005 became first brand to package green meetings. Gained clients such as Microsoft and Aveda. Uses EarthCare Meetings nine-point standard. Standards include the following: 100% recycled paper; all meeting correspondence is electronic; catering ingredients sourced locally; eco-friendly cleaning products; organic tea at coffee stations; motion-controlled lighting in all meeting spaces; unused food donated. They have found that green meetings do not cost more—in fact cost less.
- *Fairmont Hotels & Resorts:* Eco-Meet program was initiated in 2007. It focuses on four main areas.
  - Eco-accommodation: Information to guests about how to be more environmentally conscious during stay; all rooms with recycling bins; energy-efficient lighting; water-conservative plumbing.
  - Eco-service: dishes/cutlery instead of disposable plates/plastic untensils; recycling bins; reusable items such as silk flowers and linen napkins.
  - Eco-cuisine: local, seasonal, organically grown foods from within 100 miles; 50% reduction in animal proteins (use vegetable proteins instead).
  - Eco-programming: electronic registration, check-in, paper reduction efforts. Carbon offsets, energy certificates (planting trees, lower-carbon technologies).
- Fairmont's results per person: three fewer plastic water bottles, two fewer aluminum cans, three fewer paper plates, two fewer sets of disposable cutlery.
- *Hilton:* LightStay: analyzes 200 operational practices. Helps planners estimate environmental impact. Gives planners options.
- *Hyatt:* Meet and Be Green Initiative: 3% rebate for following 10-point green guidelines. Requires hotel and attendees to consciously lower impacts.
- *Marriott:* Has offered green meetings since 2008. 3,600 employees are certified Marriott Green Planners.

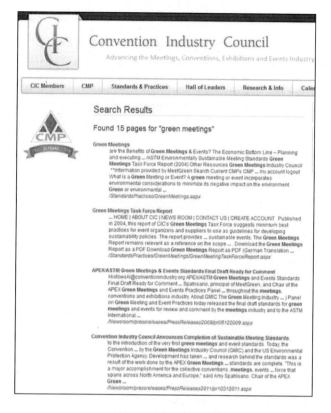

thousands of professionals on any given topic. Notice in Figure 12.12 the many options that Jeff has to choose from. Each of these groups holds dozens of ongoing converations about current practices in the industry.

- *Search beyond text-based information.* Increasingly, you can access a wealth of information in video and audio format. For example, when Jeff is seeking information about green meetings, a few simple searches yield thousands

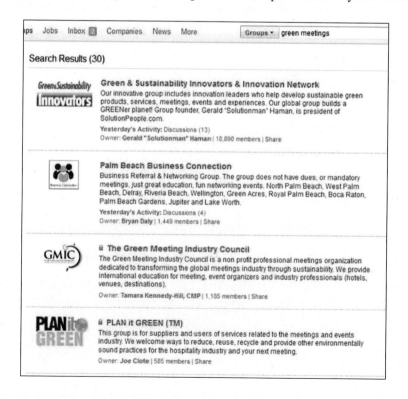

**FIGURE 12.13**

Using Online Videos
for Research

*Source:* YouTube.com

of online videos on YouTube (see Figure 12.13). By viewing a few of these videos, he identifies many green meeting practices that hotels are using. He also gets information from speeches and presentations that he could not find elsewhere.

- *Be persistent.* In the age of the Internet, many of us are accustomed to quick answers. Getting solid business information, however, rarely involves quick answers. Try as many approaches as you can to find the data you need.

## Applying the FAIR Test to Your Research Data and Charts

As you conduct research for your reports, frequently evaluate whether you are being fair. For example, whether you are doing primary or secondary research, make sure you are examining all the available facts and interpreting them from various perspectives. A common problem is that business professionals may enter into research with preexisting assumptions or even conclusions. In primary research, such assumptions may lead you to ask the wrong questions or interpret the data incorrectly. In secondary research, they may lead you to gather only information that matches your assumptions and conclusions. For example, if Jeff already assumes that developing and marketing green meetings makes business sense for the Prestigio, he may inadvertently gravitate to information that supports his position and avoid information that does not, thus misleading his readers.

Another way you may unintentionally mislead a reader is with numerical data. However, you can take a few steps to ensure that you represent data fairly and avoid losing credibility. First, whenever you are unsure of a data relationship, discuss it with your colleagues. Collectively, you will often arrive at a fair way to represent the information. Also, ask yourself if you have provided enough information for your readers and audience members to make informed and accurate judgments.

Some business professionals show only the data that supports their points. In other words, they cherry-pick the data in their favor. This practice is deceptive. Furthermore,

**LO12.7** Evaluate research data, charts, and tables for fairness and effectiveness.

# Chapter Takeaway for *Research and Business Proposals and Planning for Business Reports*

**LO12.1 Explain how planning and conducting business research for reports impacts your credibility. (pp. 369–371)**

Planning and conducting research for business reports demonstrates **your personal credibility**.

| | | |
|---|---|---|
| It shows **competence** when you can collect, analyze, and present business research. | It shows **caring** when you collect business research that fills an unmet need for others. | It shows **character** when you collect, analyze, and report your research data fairly. |

**LO12.2 Create research objectives that are specific and achievable. (p. 371)**

See *examples of research objectives* in Table 12.1.

**LO12.3 Explain principles of effective design for survey questions and choices. (pp. 371–376)**

| Principles for Survey Question Design | |
|---|---|
| • Simple to answer | • Exhaustive and unambiguous |
| • Non-leading | • Single idea |

See *examples of survey question design* in Tables 12.2 through 12.5. See a *complete online survey* in Figure 12.1.

**LO12.4 Develop charts and tables to concisely display data and accentuate key messages. (pp. 376–387)**

| Criteria for Evaluating Charts | |
|---|---|
| • Title descriptiveness | • Ease of processing |
| • Focal points | • Takeaway message |
| • Information sufficiency | |

See *examples of charts and tables* in Figures 12.2 through 12.6.

**LO12.5 Evaluate the usefulness of data sources for business research. (pp. 387–389)**

| Criteria for Evaluating Data Quality | |
|---|---|
| • Reliability | • Expertise |
| • Relevance | • Biases |
| • Adaptability | |

**LO12.6 Conduct secondary research to address a business problem. (pp. 389–395)**

| Principles for Secondary Research |
|---|
| • Use business databases such as EBSCO, IBISWorld, and Hoover's. |
| • Document your research. |
| • Conduct online research carefully, strategically, and creatively. |

See an *example of documenting research during the note-taking stage* in Figure 12.10.

**LO12.7 Evaluate research data, charts, and tables for fairness and effectiveness. (pp. 395–397)**

**Facts:** Present all relevant facts, even when they don't fit nicely into convenient conclusions. Avoid exaggeration or any other distortion of the facts.
**Access:** Grant access to your data to decision makers and others affected by your report. Focus on transparency and disclosure.
**Impacts:** Consider how the data in your report will impact stakeholders.
**Respect:** Ensure that your presentation of the data demonstrates respect for stakeholders.

# Key Terms

adaptability, 387

bar charts, 377

biases, 388

business and management books, 389

business periodicals, 389

closed questions, 371

exhaustive, 373

expertise, 388

external blogs, 389

industry publications, 388

line charts, 377

non-leading, 372

open-ended questions, 371

pie charts, 377

primary research, 371

relevance, 387

reliability, 387

scholarly journals, 389

secondary research, 371

unambiguous, 373

white papers, 388

# Discussion Exercises

**12.1 Chapter Review Questions** (LO12.1, LO12.2, LO12.3, LO12.4, LO12.5)

A. Explain the features that distinguish reports from other types of business correspondence.

B. Describe ways in which you can enhance your credibility by creating reports.

C. Discuss the advantages and drawbacks of both primary and secondary business research.

D. Describe strategies for understanding the needs of your audience for reports.

E. Explain why developing clear research objectives is so crucial to business research.

F. Describe principles for effective survey questions.

G. Summarize the primary reasons for using charts and tables.

H. Explain at least three general design principles for charts.

I. Describe unique design and formatting principles that apply to line charts, pie charts, and bar charts.

J. Explain the criteria for judging the quality of research data.

**12.2 Communication Q&A Discussion Questions** (LO12.4, LO12.7)

In the Communication Q&A section, when asked about choosing when to use tables and charts, John Phillip stated, "All communications need to be appropriately tailored to the audience. Tables are effective when I want the audience to know the numbers. I often use tables in less formal communications, especially with my level of the organization and below. Charts are a great way to visually show comparative data and trends."

A. Based on this statement as well as your own experience, list and elaborate on three or four general guidelines for choosing between tables and charts.

B. Consider John Phillip's answers, and in two or three paragraphs, explain why simpler is better when it comes to charts. Also, explain the strategy behind developing effective charts.

C. Mark Twain is famously quoted as saying, "Figures often beguile me, particularly when I have the arranging of them myself; in which case the remark attributed to Disraeli would often apply with justice and force: 'There are three kinds of lies: lies, damned lies, and statistics'" (from Twain's autobiography). Do you believe this is the case with charts? Explain in three to five paragraphs specific approaches you can use to ensure that your charts are considered credible.

**12.3 Combining Quantitative and Communication Skills** (LO12.1, LO12.4, LO12.5, LO12.6)

Lloyd C. Blankfein, chair and CEO of Goldman Sachs, was asked, "What would you like business schools to teach more of, or less of?" He responded:

Look, I think it's very important to teach people to have a healthy respect for facts and information. And you know, to paraphrase Keynes, "to change minds when facts change." That's why I think certain careers—and maybe not intuitive careers—do very well. There's a lot of lawyers floating around Wall Street. There's a lot of engineers. A lot of people who deal in facts and have an appreciation for facts. A quantitative thing is very helpful. I was a social studies major, but you need to be numerate. If you have those good quantitative skills, it's very, very helpful.[6]

Based on Blankfein's comments and your own opinions, respond to the following questions:

A. Why are quantitative skills so highly valued in various business disciplines?

B. How important do you think quantitative skills will be to your career? In what ways?

C. What are your strongest areas in terms of quantitative skills? Weakest areas?

D. What are your strongest areas in terms of spreadsheet software? Weakest areas?

E. What are five goals you have for improving your quantitative skills?

# Evaluation Exercises

**12.4 Evaluating Charts and Tables in Annual Reports**
(LO12.4)

Choose an annual report from a company that interests you. Select several tables and graphs from the report. Evaluate each in terms of design. Describe at least three effective and less effective aspects

for each chart and graph. Also, make one recommendation for improving them.

**12.5 Evaluating Charts about Exports** (LO12.4)

Examine each of the following charts (Figures 12.14A, B, and C) and respond to the questions below:[7]

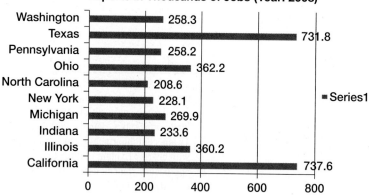

**Ten States with Most Jobs Related to Manufacturing Exports in Thousands of Jobs (Year: 2008)**

**FIGURE 12.14A**

Ineffective Bar Chart

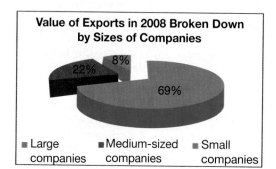

**Value of Exports in 2008 Broken Down by Sizes of Companies**

**FIGURE 12.14B**

Ineffective Pie Chart

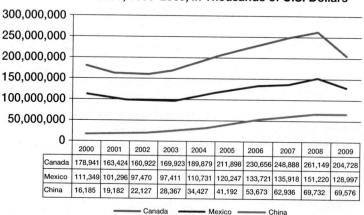

**Value of Exports to Top Three Export Partners of the United States, 2000–2009, in Thousands of U.S. Dollars**

|        | 2000    | 2001    | 2002   | 2003   | 2004    | 2005    | 2006    | 2007    | 2008    | 2009    |
|--------|---------|---------|--------|--------|---------|---------|---------|---------|---------|---------|
| Canada | 178,941 | 163,424 | 160,922| 169,923| 189,879 | 211,898 | 230,656 | 248,888 | 261,149 | 204,728 |
| Mexico | 111,349 | 101,296 | 97,470 | 97,411 | 110,731 | 120,247 | 133,721 | 135,918 | 151,220 | 128,997 |
| China  | 16,185  | 19,182  | 22,127 | 28,367 | 34,427  | 41,192  | 53,673  | 62,936  | 69,732  | 69,576  |

━━━ Canada ━━━ Mexico ━━━ China

**FIGURE 12.14C**

Ineffective Line Chart

For each of the above charts, describe their weaknesses in terms of the following: (a) title descriptiveness, (b) focal points, (c) information sufficiency, (d) ease of processing, and (e) takeaway message.

# Application Exercises

## 12.6 Developing Research Objectives (LO12.2)

Choose three topics of interest that you could research. Write three specific research objectives that could provide a clear direction for you to collect primary data or gather secondary research.

## 12.7 Conducting Survey Research (LO12.3)

Individually or in groups, select a business problem that you can learn more about by conducting survey research. You will create an online survey for all of your classmates to take, so design your project around the assumption that you are finding out what university-aged students think or feel about the topic. Design the survey so that it can be completed in three to five minutes. Do the following:

A. Create the survey with between 5 and 15 survey questions.

B. Administer the survey.

C. Identify the major findings and conclusions.

D. State related recommendations.

E. Create two tables that summarize findings from the survey.

F. Create two charts that display key messages related to the data.

G. Write a report that includes your objectives, methodology, findings, conclusions, and recommendations.

## 12.8 Learning about Online Business Databases at Your Library (LO12.6)

Identify five online business databases available through your library. For each, explain what the key advantages are and provide one limitation. When you have written about each database, write a concluding statement that identifies which databases are most useful for your business interests.

## 12.9 Evaluating Data Quality (LO12.5)

Find five data sources related to a topic that interests you. Analyze reliability, relevance, adaptability, expertise, and biases.

## 12.10 Creating Charts from the Apple Annual Report[8] (LO12.4)

Assume you are working for Apple and are summarizing key financial and sales data for presentation to an external audience, such as potential investors or media reporters. You would like to create charts to quickly summarize your performance and allow others to compare your performance across operating segments and product lines.

Use the two tables below to create the following charts. Remember to follow effective design principles.

A. Create a line chart to show net sales growth from 2009 to 2013.

B. Create a line chart to show unit sales of the top four product groups from 2011 to 2013.

C. Create a bar chart to show net sales for the top six product groups in 2013.

D. Create a pie chart to show net sales for all product groups in 2013.

E. Create a bar chart to show unit sales by product groups in 2013.

F. Identify two key relationships or comparisons from the table. Create charts that best illustrate these relationships or comparisons.

G. As directed by your instructor, exchange your charts with a partner from your class. Evaluate one another's chart designs in terms of title descriptiveness, focal points, information sufficiency, ease of processing, and take-away message.

## Selected Financial Data, 2009–2013

| | 2013 | 2012 | 2011 | 2010 | 2009 |
|---|---|---|---|---|---|
| Net sales | $ 170,910 | $ 156,508 | $ 108,249 | $ 65,225 | $ 42,905 |
| Net income | $ 37,037 | $ 41,733 | $ 25,922 | $ 14,013 | $ 8,235 |
| Earnings per common share: | | | | | |
| Basic | $ 40.03 | $ 44.64 | $ 28.05 | $ 15.41 | $ 9.22 |
| Diluted | $ 39.75 | $ 44.15 | $ 27.68 | $ 15.15 | $ 9.08 |
| Cash dividends per common share | $ 11.40 | $ 2.65 | $ — | $ — | $ — |
| Earnings per common share: | | | | | |
| Basic | $ 925,331 | $ 934,818 | $ 924,258 | $ 909,461 | $ 893,016 |
| Diluted | $ 931,662 | $ 945,355 | $ 936,645 | $ 924,712 | $ 907,005 |
| Total cash, cash equivalents and marketable securities | $ 146,761 | $ 121,251 | $ 81,570 | $ 51,011 | $ 33,992 |
| Total assets | $ 207,000 | $ 176,064 | $ 116,371 | $ 75,183 | $ 47,501 |
| Long-term debt | $ 16,960 | $ — | $ — | $ — | $ — |
| Long-term obligations | $ 20,208 | $ 16,664 | $ 10,100 | $ 5,531 | $ 3,502 |
| Total liabilities | $ 83,451 | $ 57,854 | $ 39,756 | $ 27,392 | $ 15,861 |
| Shareholders' equity | $ 123,549 | $ 118,210 | $ 76,615 | $ 47,791 | $ 31,640 |

*Notes:* Currency figures in millions of dollars; share amounts in thousands; dividends are actual figures.

Table Net Sales, 2011–2013

| | 2013 | Change | 2012 | Change | 2011 |
|---|---|---|---|---|---|
| **Net Sales by Operating Segment:** | | | | | |
| Americas | $ 62,739 | 9% | $ 57,512 | 50% | $ 38,315 |
| Europe | 37,883 | 4% | 36,323 | 31% | 27,778 |
| Greater China (a) | 25,417 | 13% | 22,533 | 78% | 12,690 |
| Japan | 13,462 | 27% | 10,571 | 94% | 5,437 |
| Rest of Asia Pacific | 11,181 | 4% | 10,741 | 8% | 9,902 |
| Retail | 20,228 | 7% | 18,828 | 33% | 14,127 |
| Total net sales | $ 170,910 | 9% | $ 156,508 | 45% | $ 108,249 |
| **Net Sales by Product:** | | | | | |
| iPhone (b) | $ 91,279 | 16% | $ 78,692 | 71% | $ 45,998 |
| iPhone (b) | 31,980 | 3% | 30,945 | 61% | 19,168 |
| Mac (b) | 21,483 | −7% | 23,221 | 7% | 21,783 |
| iPod (b) | 4,411 | −21% | 5,615 | −25% | 7,453 |
| iTunes, software and services (c) | 16,051 | 25% | 12,890 | 38% | 9,373 |
| Accessories (d) | 5,706 | 11% | 5,145 | 15 | 4,474 |
| Total net sales | $ 170,910 | 9% | $ 156,508 | 45% | $ 108,249 |
| **Unit Sales by Product:** | | | | | |
| iPhone | 150,257 | 20% | 125,046 | 73% | 72,293 |
| iPad | 71,033 | 22% | 58,310 | 80% | 32,394 |
| Mac | 16,341 | −10% | 18,158 | 9% | 16,735 |
| iPod | 26,379 | −25% | 35,165 | −17% | 42,620 |

*Notes:* Currency figures in millions of dollars; share amounts in thousands; dividends are actual figures.
(a) Greater China includes China, Hong Kong, and Taiwan.
(b) Includes deferrals and amortization of related non-software services and software upgrade rights.
(c) Includes revenue from sales on the iTunes Store, the App Store, the Mac App Store, and the iBooks Store, and revenue from sales of AppleCare, licensing, and other services.
(d) Includes sales of hardware peripherals and Apple-branded and third-party accessories for iPhone, iPad, Mac, and iPod.

**12.11 Revising Charts about Exporting** (LO12.4)

A. Revise the ineffective bar chart from Exercise 12.5.

B. Revise the ineffective pie chart from Exercise 12.5.

C. Revise the ineffective line chart from Exercise 12.5.

D. With your instructor's direction, consider evaluating your charts against those of your peers in the class. Decide which charts are most effective and share them with the class.

**12.12 Evaluate Various Types of Secondary Research Data** (LO12.5)

Based on a topic of interest, find at least one of each of the following types of sources: white paper, industry publication, business periodical, scholarly journal, external blog, and business book. Evaluate each of the sources in the following areas: reliability, relevance, adaptability, expertise, and bias.

**12.13 Planning Research at the Prestigio** (LO12.2, LO12.3, LO12.5, LO12.6)

A. Assume the role of Jeff Anderton and conduct research about green meetings. Specifically, your assignment is to identify best practices for green meetings from the perspective of vendors, compare marketing approaches, and evaluate the strategic and financial importance of offering green meetings. Do the following: Write three specific research objectives.

B. Explain strategies for collecting research for each objective.

C. Write three research questions that you could ask conference attendees that would help you understand what consumers think about green meetings.

D. Identify three online sources about green meetings. Evaluate each in terms of the following: reliability, relevance, adaptability, expertise, and biases.

# Language Mechanics Check

**12.14** **Review all rules in Appendix A about punctuation, number usage, and grammar. Then, rewrite each sentence to make all needed corrections.**

A. The majority of the marketing managers have argued for a strategy that differentiates the hotel from local, high end hotels.

B. These managers have focused on a strategy that positions the hotel as an eco friendly sustainable operation.

C. Other managers especially those in finance worries that this strategy will negatively effect profits.

D. In fact a few finance managers have all ready complained to the senior leadership team.

E. These managers say that the hotel needs to cautiously evaluate a variety of strategic options, before settling for a green strategy.

F. They also think the hotel faces more pressing threats such as employee moral union demands and outdated, in room technologies.

G. They say that the hotel should improve employee development programs and invest in inroom technologies not focus on unproven green strategies.

H. They also say that pay is an important issue and expect significant employee turnover unless the hotel increases compensation rates.

I. The senior leadership team seems to be taking their time as they consider how to resolve the differences between the marketing team and the finance team.

J. One board member said she will encourage the board to hold a meeting to weigh strategic options evaluate current plans and advice the senior leadership team.

# Endnotes

1. David Kintler and Bob Adams, *Independent Consulting: A Comprehensive Guide to Building Your Own Consulting Business* (Avon, MA: Streetwise, 1998).

2. Roly Grimshaw, "Communication by Numbers," *Harvard Management Communication Letter* 8, no. 3 (2005): 3–4.

3. Grimshaw, "Communication by Numbers"; Dona M. Wong, *The Wall Street Journal Guide to Information Graphics: The Dos and Don'ts of Presenting Data, Facts, and Figures* (New York: W. W. Norton & Company, 2010).

4. Wong, *The Wall Street Journal Guide to Information Graphics*, 13; Stephen Few, *Show Me the Numbers: Designing Tables and Graphs to Enlighten* (Oakland, CA: Analytics Press, 2004).

5. Kirsten D. Sandberg, "Easy on the Eyes: A Design Legend Tells How to Turn Complex 'Real World' Information into Clear Visual Messages," *Harvard Management Communication Letter* 5, no. 8 (2002): 3–5.

6. Adam Bryant, "Lessons Learned at Goldman," *Corner Office* (blog), *The New York Times,* September 12, 2009, retrieved from www.nytimes.com/2009/09/13/business/13corner.html.

7. Based on data retrieved June 15, 2010, from www.trade.gov/mas/ian/Jobs/Reports/2008/jobs_by_state_totals.html.

8. Timothy D. Cook and Peter Oppenheimer, 2013 *Apple Annual Report and Filing for Apple* (Form 10-K/A filed to the United States Securities and Exchange Commission, October 29, 2013), retrieved September 12, 2014, from www.apple.com/investor/.

Andrea has asked Jeff to write a report about the future of green meetings. She views this as an area of strategic concern. Jeff has collected secondary research and interviewed several hotel managers who have successfully marketed green meetings. Now, he needs to think about how to put all of the information together.

**TASK**

**1**
Shania will write a formal business proposal to gain the Prestigio as a client. She knows that several other vendors are competing for this project.

**2**
Jeff will compose a report about the current market for green meetings and recommend courses of action for the Prestigio.

**3**
Shania will write a report about the results of the guest satisfaction survey and deliver it to the Prestigio. She knows her future opportunities depend on the quality of this report.

## Developing Business Proposals

**LO13.2** Create specific and persuasive proposals.

Prior to examining reports in depth, we briefly discuss business proposals. Some proposals lead to business reports. For example, you'll notice that the proposal in Figure 13.1 leads to the report in Figure 13.7. You will likely have many opportunities to write proposals. If you're good at it, you gain resources—financial resources and organizational support—to follow through on your business goals and objectives.

Most proposals deal with decisions about allocating resources for various business activities. Proposals generally explain why business goals are beneficial and how you will use resources (people, time, partnerships, finances, etc.) to reach these goals. Proposals vary substantially in length and format. They range from a page or two to several hundred pages. Some proposals require a standard format, whereas others are more flexible.

### Components of a Business Proposal

- Cover Page
- Executive Summary
- Current Situation
- Specific Objectives
- Deliverables Overview
- Timeline
- Results Enhancers
- Pricing/Budget

Some of the most common elements of proposals, especially for consulting, include an explanation of the current situation (usually addressing an unresolved problem), specific objectives, a deliverables overview, a timeline, results enhancers (why you or your organization is positioned to add value), and pricing or budget (if appropriate). Most successful proposal writers speak to decision makers (supervisors, clients, or others) before submitting an official proposal. By negotiating some of the details ahead of time, proposal writers have a better sense of what decision makers want and expect. This helps proposal writers make decisions about how to structure the proposal to persuade decision makers. In Figure 13.1, you can see a simple proposal from Shania Baker for a relatively small project. As you view this proposal, notice the focus on action. One common mistake of proposal writers is to leave out details about deliverables and timelines.

## Demonstrating Excellent Thinking by Applying a Precision-Oriented Style

**LO13.3** Demonstrate excellent thinking by applying a precision-oriented style to reports.

The most basic and critical component of any report is precision in thinking as reflected in style—meaning that it offers accurate, well-documented facts; good reasoning for conclusions; and a solid basis for recommendations (see Figure 13.2). The foundation for these facts, conclusions, and recommendations must be a well-stated business problem or challenge. In short, a report that facilitates effective decision making must demonstrate excellence in thinking.

**FIGURE 13.1**

Proposal to Conduct a Guest Satisfaction Survey

# Proposal to Conduct Guest Satisfaction Survey for the Prestigio Hotel and Resort

Submitted by Shania Baker, Baker Consulting
October 1, 2016

## Executive Summary

> The *Executive Summary* provides the most essential points from the proposal.

Baker Consulting proposes conducting a guest satisfaction analysis for the Prestigio Hotel and Resort. Baker Consulting will provide the following: (1) design and administration of a guest satisfaction survey; (2) a written guest satisfaction report; and (3) a guest satisfaction briefing to the marketing team. Prior to conducting the survey, the Prestigio Hotel and Resort will provide an email list of recent conference attendees and other requested information. The proposed price is $5,000, which includes a $2,000 up-front fee prior to conducting the guest satisfaction survey and a $3,000 final payment once the final guest satisfaction report is completed and delivered.

## Current Situation

Guest satisfaction has always been the foundation for repeat business at the Prestigio. With so many online reviews of hotels readily available to meeting planners, the importance of achieving high guest satisfaction ratings is more important now than ever. Since 2010, the Prestigio has evaluated guest satisfaction and future intentions among conference attendees with an annual survey to help determine priorities in improving guest satisfaction. In the past four years, the Prestigio has evaluated conference attendees' views in the following areas: overall satisfaction, intent to return, intent to recommend, conference meals, meeting rooms, and staff and service.

Past surveys of guest satisfaction have not addressed several areas of interest to the Prestigio: (1) guests' views of Internet pricing and the business center and (2) guests' actual use of conference services and amenities. Also, prior analysis of guest satisfaction has not differentiated guest satisfaction by gender and income.

## Specific Objectives

> The *Current Situation* section describes the basic challenges that need to be addressed and solved.

1. Conduct a survey of conference attendees in the following areas:

   A. Satisfaction with conference services and amenities
   B. Actual use of services and amenities by conference guests
   C. Repeat business indicators: overall satisfaction, intent to return, and intent to recommend

2. Complete a guest satisfaction report:

   A. Provide complete analysis of each survey area
   B. Analyze based on income level and gender
   C. Provide realistic recommendations

> The *Specific Objectives* section provides clear statements about outcomes of the proposed work.

3. Provide a guest satisfaction briefing to the marketing team

**FIGURE 13.1**

*(Continued)*

### Deliverables Overview

> The *Deliverables section* describes the items and services that will be provided.

Baker Consulting will provide the following deliverables:

1. *A guest satisfaction briefing and discussion.* Baker Consulting will provide a written report, a 2-hour presentation and discussion, and a digital file with raw data from completed surveys.
2. *A written guest satisfaction analysis.* The report will include all survey findings. The report will be roughly ten pages.
3. *Raw data from the online survey.* Baker Consulting will provide a spreadsheet with all original survey responses.

The Prestigio Hotel and Resort will provide the following:

1. Two meetings between Baker Consulting and Prestigio Hotel and Resort to provide needed information for the research.
2. Email addresses to conference attendees during 2016.

### Timeline

> The *Timeline* section clearly states when key activities will occur and when deliverables are due.

| Date to Complete | Activity |
|---|---|
| November 15 | Kick-off meeting at Baker Consulting office with the Prestigio marketing team (estimate: 1-1/2 hours). |
| December 15 | Follow-up meeting to discuss survey design (estimate: 1 hour). |
| January 15 | The Prestigio will provide all available email addresses of conference attendees during 2016. |
| February 1 | Guest satisfaction report and raw data provided to the Prestigio. |
| February 15 | Guest satisfaction briefing to the Prestigio marketing team. |

### Pricing and Payment Plan

The following table summarizes the price for this project based on my standard rates for soliciting survey responses and completing customer satisfaction reports.

| Activity | Rate | Total |
|---|---|---|
| Survey design and administration | Standard rate for 10-item survey | $2,000 |
| Data analysis | $150 per hour (10 hours) | $1,500 |
| Guest satisfaction report | $150 per hour (10 hours) | $1,500 |
| | | $5,000 |

The total pricing for conducting the guest satisfaction research and creating a guest satisfaction report is $5,000. This includes two payments: an up-front fee of $2,000 and a final payment of $3,000 when the guest satisfaction report is delivered.

> The *Pricing and Payment Plan* section states the pricing for products and/or services and expectations for payment.

**FIGURE 13.2**

Excellence in Thinking
for Reports

In Jeff's case, he spends several months working from start to finish on his two research projects. After clearly articulating the business problem, he collects all the necessary information, carefully checks the reliability of each of his sources, examines the facts from many angles as he develops conclusions and recommendations, and asks various colleagues about their perspectives. His critical thinking skills allow him to apply a precision-oriented style to his reports.

Visit http://connect.
mheducation.com for an
exercise on this topic.

### Start with a Clear Statement of the Business Problem or Challenge

Placing a clear statement of the central business problem or challenge at the beginning helps establish the purpose and value of the report. Without such a statement, reports lack direction and may be perceived as unimportant.

Problem statements are most effective when they provide the unique context of the problem for the organization and reflect an appropriate sense of urgency. Typically, such statements should be one to three paragraphs long. Notice how Jeff establishes the direction of his green meetings report in Table 13.1.

### Use Fact-Based Language

Precision in reports relies on facts. You can raise the credibility of your report by (1) supplying the facts with precision; (2) providing supporting details for your conclusions; (3) carefully dealing with predictions and cause/effect statements (see Table 13.2); and (4) responsibly citing your research sources (see the next section about documenting secondary research).

### Document Secondary Research and Avoid Plagiarism

By nature, decision makers adopt a methodical and skeptical approach to making investments, changing strategies, and making other substantial changes. They expect quality information to make these decisions. By documenting your sources, you allow decision makers to judge the quality of your data. Decision makers are also looking for signals that you have been methodical in collecting, analyzing, and reporting findings. By documenting your sources, you display your thorough, detail-oriented approach.

Typically, you should provide a reference list at the end of the report that contains all your sources. Also, throughout your document, you should provide citations to indicate the information you have drawn from other sources. You can use a variety of *documentation* systems, including APA and MLA styles. You can see examples of these two styles in Table 13.3. You should, however, use an official style guide to document with precision. Style guides contain hundreds of rules for various types of sources. Additionally, many websites contain the most current documentation guidelines, including

**TABLE 13.1**

Problem Statement or Business Challenge

| Less Effective | More Effective |
|---|---|
| Since 2011, our revenues from conventions and meetings have declined by roughly 23 percent. One reason that we may not have rebounded is that we still do not provide options for clients who want green meetings. | Since 2011, our revenues from conventions and meetings have declined by roughly 23 percent. Since meetings constitute nearly 60 percent of our total revenues and form the basis for our reputation as a high-class provider of events, we need to seek new ways of rebuilding our conventions and meetings business.<br><br>The Great Recession that began in late 2007 led to lost revenue for nearly all hotels and organizations dependent on business travel. However, by 2011, the hotel industry had recovered. Since 2011, nationwide growth in revenue for conventions and meetings has increased by an average of 2.8 percent per year (Morea, 2016). Unlike other hotel venues in the conventions and meetings industry, the Prestigio has not rebounded in the past few years.<br><br>One reason we may not have rebounded is we still do not provide options for clients who want green meetings. Our director of conventions and meetings, Barbara Brookshire, has noticed that many meeting planners inquire about green meeting options. She is certain that we have lost business because we do not provide such meetings, and she expects that meeting planners will increasingly request these options. |
| This brief statement does suggest one reason revenues may have dropped. However, it lacks contextual details that provide the urgency to solve this problem. | This problem statement provides sufficient context to communicate the severity of the situation. Not only has the Prestigio lost revenue in meetings, but also meetings constitute the most important element of its business, and the recession cannot be used as an explanation for the continued fall in revenue. Furthermore, anecdotal evidence suggests a reason for the lost revenue. |
| Since 2010, we have evaluated guest satisfaction and future intentions among conference attendees with an annual survey. This report provides the results of this year's survey as well as year-to-year comparisons for the past five years. | Guest satisfaction has always been the foundation for repeat business. With so many online reviews of hotels readily available to meeting planners, achieving high guest satisfaction ratings is more important now than ever. Since 2010, we have used an annual survey to evaluate guest satisfaction, assess future intentions of conference attendees, and determine how we can improve guest satisfaction. This report provides the results of this year's survey as well as year-to-year comparisons for the past five years. |
| This statement fails to explain the basic purpose and value behind conducting the surveys. | By adding a few additional thoughts in just two sentences, this problem statement establishes the importance of using the survey to improve guest satisfaction and, consequently, repeat business. Furthermore, it explains the increased urgency of this effort. |

the APA style website (www.apastyle.org) and the Purdue Online Writing Lab (http://owl.english.purdue.edu). Also, if you will spend a lot of time writing reports that need documentation, you might explore some of the available software to help in this process (see the Technology Tips box in the "Achieving Objectivity and Positivity of Tone" section in this chapter).

Although you will generally base your reports on secondary research, you must still demonstrate your originality in thought. That is, your goal is to combine information from your various sources in novel and insightful ways and thereby generate your own conclusions and recommendations.

**TABLE 13.2**

Using Fact-Based Language

| Less Effective | More Effective |
|---|---|
| Nearly all of our respondents reported satisfaction with their conference experiences. | Overall, the vast majority (84 percent) of our respondents reported satisfaction with their conference experiences. |
| This fact is imprecise and open to interpretation. | By providing the exact percentage in parentheses, this fact is precise. |
| One of the strongest indicators that meeting planners expect green meeting options is that they increasingly inquire about such meetings in RFPs. | One of the strongest indicators that meeting planners expect green meeting options is that they increasingly inquire about such meetings in RFPs. A recent survey showed that *71 percent of meeting planners already do or plan to inquire about green initiatives on RFPs for meeting venues* (Shapiro, 2009). |
| Without a supporting fact, this conclusion may be viewed as unsubstantiated or merely the writer's opinion. | This conclusion is immediately substantiated with a supporting statistic (fact). Because the author provides a citation, decision makers can view the original research if they want to. |
| The return on investment for providing green meeting options is guaranteed to be at least 300 percent and potentially as high as 500 percent. Investing in green meetings would certainly be a wise choice moving forward. | Based on our conversations with three individuals who have introduced green meeting options at hotels comparable to ours, we concluded that the return on investment for developing a basic infrastructure for green meetings is strong—as high as 500 percent. Each hotel has invested $150,000 to $250,000 annually to build green meeting infrastructures. Although precisely determining how much return is due to new green meeting options is difficult, each of these individuals attributes between $500,000 and $1.3 million in additional revenue to providing green meeting options (J. Hardaway, personal communication, October 14, 2016; K. Cafferty, personal communication, October 15, 2016; M. Dipprey, personal communication, October 14, 2016). |
| This statement guarantees that the investment will bring a return. Many decision makers would view the statement as naïve. | This set of statements demonstrates a cautious but confident analysis that the investment may reap substantial returns. It treats statements about prediction and cause and effect carefully, and it includes source information. |

To develop original reports, make sure that you avoid all forms of **plagiarism**. According to the Merriam-Webster dictionary, to plagiarize is to "steal and pass off (the ideas of another) as one's own" and "to commit literary theft."[1] Thus, plagiarism is serious; it is literally stealing the ideas of others.

To avoid plagiarism on a sentence and paragraph level, document all references to the ideas of others, including (1) direct quotations, (2) paraphrases, and (3) other instances in which you borrow or reference the ideas of others. **Direct quotations** are verbatim restatements from another source. Use direct quotations only when the quotation contains a particularly compelling combination of words, flows effectively with your paper, and emphasizes the credibility of the original speaker or writer. In most situations, you should paraphrase rather than use direct quotations. **Paraphrasing** involves using your own words to express the meaning of the original speaker or writer. When you paraphrase, you significantly alter the original words and sentence structure, but you still need to give credit to the original speaker or writer for the idea. Notice Table 13.4 for examples of using direct quotations and paraphrasing in ways that avoid plagiarism.[2]

**TABLE 13.11**

Striking an Objective Tone while also Projecting Positivity

| Less Effective | More Effective |
|---|---|
| Generally, the research indicates that market demand for green meetings is growing, with the majority of meeting planners showing interest. The following features define the increasing demand: (a) many public sector organizations are required to hold green meetings; (b) many private sector organizations seek green meetings as part of CSR efforts; and (c) many organizations are pursuing more local options for meetings. Currently, demand far outstrips supply. This provides us with a golden opportunity to gain market share before other meeting venues develop green meeting options. | Generally, the research indicates that market demand for green meetings is growing, with the majority of meeting planners showing interest. The following features define the increasing demand: (a) many public sector organizations are required to hold green meetings; (b) many private sector organizations seek green meetings as part of CSR efforts; and (c) many organizations are pursuing more local options for meetings. Right now is a good time to develop green meetings because demand far outstrips supply. |
| Hotels of comparable size to the Prestigio have reported phenomenal return on investment for next to nothing as far as developing and marketing green meetings. Even though we can't predict the future market with certainty, the exponential growth of this market shows its forward trajectory, and we should make sure we're not the latecomers for this trend. As a result, the Prestigio should make short-term investments to provide some green meeting options, and also position us to invest heavily to meet future long-term demand. We should immediately take the following actions to break into the green meetings market before it's too late: | Hotels of comparable size to the Prestigio have reported strong return on investment for minimal investments in developing and marketing green meetings. However, the future demand is neither clear nor certain. As a result, the Prestigio should make relatively small, short-term investments to provide some green meeting options. This will position us to invest more heavily as we learn more about the long-term demand. In particular, we recommend the following actions during the next year: |
| 1. Hire a green meetings specialist. | 1. Hire a green meetings specialist. |
| 2. Get a fleet of hybrid or alternative fuel vans. | 2. Get a fleet of hybrid or alternative fuel vans. |
| 3. Gain recognition and certification as a green meetings venue from reputable third-party organizations. | 3. Gain recognition and certification as a green meetings venue from reputable third-party organizations. |
| 4. Adjust marketing strategy to focus more extensively on local organizations. | 4. Adjust marketing strategy to focus more extensively on local organizations. |
| 5. Reevaluate prospects in the public sector. | 5. Reevaluate prospects in the public sector. |
| 6. Feature our green meeting options prominently in marketing materials. | 6. Feature our green meeting options prominently in marketing materials. |
| The tone of this passage projects excessive enthusiasm and perhaps a rush to action. Some of the adjectives are exaggerated, perhaps displaying an imprecise, unprofessional approach to the report. | The tone of this passage projects objectivity. The adjectives are businesslike and measured. A tempered *can-do* attitude emerges without sacrificing the sense that the research is methodical, thorough, and unrushed. |

your enthusiasm and strong positive emotion do not appear to cloud your judgment. In Table 13.11, notice the comparisons between two alternative approaches to writing an executive summary. As you read through these passages, consider how to strike the right balance between objectivity and positivity.

## Assessing Key Features of a Completed Report

In the upcoming pages, you can see two examples of business reports. The first (Figure 13.6) is based on secondary research. It can be classified as a *business trend* or *business issue* report. The second (Figure 13.7) is based on survey results, which is primary research. Although you will find that reports vary greatly in purpose and

**FIGURE 13.6**

Business Report with Secondary Research

# Should the Prestigio Hotel Develop and Market Green Meetings?

Prepared by Jeff Anderton and Barbara Brookshire
October 2016

## Executive Summary

> *The executive summary tells the story of the report so the busy reader can get the gist of the content.*

In the past few years, potential clients have increasingly requested green meeting options. As a result, Prestigio managers have increasingly wondered whether providing such options could increase revenues in our conventions and meetings business. This report addresses whether the Prestigio should develop and market green meeting options. It contains analysis in the following areas: (a) market demand for green meetings; (b) risks of marketing green meetings; (c) standards and best practices for green meetings; (d) return on investment for green meetings; and (e) recommendations.

Generally, the research indicates that market demand for green meetings is growing, with the majority of meeting planners showing interest. The following features define the increasing demand: (a) many public sector organizations are required to hold green meetings; (b) many private sector organizations seek green meetings as part of CSR efforts; (c) many organizations are pursuing more local options for meetings; and (d) many conference attendees want green meetings. Right now is a good time to develop green meetings because demand far exceeds supply for small- to medium-sized meetings.

Hotels of comparable size to the Prestigio have reported strong return on investment for minimal investments in developing and marketing green meetings. However, the future demand is neither clear nor certain. As a result, the Prestigio should make relatively small, short-term investments to provide some green meeting options. This will position us to invest more heavily as we learn more about the long-term demand. In particular, we recommend the following actions during the next year:

> *The executive summary concludes with recommendations.*

1. Hire a green meetings specialist.
2. Get a fleet of hybrid or alternative fuel vans.
3. Gain recognition and certification as a green meetings venue from reputable third-party organizations.
4. Adjust marketing strategy to focus more extensively on local organizations.
5. Re-evaluate prospects in the public sector.
6. Feature our green meeting options prominently in marketing materials.

## Introduction to Green Meetings

> *Introduction begins with statement of and brief background to the problem.*

Since 2011, our revenues from conventions and meetings have declined by roughly 23 percent. Since meetings constitute nearly 60 percent of our total revenues and form the basis for our reputation as a high-class provider of events, we need to seek new ways of rebuilding our conventions and meetings business.

The Great Recession that began in late 2007 led to lost revenue for nearly all hotels and organizations dependent on business travel. However, by 2011, the hotel industry had recovered. Since 2011, nationwide growth in revenue

**FIGURE 13.6**

*(Continued)*

for conventions and meetings has increased by an average of 2.8 percent per year (Morea, 2016). Unlike other hotel venues in the conventions and meetings industry, the Prestigio has not rebounded in the past few years. One reason we may not have rebounded is we still do not provide options for clients who want green meetings. Our director of conventions and meetings, Barbara Brookshire, has noticed that many meeting planners inquire about green meeting options. She is certain that we have lost business because we do not provide such meetings, and she expects that meeting planners will increasingly request these options.

The purpose of this report is to examine the following aspects of green meetings: (a) market demand for green meetings; (b) risks of developing and marketing green meetings; (c) standards and best practices for green meetings; and (d) potential return on investment. We conclude the report with recommendations about the degree to which the Prestigio Hotel should develop and market green meetings.

> *Introduction concludes with a preview of report contents.*

> *Headings clearly state section content.*

### Market Demand for Green Meetings

Increasingly, meeting planners expect green meeting options (Boo & Park, 2013; Edelstein, 2015; Mykletun, Bartkeviciute, & Puchkova, 2014). Just seven to eight years ago, surveys of meeting planners showed that a *minority* showed strong interest in green meetings, with roughly 18 to 43 percent in various surveys deeming them important (Drammeh, 2009; Gecker, 2008). Around 2009, the market demand for green meetings quickly accelerated. Within the past few years, surveys show that the *majority* of meeting planners expect green meeting options or discuss green meeting options during pre-event planning. For example, the following survey results are typical over the past few years:

- 60 percent of meeting planners reported that green policies were *very important* or *somewhat important* when selecting a meeting venue (Edelstein, 2015).
- 64 percent of meeting professionals stated that green meeting options were *fairly important* or *critically important* in their venue choices (Mason, 2014).
- 86 percent of meeting planners discussed green meeting options during pre-event planning with sales teams at conference and exhibition centers (Simons & Unterkofler, 2015).

> *In-text citations allow readers to know exactly where the information came from.*

Venues that offer a wide variety of green meeting options are in a strong competitive position. Several industry analysts have reported that the demand for green meetings is far greater than the supply, especially for hotel venues that host small- to medium-sized events of 50 to 100 hotel rooms (Koenig, 2014). In our local event market (within 500 miles), just 20 to 25 percent of small- to medium-sized meeting venues offer significant options for green meetings (J. Hardaway, personal communication, October 14, 2016; K. Cafferty, personal communication, October 15, 2016).

While surveys of meeting planners and forecasts by industry analysts point to a continuing and increasing demand, not much detailed information is available about the market size for green meetings. In our research, we found that the following trends will increasingly impact market size: (a) many public sector organizations are required to hold green meetings; (b) many private sector organizations seek green meetings as part of corporate social responsibility (CSR) efforts; (c) many organizations are pursuing local options for meetings; and (d) conference attendees are increasingly expecting green meetings

**FIGURE 13.6**

*(Continued)*

*Many Public Sector Organizations Are Required to Hold Green Meetings*

Government agencies are leading the way in demanding green meetings (Torrence, 2010). Many government groups are increasingly required to abide by *Environmentally Preferable Purchasing* (EPP). The following EPP standards are the overarching principles that apply to green meetings:

- Include environmental factors as well as traditional considerations of price and performance as part of the normal purchasing process.
- Emphasize pollution prevention early in the purchasing process.
- Examine multiple environmental attributes throughout a product's or service's life cycle.
- Compare relative environmental impacts when selecting products and services.
- Collect and base purchasing decisions on accurate and meaningful information about environmental performance. (Environmental Protection Agency, 2016)

The application of these EPP principles demonstrates that the major sources of waste and pollution for meetings are the following: marketing of events and registration; travel to the event; hotel stays; food services; exhibition halls; and local transportation. As a result, government meeting planners increasingly emphasize green meetings with the following components: location that minimizes travel; eco-friendly meeting facilities and processes; local transportation; eco-friendly catering; and eco-friendly promotion, marketing, and registration practices (Environmental Protection Agency, 2016).

*Many Private Sector Organizations Seek Green Meetings as Part of CSR Efforts*

> These level-2 headings allow rapid comprehension of key supporting points.

One of the primary motivations for planning green meetings is to fulfill corporate CSR initiatives. Nearly all Fortune 500 organizations have developed CSR plans that include green initiatives, and, increasingly, small- and medium-sized organizations emphasize green initiatives as part of CSR plans. Many stakeholders expect that being a good corporate citizen must include these green initiatives (Gecker, 2009). Meeting planners, then, often seek out green meetings to satisfy CSR plans. In fact, 42 percent of meeting planners reported that they plan green meetings with CSR in mind (Meeting Professionals International, 2011).

With the prominent role of green initiatives as part of CSR efforts, green meetings will continue to be a focus because meetings are among the least eco-friendly activities for many organizations. According to MeetGreen, a three-day conference with 300 attendees creates 3,800 pounds of solid waste and 350,000 pounds of carbon emissions. It creates the waste equivalent to water resources that would fill half of an Olympic-sized swimming pool and greenhouse gases to fill 25 million basketballs (MeetGreen, 2015; Torrence, 2010).

*Many Organizations Are Pursuing Local and Hybrid Options for Meetings*

The major cause of pollution for meetings is travel to and from these events. As a result, many organizations that are seeking to minimize carbon footprints are holding meetings that are located closer to their headquarters. Because of increased demand for green meetings combined with the impact of higher fuel costs, 32 percent of meeting planners say they are planning more local events (American Express Meetings & Events, 2015; Edelstein, 2011a).

Similarly, many meetings planners seek virtual options at meetings to reduce travel for some attendees. Roughly 29 percent of meeting planners say they will hold more hybrid meetings that include virtual options for attendees

**FIGURE 13.6**

*(Continued)*

not traveling to the meeting (American Express Meetings & Events, 2015). Furthermore, 52 percent of meeting planners predict an increase in virtual events in the upcoming years (Braley, 2015).

*Conference Attendees Are Increasingly Expecting Green Meetings*

While meeting planners most directly impact demand, conference attendees influence the expectations of meeting planners. A variety of studies have shown that conference attendees generally expect greener meetings (Aksu, Sahin, Ozturk, & Gulteken, 2016; Bongkosh & Mair, 2012). Furthermore, once conference attendees have experienced a green meeting, they are more likely to expect them in the future (Boo & Park, 2013; Mykletun, Bartkeviciute, & Puchkova, 2014). Conference attendees are particularly likely to expect future green meetings when they have attended a green meeting with excellent customer service. (Gao & Mattila, 2014).

> *Headings support common storylines and rationales in business decision-making, including terms such as benefits, risks, and best practices.*

### Risks of Marketing Green Meetings

Although the demand for green meetings is growing, developing and marketing green meetings is not without risks. While meeting planners increasingly ask about green meetings in RFPs, little evidence shows the impact of such options on the ultimate selection of a meeting venue. In particular, clients resist green meetings for the following reasons (Campbell, 2008):

- *Many meeting planners incorrectly believe green meetings are more expensive.* In reality, most green meetings cost less than non-green meetings (Clarke, 2015). Yet, many meeting planners and other decision-makers perceive that green meetings cost more (D'Elsa, 2013; Gecker, 2009; Lowe, 2010; MeetGreen, 2010).
- *Some executives and senior managers are not interested in green meetings.* Although meeting planners organize and coordinate most of the communication between their organizations and meeting venues, they are rarely the final decision-makers. Sometimes meeting planners express interest in green meetings only to lack support from decision-makers in their organizations (Campbell, 2008).
- *Many potential clients view green meetings as lower-quality experiences.* Many meeting planners worry that although green meetings are eco-friendly and may even save money, they provide a lower-quality experience. This is largely a misperception. Many studies have shown that green meeting practices were correlated with higher satisfaction among convention attendees (Aksu, Sahin, Ozturk, & Gulteken, 2016; Bongkosh & Mair, 2012; Boo & Park, 2013; Campbell, 2008; Gao & Mattila, 2014; Lee, Brieter, & Choi, 2011; Mykletun, Bartkeviciute, & Puchkova, 2014).
- *Some meeting planners are unaware of green meeting options.* Because of the limited supply of small- to medium-sized venues that offer legitimate green meeting options, some meeting planners assume that they will not find a venue up to their expectations. Similarly, many meeting planners are unaware of the dozens of green meeting options that many venues offer (Campbell, 2008; Simons & Unterkofler, 2015).

Many of the risks of marketing green meetings are based on misperceptions. Thus, any successful development and marketing of green meetings must focus on educating the client base about the actual costs and actual quality of green meetings (Campbell, 2008; Simons & Unterkofler, 2015).

Even when green meetings are requested or desired, they are seldom prioritized. In a recent survey of meeting planners, green meetings were least likely to be identified as the top concern (American Express Meetings & Events, 2015). Furthermore, while meeting planners and conference attendees prefer green meetings, the vast majority are not willing to pay more for green meetings (Edelstein, 2015; Millar & Baloglu, 2011; Rittichainuwat & Mair, 2012). In fact, a recent survey of meeting planners showed 65 percent said they never implement green meeting initiatives that add cost (Edelstein, 2015). One exception is that some meeting planners are willing to pay a premium for distinctive eco-friendly services such as sourcing local food (Lee & Slocum, 2015).

– Page 4 –

**FIGURE 13.6**

*(Continued)*

### Standards and Best Practices for Green Meetings

During the past five years, various third-party organizations have developed concrete standards for green meetings. These organizations provide many levels of certification to green meeting venues. Also, the government and major hotel venues have contributed to emerging standards for green meetings. Finally, meeting planners have contributed to the acceptance of standards by prioritizing some standards over others.

*Certifications for Green Meeting Standards*

Over three years, the Environmental Protection Agency (EPA) and the Green Meeting Industry Council developed the most well-known and respected set of green meeting standards: the APEX/ASTM Environmentally Sustainable Event Standards. These standards are the most comprehensive in the industry (Braley, 2013; Green Meeting Industry Council, n.d.; Spatrisano, 2014).

The APEX/ASTM standards address nine areas: (a) accommodation; (b) audiovisual and production; (c) communications and marketing; (d) destinations; (e) exhibits; (f) food and beverage; (g) meeting venues; (h) on-site offices; and (i) transportation. These nine standards involve four levels of compliance from minimal to zero-waste meetings (level one to level four). Currently, there are about 30 pages of standards. Some meeting planners view the standards as most applicable to large conventions (Braley, 2013; Convention Industry Council, n.d.; Green Meeting Industry Council, n.d.; Torrence, 2010).

While the APEX/ASTM standards are the most reputable and well known, over 800 green certifications are available (Strick & Fenich, 2013). Aside from APEX/ASTM standards, the most important certifications for green meetings are Green Key, Green Seal, Green Glob, and Energy Star (Braley, 2013).

Green certifications are important to many meeting planners. In a 2013 survey of meeting planners, about 30 percent of meeting planners said that green certifications are a factor in venue selection to a *great extent* or to *somewhat of an extent*. On the flip side, 39 percent said they were not a factor at all (Edelstein, 2013). Other research has shown some meeting planners are willing to pay more for green meetings from a certified provider (Sox, Carpenter, & Strick, 2013)

*Standards from the Public Sector and Major Hotel Venues*

Another set of standards that are particularly relevant for public sector meetings was developed by the Environmental Protection Agency (EPA). The EPA requires government agencies to include the following questions in RFPs for meetings:

1. Do you have a recycling program? If so, please describe.
2. Do you have a linen/towel reuse option that is communicated to guests?
3. Do guests have easy access to public transportation or shuttle services at your facility?
4. Are lights and air conditioning turned off when rooms are not in use? If so, how do you ensure this?
5. Do you provide bulk dispensers or reusable containers for beverages, food, and condiments?
6. Do you provide reusable serving utensils, napkins, and tablecloths when food and beverages are served?
7. Do you have an energy-efficiency program? Please describe.
8. Do you have a water-conservation program? Please describe.
9. Does your facility provide guests with paperless check-in and checkout?
10. Does your facility use recycled or recyclable products? Please describe.
11. Do you source food from local growers or take into account the growing practices of farmers that provide the food? Please describe.
12. Do you use bio-based or biodegradable products, including bio-based "cafeteriaware"? Please describe.
13. Do you provide training to your employees on these green initiatives? Please describe.
14. What other environmental initiatives have you undertaken, including any environment-related certifications you possess, EPA voluntary partnerships in which you participate, support of a green supplier's network, or other initiatives? (Environmental Protection Agency, 2016)

– Page 5 –

**FIGURE 13.6**

*(Continued)*

Various websites, such as Travelocity and Yahoo, designate hotels as green hotels. In some cases, even travel companies and agencies have created measures of green compliance. For example, American Express Meetings and Events created a metric that measures carbon, water, and waste for each meeting venue (Edelstein, 2011b). In addition to venue certification, some hotel chains provide in-house certification for green planners. For example, Marriott has certified employees as Marriott Green Planners for nearly a decade. Thousands of these certified employees work directly with meeting planners to make meetings more sustainable (Braley, 2014; Lowe, 2010).

*Most Sought After Standards by Meeting Planners*

Meeting planners also contribute to green meeting standards based on their priorities. Several studies have highlighted some of their most sought after green initiatives. For example, Edelstein (2013) provided *Meetings & Conventions* research about meeting planners' preferences. As displayed in Table 1, meeting planners are most interested in managing food sustainably and recycling paper and other solid products. Meeting planners appear less concerned about water management issues. Christensen (2015) similarly reported that the top three green procedures sought after by meeting planners were donation of leftover food, local food sourcing, and recycling bins in guest rooms. Another study of meeting planners showed that the three most common practices to achieve green meetings were the following: reducing paper by using digital alternatives (79%); providing onsite recycling programs (61%); and selecting host cities that require less travel (48%) (Richard K. Miller & Associates, 2010).

> Table is sorted to clearly show the priorities of meeting planners.

*Table* 1. Preferences of Meeting Planners for Green Meeting Initiatives.

| Green initiative | Require or Prefer | No Preference | Prefer Not to Have |
|---|---|---|---|
| Donation of leftover food | 73% | 23% | 4% |
| Local food sourcing | 67% | 30% | 3% |
| Recycling bins in guest rooms | 67% | 27% | 6% |
| Towel reuse policy | 65% | 25% | 10% |
| Linen reuse policy | 62% | 28% | 10% |
| Low-flush toilets | 46% | 42% | 12% |
| Low-flow shower heads | 44% | 31% | 25% |
| Soap and shampoo dispensers | 26% | 42% | 32% |

**Return on Investment for Green Meetings**

Although surveys of meeting planners show growing interest in green meetings, little is known about the return on investment for developing and marketing green meetings. Furthermore, little is known about how often green meeting options are a deciding factor for meeting planners. Rather, much of the research and advice about green meetings focuses more on social responsibility than profitability.

We talked to three individuals during the past month who have initiated green meetings in their hotels as a marketing strategy: Jack Hardaway, Director of Meetings at Lionwood Hotels; Melanie Dipprey, General Manager of Silver Lake Hotel and Resort; and Kirsley Cafferty, Director of Sales at the Easton Inn. Each of these individuals is extensively involved in marketing meetings at their hotels, all of which are similar in size to our hotel. Each has initiated green meetings during the past 2 to 3 years.

Based on our conversations with them, we concluded that the return on investment for developing a basic infrastructure for green meetings is strong – as high as 500 percent. Each hotel has invested approximately $150,000 to $250,000 annually to build their green meetings infrastructures. Although precisely determining how much return is due to new green meeting options is difficult, each hotel attributes between $500,000 and $1.3 million in additional revenue due to providing green meeting options (J. Hardaway, personal communication, October 14, 2016; K. Cafferty, personal communication, October 15, 2016; M. Dipprey, personal communication, October 14, 2016).

– Page 6 –

> Report relies on firsthand interviews in addition to secondary research. The firsthand information addresses difficult-to-find secondary information.

**FIGURE 13.6**

*(Continued)*

These hotels have taken the following actions, which require little investment, to develop and market their green meetings: (a) hired or trained full-time green meetings specialists; (b) sought out public sector organizations; (c) gained Green Seal certification; and (d) created a webpage about green meeting options (J. Hardaway, personal communication, October 14, 2016; K. Cafferty, personal communication, October 15, 2016; M. Dipprey, personal communication, October 14, 2016). In addition, Lionwood Hotels has started ensuring that at least half of all catered food is sourced from within fifty miles of their hotels. Lionwood managers believe their focus on local, organic foods has been the deciding factor in two groups selecting their hotel for conventions (J. Hardaway, personal communication, October 14, 2016)

> *Report relies on firsthand interviews in addition to secondary research. The firsthand information addresses difficult-to-find secondary information.*

### Recommendations

With the majority of meeting planners in the public and private sectors to some extent expecting green meetings, we should move immediately to develop and market green meetings. However, because the future demand for green meetings and related services is not well understood (even among the major hotel chains), we recommend a short-term strategy. An initial one-year strategy requires little initial investment but positions us to move forward aggressively in years to come as we gain a clearer understanding of the market demands. Specifically, we recommend the following actions in the next year:

1. *Hire a green meetings specialist.* An experienced green meeting planner or marketer could help us develop green meeting options and provide the needed expertise to develop longer-term plans.

2. *Get a fleet of hybrid or alternative fuel vans.* Many meeting planners on RFPs request that hotels provide energy-efficient transportation options. Providing local transportation with energy-efficient vans can significantly lower the overall carbon footprint of conferences held at our hotel and serve as a high-profile illustration of our commitment to eco-friendly meetings. Our initial estimates suggest that we could replace our four-van fleet for roughly $100,000 (after trade-in or sale of our existing fleet).

3. *Gain recognition and certification as a green meetings venue from reputable third-party organizations.* Gaining certification will immediately place us in a select group of venues. Moreover, the process of gaining certification will help us develop knowledge about providing green meetings. This effort also allows us to meet evolving industry standards and promote ourselves with these third-party endorsements. Specifically, we can accomplish the following actions in the upcoming year:

    a. Achieve Level 1 compliance for each of the nine standards in the APEX/ASTM green meeting standards.
    b. Gain Green Seal certification as a green meetings provider.
    c. Gain recognition as a green hotel on websites such as Expedia and Travelocity.
    d. Join the Green Meeting Industry Council.

4. *Adjust our marketing strategy to focus more extensively on local organizations.* Most organizations are realizing that travel to and from the host city of an event is the least eco-friendly aspect of meetings. Furthermore, more organizations are seeking to save money by holding more local meetings. As a result, we suggest increasing our marketing efforts to organizations located within five hundred miles.

5. *Re-evaluate prospects in the public sector.* Government agencies are among the most progressive organizations that are seeking green meeting options. As we position ourselves as a green meetings provider, we should market aggressively to public sector organizations.

6. *Feature our green meeting options prominently in marketing materials.* We should feature our new options prominently on our website and develop contract language that favors green meetings. On the website, we should address frequently asked questions and address frequent misperceptions about green meetings.

> *Recommendations are specific and achievable. They are based on needs and opportunities described in the body of the paper.*

– Page 7 –

> *Enumerated list contains recommendations. They are set apart in italics followed by a short rationale to allow decision-makers to understand the ideas clearly.*

**FIGURE 13.6**

*(Continued)*

# References

Aksu, A., Sahin, I., Ozturk, A., & Gulteken, S. (2016). Analysing green meeting perceptions of medical meeting participants: An exploratory research in the Anatalya region of Turkey. *European Journal of Tourism Research*, 12, 114-132.

American Express Meetings & Events. (2015). 2015 *global meetings & events forecast*. USA: Author.

Bongkosh, R., & Mair, J. (2012). An exploratory study of attendee perceptions of green meetings. *Journal of Convention & Event Tourism*, 13(3), 147-158.

Boo, S., & Park, E. (2013). An examination of green intention: The effect of environmental knowledge and educational experiences on meeting planners' implementation of green meeting practices. *Journal of Sustainable Tourism*, 21(8), 1129-1147.

Braley, S. J. F. (2013, October 1). *Making sense of green hotel certifications*. Retrieved from http://www.meetings-conventions.com/News/Features/Making-Sense-of-Green-Hotel-Certifications/

Braley, S. J. F. (2014, May 28). *Marriott wants to help planners go paperless*. Retrieved from http://www.meetings-conventions.com//Blogs/Green-Standard/Meetings%20and%20Conventions-%20The%20Green%20Standard/post/2014/05/28/Marriott-Wants-to-Help-Planners-Go-Paperless

Braley, S. J. F. (2015, December 1). *MPI research: Quarterly survey points to improving business conditions*. Retrieved from http://www.meetings-conventions.com/News/Research/MPI-Research-Meetings/

Campbell, S. (2008, January). *Shades of green*. Retrieved from www.elitemeetings.com/docs/shades-of-green.php

Clarke, K. (2015, April 15). *Five green meeting myths: Busted!* Retrieved from http://conventionforum.com/five-green-meeting-myths-busted/

Convention Industry Council. (n.d.). *APEX/ASTM sustainable event standards*. Retrieved from http://www.gmicglobal.org/?page=APEX

Cumming, P., & Pelham, F. (2010). *Making events more sustainable: A guide to BS* 8901. London, UK: BSI Group.

D'Elsa, L. (2013, September 24). *Don't talk to me*. Retrieved from http://www.meetings-conventions.com/Blogs/Guest-Stars/post/2013/09/24/Dont-Talk-Green-to-Me!

Drammeh, J. (2009, February 15). *Green meetings good for business*. Retrieved from www.connectyourmeetings.com/2009/02/15/green-meetings-good-for-business/

Draper, J., Dawson, M., & Casey, E. (2011). An exploratory study of the importance of sustainable practices in the meeting and convention site selection process. *Journal of Convention & Event Tourism*, 12(3), 153-178.

Edelstein, L. G. (2011a, May). Slammed by fuel costs: Planners say oil prices are directly affecting meetings. *Meetings and Conventions*, 46(5), 20-21.

Edelstein, L. G. (2011b, October 18). *American Express releases green meetings measurement tool*. Retrieved from www.meetings-conventions.com/articles/american-express-releases-green-meetings-measurement-tool/c44242.aspx

Edelstein, L. G. (2013, October 1). *How Important is green? On-site conservation efforts preferred but not a priority*. Retrieved from http://www.meetings-conventions.com/News/Research/How-Important-is-Green-/

Edelstein, L. G. (2015, November 1). *Green meetings: Low priority?* Retrieved from http://www.meetings-conventions.com/News/Research/Green-Meetings-policy-recycling-survey/

Environmental Protection Agency. (2016, April 27). *Identifying greener meetings and conferences*. Retrieved from www.epa.gov/greenerproducts/identifying-greener-meetings-and-conferences

Gao, Y. L., & Mattila, A. S. (2014). Improving consumer satisfaction in green hotels: The roles of perceived warmth, perceived competence, and CSR motive. *International Journal of Hospitality Management*, 42, 20-31.

Gecker, R. (2009, July). Lean and green: How companies that are cutting budgets still manage to make their meetings sustainable. *Corporate Meetings & Incentives*, 28(7), 16-20.

*Reference list (in APA style) allows decision-makers and other readers to follow up on information and make judgments about data quality. It also inspires confidence in the writer as organized and detail-oriented.*

**FIGURE 13.6**

*(Continued)*

Green Meeting Industry Council. (n.d.). *APEX/ASTM sustainable event standard overview*. Retrieved from http://www.gmicglobal.org/?page=APEX

Kim, Y., & Han, H. (2010). Intention to pay conventional-hotel prices at a green hotel – a modification of the theory of planned behavior. *Journal of Sustainable Tourism*, 18(8), 997-1014.

Koenig, C. (2014, October 24). *Small meetings: Big Influence*. Retrieved from http://www.smartmeetings.com/meeting-planning/13433/small-meetings-big-influence

Lee, J., Breiter, D., & Choi, Y. (2011). Quality of a green destination as perceived by convention attendees: The relationships between greening and competitiveness. *Proceedings of the 16th Graduate Students Research Conference in Hospitality and Tourism*.

Lee, S., & Slocum, S. (2015). Understanding the role of local food in the meeting industry: An exploratory study of meeting planners' perception of local food in sustainable meeting planning. *Journal of Convention & Event Tourism*, 16(1), 45-60.

Lowe, M. C., (2010, October). The greening of hotels: A look at what major chains are doing to support eco-friendly meetings. *Meetings & Conventions*, 45(10), 45-56.

MeetGreen. (2010). *Oracle Open World sustainable event report*. Portland, OR: Author.

MeetGreen. (2015, May). *The environmental footprint of an event*. Retrieved from http://meetgreen.com/wp-content/uploads/2015/05/eventfoot.pdf.

Millar, M., & Balogu, S. (2011). Hotel guests' preferences for green guest room attributes. *Cornell Hospitality Quarterly*, 52(3), 302-311.

Morea, S. (2016). *IBISWorld industry report* 56192: *Trade show and conference planning in the US*. Los Angeles, CA: IBISWorld.

Mykletun, R.J., Bartkeviciute, M., & Puchkova, Y. (2014) Green meetings – do they matter to their closest stakeholders? *Scandinavian Journal of Hospitality and Tourism*, 14(3), 211-233.

Pizam, A. (2009). Green hotels: A fad, ploy or fact of life? *International Journal of Hospitality Management*, 28(1), 1-5.

Richard K. Miller & Associates (2010). 2010 *Travel & Tourism Market Research Handbook*. Loganville, GA: Author.

Rittichainuwat, B., & Mair, J. (2012) An exploratory study of attendee perceptions of green meetings. *Journal of Convention & Event Tourism*, 13, 147-158.

Simons, A., & Unterkofler, C. (2015). *Green venue report* 2015: *The state of convention & exhibition center sustainability*. Portland, OR: Greenview.

Sox, C., Benjamin, S., Carpenter, J., & Strick, S. (2013). An exploratory study of meeting planners and conference attendees' perception of sustainable issues in convention centers. *Journal of Convention & Event Tourism*, 14, 144-161.

Spatrisano, A., & Wilson, N. J. (2007). *Simple steps to green meetings and events: The professional's guide to saving money and the earth*. Portland, OR: Meeting Strategies Worldwide.

Spatrisano, A. (2014). *What you need to know about green meetings standards*. Retrieved from www.greenbiz.com/blog/2014/01/21/epaapproved-standards-green-meetings

Strick, S., & Fenich G. C. (2013). Green certifications and ecolabels in the MEEC industry. *Journal of Convention & Event Tourism*, 14, 162-172.

Torrence, S. (2010, November). Change the world one meeting at a time: APEX/ASTM sustainability standards nearly set. *Corporate Meetings & Incentives*, 29(11), 18-21.

Travel Portland and Oregon Convention Center. (2011, October 23, 2011). *Green meetings*. Retrieved from www.greenmeetings.travelportland.com/

**FIGURE 13.7**

Business Report with Primary Research in Slide Deck Format

**Guest Satisfaction among Conference Attendees
at the Prestigio Hotel & Resort**

baker consulting • *Prepared by Shania Baker* • February 2017

© Andersen Ross/Blend Images LLC RF

The title page—visually and textually—rapidly shows the key theme: guest satisfaction among conference attendees.

In slide deck format for reports, analysts can focus slightly more on the visual and aesthetic nature of reports. However, the most important issues still relate to the strength of the research.

## Executive Summary

*Survey Details*

Baker Consulting surveyed 264 convention attendees who participated in three- or four-day conventions between January and December 2016.

*Key Findings*

- Satisfaction ratings for key guest services and amenities: conference meals, 76 percent; meeting rooms, 75 percent; staff and service, 69 percent.

- Key indicators of repeat business: overall guest satisfaction, 84 percent; willingness to recommend the Prestigio, 57 percent.

- Overall satisfaction ratings by gender and income: women, 78 percent; men, 89 percent; higher-income, 66 percent; lower-income, 88 percent.

- Overall satisfaction in the past five years: 2012, 87 percent; 2013, 81 percent; 2014, 79 percent; 2015, 79 percent; 2016, 84 percent.

*Key Conclusions*

- The Prestigio fell short of 85 percent satisfaction targets in the following areas: conference meals, meeting rooms, and staff and service.

- The Prestigio received high ratings for its restaurants, which are the most popular guest service and amenity.

*Key Conclusions (continued)*

Preferences for other guest services and amenities are highly variable based on gender and income.

- The Prestigio fell short of its goals for overall satisfaction and willingness to recommend.

- Women and higher-income guests tend to be less satisfied, less willing to return, and less willing to recommend the Prestigio. Similarly, women and higher-income guests are also less satisfied with conference meals and staff and service.

- The Prestigio has made significant improvement over the past year in nearly all satisfaction ratings following four years of declines.

*Recommendations*

- Examine ways to raise satisfaction among women and higher-income conference attendees.

- Adapt the marketing of meetings to the group composition of prospects.

- Continue customer service initiatives to improve staff and service ratings.

- Reexamine catering services to improve conference meals.

This executive summary is in *structured format* (compared to the narrative format of the executive summary in the prior report). The headings allow decision makers and other readers to easily distinguish between survey details, findings, conclusions, and recommendations.

**FIGURE 13.7**

*(Continued)*

### Introduction

Guest satisfaction has always been the foundation for repeat business. With so many online reviews of hotels readily available to meeting planners, the importance of achieving high guest satisfaction ratings is more important now than ever. Since 2012, the Prestigio has evaluated guest satisfaction and future intentions among conference attendees with an annual survey to help determine priorities for improving guest satisfaction. This report provides the results of this year's survey as well as year-to-year comparisons for the past five years.

### Survey Purpose and Administration

This guest satisfaction survey addressed the following broad questions:

- How satisfied are conference attendees with conference services and amenities?
- What hotel amenities do conference attendees use during their conference stays?
- How likely are our conference attendees to contribute to future business?

Most of the survey questions have remained identical since annual surveys were started in 2012. Some unique questions are inserted into the survey each year to address particular areas of strategic concern. Survey questions are provided in the Appendix of Survey Questions.

The survey was administered online. The survey link was sent to 534 guests who had participated in three- or four-day conferences between January 2016 and December 2016. Altogether, 236 respondents completed the survey, garnering a participation rate of roughly 44 percent.

### Results from This Year's Survey

Findings and conclusions can be grouped into three broad areas: (1) satisfaction with conference services and amenities; (2) use of Prestigio guest services and amenities during conference stays; and (3) overall satisfaction and future intentions among conference attendees.

#### Satisfaction with Conference Services and Amenities

Between two-thirds (64%) and three-fourths (76%) of respondents expressed satisfaction with various conference services and amenities (see Table 1). These results indicate the following:

- *The Prestigio fell short of its goals in the following areas: conference meals, meeting rooms, and staff and service.* In January 2016, the Prestigio marketing team set goals to reach at least 85 percent satisfaction for these three key areas. Barbara Brookshire has indicated that 85 percent satisfaction in these areas would place the Prestigio in the elite category compared to our competitors. The Prestigio fell between 9 and 16 percent short of these goals.
- *Prestigio guests are most satisfied with conference meals and meeting rooms.* While the goal remains to reach 85 percent satisfaction for all conference services and amenities, the Prestigio marketing team generally views 75 percent satisfaction as good performance. Therefore, satisfaction with conference meals and meeting rooms is acceptable. However, the Prestigio may not have the unique competitive advantage in this area that it did five years ago.
- *Many of Prestigio guests are unhappy with Internet pricing and the business center.* Roughly one in three respondents was not satisfied with these services.

Headings and bulleted items allow readers to fairly rapidly read this report. This is particularly helpful for data-intensive reports such as this one.

Italicized conclusions help decision makers recognize what big ideas emerge from the report.

**Table 1.** Satisfaction with Conference Services and Amenities.

| | Conference Meals | Meeting Rooms | Staff and Service | Internet Pricing | Business Center |
|---|---|---|---|---|---|
| *All Respondents* | 76% (179) | 75% (178) | 69% (163) | 66% (155) | 64% (152) |
| *Gender* | | | | | |
| Male | 85% (108) | 76% (97) | 72% (91) | 73% (93) | 56% (71) |
| Female | 65% (71) | 74% (81) | 66% (72) | 57% (62) | 74% (81) |
| *Income* | | | | | |
| Under $40,000 | 73% (94) | 77% (56) | 78% (57) | 38% (28) | 64% (47) |
| $40,000–$75,000 | 62% (79) | 76% (97) | 68% (87) | 76% (97) | 66% (84) |
| Over $75,000 | 57% (20) | 71% (25) | 54% (19) | 86% (30) | 60% (21) |

*Note*: Altogether, 236 respondents took the survey. Percentages and number of respondents (in parentheses) refer to those who responded *satisfied* or *extremely satisfied* on the survey.

Tables allow decision makers to examine the data themselves and make their own judgments.

**Table 2.** Use of Prestigio Guest Services and Amenities during Conference Stay.

| | Prestigio Restaurants | Comedy Club | Fitness Center | Swimming Pool | Spa | Golf Course |
|---|---|---|---|---|---|---|
| *All Respondents* | 53% (126) | 39% (92) | 35% (82) | 31% (73) | 19% (45) | 8% (18) |
| *Gender* | | | | | | |
| Male | 46% (59) | 53% (67) | 38% (48) | 29% (37) | 2% (3) | 11% (14) |
| Female | 61% (67) | 23% (25) | 31% (34) | 33% (36) | 39% (42) | 4% (4) |
| *Income* | | | | | | |
| Under $40,000 | 33% (24) | 22% (16) | 18% (13) | 33% (24) | 1% (1) | 3% (2) |
| $40,000–$75,000 | 62% (79) | 50% (64) | 39% (50) | 30% (39) | 17% (22) | 7% (9) |
| Over $75,000 | 66% (23) | 34% (12) | 43% (15) | 29% (10) | 63% (22) | 20% (7) |

*Note*: Altogether, 236 respondents took the survey. Percentages and number of respondents (in parentheses) refer to those who responded *satisfied* or *extremely satisfied* on the survey.

Several pictures help readers visualize what survey respondents are providing feedback about.

Photos: (top) © Thinkstock/Jupiterimages RF; (bottom) © Ingram Publishing/SuperStock RF

**FIGURE 13.7**

*(Continued)*

### Use of Prestigio Guest Services and Amenities during Conference Stays

By far, the most used guest services and amenities by conference attendees are the Prestigio restaurants, with over half (53%) of our respondents stating they ate at Prestigio restaurants during their conference stays. Roughly 30 to 40 percent of respondents reported using the comedy club (39%), the fitness center (35%), or the swimming pool (31%). Relatively few of our conferences guests reported using the spa or golf course (see Table 2). These results indicate the following:

- *The restaurants are most convenient for use during conference stays.* Other internal surveys show that our non-conference guests tend to frequent the fitness center, the swimming pool, and the golf course more so than our restaurants. This implies that conference attendees most likely use the restaurants more than other services and amenities because of their busy conference schedules.
- *Use of guest services and amenities is highly variable based on gender and income.* This is discussed further in the *Differences by Gender and Income* section.

### Overall Satisfaction and Future Intentions among Conference Attendees

Overall, the vast majority (84%) of respondents reported satisfaction with their conference experiences. Nearly three out of four (73%) respondents stated that they would want to attend another conference at the Prestigio, and nearly six in ten respondents (57%) said they would recommend the Prestigio as a good site for a business conference

(see Table 3). These results indicate the following:

- *The Prestigio fell short of its goals for guests' overall satisfaction and willingness to recommend the Prestigio.* In January 2016, the Prestigio marketing team set goals for overall satisfaction at 90 percent and willingness to recommend the Prestigio at 65 percent. The Prestigio fell short by 6 to 8 percentage points.
- *Overall satisfaction, desire to return to the Prestigio, and willingness to recommend the Prestigio are highly variable on gender and income.* This is discussed further in the *Differences by Gender and Income* section.

**Table 3.** Overall Satisfaction and Future Intentions among Conference Attendees.

|  | Overall Satisfaction | Want to Return | Would Recommend |
|---|---|---|---|
| *All Respondents* | 84% (198) | 73% (173) | 57% (135) |
| *Gender* | | | |
| Male | 89% (113) | 77% (98) | 66% (84) |
| Female | 78% (85) | 69% (75) | 47% (51) |
| *Income* | | | |
| Under $40,000 | 88% (64) | 81% (59) | 67% (49) |
| $40,000–$75,000 | 87% (111) | 74% (95) | 57% (73) |
| Over $75,000 | 66% (23) | 54% (19) | 37% (13) |

*Note:* Altogether, 236 respondents took the survey. Percentages and number of respondents (in parentheses) refer to those who responded *satisfied* or *extremely satisfied* on the survey. The full wording for survey items was as follows: Overall, I was satisfied with the conference experience; I would like to attend another business conference held at the Prestigio; I would recommend the Prestigio as a good site for a business conference.

### Differences by Gender and Income

For the first time, this year's guest satisfaction survey includes breakdowns by gender and income. The results indicate the following:

- *Women and higher-income guests tend to be less satisfied, less willing to return, and less willing to recommend* (see Figure 1). A review of findings in Table 3 reveals that women and higher-income guests are far less likely to express satisfaction on those items that we consider barometers of future and repeat business. On the issue of willingness to recommend, roughly half (47%) of women reported that they are willing to recommend, whereas roughly two-thirds (67%) of men said they would recommend the Prestigio. The difference is even larger by income level. Just one-third (37%) of high-income respondents said that they would

recommend the Prestigio, whereas roughly two-thirds (67%) of lower-income respondents said that they would do so.

- *Women and higher-income guests are less satisfied with conference meals and staff and service.* A review of Table 1 reveals that women and higher-income guests are less satisfied with conference meals and staff and service. In past years, we have identified these as key factors leading to overall satisfaction. The gaps are especially wide for conference meals. Whereas the vast majority (85%) of men were satisfied with conference meals, just two-thirds (65%) of women were satisfied. The gap is wider when considering income level. Whereas nearly all (89%) lower-income respondents were satisfied with conference meals, just over half (57%) of higher-income respondents felt this way.

**Figure 1.** Guest Satisfaction by Gender.

**Percentage of Agreement**

**Figure 2.** Guest Satisfaction by Income.

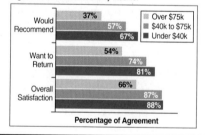

**Percentage of Agreement**

Formatting allows readers to quickly grasp the key ideas.

Table notes give additional information to decision makers to evaluate the data quality and relevance.

A section focused on gender and income emphasizes some of the key differences in satisfaction levels. These conclusions directly lead to some of the recommendations.

Charts reveal the key findings. Readers can rapidly see the differences by gender and income.

**FIGURE 13.7**

*(Continued)*

- *Women conference attendees tend to disproportionately choose Prestigio restaurants and the spa. Men conference attendees disproportionately choose the comedy club and the golf course.* Women attendees' top two choices of guest services and amenities are Prestigio restaurants (61%) and the spa (39%), whereas men attendees' top two choices are the comedy club (53%) and the Prestigio restaurants (46%). Men are roughly three times as likely to use the golf course (11% to 4%).

- *Higher-income guests tend to disproportionately choose the spa and the golf course; middle-income guests tend to disproportionately choose the comedy club; and lower-income guests tend to utilize all hotel services and amenities less with the exception of the swimming pool.* Higher-income guests are three to four times more likely to use the spa and golf course compared to middle-income guests. Lower-income guests rarely if ever use the spa and golf course.

These conclusions regarding the experiences of women and higher-income guests are quite concerning. The Prestigio deals mostly with meeting planners who are women, and our women respondents likely reflect the expectations of these meeting planners. Furthermore, the Prestigio brands itself as providing high-class conference experiences—those that would by assumption cater to the tastes of higher-income guests.

### Comparison of Guest Satisfaction Rates over the Past Five Years

Comparisons of survey results over the past five years reveal several basic trends (see Table 4 for complete results):

- *Overall satisfaction and willingness to recommend have increased over the past year.* From 2012 to 2015, overall satisfaction and willingness to recommend fell 10 and 13 percentage points, respectively. However, in the past year (2015 to 2016), overall satisfaction and willingness to recommend improved 5 and 8 percentage points, respectively (see Figure 3).

**Figure 3.** Five-year Trends in Indicators of Repeat Business.

The report provides perspective by comparing current satisfaction rates with those of past years.

A line chart rapidly allows readers to see a trend: slight declines over the 2012–2015 period and slight improvements during the past year.

---

- *Satisfaction with conference meals and staff and service has increased over the past year.* From 2012 to 2015, satisfaction with conference meals and staff and service decreased 19 and 3 percentage points, respectively. However, in the past year (2015 to 2016), satisfaction with conference meals and staff and service increased 8 and 7 percentage points, respectively.

- *Most indicators of satisfaction have returned to levels from five years ago.* In general, nearly all indicators of satisfaction showed steady deterioration from 2012 to 2015, with the past year showing improvement back to near-2000 levels of satisfaction.

|  | 2012 | 2013 | 2014 | 2015 | 2016 |
|---|---|---|---|---|---|
| *Indicators of Repeat and Referral Business* |  |  |  |  |  |
| Overall Satisfaction | 87% | 81% | 79% | 79% | 84% |
| Want to Return | 72% | 74% | 71% | 72% | 73% |
| Would Recommend | 62% | 59% | 55% | 49% | 57% |
| *Conference* |  |  |  |  |  |
| Conference Meals | 87% | 76% | 74% | 68% | 76% |
| Meeting Rooms | 77% | 71% | 74% | 76% | 75% |
| Staff & Service | 65% | 64% | 61% | 62% | 69% |
| Internet Pricing | - | - | - | - | 66% |
| Business Center | - | - | - | - | 64% |

*Note:* Altogether, 236 respondents took the survey. Percentages and number of respondents (in parentheses) refer to those who responded *agree* or *strongly agree* on the survey. The items for Internet pricing and the business center were introduced for the first time in this year's survey.

Table with five years of data allows readers to quickly see the trend for all survey items.

**FIGURE 13.7**

*(Continued)*

### Recommendations

1. *Examine ways to raise satisfaction among women and higher-income conference attendees.* Women and higher-income guests are particularly important to the Prestigio's brand and financial success. Most meeting planners the Prestigio works with are women and likely reflect the perspectives of female guests more so than our male guests. Furthermore, since the Prestigio brand stands for providing high-end conference services, the fact that higher-income guests are less satisfied is concerning. To better understand how to raise guest satisfaction among women and higher-income conference attendees, the Prestigio should take the following actions:

   a. Set up focus groups with women and higher-income guests to gain a more in-depth understanding of their concerns and suggestions for improvement.

   b. Informally talk to women and higher-income guests during conferences and catalog these guests' feedback in a lessons-learned database.

2. *Adapt the marketing of meetings to the group composition of prospects.* With a much better understanding of how the gender and income level of our guests impact which amenities and services they use, marketing materials can be developed to appeal more strongly to certain groups.

For example, each year the Prestigio hosts meetings for the Northern Hunters Association, with over 90 percent male membership, and the Farmers Healthcare Group, comprised mostly of female nurses.

3. *Continue customer service initiatives to improve staff and service ratings.* The recent initiatives to improve personalized guest service appear to have been successful. Given the emphasis on guest service as a foundation for all improvements, the Prestigio should maintain a high staff-to-guest ratio, provide incentives for exceptional guest service, and continue the intensive two-month mentoring and training program for new guest attendants.

4. *Reexamine catering services to improve conference meals.* Five years ago, Prestigio guests were overwhelmingly satisfied with conference meals. In fact, many guests recommended repeat business in large part due to the excellent meals. To cut costs, the Prestigio changed catering services over the past five years, and the result has been far lower guest satisfaction with meals. To strengthen or regain a reputation for high-end conference experiences, the Prestigio should identify ways to return to 2010-level guest satisfaction for conference meals.

Recommendations emerge directly from the survey findings and conclusions.

These recommendations serve as a good way to prioritize initiatives to improve guest satisfaction.

---

length, as you glance through these examples, consider the key features to strive for in all your reports: value to decision makers, precision, documentation, easy navigation, and objectivity. Also, notice how the report in Figure 13.7 is in slide deck format. Many reports, particularly survey reports, are increasingly created in slide deck format. This allows writers to create visually stronger and more creative reports. Yet, the same principles of strong report writing apply to this format. Notice that the report in slide deck format is for reading, not for a presentation. As you'll see in the upcoming chapters, your slides for presentations should contain far less content.

## Reviewing Your Reports for Fairness and Effectiveness

**LO13.6** Review reports for effectiveness and fairness.

As with other written documents, you will always review your reports to ensure that you have been fair to yourself and your readers. Also, you want to make sure the report is as effective as possible.

Since research-based reports are generally commissioned for high-stakes decisions, you have likely worked collaboratively with others. If you've developed the report by yourself, you should still try to get other perspectives before you officially submit it. When possible, discuss the report with the ultimate decision makers so that you can best tailor the final product to their needs.

As you review the report by yourself and with others, run through it numerous times, each time considering a different perspective. For example, review the entire document several times for accuracy and precision in logic. Review it at least once, imagining yourself in the position of decision makers to improve it based on what you perceive as their needs. Also, review it at least once for typos or mechanical errors. Make sure you review the report over several sittings and several days if possible, since you are unlikely to catch all of the changes you would ideally make in just one sitting. And for the perspective of an experienced business professional on writing reports, see the Communication Q&A with Rich Harrill.

## 💬 COMMUNICATION Q&A

### CONVERSATIONS WITH CURRENT BUSINESS PROFESSIONALS

**Pete Cardon: What are some keys to writing effective reports?**

**Rich Harrill:** Reports should be comprehensive in their presentation of data and information, but should also have a strong, succinct executive summary for busy industry and community leaders. The report should be well organized with a table of contents. Tables, graphs, and charts need to be used only where relevant to illustrate an example. The same rule goes for appendixes. I always provide a brief PowerPoint presentation to go with the document. It is often this presentation that is circulated among interested parties rather than the report itself. Project reports should be attractive. I now prefer "perfect" bound documents to messy, spiral binding. A writing and editing mentor once told me that you should write so that the reader can understand every word. He offered very simple but very effective advice in a world that sometimes uses esoteric words and concepts as a replacement for simple and direct communication.

**PC: How do you facilitate effective team writing on reports?**

**RH:** I believe it is best to let individual team members write in their own voice and style. In some cases, I might provide a very loose style sheet to guide certain requirements. However, I generally suggest structural or content changes to the authors. When the manuscript comes back after this first pass, an experienced editor and I will edit thoroughly and try to integrate the different styles. It is a good editor's job to weave the submissions together in a way that results in a coherent document with consistent style and tone.

**PC: Has report writing changed during your career?**

**RH:** Yes, and quite drastically. Increasing competition among individuals and firms has upped the ante on report writing. Years ago, a report that was technically great was held to minimal aesthetic standards. Today, a report must have both style and substance. The data or information must be great, the document must look appealing, and it must be accessible to many different clients and constituents—from laypersons or reporters to politicians and bureaucrats. No matter how good the methodology or analysis used to produce the report, it will go unnoticed if it is not interesting, compelling, and even "sexy." This trend is now the rule rather than the exception in the age of viral marketing and social media.

**PC: For young professionals, what concluding advice would you give about creating business proposals and reports?**

**RH:** Cultivate your own sense of style and substance. Be technically proficient but also confident and appealing. The report should be an extension of your own brand—classy and attractive to people who work with you and would like to work with you. Shoot for timeless qualities in composition. Develop an ear for pauses and breaths, the same way you develop good conversational skills that make you popular with friends and colleagues. Good technical report writing is not much different; the researcher is disseminating information in a way that defies fad and will be relevant to readers many years from now.

***Rich Harrill*** *is director of the Alfred P. Sloan Foundation Travel and Tourism Industry Center and the International Tourism Research Institute at the University of South Carolina. He has written dozens of reports for government and private-sector clients.*

Courtesy of Rich Harrill

# Chapter Takeaway for *Completing Business Proposals and Business Reports*

**LO13.1 Explain how completed reports affect your credibility. (pp. 405–406)**

It shows **competence** when you provide facts, conclusions, and positions that help decision making.

It shows **caring** when you involve decision makers and address their needs.

It shows **character** when you report all information honestly and provide access to your rationale.

**LO13.2 Create specific and persuasive proposals.** See *example of a proposal* in Figure 13.1. **(p. 406)**

**LO13.3 Demonstrate excellent thinking by applying a precision-oriented style to reports. (pp. 406–415)**

**Style:** Apply precision-oriented language and display excellence in thinking.

See *examples of a clear problem statement* (Table 13.1), *fact-based language* (Table 13.2), *citations to avoid plagiarism* (Table 13.4), *recommendations based on facts and conclusions* (Figure 13.3), and *specific and actionable recommendations* (Table 13.5).

**LO13.4 Design your reports to aid in decision making. (pp. 415–420)**

**Design:** Provide easy navigation so that decision makers can quickly identify key points and themes.

See *examples of common headings/sections in reports* (Figure 13.4), *common components of formal reports* (Figure 13.5), *use of headings as a story line device* (Table 13.6), *wording for headings* (Table 13.7), *use of preview statements* (Table 13.8), *effective charts* (Table 13.9), and *bulleting and enumerated lists* (Table 13.10).

**LO13.5 Project objectivity in reports. (pp. 420–436)**

**Tone:** Emphasize objectivity and project a tempered can-do attitude.

See *examples of objective tone* (Table 13.11).

**LO13.6 Review reports for effectiveness and fairness. (pp. 436–437)**

**Feedback:** Involve as many trusted colleagues and partners as possible. Ideally, involve decision makers.

**FAIR Test:** Make sure facts, conclusions, and positions are as objective as possible. Make any of your biases apparent.

**Proofreading:** Check for precision and excellence in your thinking. Ensure your report is complete but easy to navigate.

# Key Terms

direct quotations, 411 paraphrasing, 411 plagiarism, 411

# Discussion Exercises

**13.1 Chapter Review Questions** (LO13.1, LO13.2, LO13.3, LO13.4)

For each of the following items, respond with one or two paragraphs.

A. Explain the significance of stating the business problem or challenge at the beginning of a report.

B. Discuss the various ways in which reports should be precise.

C. Describe the value of good documentation in your research reports.

D. Explain what it means for recommendations to be specific and actionable.

E. Discuss how charts should be used in reports.

F. Describe how you can strike a tone of objectivity in a report and also project positivity.

G. Explain various approaches for reviewing reports.

**13.2 Communication Q&A Discussion Questions** (LO13.1, LO13.2, LO13.3)

Read the Communication Q&A section with comments from Rich Harrill. Respond to the following questions:

A. What does Harrill offer as keys to writing effective reports?

B. According to Harrill, how should you lead a team writing effort?

C. How has report writing changed in recent years, according to Harrill? What does this mean for your approach to report writing?

D. Harrill repeatedly mentions getting advice and feedback from others. In some cases, he relies on hired editors. In other cases, he gets informal feedback. Why is it so important to get feedback for your report writing? What steps can you take in your report writing to get more feedback from others? How should you select others you will approach for advice?

**13.3 Complete SBA Training for Business Plans** (LO13.1, LO13.2, LO13.3)

Go to the Small Business Administration website (www.sba.gov) and complete the online training for "Starting a Business" (www.sba.gov/training/index.html), which takes about 30 minutes. In three to five paragraphs, describe the key points of developing a business plan that apply to writing effective reports.

# Evaluation Exercises

**13.4 Evaluating a Business Report** (LO13.1, LO13.2, LO13.3, LO13.4)

Choose a business report to evaluate. Answer the following questions related to it:

A. How effectively does the report tell a story?

B. How effectively are headings used?

C. How effectively are charts, figures, and/or other graphics used?

D. How effectively are research results presented?

E. Overall, how reliable and useful is this report? Explain.

F. What three aspects of the report would you like to model in your report writing?

G. What three aspects of the report do you think should be improved?

You can find numerous reports online; often these are white papers. Ideally, search for a topic of interest. For example, if you are interested in the future of shopping malls, you could conduct an Internet search with a search phrase such as *future of shopping malls "white paper,"* and you will likely find dozens of options to choose from. Spend 10 to 15 minutes to find a report that is interesting to you.

# Application Exercises

**13.5 Writing a Survey Report and Marketing Plan for an Ice Cream Shop** (LO13.1, LO13.2, LO13.3)

Assume you are planning to open an ice cream shop on campus. There are currently no ice cream shops within three miles of your campus. You are deciding between leasing space in the student center or opening a stand-alone shop on the outskirts of campus. You recently surveyed just over 400 university students to identify their preferences. The following table contains the results.

| Gender | | | | | |
|---|---|---|---|---|---|
| **Female** | | **Male** | | **Total** | |
| # | % | # | % | # | % |
| *How often do you go to an ice cream parlor in a given month?* | | | | | |
| 0 times | 26 | 14% | 40 | 19% | 66 | 16% |
| 1 time | 73 | 38 | 112 | 53 | 185 | 46 |
| 2 to 4 times | 83 | 43 | 57 | 27 | 140 | 35 |
| 5 or more times | 9 | 5 | 4 | 2 | 13 | 3 |
| *Would you prefer a drive-through versus sit-down?* | | | | | |
| Drive-through | 51 | 27 | 95 | 45 | 146 | 36 |
| Sit-down | 140 | 73 | 118 | 55 | 258 | 64 |
| *Which do you prefer?* | | | | | |
| Ice cream | 77 | 40 | 170 | 80 | 247 | 61 |
| Frozen yogurt | 102 | 53 | 43 | 20 | 145 | 36 |
| Sherbet | 12 | 6 | 0 | 0 | 12 | 3 |
| *How do you like your ice cream prepared?* | | | | | |
| Sundae | 57 | 30 | 38 | 18 | 95 | 24 |
| Cone | 47 | 25 | 40 | 19 | 87 | 22 |
| Cup | 64 | 34 | 67 | 31 | 131 | 32 |
| Milkshake | 23 | 12 | 68 | 32 | 91 | 23 |
| *What's your favorite condiment?* | | | | | |
| Candy | 35 | 18 | 93 | 44 | 128 | 32 |
| Cookies | 31 | 16 | 49 | 23 | 80 | 20 |
| Flavored syrup | 57 | 30 | 52 | 24 | 109 | 27 |
| Nuts | 45 | 24 | 19 | 9 | 64 | 16 |
| Fruit | 23 | 12 | 0 | 0 | 23 | 6 |
| *Have you bought store novelties in the past (i.e., shirts, hats, etc.)?* | | | | | |
| Yes | 111 | 58 | 178 | 84 | 289 | 72 |
| No | 80 | 42 | 35 | 16 | 115 | 28 |
| *How many scoops do you typically prefer?* | | | | | |
| 1 | 112 | 59 | 42 | 20 | 154 | 38 |
| 2 | 71 | 37 | 140 | 66 | 211 | 52 |
| 3 | 8 | 4 | 31 | 15 | 39 | 10 |
| *How much are you willing to pay for a one-scoop ice cream cone?* | | | | | |
| $1.00–$1.50 | 67 | 35 | 45 | 21 | 112 | 28 |
| $1.51–$2.00 | 105 | 55 | 64 | 30 | 169 | 42 |
| $2.01–$2.50 | 13 | 7 | 62 | 29 | 75 | 19 |
| $2.51 or more | 6 | 3 | 42 | 20 | 48 | 12 |
| *How much are you willing to pay for a two-scoop ice cream cone?* | | | | | |
| $1.51–$2.25 | 73 | 38 | 43 | 20 | 116 | 29 |
| $2.26–$3.00 | 76 | 40 | 40 | 19 | 116 | 29 |
| $3.01–$3.50 | 31 | 16 | 84 | 39 | 115 | 28 |
| $3.51 or more | 11 | 6 | 46 | 22 | 57 | 14 |
| *Would you prefer an all-you-can-eat ice cream shop?* | | | | | |
| Yes | 25 | 13 | 158 | 74 | 183 | 45 |
| No | 166 | 87 | 55 | 26 | 221 | 55 |

Write a marketing report that includes your survey objectives, methodology, findings, and conclusions. Also, provide your related marketing recommendations.

### 13.6 Writing a Proposal for a Student Club (LO13.1, LO13.2, LO13.3)

Assume your university has recently developed a grant program for student clubs. The goal of the program is to award between $5,000 and $10,000 per club for activities that promote academic research and/or travel to industry conferences.

Choose a student club of interest and write a proposal that describes the purpose of your club and a specific project that the grant money would support. Provide a rationale for how you will use the money, a timeline for completing your project (or travel), and a description of deliverables. (Look at the proposal in the Bonus Appendix as a guide.)

### 13.7 Writing a Survey Report about Mobile Phone Use in the Workplace (LO13.1, LO13.2, LO13.3)

Ashley Foxe works for Process Leadership, a large consulting group that advises companies in North America, Europe, and Asia. It typically works on one- to six-month projects with companies that are trying to develop more open and collaborative work environments. The Process slogan is *leading with culture*, implying that entire companies need to share work values to maximize their productivity.

Ashley's role with Process Leadership is to write research reports or white papers that are available free of charge. These research reports are distributed on the Process Leadership home page and are intended to reinforce the Process brand of improving corporate culture. Process generally disseminates press releases about the research. Often, the research is picked up in newspapers, business magazines, and other professional publications. Each time the research is mentioned, it serves as free marketing and advertising for Process Leadership.

Ashley recently conducted a survey project about mobile phone use in the workplace. She conducted a nationwide survey of full-time business professionals with annual salaries over $30,000. She compiled the following data tables from the survey.

**TABLE A**

## Demographics of Survey Respondents

| Gender | Count | Percentage |
|---|---|---|
| Male | 186 | 53.1% |
| Female | 164 | 46.9 |
| **Age Group** | | |
| 21–30 | 35 | 10.0 |
| 31–40 | 95 | 27.1 |
| 41–50 | 87 | 24.9 |
| 51–65 | 133 | 38.0 |
| **Income** | | |
| $30,000 to $39,999 | 41 | 11.7 |
| $40,000 to $49,999 | 46 | 13.1 |
| $50,000 to $59,000 | 53 | 15.1 |
| $60,000 to $69,999 | 31 | 8.9 |
| $70,000 to $79,999 | 40 | 11.4 |
| $80,000 to $89,999 | 33 | 9.4 |
| $90,000 to $99,999 | 29 | 8.3 |
| $100,000 to $149,999 | 50 | 14.3 |
| $150,000 or more | 27 | 7.7 |
| **Total** | 350 | 100 |

**TABLE B**

## Appropriateness of Mobile Phone Use in Meetings by Gender

| | Male | | Female | | Total | |
|---|---|---|---|---|---|---|
| | **Rarely** | **Never** | **Rarely** | **Never** | **Rarely** | **Never** |
| Bringing phone to meeting | 34.5% | 11.4% | 33.7% | 24.0% | 34.0% | 21.7% |
| Checking time with phone | 26.9 | 30.6 | 27.4 | 30.5 | 27.1 | 30.6 |
| Checking incoming calls | 26.3 | 25.8 | 31.1 | 21.3 | 28.6 | 27.4 |
| Checking text messages | 30.1 | 41.4 | 30.5 | 50.6 | 30.3 | 45.7 |
| Answering a call | 35.5 | 41.3 | 25.6 | 64.0 | 30.9 | 56.3 |
| Excusing self to answer call | 36.0 | 18.8 | 30.5 | 23.8 | 33.4 | 21.1 |
| Writing and sending texts | 26.9 | 54.3 | 22.0 | 65.2 | 24.6 | 51.3 |
| Browsing the Internet | 28.5 | 43.5 | 26.8 | 53.0 | 27.7 | 48.0 |

**TABLE C**

Appropriateness of Mobile Phone Use in Meetings by Gender

| | 21–30 | | 31–40 | | 41–50 | | 51–65 | |
|---|---|---|---|---|---|---|---|---|
| | **Rarely** | **Never** | **Rarely** | **Never** | **Rarely** | **Never** | **Rarely** | **Never** |
| Bringing phone to meeting | 20.0% | 8.6% | 28.4% | 12.6% | 35.6% | 28.7% | 40.6% | 27.1% |
| Checking time with phone | 37.1 | 2.9 | 22.1 | 26.3 | 28.7 | 34.5 | 27.1 | 38.3 |
| Checking incoming calls | 25.7 | 5.7 | 24.2 | 24.2 | 27.6 | 32.2 | 33.1 | 32.3 |
| Checking text messages | 28.6 | 20.0 | 30.5 | 37.9 | 32.2 | 50.6 | 21.3 | 54.9 |
| Answering a call | 22.9 | 42.9 | 36.8 | 42.1 | 34.5 | 51.4 | 26.3 | 67.7 |
| Excusing self to answer call | 31.4 | 11.4 | 23.2 | 16.8 | 313.1 | 25.3 | 37.6 | 24.1 |
| Writing and sending texts | 22.9 | 34.3 | 30.5 | 45.3 | 28.7 | 51.4 | 18.0 | 75.9 |
| Browsing the Internet | 28.6 | 20.0 | 32.6 | 32.6 | 24.1 | 57.5 | 26.3 | 60.2 |

**TABLE D**

Attitudes toward Texting and Making Calls with Mobile Phones

| | **Males** | **Females** | **21–30** | **31–40** | **41–50** | **51–65** | **Total** |
|---|---|---|---|---|---|---|---|
| Overall, using mobile phones for *TEXTING* in the workplace . . . | | | | | | | |
| Reduces miscommunication. | 37.6% | 34.8% | 54.3% | 42.1% | 33.3% | 21.3% | 36.3% |
| Makes communication more efficient. | 41.4 | 45.7 | 71.4 | 55.8 | 41.3 | 34.6 | 47.7 |
| Improves relations with colleagues. | 32.3 | 21.3 | 60.0 | 37.9 | 28.7 | 11.4 | 30.9 |
| Improves relations with clients. | 36.6 | 26.8 | 54.3 | 34.7 | 31.0 | 24.8 | 32.0 |
| Makes work easier. | 43.5 | 40.2 | 65.7 | 56.8 | 35.6 | 21.3 | 42.0 |
| Overall, using mobile phones for *CALLS* in the workplace . . . | | | | | | | |
| Reduces miscommunication. | 64.0 | 53.7 | 77.1 | 74.7 | 55.2 | 45.9 | 51.3 |
| Makes communication more efficient. | 70.4 | 65.2 | 88.6 | 81.1 | 66.7 | 54.1 | 68.0 |
| Improves relations with colleagues. | 51.3 | 51.3 | 88.6 | 70.5 | 60.9 | 42.1 | 51.3 |
| Improves relations with clients. | 66.1 | 61.6 | 88.6 | 82.1 | 60.9 | 46.6 | 64.0 |
| Makes work easier. | 65.6 | 64.0 | 88.6 | 75.8 | 63.2 | 51.9 | 64.9 |

Take the role of Ashley and write a white paper on mobile phone use in the workplace. You can include any other information you find useful. Include sections for data collection, survey findings and conclusions, and recommendations. Make sure to include at least a few charts or figures that illustrate compelling points. Remember your corporate slogan as you develop the report.

**13.8 Write a Business Plan for a Franchise** (LO13.1, LO13.2, LO13.3)

Choose a franchise that interests you. Write a business plan for the franchise in your location (or location of your choice) that includes the following:

- Executive summary
- Introduction
- Management
- Marketing
- Financial projections
- Financial needs

Be creative with your management and marketing ideas. You may not be familiar with creating financial projections, but do your best and simplify this step if necessary. The point of this assignment is to practice writing the plan. Work with your instructor to decide what is acceptable.

You can find possible franchises for this project by searching online for franchising opportunities. Most franchisors supply plenty of information about requirements to open a franchise.

You may want to consult several online articles about writing business plans. You can find many good resources. For example, consider the following article: Jeff Elgin, "Writing the Franchise Business Plan," *Entrepreneur*, September 5, 2005, retrieved from www.entrepreneur.com/franchises/buyingafranchise/franchisecolumnistjeffelgin/article79626.html.

**13.9 Conducting Survey Research** (LO13.1, LO13.2, LO13.3)

Individually or in groups, select a business problem you can learn more about by conducting survey research. You will create an on-line survey for all of your classmates to take, so design your project around the assumption that you are finding out what university-aged students think or feel about the topic. Design the survey so that respondents can complete it in three to five minutes. Once you have conducted the survey, write a report that includes your objectives, methodology, findings, conclusions, and recommendations.

**13.10 Write a Report about a Business Trend** (LO13.1, LO13.2, LO13.3)

Using research from your university library, write a report in APA or MLA documentation style that accomplishes the following:

A. States a business problem or challenge (you might imagine yourself in a position within a company of interest).

B. Describes and substantiates a trend that impacts business.

C. Provides recommendations for how your company can respond to the trend to become more competitive.

# Language Mechanics Check

**13.11 Review all rules in Appendix A about punctuation, number usage, and grammar. Then, rewrite each sentence to make all needed corrections.**

A. Frequent flier programs have traditionally awarded miles based on the number of miles in a flight not on the price of air tickets.

B. Some airlines are now changing these loyalty programs, to reward miles based on ticket prices which makes many bargain hunters upset.

C. These airlines say that dollars spent is a better indicator of loyalty than miles traveled but many long time loyalty program members disagree.

D. Some airlines have all ready expanded the options, for members to use their miles.

E. In addition to using miles to purchase flights they will now be able to purchase extra legroom, check in baggage and even in flight food and services.

F. Overall these policies are aimed at rewarding travelers who spend more money on flights and in flight services.

G. Most travelers, who purchase primarily based on ticket prices, are disappointed with the new changes, because they reduce the benefits of getting the best deal.

H. Many airlines now sell annual, checked baggage subscriptions for around 300 to 400 dollars.

I. Airlines brought in about forty billion dollars last year in baggage fees, most airlines are using these fees to significantly improve profitability.

J. Many budget airlines make more money from fees, than they do from ticket prices.

# Endnotes

1. "Plagiarize," retrieved March 1, 2012, from *Merriam-Webster Online Dictionary* at www.merriam-webster.com/dictionary/plagiarize.

2. "What Is Citation?" retrieved March 1, 2012, from *Plagiarism.org* website at www.plagiarism.org/plag_article_what_is_citation.html; "Plagiarism FAQs," retrieved March 1, 2012, from *Plagiarism.org* website at www.plagiarism.org/plag_article_what_is_citation.html; "What Is Plagiarism?" retrieved March 1, 2012, from *Plagiarism.org* website at www.plagiarism.org/plag_article_what_is_citation.html.

3. David Kintler and Bob Adams, *Independent Consulting: A Comprehensive Guide to Building Your Own Consulting Business* (Avon, MA: Streetwise, 1998); Brian R. Ford, Jay M. Bornstein, and Patrick T. Pruitt, *The Ernst & Young Business Plan Guide* (Hoboken, NJ: John Wiley & Sons, 2007); Small Business Administration,

"Write a Business Plan," retrieved September 15, 2010, from Small Business Administration website at www.sba.gov/smallbusinessplanner/plan/writeabusinessplan/index.html.

4. Roberta Moore, Patricia Seraydarian, and Rosemary Fruehling, *Pearson Business Reference and Writer's Handbook* (Upper Saddle River, NJ: Pearson Education, 2010).

5. Joy Roach, Daniel Tracy, and Kay Durden, "Integrating Business Core Knowledge through Upper Division Report Composition," *Business Communication Quarterly* 70, no. 4 (2007): 431–449.

6. Joseph Covello and Brian Hazelgren, *Your First Business Plan*, 5th ed. (Naperville, IL: Sourcebooks, 2005): 12.

7. Ibid.

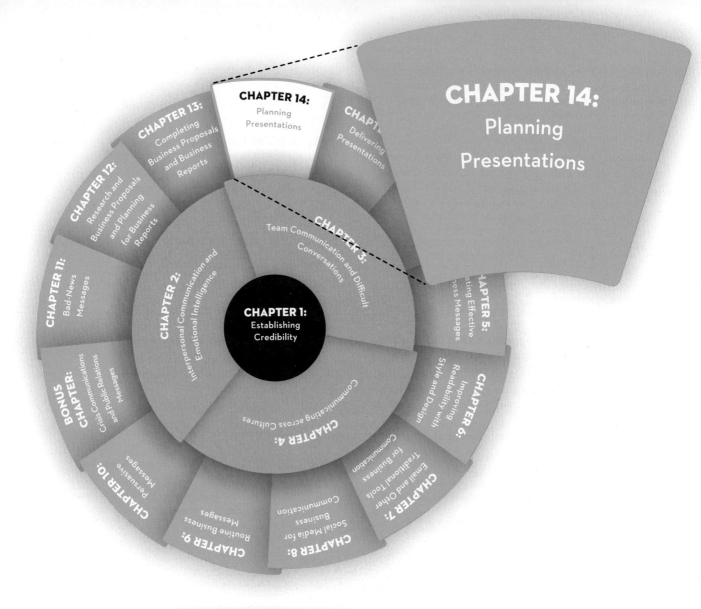

# CHAPTER 14:
## Planning Presentations

CHAPTER 14:
Planning Presentations

 ESTABLISHING CREDIBILITY

 PRINCIPLES OF INTERPERSONAL COMMUNICATION

 PRINCIPLES FOR & TYPES OF BUSINESS MESSAGES

 Learning Objectives

After studying this chapter, you should be able to do the following:

**LO14.1** Describe how planning your presentations leads to credibility.

**LO14.2** Analyze presentation audiences in terms of message benefits, learning styles, and communicator styles.

**LO14.3** Organize and gather content for a preview, view, and review.

**LO14.4** Develop effective slide presentations.

**LO14.5** Use the story line approach to presentations.

**LO14.6** Evaluate your presentations for fairness and effectiveness.

Presentations have many purposes, including promoting a new business or idea, reporting on the status of projects or product performance, helping management and employees stay informed about business policies, or selling a product or service. Presentations give you opportunities to connect deeply with your audiences and convey and control your messages carefully.

Presentations place a spotlight on you and allow you to maintain and even build your credibility. When you clearly know what you're talking about, audiences judge you as competent. When you show that you are interested in the needs of your audience, they judge you as caring. When you offer your views honestly and transparently, audiences judge you as having character.

Although speaking is a normal part of every day for you, making business presentations is not necessarily automatic or natural. As speech expert Thomas Leech explained, "Developing proficiency in oral communications doesn't occur automatically. The ability to speak may have come much as did walking and breathing, but speaking well to groups is another matter."[1] As you read this chapter, identify the areas that will help you most in developing your presentation skills. This chapter focuses on planning your content. The next one focuses on delivering that content effectively.

Read the chapter case about Latisha Jackson and her plans to develop a presentation about transitioning from annual performance reviews to continuous reviews.

**Hear Pete Cardon explain why this matters.**

**bit.ly/cardon14**

**LO14.1** Describe how planning your presentations leads to credibility.

## CHAPTER CASE: PLANNING A PRESENTATION AT EASTMOND NETWORKING

*Latisha Jackson, HR intern*

*Jeff Brody, personnel director*

**WHO'S INVOLVED**

- Hired for a summer internship to work on employee programs
- Double majoring in business administration and health education

- Worked as HR director at Eastmond Networking for the past five years

Eastmond Networking holds performance evaluations for employees once per year. Jeff sees the results of the company's internal, anonymous employee survey each year. Each year, he notices that employees do not like the performance evaluations. They think the evaluations are not fair and do not help them improve. Jeff has talked to several human resources (HR) directors and learned that many companies now use continuous performance reviews with a lot of success. To learn more about and help transition to continuous performance reviews, he asked Latisha Jackson to help formulate a plan for this transition.

**THE SITUATION**

Over an approximately six-week period, Latisha collected information about continuous reviews from other companies and software vendors. She also ran a few employee focus groups and helped conduct a detailed employee survey about performance reviews. Jeff has asked her to develop a presentation about continuous reviews to deliver at a senior management meeting. The meeting will include roughly 15 of the company's leaders, most of whom Latisha has not met in person. Jeff recently told Latisha that he was so impressed with her performance that he might be able to open a permanent position for her. Latisha hopes that a strong presentation will improve her chances of getting a permanent spot on the Eastmond team.

Jeff tells Latisha that the senior managers will most likely have the following major objections to continuous reviews: (1) they won't promote candid feedback, (2) they won't get support from managers, and (3) they will cost too much. Jeff believes that senior managers will support initiatives that improve employee engagement because a consulting firm recently surveyed employees and concluded that Eastmond's employees were below average in all measures of engagement.

**TASK**

**1** Prepare the basic content of the presentation to explain the benefits of continuous reviews while also addressing concerns.

**2** Develop slides to supplement the presentation and reinforce the key messages.

## Applying the AIM Planning Process for Presentations

As you design your presentations and speeches, the AIM planning process will help you, just as it does in the writing process. You'll analyze your *audience* to make sure you're addressing audience members' needs and speaking to them in the way that is most appealing and easy to learn. You'll gather and develop your *information* and ideas by identifying the key facts and conclusions related to your topic. You'll also develop your *message* to focus on the key takeaway concepts and to provide supporting points throughout. In this chapter, we do not focus on developing your ideas, since this process is largely similar to that for writing. We instead discuss analyzing your audience and structuring your message since these processes have some unique features for presentations. Then, we discuss designing electronic slides since these are commonly included in many professional presentations.

**LO14.2** Analyze presentation audiences in terms of message benefits, learning styles, and communicator styles.

Visit http://connect.mheducation.com for an exercise on this topic.

### Analyze Your Audience and Gather the Right Information

Understanding the needs of your audience is one of your first tasks as you develop your presentations. Of course, this is complicated by a variety of factors. Your audiences for presentations may differ in size and makeup, and in some cases, you won't know who they will be. As you do your homework about the audience, answer the following questions to the degree possible:

**How Will Audience Members Benefit from the Product, Service, or Ideas I Am Proposing?** This is the single most important question you can use to guide you as you design your presentation. In particular, focus on benefits that fulfill an unmet need.[2]

In Latisha's case, she will focus primarily on improving employee engagement. Senior managers know this is a problem at Eastmond. She will explain that annual reviews lower engagement and continuous reviews improve engagement.

**What Do the Audience Members Already Know about My Product, Service, or Ideas?** Find out whatever you can about your audience members' knowledge level. If people know little about your product, you will need to spend a proportionately higher amount of your presentation time to inform them. Also, try to find out where they have gotten their information or how they have developed their perceptions about the topic. Knowing this allows you to more effectively deal with misinformation.

In Latisha's case, she thinks that senior managers don't know much about continuous performance reviews. She will need to explain the benefits clearly. Also, since continuous reviews depend on software platforms, she'll need to show the managers how these platforms operate. She assumes that these managers may not be able to visualize how the systems work unless she shows pictures or does a live demo.

**What Are My Audience Members' Chief Concerns?**   Considering this question is particularly important for presentations. Whereas you can take time to gather your thoughts when responding in writing to someone's concerns, in presentations and other face-to-face communications you must respond immediately.

Latisha was wise to ask Jeff about the senior managers' chief concerns. Jeff told her they'd be worried about the candidness or accuracy of continuous reviews, support from managers, and cost.

**Who Are the Key Decision Makers?**   Your presentation is generally intended to draw support from your whole audience. Typically, however, some people in your audience have more impact on your ability to achieve your work objectives than do others. These key decision makers are the ones you want to influence the most.

For internal presentations, think about those individuals who have the most influence and authority to act on your ideas. For presentations to clients, customers, and prospects, think about which individuals are the decision makers for their organizations or who you perceive as the most likely prospects for future business. Focus most of your attention on them.[3]

Once again, Latisha can rely on Jeff to identify which senior managers will have the most impact on whether continuous reviews get support. Latisha can think of ways to tailor her presentation to these individuals.

**What Will Appeal to Your Audience?**   You can influence your audience by employing a combination of emotional and analytical appeals. Oral communications, especially speeches and presentations, are well suited to strong emotional appeal, as they create bonds between the speaker and the audience and emotional connections with products, services, and ideas. At the same time, your speeches and presentations will include a set of ideas that you want your audience to appreciate analytically. Plan to make both emotional and analytical connections with your audience.

As you're thinking about emotional and analytical appeals, consider the motivational value systems (MVSs) of your audience members (see Chapter 2). Professionals with red MVSs will appreciate your ability to stay on point and discuss immediate goals. Emotionally and analytically, they are attracted to action-oriented and results-oriented language and logic. They generally think concise and confident presentations are more persuasive.

Professionals with blue MVSs will appreciate your ability to discuss business relationships—such as benefits to work teams and colleagues and loyalty to customers and clients. Emotionally, blues will connect to you with your use of "we" language and other relationship-centered terms. Analytically, blues will connect with your holistic approach to business benefits. They are attracted to business logic that includes more than just bottom-line measures of performance.

Professionals with green MVSs will appreciate your ability to provide all of the facts and avoid rushing to judgment about conclusions. Greens generally pride themselves on a dispassionate (nonemotional) approach to decision making and may be turned

> **Principles of Audience Analysis**
>
> Identify the following:
> - Audience benefits
> - Existing knowledge
> - Concerns
> - Decision makers
> - Appeals
> - Communicator style
> - Learning style

off by what they consider blatant and irrelevant appeals to emotion. However, this in no way implies that emotional appeal is unimportant to thinkers. Greens are often emotionally connected to precise language; well-designed and conceptualized charts, models, and other figures; and the ability to handle tough questions.

Professionals with hub MVSs are most common. Hubs are by nature pragmatic and flexible. They prefer a presentation that holds clear business logic with an emphasis on benefits to people—clients, customers, colleagues, and others. They prefer option-oriented language. Excessively confident language is often interpreted by hubs as arrogant or rigid.

**What Is the Learning Style of Your Audience?** As with motivational value systems, audience members have different learning styles. **Visual learners**, who make up about 40 percent of the population, learn best from illustrations and simple diagrams that show relationships and key ideas. They also enjoy gestures and metaphors. Ironically, text-based PowerPoint slides do not appeal to them much. On the other hand, PowerPoint slides rich in images and figures do help visual learners respond to your message. **Auditory learners**, who also comprise roughly 40 percent of the population, like loud, clear voices and believe emotion is best conveyed through voice. **Kinesthetic learners**, who make up about 20 percent of the population, need to participate to focus their attention on your message and learn best. They need group activities, hands-on activities, or breaks at least every 20 minutes.[4]

Latisha can plan a presentation that appeals to all types of learners. She can use a variety of images and diagrams to appeal to visual learners, speak with energy and conviction to appeal to auditory learners, and provide handouts for participants to fill out to appeal to kinesthetic learners.

**What Information Do I Need to Gather?** As you ask questions about your audience, you'll naturally create of list of information you need. As with other types of messages, make sure to also create a list of research questions that helps you develop the content of your presentation. As mentioned in the opening case to this chapter, Latisha spent about six weeks gathering information about annual performance reviews versus continuous reviews.

## Develop Your Message

As with written reports, successful presentations rely on well-developed takeaway messages, supporting information, and structure. You'll get lots of advice during your career about how to deliver a successful presentation. Much of this advice is good because delivery is important. However, developing your content is still the most critical factor in presentation success, so prepare your content before you spend too much time on your delivery.[5]

**Identify a Few Takeaway Messages** Your first task is to identify the two or three key messages you want to convey. Once you've developed these key messages, everything in the presentation should lead back to them.[6] Particularly for presenting to busy executives, summarize your key takeaway messages at the outset and reemphasize them several times.[7]

Overall, your presentation will be most effective if you focus on how your key messages relate to the common interests of your audience. At the same time, be cautious about trying to please everyone. Some presenters broaden their messages in an attempt to appeal to everyone in the audience. This approach is risky, however, since broadening the message so much may dilute its impact and power.[8]

In Latisha's case, she frames her message in the following way: Continuous reviews increase employee engagement. She has a few key takeaway messages to support this idea: Continuous reviews provide more accurate and more motivating feedback; continuous reviews make managers' jobs easier; and continuous reviews are relatively inexpensive.

**Components of Presentations**

- Preview (10–15 percent of time)
  - Attention-getter
  - Positioning statement
  - Overview: Takeaway messages
- View (85–90 percent of time)
  - Takeaway message #1
  - Takeaway message #2
  - Takeaway message #3
- Review (5 percent of time)
  - Recap
  - Call to action

Structure Your Presentation with a Clear Preview, View, and Review[9]
Most audience members expect your presentation to include a **preview**, view, and review (analogous to the introduction, body, and conclusion in written documents). Typically, your preview occupies roughly 10 to 15 percent of your presentation time, your view takes up the vast majority (85 to 90 percent) of your time, and the review takes up the least time (5 percent).

**LO14.3** Organize and gather content for a preview, view, and review.

## Provide a Compelling Preview

The beginnings of your presentations and speeches are critical. Audience members who do not know you well often form quick impressions about you and your message. Even people who know you fairly well generally decide quickly if your message is important to them. Dana LaMon, who lost his sight at the age of four but went on to achieve a highly successful career as a judge and professional speaker, suggests that audiences make up their minds in the first minute or two of the presentation:

**connect**

Visit http://connect. mheducation.com for an exercise on this topic.

> As an administrative law judge for 26 years, I have heard and written decisions in about 6,400 cases. My unscientific estimate is that in about 95 percent of them, I knew what I would decide before the hearing was over. After 19 years in Toastmasters and 16 years as a professional speaker, I have learned that the audience, too, will make quick decisions. They will judge a speaker and his or her speech well before the presentation is done. That is why I have come to believe that the most important part of my speech is the opening.[10]

In other words, during that first few minutes, audience members have their answers to the following questions: Am I going to listen? Am I going to benefit from what is said? Will it be valuable enough to take with me? Am I going to act on what I hear?

The *preview* should generally include an attention-getter, a positioning statement, and an overview. The preview should accomplish the following: create interest, show benefits, demonstrate value, and encourage action (all related to the four questions in the prior paragraph).

**Choose an Effective Attention-Getter**   In research among executives, the factors most likely to attract their attention were the following: The message was personalized, it evoked an emotional response, it came from a trustworthy source, and it was concise. In particular, personalized and emotion-evoking attention-getters led executives to pay close attention to presentations more than twice as often.[11]

Stephen Denning, one of the world's foremost authorities on leadership communication, spent decades working for the World Bank. While leading World Bank initiatives and meeting leaders throughout the world, he learned that influence in presentations depends heavily on first garnering attention. He explained:

> Successful leaders communicate very differently from the traditional, abstract approach to communication. In all kinds of settings, they communicate by following a hidden pattern: first, they get attention. Then they stimulate desire, and only then do they reinforce with reasons.[12]

The primary goals of attention-getters are to get your audience members emotionally invested in your presentation and engaged in thinking about your ideas. Table 14.1 focuses on seven types of attention-getters that Latisha could use in her presentation: rhetorical questions, vivid examples, dramatic demonstrations, testimonials or quotations, intriguing statistics, unexpected exercises, and challenges. This is not a comprehensive list; however, these strategies are among the most effective.[13] Think about how you might use each option in a presentation.

People enjoy humor in presentations. Generally, however, avoid opening with jokes. Few people do well when they open with jokes. Communication specialist Nick Morgan explains:

> You need to start with something clever enough to catch everyone's attention, but you're at your most nervous, and thus it's hard to shine like you want to. So how to get started? The traditional advice—still followed by many business speakers—is to begin with a joke. . . .

**TABLE 14.1**

Types of Effective Attention-Getters

| Attention-Getter | Example |
|---|---|
| Rhetorical question | Have any of you ever thought your performance review wasn't fair? Or, have you ever dreaded delivering a performance review? As we started looking at research about annual reviews, we found that most employees *and* managers don't think annual reviews improve performance.<br><br>This attention-getter immediately evokes thinking about personal experiences for audience members. It focuses on an unmet need (using performance reviews to improve performance). It is also concise: It takes roughly 20 seconds to deliver (42 words). |
| Vivid example | We held two focus groups with employees about their views of annual reviews. Right at the start of the first focus group, one of the employees whom everyone recognizes as devoted, reliable, and friendly, simply said, "The reviews don't help us at all." Every person in the group nodded their heads. Nearly every comment I heard from employees came back to this simple theme: Annual reviews don't help the employees perform better, be more motivated, or be more invested in their work.<br><br>This example captures the attention of the audience with its vivid, story-based description of what employees really think. Many audience members would take this example seriously. This example would take roughly 30 to 35 seconds to deliver (82 words). |
| Dramatic demonstration | (Live demo of the software) Some of you are probably wondering what makes continuous reviews possible. We can do it with a variety of software platforms. If you look at the screen, I'm going to take two to three minutes to demo how the platform works. You'll see how employees get immediate, helpful, and accurate feedback . . .<br><br>This attention-getter gives the audience a tangible sense of how the platform can produce continuous, helpful feedback. This demonstration is delivered in a few minutes. Latisha should be prepared to demonstrate the technology rapidly or she'll lose the interest of audience members. |
| Testimonial or quotation | Managers at many companies say transitioning to continuous reviews has dramatically improved performance and morale. I talked to three HR directors who started using continuous review systems in the past few years. Janna Leahy, the HR director at Peakster Computing, told me that the company has increased billable hours in the consulting division by 35 percent. She attributes this to the coaching and motivating environment of continuous reviews. She said continuous reviews create an "enjoyable culture of performance."<br><br>This short statement focuses on the testimonial of an HR manager who implemented a similar solution. The statement emphasizes a dramatic rise in profitability, which appeals to senior managers emotionally and rationally. It would take just 30 seconds to deliver (77 words). Ideally, a compelling video testimonial would be provided as well. |
| Intriguing statistic | It's no secret that employees don't think annual reviews are accurate indicators of their performance. In fact, roughly 50 to 75 percent of employees say this in various surveys. But, did you know that nearly 50 percent of HR managers don't even think annual reviews are accurate?<br><br>This attention-getter focuses on a compelling but likely expected statistic about employees (50 to 75 percent don't think annual reviews are accurate indicators of their performance) and an unexpected statistic about HR managers (nearly 50 percent of HR managers don't even think annual reviews are accurate). These statistics rapidly create the message that annual reviews aren't considered reliable by all parties involved—the employees who receive them or managers who administer them. This concise statement takes roughly 20 seconds to deliver (47 words). |
| Unexpected exercise | As we get started, I'd like each of you to answer two questions with the person sitting next to you. First, ask your partner, "What was the worst experience you've had getting a performance review?" Then ask, "What was the best experience you've had getting a performance review?"<br><br>This quick exercise gets participants talking right away about topics that are central to the presentation: performance, motivation, and management. This exercise may also get participants to open up and relax. Another benefit for Latisha is she can now adapt her presentation to the needs of her audience more effectively. This is a great approach for kinesthetic learners. |

**TABLE 14.1**

*(Continued)*

| Attention-Getter | Example |
|---|---|
| Challenge | Today I'm going to talk about transitioning from annual reviews to continuous reviews. I'm going to show you some new tools to provide feedback and coaching on a daily basis. Once I explain the tools, I'm going ask each of you to describe how you think this would impact your teams. |
| | This is a direct challenge to audience members to conceptualize and envision how the tools apply to their own teams. This approach will help many of the audience members become more engaged and active during the presentation. This is a concise opening at just 20 seconds or so (51 words). |

For everyone except the professional comedian, this is bad counsel indeed. You're at your worst in terms of nerves. Don't compound the problem by setting for yourself one of the most difficult public speaking chores of all right off the bat: Delivering a punch line with brilliant comic timing. It's extremely difficult to do under the best of circumstances—even for seasoned professionals.[14]

Even if you're one of the rare breed of people who can consistently pull them off, opening jokes may have unintended consequences. Audience members may remember your jokes more than your key messages, so if you choose a humorous opening, tie it to your key messages.

Starting with an overwhelming set of facts and numbers or telling the story of your company may not be particularly effective either. If you choose to give background on your company, do so concisely, and make sure you connect the story of your company to the needs of your audience.[15]

**Creating a Positioning Statement** A **positioning statement** frames your message in appealing terms to your audience members and demonstrates clear and valuable benefits to them. The positioning statement should be as concise as possible—ideally one to two sentences. With the attention-getter, you engage and capture interest. With the positioning statement, you demonstrate that your presentation is worth paying close attention to for its entirety.

In Latisha's case, she selects the following positioning statement: "Today I'm going to discuss how continuous reviews can significantly increase employee engagement. I'm also going to share our plan to implement continuous reviews throughout the company by January 2016." This positioning statement speaks directly to the needs of the senior managers. It employs positive and upbeat language.

**Providing an Overview Statement** The final part of the preview is the overview. Ideally, you can state your overview in one to three sentences in simple, conversational language. Immediately after Latisha makes her positioning statement, she provides an overview: "We'll discuss how continuous reviews provide more accurate and more motivating feedback; how continuous reviews make managers' jobs easier; and how continuous reviews are relatively inexpensive." This overview segments the presentation in terms of three key benefits or takeaway messages. These benefits are easy to remember and help audience members think about the benefits to their units within the company.

## Justify Your Views

The majority of your presentation will be devoted to expressing and supporting your **views**—your two, three, or four key messages. Recognize that many of your audience members are skeptical. After all, you will likely be asking them to commit to your products, services, or ideas at the expense of their time, money, or other resources. In other words, you are generally asking people to take some type of professional and/or personal risk. Make sure you can back up your main positions with strong support material, including specific cases or examples, stories and illustrations, analogies, statistics and facts, quotations, or your own professional experiences.[16]

Use support materials in moderation, however. You can easily overwhelm your audience. Furthermore, most audience members prefer certain types of supporting material during presentations. For example, personalized case studies are more likely to influence audience members than statistics. At the same time, avoid any weak evidence, since that will undermine your case, and be prepared with additional support material if audience members request it.[17] Furthermore, gain a sense of your audience members' preferences. For example, professionals with green MVSs are typically more influenced by quantitative information whereas professionals with blue MVSs are typically more influenced by personal experiences.

Executive communication coach Roly Grimshaw observes that the most serious mistake business managers make is to present the evidence (numbers, statistics, facts) first, or only the evidence, and leave out their primary conclusions or central positions.[18] A more successful approach is the **PREP method,** which involves stating your *position,* providing the *reasons,* giving an *example* or providing evidence, and then restating your *position.*[19] Table 14.2 provides an instance of the PREP method from Latisha's presentation. As you read through this example, think about what Latisha gains from starting and ending with her position.

### Conclude with an Effective Review

The **review** comprises a small percentage of your presentation time. However, make sure to have a strong finish—this is the place where you are hoping to gain buy-in on specific actions. First, you will recap your message in just a few sentences. Then, you'll provide a call to action, where you'll ask the audience members to make specific commitments. For example, Latisha ends with the following call to action: "Thank you for your time and thoughts today. Jeff and I want to continue getting your feedback as we select a software vendor and start the pilot phase. We'll send updates and requests for feedback every few weeks. Please feel free to contact us with more of your ideas about making continuous reviews work effectively." This call to action is polite and sincere. It shows genuine interest in getting the input of others.

### Design Appealing Slides

Businesspeople frequently use PowerPoint or other electronic slide presentations as visual aids for their presentations (see the Technology Tips feature for alternatives to PowerPoint). The reason for doing so is compelling. Good visuals can increase communication effectiveness and persuasiveness by about 50 percent.[20] After all, about 75 percent of what people learn comes visually; 12 percent through hearing; and 12 percent through smell, taste, and touch.[21]

However, poorly designed or poorly selected visuals can actually detract from presentation effectiveness.[22] While the use of electronic slides is often effective and nearly ubiquitous for business presentations, take caution. People in the workplace sometimes mock poor electronic slide presentations as *suffering death by PowerPoint.* Consider some of the comments in Figure 14.1 from business leaders.[23]

While well-designed electronic slide presentations can dramatically increase audience learning, poorly designed ones can draw intense negative reactions, as evidenced by the quotations in Figure 14.1. Make sure your electronic slide presentations aid rather than detract from your presentation objectives. Consider the following advice as you design your slides:

**Components of PREP Method**

- Position
- Reasons
- Example
- Position

**LO14.4** Develop effective slide presentations.

Visit http://connect.mheducation.com for an exercise on this topic.

**TABLE 14.2**

The PREP Method

| | Sample Statements |
|---|---|
| Step 1: **Position** | With annual reviews, our employees often get feedback when it's too late to make any changes. With continuous reviews from managers and peers, our employees will receive constant feedback—positive and negative—that will help them improve their performance right away. |
| Step 2: **Reasons** | Many HR professionals in recent years have found that the timing of feedback, the amount of positive feedback, and feedback from a variety of colleagues all contribute to better performance. |
| Step 3: **Example** | Let me give you a quick example at Peakster Computing. Janna Leahy, the HR director, estimated that productivity increased by 15 to 20 percent because of continuous reviews. After using continuous reviews for one year, Janna conducted a complete evaluation of the types of feedback that employees received. Here's what she found. |
| | First, employees said that feedback was "actionable." Before implementing continual reviews, employee surveys showed that only 23 percent of employees agreed with the statement *I've improved my performance due to performance reviews*. After a year of continuous reviews, employee surveys showed that 92 percent of employees agreed with the statement *I've improved my performance due to continuous reviews*. Clearly, the employees see value in this feedback. |
| | The next point is that employees get feedback from many sources. Before the continuous review system was implemented, Janna estimates that most employees received documented feedback from two to three people per year. This feedback was almost entirely from managers. With the new continuous review system, employees get feedback from an average of 15 colleagues per year. |
| | Finally, the amount of positive and negative feedback makes a huge difference. Janna estimates that employees now receive approximately 55 times more feedback throughout the course of a year! Of this feedback, roughly 80 percent is positive feedback and roughly 20 percent is negative or suggestion-based. She thinks that the positive feedback serves as motivation and confirmation of employee strengths. |
| | One concern many people have of continual feedback is that colleagues won't be candid about suggestions for one another's improvement. Janna has found this simply isn't the case. It's true most comments are positive. But, employees at her company regularly give tough love to each other. Janna estimates that the average employee last year received 22 clear recommendations about how to improve performance from fellow managers and employees. Now, compare that to an annual review from a single manager's viewpoint where an employee might get three to four suggestions. |
| Step 4: **Position** | So, we anticipate the same results here at Eastmond. Continuous reviews will ensure each employee gets more constructive feedback more often. We expect this helpful feedback will increase the performance level of our employees. |

I actively despise how people use PowerPoint as a crutch. I think PowerPoint can be a way to cover up sloppy thinking, which makes it hard to differentiate between good ideas and bad ideas. I would much rather have somebody write something longhand, send it in ahead of the meeting and then assume everybody's read it, and then you start talking, and let them defend it. The question from the beginning of the meeting to the end of the meeting is, "Have we added value: yes or no?" And I would say that if the meeting is mostly the presentation of a deck of PowerPoint slides, you conveyed information, but you didn't actually add value.

**—Cristóbal Conde, former CEO of SunGard**

I prefer that people not go through a slide deck. If you're working in an area, and you are running a business, you ought to be able to stand up there and tell me about your business without referring to a big slide deck. When you are speaking, people should focus on you and focus on the message. They can't walk away remembering a whole bunch of different things, so you have to have three or four really key messages that you take them through, and you remind them of what's important.

**—James J. Schiro, director at PepsiCo**

*Death by PowerPoint* occurs because of the bullet trap. Speakers and presenters often reduce their presentations to series of bullets and thoughts in outline form. As a result, they often bore their audiences and lose connection with their audiences.

**—Ellen Finkelstein, communication specialist**

**FIGURE 14.1**

Avoiding Death by PowerPoint

**You Are the Focus of Your Presentation** From the beginning of the design process, resist the urge to make your slides the primary focal point; they are just an aid. Ideally, audience members will focus their eyes on you for the majority of the presentation. Consider the comments of Judith Humphrey, a prominent executive trainer:

> Great leaders understand that they are the best visual. They instinctively know that their message will come through best if the audience looks at them and listens to them—with no distractions. Audiences that divide their attention will only be able to partially commit to you. PowerPoint slides are usually a dumbed-down version of the narrative script you are delivering. Visuals rely on bullet points; you speak in full sentences, with illustrations and stories. Slides are dispassionate; your voice and gestures provide passion and emphasis. So in deflecting the audience's attention away from you to the bullet points, you're reducing the quality of your material and its impact on the audience.[24]

**Create a Storyboard with Your PowerPoint Slide Titles** Make sure that your presentations *tell a story* to your audience. To check whether your slides provide a flowing narrative rather than a disjointed set of ideas, line up your slide titles (see Table 14.3). Ask yourself whether the slide titles move naturally through the narrative of your presentation.[25]

**TABLE 14.3**

Setting Up Slide Titles to Help You Make a Smooth, Logical Presentation

| Slide # | Title | Story Line |
|---|---|---|
| 1 | Improving Employee Engagement: Transitioning to Continuous Reviews and Recognition | *Positive overarching theme in the title slide:* higher employee engagement |
| 2 | Benefits of Employee Engagement | *Attention:* shows the benefits of increasing employee engagement |
| 3 | Problems with Annual Reviews | *Need:* shows how the current approach of annual reviews does not improve employee engagement |
| 4 | Our Employees' Views of Annual Reviews | *Need:* shows current disenchantment with annual reviews at this company |
| 5 | Benefits of Continuous Reviews | *Solution:* shows how continuous review systems overcome the problems of annual reviews and increase employee engagement |
| 6 | Our Employees' Views of Continuous Reviews | *Solution:* shows how continuous review systems have support from the employees |
| 7 | Positive, Helpful, and Candid Feedback | *Rationale/counterpoints:* describes the nature of feedback; addresses concerns that a new system won't promote candid feedback |
| 8 | Ease of Use for Managers | *Rationale/counterpoints:* describes how the system gets buy-in from managers; addresses concerns that a new system won't get support from managers |
| 9 | Cost-Effectiveness | *Rationale/counterpoints:* describes the costs of a system; addresses concerns that a new system costs too much |
| 10 | Proposed Implementation | *Call to action:* uses a timeline to identify implementation |

Latisha sets up her slides in a pattern that is solution-oriented. The order of these slides includes the elements of a classic narrative of persuasion: attention, need and solution, rationale, counterpoints, and call to action (see Chapter 10). Also, notice how the slides position Latisha to tell the story of continuous reviews. Stories contain answers to the questions *who? what? when? where?* and *why?* Latisha will engage her audience with responses to all these types of questions.

Setting out the titles in this storyboard approach helps you see which slides you really need. A common misperception of electronic slide presentations is that more is better. In fact, using fewer slides can help you tell the story more effectively. As one recruiter in a recent *Wall Street Journal* study stated, "Students seem to think a better grade is assigned based on the number of slides in a presentation. In real life, you have 10 minutes to present to management. If you can't get the whole story in that time on two or three slides, you're dead in your career."[26]

In Latisha's presentation (see Figure 14.2), she uses a total of ten slides—one slide for every two minutes or so of her 20-minute presentation. As a rule, avoid showing more than one slide for every minute to two minutes of a presentation.

**Design Your Slides for Ease of Processing**   In relation to speeches and presentations, you have likely heard of the KISS method: *Keep it simple, stupid.* Creating simple presentations is a good strategy. However, a more overarching and effective strategy is to focus on ease of processing. Your goal is to take your often complex data, relationships, and ideas and illustrate and depict them in easy-to-learn ways. Consider the following approaches to facilitate ease of processing:[27]

- *Limit the amount of information on any given slide.* Readers should be able to grasp the content within 10 to 15 seconds. For text, rarely should you use more than ten words per line and more than five to six lines.
- *Use font sizes that all audience members can read easily.* For titles, use at least 24-point fonts; for body text, use at least 18-point fonts.
- *Focus on and highlight key information.* Use bold, italics, and other formatting features to make key phrases or key components in figures stand out.
- *Use plenty of white space.* White space is effective for borders and between items and text on slides; it provides an uncluttered appearance.
- *Use high-contrast backgrounds and colors.* Make sure backgrounds do not obscure text. For dark text, use light backgrounds. For light text, use dark backgrounds.
- *Use compelling images in moderation.* One of the basic reasons to use electronic slide presentations in the first place is to display images. You can use these images to convey powerful messages efficiently and with emotional power, especially for the visual learners in your audience. But make sure you are selective. Too many pictures, poor-quality pictures, or off-message pictures may detract from your message.
- *Develop simple charts and diagrams.* Charts and diagrams can be particularly helpful for simplifying complex data relationships. Make sure to use charts and figures that the audience can process in a matter of seconds. Otherwise, they have to spend an excessive amount of time trying to understand the chart or diagram and they're not paying attention to you. In some cases, they may give up and become annoyed.
- *Get professional design help when possible.* For high-stakes presentations, consider getting help from public relations or design specialists. If you are part of a large organization, you can often get this help internally. In many cases, well-designed templates may already exist. For smaller organizations, you may need to hire outside help.

To this point, most of the tips are based on the creation of PowerPoint slides (PowerPoint is clearly the most used slide software). However, you have many

**FIGURE 14.2**

Less Effective and More Effective Slides for Presentation

**Less Effective Opening Slide**

TRANSITIONING TO CONTINUOUS REVIEWS AND RECOGNITION

Latisha Jackson
August 14, 2017

Key message does not stand out clearly; most prominent text is the presenter's name.

Clip art on title slide does not convey professional image.

**Less Effective Slide #2**

**Research about Employee Engagement**

- A 2013 meta-analysis of 263 studies of engagement involving 1.3 million employees found the following:
  - ○ 47% fewer safety accidents
  - ○ 21% higher productivity
  - ○ 22% higher profitability
  - ○ 41% higher quality
  - ○ 37% reduced absenteeism

**Source:** Cameron, Yvette. (2013 December). *Social employee recognition systems reward the business with results.* Stamford, CT: Gartner.

The key messages of this slide take too long to process because of cluttered text, too much text at the beginning of the slide, and too many statistics.

**More Effective Opening Slide**

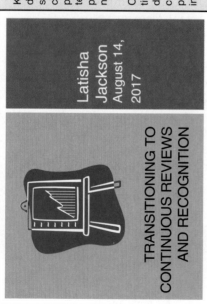

Improving Employee Engagement
*Transitioning to Continuous Reviews and Recognition*
Latisha Jackson | HR Intern | August 14, 2017

Key message (improving employee engagement with continuous reviews) stands out clearly.

A professional photograph reinforces the theme of employee engagement.

**More Effective Slide #2**

**Benefits of Employee Engagement**

- 21% higher productivity
- 22% higher profitability
- 37% reduced absenteeism

**Source and note:** Cameron, Yvette. (2013 December). *Social employee recognition systems reward the business with results.* Stamford, CT: Gartner. These figures are based on the top quartile of employees in a 2013 meta-analysis of 263 studies involving 1.3 million employees.

These statistics tell the story of benefits of employee engagement. Most audience members would understand these statistics within seconds. Because the slide is so easy to process, it does not distract attention from the presenter.

FIGURE 14.2

*(Continued)*

**Less Effective Slide #3**

## Problems with Annual Reviews

- Most employees think annual reviews are not accurate.

- Most employees think the feedback is too late to make changes.

- Most employees think annual reviews feel like punishment.

Without any special formatting, audience members must work too hard to read each sentence. This will draw attention away from the presenter.

**Less Effective Slide #4**

## Results of Our Employee Survey

| Annual reviews are . . . | Strongly Disagree | Disagree | Neutral | Agree | Strongly Agree |
|---|---|---|---|---|---|
| accurate indicators of my performance. | 12.6% | 30.0% | 14.8% | 26.9% | 15.7% |
| a productive experience. | 21.5% | 37.2% | 9.4% | 22.0% | 9.9% |
| a forward-looking process. | 21.1% | 28.3% | 14.3% | 23.8% | 12.6% |
| good recognition of my achievements. | 25.6% | 26.5% | 19.3% | 20.6% | 8.1% |
| helpful in my career development. | 18.4% | 35.0% | 10.8% | 23.8% | 12.1% |
| motivating. | 22.9% | 43.9% | 12.6% | 15.7% | 4.9% |

This table is accurate but difficult for audience members to process quickly. This much information would likely distract attention from the presenter.

**More Effective Slide #3**

## Problems with Annual Reviews

- **Fairness:** most employees think annual reviews are not accurate.
- **Motivation:** most employees think the feedback is too late to make changes.
- **Morale:** most employees think annual reviews feel like punishment.

Key problems with annual reviews are recognizable within seconds.

The picture accentuates the message that annual reviews are dissatisfying to employees.

**More Effective Slide #4**

## Our Employees' Views of Annual Reviews

*Annual reviews are . . .*

| | |
|---|---|
| accurate indicators of my performance. | 43% |
| helpful in my career development. | 36% |
| a forward-looking process. | 32% |
| a productive experience. | 32% |
| good recognition of my achievements. | 29% |
| motivating. | 21% |

**Note:** Percentages refer to number of employees who stated "agree" or "strongly agree" on our July 2017 survey of 223 Eastmond employees.

This chart is easier to process because it contains condensed information without sacrificing accuracy.

457

**FIGURE 14.2**

*(Continued)*

---

**Less Effective Slide #5**

## Continuous Reviews

- Peers and managers give daily feedback and recognition.
- Feedback and praise can be private or public.
- Features to improve rewards and recognition programs.
- Features for goal development and tracking.

Complete sentences without any special formatting require too much work for audience members.

---

**Less Effective Slide #6**

## What Our Employees Are Saying

| For performance reviews, I prefer... | Strongly Disagree | Disagree | Neutral | Agree | Strongly Agree |
|---|---|---|---|---|---|
| frequent feedback. | 4.9% | 14.3% | 16.1% | 40.8% | 23.8% |
| more feedback from my supervisors. | 7.2% | 16.6% | 17.0% | 37.7% | 21.5% |
| more feedback from my peers. | 5.8% | 8.1% | 11.7% | 46.6% | 27.8% |
| more recognition from my supervisors. | 3.1% | 4.0% | 6.3% | 38.6% | 48.0% |
| more recognition from my peers. | 4.0% | 6.3% | 10.3% | 35.4% | 43.9% |
| crowdsourced input on my evaluations. | 3.6% | 9.4% | 17.5% | 43.9% | 25.6% |
| more coaching from my supervisors. | 4.0% | 5.4% | 9.4% | 35.0% | 46.2% |
| more coaching from my peers. | 4.9% | 4.9% | 18.8% | 36.3% | 35.0% |

This table provides far too much information for audience members to process. If the presenter wants the audience to see all this information, he or she can do it with a handout.

---

**More Effective Slide #5**

## Benefits of Continuous Reviews

- **Multisource:** Peers and managers give daily feedback and recognition.
- **Private and public options:** Feedback and praise can be private or public.
- **Frequent recognition:** Features to improve rewards and recognition programs.
- **Goal-oriented:** Features for goal development and tracking.

© Ariel Skelley/Getty Images RF

Bolded keywords and phrases allow audience members to rapidly understand the key benefits.

---

**More Effective Slide #6**

## Our Employees' Views of Continuous Reviews

*For performance reviews, I prefer...*

- more recognition from my supervisors. — 87%
- more coaching from my supervisors. — 81%
- more recognition from my peers. — 79%
- more feedback from my peers. — 74%
- more coaching from my peers. — 71%
- crowdsourced input on my evaluations. — 70%

**Note:** Percentages refer to number of employees who stated "agree" or "strongly agree" on our July 2015 survey of 223 Eastmond employees.

This chart captures the key ideas from the survey fairly concisely. It still contains a lot of information, so the presenter needs to take time on this slide, put the information in context, and provide interesting commentary.

FIGURE 14.2

*(Continued)*

## Less Effective Slide #7

**The Continuous Review Systems Allows Positive, Helpful, and Candid Feedback**

- Supervisors can provide regular and constant feedback for their employees via comment boxes (these can then be sent with email or posted to public spaces).
- Peers can also post comments.

This slide contains far too much text. By this point in the presentation, audience members are tiring. Typically, the slides need to get simpler near the end of the presentation.

## Less Effective Slide #8

**The Continuous Review System Helps Managers in Many Ways**

- Managers can track feedback for their employees.
- Managers can create many types of reports.
- Managers can use the data to coach employees more effectively.

This slide contains far too much text. Audience members are getting more tired from trying to process this much text over the course of many slides.

## More Effective Slide #7

**Positive, Helpful, and Candid Feedback**

**Evaluation and Critique from Managers**

**Positive Feedback and Suggestions from Peers**

This slide is essentially a mock-up of the continuous review software. It allows audience members to visualize how the system works. It also positions the presenter to explain various functions depicted in the picture.

## More Effective Slide #8

**Ease of Use for Managers**

Convenient Tracking        Easy Reporting        Effective Coaching

This slide provides simple statements about functions of the software. This positions the presenter to take center stage describing how managers accomplish these objectives.

**FIGURE 14.2**

*(Continued)*

**Less Effective Slide #9**

## Costs of a Continuous Review System

- $10 to $20 per month per user (determined by the number of employees).
- Annual software administration fees of $1,600 to $2,100.
- Other indirect costs of around $2,000.
- Final costs will depend on the vendor we choose.

This slide provides a lot of data but almost no meaning or appropriate frame of reference. It mixes monthly and annual figures. It does not contain any summary totals to provide audience members with perspective.

**More Effective Slide #9**

## Cost-Effectiveness (Annual Figures)

| Item | Amount* |
|------|---------|
| Software user costs | $2,750 to $5,500 |
| Software administration fees | $1,600 to $2,100 |
| Other indirect costs | $1,000 to $2,000 |
| **TOTAL** | **$5,350 to $9,600** |

*Variation in costs depend on the software vendoe we choose.

This slide includes summary totals on an annual basis. This provides decision makers with valuable and easy-to-process information.

**Less Effective Slide #10**

## Implementation

- Phase I (August to September 2015)
  - Vendor selection
- Phase II (October to December 2015)
  - Pilot in the HR department
- Phase III (December 2015)
  - Companywide training
- Phase IV: (January 2016)
  - Companywide adoption
- All activities conducted by HR department

This slide contains slightly too much text. It presents the timeline and related activities in vertical format. Most people can process timeline information more easily in a horizontal format.

**More Effective Slide #10**

## Proposed Implementation

| Time Frame | Activities |
|------------|------------|
| Aug to Sept 2017 | Vendor selection |
| Oct to Dec 2017 | Pilot in the HR dept |
| Dec 2017 | Companywide training |
| Jan 2018 | Companywide adoption |

This slide allows readers to rapidly recognize key time frames and related activities.

# ⏻ TECHNOLOGY TIPS

### ALTERNATIVES TO POWERPOINT

In many work environments, PowerPoint slides have become the standard visual aid for presentations and meetings. Even if you're great at using them, you might consider other types of visual aids and props to add impact, creativity, or simply variety to your presentations.

*Try other electronic slide and presentation software.* Consider trying Prezi, Google Docs, SlideRocket, 280 Slides, or other software packages to see what you're most comfortable with. Many presenters find that presentation software such as Prezi does not box them into bullet-point-based, linear presentations and provides more flexibility.

*Use smartboards, whiteboards, or chalkboards.* The act of writing as you go with keyboards, markers, or chalk may allow you to engage your audience more effectively because you are presenting in the moment, avoiding the structure or order of electronic slides, and getting input from your audience as you go. Furthermore, you may find that drawing objects freehand allows you to depict ideas more accurately and forcefully than you can with the drawing tools in PowerPoint. Still, make sure you avoid spending too much time facing away from the audience.

*Experiment with new presentation technologies.* Hundreds of new and emerging presentation technologies are *social*. In other words, they allow you to get information and feedback from your audience that you can incorporate into your presentation. By experimenting with these technologies, you'll learn to tap into the incoming messages while also controlling your message or the conversation.

© Stockbyte/Getty Images RF

other options (see the "Alternatives to PowerPoint" Technology Tip). One appealing alternative is Prezi, presentation software that focuses less on slides and more on movement across a canvas. In contrast to PowerPoint, Prezi presentations are less linear. In other words, PowerPoint presentations typically contain one order to present slides (there are ways around this but few professionals use them). Prezi presentations allow more flexibility to use paths and focal points in unique ways during a presentation. You've probably seen a Prezi presentation before. If you haven't, you can go to the Prezi website (prezi.com) to see several examples.

Prezi allows you to really "wow" your audience with stunning imagery and movement. It is a good choice when you want to creatively and visually display your key messages. It is particularly appropriate when one of your major goals is to leave an emotional impact on your audience. Typically, Prezi presentations are less ideal when you plan to stop frequently during a presentation for discussion and interaction. Like PowerPoint presentations, one major goal is still to focus on ease of processing. Compared to PowerPoint presentations, keep in mind these tips:

- *Practice, practice, practice.* Prezi presentations can turn into a mess quickly if you're a novice at the software. Spend enough time practicing so that you can use the software smoothly in front of a group.

- *Create a sense of adventure and enthusiasm.* Prezi presentations equip you with tools to get your audience emotionally invested in the content of your presentation. Most audience members raise their expectations for an engaging presentation as soon as they notice it's a Prezi presentation. Be prepared to meet these expectations.

- *Use motion effectively.* Prezi presentations allow you to move around your canvas by panning from one place to another, rotating views, and zooming in and out on various focal points. This motion allows you to capture your audience's attention. Yet, panning, zooming, and rotating too often and too quickly can disorient some audience members. Some audience members even report getting dizzy in Prezi presentations.

- *Integrate video, pictures, graphics, and other images.* Prezi presentations typically allow easier integration of many types of multimedia than do PowerPoint presentations. To really make use of Prezi, you should invest a lot of effort in developing outstanding graphics and video. You can often do this by using other software programs such as Photoshop and Illustrator. Similarly, you should generally use even less text in Prezi presentations than in PowerPoint presentations.

- *Make sure your key messages are the emphasis.* While many people consider PowerPoint presentations dull in comparison to Prezis, most people also find it easier to recall key messages from the linear, more text-based format of PowerPoint presentations. In your effort to create a visually powerful presentation with Prezi, never lose sight of the primary goal: emphasizing your key messages often.

For advice from an expert, read the Communication Q&A with James Robertson.

## Applying the Story Line Approach to Your Presentations

**LO14.5** Use the story line approach to presentations.

**connect**

Visit **http://connect. mheducation.com** for an exercise on this topic.

Earlier in this chapter, you learned about the PREP method of providing rich examples to support your positions. You also learned that you should create electronic slides with a story line approach. This section explains how you can apply a story line approach to your entire presentation and enhance your ability to connect with and influence others.

The story line approach is useful for various types of presentations because it allows your listeners to engage on a deeper level emotionally and intellectually. Emotionally, they often feel a bond with you as a speaker. Furthermore, they tend to internalize stories, even developing their own parallel stories that evoke commitment, determination, sympathy, and other emotions. However, stories are far more than emotional tools. Research shows that people remember stories more easily than they do abstract information, and they are more likely to act on what they hear via stories.[28]

When James E. Rogers, president and CEO of Duke Energy, was asked "What would you like business schools to teach more of, or less of?" he had this to say:

> What I would really teach is how to write, and how to speak and make presentations. I've overused this term in this conversation, but *it's the ability to pull the salient facts together and tell a story, so that people feel it, sense it, they're convinced by it, and want to do something because of it.*
>
> My first full-time job, I worked at night as a newspaper reporter, going to school during the day. So, I really started out covering police news, and then federal courts and political news. And I really kind of developed a sense of the importance of trying to find the essence of the story and trying to arrange the facts in some chronology to make sense out of it. In a sense, as a CEO, part of my job is not only to help develop direction but to teach the storytelling. Those early years as a reporter gave me a sense of that in terms of how to tell the story, how to communicate.[29]

Rogers is not the only business professional who emphasizes storytelling. Jathan Janove, who did extensive HR training about sexual harassment in the early to mid-1990s, described his transition to storytelling for presentations. Penalties to employers and employees had increased substantially, and his job was to explain new laws governing appropriate behavior. As he lectured employees, he found that they often resented the perceived intrusiveness of the new laws and the fear tactics of describing harsh penalties. And they found the lectures boring. Here is what Janove did:

> It didn't take a great leap to realize that this training wasn't working, so I adopted a new approach, jettisoning scare-you-straight legal points. I substituted stories illustrating types of behaviors employees should avoid and how they unwittingly get themselves in trouble. Something amazing happened: Suddenly, the rooms were full of bright eyes. Discovering that telling stories is an excellent way to train employees about workplace law, I began collecting parables.[30]

Janove further explained that once he adopted a story-based approach to business training, he became far more influential. Audiences listened more attentively, learned more, and changed their behaviors.

You can use stories in many kinds of business presentations. For example, Sally Herigstad, a CPA and consultant to *MSN Money,* spoke about using this strategy for delivering financial presentations:

> Financial presentations tell a story. You're not just showing a collection of profit-and-loss statements and balance sheets—you're telling a story that your audience needs to hear. It may be a story of a new company with promising growth. Or maybe it's a story about meeting market challenges. Whatever your story is, stick to it: Toss everything that doesn't help you tell it in a compelling, easy-to-follow way. Tell your story with simplicity and clarity.[31]

Typically, stories for business connect facts with people and their business goals. Ideally, they are true, factual, and based on real events. In some cases, they may be hypothetical, but listeners still must find them realistic and relevant.[32] Generally, stories for business include the following components:[33]

- *Plot:* a business situation that involves challenges or tensions to overcome and a clear beginning and end.
- *Setting:* the time, place, characters, and context of the business situation.
- *Resolution:* a solution to the challenges or tensions.
- *Moral or lesson:* a point to the story.

In Figure 14.3, you'll find a story Latisha uses to explain how continuous review systems allow for better employee recognition and rewards. The story contains a plot, a setting, a resolution, and a moral. It speaks directly to a concern senior managers have—high employee turnover. This story is part of a larger story line that Latisha carries across her entire presentation.

Keep in mind that stories should be short. Even when audience members are engaged, their patience is limited. They expect to get the point quickly. Typically, stories should last 30 seconds to one minute. In some cases, a story can last two to three minutes. Use your judgment and pay attention to your audiences. To help you identify how long a story is, time it while you rehearse. Or write it out and estimate how much time it will take to tell. Most people are comfortable with speaking at about 150 to 160 words per minute (this is the pace of most audio books). So, a 75-word story takes roughly 30 seconds, and a 150-word story takes about one minute.

It takes time to gather true stories for your presentations, so be alert for good ones. Remember, the purpose is always to make a point, not to entertain. If the stories have entertainment value, that's an added bonus.

**FIGURE 14.3**

Telling Stories to Connect with and Influence Audience Members

One of the pressing issues we're facing is high turnover among our employees. In the past three years, our annual turnover rate has been nearly 25 percent — nearly twice that of companies in our industry. As we've considered our strategies to address this problem, we've recognized that continuous review systems with frequent recognition and rewards are an effective way to reduce employee turnover.

Let me share with you what happened at Peakster Computing, a company that was in a similar situation five years ago. Its annual employee turnover was roughly 18 percent. It estimated that replacing each employee cost about $25,000. Across Peakster locations, it estimated excessive turnover was costing at least $35 million per year.

Janna, Peakster's HR director, tried a variety of approaches to learn about the high employee turnover. She used exit surveys and focus groups, and even contacted past employees. The message she kept getting from former employees was this: "No one appreciated us."

As a result, Peakster started instituting a variety of employee recognition programs. After several years of these programs, the company concluded the programs hadn't made any difference. Why? Because recognition and rewards still occurred only every six months or so. In other words, the recognition and rewards simply did not occur frequently enough.

Then, Janna adopted a continuous review system with the ability to give frequent recognition and rewards. Employees were getting highly visible compliments and kudos from managers and peers. Many employees got some type of recognition almost daily. Instead of employee recognition awards that arrived every six months, every year, or even every five years, employees were now getting smaller but more frequent rewards. Part of the rewards program involved receiving redeemable rewards points. On average employees were redeeming these points every five to six weeks for movie tickets, meals, other prizes, and even cash.

The results have been dramatic. Employee turnover is now around 11 percent. Janna says the drop in turnover alone accounts for millions of dollars in savings. She also says that improved morale is leading to far higher productivity. What Janna says makes all the difference is a "culture of appreciation."

What we've learned from Janna is that continuous review systems with options for frequent recognition and rewards lead to lower employee turnover. The main reason is that employees respond best to frequent recognition and small rewards more so than infrequent recognition and more prestigious rewards.

**Plot:** This plot is about how continuous review systems can lower employee turnover.

**Setting:** The setting focuses on Peakster Computing, where high employee turnover was costing the company millions of dollars. The company tried a variety of strategies to reduce employee turnover.

**Resolution:** By using continuous review systems, Peakster Computing was able to dramatically reduce employee turnover.

**Moral or lesson:** Frequent recognition and small rewards reduce employee turnover more effectively than infrequent recognition and large rewards.

*At 399 words, this story would take roughly 2½ minutes.*

# Reviewing Your Presentations for Fairness and Effectiveness

Review your presentations in the same way you review your written communications. In the first place, double-check every aspect of your supplementary materials as well as the technology you will use to ensure that it is perfect and working. Typos on electronic slides can be a glaring display of carelessness. Also, seek feedback from colleagues and clients before and after your presentations. Ask them how they would change the presentation to better meet their needs.

As with all of your communications, ask yourself how fair your business presentations are. Is the content based on *facts*? Have you granted others *access* to your real motives and reasoning? Have you been forthright about *impacts* on audience members and other stakeholders? Have you ensured that you show *respect* for audience members (see Figure 14.4)?

In Latisha's case, she evaluates her presentation in each regard. In particular, she has provided claims about the impacts of continuous review systems on employee engagement. Latisha is comfortable with these claims. She has researched these impacts carefully. She provides access to the sources of her information so senior managers can make judgments about the reliability of the information. She discusses impacts on stakeholders and explains that these changes require a new approach to managing employees. Finally, she should be respectful in every way as senior managers ask tough questions (you'll see some of these tough questions in Chapter 15). For additional thoughts on delivering presentations from an experienced professional, read the Communication Q&A with James Robertson.

**LO14.6** Evaluate your presentations for fairness and effectiveness.

---

**FIGURE 14.4**

## Are Your Presentations FAIR?

**Facts** (How *factual* is your presentation?)

- Have you presented *all* the facts correctly?
- Have you presented information that allows colleagues, customers, and consumers to make informed decisions that are in their best interests?
- Have you carefully considered various interpretations of your data? Have you assessed the quality of your information?

**Access** (How *accessible* or *transparent* are your motives, reasoning, and information?)

- Are your motives clear, or will others think you have a hidden agenda? Have you made yourself accessible to others so that they can learn more about your viewpoints?
- Have you fully disclosed information that colleagues, customers, or consumers should expect to receive?
- Are you hiding any information to cast your recommendations in a better light or real reasons for making certain claims or recommendations?

**Impacts** (How does your communication *impact* stakeholders?)

- Have you carefully considered how your ideas, products, and services will impact colleagues, customers, and consumers?
- Have you made recommendations to colleagues, customers, and consumers that are in their best interests?

**Respect** (How *respectful* is your presentation?)

- Does the message offend or pressure in any way? Does it show that your colleagues' and customers' needs are important?
- Would a neutral observer consider your communication respectful?

# COMMUNICATION Q&A

## CONVERSATIONS WITH CURRENT BUSINESS PROFESSIONALS

**Pete Cardon: What types of presentations do you give?**

**James Robertson:** In the course of a year I typically give two or three "keynote" presentations at conferences or conventions and many internal presentations on strategy, business plans, or technology directions to people above and below me in the organization. Many of my presentations come in the form of general communication and update meetings to staff teams or working groups where I need to deliver a consistent and accurate message on a topic as their leader.

**PC: How do you prepare for the presentations?**

**JR:** The key to a successful presentation is knowing your audience and practicing your message. Regardless of how big or small the group, make sure you spend plenty of time preparing. I dedicate many hours of practice to making sure that the 20 or 30 minutes I'll have in front of them comes off without a hitch. The audience is always the wild card, but anticipating their response is important.

**PC: In what ways do you see PowerPoint used effectively in the workplace?**

**JR:** Presentations resonate with me more when they convey a simple message. There is an old saying "a picture says a thousand words." I recently delivered a presentation where I did not have a single word on any of the slides, but the pictures on those slides conveyed the message. Humans are very visual and experiential, and they retain visuals in memory more easily than they do words. While not all presentations are purely visual, the best ones I've ever seen, or have given, involved more use of graphics and pictures and less use of words and text.

**PC: In what ways do you see PowerPoint used ineffectively in the workplace?**

**JR:** I hate presentations where the slides consist only of words or numbers or very complicated charts I can't read at a distance or really understand. That's the ultimate turnoff and will put your audience to sleep in a hurry.

*See more of James Robertson's comments about presentations at the end of the next chapter.*

***James Robertson*** *is the chief technology officer at Time Warner Enterprise Infrastructure Services. He has worked at Turner Broadcasting for nearly 20 years in various executive and management positions.*

© Courtesy of James Robertson

# Chapter Takeaway for *Planning Presentations*

**LO14.1 Describe how planning your presentations leads to credibility. (pp. 445–446)**

Planning presentation content demonstrates **your personal credibility.**

| | | |
|---|---|---|
| It shows **competence** when you demonstrate that you know what you're talking about. | It shows **caring** when you provide content that meets the needs of others. | It shows **character** when you provide honest and transparent content. |

**LO14.2 Analyze presentation audiences in terms of message benefits, learning styles, and communicator styles. (pp. 446–448)**

| Principles of Audience Analysis | | |
|---|---|---|
| **Identify the following:** | | |
| • Audience benefits | • Decision makers | • Communicator style |
| • Existing knowledge | • Appeals | • Learning style |
| • Concerns | | |

| Learner Types |
|---|
| • Visual |
| • Auditory |
| • Kinesthetic |

**LO14.3 Organize and gather content for a preview, view, and review. (pp. 449–452)**

**Audience:** Identify how your message benefits your audience and make your message easy to understand.

**Information:** Gather the right information to support your key message.

**Message:** Give a preview of your message, justify your views, and end with a review.

**Components of Presentations:** Preview, View, Review

**Types of Attention-Getters:** Rhetorical Question, Vivid Example, Dramatic Demonstration, Testimonial or Quotation, Intriguing Statistic, Unexpected Exercise, Challenge

See *examples of attention-getters* in Table 14.1.

**PREP Method:** Position, Reasons, Example, Position

See an *example of a PREP statement* in Table 14.2.

**LO14.4 Develop effective slide presentations. (pp. 452–462)**

| Principles for Developing Slides | |
|---|---|
| • Create a storyboard with your PowerPoint slide titles. | • Use plenty of white space. |
| • Design your slides for ease of processing. | • Use high-contrast backgrounds and colors. |
| • Limit the amount of information on any given slide. | • Use compelling images, charts, and figures. |
| • Use font sizes that all audience members can read easily. | • Get professional design help when possible. |
| • Focus on and highlight key information. | |

See *less effective and more effective examples of slides* in Figure 14.2.

| Statement | 1 – Rarely/Never | 2 – Sometimes | 3 – Usually | 4 – Always |
|---|---|---|---|---|
| I carefully select two or three key messages that I want to get across for my presentations. | 1 | 2 | 3 | 4 |
| I design my presentations so that nearly every aspect leads back to one of my main points. | 1 | 2 | 3 | 4 |
| I repeat my main points at least several times during a presentation. | 1 | 2 | 3 | 4 |
| I provide an overview at the beginning of my presentations that includes my key messages. | 1 | 2 | 3 | 4 |
| I think carefully about how my key messages meet the needs of my audiences. | 1 | 2 | 3 | 4 |
| I think carefully about how to adapt my key messages to the preferred communicator styles of my audience members. | 1 | 2 | 3 | 4 |
| I think carefully about how to adapt my key messages to the preferred learning styles of my audience members. | 1 | 2 | 3 | 4 |
| I provide enough support materials to make my key messages convincing. | 1 | 2 | 3 | 4 |
| I speak with confidence about my key messages. | 1 | 2 | 3 | 4 |
| I conclude with a call to action that is built upon my key messages. | 1 | 2 | 3 | 4 |

Add up your score and consider the following advice:

35–40: You are a *strategic, other-oriented presenter.* You think about how to prepare and deliver a presentation that meets the needs of others. Continue with such awareness of the impact of your written messages.

30–34: You are a *careful, considerate presenter.* You spend some time thinking about the content of your message and the needs of your audience members. Take time to think your message through even more carefully and pay close attention to the needs and potential responses to your written messages by audience members.

25–29: You are an *average* presenter. Sometimes you are careful about developing your message and considerate of the needs and reactions of others. Other times you are not. Get in the habit of taking time to carefully craft your message.

Under 25: You *need to improve* your approach to presenting. You likely don't spend enough time thinking through the key messages and their impacts on others. You will be far more influential if you spend more time preparing your messages and delivering them with your audience members in mind.

Once you complete the assessment, write three paragraphs about the three specific ways in which you can improve your ability to prepare and deliver your key messages in presentations.

**14.8 Evaluating Learning and Communicator Styles** (LO14.2)

Based on the descriptions of communicator styles (professionals with red, blue, green, and hub MVSs) and learning styles (visual, auditory, kinesthetic) described in the "Analyze Your Audience" section of this chapter, do the following:

A. Describe your learning and communicator styles (you may consider yourself a combination of various styles).

B. Discuss how your learning and communicator styles may impact how you prefer to receive presentations.

C. Discuss how your learning and communicator styles may impact how you plan and deliver presentations.

D. Explain a few ways you can adapt your presentation style to learning and communicator styles other than your own.

**14.9 Interviewing a Business Professional about Planning for Presentations** (LO14.1, LO14.2, LO14.3, LO14.4)

Interview a business professional about best practices in planning business presentations. Write four to five paragraphs about the interview and address the following issues:

A. Planning themes and key points.

B. Adapting the presentation to the needs and preferences of the audience.

C. Using attention-getters or other strategies to engage the audience in the opening moments.

D. Preparing examples and support for key ideas.

E. Developing electronic slides and handouts.

F. Using technology.

**14.10  Conducting a FAIR Test of a Recent Presentation** (LO14.6)

Think about a presentation you made recently. Assess how you did in terms of the following:

A. Did you present the facts correctly?

B. Did you present all the relevant facts?

C. Did you present any information that would be considered misleading?

D. Did you make your motives clear, or will others perceive that you have a hidden agenda?

E. Did you hide any of the real reasons for making certain claims or recommendations?

F. Did you seek the opinions and ideas of those impacted by your communication?

G. Did you think about how your communication will help or even hurt others?

H. Would others consider your presentation respectful?

# Application Exercises

**14.11  Planning Attention-Getters** (LO14.3)

Using Table 14.1 as a guide, do the following:

A. Identify a topic for a presentation.

B. Write how you could use each type of attention-getter: rhetorical question, vivid example, dramatic demonstration, testimonial or quotation, intriguing statistic, unexpected exercise, and challenge.

C. Explain the three approaches you believe would be most effective.

**14.12  Creating Positioning and Preview Statements** (LO14.3)

A. Identify a topic for a presentation.

B. Write a positioning statement.

C. Write a preview statement.

**14.13  Employing the PREP Method to Take Positions** (LO14.3)

Identify a key position that you intend to make during your presentation. Using Table 14.2 as a guide, write out how you could use the PREP (Position–Reasons–Example–Position) method to effectively convey this position to your audience.

**14.14  Creating a Storyboard for Your Presentation** (LO14.4)

Identify a topic of interest. Create a storyboard (similar to the one displayed in Table 14.3) to outline the titles, content, and related story line of your PowerPoint slides.

**14.15  Creating Electronic Slides** (LO14.4)

Create an electronic slide presentation for your topic of interest. Ensure that it conveys your key messages effectively.

**14.16  Creating Electronic Slides from Reports** (LO14.4)

Many times in the workplace, you will create a written report and provide an oral presentation as well. Select a written report and develop a set of electronic slides that could be used to present it. If you have not developed your own report, consider the following options:

- A report or other written message in the textbook. For example, you could consider the following: "Should the Prestigio Hotel Develop and Market Green Meetings?" in Chapter 13 or "Guest Satisfaction among Conference Attendees" in Chapter 13.

- An annual report from a company of interest.

- A white paper from a company of interest.

# Language Mechanics Check

**14.17  Review all rules in Appendix A about punctuation, number usage, and grammar. Then, rewrite each sentence to make all needed corrections.**

A. Jim I'm disappointed that many of our job candidates have rejected our high compensation attractive job offers during the past year.

B. I believe we're facing a crisis if we can't hire top tier candidates, soon we may face a major talent gap.

C. Job candidates may be dissatisfied with some of the following issues career path, office locations, perceived work hours, sign on bonus and/or benefits.

D. I think we should organize a committee which should include some of our more recent hires, to examine the reasons these job candidates are not accepting our offers.

E. I'd like you to give me some advice about the following (1) employees to place on this committee, (2) charges to give the committee, (3) information to give the committee and (4) timeline for the committee to complete their work.

F. Also I'd like you to send me your impressions of the last five job candidates, who declined our offers.

G. Since you got to know them so well perhaps you could contact them personally, and ask them directly why they chose not to accept our offers.

H. I think they will give you their candid views since you seemed to really connect with them.

I. I'm hoping that we make adjustments before our next recruiting season, because we can't afford to continue this hiring slump.

J. Thanks, Jim for your efforts on behalf of the firm, you make a tremendous difference for us.

# Endnotes

1. Thomas Leech, *How to Prepare, Stage, and Deliver Winning Presentations,* 3rd ed. (New York: American Management Association, 2004): 9–10.

2. Lin Grensing-Pophal, "Presentations That Sell without Offending," Society for Human Resource Management website (July 1, 2004).

3. Harry Mills, *Power Points! How to Design and Deliver Presentations That Sizzle and Sell* (New York: AMACOM, 2007).

4. Nick Morgan, "Reach Audience Members Where They Learn," *Harvard Management Communication Letter,* May 2002: 9.

5. Mills, *Power Points! How to Design and Deliver Presentations That Sizzle and Sell.*

6. Leech, *How to Prepare, Stage, and Deliver Winning Presentations.*

7. Ibid.

8. Mills, *Power Points! How to Design and Deliver Presentations That Sizzle and Sell.*

9. This section is adapted from the work of Mills, *Power Points! How to Design and Deliver Presentations That Sizzle and Sell.*

10. Dana LaMon, "Making the Moment Meaningful," *Toastmaster* online (November 2007), available at www.toastmasters.org/ ToastmastersMagazine/ToastmasterArchive/2007/November/ MomentMeaningful.aspx.

11. Stephen Denning, *The Secret Language of Leadership: How Leaders Inspire Action through Narrative* (San Francisco: John Wiley & Sons, 2007).

12. Denning, *The Secret Language of Leadership.*

13. Ibid.

14. Nick Morgan, "Opening Options: How to Grab Your Audience's Attention: Six Great Ways to Begin a Presentation," *Harvard Management Communication Letter,* June 2003: 3–4.

15. Denning, *The Secret Language of Leadership: How Leaders Inspire Action through Narrative.*

16. Leech, *How to Prepare, Stage, and Deliver Winning Presentations.*

17. Mills, *Power Points! How to Design and Deliver Presentations That Sizzle and Sell.*

18. Roly Grimshaw, "Communication by Numbers," *Harvard Management Communication Letter* 8, no. 3 (2005): 3–4.

19. Nick Morgan, "How to Put Together a Great Speech When You're Under the Gun," *Harvard Management Communication Letter,* September 2003: 3–4.

20. Leech, *How to Prepare, Stage, and Deliver Winning Presentations*; Mills, *Power Points! How to Design and Deliver Presentations That Sizzle and Sell.*

21. Mills, *Power Points! How to Design and Deliver Presentations That Sizzle and Sell.*

22. Leech, *How to Prepare, Stage, and Deliver Winning Presentations.*

23. Adam Bryant, "Structure? The Flatter, the Better," *Corner Office* (blog), *The New York Times,* January 16, 2010, retrieved from www.nytimes.com/2010/01/17/business/17corner.html; Adam Bryant, "The C.E.O., Now Appearing on YouTube," *Corner Office* (blog), *The New York Times,* May 9, 2009, retrieved from www. nytimes.com/2009/05/10/business/10corner.html; Stephen M. Kosslyn, *Clear and to the Point: 8 Psychological Principles for Compelling PowerPoint Presentations* (Oxford: Oxford University Press, 2007): 1; Ellen Finkelstein, "Sidestep the PowerPoint Trap," *Toastmaster* online (May 2009), available at www.toastmasters. org/ToastmastersMagazine/ToastmasterArchive/2009/May/ SidestepPowerPoint.aspx.

24. Judith Humphrey, "You Are the Best Visual," *Harvard Management Communication Letter,* October 2011: 10–11.

25. Grimshaw, "Communication by Numbers."

26. Ronald Alsop, "Poor Writing Skills Top M.B.A. Recruiter Gripes," *The Wall Street Journal,* January 17, 2006.

27. Kosslyn, *Clear and to the Point: 8 Psychological Principles for Compelling PowerPoint Presentations*; Leech, *How to Prepare, Stage, and Deliver Winning Presentations*; Sally Herigstad, "Giving Effective Financial Presentations with PowerPoint," *Toastmaster* online (July 2008), available at www.toastmasters.org/ToastmastersMagazine/ ToastmasterArchive/2008/July/PresentationswithPowerPoint.aspx; Mills, *Power Points! How to Design and Deliver Presentations That Sizzle and Sell.*

28. John Seely Brown, Stephen Denning, Katalina Groh, and Laurence Prusak, *Storytelling in Organizations: Why Storytelling Is Transforming 21st Century Organizations and Management* (Burlington, MA: Elsevier Butterworth-Heinemann, 2005); Roger C. Schank, *Tell Me a Story: A New Look at Real and Artificial Memory* (New York: Charles Scribner's Sons, 1990); Walter Swap, Dorothy Leonard, Mimi Shields, and Lisa Abrams, "Using Mentoring and Storytelling to Transfer Knowledge in the Workplace," *Journal of Management Information Systems* 18, no. 1 (2001): 95–114; Michael W. McLaughlin, "Getting Clout from Speaking Engagements," *Society for Human Resource Management* website (May 5, 2010); Judith Tingley, "Walking a Fine Line: How Much Personal Information Should Speakers Share?" *Toastmaster*

online (March 2009), available at www.toastmasters.org/ToastmastersMagazine/ToastmasterArchive/2009/March/Walking-a-Fine-Line.aspx; Jathan Janove, "A Story Is Worth a Thousand Lectures," *HR Magazine* 54, no. 7 (July 1, 2009) [online version]; Mills, *Power Points! How to Design and Deliver Presentations That Sizzle and Sell.*

29. Adam Bryant, "The C.E.O. as General (and Scout)," *Corner Office* (blog), *The New York Times*, October 10, 2009, retrieved from www.nytimes.com/2009/10/11/business/11corner.html.

30. Janove, "A Story Is Worth a Thousand Lectures."

31. Herigstad, "Giving Effective Financial Presentations with PowerPoint."

32. David Armstrong, *Managing by Storying Around* (New York: Doubleday, 1992).

33. Adapted from Robert F. Dennehy, "The Executive as Storyteller," *Management Review* 88, no. 3 (1999): 40–43; Schank, *Tell Me a Story: A New Look at Real and Artificial Memory.*

34. Stephen Denning, "Stories in the Workplace," Society for Human Resource Management website (October 1, 2008).

35. Bryant, "The C.E.O. as General (and Scout)."

**ESTABLISHING CREDIBILITY**

 **PRINCIPLES OF INTERPERSONAL COMMUNICATION**

 **PRINCIPLES FOR & TYPES OF BUSINESS MESSAGES**

## Learning Objectives

After studying this chapter, you should be able to do the following:

**LO15.1** Describe how presentation delivery impacts your credibility.

**LO15.2** Deliver presentations with authenticity, confidence, and influence.

**LO15.3** Apply the SOFTEN model of nonverbal communication for presentations.

**LO15.4** Use slides and handouts to supplement your presentation effectively.

**LO15.5** Interact effectively with your audience.

**LO15.6** Prepare to present effectively in teams.

Once you've settled on the content of your presentation, you turn to preparing for the delivery. Delivering great presentations involves art and skill. With each of your professional presentations, you'll fine-tune your abilities. In this chapter, we focus on making your delivery as smooth and engaging as possible so that you will successfully connect with your audiences. Read the chapter case, which is a continuation from Chapter 14 and is the basis for many examples in this chapter.

**Hear Pete Cardon explain why this matters.**

**bit.ly/cardon15**

## CHAPTER CASE: DELIVERING A PRESENTATION AT EASTMOND NETWORKING

Latisha Jackson, HR intern

**WHO'S INVOLVED**

- Hired for a summer internship to work on employee programs
- Double majoring in business administration and health education

Latisha has prepared a presentation to deliver to the senior management team about transitioning from annual performance reviews to continuous performance reviews. She hopes the presentation will provide her with more professional opportunities at Eastmond Networking. She's nervous, though, and uncertain of the outcome.

**THE SITUATION**

© LWA/Larry Williams/Blend Images LLC RF

**TASK**

1

2

Connect with the audience, gaining their trust and confidence.

Deliver a persuasive and memorable explanation of the benefits of continuous reviews.

## Establishing Presence

Presenting gives you an excellent opportunity to connect deeply with your colleagues, your clients, and your other contacts. It allows you to express your views in a rich, two-way environment. As you do with your written communication, you will aim to strike the right style and tone in your presentations. Moreover, you will strive to establish a "presence," something great speakers and presenters are often described as doing. Having presence means commanding attention, garnering respect for your ideas, engaging your listeners, and even inspiring your audiences to action. In this section, we focus on strategies you can use to enhance your presence as you deliver your presentations.

they have the least-certain outcome. Sometimes, out of nervousness, presenters do not follow through completely at these moments. If nervousness means you short-change yourself at those critical moments, use techniques to help you manage your nervousness.[6]

Consider some of the following recommendations:[7]

**Engage in Relaxation Techniques**   Consider some of the following options:

- Stretching.
- Meditating.
- Going hiking or exercising (a day or so before your presentation).
- Listening to music.
- Going to a movie.

- Watching a sunset.
- Thinking about the things in your life you are grateful for, such as your cherished relationships.
- Letting your mind go blank.
- Counting backward from 100.

**Become Aware of Your Breathing**   Taking several deep breaths is a great technique to quickly alleviate anxiety. Also, consistently taking full breaths leads to improved tone and timber of your voice as well as better, more confident posture.

**Practice Visualization**   Envision yourself speaking with confidence and ease. Imagine making nonverbal connections with your audience. Think about how you will respond to audience questions. In your mind, play out your presentation and see yourself succeeding.

**Focus on Friendly Faces Initially to Gain Composure and Confidence**
Inevitably, the presence of some audience members will make you more nervous than others. It may be a critical boss, a skeptical client, a person you disagree with often, or someone who intimidates you for other reasons. In the opening moments of your presentation, when you are most apt to suffer from nervousness, look at those in the audience with whom you are most friendly. This will help calm you during those ever-important first moments.

**Watch Your Food and Beverage Intake**   Pay attention to foods and beverages that impact your nervousness. Some people avoid or minimize caffeine intake on speech days to avoid jitters. Others avoid dairy products since they can coat the mouth and throat and make speaking feel less smooth. Notice how various foods and beverages affect your body and adjust accordingly.

**Get Comfortable with Audience Members before Starting Your Presentation**   One of the best ways of relaxing immediately before your presentation is to speak with audience members. Greet them at the door, walk around the room, engage in small talk, and find other ways to break the ice and help you and your audience members warm up to each other.

## Focus on People

If you make your speech about people, your audience members are more likely to trust your commitment to them and others: People like to hear about people. Also, a strong people-focus will allow you to liven up dry facts and statistics. Try the following methods of making your speech about people.[8]

**Make People the Subject of Your Sentences**   Especially when you present numerical information, using people as the subjects of your sentences humanizes your presentation. Notice how Latisha does this in Table 15.1.

**TABLE 15.1**

Making People the Subject of Your Sentences

| Less Effective | More Effective |
|---|---|
| The survey showed just 43 percent of respondents believe that annual reviews are accurate indicators of performance. | Jeff, Steve, and I developed the survey after holding focus groups with our employees to learn about their views of annual reviews. Of the 223 employees who took the survey, just 43 percent believed that annual reviews are accurate indicators of performance. |
| This statement is compelling but dry and impersonal to some audience members. | This statement is more compelling by introducing the people involved: the HR personnel who designed the survey based on what they heard from employees and the larger group of employees who ultimately took the survey. |

**TABLE 15.2**

Introducing Colleagues by Name

| Less Effective | More Effective |
|---|---|
| I'll be presenting research conducted by the HR team. | Our HR team, including Jeff Brody and Steve Choi, spent the last two months gathering information about annual reviews and continuous reviews. We've talked to HR directors at other companies, software vendors who provide new continuous review tools, and our own employees. Today we'll share this research with you. |
| This statement is good but could be improved by elaborating on who the members of the HR team are and why they're positioned to provide good advice. | This statement is stronger with its focus on the members of the HR team and why they are positioned to provide strong advice. |

**TABLE 15.3**

Using Names of Audience Members

| Less Effective | More Effective |
|---|---|
| It's common for managers to continue conducting annual performance reviews even though they think there should be better ways of evaluating and motivating performance. | Just before we started the meeting this morning, Cynthia, John, and I were chatting about annual performance reviews. They each mentioned great managers they knew here in this company who conduct annual performance reviews as a matter of routine but don't think they work. These managers think there should be better ways of evaluating and motivating performance. |
| This statement is good but is not personalized. It is essentially a "faceless" comment that may be less persuasive without talking about "real" people. | This statement makes the point in a personalized, relatable manner. It shows the presenter is connected to the experiences of the audience. |

**Introduce Colleagues and Refer to Them by Name during Your Presentation**   By naming members in your organization or other relevant people, you help your audience members feel they are getting to know these important individuals (see Table 15.2).

**Use Names of Audience Members as Appropriate**   When you know the names of those in your audience, consider using their names from time to time to personalize your presentation (see Table 15.3).

## Stay Flexible

Presentations rarely go as planned. Knowing your content perfectly will help you adapt to unexpected circumstances. Maintaining a flexible approach will help you think on your feet for unanticipated events. Consider the following ways of staying flexible.

**Arrive Early**    Arriving early lets you notice if you have any surprises in terms of equipment, room layout, or people in attendance. If so, you may be able to make adjustments before the presentation begins. When presenting in a place you've never been before, arrive at least an hour or two early.

**Focus on the Needs of Your Audience**    Some presentations can get off course when audience members raise questions or make comments. If you are preoccupied with your own agenda only, you can become flustered or disorganized if someone poses a question. Be ready to adapt to the immediate needs of your audience so you can quickly modify your presentation based on their requests. If you spend time anticipating possible questions, you will generally be prepared to answer them at any point in your presentation and segue back into the flow.

**When You Lose Your Place, Don't Panic**    All presenters inevitably lose their train of thought from time to time. When this happens, you can try a few strategies. One is simply to pause until you regain your composure and your line of thinking. Within a few seconds, you will often get back on target. What seems like an eternity to you will be but a short pause to audience members. Many audience members will not even notice you lost your place. Another strategy is to repeat the last statement you made (five or six words). Doing so will help you regain your thought process.

**Never Tell Your Audience Things Haven't Gone as Expected**    Many presenters instinctively tell the audience about problems that have disrupted the presentation (i.e., technology failures, misplaced handouts). Resist the urge to mention these mishaps. To many audience members, this sounds like excuse-making and detracts from your key messages and/or your credibility. Most audience members will never know that anything out of the ordinary happened if you simply proceed with slightly modified plans.

**Always Have a Plan B**    If you have electronic slides to display, be prepared for a situation where the projector does not work and you need to speak without them. If you recognize factual problems in your handouts at the last moment, be prepared to present without them. Know ahead of time how you'll present under these situations.

**Know What Your Key Messages Are**    You can often leave out parts of your presentations as necessary with little change in impact as long as you know your three or four key messages and accentuate them throughout your presentation.

## Use the Room to Your Advantage

You will inevitably present in rooms of various sizes and layouts. Generally, you connect with your audiences best if you position yourself close to them and establish eye contact with them. Consider the following advice.

**Position Yourself Where People Can See You Easily**    Walk around the room before your presentation to check the vantage points that various audience members will have. After you do this, you can generally determine where you can stand to get the most eye contact with your audience. Also, think about how you can be closest to them. If your audience members have taken all the back seats and left the front seats empty, move closer to them to reduce the spatial barrier. Or, politely ask your audience members to move forward to the front of the room.

**Move Around but Avoid Distracting the Audience**   During presentations of more than five to ten minutes, you can keep the audience more engaged by moving around the room. This draws the focus to you and allows you to gain spatial proximity with most of your audience members at some point during your presentation. However, some movements can be distracting. For example, excessive pacing may show that you're nervous. Or, since you will likely be standing and your audience members will likely be seated, getting too close may make them feel that you are hovering over them.

**Use Podiums and Tables Strategically**   Many rooms are set up with podiums or tables, where presenters can place notes and other materials. Standing behind a podium or table can help you project authority and add to the formality of the presentation. If you do use a podium to achieve these goals, make sure you stand upright. Avoid leaning on or gripping the podium, which indicates nervousness. Also, consider whether a podium, table, or other object placed between you and your audience creates a barrier to connection. If you stand in front of the podium or table, you can get closer to your audience physically. As a result, you may achieve a more friendly, accessible, and casual tone.

## Communicate Nonverbally

Your audience members consciously and subconsciously make a variety of judgments about your credibility and your message based on your nonverbal behavior. Gary Genard, president of Public Speaking International, had this to say about nonverbal communication:

> How comfortable a speaker is in his own skin, how he stands and moves, how he looks at others in the room, his tone of voice, even the clothes he wears—together, these variables constitute a constant flow of data running underneath whatever the speaker is saying . . . leaders know how to move boldly and decisively. There is nothing tentative about their movements and gestures—instead, they literally command the space through which they move.[9]

**LO15.3** Apply the SOFTEN model of nonverbal communication for presentations.

Consider the **SOFTEN model of nonverbal communication** in your presentations: *s*mile, *o*pen stance, *f*orward lean, *t*one, *e*ye contact, and *n*od. By focusing on these nonverbal behaviors, you can display confidence and strength while also showing warmth and concern.[10]

**Smile**   Use your facial expressions to connect with your audience members and show your enthusiasm for your topic. Audience members are more likely to warm up to you when you put forth positive, can-do emotion.

**Open Stance**   Most people consider an open stance as more warm and inviting. Excessively putting your hands on your hips, folding your arms, crossing your legs, and gripping a podium or other objects closes you off from some people and implies less warmth. Keeping your arms to your sides or gesturing with palms up is more inviting to the audience.

**Forward Lean**   Facing your audience directly with a slight forward lean and upright posture shows confidence and interest. By contrast, leaning back, slouching, and lowering one's shoulders imply timidity and lack of confidence.

**Tone**   Use your voice to express enthusiasm or other intended emotion. To make sure everyone in the room can hear the confidence of your message, project your voice adequately. Also, speak at a reasonable pace. Rushing your presentations is often a sign of nervousness. First impressions of self-confidence and empathy often come from a slower rate of speaking with fewer gestures.[11] On the other hand, many audience members tune out when you speak too slowly and may even think you are unprepared.

Evaluating your own voice is difficult, since the voice you hear is not what your listeners hear.[12] Consider recording your voice so you can evaluate your tone and pace. Also, ask people you trust to evaluate the tone, pace, and emotion conveyed by your voice during presentations.

**Eye Contact**  Maintaining eye contact with your audience is among the most important forms of nonverbal communication. It creates an immediate sense of connection when you meet audience members eye to eye. The very act of keeping eye contact forces you to think about your listeners. It helps you evaluate and adjust your presentation as you observe your audience members' reactions. Perhaps most important, eye contact facilitates trust. Many people partially judge the truthfulness of a message from eye contact.[13]

**Nod**  Use gestures that show affirmation and acceptance of your audience members. For example, nodding indicates that you agree or recognize the value of what others say. Gesture with your hands, arms, body, and head to achieve positive connections with your audience. Attempt to read your audience and get a sense for how much energy they have. Research shows that morning speakers should have medium energy and match most audiences' lower energy levels with a conversational tone. Afternoon and evening speakers can increase their expressiveness and energy.[14]

Remember to be natural. While you can improve your nonverbal communication to better connect with your audience, it takes time. Try out new forms of nonverbal communication incrementally. And be aware that people often misread body language. The more you pay attention to your audience's reactions, the more you will be able to identify how people respond to your nonverbal communication.[15]

## Dress for Success

Business professionals are frequently advised to *dress for success,* especially for important events such as speeches and presentations. How you dress can make a big impact on how others perceive you. In a recent survey, 41 percent of employers stated that employees who dressed professionally were more likely to be promoted. This figure rises to 55 percent in certain industries, such as financial services.[16]

Most attire can be placed on a continuum from formal to casual. Common categories along this continuum are formal business, business casual, and casual. **Formal business dress,** at one end of the continuum, is intended to project executive presence and seriousness. It is distinguished by business suits, typically dark and conservative, accompanied by collared, button-down dress shirts. For men, neckties are essential.

**Business casual dress** is one step down in formality along the continuum. It is intended to project a more comfortable, relaxed feel while still maintaining a high standard of professionalism. Business casual dress is interpreted broadly and varies significantly by location and company. As a result, business casual can be divided into *high-level business casual* and *low-level business casual.* In Figure 15.2, you can see three levels of attire: formal business, high-level business casual, and low-level business casual. Business casual dress is probably the most common form of dress in the workplace today, with 43 percent of adults in a recent survey identifying that as their typical workplace attire.[17]

**Casual dress** is the least formal option. It is rare in a business-related setting.[18] While some companies have implemented casual Fridays, nearly half of executives and managers feel that employees dress too casually on these days.[19] If your company allows casual Fridays, make sure your attire continues to project a professional image.

**FIGURE 15.2**

Formality of Workplace Attire

**Formal Business**

*Men*
Tailored business suits
Dress shirts
Neckties
Leather shoes

*Women*
Tailored business suit with pants or skirt
Dress shirts
Hosiery or socks
Leather shoes

**Business Casual (high-level)**

*Men*
Suit coats, sports coats, or blazers
Button-down collar shirts
Neckties optional
Leather shoes

*Women*
Pantsuits and tailored separates
Closed-toe or closed-heel shoes

**Business Casual (low-level)**

*Men*
Button-down collar shirts or polo-type shirts
Khakis or chinos
Leather belts and shoes
Conservative footwear

*Women\**
Dress shirt
Dress pants or skirt
Conservative footwear

*Standards for women vary more than for men.

Photos (left to right from top left): © Justin Horrocks/Getty Images RF; © Neustockimages/Getty Images RF; © 4x6/Getty Images RF; © drbimages/Getty Images RF; © g_studio/Getty Images RF; © Ann Marie Kurtz/Getty Images RF

Your attire, and the level of formality you choose, projects a range of messages (see Figure 15.3). Generally, formal business attire projects authority and competence, high-level business casual is associated with productivity and trustworthiness, and low-level business casual is associated with creativity and friendliness.[20]

For business presentations, you should generally dress up slightly more formally than your audience. Also, consider the messages you intend to send. Younger professionals may not yet have established traits such as authority and competence, whereas they are often assumed to be friendly. So, younger professionals can gain significantly by dressing more formally.

**FIGURE 15.3**

Messages Sent
by Formality of
Workplace Attire

*Source:* Peter W. Cardon and
Ephraim A. Okoro, "Professional
Characteristics Communicated
by Formal versus Casual Workplace Attire," *Business Communication Quarterly* 72, no. 3 (2009):
355–360.

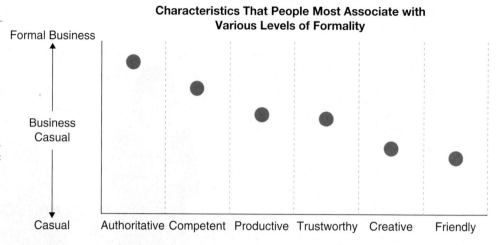

Characteristics That People Most Associate with
Various Levels of Formality

## Using Visual Aids and Handouts

**LO15.4** Use slides and
handouts to
supplement your
presentation
effectively.

You can powerfully supplement your presentations with visual aids and handouts. In
fact, many audiences expect both. In this section, we discuss how to use these items to
increase your presentation effectiveness.

### Use Visuals without Losing Focus on You

In Chapter 14, we discussed the design of electronic slides. Another option for
presentations is the screencast video, described in the Technology Tips feature.
Regardless of the technology you use, your goal is to keep yourself as the main focus
of the presentation. Even with well-designed slides or videos, however, keeping the
focus on you during the presentation can be challenging. Keep in mind the following
tips as you present:

**Avoid Turning Out the Lights in Most Cases**   Many presenters turn out the
lights so that the audience can more easily view the slides. This makes the slides,
rather than you, the focal point for the duration of the presentation. Some audience
members may also get drowsy in low light. In some rooms, you can dim the lights next
to the screen, but if you do, make sure that you are in full light to your audience.

**Don't Start Your Slides Right Away**   The opening moments of your presentation
are too valuable to devote to slides. Use at least the opening one to two minutes to
make a personal connection with your audience. Then begin your slides.

**Speak to Your Audience, Not the Screen**   The single most important strategy
is to face your audience. Presenters often spend too much time looking at their slides
with their back or side to the audience.

**Interpret, Don't Read Your Slides**   When you simply read your slides, you reduce yourself to nothing but a narrator. Since audience members can read your slides
more quickly than you can recite what they say, the slides become the primary source
of information. When you explain and elaborate on the content in your slides, you draw
your audience's attention to you as the primary source of information.

**Preview the Slides before Showing Them**   To keep the focus on you and more
effectively control the timing of your message, introduce your slides before you show

## ⏻ TECHNOLOGY TIPS

### CREATING SCREENCAST VIDEOS

Business professionals—especially executives, human resource professionals, and sales and marketing professionals—increasingly use screencast videos to reach audiences remotely. Many software packages, such as Camtasia, Adobe Captivate, and Jing, allow you to develop presentation videos that record the activity on your computer screen and combine it with video, audio, and other files. As you develop these screencast videos, keep in mind the following tips:

*Plan your production and make several trial runs.* A screencast video requires you to take the roles of producer, director, and actor all in one. You can choose elements to display on your screen, such as PowerPoint slides, spreadsheets, word processing documents, or other types of files. Simultaneously, you can narrate as you display the content and can even provide video of yourself. After recording, you have many tools available to edit your production.

*Create short, concise videos.* Most screencast videos are short. For example, most how-to videos created by companies and posted on YouTube or their own websites last one to five minutes.

© digitalskillet/iStock/Getty Images RF; © Dougal Waters/Digital Vision/Getty Images RF;© LWA/Larry Williams/Blend Images LLC RF; © Polka Dot Images/Jupiterimages RF; © Brand X Pictures/PunchStock RF

*Use the right resources.* You can use free screencast software and inexpensive video cameras and microphones to make screencasts; however, it's generally worth the investment to purchase state-of-the-art screencast software and the right cameras and microphones, especially if you intend to create professional-grade screencasts.

them. When you move to a slide without any introduction, the audience automatically focuses on the slide more than on you.

**Use a Remote Control to Advance Slides When Possible**   Using a remote control to move from slide to slide allows you to move around as you talk and more effectively engage with your audience. It also allows you to maintain more eye contact, since using a keyboard requires glancing down.

**Avoid Standing in Front of the Slide Projection**   Make sure to stand to the side of the slide projection area. Standing in front of the projection causes two problems. It makes the slide more difficult to view. But, perhaps worse, it distorts your appearance.

**Use Blank Slides Strategically**   If you plan to speak for lengthy periods without referencing your slides, consider displaying a blank slide so that the screen does not become a distraction.

### Use Handouts Effectively

Handouts generally make sense for detailed, numerical, and other information that is difficult to project adequately onto a screen. Also, you may want audience members to complete certain handouts during or after the presentation. For example, Shannon provides a handout on which seminar participants describe a manufacturing project they want to outsource.

However, handouts can distract your audience and take attention away from you. One primary advantage of presentations is that you have high control over what message your audience members hear, especially compared to written communications. As soon as you distribute handouts, you may lose this control since some audience members will immediately begin looking through the handouts and lose their focus on you.

If you can, wait until the end of your presentation to distribute handouts. This allows you to maintain more control over the message. If you need to use handouts during the presentation, consider how you might distribute them without losing control, especially during the opening one to two minutes of your presentation. Recall that audience members form many of their deepest impressions during this initial part of your presentation. Many presenters have lost the opportunity to connect effectively during their openings because of rustling handouts.

## Interacting with Your Audience

**LO15.5** Interact effectively with your audience.

Visit **http://connect.mheducation.com** for an exercise on this topic.

Good speakers involve the audience as much as possible without getting off message and taking too much time. A few ways to interact with your audience include fielding questions during the presentation as well as mingling and following up with audience members afterward.

### Field Questions

Many of your presentations will involve a question-and-answer (Q&A) portion. You may ask for questions at the conclusion of your presentation or invite questions throughout. When you take questions, you show you are interested in your listeners' real concerns and needs. You also have an opportunity to clarify points you may have misstated or omitted. Of course, fielding questions involves a number of risks: Your audience members may ask you difficult ones and may even get you off topic. The solution is to reinforce your key messages while also addressing the needs of your questioners. Practice the following strategies to make the Q&A go as smoothly and effectively as possible:[21]

**Pause before Answering**   This gives you time to reflect and quickly develop the best response. It also gives the impression that you are thoughtful. In some cases, you may feel under pressure during questioning. Pausing helps you stay calm and collected.

**Be Honest**   During questioning, many presenters are so committed to supporting their own positions that they respond with exaggeration or with excessive confidence. This is a mistake. Admit when you do not know the answer. Explain that you would like to get an answer to the question and seek an opportunity to continue the conversation later on. Notice in Table 15.4 how Latisha responds when she doesn't have a firm answer to a question.

**Show Appreciation**   Fielding questions allows you to develop an emotional bond with the questioner. You can do so by sincerely showing thanks, recognizing the importance of the question, and otherwise validating the questioner, as Latisha does in the more effective example in Table 15.5.

**TABLE 15.4**

Be Honest

| Less Effective | More Effective |
|---|---|
| **Q.** *I know you've said that managers will like this new system, but you haven't really talked about what managers wouldn't like about the system. For me, I'd worry about this system eroding my authority to ask for real changes, especially if other employees are giving so much positive feedback. So, don't you think this could actually upset some managers?* | |
| **A.** I guess that I haven't really heard that concern yet. I think that managers might have a concern like that initially, but as they continue using the system they'll notice they are actually empowered rather than having their authority eroded. | **A.** I'm not prepared to give a good answer to that question right now, but I think we certainly need to address it. Perhaps the HR team can ask some of our contacts at companies using continuous reviews to tell us their experiences with the challenges that managers face with these systems. If it's okay with you, the HR team and I will get some answers to your question and email the entire senior management team within a week. |
| Lathisha's response glosses over the fact that she is not informed enough to give an accurate answer. Although she attempts to put a positive spin on the problem, she may appear dismissive of some listeners' genuine concerns. | Latisha states that she is uncertain. However, she demonstrates a willingness to get the answer from reliable sources and promises to provide that information within a week. Overall, she gains credibility with her up-front, helpful response. |

**TABLE 15.5**

Show Appreciation

| Less Effective | More Effective |
|---|---|
| **Q.** *Do you think there's a risk that because the feedback is public, managers and employees will avoid sharing their candid and real views of one another's performance?* | |
| **A.** Actually, the system allows private feedback so that . . . | **A.** That's a good question. We talked to four or five HR directors who have implemented continuous reviews, and they each initially had this concern. In practice, employees and managers use the private feedback feature when they offer negative or sensitive feedback. . . . |
| This is a good, rational response but could be improved with additional validation of the questioner. | By briefly validating the importance of the question, Latisha is able to demonstrate that she relates directly to this concern and that Eastmond Networking is committed to facilitating this communication. The response is strong rationally and emotionally. |

**Be Concise**  Short responses are effective for several reasons. First, the question may be of interest to just one or a few of your audience members. Second, the longer your response, the more likely you are to stray from your key messages or excessively repeat them. As a rule of thumb, keep most responses to between 20 and 45 seconds. Pay close attention to your audience members during Q&A to see if they are remaining interested and engaged. Notice Table 15.6 to compare Latisha's less and more concise responses.

**Reframe the Question to Match Your Agenda**  You should have fairly clear objectives for your presentation. When your listeners ask questions that could derail your agenda, find ways to tactfully reframe the conversation in favor of your objectives, as Latisha's does in the examples in Table 15.7.

## Mingle and Follow Up

When you complete your presentation, your work is not complete. In most cases, this is a good opportunity to work the room, further connecting with your audience. You can get additional feedback and discuss future endeavors with your listeners.

**TABLE 15.6**

Be Concise

| Less Effective | More Effective |
|---|---|
| **Q.** *You've mentioned a few success stories at Peakster Computing. Could you mention some examples at other companies you've talked to?* | |
| **A.** Sure. I could give you lots of examples. Let me tell you about three other companies . . . (continues on for three to four minutes largely repeating the same key points). | **A.** Momentarily, I'll distribute a handout with more comprehensive information from our research. The handout provides cases for four companies we worked with, so you'll be able to see that the results at Peakster Computing are quite similar to those at the other three companies. |
| By providing such a lengthy answer, Latisha may inadvertently disengage some of her audience members who have already gotten her key points. | In this brief response (roughly 20 seconds), Latisha provides new information (that will be in a handout) and touches on but does not belabor key take-away points. This response has broad appeal since it allows audience members to locate additional results from other companies. |

**TABLE 15.7**

Reframe the Question to Match Your Agenda

| Less Effective | More Effective |
|---|---|
| **Q.** *I'm quite skeptical that our company will get the dramatic results you've suggested. Do you really think a software program will help us reduce employee turnover?* | |
| **A.** Well, actually, I can't guarantee anything. But, I can tell you with certainty that these types of software platforms have made dramatic differences in each company we've talked to. I think we'll have similar results here. | **A.** I think it's fair to say that we can reduce employee turnover by focusing on performance in a more positive and motivating way. What we've learned from these other companies is that they used the software successfully because they created a culture of performance where managers and employees are giving one another more frequent, more positive, and more candid feedback. This energizing environment is what reduced employee turnover. So, I'd say creating this culture with the help of these software tools will help us reduce employee turnover. |
| This question challenges the basic premise that technology (a software platform) can make a difference. It may raise this doubt among other audience members as well. While the response is true, it fails to reframe the question in a way that focuses on how managers and employees help each other. | This response reframes the conversation by emphasizing how managers and employees encouraging one another to improve is the key driver of lower employee turnover. This response is successfully reframed to address the questioner's real concern: Technology isn't the solution. |

Similarly, in the days following the event, you can reach out to your audience members. Follow up on any promises you made about providing additional information. If possible, send a quick email note to thank people for attending. Set in motion steps that turn a onetime presentation into an ongoing professional relationship.

# Present Effectively in Teams

**LO15.6** Prepare to present effectively in teams.

You'll often have the opportunity to present in teams. Delivering an effective team presentation involves the same principles as an individual presentation with a few complications to address. The key is to plan for these issues well ahead of the presentation. Keep in mind these tips:

### Be Clear with One Another about Your Objectives and Key Messages

The primary challenge for a team presentation is ensuring that it is cohesive. If you're united in your objectives and key messages, your team will present far more cohesively, smoothly, and influentially. As you prepare, make sure you and your team explicitly mention your key objectives and messages often.

### Decide on Your Presentation Roles

Early in your planning, you should make decisions about how you and your team members will gather information, analyze it, and present it. Similarly, you should make decisions about which team members will deliver various portions of the presentation. Consider which team members are best suited to explain certain types of information and which team members should open and close the presentation. While roles are important, remember that you will need to hold team discussions and make team decisions during the entire process leading up to the presentation. One common mistake teams make is to assign information gathering to various team members early in the process and then work independently up until the presentation. This generally leads to disjointed, disorganized presentations. Also, an often overlooked issue for team presentations is assigning roles for responding to questions from the audience. Make sure you plan which team members will respond to various types of questions.

### Stand Together and Present a United Front

Your team is far more effective when you maintain a united front. As much as possible, stand close to one another. Stay interested in your teammates as they present, nodding in agreement and interest periodically. Similarly, maintain eye contact with the audience to show your interest in them, even when you're not presenting. Coordinate with one another to make sure you all wear the same formality of attire.

### Refer to One Another's Points

By referring to one another throughout the presentation, you make sure your comments connect with your teammates and you also show that your team is united. Phrases such as "As Latisha mentioned . . ." or "Jeff's point about . . ." are signals that your team has prepared its ideas carefully.

### Transition Effectively

You and your team members should smoothly pass speaking roles from one to the next. Simple phrases such as the following allow effective transitions from one person to the next: "I've shared with you how employee engagement increases productivity and profitability. Now, Latisha will share some ways we can improve employee engagement." As you make transitions, however, be careful about taking opportunities away from your teammates to showcase their best points. For example, consider the following transition: "Now, Latisha will share how continuous reviews increase employee engagement. She will show you software tools that allow multi-source feedback and recognition. She'll even explain how for under $10,000 per year, we can substantially increase employee engagement with these tools." Notice how this transition doesn't allow Latisha to choose the timing of her key messages and key points. In short, use transitions that set your teammates up for success and avoid stealing their thunder.

## Being a Supportive Audience Member

You will likely be an audience member more often than you are a presenter. Take this role seriously. Do all you can to support the presenter. Show interest by maintaining eye contact and sitting up straight. Avoid behaviors that may distract the presenter,

## COMMUNICATION Q&A

### CONVERSATIONS WITH CURRENT BUSINESS PROFESSIONALS

**Pete Cardon: Do presentations generally go as expected?**

**James Robertson:** You can have many things working against you when presenting. Everything from the audiovisual equipment not behaving to the slide deck not working as expected, and then there's the dynamics of the audience. Many technical problems can be corrected by spending a few minutes beforehand making sure everything works, but always be aware of the presenting "gremlins," and always have a plan if something does trip you up. The key to overcoming these problems is to know the subject, know the audience, and practice the presentation so that even if the technology fails, you still deliver on message.

**James Robertson** *is the chief technology officer at Time Warner Enterprise Infrastructure Services. He has worked at Turner Broadcasting for nearly 20 years in various executive and management positions.*

Courtesy of James Robertson

The hardest thing to plan for is the human factor: *How will the audience react to your message? Will they agree or disagree with your point of view?* and *Will they speak up or keep quiet during Q&A?* Be prepared by thinking about some of the questions you'd ask if you were looking at the information presented. Anticipating and planning the answers will help you get all the way to closure.

**PC: What are some of the keys to connecting with your audience?**

**JR:** I've found that you need to set the stage with a scenario or situation that's applicable to the subject you're discussing. Linking this topic back to your message provides a powerful opening and grabs the audience attention from the start. This can be as simple as opening with something you've read in a magazine or a newspaper or something you've seen on TV or a life experience you've had. The key is to make sure you bridge between the experience you're opening with and the topic you're presenting on.

During the presentation, always talk to the audience and not to the slides. Practice makes perfect.

At the end of the presentation, leave them with a closing that reinforces the message. Again, it can be an experience or just a good summary of what you discussed, but with a punch that they remember. I try and leave my audience with no more than three points they can take away with them, but those three points should encapsulate the essence of the message.

**PC: For young professionals, what concluding advice would you give about developing skills to give great presentations?**

**JR:** Much of real success in business is being able to "tell your story" well. Whether presenting a project to gain financial funding or rolling out goals to staff, it's critical that you are confident and persuasive. People will follow a leader they believe in, so it's important to cultivate your credibility. Being able to connect to any audience is a critical skill, so look for any opportunity to present and hone your presentation skills. It will become one of your most important skill sets.

such as glancing at your mobile phone or yawning. Make comments and ask questions that help the presenter stay on message. Publicly express appreciation for the merits of the presentation. Privately offer advice for making the presentation more useful.

Being a supportive audience member has many advantages. In most cases, you share professional interests with the presenter. As a result, the success of the presentation is a team effort. Furthermore, your reputation for being a supportive audience member may be reciprocated when you take the role of presenter. For further insights on delivering presentations, read the Communication Q&A with James Robertson.

# Chapter Takeaway for *Delivering Presentations*

**LO15.1 Describe how presentation delivery impacts your credibility. (p. 476)**

Delivering presentations demonstrates **your personal credibility**.

| | | |
|---|---|---|
| It shows **competence** when you know and provide valuable content. | It shows **caring** when you are responsive to the expectations of your audience. | It shows **character** when you display complete openness and honesty. |

**LO15.2 Deliver presentations with authenticity, confidence, and influence. (pp. 476–481)**

| Principles for Establishing Presence | | |
|---|---|---|
| • Establish credibility. <br> • Maintain authenticity. <br> • Know your material. | • Speak with confidence. <br> • Focus on people. <br> • Stay flexible. | • Use the room to your advantage. <br> • Communicate nonverbally. <br> • Dress for success. |

| Principles for Focusing on People | |
|---|---|
| • Make people the subject of your sentences. <br> • Introduce colleagues by name. | • Use names of audience members. |

See *examples of focusing on people* in Tables 15.1, 15.2, and 15.3.

| Principles for Staying Flexible | | |
|---|---|---|
| • Arrive early. <br> • Focus on the needs of the audience. | • When you lose your place, don't panic. <br> • Never tell your audience things haven't gone as expected. | • Always have a plan B. <br> • Know what your key messages are. |

**LO15.3 Apply the SOFTEN model of nonverbal communication for presentations. (pp. 481–484)**

| Principles of the SOFTEN Model | | |
|---|---|---|
| • *S*mile <br> • *O*pen stance | • *F*orward lean <br> • *T*one | • *E*ye contact <br> • *N*od |

**LO15.4 Use slides and handouts to supplement your presentation effectively. (pp. 484–486)**

| Principles for Using Slides | | |
|---|---|---|
| • Avoid turning out the lights in most cases. <br> • Don't start the slides right away. <br> • Speak to your audience, not the screen. | • Interpret, don't read your slides. <br> • Preview the slides before showing them. <br> • Use remotes to advance slides. | • Avoid standing in front of the slide projection. <br> • Use blank slides strategically. |

**LO15.5 Interact effectively with your audience. (pp. 486–488)**

| Principles for Fielding Questions | | |
|---|---|---|
| • Pause before answering. <br> • Be honest. | • Show appreciation. <br> • Be concise. | • Reframe the question to match your agenda. |

See *examples of fielding questions* in Tables 15.4, 15.5, 15.6, and 15.7.

**LO15.6 Prepare to present effectively in teams. (pp. 488–490)**

| | | |
|---|---|---|
| • Be clear with one another about your objectives and key messages. | • Decide on your presentation roles. <br> • Stand together and present a united front. | • Refer to one another's points. <br> • Transition effectively. |

# Key Terms

business casual dress, 482

casual dress, 482

formal business dress, 482

SOFTEN model of nonverbal
communication, 481

# Discussion Exercises

**15.1 Chapter Review Questions** (LO15.1, LO15.2, LO15.3, LO15.4, LO15.5)

For each of the following items, respond with one or two paragraphs.

A. Discuss how you can establish and build credibility before, during, and after your presentations.

B. Describe the importance of authenticity for presentations. Discuss how you can plan and rehearse for presentations and also maintain authenticity.

C. Discuss some strategies for overcoming nervousness and fear before and during presentations. Describe the three strategies you believe are most effective for you.

D. Describe strategies for making people the focus of your presentations.

E. Explain the SOFTEN model of nonverbal communication.

F. Describe strategies for using slides and handouts without distracting the audience from what you have to say.

G. Describe strategies for effectively fielding questions during or after your presentation.

**15.2 Communication Q&A Discussion Questions** (LO15.1, LO15.2, LO15.4, LO15.5)

Read the comments from James Robertson in the Communication Q&A. Respond to the following questions:

A. What is Robertson's advice for when things go awry with technology?

B. What tips does he give for connecting with your audience?

C. What does he say is the hardest thing to prepare for and why?

D. What does he explain about how to start and end a presentation?

# Evaluation Exercises

**15.3 Evaluating an Effective Presentation** (LO15.2, LO15.3, LO15.4)

Think about a recent presentation you attended that you found effective. In three to five paragraphs, describe why it was effective. Include the following aspects in your analysis, referring to Chapter 14 if necessary for a refresher on preview-view-review:

A. Description of the presentation.

B. Key points.

C. Preview.

D. View.

E. Review.

F. Electronic slides or other visual aids.

G. Nonverbal behavior.

**15.4 Evaluating a Corporate Presentation** (LO15.2, LO15.3, LO15.4)

Go online and find a business presentation that interests you. You can generally find presentations easily on company websites (usually in the Media, Newsroom, or Investors sections), YouTube, or business websites (e.g., CNBC). Evaluate the presentation and

include the following in your analysis, referring to Chapter 14 if necessary for a refresher on preview-view-review:

A. Description of the presentation.

B. Key points.

C. Preview.

D. View.

E. Review.

F. Electronic slides or other visual aids.

G. Nonverbal behavior.

**15.5 Assessing One of Your Recent Presentations** (LO15.1, LO15.2, LO15.3, LO15.4, LO15.5)

Think about a presentation you delivered recently. In three to five paragraphs, address the following issues, referring to Chapter 14 if necessary for a refresher on preview-view-review:

A. Description of the presentation.

B. Key points.

C. Preview.

D. View.

E. Review.

F. Electronic slides or other visual aids.

G. Nonverbal behavior.

H. Three improvements you would make if you did the presentation again.

**15.6 Video Recording Your Presentation** (LO15.1, LO15.2, LO15.3, LO15.4, LO15.5)

Record one of your presentations and then do the following:

A. Immediately following your presentation, draft your basic impressions of your performance.

B. Watch the video recording three times as follows:

- On the first viewing, observe the overall impact of your presentation.

- On the second viewing, turn the volume off and observe your nonverbal behaviors.

- On the third viewing, close your eyes and listen. Pay attention to the speed, volume, pitch, variety, and enthusiasm in your voice.

After completing steps A and B above, answer the following questions about your presentation:

C. How effective was your opening?

D. How effective was your nonverbal communication (e.g., voice quality, eye contact with audience)?

E. How effective was the content of your presentation (e.g., relevance to audience, logical order, impact)?

F. How persuasive was your presentation?

G. How well did you connect with your audience?

H. Overall, name two major strengths and two major weaknesses of your oral presentation.

I. If you were going to deliver this same presentation again, what three adjustments would you make?

J. What are the two presentation skills you believe you most need to improve? Explain.

# Application Exercises

For Exercises 15.7 through 15.10, prepare five- to ten-minute presentations. Make sure you first identify your key messages and analyze your audience based on information in the textbook. Create a clear and compelling preview, view, and review (see Chapter 14). If directed by your instructor, create electronic slide presentations.

**15.7 Presentation to the Board about Changing Direction at Better Horizons Credit Union** (LO15.1, LO15.2, LO15.3, LO15.4, LO15.5)

Assume the role of Christine Russo (see Chapter 10). Based on the information in Chapter 10, create a presentation to the board about building marketing strategies and product offerings for younger members. You could base a large part of the presentation on Figure 10.4.

**15.8 Presentation to College Students about Joining Better Horizons Credit Union** (LO15.1, LO15.2, LO15.3, LO15.4, LO15.5)

Assume the role of Haniz Zogby (see Chapter 10). Based on the information in Chapter 10, create a presentation to

university students to persuade them to join Better Horizons Credit Union. You could base part of the presentation on Figure 10.6.

**15.9 Presentation Asking for Participation in the Hope Walkathon** (LO15.1, LO15.2, LO15.3, LO15.4, LO15.5)

Assume the role of Haniz Zogby (see Chapter 10). Based on the information in Chapter 10, create a presentation to encourage credit union members to participate in the Hope Walkathon. You could base part of the presentation on Figure 10.8.

**15.10 Presentation about Changes at Marble Home Makeovers** (LO15.1, LO15.2, LO15.3, LO15.4, LO15.5)

Assume the role of Juan Hernandez (see Chapter 11). Based on the information in Chapter 11, create a presentation to employees about temporary changes in work shifts. You could base the presentation on Figure 11.4.

# Language Mechanics Check

**15.11 Review all rules in Appendix A about punctuation, number usage, and grammar. Then, rewrite each sentence to make all needed corrections.**

A. To gain experience as a public speaker, you can find many opportunities, to develop your abilities.

B. Many professionals join training groups or organizations such as Toastmasters, which focus on public speaking.

C. Once you're part of one of these groups you and the other members practice intensively, and give supportive and helpful feedback to one another.

D. Most of these organizations provide training materials, magazines, guidebooks and development plans.

E. You can also join organizations, which frequently hold public speeches that you can observe or even deliver.

F. Many civic organizations such as the Rotary Club hold weekly meetings, where community members are invited to speak.

G. You might consider volunteering to speak in classes, at clubs or at other events to increase your experience speaking, in uncomfortable and uncertain situations.

H. Many people, who aspire to develop public skills, regularly watch Ted Talks so they can see the delivery style of great speakers.

I. Surprisingly most expert public speakers get nervous nearly each time they speak.

J. Yet most audience members don't even notice these expert speakers are nervous, which shows how well these speakers have learned to control their emotions during public events.

# Endnotes

1. Barbara De Angelis, "Communicating with Authenticity," *Toastmaster* online (June 2007), available at www.toastmasters. org/ToastmastersMagazine/ToastmasterArchive/2007/June/ Authenticity.aspx.

2. Found in Nick Morgan, "How to Put Together a Great Speech When You're Under the Gun," *Harvard Management Communication Letter,* September 2003: 3. He was citing Phillip Khan-Pami, *Blank Page to First Draft in 15 Minutes: The Most Effective Shortcut to Preparing a Speech or Presentation* (Miami, FL: How To Books, 2002).

3. www.time.com/time/magazine/article/0,9171,994670-1,00.html.

4. Geoffrey Brewer, "Snakes Top List of Americans' Fears: Public Speaking, Heights and Being Closed in Small Spaces Also Create Fear in Many Americans" (March 19, 2001), retrieved August 22, 2010, from *Gallup* online: www.gallup.com/poll/1891/ Snakes-Top-List-Americans-Fears.aspx.

5. Karen L. Twichell, "Stage Fright—Why Now?" *Toastmaster* online (January 2010), available at www.toastmasters.org/ ToastmastersMagazine/ToastmasterArchive/2010/January/ Stage-Fright.aspx.

6. Thomas Leech, *How to Prepare, Stage, and Deliver Winning Presentations,* 3rd ed. (New York: American Management Association, 2004).

7. Twichell, "Stage Fright—Why Now?"; Judi Bailey, "Beauty and the Beast: Changing Your Fear from Fiend to Friend," *Toastmaster* online (December 2007), available at www.toastmasters.org/ToastmastersMagazine/ ToastmasterArchive/2007/December/BeautyandtheBeast. aspx; Gabrielle B. Dahms, "Good Posture = Good Breathing," *Toastmaster* online (June 2008), available at www.toastmasters. org/ToastmastersMagazine/ToastmasterArchive/2008/June/ Departments/HowToPDF.aspx; Harry Mills, *Power Points! How to Design and Deliver Presentations That Sizzle and Sell* (New York: AMACOM, 2007).

8. Kevin Johnson and Tennille-Lynn Millo, "Put Your Audience in Your Speech," *Toastmaster* online (August 2007),

available at www.toastmasters.org/ToastmastersMagazine/ ToastmasterArchive/2007/August/Audience.aspx.

9. Gary Genard, "Leveraging the Power of Nonverbal Communication," *Harvard Business Management Communication Letter* (2004): 3–4.

10. Mills, *Power Points! How to Design and Deliver Presentations That Sizzle and Sell.*

11. Dave Zielinski, "Body Language Myths," *Toastmaster* online (September 2007), available at www.toastmasters.org/ ToastmastersMagazine/ToastmasterArchive/2007/September/ Myths.aspx.

12. Nancy Sebastion Meyer, "That's Not My Voice—Is It?" *Toastmaster* online (February 2009), available at www.toastmasters. org/ToastmastersMagazine/ToastmasterArchive/2009/February/ Departments/Manner-of-Speaking.aspx.

13. Mike Landrum, "Speaking Eye to Eye: A Meeting of the Eyes Denotes a Meeting of the Minds," *Toastmaster* online (December 2009), available at www.toastmasters.org/ ToastmastersMagazine/ToastmasterArchive/2009/December/ Articles/Speaking-Eye-to-Eye.aspx.

14. Zielinski, "Body Language Myths."

15. Ibid.

16. R. Haefner, "How to Dress for Success for Work," retrieved January 27, 2009, from www.cnn.com/2008/ LIVING worklife/07/30/cb.dress.for.success/index.html (July 30, 2008).

17. Joseph Carroll, "Business Casual Most Common Work Attire," *Gallup Poll,* October 4, 2007.

18. Thomas Kiddie, "Recent Trends in Business Casual Attire and Their Effects on Student Job Seekers," *Business Communication Quarterly,* September 2009: 350–354; Beverly Langford, *The Etiquette Edge: The Unspoken Rules for Business Success* (New York: American Management Association, 2005).

19. Accountemps, "Survey Shows Relaxed Attire May Be Too Relaxed at Many Firms," May 25, 2000, www.accountemps com/ PressRoom?id=151 (accessed January 10, 2010).

20. Based on studies from the following sources: Peter W. Cardon and Ephraim A. Okoro, "Professional Characteristics Communicated by Formal versus Casual Workplace Attire," *Business Communication Quarterly* 72, no. 3 (2009): 355–360; J. V. Peluchette and K. Karl, "The Impact of Workplace Attire on Employee Self-Perceptions," *Human Resource Development Quarterly* 18, no. 3 (2007): 345–360; J. V. Peluchette and K. Karl,

"Dressing to Impress: Beliefs and Attitudes regarding Workplace Attire," *Journal of Business and Psychology* 21, no. 1 (2006): 45–63.

21. Granville N. Toogood, *The New Articulate Executive: Look, Act, and Sound Like a Leader* (New York: McGraw-Hill, 2010).

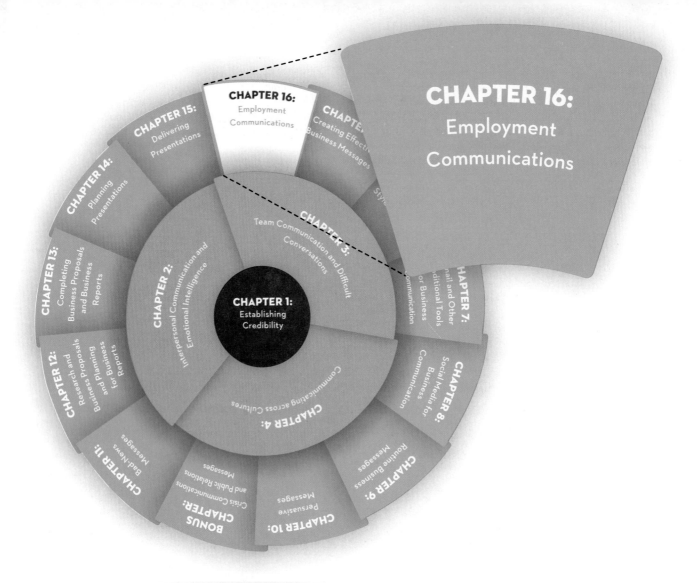

**CHAPTER 16:**
Employment Communications

ESTABLISHING
CREDIBILITY

PRINCIPLES OF INTERPERSONAL
COMMUNICATION

PRINCIPLES FOR & TYPES OF
BUSINESS MESSAGES

 **Learning Objectives**

After studying this chapter, you should be able to do the following:

**LO16.1** Identify your key selling points for the job application process.

**LO16.2** Evaluate the primary needs of employers for positions of interest.

**LO16.3** Set up the message structure for résumés and cover letters.

**LO16.4** Highlight your qualifications with effective tone, style, and design.

**LO16.5** Create chronological and functional résumés to highlight your key selling points.

**LO16.6** Use LinkedIn as part of the job search process and to network professionally.

**LO16.7** Develop a list of references that will improve your employment prospects.

**LO16.8** Compose effective cover letters that highlight your key selling points.

**LO16.9** Review your job application documents for effectiveness and fairness.

**LO16.10** Develop strategies for responding to common job interview questions.

**LO16.11** Explain etiquette for following up after job interviews.

**LO16.12** Explain etiquette for leaving an organization with grace and foresight.

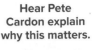

## WHY DOES THIS MATTER?

Searching for jobs can be exhilarating. It involves hopes for new beginnings and possibilities! Many job applicants also find the process stressful, intimidating, and scary. In recent years due to the recession, one reality is that the number of applicants exceeds the number of positions. However, with determination, patience, and planning, you can land a job that will help you move forward in your career. In this chapter, you will focus on developing a job application package that allows you to identify and highlight your key selling points in a way that meets the needs of employers. Quickly read the following case that is the basis for examples you will see throughout the chapter.

**Hear Pete Cardon explain why this matters.**

**bit.ly/cardon16**

## CHAPTER CASE: HANIZ AND JACLYN APPLY FOR JOBS

**Haniz Zogby**

**Jaclyn Peha**

**WHO'S INVOLVED**

**Marketing specialist and loan officer at Better Horizons Credit Union**
**Florida State University, Class of 2015**
*Major:* **Finance;** *Minor:* **Event Management**

**Technology intern at Better Horizons Credit Union**
*Major:* **Business Information Systems**

Haniz Zogby will graduate soon. She has worked for Better Horizons Credit Union for five years and feels a high level of job security. At Better Horizons, she has been given many opportunities to assist and, in some cases, direct promotional campaigns. However, she typically spends less than half of her time involved in marketing. Haniz wants a job where she has more responsibility, spends more of her time on innovative marketing campaigns, and makes more money. Jaclyn is also applying for positions. Like Haniz, she is soon graduating. Unlike Haniz, she has less work experience.

**THE SITUATION**

(Haniz Zogby character): © Ingram Publishing RF; (Jaclyn Peha character): © Onoky/SuperStock RF

**TASK**

**1**
Haniz and Jaclyn want to write résumés that effectively portray their selling points.

**2**
Haniz wants to write cover letters that introduce her to employers and explain her value to them.

**3**
Haniz wants to interview effectively and show she's ready for the job.

## Applying the AIM Planning Process to Résumés and Cover Letters

Preparing for the job application process is similar to preparing for other forms of business communication: It involves analyzing your audience (meeting the needs of your employers), gathering the right information (identifying your key

**LO16.1** Identify your key selling points for the job application process.

selling points), and developing your message. Your end products—cover letters and résumés—are persuasive messages that show how you meet the needs of your prospective employers.

## Identify Your Key Selling Points

To create résumés and cover letters that serve your long-term career interests, your first step should be to carefully evaluate your career ambitions and qualifications. In this process, you clarify your professional goals for the short term (one to two years) and long term (five to ten years), identify the skills you have developed at school and work, and sort out the attributes that define who you are as a professional. As with other business communications, you attempt to identify your most important and strongest features so you can develop a concise and compelling message about the value you will bring to your prospective employers.

To help you identify your interests, abilities, and attributes, you might consider completing a self-inventory (see Figure 16.1 with an example of Haniz's self-inventory). Start by writing your career goals. Even if you don't yet have clear ones in mind, do your best to imagine the type of work you would like to be doing in five and ten years. Allow yourself enough time to do some soul-searching and research about careers as you develop your goals.

Identifying your career goals helps you accomplish several things in the job search process. First, it helps you frame your résumé and cover letter to project your career hopes. Second, it helps you evaluate how well your abilities and attributes prepare you for your desired career. This process allows you to address those areas where you most need improvement. Finally, it shows employers that you are serious, as well-defined career goals imply seriousness in your approach to work.

Once you have written down your career goals, identify your abilities and attributes.[1] **Abilities** are skills and knowledge that can be applied to accomplishing work tasks. **Attributes** are personal traits or characteristics. In the job application process, employers are often looking for more than your abilities. They're trying to figure out the kind of person you are. These judgments often come in the form of adjectives, such as *reliable*,

## FIGURE 16.1

Self-Inventory of Career Interests and Job-Related Abilities and Attributes

Haniz Zogby
April 1, 2017

**My Career Goals**
1. To act in a leadership role to develop and marked financial services for credit unions
2. In five to ten years, to hold an influential marketing position within a credit union group

**My Strongest Professional Abilities**
1. Developing strong professional relationships with clients and venders
2. Attracting new members to credit unions through referrals, seminars, mailings, and online social networking
3. Organizing members to participate in credit union-sponsored financial workshops and community events

**My Strongest Professional Attributes**
1. Trusted and reliable on important campaigns
2. Innovative and creative in approach to marketing and promotions
3. Passionate about the credit union industry

**Areas Where I Need to Improve**
1. Conducting customer surveys, statical analysis, and survey reporting
2. Earning a reputation for excellence outside of my local community

**TABLE 16.1**

Abilities and Attributes That Establish Credibility in the Job Application Process

| | Abilities (*Skills and/or Knowledge*) | Attributes (*Enduring Approaches to Work*) | | |
|---|---|---|---|---|
| **Competence** (*Task*) | Function-specific (e.g., marketing, finance) Company/industry Technology Analysis/research | Achievement-oriented Ambitious Analytical Assertive Creative Can-do attitude Curious | Decisive Detail-oriented Entrepreneurial Independent Inquisitive Passionate | Problem solver Resourceful Results-oriented Seeks challenges Takes initiative Visionary |
| **Caring** (*Relationships*) | Communication/interpersonal Teamwork Emotional intelligence Leadership Intercultural | Customer-oriented Diplomatic Empathetic Flexible Generous | Inspiring Loyal Motivational People-oriented Persuasive | Responsive Sensitive Supportive Team-oriented Tolerant |
| **Character** (*Values*) | Familiarity with corporate culture and values Dedication to the success of the company Knowledge of business ethics | Accountable Committed Constant Dedicated Dependable | Fair Hardworking Honest Open-minded Optimistic | Reliable Responsible Straightforward Trustworthy Unbiased |

*analytical*, or *people-oriented*. These attributes are difficult to measure precisely, but they indicate how well you'll fit into the company culture, how much effort and commitment you'll put into your work, and how you'll impact the work of others.

Employers consider your mix of attributes as they try to determine if you have the right *chemistry*—an intangible that human resource professionals say they weigh heavily in the decision to hire. Fifteen percent of HR professionals say it accounts for 75 percent or more of the decision. Nearly four in ten (39 percent) say it accounts for about 50 percent of the decision.[2]

One useful way of analyzing your *abilities* and *attributes* is in terms of credibility. To do so, consider the features of competence (ability to accomplish work tasks), caring (ability to maintain effective workplace relationships), and character (ability to uphold corporate norms and standards). Competence focuses on the technical skills to achieve work tasks. In Table 16.1, you can see examples of abilities and attributes associated with competence, caring, and character.

## Understand the Needs of Your Potential Employers

When hiring you, employers are making a huge investment. They will make this investment only when you demonstrate that you meet *their* needs. You can learn how well you fit the needs of employers by conducting a thorough job search and carefully analyzing those positions that are most compatible with your abilities and attributes.

**LO16.2** Evaluate the primary needs of employers for positions of interest.

**Completing a Thorough Job Search Process**  Looking for jobs takes a lot of time. It's not uncommon for the process—from finding a position announcement to application to offer—to take three to six months (or even longer in some industries). Your thorough search for the best potential positions at the initial stages can save you a lot of time and increase the likelihood you'll get a position that is in your long-term interests.

Use all the resources available to learn about your options and ensure that you apply for the jobs that are good fits for you. You likely have a career center located in your college or university. Spend some time talking to experts there and make a plan for exhaustively searching for jobs that match your interests and qualifications. Where possible, contact and get involved with professional organizations and visit organizational websites to learn about options. Go to job fairs on and off campus to see what opportunities are open and to practice networking in a competitive environment.

Certainly you're aware of the many job websites to search for positions (e.g., monster.com, careerbuilder.com, collegerecruiter.com). Your college or university may even recommend particular websites. Use all the available online options, but also make sure you are networking in the traditional sense as well—talking to friends, relatives, and colleagues. Even in the Social Age, the most common forms of networking for employment opportunities remain people you know well.[3]

**Analyze the Needs of Potential Employers**  One of the best ways to understand an employer's needs is to carefully read and analyze the job position announcement. Then, group the requests in the announcement in terms of abilities and attributes (for an example, see Figure 16.2, where Haniz did this for a job announcement). Once you've done this, you're in a good position to decide whether you match these criteria and, if so, to frame your résumé and cover letter to highlight these abilities and attributes.

In addition to analyzing the job position announcements, consider other strategies to gain insight about what the company is seeking. Some job announcements include contact information for a company representative. You might call this person, express your interest, and find out more. By doing this, you connect with an influential company representative and gain insight not provided in the job announcement.

Also, learn all you can about the company. Spend time researching its strategic goals. Find out about its unique challenges, and think about how you might fit into the company's plans to face these challenges.

## Develop Your Message for Résumés and Cover Letters

**LO16.3** Set up the message structure for résumés and cover letters.

Your résumé should tell a story of the value you can provide to a company. Like other persuasive messages, it is stronger if you have a central sales theme. By choosing two or three abilities and attributes to highlight, you can craft a compelling document that shows how you meet the needs of employers.

A mistake that many job applicants make is trying to display everything they do well. This approach often ends up sending a scattered message and diluting a central sales theme about your key abilities and attributes.

Generally, employers prefer single-page résumés, although it is increasingly acceptable to create two-page résumés.[4] As a university student, however, aim for a single page. If you find yourself using more than one page, you are likely weakening the message about your key selling points. Condensing all your experience may be painful, but keep in mind that executives are more than three times as likely to complain about résumés that contain too much information than they are about résumés that contain too little.[5] Typically, résumés contain the following major sections: name block, career summary or objective, education, and experience.

**Name Block**  Most résumés begin with your name and contact information. This section allows recruiters to easily find your contact information (i.e., address, phone, email). This section should not contain any distracting information, such as an unprofessional email address.

**Summary or Objective (Optional)**  Many professionals now create a short section just following the name block about their overall qualifications. They often label this section "Qualifications Summary," "Skills Summary," "Career Summary," or

**FIGURE 16.2**

Analyzing a Job Posting for Key Needs

| Job Summary | Credit Union Field Marketing Specialist |
|---|---|
| **Location**<br>84341<br><br>**Job Type**<br>Full-time<br><br>**Reference Code**<br>831481809 | **Organization:** Anchor Federal Credit Union Network<br>**Education Required:** College degree<br>**Experience Required:** 1–3 years<br>**Position Description:** |

**Position Description:**

Works with managers throughout the Anchor Federal Credit Union network to develop local marketing events to promote Credit Union membership. Coordinates all activities for each event, including supply distribution, prizes, and duration of campaign, budget, marketing support, and staffing. Responsible for tracking results and providing recommendations for future events. Also is responsible for collecting and maintaining data related to market conditions of each proposed site. Performs various other marketing and support functions when not traveling including general promotional development, membership surveys, collateral production and tracking, retiree package mailings, and other projects as assigned by the VP of Marketing.

**Position Requirements:**

Develops individual marketing activities to support branch growth and/or agency events.
Travels to various locations throughout the country to organize events.
Analyzes market conditions to ensure that the marketing activity is in line with the demographics of that particular region. Provides annual profile of demographics for each region.
Oversees budget for each activity. Is responsible for reporting variances on a monthly basis.
Works with outside vendors to solicit participation in marketing activities. Actively promotes the participation of both staff and monetary contributions from these outside sources.
Works with VP and AVPs of branches to set priorities and establish goals for each event. Tracks results of each event and analyzes the success/shortfall of each. Distributes reports for review.
Tracks marketing collateral inventory for branches and DMs. Ensures timely distribution and proper inventory controls.
Develops mailings for account generation and retention.
Develops ongoing mail programs to DMs and BCO managers for relationship development throughout the agency side of the business.
Makes routine phone calls to HR managers, DMs, and BCO managers to establish event schedules, coordinate Financial Finesse seminars, and maintain relationships throughout the organization.
Performs other duties as assigned.

**Position Attributes:**

*Candidate must be able to travel 25–30% domestically.
*A minimum of 2 years of field marketing and sales experience.
*Candidate must have presentation skills and experience.

**Abilities wanted**
*Marketing:* local marketing events, market analysis, marketing reports (written and oral), sales letters and other mailings to generate membership, seminars.
*Relationship management:* work with branch managers to organize local events and set marketing strategies; staffing for events; maintain intra-organizational relationships and relationships with outside vendors.
*Communication:* distribute event schedules, disseminate marketing reports, encourage participation, make sales presentations.

**Attributes wanted**
*Ambitious:* must be able to take initiative on organizing many events and meet deadlines.
*Creative:* must develop attractive and compelling marketing events and campaigns.
*Organized:* must be able to manage many simultaneous projects, events, and relationships.

other similar phrases. In five to ten sentences, this section generally states the candidate's primary accomplishments, abilities, and attributes. This summary should stick to the central selling theme.

Instead of a summary, some professionals write a job objective in one to two sentences. Until about five to ten years ago, a job objective was expected by most HR professionals. Increasingly, however, a job objective statement is not expected. From a 2014 survey of HR professionals, just 7 percent of them said a job objective is important.[6]

**Education** This section summarizes your experiences in higher education and professional training. Most university students place the education section before the work experience section, since it generally highlights studies in a discipline directly related to the jobs they are seeking.

Consider providing some information that distinguishes or explains the uniqueness and value of your education. For example, a short list of related coursework helps employers understand the content of your program. You might also include class projects, practicum, service learning projects, or other educational experiences that highlight your key abilities and attributes.

Include your GPA if it is high (3.5 or higher) or required. Also, if you have achieved any academic credentials or awards, mention them. For example, being on the dean's list or graduating summa cum laude are well-recognized honors. If you received scholarships or other academic awards that employers may not recognize, include a short note that explains why the awards are significant.

Generally, do not include information about your high school education. Employers are not interested. However, during your high school years, you may have been involved in work or other relevant activities that emphasize your key abilities and attributes. This type of information may be appropriate for the work experience or "additional information" sections of your résumé.

**Work Experience** In this section, also called *employment history or experience*, list your accomplishments and responsibilities from prior jobs in chronological order beginning with your current or most recent one.

Some students wonder if they should include unpaid internships in this section. Typically, you should, since they are relevant and legitimate professional experiences. In fact, the abilities and attributes students gain from internships are often more relevant and transferable to sought-after positions than those from their previous paid positions.

If you have little or no work experience, you shouldn't panic. You can highlight your abilities and attributes by listing achievements and experiences in school and community activities. In Figures 16.6 and 16.7, you can see ineffective and effective examples of résumés for Jaclyn Peha, who doesn't have a lot of work experience. You can see how she shows her strengths convincingly. Of course, you should make a priority of establishing a job history right away to bolster your credibility in the eyes of potential employers.

**Additional Information** Education and work experience often account for the majority of your résumé content. You can provide a variety of other information, however, to accentuate your key abilities and attributes. In fact, some of the additional information may be critical to showing who you are as a person—your attributes. You have a great deal of flexibility with other information you display. You might consider including some of the following sections:

- Technology Skills
- Professional Associations
- School Clubs
- Honors and Awards
- Certifications and Licensure
- Community Activities
- Volunteer Work
- Training
- Language Abilities

As you think about additional information to provide, the standard is simple: *Does providing this information carry on a narrative of your key abilities and attributes?* Keep in mind that many employers are particularly looking for job candidates with strong technology and interpersonal skills.[7] You can highlight these skills when you showcase your community and volunteer work, professional and student affiliations, and computer skills. Do not include such personal information as marital status, age, religion, or sexual orientation, as none of this is relevant.

## Getting the Tone, Style, and Design Right for Résumés and Cover Letters

Once you've analyzed your key abilities and attributes and gathered information to place in your résumé, you're ready to present the information in a compelling manner. The tone, style, and design must be perfect. Employers often skim your résumé on the first pass. Unless you can present your main credentials within 15 to 30 seconds, you may be eliminated from the job pool. Even if potential employers reward your well-designed résumé with a second look, they are unlikely to spend a lot of time. In one survey of hiring managers, 24 percent said they spent less than two minutes reviewing a résumé, 32 percent spent three to five minutes, 23 percent spent six to ten minutes, and just 16 percent spent more than ten minutes.[8]

This section is about developing your résumé so that you can make the most of the small window you have with potential employers. What can you do to show your distinctive combination of abilities and attributes? What can you do to make your experience stand out? What can you do to persuade prospective employers that you will be a good investment for them? In short, how can you make sure that potential employers rapidly understand your story: the unique abilities and attributes that will deliver value to them?

### Emphasize Accomplishments with Action Verbs

As you describe your accomplishments and experiences, begin your statements with action verbs (see Table 16.2 for a list). By doing so, you highlight your abilities and attributes in a way that emphasizes action and results.

Select your action words strategically. Without exaggerating, choose verbs that make your key abilities and attributes jump off the page. For example, if you want to show that you are a leader, a series of statements beginning with action verbs such as *guided, initiated,* and *led* paint a more vivid picture than the statement *I am a good leader.*

By the same token, avoid verbs that undersell your abilities and attributes. Many university students use weak verbs when describing their significant customer service and administrative experiences. Phrases such as *answered calls, entered information in the computer,* and *waited tables* do not emphasize transferable abilities and attributes. Rather, they focus on menial duties and do not focus on professional outcomes. Read through some of the less effective and more effective statements in Table 16.3 and notice how action verbs can bolster your credibility.

### Quantify Accomplishments Where Possible

Your potential employers want to know how valuable your contributions have been in your prior jobs. So, where possible, describe key contributions and how they affected the bottom line. Often, even when you can't say for certain how much you affected financial results, you can provide numbers that show the significance of your work. Notice the contrasts between less effective and more

**LO16.4** Highlight your qualifications with effective tone, style, and design.

### Principles of Effective Résumés

- Emphasize accomplishments with action verbs.
- Quantify accomplishments where possible.
- Position your most important contributions first.
- Remove irrelevant details.
- Avoid buzzwords and jargon.
- Be exact and avoid any errors.
- Group and label information to improve ease of reading.
- Format to distinguish pieces of information.
- Select a simple yet visually appealing layout.

**TABLE 16.2**

Action Verbs for Résumés

| Management/ Supervision | Contracted | Explained | Reorganized |
|---|---|---|---|
| Assigned | Demonstrated | Informed | Reviewed |
| Evaluated | Developed | Mediated | Screened |
| Executed | Exceeded | Negotiated | Streamlined |
| Facilitated | Excelled | Persuaded | Systematized |
| Hired | Gained | Presented | Updated |
| Managed | Generated | Promoted | |
| Mentored | Improved | Publicized | **Customer Service** |
| Monitored | Increased | Reported | Assisted |
| Motivated | Launched | Specified | Clarified |
| Organized | Marketed | Summarized | Confronted |
| Oversaw | Proposed | Supported | Delivered |
| Planned | Raised | Teamed with | Greeted |
| Scheduled | Secured | | Handled |
| Screened | Sold | **Analysis/Research** | Maximized |
| Selected | | Analyzed | Met |
| Strengthened | **Finance/Accounting** | Compiled | Minimized |
| Supervised | Allotted | Conducted | Performed |
| Trained | Appraised | Detected | Provided |
| | Assessed | Diagnosed | Resolved |
| **Leadership** | Audited | Explored | Responded |
| Authorized | Averted | Gathered | Served |
| Decided | Balanced | Identified | Settled |
| Delegated | Budgeted | Inspected | Treated |
| Directed | Controlled | Interpreted | Worked with |
| Enabled | Corrected | Operated | |
| Encouraged | Cut | Performed | **Innovation/Creativity** |
| Enlisted | Earned | Proved | Built |
| Executed | Estimated | Quantified | Completed |
| Formed | Evaluated | Researched | Conceptualized |
| Guided | Forecasted | Reviewed | Created |
| Implemented | Interpreted | Solved | Defined |
| Influenced | Prepared | Studied | Designed |
| Initiated | Preserved | Surveyed | Developed |
| Instituted | Projected | Tested | Devised |
| Led | Reconciled | | Formulated |
| Set goals | Reduced | **Administration** | Innovated |
| | | Administered | Invented |
| **Marketing/Sales** | **Teamwork/ Communication** | Arranged | Modernized |
| Accumulated | Coached | Edited | Ranked |
| Advertised | Collaborated | Installed | Received |
| Attained | Coordinated | Maintained | Recognized |
| Boosted | Described | Processed | Revolutionized |
| Broadened | Encouraged | Purchased | |
| | | Recorded | |

effective examples in Table 16.4 and how quantification strengthens the more effective statements.

## Position Your Most Important Contributions First

The order in which you place your accomplishments and other supporting details shows how you prioritize them. The supporting details you place first or second under each heading in your résumé form the deepest impressions about your abilities and attributes. Furthermore, because most potential employers skim, they may only see

**TABLE 16.3**

Using Action Words to Emphasize Accomplishments

| Less Effective | More Effective |
|---|---|
| Responsible for marketing efforts for younger members. | Developed and ran marketing campaigns targeting young professionals and university students that resulted in approximately 55 new members in the past year. |
| Without an action word, this statement sounds unnecessarily weak and passive. | By starting with strong action words, this statement illustrates a sense of goal setting and achievement. |
| Answered phones. | Greeted clients and scheduled appointments in person and by phone. |
| Although this statement starts with an action word, it emphasizes a menial, nonskilled effort. | This action word immediately draws attention to Haniz's focus on her customer orientation and value for a business. |
| Kept track of tanning products. | Took inventory of all items sold in the store. |
| This statement emphasizes a duty without any reference to the business importance of the task. | This statement illustrates a sense of purpose in accomplishing an important business task. |

**TABLE 16.4**

Quantifying Accomplishments

| Less Effective | More Effective |
|---|---|
| Supervised other tellers in the teller department. | Supervised six tellers—responsible for the overall direction, coordination, and evaluation of unit. |
| Without a quantity, potential employers might assume a rather inconsequential set of supervision duties. | With a number of tellers noted, potential employers see that the applicant has supervised a team. |
| In charge of effort to support local breast cancer awareness event. | Organized a group of 83 members to participate in a local breast cancer walkathon. |
| Without quantification and an action word to begin this statement, this phrase emphasizes responsibilities rather than accomplishments. | By quantifying the performance (recruiting 83 members), this accomplishment stands out as exceptional. |

the first one or two supporting details for each heading. So, strategically arrange this information to highlight your best features (see Table 16.5).

## Remove Irrelevant Details

Writing résumés and cover letters requires the discipline to tell a story of how your key abilities and attributes will provide value to an employer. You should generally avoid details about your personal life, especially those that some people may find objectionable or unprofessional (e.g., politics or religion). Other information—although technically okay on a résumé—should be provided only if it helps develop your narrative.

**TABLE 16.5**

Positioning Your Most Important Contributions First

| Less Effective | More Effective |
| --- | --- |
| • Greeted clients and scheduled appointments in person and by phone<br>• Assisted with purchasing of medical supplies and processing of client orders<br>• Managed financial bookkeeping for the company using QuickBooks | • Managed financial bookkeeping for the company using QuickBooks<br>• Assisted with purchasing of medical supplies and processing of client orders<br>• Greeted clients and scheduled appointments in person and by phone |
| This list emphasizes customer skills and de-emphasizes financial bookkeeping skills. If the goal is to display financial abilities, then the list is not effective. | This list emphasizes financial abilities with less emphasis on purchasing and customer service. |

**TABLE 16.6**

Removing Unnecessary Details

| Less Effective | More Effective |
| --- | --- |
| *Community Activities and Accomplishments*<br>Volunteer, VITA, Columbia, SC (giving up my Saturdays in support of a good cause)<br>Church Choir (my church choir contains professional-level talent and tours internationally)<br>Member of the National Association of Federal Credit Unions<br>Volunteer Gymnastics Coach, Columbia, SC<br>Varsity Basketball Overall MVP (2005–2006), Team Captain (2005–2006) | **PROFESSIONAL ASSOCIATIONS AND COMMUNITY ACTIVITIES**<br>**Member,** National Association of Federal Credit Unions, Arlington, VA, 2010 to present<br>**Volunteer Tax Consultant,** Volunteer Tax Assistance Program (VITA), Columbia, SC, 2008 to present<br>**Volunteer Coach,** Elite Gymnastics Summer Camp, Columbia, SC, 2003 to 2007 (summers) |
| This list contains several unnecessary pieces of information. The references to the church choir and high school sports are interesting; however, in limited space, they do little to highlight Haniz's key abilities and attributes. | This condensed list better frames the activities in a professional light and in terms of Haniz's key abilities and attributes. She retains one sports item (gymnastics coach) to show her leadership abilities and commitment to the community. |

Generally, avoid listing personal interests and hobbies unless this information takes up little space and accentuates your key abilities and attributes (see Table 16.6).

### Avoid Clichés, Buzzwords, and Jargon

As you craft your job application, show enthusiasm for potential positions without resorting to clichés. Many clichés, such as *dream job* or *track record of success,* fail to highlight your abilities and attributes for a few reasons. First, they do not communicate your specific accomplishments. Second, many potential employers perceive these statements as showing unrealistic or naïve expectations about a job or inflated beliefs about abilities (see Table 16.7).

### Be Exact and Avoid Errors

Potential employers examine your résumé with intense scrutiny. On the first pass, many discard it immediately if it contains typos or other careless errors. In one recent survey, roughly three out of four financial executives (76 percent) said they would

**TABLE 16.7**

Avoiding Clichés

| Less Effective | More Effective |
|---|---|
| The Credit Union Marketing Specialist position you posted is my dream job. | My successes in attracting new credit union members would translate well into the requirements of your Credit Union Marketing Specialist position. I am eager to speak with you by phone or in person to learn more about the position and explain how I can contribute. |
| This statement is inherently me-centered and naïve. | This statement projects credibility and shows an interest in dialogue about the position. |

**TABLE 16.8**

Proofreading for Typos and Misspellings

| Less Effective | More Effective |
|---|---|
| Increased the moral of the unit and gained incite into managing frontline employees. | Increased the morale of the unit and gained insight into managing frontline employees. |
| These spelling errors (moral, incite) would not be detected with spell-check software. | The spelling is correct in this case. |

eliminate job applicants with just one or two typos on their résumés (see Figure 16.3).[9] In other words, the standard is high, and few potential employers are forgiving. For an example of poor proofreading, see Table 16.8.

Throughout the job application process, potential employers will apply exacting attention to all of the information in your documents and interviews. Any inconsistency or questionable information may damage or disqualify your chances. Often, potential employers judge your character when they see seemingly contradictory information. So be accurate and precise in setting out dates of employment, job responsibilities and accomplishments, educational background, and all other aspects of the résumé and cover letter.

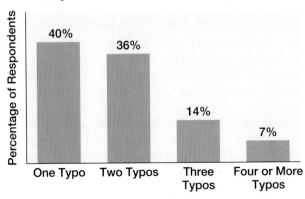

**Responses from Senior Financial Executives**

**FIGURE 16.3**

How Many Typos in a Résumé Does It Take for You to Decide Not to Consider a Job Candidate for a Position in Your Company?

*Source:* Accountemps, "One or Two Resume Mistakes Enough for Majority of Managers to Pass on a Job Candidate; Still, Managers More Lenient Than They Were Five Years Ago," May 15, 2014, http://accountemps.rhi.mediaroom.com/2014-05-15-Survey-One-or-Two-Resume-Mistakes-Enough-for-Majority-of-Managers-to-Pass-on-a-Job-Candidate-Still-Managers-More-Lenient-Than-They-Were-Five-Years-Ago .

**TABLE 16.9**

Grouping and Labeling to Highlight the Employment Narrative

| Less Effective | More Effective |
|---|---|
| Computer Skills: MS Word, MS Excel, MS Access, MS PowerPoint, Prezi, MS Publisher, MS Project, QuickBase, MS Outlook, QuickBooks, Powerscan Loan Display, WebEx | *Project Management/Scheduling:* QuickBase, MS Project, MS Outlook<br>*Finance/Accounting:* QuickBooks, Powerscan Loan Display<br>*Spreadsheets and Databases:* MS Excel, MS Access<br>*Presentations/Publishing:* WebEx, MS PowerPoint, Prezi, MS Publisher, MS Word |
| Since the list contains 12 items, recruiters are unlikely to read through it. Furthermore, they are unlikely to distinguish the various types of software skills. | Once the list is grouped, recruiters can quickly (within three or four seconds) recognize the types of software skills involved. |
| Major coursework: ECON 2013, 2023; ACG 2021, 2071, 3171, 3331; FIN 3244, 4424, 4324, 4329, 4453; MAN 3240, 4720 | *Primary coursework:* bank administration, investments, marketing of financial services, event management |
| This list of major courses provides little meaningful information and does not feed into an employment narrative. | Because these courses are grouped into three or four areas that feed into an employment narrative, potential employers understand the gist of the academic program rapidly and see its place in Haniz's set of abilities and attributes. |

### Group and Label Information to Improve Ease of Reading

When you have long lists of items, consider grouping the information to help recruiters quickly grasp your abilities (see Table 16.9). If you don't group lists of four or more items, recruiters will often skip or gloss over them. Furthermore, by grouping items on your résumé, you show your understanding of related skill sets.

### Format to Distinguish Pieces of Information

As you format your résumé, focus on ease of processing and consistency. Imagine recruiters who are reviewing dozens if not hundreds of résumés in a day. They are likely skimming on the first pass to see if your résumé deserves more attention. So make sure they can gather the most pertinent information quickly. By formatting your document effectively with bold, italics, spacing, and other features, you can help recruiters understand your primary abilities and attributes within 20 to 30 seconds (see Table 16.10).

### Select a Simple Yet Visually Appealing Layout

The last step in the résumé process is choosing a layout. Many job candidates instinctively worry about the appearance in the early stages of résumé writing, especially when they are working from model documents or templates. Resist this natural urge and focus on planning your message first and fine-tuning its tone and style. Then, select an appealing layout.

You can choose from dozens of layout options and even design your own. Generally, seek layouts with a lot of white space so that your résumé does not appear cluttered. Also, choose designs that contain a clear scheme for headings and formatting. Make sure that the content is balanced across the page rather than clustered on one side.

**TABLE 16.10**

Formatting to Distinguish Key Pieces of Information

| Less Effective | More Effective |
|---|---|
| *Work Experience*<br>Better Horizons Credit Union, Pescaloosa, FL<br>Marketing Specialist/Loan Officer Jan 2011 to present | **WORK EXPERIENCE**<br>BETTER HORIZONS CREDIT UNION, Pescaloosa, FL<br>**Marketing Specialist/Loan Officer Jan 2011 to present** |
| With formatting the same for company, position, and dates, this information is difficult to pick out quickly. This problem is amplified over an entire document. | With unique formatting applied to section headings (centered, capitalized, bolded), company (capitalized, left aligned), position (bolded, left aligned), and dates (bolded, right aligned), employers can pick out key pieces of information rapidly and within seconds gain a good sense of employment and education histories. |

## Creating Chronological and Functional Résumés

One of your first choices as you assemble your résumé is the format. The two major options are **chronological résumés**, which present the information grouped by work and education over time, and **functional résumés**, which present the information in terms of key skills. The most common and generally preferred format, especially for young professionals, is the chronological résumé. One recent survey showed that 75 percent of hiring managers preferred them, whereas 17 percent preferred functional résumés, and 8 percent had no preference.[10]

Functional résumés draw special attention to your key skills. They are most often used by professionals with extensive (more than 15 years) experience and individuals with little or no work experience. Experienced professionals use them as a way to streamline a lengthy list of jobs, many of which involved similar accomplishments and experiences. Inexperienced individuals often use them to emphasize key skills developed through a combination of school, community, volunteer, and other types of activities while de-emphasizing a lack of work experience.

Consider creating both a chronological and a functional résumé to determine which format is more effective at selling your key abilities and attributes. The process of creating both types may even give you insight about how to present your selling points. So, even if you don't think you'll use a functional résumé, writing one will likely give you ideas to improve and refine your chronological résumé (or vice versa). Notice the ineffective chronological résumés in Figures 16.4 and 16.6 and the effective chronological résumés in Figures 16.5 and 16.7. Then, notice the example of an effective functional resume in Figure 16.8.

For some positions, you may be asked to provide text or scannable résumés (examples of these are provided in the online resources for the textbook). Generally, these formats allow employers to upload data into a database and search a set of résumés electronically. A few strategies can increase the effectiveness of these types of résumés. For example, when you convert your standard résumé into a scannable one, adjust the content to gain success with the robot. Typically, you can do this by using nouns instead of verbs for job duties and accomplishments and packing keywords early in your résumé.[11]

Generally, employers prefer to receive résumés in standard format through electronic channels. In a recent survey of employers, 71 percent stated a preference for standard résumés, 21 percent for standard résumés in text format, 3 percent for scannable résumés, and 5 percent expressed no preference.[12] In terms of delivery, about 68 percent of organizations expect you to submit your résumé through their websites. Roughly 14 percent of organizations prefer you to send your résumé as an attachment to an email.[13]

**LO16.5** Create chronological and functional résumés to highlight your key selling points.

**Components of Chronological Résumés**

- Name block
- Summary of qualifications *or* Career objective (optional)
- Education
- Work experience
- Additional information

**Components of Functional Résumés**

- Name block
- Summary of qualifications *or* Career summary
- Skills
- Additional information

**FIGURE 16.4**

An Ineffective Chronological Résumé

Haniz Zogby
164 Founders Ridge Court, Havana, FL 32333
Phone: 850-784-7391; email: hanizzogby@gmail.com

Education
Florida State University, Tallahassee, Florida, Graduation: May 2017, BS in Finance, Minor in
Event Management GPA: 3.714 (Magna Cum Laude)
Major coursework: ECON 2013, 2023; ACG 2021, 2071, 3171, 3331; FIN 3244, 4424, 4324, 4329,
4453; MAN 3240, 4720 3.924 GPA at Woodbridge High School (7th in Class), Palmetto Scholarship

Work Experience
Better Horizons Credit Union, Irmo, SC
Marketing Specialist/Loan Officer, Oct 2015 to present
- Extend business and personal loans to credit union members
- Assist with promotional programs
- Responsible for marketing efforts for younger members
- In charge of effort to support local breast cancer awareness event
Teller Supervisor, Oct 2014 to Oct 2015
- Responsible for all cash reserves at the credit union
- Helped with referral and sales programs
- Balanced monthly general ledgers
- Supervised other tellers in the teller department
- In charge of the entire unit and its activities
Teller, July 2012–Oct 2014
- Managed banking transactions for members in a helpful and efficient manner
- Recognized as the top referral getter among the tellers
Palmetto Home Medical, Columbia, SC
Receptionist/Billing Assistant, May 2009–May 2012 (summers)
- Answered phones
- Data entry into the computer
Ultra Tan, Blythewood, SC
Salon Attendant, September 2011 to May 2012
- Cleaned the salon
- Answered questions that customers had
- Kept track of tanning products
Computer Skills
MS Word, MS Excel, MS Access, MS PowerPoint, Prezi, MS Publisher, MS Project, QuickBase,
MS Outlook, QuickBooks, Powerscan Loan Display, WebEx

Community Activities and Accomplishments
Volunteer, VITA, Columbia, SC (giving up my Saturdays in support of a good cause)
Church Choir
Member of the National Association of Federal Credit Unions
Volunteer Gymnastics Coach, Columbia, SC
Varsity Basketball Overall MVP (2009–2010), Team Captain (2009–2010)

Study Abroad
Cass Business School, Dubai, United Arab Emirates
- Took business classes in a multicultural environment
- Observed one of the most dynamic business environments in the world
- Took Arabic language courses

---

The excessively plain appearance of this résumé does not create a positive initial impression.

Recruiters will have a challenging time identifying key attributes and abilities.

Text appears cluttered because it is mostly on the left-hand side of the page without space in between.

The lack of **bold,** *italics,* or other formatting features makes it difficult to rapidly identify key pieces of information.

The focus on responsibilities as opposed to accomplishments fails to sufficiently highlight abilities.

Weak verbs do not emphasize high-order thinking and transferable skills for business.

Sections with additional information do not effectively highlight key attributes and abilities.

**FIGURE 16.5**

## An Effective Chronological Résumé

**Haniz Zogby** | 164 Founders Ridge Court, Havana, FL 32333 ● 850-784-7391 ● hanizzogby@gmail.com
*LinkedIn*: linkedin.com/in/hanizzogby ● *Online Portfolio*: sites.google.com/site/hanizzogby

### EDUCATION

FLORIDA STATE UNIVERSITY, Tallahassee, Florida
**Bachelor of Science in Finance, Minor in Event Management**    **Graduation: May 2017**
- *Primary coursework*: bank administration, investments, marketing of financial services, event management
- *Study abroad*: one semester at Cass Business School in Dubai focusing on international finance and marketing
- *GPA*: 3.7; *Awards*: Magna Cum Laude

### WORK EXPERIENCE

BETTER HORIZONS CREDIT UNION, Pescaloosa, FL
**Marketing Specialist/Loan Officer**    **Jan 2015 to present**
- Developed and ran marketing campaigns targeting young professionals and university students that resulted in approximately 55 new members in the past year
- Established a reward points program that was adopted by nearly 30 percent of members
- Organized a group of 83 members to participate in a local breast cancer walkathon
- Extend business and personal loans to credit union members

**Teller Supervisor**    **Dec 2013 to Jan 2015**
- Implemented and tracked referral and sales programs in the teller department
- Balanced monthly general ledgers, including branch and teller over/short
- Managed all cash reserves at the credit union
- Supervised six tellers; responsible for the overall direction, coordination, and evaluation of unit

**Teller**    **July 2012 to Dec 2013**
- Handled banking transactions for members in a helpful and efficient manner
- Obtained the most referrals in the teller unit during the entire year (2013)

PALMETTO HOME MEDICAL, Columbia, SC
**Receptionist/Billing Assistant**    **May 2010 to July 2012 (summers)**
- Managed financial bookkeeping for the company using QuickBooks
- Assisted with purchasing of medical supplies and processing of client orders
- Greeted clients and scheduled appointments in person and by phone

ULTRA TAN, Blythewood, SC
**Salon Attendant**    **Sept 2011 to May 2012**
- Sold tanning packages and tanning lotions
- Took inventory of all items sold in the store
- Resolved customer concerns related to products, billing, and scheduling

### COMPUTER SKILLS

*Project Management/Scheduling*: QuickBase, MS Project, MS Outlook
*Presentations/Publishing/Word Processing*: WebEx, MS PowerPoint, Prezi, MS Publisher, MS Word
*Finance/Accounting*: QuickBooks, Powerscan Loan Display; *Spreadsheets and Databases*: MS Excel, MS Access

### PROFESSIONAL ASSOCIATIONS AND COMMUNITY ACTIVITIES

**Member,** National Association of Federal Credit Unions, Arlington, VA, 2014 to present
**Volunteer Tax Consultant,** Volunteer Tax Assistance Program (VITA), Pescaloosa, FL, 2012 to present
**Volunteer Coach,** Elite Gymnastics Summer Camp, Columbia, SC, 2007 to 2011 (summers)

---

This simple but nicely formatted résumé allows recruiters to rapidly identify key abilities and attributes.

Distinctive and consistent formatting for headings (centered **BOLD CAPS**), organizations (CAPS), position (**bold**), and dates (right-aligned **bold**) make information easy to identify.

Specific accomplishments enhance credibility of claims.

Strong action verbs emphasize transferable management and marketing abilities.

Grouping helps rapidly display key computer skills.

Selective display of associations and community activities highlights key abilities and attributes.

**FIGURE 16.6**

Ineffective Chronological Résumé

Jaclyn Peha
1832 Weston Avenue, Pescaloosa, FL 32333
*Email*: jpeha@betterhorizons.net

Skills & Qualifications

Proven web developer with track record of success. Specialties in all areas of web development. Experience with many programming languages and web development tools. Strong communicator with excellent multitasking abilities.

Education and Coursework

**Associate of Applied Science in Information Technology**
*Pescaloosa Community College*, Pescaloosa, FL
April 2017

*Classes*

- Composition I & II
- Web & Multimedia Development
- Psychology
- Web Analytics & Search Engine Optimization
- Networking Basics
- Interactive Web Design
- Web Security
- Internet Commerce
- ActionScript Programming
- Introduction to Management
- Creative Writing
- College Algebra I

- Oral Communication
- Technical Communication
- Introduction to Databases
- Web Content Management
- Advanced Website Design
- Audio-Video Editing
- HTML Programming
- Web Scripting
- Server-Side Programming
- Microeconomics
- Macroeconomics
- College Algebra II

High School Degree
Joaquin Jacobi High School
May 2013, 3.69 GPA

Work Experience

IT Intern

*Better Horizons Credit Union*, Pescaloosa, FL
April 2017 to present

- Tech support
- Identify strategies for SEO
- Development of website

Personal Interests

Puzzles, video games, photography, hiking, camping, outdoor sports, hunting

---

Formatting does not allow recruiters to rapidly identify key abilities and attributes.

Words and phrases such as "proven," "track record of success," and "expertise in all areas of web development" are exaggerated and diminish credibility.

Jaclyn tends to provide too much information just for the sake of filling the page. For example, she lists nearly all courses she's taken as well as her high school degree. This strategy does not help sell her web development skills.

The most significant missed opportunities involve not emphasizing her web development experience. Jaclyn fails to provide enough detail about her activities at her current internship. She also fails to mention web development projects she's participated in.

**FIGURE 16.7**

Effective Chronological Résumé

## Jaclyn Peha
1832 Weston Avenue, Pescaloosa, FL 32333
*Email*: jpeha@betterhorizons.net

### WEB DEVELOPMENT SKILLS
Creative and talented web developer with skills in the following areas:
- *Web specialties*: Website design, web analytics, user interaction, search engine optimization
- *Programming languages*: JavaScript, Java, CSS, HTML, XHTML
- *Adobe Suite*: Dreamweaver, Muse, Fireworks, Flash Professional, Photoshop

### EDUCATION AND COURSEWORK
**Associate of Applied Science in Information Technology**
*Pescaloosa Community College*, Pescaloosa, FL
September 2015 to April 2017

*Web Development Coursework:*

- Web & Multimedia Development
- Web Analytics & Search Engine Optimization
- Interactive Web Design
- Web Security
- Internet Commerce
- ActionScript Programming

- Web Content Management
- Advanced Website Design
- Audio-Video Editing
- HTML Programming
- Web Scripting
- Server-Side Programming

### WORK EXPERIENCE
**IT Intern**

*Better Horizons Credit Union*, Pescaloosa, FL
April 2017 to present

- Assist in developing the branding and communication strategies for the website
- Develop multimedia content for the "Members" section of the website
- Identify strategies for search engine optimization
- Provide tech support for public relations events

### PROJECTS
- Co-developed the "Career Resources" section on the Pescaloosa Community College website
- Developed the website of a local nonprofit (*Foundation for Consumer Fairness*)
- Created and maintained Joaquin Jacobi High School's Debate Club website for two years

### PERSONAL INTERESTS
Sudoku and crossword puzzles, travel photography, travel documentaries, hiking

Formatting allows recruiters to rapidly identify key abilities and attributes. Recruiters can gather the main messages (Jaclyn's abilities and attributes) in each section in a matter of 10 to 15 seconds.

Despite relatively limited experience, Jaclyn portrays herself as skilled in many areas of web development. Her confident, but not exaggerated, language shows her strong potential.

Compared to the ineffective example, this résumé provides far more relevant details, particularly in the "Work Experience" and "Projects" sections

**FIGURE 16.8**

## An Effective Functional Résumé

**Haniz Zogby**

164 Founders Ridge Court, Havana, FL 32333 • 850-784-7391 • hanizzogby@gmail.com
*LinkedIn:* www.linkedin.com/hanizzogby • *Online Résumé:* https://sites.google.com/site/hanizzogby

**Qualifications Summary**

Ambitious credit union professional with record of successful marketing through local events, seminars, mailings, online social networking, and referrals. Knowledgeable of best practices in marketing for credit unions and innovative financial services for credit unions. Committed to leading marketing efforts to increase credit union membership and empower those who use local credit unions.

**Skills**

*Marketing for Credit Unions*
- Developed and ran marketing campaigns targeting young professionals and university students that resulted in approximately 55 new members in the past year
- Established a reward points program that nearly 30 percent of members adopted
- Implemented and tracked referral and sales programs in the teller department

*Event Management*
- Organized a group of 83 members to participate in a local breast cancer walkathon
- Set up regular seminars about retirement plans, investing, and business loans for credit union members
- Minored in Event Management and completed team projects for a charity fund-raiser (organized a music concert), a sports event (set up a kids' night), and a wedding

*Leadership*
- Participated in all major decisions for Better Horizons Credit Union during the past year as assistant manager
- Supervised six tellers; responsible for the overall direction, coordination, and evaluation of entire teller unit
- Involved in leadership roles at work, school, and community for the past ten years

*Technology*
- Excel at using software to facilitate project management and scheduling (QuickBase, MS Project, MS Outlook)
- Comfortable with a variety of online and face-to-face presentation software platforms (WebEx, MS PowerPoint, Prezi)
- Advanced-level use of a variety of finance, accounting, spreadsheet, and database software (QuickBooks, Powerscan Loan Display, MS Excel, MS Access)
- Expert at word processing and publishing software (MS Publisher, MS Word)

**Employment History**

| | |
|---|---|
| 07/2012–present | BETTER HORIZONS CREDIT UNION, Pescaloosa, FL *Marketing Specialist/Loan Officer* (01/2015–present), *Teller Supervisor* (12/2013–01/2015), *Teller* (07/2012–12/2013) |
| 05/2009–07/2012 (summers) | PALMETTO HOME MEDICAL, Columbia, SC, *Receptionist/ Billing Assistant* |
| 09/2011–05/2012 | ULTRA TAN, Blythewood, SC, *Salon Attendant* |

**Education**

*Bachelor of Science in Finance, Minor in Event Management,* FLORIDA STATE UNIVERSITY, Tuscaloosa, FL, Graduation: 05/2017.

*Study Abroad,* one semester of business classes at CASS BUSINESS SCHOOL, Dubai, UAE

**Community Involvement**

*Volunteer Tax Consultant,* VOLUNTEER TAX ASSISTANCE PROGRAM (VITA), Columbia, SC, 2012–present.

*Volunteer Coach,* ELITE GYMNASTICS SUMMER CAMP, Columbia, SC, 2007–2011 (summers).

---

This cleanly formatted résumé sends signals of professionalism and orderliness.

The "Qualifications Summary" section contains a concise statement that highlights key abilities and attributes.

By grouping skills, Haniz demonstrates what she has to offer in a matter of seconds.

A brief "Employment History" section helps recruiters judge the depth and consistency of her experience.

The "Education" and "Community Involvement" sections contain only a few strategically selected items that focus on her key messages.

## Using LinkedIn Strategically

Social media platforms give you many opportunities to network and reach you professional goals. LinkedIn is the most popular professional networking platform. Approximately 54 percent of HR professionals say it is *very important* and another 33 percent say it is *somewhat important* to manage your professional reputation on LinkedIn.[14]

**LO16.6** Use LinkedIn as part of the job search process and to network professionally.

A strong presence on LinkedIn can help you in a variety of ways in the job search process. Most often, your LinkedIn profile serves as a supplement to the materials you provide to a prospective employer. Many HR professionals will view your LinkedIn profile after seeing your cover letter or résumé. Just before a job interview, your interviewer may look at your profile to learn more about you. The company representative you met at a job fair may look at your profile to decide whether to follow up with you. In some cases, HR professionals may contact you after seeing that you match what they're looking for in certain positions.

You should consider using LinkedIn for many purposes, not just to find job opportunities. You can expect that many of your professional contacts—colleagues, partners, clients, customers, and others—will check your profile to learn more about you. Increasingly, LinkedIn is a professional learning platform. By following the posts of thought leaders, business leaders, companies of interest, and curated newsfeeds in specific topics, you can consistently learn and stay up to date with business and industry knowledge.

You should approach your LinkedIn profile in the same way you approach your résumé. By identifying a professional narrative of your key selling points, you're ready to set up a profile that is persuasive to your professional contacts. Typically, your LinkedIn profile is an elaborated version of your résumé. With fewer space constraints, you can provide additional types of information. Notice Haniz's LinkedIn profile in Figure 16.9. In addition to providing information about her education and work experience, she has dedicated space to list personal interests, languages, volunteer experience, certifications, courses, and other items. She also displays the people, organizations, and curated newsfeeds she follows. As long as these additional items reinforce her intended professional narrative, she should display them. Keep in mind these tips as you manage your LinkedIn presence.

*Provide a professional photo.* Unlike résumés, the first item most LinkedIn viewers see is your profile picture. Make sure you upload a high-resolution, warm, and professional photo.

*Create a personalized URL.* LinkedIn allows you to create a unique web address. Personalizing your link to include your name makes your profile more memorable and professional.

*Complete the summary space.* A common missed opportunity among LinkedIn users is failing to use the summary space. In one to three paragraphs, you can brand yourself with your key abilities and attributes and major accomplishments. Use concise, confident, natural, and cliché-free language.

*Use multimedia.* Increasingly, LinkedIn allows you to upload a variety of file types, including video and pictures. If you have appropriate multimedia to highlight your accomplishments, you can set yourself apart from others on LinkedIn.

*Choose sections wisely.* LinkedIn allows you to choose from well over 20 types of sections, including categories such as causes you care about, test scores, projects, honors and awards, publications, and so on. Choose to add information when these new sections add to your professional narrative. While you have more space than a résumé, you should still selectively choose content that highlights your key selling points.

*Manage your recommendations and endorsements strategically.* LinkedIn allows you to give and receive recommendations and endorsements. If you choose to display them, you should generally limit the number of recommendations to two or three per position or section. LinkedIn automatically gives your connections the option to endorse you for various skills. You can choose to display only those endorsements that are most accurate and align with your key selling points.

**FIGURE 16.9**

An Example of a Well-Developed LinkedIn Profile

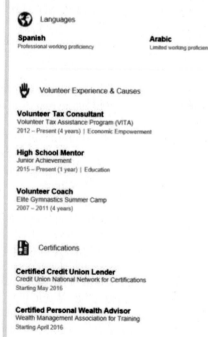

*Photos:* (left) © Ingram Publishing RF; (right) © Images-USA/Alamy

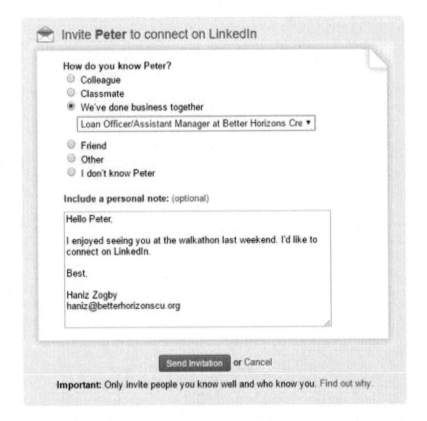

**FIGURE 16.10**

A Less Effective,
Nonpersonalized
LinkedIn Invitation

*Build a network of important connections.* LinkedIn prominently displays the number of connections you have in your network. As you build your LinkedIn connections, resist the urge to focus on the quantity of your connections. Rather, focus on the quality of your connections. Typically, connect with professionals and peers with whom you share professional interests. Make sure to personalize your invitations when you hope to connect with others. Notice Figure 16.10 in which the invitation is generic and nonpersonalized. By contrast, the invitation in Figure 16.11 is personalized. Taking 30 seconds to 1 minute to personalize the invitation shows your genuine interest in connecting with others.

**FIGURE 16.11**

A More Effective,
Personalized LinkedIn
Invitation

*Show some personality and be positive.* While you should maintain professionalism on LinkedIn, you have more flexibility in how you portray yourself and interact with others than with résumés and cover letters. Find ways to show your personality in positive and warm ways.

*Maintain a giver mentality.* As discussed in Chapters 1 and 2, an important principle of networking is maintaining a giver mentality as opposed to adopting a taker mentality. The same principle applies to online networking. As you gain a reputation for helping and providing value to others, you will find many opportunities open up to you. LinkedIn allows you to provide others with recommendations, endorsements, likes, and lots of helpful information.

*Stay active on LinkedIn.* Make sure to consistently update your LinkedIn information. Use LinkedIn as a professional learning platform. Pay attention to the accomplishments of those in your network and congratulate them. Periodically share status updates. Join some communities and groups. As you invest an hour or two per week on LinkedIn, you'll find that professional opportunities will arise through your networking and learning.

## Developing a Reference List

**LO16.7**   Develop a list of references that will improve your employment prospects.

You will need to provide a list of personal references as part of most job applications. Some job applicants put off this task until the last minute, often underestimating its significance. In fact, your references may be among the most important factors in gaining a new position.

One recent study showed that for professional positions, 62 percent of employers call three or more references from applicants' lists of references, 18 percent call two references, 3 percent call just one reference, 8 percent call more than three references, and just 9 percent do not contact any references.[15] As you construct your list of references, consider these tips:

### Develop Relationships with Potential References over Time

Well before you need to apply for a position, compile a list of people who can provide credible accounts of your qualifications. Consider people who work in fields and industries that interest you. Also consider professors with whom you have established a relationship over several semesters, ideally in classes directly related to your sought-after positions.[16]

### Contact Your References Ahead of Time

Before you place any names on your list, reach out to those individuals and, as a courtesy, ask permission to use their names. A short email may be enough to accomplish this request, but consider meeting in person or calling to explain the positions you are applying for and recent experiences you've had. These short conversations allow your references to speak about you with enthusiasm and up-to-date information. Also, these conversations give you a chance to seek advice about how to handle the job application process. Generally, also send these individuals your most updated résumé so they are aware of the information that potential employers have.

Some of your references will be former supervisors. Forward-thinking job applicants stay in touch with past supervisors from time to time to keep them updated with their career developments. Even small but sincere gestures such as sending yearly holiday cards can lead to favorable comments when these former supervisors speak with your potential employers.[17]

Think about whether you should include your current supervisor as a reference. In some cases, she or he will understand and even encourage your efforts to seek new positions and will serve as an excellent reference. In other cases, however, your supervisors may be unhappy that you want to leave your current position. For example, if

**FIGURE 16.12**

References List

---

**Haniz Zogby** | 164 Founders Ridge Court, Havana, FL 32333 • 850-784-7391 • hanizzogby@gmail.com
*LinkedIn*: linkedin.com/in/hanizzogby • *Online Résumé*: sites.google.com/site/hanizzogby

**REFERENCE LIST**

Christine Russo
**CEO and President**
BETTER HORIZONS CREDIT UNION
*Address*: 1488 Altura Dr.
Pescaloosa, FL 32315
*Phone*: 850-971-0234
*Email*: russo@betterhorizons.com
*Relationship*: Ms. Russo has been my supervisor for the past five years. She is intimately familiar with my work in the following positions: marketing specialist, loan officer, teller supervisor, and teller.

Jim Harrill, CPA
**Owner**
HARRILL TAX ASSOCIATES
*Address*: 3419 Main Street
Havana, FL 32333
*Phone*: 850-972-3188
*Email*: jamesharrilljr@harrilltax.com
*Relationship*: Mr. Harrill trained me and supervised my work as a volunteer tax consultant for the VITA program. He is familiar with my work ethic and commitment to the community.

Jamie McPherson, PhD
**Associate Professor of Finance**
FLORIDA STATE UNIVERSITY
*Address*: 719-C Thurmond Tower
Tallahassee, FL 32302
*Phone*: 850-777-1848
*Email*: mcpherson@fls.edu
*Relationship*: Dr. McPherson taught two of my courses and served as an advisor for my honors thesis about emerging financial services in credit unions.

Jack Gerardi
**Owner and President**
PALMETTO HOME MEDICAL
*Address*: 18 Foxborough Lane
Columbia, SC 29201
*Phone*: 803-798-1312
*Email*: jgerardi@palmettohomemed.com
*Relationship*: Mr. Gerardi supervised my work as a receptionist and billing assistant for 3-1/2 summers.

> Consistent formatting allows recruiters to quickly gather key information.
>
> Formatting that matches the résumé formatting shows attention to detail and a touch of class.
>
> A brief statement about relationships with references demonstrates professionalism and helps recruiters make judgments about the value of each one.

---

your supervisor thinks your job search indicates a lack of dedication to your current job, you may find your professional opportunities diminishing. If you're uncomfortable telling your supervisor that you're searching for a new position, you likely should not provide him/her as a reference.

## Thank Your References

Your references will undoubtedly wonder how your job search fares. Stay in touch with them about progress you've made. When your job search is over, thank them for their participation in the process. These shows of goodwill may come in handy over the years as you ask these same individuals for assistance in future job searches.

## Complete a Consistently Formatted, Well-Detailed Reference List

When you construct the list of references, check the job announcement to see how many references are required. If it does not provide a number, list three to five individuals. Make sure you provide current contact information. In addition, consider providing a brief (one or two sentences) description of your professional or school relationship to each reference. Finally, format the list of references to be compatible with your résumé (see Figure 16.12).

# Constructing Cover Letters

**LO16.8** Compose effective cover letters that highlight your key selling points.

**Components of Cover Letters**

- Interest in position.
- Match with position.
- Call to action.

Cover letters describe your interest in and qualifications for a position. Whereas you may have one, two, or at most three versions of your résumé for various positions, you must uniquely tailor each cover letter to a particular position. No two cover letters should be the same.

The role of cover letters has changed in recent years. Some hiring managers no longer read them. One recent survey showed that only about 20 percent of private-sector companies expect them. Yet, even with this slightly declining interest, you should write perfect cover letters because almost half (41 percent) of HR professionals still say a cover letter is important.[18]

Your primary goal for cover letters is to sell your key abilities and attributes in a way that matches the needs of the employer for a particular position. As you do with sales letters, you build excitement and optimism that you can excel in the posted position. Unlike mass sales letters, however, cover letters deliver the message that you are writing to one particular employer, and only that employer.

Keep in mind the following advice:[19]

## The Cover Letter Often Forms the First Impression

Since many potential employers read your cover letter (or a condensed version of it as an email) first, it forms the first impression of you. Therefore, it must be perfect. As an error-free message, the cover letter can immediately place you in the upper echelons. A New York tutoring company, Inspirica, recently sought out writing tutors. In 93 percent of the 220 cover letters, HR specialists found writing errors.[20]

## Clearly Identify the Position You Are Applying For

Your potential employer is likely reviewing applications for many—sometimes hundreds or thousands—of positions at the same time. Many employers use electronic application systems to clearly identify the positions that applicants are seeking. In any case, clearly and prominently identify the position you are applying for in your cover letter. The subject line is often a good location for this information.

## Be Focused and Concise

In recent years, potential employers have come to expect shorter, more concise cover letters. This is in part due to larger application pools for each position. Thus, you should generally aim for three to five targeted paragraphs.

In such limited space, focus on your main selling points—your key abilities and attributes—and how these selling points match the needs of your employer. By taking this focused approach, you create a prism from which the employer will interpret your résumé, thus strengthening the story you are telling of your qualifications.

## Show a Confident and Enthusiastic Tone without Exaggerating or Displaying Arrogance

One of the most challenging aspects of the cover letter is getting the tone right. Employers are looking for employees who can contribute, so you should mention how your unique abilities can help the company. Yet, hiring managers may view excessive self-praise as arrogance.

Also, you should show your interest in the position and the company, as hiring managers will be trying to gauge your enthusiasm and commitment levels. At the same time, you will want to avoid flowery language, which hiring managers may find off-putting and not businesslike.

**FIGURE 16.13**

## An Ineffective Solicited Cover Letter

Haniz Zogby
164 Founders Ridge Court, Havana, FL 32333
850-784-7391
hanizzogby@gmail.com

May 15, 2017

Human Resources Department
Anchor Federal Credit Union Network
158 Anchor Loop
Raleigh, NC 27601

Hello Hiring Committee:

Please consider my application for the Credit Union Marketing Specialist position. I think you will find that I possess the skills that you are looking for.

My mother always has said, "The sky's the limit." I have always admired her sense of optimism. One reason I admire the credit union model is because of my mom. My mother was a teller for nearly 20 years, and I followed in her footsteps. She always felt that she was doing good for the community by working in a credit union, and I have gained this deep sense of commitment to the community through credit unions as well. In my current workplace, I have been promoted more quickly than any other employees. You will find that I am ambitious, organized, and I am passionate about marketing credit unions. My passion has driven me to success at Better Horizons Credit Union and will propel me to success at Anchor Federal Credit Unions if you give me a chance.

I want to illustrate to you the kind of abilities I can bring to Anchor Federal Credit Union Network by describing a recent marketing campaign that I ran. About one year ago, our CEO, Christine Russo, determined that we needed to gain younger members. She has relied on me often to help come up with ideas for important marketing campaigns, and she turned to me in this instance as well. After thoroughly examining best practices throughout the industry, we came up with a set of financial services and advertising ideas that resulted in approximately 55 new members. Our branch manager recognized this campaign as the most effective marketing effort during her 15 years at the credit union. I'm proud of this kind of effort and I can deliver this level of result at Anchor Federal Credit Union if you give me the chance.

The job you posted is my dream job. It combines my love of credit unions with my skills and interests in event management. You will notice on my résumé that not only do I have training in event management, but I also have experience using events as marketing tools for Better Horizons Credit Union. I thrive in these environments where I need to bring people together for fun and exciting events. Thank you for your attention to this letter. I hope that we can meet to further our discussions.

Sincerely,

Haniz Zogby

*Margin notes:*

This letter contains too much text and long paragraphs. The body has 405 words and two long paragraphs of 138 and 143 words. Many busy recruiters will not read it carefully.

Because of excessive personal information and emotion, this cover letter lacks a professional and serious tone.

The use of clichés, such as "the sky's the limit" and "dream job," shows naïveté.

The closing does mention future contact but is vague.

## Tailor Your Cover Letter to the Job Posting and Needs of the Employer

By carefully reading the job announcement, you can prioritize your selling points so they are tailored to the position of interest. This approach not only accentuates your ability to do the job, it also shows that you have researched the position and are responsive to the needs of the company. The Internet provides many avenues for job seekers to learn about companies. Read the Technology Tips feature to learn about one approach.

## Adapting for Unsolicited Letters

Most people gain their positions through formal job announcements—that is, jobs *solicited* by companies. When applying for these jobs, you will write a **solicited cover letter** since it is for an open position that a company advertises (see Figures 16.13 and 16.14 for examples of ineffective and effective solicited cover letters). In some cases,

**FIGURE 16.14**

## An Effective Solicited Cover Letter

Haniz Zogby
164 Founders Ridge Court, Havana, FL 32333
850-784-7391
hanizzogby@gmail.com

May 15, 2017

Mr. Jacob Garcia, Director of Human Resources
Anchor Federal Credit Union Network
158 Anchor Loop
Raleigh, NC 27601

**RE: Credit Union Marketing Specialist Position (Job Posting #831481809)**

Dear Mr. Garcia:

My successes in attracting new credit union members would translate well into meeting the requirements of your Credit Union Marketing Specialist position. I am eager to speak with you by phone or in person to learn more about the position and explain how I can contribute.

During nearly five years at Better Horizons Credit Union, I have excelled at many of the responsibilities you are seeking, including marketing to increase membership, tracking the success of marketing activities, coordinating marketing events and efforts, and delivering presentations to partners and potential clients. I have helped gain new credit union members by developing marketing campaigns with many of the techniques you are seeking, including event marketing, mailings, referral programs, seminars, and online social networking.

One of my most successful marketing campaigns occurred last year when I was given the responsibility of increasing membership among young professionals and university students. I developed mailings, an online social networking campaign, and seminars that resulted in approximately 55 new members. Our branch manager, Ms. Christine Russo, recognized this campaign as the most effective marketing effort during her 15 years at the credit union.

During my time working at Better Horizons Credit Union, I have been rapidly promoted and given critical marketing responsibilities due to my leadership, initiative, creativity, and performance. I can make these same contributions to the Anchor Credit Union Network.

Please call me at your convenience to arrange an interview. You can reach me at my mobile phone (850-784-7391) between 9 a.m. and 6 p.m. daily.

Sincerely,

*Haniz Zogby*

Haniz Zogby

---

This cover letter is brief but focused, stating key abilities and attributes in a professional and confident manner. The body contains 257 words. The longest paragraph is 75 words. Recruiters are far more likely to read this letter.

The letter demonstrates awareness of the needs of the employer and how her skills match those needs.

This letter conveys a professional and confident tone.

The closing statement is assertive and specific in requesting contact. Yet, it is not overbearing or pushy.

---

however, you may seek employment with a company that does not even have an open position. In these cases, you will submit an **unsolicited cover letter** since the company has not requested job applications.

When writing unsolicited cover letters, you make several modifications. You must first find out as much as possible about the employer so that you can explain how you fit the employer's needs. Also, you should open immediately with a proposition about how you can add value, and summarize your key abilities and attributes quickly, often in bulleted form (see Figure 16.15 for an example of an unsolicited cover letter in email form).[21]

**FIGURE 16.15**

## An Unsolicited Referral Cover Letter

| To: | Lucy Sharapova <l.sharapova@easterncu.org> |

| Subject: | Expansion Plans for the Eastern Credit Union Network |

📎 Zogby_Haniz_Resume.docx (48.00

**B** *I* <u>U</u> F ᴛ**T** T ²⁻₃⁻ ▢ ▤ ▤ <u><<**Plain Text**</u>

Dear Ms. Sharapova:

After reading about your credit union network's expansion plans in the *Credit Union Leadership Journal*, I am eager to join your marketing team. My skills in attracting new credit union members through event marketing, mailings, referral programs, seminars, and online social networking could help you achieve your ambitious growth plans.

I am an experienced credit union professional with extensive marketing experience and financial background. My marketing successes include the following:

- Attracting 55 new members within one year in a marketing campaign targeting young professionals and university students
- Developing a reward points program that was adopted by nearly 30 percent of our members
- Establishing referral and sales programs in our teller department that significantly increased membership and member use of financial services

You can learn more about my qualifications by reading my attached résumé. Also, please see my online résumé and LinkedIn profile. My online résumé contains actual samples from marketing campaigns I have led. It contains mailings, content from the Better Horizons website, and video of two marketing seminars that I organized and presented.

I am seeking an entry-level marketing position in a credit union network with potential for advancement based on performance. As far as location, I am flexible and willing to relocate anywhere. I am seeking an opening salary range of $50,000 to $60,000.

Please give me a call at your convenience to arrange an interview. You can reach me on my mobile phone (850-784-7391) between 9 a.m. and 6 p.m. daily. Also, I plan to give you a call within the next two weeks to learn more about potential job openings and explore the possibility of a job interview.

Best regards,

Haniz Zogby

Mobile Phone: 850-784-7391
Email: hanizzogby@gmail.com
Online Résumé: linkedin.com/in/hanizzogby
LinkedIn Profile: sites.google.com/site/hanizzogby

---

The message is concise. The body has just 276 words. Further, the short paragraphs and bulleted items allow the recruiter to get the gist within 15 to 30 seconds.

The subject line focuses on the needs and ambitions of the employer.

Links to Haniz's online résumé and LinkedIn profile allow the recruiter to learn more if she is interested.

The tone is confident and assertive without being demanding.

As an unsolicited request for a job interview, this message is more up front about issues such as salary and promotional opportunities.

## Reviewing Your Résumés and Cover Letters

Your job application must be perfect. Recruiters rarely have any tolerance for inaccuracies in a résumé. Furthermore, they won't hire you unless you present your selling points effectively.

On the most basic level, you should make sure every element of your job application correctly portrays your abilities and attributes, so you must avoid any urge to exaggerate. You should also review your documents over and over to ensure they emphasize your selling points in a compelling manner. Consider getting the opinions of many people about your résumé. You might start with some individuals in the career center and a few of your professors.

**LO16.9** Review your job application documents for effectiveness and fairness.

**TECHNOLOGY TIPS**

### GETTING AN INSIDER'S VIEW OF POTENTIAL EMPLOYERS

Most job seekers use Internet job postings and advertisements to find and apply for jobs. Most also have used LinkedIn and other professional networking websites to find opportunities. However, few job seekers get an inside look at the companies that interest them.

A variety of websites can help you get insiders' perspectives about companies. One example of this type of website is Glassdoor.com, where you can find reviews about any company of interest from its current and former employees. You can learn how satisfied employees are with the company, what the company culture is like, what advancement opportunities there are, and even salary ranges for various positions.

By getting as much inside information about a company as possible, you can determine if the company culture and job opportunities match your expectations before you ever apply. Furthermore, this inside information can help you prepare for the job application and interview process. It may even help you in the salary negotiations once you have a job offer.

*Source:* Glassdoor.com

Also, try to get the opinions of some people in positions that match your career interests. Since business professionals interpret résumés quite differently, you may get some conflicting advice. This is normal. Even all hiring managers won't agree about what makes the best résumé. However, by getting many opinions, you'll be able to make decisions about strategies that enhance your likelihood of success in the job search process.

## Acing the Job Interview

Your cover letter, résumé, list of references, and other pieces in your job application package set the stage for the most consequential part of the process—the interview. When you have secured an interview, you have made the initial cut and are likely deemed a good candidate. You are now competing against the best candidates for the position.

Many job applicants spend little time preparing for the interview, essentially winging it. At this crucial stage—where hiring managers are making their decisions—preparation often sets apart those who receive offers and those who do not. In this section, we focus on a few parts of the job interview: dressing appropriately, using appropriate etiquette, responding to interview questions, and following up.

**FIGURE 16.16**

## Most Serious Problems in the Job Application/Interview Process

**Nationwide Survey of Hiring Managers**

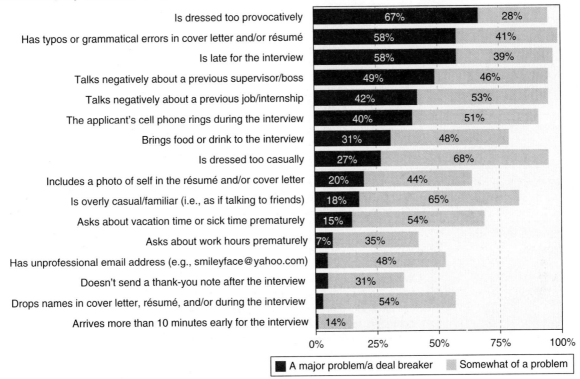

| | A major problem/a deal breaker | Somewhat of a problem |
|---|---|---|
| Is dressed too provocatively | 67% | 28% |
| Has typos or grammatical errors in cover letter and/or résumé | 58% | 41% |
| Is late for the interview | 58% | 39% |
| Talks negatively about a previous supervisor/boss | 49% | 46% |
| Talks negatively about a previous job/internship | 42% | 53% |
| The applicant's cell phone rings during the interview | 40% | 51% |
| Brings food or drink to the interview | 31% | 48% |
| Is dressed too casually | 27% | 68% |
| Includes a photo of self in the résumé and/or cover letter | 20% | 44% |
| Is overly casual/familiar (i.e., as if talking to friends) | 18% | 65% |
| Asks about vacation time or sick time prematurely | 15% | 54% |
| Asks about work hours prematurely | 7% | 35% |
| Has unprofessional email address (e.g., smileyface@yahoo.com) | | 48% |
| Doesn't send a thank-you note after the interview | | 31% |
| Drops names in cover letter, résumé, and/or during the interview | | 54% |
| Arrives more than 10 minutes early for the interview | 14% | |

*Source:* "SHRM Poll: Interviewing Do's and Don'ts for Job Seekers," September 15, 2009.

### Dress for the Interview and Pay Attention to Etiquette

One of the first signals of professionalism you give at a job interview relates to your clothing choices. (Notice, for example, the items related to dress in Figure 16.16. Also, notice how the first item in the survey may be considered sexist or unfair. Some gender biases continue to affect judgments made about job applicants.)[22] As much as possible, gain a sense ahead of time about the dress standards at the company where you are interviewing. Generally, you should dress up, even when the company has a fairly casual environment. Typically, err on the side of conservative dress—that is, wear well-pressed, clean, and nicely fitted clothes. Avoid overaccessorizing with too much jewelry, flashy glasses, or other items. Consider a dress rehearsal at home to feel at ease in your chosen outfit.[23]

During your visit to the company—before, during, and after the formal interview—pay attention to appropriate etiquette. Most hiring managers expect you to maintain a certain level of formality. Greet those you meet with handshakes and enthusiasm.

### Respond Effectively to Interview Questions

The moment of truth for hiring managers generally occurs during the job interview. Many make fairly quick judgments about your abilities and attributes. In a recent survey of 498 human resource professionals, one-third (33 percent) made not-to-hire decisions within 5 minutes, and another third (30 percent) made that decision within 15 minutes.[24] Your window may be brief to make the case that you are a good fit for the company. To prepare for the questions you may be asked, consider the following tips:

**Respond to Questions Strategically, Confidently, and Concisely**  As you crafted your cover letter and résumé, you identified those professional abilities and attributes that meet the needs of your employer. These are your selling points, and you

**LO16.10** Develop strategies for responding to common job interview questions.

**connect**

Visit **http://connect. mheducation.com** for an exercise on this topic.

**TABLE 16.11**

Common Job Interview Questions for Entry-Level Business Positions

| Type of Interview Question | Examples |
|---|---|
| Introduction questions | • Tell me about yourself.<br>• How was your flight here? Did you find this office easily?<br>• How was your flight here? How do you like living in _____? |
| Education and training | • Why did you choose your school?<br>• Why did you choose your major?<br>• What was your favorite part of your program? Least favorite? |
| Knowledge of company and industry | • What do you know about our company?<br>• What do you think are some of our main business challenges? How can you help?<br>• What trends do you see in this industry? |
| Work experience | • How did you get your last job?<br>• Why did you leave your last job? Have you ever been fired?<br>• What did you like least about your last job? |
| Approaches to work, goals, and successes | • Why did you apply for this job?<br>• What are you looking for in a job?<br>• How will you be successful in this position?<br>• What were some tough decisions you had to make at your last job?<br>• What are your biggest accomplishments?<br>• Tell me about a project you worked on in your most recent job. How did you contribute to its success?<br>• What do you wish you had accomplished but were unable to?<br>• Can you tell me about a difficult situation you encountered at work? How did you respond? How did you get your team to work effectively?<br>• Can you tell me about a situation where you had to work under pressure and deal with deadlines? |
| Personal attributes | • What are your strengths? Weaknesses?<br>• What would your current boss say are your greatest strengths and weaknesses?<br>• Are you creative? Hardworking? Ambitious?<br>• What have you learned from your past jobs? |
| Interpersonal, team, management, and leadership skills | • What types of people do you like to work with?<br>• What types of people do you think are most difficult to work with?<br>• What is your leadership/management style?<br>• Do you have top management potential?<br>• How well do you work in teams?<br>• What is your communication style when working with others?<br>• Have you had to make an unpopular decision or announcement? How did you do it? |

should find ways throughout the interview to emphasize them. You are strategic to the degree that you find ways to bring up these selling points.

Also, show confidence. While you should avoid bragging, you need to emphasize your abilities and attributes. Some job applicants are uncomfortable doing this. Claim credit for work you have accomplished. Say "I" instead of "we" during the job interview more often than you would otherwise as you talk about accomplishments at work. Yet, at the same time, maintain a balance between taking credit for your individual accomplishments and demonstrating your team orientation.[25]

Finally, give concise answers. Most responses should be between 30 seconds and two minutes. Briefer answers are generally too abrupt, and longer answers are often unfocused. Also, longer answers disrupt the conversational nature of the job interview.

In Table 16.11, you'll find many common types of interview questions. Be prepared to respond to any of them strategically, confidently, and concisely. In Table 16.12,

**TABLE 16.12**

## Responses to Common Job Interview Questions

| Less Effective | More Effective |
|---|---|
| **Q.** *Tell me about yourself.* | **Q.** *Tell me about yourself.* |
| **A.** Well, I'm a recent graduate with a degree in finance. I also minored in event management. I have worked for a credit union for the past five years. I started out as a teller and moved up from there. Prior to working at the credit union, I worked at a medical supplies company and a tanning salon. Outside of that, I've been heavily involved in sports my whole life. And, that brings me right up until now, ready to move into a new position. | **A.** About five years ago, I took a position as a teller at a credit union. I found that I really loved the credit union approach to providing financial services. Within months, I realized that this was a career direction for me. I was fairly quickly promoted into other positions—first as a teller supervisor and then as loan officer and marketing specialist. While working at the credit union, I also went to Florida State University, where I majored in finance and minored in event management. I focused all of my studies on my deep interest in marketing financial services for credit unions. One reason I'm so intrigued by the position is that it combines several of my key interests. |
| This response is factual but does not directly lead into a coherent, inspiring account of Haniz's selling points. | This statement captures Haniz's background, naturally describes several of her selling points, and ties her selling points to the needs of the position. At 115 words, this statement would take roughly 45 seconds to one minute to state. |
| **Q.** *It looks like you just graduated. Tell me about your university experience.* | **Q.** *It looks like you just graduated. Tell me about your university experience.* |
| **A.** I had a great time in school. I had great professors all the way through my program in finance. I made great friends. One of the most exciting parts of my schooling was studying in Dubai for a semester, which really opened my eyes to the world. The only part I didn't like about school was the pressure of working full-time for most of my four years and also studying on the side. But, I think I grew a lot from the experience. | **A.** Going to Florida State University was a great experience and helped me improve my skills in marketing financial services. Early on in my finance program, I took a variety of classes about banking and investments that helped me think about financial services we could offer at Better Horizons. Also, I used a lot of what I learned in my event management minor to think about events we could run at the credit union. I think my favorite semester was when I went abroad to Dubai. I was fascinated to see that the businesses in that country are using so many creative and innovative approaches to event marketing. I've tried to use some of those techniques I saw in Dubai at Better Horizons. |
| This response provides a general overview of Haniz's experience but fails to provide a sense that she was pursuing a set of goals. The response does not contain selling points. | This response ties Haniz's university experiences into her professional goals and accomplishments. It highlights her key selling points and shows her goal-directed approach to work. |
| **Q.** *Why do you want to leave your current job?* | **Q.** *Why do you want to leave your current job?* |
| **A.** My job at Better Horizons Credit Union has given me many opportunities, but I am often frustrated with the conservative approach that our Board has taken to developing new services. My immediate supervisor usually agrees with my ideas, but she understands that the Board will not approve our most ambitious ideas. So, she falls in line. Better Horizons has been a great learning experience, but I'm simply ready to move on to a more ambitious work environment. | **A.** Leaving Better Horizons Credit Union will not be easy for me. I've enjoyed working closely with so many of my colleagues, and getting to know the community has been wonderful. Last year, when I helped run our campaign that brought in so many younger members, I realized that I wanted to be part of a larger credit union network in a position where I could spend more of my time developing marketing events and facilitating coordination between branches. I think this is where my strengths lie, and as far as I can tell, would be a good match for your position. |

TABLE 16.12

(*Continued*)

| Less Effective | More Effective |
|---|---|
| By stating her displeasure with the Board and the less than ambitious work culture, Haniz makes a risky statement. Some hiring managers will worry that Haniz does not work well with others. | By focusing on the satisfying aspects of the position she intends to leave, Haniz is more likely to give the impression that she is a committed, team-oriented employee. She segues her response into the needs of the current position. |
| **Q.** *How well do you work in teams?*<br><br>**A.** I take a win-win mentality into all team projects. I really believe that one plus one can make three if you work together as a team. I think if you ask anyone whom I've worked with, they'll tell you that I facilitate a productive work environment where we're feeding off one another's ideas and where the end result is a creative and effective solution. | **Q.** *How well do you work in teams?*<br><br>**A.** I enjoy working in teams to meet marketing objectives. Last year's marketing campaign that resulted in 55 new members was the result of a five-member team at Better Horizons. I was asked to head up the team and focused on events and social media, while the other team members worked on their specialty areas, such as market research, print advertising, and radio spots. Even though we each had our specialties, we had to work together extensively to make sure we created a unified marketing message. We also pushed one another to come up with better ideas. I don't think we could have achieved such a successful campaign without one another. |
| This clichéd, vague response does little to convey Haniz's real ability to work in teams. | This response shows Haniz's ability to work in teams through a concrete example. It inspires confidence that Haniz is a team player and genuinely understands the economic value of working in teams. |
| **Q.** *Do you have management experience? What is your approach to managing others?*<br><br>**A.** Yes. As a teller supervisor, I supervised a unit of six tellers. I was responsible for coordinating, scheduling, and the overall performance of the group. I think the most important part of managing is being open. The tellers always knew where I was coming from and vice versa. | **Q.** *Do you have management experience? What is your approach to managing others?*<br><br>**A.** Yes. At Better Horizons, I've managed the teller department and led a variety of marketing campaigns that required bringing together the ideas and resources of credit union employees and members. I have been most successful when I've followed several principles. First, I think it's important to set a vision and articulate the big goals. Second, I think it's critical to get everyone's ideas about how to achieve the goals. Finally, I think you have to find ways to gain buy-in and create incentives for others to engage in the goals. Here's how I did this with our mailing campaign to attract more members . . . |
| This response is too short. While the response is positive, it fails to lead into Haniz's selling points of developing marketing campaigns. | This response answers the question and also transitions to Haniz's selling points. |
| **Q.** *What are your weaknesses?*<br><br>**A.** I can't really think of any weaknesses off the top of my head. Well, I guess one thing is that I never settle for anything less than excellence. Some people who accept mediocrity sometimes say I'm a control freak, but I get the job done. So, in one way you could view this as a weakness, but from the business viewpoint, it's a net plus. | **Q.** *What are your weaknesses?*<br><br>**A.** One of the things I noticed in the job posting is that you are looking for someone with the ability to conduct member surveys. I wish I could say that I had experience doing surveys in my current job. I think it is critical to include surveys as part of market analysis. I took several courses about conducting surveys and statistical analysis, yet I haven't applied this knowledge to real business problems. I look forward to developing my abilities in this regard and would welcome any training or mentoring. |
| This question is common in job interviews. Many job candidates view it as a trick question and evade it or state a weakness that could really be viewed as a strength. This response does not show that Haniz is self-aware enough to improve quickly on the job. | This response shows that Haniz is self-aware. It also reveals her ambitious, goal-setting nature and recognition of what she needs to do to provide value for her potential employer. |

you'll see some sample responses from Haniz. As you read these questions, think about how the hiring manager is likely responding.

### Be Perceptive about What Hiring Managers Are Evaluating

Hiring managers ask most questions with specific goals in mind. They are trying to evaluate how well your abilities and attributes match the needs of the position and fit into the corporate culture. Thus, they will ask a variety of questions about your education, work experience, and knowledge of their company. In most questions, you can fairly easily discern what they are trying to find out about you.

Other interview questions, however, may be more difficult to "read." With such questions, think about what kinds of judgments the interviewer might make. For example, when hiring managers ask you to introduce yourself, they want to know how you see yourself; it gives them a glimpse into your sense of your life and career direction, your priorities, and your work values. When they ask you what your weaknesses are, they are generally less concerned about what you can't do now but rather what you can do later. They are trying to see how self-aware you are and if you are likely to improve over time. Even questions in small talk—such as how your flight was, how your hotel room is, or how your football team is doing—are asked by hiring managers to make judgments about your emotional intelligence.

### Tell Success Stories

Throughout this book, we've discussed the importance of stories. During job interviews, telling stories about your successes can create a positive connection between you and your potential employers. By telling success stories, you provide specific and concrete examples as evidence of your abilities and attributes. Also, these stories often offer a glimpse into who you are as a person.[26]

One approach to telling success stories is the **STAR method** (Situation—Tasks—Actions—Results). Table 16.13 shows how Haniz uses the STAR method to briefly but convincingly respond to the question *How well do you work with deadlines?* Read through this example and compare its specificity to an abstract, nonspecific response,

**TABLE 16.13**

The STAR Approach to Responding to Interview Questions

| | **Example Statements** |
|---|---|
| **SITUATION** where you created a positive outcome<br><br><br>**TASKS** you were assigned as part of a process<br><br><br>**ACTIONS** you took that led to outcome<br><br><br><br>**RESULTS** that occurred | **Q.** *How well do you work with deadlines?*<br>**A.** I'm quite used to meeting deadlines, and actually, I've done some of my best work when I had to hit a deadline. One example occurred recently in organizing a group of credit union employees and members to participate in a local walkathon to support breast cancer.<br><br>For over a decade, our credit union has been a prominent supporter of the event, but our participation has decreased almost every year. Last year, our group was comprised of just 15 people, most of whom were employees. Altogether, we raised only around $600.<br><br>Two weeks before the deadline for signing up, our president approached me and asked me if I could head up a promotional effort to get a larger group from the credit union. She suggested that I aim for at least 30 people and focus on getting more of our members on the walkathon team, especially newer members.<br><br>Within a few days, another marketing specialist and I had set up some incentives for members to participate, such as a free T-shirt and a water bottle. We developed promotional messages that we sent out by email and via our Facebook page and our website. I think what made the most difference is that we asked tellers to distribute flyers each time a member came in for a transaction.<br><br>Ultimately, we recruited 83 walkers and raised nearly $10,000 for our local breast cancer center. We also were able to get a variety of new members to join our walkathon team and connect on a deeper level with our credit union community. |

**TABLE 16.14**

Questions by Job Candidates in First Interviews

| Less Effective | More Effective |
|---|---|
| • What kind of salary are you offering for this position?<br>• How often can I work from home?<br>• Is there a strong benefits package? | • Can you tell me about the company culture?<br>• If there were any one thing you could change about the company culture, what would it be?<br>• What are you looking for in the person who takes this position?<br>• How do you evaluate employees' performance?<br>• What are the next steps in the process?<br>• Whom would I report to in this position? What management style does this person have?<br>• Do you have any concerns about my ability to succeed in this position? |

such as "I work well under pressure and deadlines. In fact, I thrive under these conditions and often produce my best results."

As you tell success stories, make sure that they respond directly to interview questions and reveal your best selling points. Also, make sure your stories stay relatively brief. Generally, responses that are longer than one to two minutes are too long. You might consider writing out five or six success stories you could use in a job interview.

**Avoid Criticizing Your Former Organizations, Supervisors, and Colleagues**
If you glance back at Figure 16.14, you will notice that among the worst offenses in job interviews is speaking negatively of your current or past employers. If you express negativity, hiring managers may wonder how well you get along with others and what attitude you bring to work. When you are asked questions such as *Why do you want to leave your current job* or *What is your least favorite part of your job*, be prepared with an honest response that is constructive, forward-looking, and complimentary if possible.

**Ask Questions**   Generally, your interviewer will ask you what questions you have. Come prepared with some. When interviewees do not ask questions, hiring managers often view them as uninterested or inexperienced. In Table 16.14, you will notice several questions that are not effective and others that are generally effective.[27]

Typically, if you ask about salary, compensation, and other perks on the first interview, you may inadvertently send the meta message "this is all about me." One survey showed that less than one-third of hiring managers thought it was OK for interviewees to bring up salary on the first interview.[28] Of course, these are considered appropriate topics on second or third interviews when a potential employer is showing strong interest in you.

## Succeed in Web Conference Interviews

Many companies are increasingly using web conferences for initial job interviews. Using Skype, Google Hangouts, or other platforms is far more convenient and less expensive—in time and money—than flying in job candidates for job interviews. Consider the following strategies for these types of job interviews:

**Do Several Trial Runs**   Make sure to do several mock job interviews via web conference. You'll notice that within 20 to 30 minutes, you'll learn a variety of ways to act professionally and feel natural. Consider asking a parent, a friend, or a professional to run the practice interview with you. As part of this process, test your equipment to make sure your video and audio work well.

**Make Sure Your Profile for the Web Conference Software Creates the Right Impressions**   The first thing that many recruiters will see is your profile on Skype or Google Hangouts. You can make a great first impression with a professional photograph and professional bio.

**Look Professional**   Some job candidates view web conference job interviews as less formal than in-person job interviews. That's simply not the case. Dress up in a suit or appropriate professional dress to show your interest in the job. Consider adjusting the temperature in your room to ensure you're comfortable with a suit on during the interview.

**Tidy Your Room or Office**   Many job interviewers form impressions of you based on the surroundings in your room or office. Make sure your room is clean, organized, and attractive.

**Look Directly at the Camera**   Holding an authentic conversation with your interviewer is one of your main goals. By looking straight into the camera, you allow eye contact to make the conversation more personable and real. To look straight into the camera and also position the web conference window so that you can see your interviewer may require several minutes of adjusting the location of your webcam.

**Smile and Express Yourself Nonverbally**   Many people find it challenging to express themselves nonverbally in web conferences. Initially, you may need to make conscious effort to smile more often and use gestures. Many people use gestures less because they rest their elbows on a desk or armchair, which hinders them from natural movements. You might consider not placing your hands or elbows on the desk in front of you to free up your hands and arms.

**Use Notes Strategically**   A major advantage of web conference interviews is you can have notes—on paper or in an open file on your computer—to give you cues during the interview. For example, you might have a list of points you want to emphasize or a few questions to ask. Use these notes sparingly, however, so that you can maintain eye contact with your interviewer and avoid the impression you're not prepared for the interview.

**Avoid Distractions**   By removing clutter on your desk and closing all windows and unneeded files on your computer, you ensure you can focus completely during your interview. Similarly, make sure there aren't any interruptions during your interview. If you have roommates, make sure they know to be quiet during your interview. If you have a pet, make sure it's not close enough to your room or office that the interviewer might hear it. If you live where it's not uncommon to hear car honks, police sirens, or other distracting noises, consider finding a better location for your job interview.

**Send a Thank-You Note**   As with any job interview, send a thank-you note soon after your interview (see the next section "Follow Up after the Job Interview").

## Follow Up after the Job Interview

Sending a note of appreciation following an interview is a good strategy. In a poll of 150 senior executives, 88 percent stated that sending a thank-you note could increase chances of employment. When asked how many job applicants actually did send thank-you notes, executives estimated that just 51 percent of candidates do so.[29]

Within a few hours to one day after your interview, send a thank-you note. Your primary goal should be to express goodwill and confirm your interest in the position (see Figure 16.17). The note should be brief and genuine. Some job applicants wonder

**LO16.11** Explain etiquette for following up after job interviews.

**FIGURE 16.17**

## Thank-You Note Following an Interview

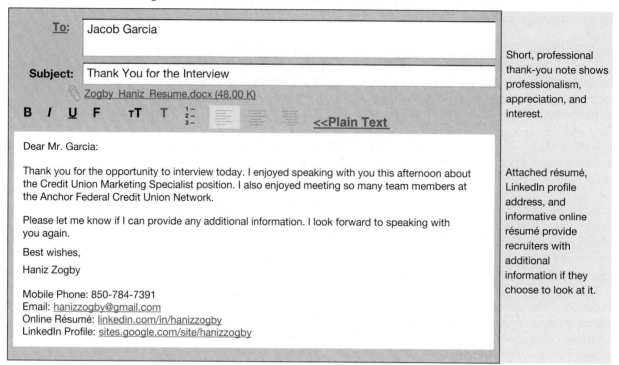

To: Jacob Garcia

Subject: Thank You for the Interview

Zogby_Haniz_Resume.docx (48.00 K)

B  *I*  U  F  ᴛT  T  1–2–3–    <<**Plain Text**

Dear Mr. Garcia:

Thank you for the opportunity to interview today. I enjoyed speaking with you this afternoon about the Credit Union Marketing Specialist position. I also enjoyed meeting so many team members at the Anchor Federal Credit Union Network.

Please let me know if I can provide any additional information. I look forward to speaking with you again.

Best wishes,

Haniz Zogby

Mobile Phone: 850-784-7391
Email: hanizzogby@gmail.com
Online Résumé: linkedin.com/in/hanizzogby
LinkedIn Profile: sites.google.com/site/hanizzogby

Short, professional thank-you note shows professionalism, appreciation, and interest.

Attached résumé, LinkedIn profile address, and informative online résumé provide recruiters with additional information if they choose to look at it.

whether they should send a thank-you email or a thank-you card. In a recent survey, 60 percent of HR professionals said that sending a thank-you email is the best way of expressing thanks. Roughly 37 percent said it's best to send a thank-you note by email *and* regular mail.[30] Clearly, the only "right" answer is that you should send one.

Unless the interviewers tell you that you should wait until they contact you, feel free to follow up with their progress in making a selection. Many job applicants feel hesitant to follow up, assuming that they may annoy or nag hiring managers. The reality is far different. Nearly half (48 percent) of HR managers say they view job candidates more favorably when they follow up. Fewer than 4 percent of HR managers say they view candidates less favorably for following up.[31] Your polite follow-ups show that you want the position and that you are persistent. As shown in Figure 16.18, most hiring managers expect you to follow up, with nearly half (43 percent) stating you should check back at least once per week.

**FIGURE 16.18**

## How Often Should You Check Back after Being Interviewed?

***Nationwide Survey of Human Resource Professionals***

Source: "SHRM Poll: Interviewing Do's and Don'ts for Job Seekers," September 15, 2009. Copyright © 2009, Society for Human Resource Management, Alexandria, VA.

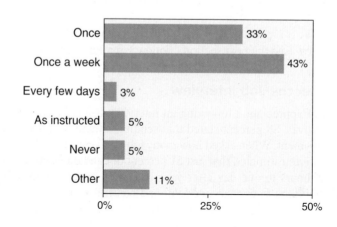

| | |
|---|---|
| Once | 33% |
| Once a week | 43% |
| Every few days | 3% |
| As instructed | 5% |
| Never | 5% |
| Other | 11% |

0%        25%        50%

## Leaving an Organization

When you accept a new position, you can extend several courtesies to your current employer and ensure that you leave on good terms so that your supervisors can provide a positive recommendation in the future if you need it. In the first place, you should inform your supervisor that you are leaving immediately, preferably in person. Show graciousness and appreciation for the professional opportunities you have been given. Be careful about bragging or boasting about your new position, which will imply to some of your colleagues that you do not appreciate the sacrifices that many of your supervisors and colleagues likely made for you.[32] In addition to telling your supervisor in person that you are leaving, you may be required to write a formal resignation. Write a brief, warm, and appreciative letter (see Figure 16.19).

**LO16.12** Explain etiquette for leaving an organization with grace and foresight.

**FIGURE 16.19**

Resignation Letter

**BETTER HORIZONS CREDIT UNION**
Est. 1937

May 14, 2017

Christine Russo, President and CEO
Better Horizons Loop, Pescaloosa, FL 91214

RE: Notice of Resignation

Dear Christine:

I am writing to inform you of my resignation from Better Horizons Credit Union effective May 31, 2017.

Leaving BHCU is an extremely difficult decision. Please accept my deep gratitude for the many professional opportunities you have provided me.

Most of all, I will miss the people of BHCU. When we say the "Better Horizons family," we are not exaggerating.

Best wishes to you and the credit union for continued growth and success!

Sincerely,

*Haniz Zogby*

Haniz Zogby
Better Horizons Credit Union

This concise letter provides all needed components: a resignation date and an expression of goodwill.

Expression of goodwill and gratitude is professional, warm, and sincere.

# COMMUNICATION Q&A

## CONVERSATIONS WITH CURRENT BUSINESS PROFESSIONALS

**Peter Cardon: What do you think are some ways students can make themselves stand out in the job application process?**

**Nancy Vaccaro:** The application process is your opportunity to promote your unique attributes and emphasize what sets you apart from other applicants. Think about how best to communicate what relevant skills you can bring to an organization. Employers are looking for applicants who are motivated for success, so be sure to highlight work that you've done in and out of the classroom setting such as internships, volunteer jobs, or class projects. While it may sound basic, you should always be thorough, neat, and pay attention to detail on the application. Avoid using overarching, generic comments such as "open to any position." As you start your job search, take a focused approach and target your application to a specific job or position.

**PC: What do you think are some keys to developing an effective résumé? What are some of the most common mistakes you see?**

**NV:** Employers typically spend just a few seconds reviewing a résumé. This means you have a very small window of opportunity to catch and hold the attention of a recruiter and, ultimately, a hiring manager. Be mindful of typos and grammatical errors. Provide as much detail as possible without being too wordy. Generally, one to two pages for your résumé is acceptable. Always provide current contact information, and stay clear of listing an email address that runs the risk of reading and sounding inappropriate or unprofessional. Make your résumé visually appealing by steering clear of fonts that clutter the page. Take a thoughtful approach and speak not only to what you've accomplished, but how you did it. As a hiring manager, I look for candidates who are motivated, forward-thinkers, and not just "doers."

As you tailor your résumé, use keywords and terminology that are directly related to the job for which you're applying. It's not uncommon for organizations to use talent management or recruiting tools that parse résumés and search for keywords electronically. But do this with care! If you're unable to demonstrate the correlation between the keywords and your own work experience and skill set, employers will know very quickly that you are not a fit for their needs or their organizations. With all this said, it's just as important to add some personality to your résumé and make it interesting so it doesn't read too much like a job description. Consider your résumé as a marketing tool or an advertisement of your skills, accomplishments, and achievements. What sets YOU apart from all other candidates? Highlight your unique tangible and intangible qualities and transferable skills. How would you apply them? How can they add value to an organization? You're branding yourself as the type of employee that employers want on their team and in their organization.

**PC: What do you think are some keys to an effective job interview? What are some of the most common mistakes you see?**

**NV:** Prepare for the interview in advance by researching and familiarizing yourself with the company and the job description. I've often interviewed candidates who weren't able to tell me what they knew about the company and couldn't articulate their understanding of the job. In the eyes of prospective employers, this is a sign that you don't care and you aren't taking your job search seriously. You should come prepared with a list of questions to ask at the end of the interview as well as questions you anticipate will be asked of you. Don't be surprised if you're asked to provide real examples of items that you've listed as accomplishments on your résumé. Stay engaged, pay attention in the interview, and take notes, as some of your prepared questions will inevitably be answered in the course of the interview, and others will arise. Lastly, always demonstrate your level of professionalism and interest in the job by sending a thank-you note or email to all those you've interviewed with.

**PC: What is the most important piece of advice for business students in gaining an entry-level business position?**

**NV:** Network! Network! Network! Build your network through social media tools like LinkedIn, Facebook, and Twitter. Understand your career goals, stay positive, and have confidence in your abilities! Good luck!

***Nancy Vaccaro*** *is a senior HR manager at NBCUniversal. She has held HR management positions for about 20 years at The Walt Disney Company, Mattel, and Easton-Bell Sports.*

Courtesy of Nancy Vaccaro

# Chapter Takeaway for *Employment Communications*

**LO16.1 Identify your key selling points for the job application process. (pp. 498–499)**

Effective résumés, cover letters, and interviews enhance **your personal credibility.**

| | | |
|---|---|---|
| It shows **competence** when you demonstrate skills and/or knowledge to complete work tasks. | It shows **caring** when you demonstrate the ability to manage effective workplace relationships. | It shows **character** when you demonstrate that you uphold high professional norms and standards. |

See *skills and attributes that reflect competence, caring, and character* in Table 16.1.

See an *example of a self-inventory* in Figure 16.1.

**LO16.2 Evaluate the primary needs of employers for positions of interest. (pp. 499–500)**

See an *example of analyzing a job posting for key needs* in Figure 16.2.

**LO16.3 Set up the message structure for résumés and cover letters. (pp. 500–503)**

| Components of Chronological Résumés | |
|---|---|
| • Name block<br>• Summary of qualifications *or* Career objective (optional) | • Education<br>• Work experience<br>• Additional information |

| Components of Functional Résumés | |
|---|---|
| • Name block<br>• Summary of qualifications *or* Career summary | • Skills<br>• Additional information |

**Audience**: Identify the abilities and attributes that add value to employers.

**Information**: Identify your career interests and job-related abilities and attributes.

**Message**: Match your abilities and attributes to the needs of employers.

**LO16.4 Highlight your qualifications with effective tone, style, and design. (pp. 503–509)**

| Principles of Effective Résumés | |
|---|---|
| • Emphasize accomplishments with action verbs.<br>• Quantify accomplishments where possible.<br>• Position your most important contributions first.<br>• Group and label information to increase ease of reading.<br>• Remove irrelevant details. | • Avoid buzzwords and jargon.<br>• Be exact and avoid any errors.<br>• Group and label information to improve ease of reading.<br>• Format to distinguish pieces of information.<br>• Select a simple yet visually appealing layout. |

See *examples of action words* in Tables 16.2 and 16.3; *quantifying accomplishments* in Table 16.4; *positioning contributions* in Table 16.5; *removing unnecessary details* in Table 16.6; *avoiding clichés* in Table 16.7; *proofreading for typos and misspellings* in Table 16.8; *grouping and labeling* in Table 16.9; and *formatting to distinguish key pieces of information* in Table 16.10.

**Tone**: Tell the story of your abilities and attributes with tempered enthusiasm and confidence. Avoid a me-first mentality.

**Style**: Display an action orientation and ensure consistency of facts throughout your employment application.

**Design**: Make sure that employers can pick out key pieces of information to understand your story quickly.

**LO16.5 Create chronological and functional résumés to highlight your key selling points. (pp. 509–514)**

See *examples of ineffective and effective chronological résumés* in Figures 16.4, 16.5, 16.6, and 16.7.

See an *example of a functional résumé* in Figure 16.8.

**LO16.6 Use LinkedIn as part of the job search process and to network professionally. (pp. 515–518)**

| Tips for Using LinkedIn: | |
|---|---|
| • Provide a professional photo.<br>• Create a personalized URL.<br>• Complete the summary space.<br>• Use multimedia.<br>• Choose sections wisely. | • Manage your recommendations and endorsements strategically.<br>• Build a network of important connections<br>• Show some personality and be positive.<br>• Maintain a giver mentality.<br>• Stay active on LinkedIn. |

See an *examples of a LinkedIn profile* in Figure 16.9.

**LO16.7 Develop a list of references that will improve your employment prospects. (pp. 518–519)**

See an *example of a reference list* in Figure 16.10.

**LO16.8 Compose effective cover letters that highlight your key selling points. (pp. 520–523)**

| Components of Cover Letters |
|---|
| • Interest in position<br>• Match with position<br>• Call to action |

See *examples of ineffective and effective solicited cover letters* in Figures 16.11 and 16.12.

See an *example of an unsolicited referral cover letter* in Figure 16.13.

**LO16.9 Review your job application documents for effectiveness and fairness. (pp. 523–525)**

**Feedback**: Ask colleagues and clients what they would like you to change about your presentation.

**FAIR Test**: Focus on presenting factual information and being clear about impacts on others.

**Proofreading**: Make sure your slides, handouts, and other supplementary materials are attractive and error-free.

**LO16.10 Develop strategies for responding to common job interview questions. (pp. 525–531)**

See *common interview questions* in Table 16.11.

See *ineffective and effective responses to interview questions* in Table 16.12.

| Components of STAR Stories | |
|---|---|
| • Situation | • Actions |
| • Tasks | • Results |

See an *example of a STAR story* in Table 16.13.

See *examples of ineffective and effective questions by job candidates* in Table 16.14.

**LO16.11 Explain etiquette for following up after job interviews. (pp. 531–532)**

See an *example of a thank-you note following an interview* in Figure 16.15.

**LO16.12 Explain etiquette for leaving an organization with grace and foresight. (pp. 533–534)**

See an *example of a resignation letter* in Figure 16.17.

# Key Terms

abilities, 498
attributes, 498
chronological résumé, 509

functional résumé, 509
solicited cover letter, 521

STAR method, 529
unsolicited cover letter, 522

# Discussion Exercises

**16.1 Chapter Review Questions** (LO16.1 to LO16.12)

A. How can identifying your job interests, abilities, and attributes help you develop an effective résumé?

B. In what ways can you categorize your key abilities and attributes to project credibility?

C. What are some ways of identifying the key abilities and attributes employers are seeking for unfilled positions?

D. What are the benefits and drawbacks of chronological and functional résumés?

E. What strategies can you use to project competence and confidence but not arrogance in your job application messages?

F. What is the underlying purpose of grouping and labeling data on your résumé?

G. What strategies can you use to develop a reliable reference list for your job searches?

H. What are the key factors in appropriate etiquette for your job interview?

I. Explain how the STAR approach to answering interview questions can help you display your key abilities and attributes.

J. What are some principles to abide by when leaving a position?

**16.2 Using All Communication Channels in the Job Search Process** (LO16.2)

Terry J. Lundgren, CEO and president of Macy's, was asked, "[Do you have] any job-seeking advice for college grads?" Here's what he had to say:

> Use whatever contact you have to try to get your résumé read. That's the most important thing—just to get it in front of people. Because we're all flooded with, of course, thousands and thousands of résumés in a company of our size, and getting your résumé read is not an automatic. And so do what you can do to get it in front of the people who matter who will read it. It's not the CEO typically, by the way; it's the HR person or the head of recruiting or head of training or whatever. Third, don't stop there. Don't just do it online, because it's easy to do it online. Do it online and then put it in an envelope and send it to the top company that you're interested in pursuing. And then follow up with a phone call, and talk to the assistant and say: "I just want to make sure that my résumé's getting read. I'm very interested in your company, and it's really important

to me. And I just want to know—can you give me advice?— is there anything that I can do to get my résumé in front of your boss?" Whatever you have to say, just to show the most important thing—that you're hungry. And to convince them, maybe you use a little of your acting skills. And I'll probably relate it to college dating—you know, use a little, "I'm really interested in you"—to say: "This is the company I want to work for. Yours is the company that I want to work for." And then once you get, hopefully, more than one opportunity, you're back in charge to say, "Where do I want to go and where do I want to work."[33]

Based on Lundgren's comments and your own perspectives, respond to the following questions:

A. Explain what Lundgren means by showing "you're hungry" for a position. Describe ways in which you can show hunger in a positive way.

B. What does he suggest about the effectiveness of relying exclusively on electronic means to submit job applications? What combination of communication channels do you consider optimal for gaining a job of interest?

C. He suggests that you should view the process like dating. In what ways does this analogy make sense to you? Explain.

**16.3 Identifying What Employers Are Seeking** (LO16.2)

Anne Berkowitch, co-founder and former chief executive of SelectMinds, discussed how her approach to hiring new employees has evolved:

> I started out recruiting for skills that I knew I didn't have and I didn't understand intuitively. I was putting way too much emphasis on skills and background and what I could see on paper. I wasn't trusting myself to evaluate whether these were the right people. I'd say I went through a spate where I made the wrong hires. Then I said, "I have to do this differently, and I'm just going to trust my instinct about the right kind of person to bring onto this team." I had to hire people who had skills and experience I needed, but who they were as a person played a much bigger role in what I looked for. The people I want to hire share a number of characteristics. They're smart. They're problem solvers. They're good at what they do. They are honest with themselves, which to me is extremely important. If you're not honest with yourself, then too much of your energy goes toward managing what you're saying to everybody else, rather than what you should be doing. They are curious and they want to do things outside their comfort zone. They're passionate—it

doesn't matter about what. It could be about theater. It could be about your kids. The other quality is they're people who want to be part of a group to build something. They're not looking for title. They're really motivated by coming on board. At this point, I feel like I could talk to somebody for five minutes and have a good sense of whether they have those qualities, and I'll be right 85 percent of the time.[34]

A. Explain what you think Berkowitch means when she says she started prioritizing hiring employees for "who they were as a person" more so than by their skills and experience?

B. What attributes does she look for in particular when hiring new employees? Are these attributes that you can demonstrate on paper? Explain.

C. She says she can judge whether a person fits her company within five minutes. Do you believe that hiring managers can do this reliably? Assuming that you have only five minutes to demonstrate your value to a hiring manager, what would you want to stand out about yourself?

# Evaluation Exercises

**16.4 Interviewing with a Hiring Manager about Job Application Best Practices** (LO16.1, LO16.2)

Contact a hiring manager (consider any person you know who is involved in the hiring process) and arrange a time to interview that person for 30 minutes to one hour. Ask the hiring manager about the following related to hiring new employees:

A. Most common mistakes on résumés and cover letters.

B. Aspects in résumés and cover letters that make successful job candidates stand out.

C. Keys to successful interviews.

D. Common mistakes at job interviews.

E. Appropriate ways to follow up after interviews.

After the interview, write a two-page report detailing best practices for successfully navigating the job application process and getting a job. Tailor your report to undergraduate students who are seeking entry-level professional positions.

**16.5 Getting Feedback on Your Résumé and Cover Letter** (LO16.3, LO16.4, LO16.5, LO16.8, LO16.9)

To determine how well you are promoting your selling points (your two or three key abilities and two or three key attributes), do the following in this order:

A. Write down your key selling points.

B. Create your résumé and cover letter to highlight these key selling points.

C. Without providing what you believe are your key selling points, ask a trusted classmate/colleague/professor to review your résumé and cover letter. Specifically, ask your peer to answer the following questions:

1. Based on these documents, what do you think my key selling points are? Ask your peer to mention abilities or skills and attributes or traits.

2. Do my key selling points stand out clearly? Do you think my résumé and cover letter provide a consistent message about my selling points?

3. What suggestions do you have for me to improve these documents?

After getting responses from your peer, answer the following questions:

A. What did your peer say were your key selling points? What did your peer say about how well your selling points stood out?

B. How closely aligned were your peer's observations with what you intended to be your key selling points?

C. Based on your peer's observations, what modifications should you make to your résumé and cover letter to better highlight your selling points?

**16.6 Getting Feedback on Your Résumé from a Professional in Your Desired Discipline/Industry** (LO16.3, LO16.4, LO16.5, LO16.9)

Find a professional in the discipline and/or industry that interests you. Ask this person to review your résumé and give you feedback about the following: (a) strength of your résumé in gaining the position you seek; (b) advice for improving the résumé; (c) areas of your résumé that may appear less credible or perhaps even exaggerated; and (d) advice for increasing career opportunities. Turn in the following:

A. Revised résumé.

B. Document detailing what you learned from the business professional and what changes you made to your résumé as a result.

**16.7 Getting Feedback on Your Résumé from Classmates** (LO16.3, LO16.4, LO16.5, LO16.9)

Form a group of three to four classmates. Read one another's résumés, spending three to five minutes per résumé. As you read, focus on how well the person communicates key abilities and attributes. Debrief by explaining the following:

A. Key abilities and attributes communicated by the résumé.

B. Two or three areas in which the résumé could be improved.

C. Any areas in the résumé that seem less substantiated than others.

Individually, write two to three paragraphs about the comments and advice you received from the other members in your group.

# Application Exercises

**16.8 Evaluating Your Key Selling Points** (LO16.1)

Using Table 16.1 and Figure 16.1 as guides, do the following:

A. State your career goals.

B. Describe the three or four abilities and three or four attributes that you want to stand out most prominently in your job application package. Why do you want these skills and attributes to stand out?

C. Name the two or three abilities and attributes you most want to develop.

**16.9 Analyzing a Job Announcement of Interest to You** (LO16.2)

Find a job announcement for a position of interest to you. Using Figure 16.2 as a guide, do the following:

A. Group and categorize the key abilities and attributes that are being sought.

B. Describe your fit with these abilities and attributes.

C. Explain how you can compensate for abilities or attributes that you have not yet fully developed.

**16.10 Using Action Words** (LO16.4)

Using Tables 16.3, 16.4, and 16.5 as guides, do the following:

A. Choose ten of the action words and create statements that you could use on your résumé with your accomplishments.

B. Make five statements of accomplishments that you could place on your résumé that include quantification (e.g., increased sales by 12 percent).

**16.11 Creating a Résumé** (LO16.3, LO16.4, LO16.5)

Create a perfectly polished résumé.

**16.12 Creating Functional and Chronological Résumés** (LO16.3, LO16.4, LO16.5)

Create two versions of your résumé—a chronological and a functional résumé. In addition to these two documents, create a separate document that describes the advantages and disadvantages of using each type.

**16.13 Creating a Reference List** (LO16.7)

Create a reference list with five individuals whom you could trust to provide good professional endorsements of your abilities. Provide all contact information and a brief statement about how each person knows you.

**16.14 Creating a Cover Letter** (LO16.8)

Choose a job announcement that interests you. Write a cover letter that is addressed to the contact person/organization in this announcement.

**16.15 Telling Stories with the STAR Method** (LO16.10)

Write down how you would answer one of the following interview questions using the STAR method: (a) Can you tell me about a challenge you overcame at work? (b) Can you give me an example of how you showed leadership at work? or (c) Can you tell me about one of your recent successes at work? You can substitute school experiences for work experiences if you'd like.

**16.16 Writing a Thank-You Note** (LO16.11)

Choose a job position that interests you. Assume you have just completed the job interview. Write a thank-you message that you think appropriately expresses gratitude and improves your chances in the hiring process.

**16.17 Writing a Resignation Letter** (LO16.12)

Assume that you will be resigning from a job (you can use a current/past position). Write a message that states when you will leave, shows your appreciation, and ensures goodwill with the employer in the future.

# Language Mechanics Check

**16.18 Review all rules in Appendix A about punctuation, number usage, and grammar. Then, rewrite each sentence to make all needed corrections.**

A. Please except my application for the Web Developer position (Job ID#4392) on your companies website.

B. For the past 4 years I have helped develop and run several websites.

C. Before I describe some of my technical abilities I want to describe the success of these websites.

D. In my current position at Better Horizons Credit Union the marketing team and several web developers have worked on a web strategy, to attract younger members.

E. I've been a significant part of these efforts to match a strategy to a web design, improve the overall aesthetic appeal of the web page and identify strategies to improve our place in internet searches.

F. I was able to oversee some design changes on the *Members* section of the website

G. After applying these design changes the web traffic has grown by 18% in the last month.

H. In each of these web development projects, I've gathered input from all people who will use the websites; managers, colleagues, customers and prospects.

I. By getting this input, I can develop websites that are user-friendly, helpful and appealing.

J. I believe my primary strength as a web developer is to understand how the user experience impacts future use, of the website.

# Endnotes

1. KSA (Knowledge, Skills, Abilities) approach for federal jobs.

2. Society for Human Resource Management, "SHRM Poll: Interviewing Do's and Don'ts for Job Seekers," September 15, 2009, retrieved from *Society for Human Resource Management* website, www.shrm.org/Research/SurveyFindings/Articles/Pages/Interviewing-DosandDonts.aspx.

3. Society for Human Resource Management, "Networking Professionally: Employee Perspective," January 12, 2009, retrieved from *Society of Human Resource Management* website, www.shrm.org/Research/SurveyFindings/Articles/Documents/OEnetworking.pdf.

4. Accountemps, "Survey Shows Longer Resumes Now More Acceptable," March 20, 2007, www.accountemps.com/PressRoom?id=1840 (accessed January 10, 2010).

5. Accountemps, "The Devil Is in the 'Resume' Details: Typos or Grammatical Errors Most Common Resume Mistake, Survey Shows," March 31, 2005, accountemps.rhi.mediaroom.com/index.php?s=189&item=250 (accessed January 10, 2010).

6. Society for Human Resource Management, *SHRM Survey Findings: Résumés, Cover Letters and Interviews* (Alexandria, VA: SHRM, April 28, 2014).

7. Accountemps, "Most Wanted: 'People' People: Survey Shows Interpersonal Skills Can Trump Technical Knowledge in Job Search," October 29, 2009, http://accountemps.rhi.mediaroom.com/index.php?s=189&item=863 (accessed January 10, 2010).

8. Accountemps, "More Than Half of Executives Surveyed Spend Five Minutes or Less Screening a Resume," January 17, 2001, http://accountemps.rhi.mediaroom.com/index.php?s=189&item=328 (accessed January 10, 2010).

9. Accountemps, "Have a Keen Eye for Derail," July 14, 2009, www.accountemps.com/PressRoom?id=2491 (accessed November 20, 2010).

10. Accountemps, "Form over Function: Three-Quarters of Executives Surveyed Prefer Chronological Resumes from Job Seekers," www.accountemps.com/PressRoom?id=2527 (accessed January 10, 2010).

11. Nicole Amare and Alan Manning, "Writing for the Robot: How Employer Search Tools Have Influenced Résumé Rhetoric and Ethics," *Business Communication Quarterly* 72, no. 1 (2009): 35–60.

12. Nancy Schullery, Linda M. Ickes, and Stephen E. Schullery, "Employer Preferences for Résumés and Cover Letters," *Business Communication Quarterly* 72, no. 2 (2009): 163–176.

13. Society for Human Resource Management, *SHRM Survey Findings*.

14. Accountemps, "Put In a Good Word for Me," August 13, 2003, www.accountemps.com/PressRoom?id=367 (accessed January 10, 2010).

15. Kim Isaacs, "Get Your References Together for Your Job Search," retrieved October 6, 2011, from http://career-advice.monster.com/job-search/getting-started/prepare-your-references/article.aspx.

16. Therese Droste, "Help Your References Help You," retrieved October 6, 2011, from http://career-advice.monster.com/job-search/getting-started/Help-Your-References-Help-You/article.aspx.

17. Society for Human Resource Management, *SHRM Survey Findings*.

18. Kim Isaacs, "Cover Letters to Recruiters," Monster.com Advice blog, retrieved January 20, 2011, from http://career-advice.monster.com/resumes-cover-letters/cover-letter-tips/cover-letters-to-recruiters/article.aspx.

19. JoAnn S. Lublin, "The Keys to Unlocking Your Most Successful Career," *The Wall Street Journal Career Journal* [online], July 6, 2010.

20. Kim Isaacs, "Cold Cover Letters," Monster.com Advice blog, retrieved January 20, 2011, from http://career-advice.monster.com/resumes-cover-letters/Cover-Letter-Tips/Cold-Cover-Letters/article.aspx.

21. Society for Human Resource Management, "SHRM Poll: Interviewing Do's and Don'ts for Job Seekers."

22. Kathy Gurchiek, "Dress to Impress, Not Stress, the Hiring Manager," *Society for Human Resource Management HR News* [online], November 1, 2010.

23. Society for Human Resource Management, "SHRM Poll: Interviewing Do's and Don'ts for Job Seekers."

24. Eve Tahmincioglu, "Avoid 'the Seven Deadly Sins of Interviewing,'" August, 29, 2010, MSNBC Careers blog, retrieved January 10, 2011, from www.msnbc.msn.com/id/38882416/ns/business-careers.

25. Harrison Barnes, "Use Personal Stories to Connect with an Employer and Get a Job," Harrison Barnes blog, retrieved January 10, 2011, from www.aharrisonbarnes.com/use-stories-to-get-a-job-and-connect-with-an-employer/.

26. Tory Johnson, "Land That Job: What Interviewers Really Want You to Ask Them," April 19, 2010, retrieved October 7, 2011, from http://abcnews.go.com/GMA/JobClub/questions-job-interview/story?id=10409243.

27. Accountemps, "Most Executives OK with Applicants Asking about Compensation by Second Interview," March 18, 2009, http://accountemps.rhi.mediaroom.com/index.php?s=189&item=165 (accessed January 10, 2010).

28. Accountemps, "Thanks, But No Thanks: Survey Shows Thank-You Notes Influence Hiring Decisions, but Only Half of Candidates Send Them," August 9, 2007, http://accountemps.rhi.mediaroom.com/index.php?s=189&item=203 (accessed January 10, 2010).

29. Mariotti et al., *SHRM Survey Findings: Résumés, Cover Letters and Interviews*.

30. Beverly Langford, *The Etiquette Edge: The Unspoken Rules for Business Success* (New York: American Management Association, 2005).

31. Adam Bryant, "Knock-Knock: It's the C.E.O.," *Corner Office* (blog), *The New York Times*, April 11, 2009, retrieved from www.nytimes.com/2009/04/12/business/12corner.html.

32.  Adam Bryant, "Learn to Lead from the Back of the Boat," *Corner Office* (blog), *The New York Times,* September 4, 2010, retrieved from www.nytimes.com/2010/09/05/business/ 05corner.html.

33.  Adam Bryant, "A C.E.O. Must Decide Who Swims," *Corner Office* (blog), *The New York Times,* August 22, 2009, retrieved from www.nytimes.com/2009/08/23/business/23corner. ready.html.

34.  Adam Bryant, "Learn to Lead from the Back of the Boat," *Corner Office* (blog), *The New York Times,* September 4, 2010, retrieved from www.nytimes.com/2010/09/05/business/ 05corner.html.

# Punctuation, Number Usage, and Grammar

This appendix includes rules that cover many common writing issues. For a complete review of language mechanics guidelines, consult a comprehensive guidebook such as the *Gregg Reference Manual*. Also, use the online resources, including exercises and assessments.

## Overview of Terms Used in This Appendix

**Nouns** are words or phrases that refer to persons, places, objects, qualities, or activities.

**Subjects** are nouns that are the primary topics of a sentence. The subject determines the verb form used in the sentence (see rule G2).

**Verbs** are words or phrases that express action or existence.

**Predicates** are verb phrases that in combination with a subject make a complete sentence.

**Adjectives** are words or phrases that modify nouns.

**Adverbs** are words or phrases that modify adjectives, verbs, or adverbs.

**Prepositions** are words that show the relationships between nouns (e.g., *at, in, by, from, with*).

**Coordinating conjunctions** connect words, phrases, or clauses; examples include *and, but, or,* and *nor*.

**Clauses** contain a subject and a predicate. **Independent clauses** express a complete thought and can stand alone, whereas **dependent clauses** cannot stand alone.

**Participles** are words that share characteristics of verbs and adjectives. *Present participles* end in *ing*; *past participles* end in *ed*; and *perfect participles* are a combination of a form of the verb "to have" and a past participle.

## Punctuation and Formatting

### Commas

Commas have two functions: (1) to set off nonessential expressions that break the flow of a sentence and (2) to separate items in a sentence so that their relationships to one another are clear. *Nonessential* expressions, if removed, do not alter the meaning of the sentence or make the sentence incomplete. Table A.1 lists ten key rules related to commas, with examples. Each rule in this section is identified by a letter (C, for comma) and a number.

**TABLE A.1**

Comma Rules

| Rules | Examples |
|---|---|
| **C1.** Use commas to distinguish essential from nonessential information (essential expressions do not require commas; nonessential expressions do require commas). | ✔ Sergey Brin and Larry Page, <u>who were attending Stanford at the time</u>, developed the initial technology for Google searches. ***Explanation:* The *who* clause is nonessential because a specific person is mentioned; the information does not narrow down who the people are.** |
| | ✔ Graduate students <u>who were attending Stanford University at the time</u> developed the initial technology for Google searches. ***Explanation:* The *who* clause is essential because it further specifies, or narrows down, who the students are—students *at Stanford*.** |
| | ✔ Google's initial public offering <u>occurred in 2004, the same year that</u> Google developed a multiyear alliance with AOL Europe. ***Explanation:* A comma is required after the year 2004 since the following expression does not further specify which year and is thus nonessential.** |
| | ✔ Google's initial public offering <u>occurred in the same year that</u> Google developed a multiyear alliance with AOL Europe. ***Explanation:* A comma is not required because the that clause further specifies which year and is thus an essential expression.** |
| **C2.** Use commas to set off interrupting expressions. | ✔ Larry, <u>rather than Sergey</u>, was listed as the inventor on the patent for Google's original search mechanism. ***Explanation:* The underlined expression interrupts the flow of the sentence from subject to verb.** |
| | ✔ Eric Schmidt, <u>the CEO at Google since 2001</u>, was previously Chairman of the Board and CEO at Novell. ***Explanation:* The underlined expression is an appositive and interrupts the flow of the sentence from subject to verb.** |
| | ✔ Google's largest market, <u>which accounts for 47 percent of revenues</u>, is the United States. ***Explanation:* The underlined expression provides further but nonessential information and interrupts the flow of the sentence from subject to verb.** |
| | ✔ Google offers a variety of applications, <u>such as Google Docs and Google Calendar</u>. ***Explanation:* The underlined expression is additional and nonessential information.** |
| | ✔ Google, <u>in my opinion</u>, is the best technology company to work for. ***Explanation:* Independent thoughts interrupt the flow of the sentence and require commas.** |
| | ✔ Google Chrome, <u>if you're looking for an open-source web browser</u>, may be a fit for you. ***Explanation:* Dependent clauses in the middle of the sentence must be set off by commas.** |
| | ✔ Double-digit annual sales growth at Google during the past three years, <u>in spite of the recession and increased competition</u>, demonstrates the strong demand for Google products and services. ***Explanation:* This nonessential prepositional phrase in the middle of the sentence interrupts the flow of the sentence.** |
| | **Note:** Many clauses that require commas in the beginning or middle of a sentence do not require one when they are at the end of the sentence. |
| | ✔ Google Chrome may be a fit for you <u>if you're looking for an open-source web browser</u>. ***Explanation:* This dependent clause at the end of the sentence does not interrupt the flow of the sentence, so no comma is needed.** |
| | ✔ Double-digit annual sales growth at Google during the past three years demonstrates the strong demand for Google products and services <u>in spite of the recession and increased competition</u>. ***Explanation:* This prepositional phrase at the end of the sentence does not interrupt the flow of the sentence, so no comma is needed.** |

**TABLE A.1**

*(Continued)*

| Rules | Examples |
|---|---|
| **C3.** Use a comma following a transitional expression. | ✔ <u>Also</u>, Google's social networking website has gained little acceptance in the United States. ***Explanation:*** **Transitional expressions such as *also* help readers relate sentences to one another. Transitional expressions are followed by commas.** |
| | ✔ <u>As a result</u>, Google purchased a new mobile display ad provider to increase its revenues in mobile advertising. ***Explanation:*** **Transitional expressions such as *as a result* help readers relate sentences to one another. Transitional expressions are followed by commas.** |
| **C4.** Use a comma between two independent clauses separated by *and*, *but*, *or*, or *nor*. | ✔ Sergey Brin is currently the President of Technology, <u>and</u> Larry Page is currently the President of Products. ***Explanation:*** **Two independent clauses are separated by a comma and coordinating conjunction.** |
| | **Exception:** When an introductory expression applies to both independent clauses, a comma is not placed between the independent clauses. |
| | ✔ Since Google's organizational restructuring in 2001, Sergey Brin has served as the President of Technology <u>and</u> Larry Page has served as the President of Products. ***Explanation:*** **A comma is not placed between the independent clauses because the introductory expression applies to both of them.** |
| | **Exception:** Short compound sentences often do not require a comma (generally less than 12 to 13 words). |
| | Sergey is in charge of technology <u>and</u> Larry is in charge of products. ***Explanation:*** **This sentence is short (13 words) and is understood easily without a comma separating the two independent clauses.** |
| **C5.** Use commas in a series with three or more items. | ✔ Google's client services include <u>Google Toolbar, Google Chrome, and Google Pack</u>. ***Explanation:*** **Each of these three items in a series is separated from one another by a comma.** |
| | ✔ Google has developed an innovative culture by <u>setting up an informal work environment, providing the top incentives in the industry, and encouraging employees to spend 20 percent of their time on their own projects</u>. ***Explanation:*** **Each of the three items in the series is separated from one another by a comma.** |
| | ✔ Google spends far above industry averages in the following areas: <u>marketing, training, and research and development</u>. ***Explanation:*** **Each item in the series is separated by commas. Notice that *research and development* is a single item.** |
| **C6.** Use a comma between two independent adjectives preceding a noun. | ✔ Google has long been recognized as an <u>innovative, unconventional</u> company. ***Explanation: Innovative* and *unconventional* each independently modifies *company.*** |
| | **Note:** There are two quick ways to identify independent adjectives. First, if you can place the word *and* between the two adjectives without changing the meaning, then they are independent (innovative and unconventional). Second, if you can reverse the order of the adjectives without changing the meaning, then they are independent (unconventional, innovative). |

**TABLE A.1**

*(Continued)*

| Rules | Examples |
|---|---|
| **C7.** Use a comma after introductory expressions. | ✔ After Google had installed solar panels at Googleplex, it continued its environmental efforts by placing herds of goats around the campus so that mowing the lawns was not necessary. ***Explanation:* Commas are always placed after introductory dependent clauses.** |
| | ✔ By installing thousands of solar panels at Googleplex, Google showed its commitment to environmental causes. ***Explanation:* Commas are always placed after introductory participial phrases.** |
| | ✔ To show its commitment to environmental causes, Google has installed thousands of solar panels at Googleplex. ***Explanation:* Commas are always placed after introductory infinitive phrases.** |
| | ✔ Under the new set of corporate policies, Google will lease only LEED-certified buildings. ***Explanation:* Commas are placed after long (five or more words) introductory prepositional phrases.** |
| | <div align="center">**Common Exceptions***</div> |
| | Short introductory adverbs that explain *when* (e.g., next week), *how often* (e.g., frequently), *where* (e.g., at the office), or *why* (e.g., for this reason) do not require commas afterward. |
| | ✔ A few years ago Google became part of the public debate over network neutrality. ***Explanation:* An introductory adverb that expresses *when* does not require a comma.** |
| | ✔ Often the company issues public statements regarding its stand on this issue. ***Explanation:* An introductory adverb that expresses *how often* does not require a comma.** |
| | ✔ At Google the leadership team believes that users should have complete control over the content they view. ***Explanation:* An introductory adverb that expresses *where* does not require a comma.** |
| | ✔ For this reason Google supports network neutrality. ***Explanation:* An introductory adverb that expresses *why* does not require a comma.** |
| | Short (less than five words) introductory prepositional phrases that do not contain a verb, a transitional phrase, or an independent comment do not require commas. |
| | ✔ In the interview Google's CEO emphasized the company's commitment to network neutrality. ***Explanation:* A comma is not required because the introductory prepositional phrase is short (three words) and does not contain a verb, a transitional phrase, or an independent thought.** |
| | ✔ In the interview with Google's CEO, he emphasized the company's commitment to network neutrality. ***Explanation:* A comma is required because the introductory prepositional phrase is long (five or more words).** |
| | ✔ In the statement he explained that broadband carriers should not be allowed to control content. ***Explanation:* A comma is not required because the introductory prepositional phrase is short (three words) and does not contain a verb, a transitional phrase, or an independent thought.** |
| | ✔ In making this statement, he demonstrated Google's position that broadband carriers should not be allowed to control content. ***Explanation:* A comma is required. Though the introductory prepositional phrase is short (four words), it contains a verb.** |
| | *A lot of variation exists in how writers apply these exceptions. Many writers use commas after all introductory expressions to avoid analyzing each situation. |

**TABLE A.1**

*(Continued)*

| Rules | Examples |
|---|---|
| **C8.** Use commas in dates. | ✔ Tuesday, May 10 ***Explanation:* A comma separates a day and a date.**<br>✔ May 10, 2011 ***Explanation:* A comma separates a date and a year.**<br>✔ May 2011 ***Explanation:* A comma does not separate a month and a year.**<br>✔ Between May 10, 2011, and May 13, 2011, there were 13 billion Google searches. ***Explanation:* A comma follows a date-year combination in the middle of a sentence.** |
| **C9.** Use commas as needed for clarity. | ✘ <u>At the Googleplex campus</u> building engineers have identified several approaches to reducing carbon emissions. ***Explanation:* Although technically correct (*At the Googleplex campus* is a short introductory adverb), many readers will wonder what the subject of the sentence is. Is it *building engineers* or just *engineers*?**<br>✔ <u>At the Googleplex campus</u>, building engineers have identified several approaches to reducing carbon emissions. ***Explanation:* The comma between campus and building clearly shows that *building* modifies *engineers*.**<br>✘ <u>In 2010</u> 37 of Google's top employees left and took positions at Facebook. ***Explanation:* Although technically correct (*In 2010* is a short introductory adverb), readers may misunderstand or become momentarily confused with two sets of numbers placed next to one another.**<br>✔ <u>In 2010</u>, 37 of Google's top employees left and took positions at Facebook. ***Explanation:* A comma between the two numbers clarifies that they do not belong together.**<br>**Alternatively:** <u>In 2010 thirty-seven</u> of Google's top employees left and took positions at Facebook. ***Explanation:* Spelling out one of the numbers clarifies that the two numbers do not belong together.** |
| **C10.** Common misuses of commas. | ✘ <u>Google, provides</u> a number of inexpensive enterprise products. ***Explanation:* Commas do not separate subjects from verbs.**<br>✘ Google <u>provides, a number</u> of inexpensive enterprise products. ***Explanation:* Commas do not separate verbs from objects.**<br>✘ Google provides a number of <u>free, services</u>. ***Explanation:* Commas do not separate adjectives from nouns.**<br>✘ The <u>CEO, of Google</u> has prioritized the launch of enterprise products to compete directly with Microsoft. ***Explanation:* Commas do not separate related prepositional phrases.**<br>✘ Sergey Brin <u>is currently the President of Technology, and is a member of the board of directors</u>. ***Explanation:* Commas do not separate two predicates with a single subject.**<br>✘ <u>Sergey Brin is currently the President of Technology, Larry Page is currently the President of Products</u>. ***Explanation:* Commas do not separate two independent clauses not connected with a coordinating conjunction (this is called a *comma splice*).**<br>✘ Google's stock price rose rapidly, <u>after it went public</u>. ***Explanation:* Commas do not separate a dependent clause at the end of a sentence.**<br>✘ <u>To acquire On2 Technologies</u>, was a key move in improving Google's video compression capabilities. ***Explanation:* Commas do not separate infinitives that serve as subjects from verbs.**<br>✘ <u>Acquiring On2Technologies</u>, was a key move in improving Google's video compression capabilities. ***Explanation:* Commas do not separate gerunds that serve as subjects from their related verbs.**<br>✘ Google's <u>nearly, limitless</u> email service is free. ***Explanation:* Commas do not separate adverbs from adjectives.** |

**TABLE A.2**

Semicolon Rules

| Rules | Examples |
|---|---|
| **S1.** Use a semicolon between two closely related independent clauses omitting *and*, *but*, *or*, or *nor*. | ✔ Google's business model focuses on providing applications free of charge to users and receiving revenue through advertising; Microsoft's business model focuses on selling applications to users without the clutter of advertising. ***Explanation:* The semicolon separates two closely related independent clauses to emphasize their relatedness.**<br><br>**Alternatively:** Google's business model focuses on providing applications free of charge to users and receiving revenue through advertising. Microsoft's business model focuses on selling applications to users without the clutter of advertising. ***Explanation:* A period separates two independent clauses.**<br><br>✘ Google's business model focuses on providing applications free of charge to users and receiving revenue through advertising, Microsoft's business model focuses on selling applications to users without the clutter of advertising. ***Explanation:* A comma does not separate two independent clauses (unless connected by a coordinating conjunction). Using a comma in this way is called a comma splice.** |
| **S2.** Use a semicolon between two independent clauses separated by transitional expressions. | ✔ Google's business model focuses on providing applications free of charge to users and receiving revenue through advertising; on the other hand, Microsoft's business model focuses on selling applications to users without the clutter of advertising. ***Explanation:* Semicolons separate two independent clauses separated by a transitional expression.**<br><br>✔ Google offers more than 30 major products and services; however, Google derives 90 percent of its revenues through Google Web Search. ***Explanation:* Semicolons separate two independent clauses separated by a transitional expression.** |
| **S3.** Use semicolons between items in a series that contains internal commas. | ✔ Google's major offices in the United States are in Mountain View, California; New York City; and Seattle, Washington. ***Explanation:* Semicolons separate items that contain internal commas in a series.**<br><br>✔ The Google delegation includes Jeff Huber, Senior Vice President of Engineering; Omid Kordestani, Senior Advisor in the Office of the CEO; and Rachel Whetstone, Vice President of Public Policy and Communications. ***Explanation:* Semicolons separate items that contain internal commas in a series.** |
| **S4.** Use semicolons in a series of long dependent clauses. | ✔ Google's excellent brand recognition is due to a variety of factors, including that it accounts for 67 percent of the global search market; that it owns the popular online video service YouTube; and that, in spite of stiff competition, it maintains a dominant market share for webmail. ***Explanation:* Semicolons add clarity by separating long items in a series.** |

## Semicolons

One major use for semicolons is to emphasize the relatedness between two independent clauses (see Table A.2). In a series, semicolons also separate items that contain internal commas or that are particularly long. Each rule in this section is identified with a letter (S, for semicolon) and a number.

## Colons

Colons precede further explanations or elaborations. This rule is identified by letters (Co, for colon) and a number (see Table A.3).

**TABLE A.3**

Colons

| Rule | Examples |
|------|----------|
| **Co1.** Use a colon for further explanation or elaboration following an independent clause. | ✔ Google faces <u>two major challenges</u>: It lacks product integration and its profitability is weakened by major currency fluctuations. ***Explanation:*** **The colon separates a complete thought with an elaboration of *the two major challenges.*** |
| | ✔ Compared to other free webmail services, Gmail provides <u>several major benefits</u>: It provides more storage than any other major competitors, it contains a more efficient search-oriented interface, and it has a superior spam filter. ***Explanation:*** **The colon separates a complete thought with elaboration of the *several major benefits.*** |
| | ✔ Google Sites has limited control of <u>various web design tools: For example</u>: you are restricted in using HTML, CSS, and JavaScript. ***Explanation:*** **Independent clauses and related series are often separated by a colon and phrases such as for *example, such as,* and *namely.*** |
| | ✘ <u>Google's seven product groups are</u>: Google.com, applications, client, Google GEO, Android and Google Mobile, Google Checkout, and Google Labs. ***Explanation:*** **The underlined introductory expression is not an independent clause, so a colon is inappropriate. It separates the verb from the object of the sentence (see C10, above).** |
| | ✔ <u>Google's seven product groups are the following</u>: Google.com, applications, client, Google GEO, Android and Google Mobile, Google Checkout, and Google Labs. ***Explanation:*** **The underlined introductory expression is an independent clause, so a colon is appropriate.** |

**TABLE A.4**

Dashes and Hyphens

| | Symbol | When to Use |
|---|--------|-------------|
| Dash (also called em dash) | — | To take the place of commas, semicolons, colons, or parentheses to add emphasis. Should be used sparingly. Consists of two hyphens with no space on either side. |
| En dash (also called figure dash) | – | To separate a range of values, such as years or page numbers |
| Hyphen | - | To combine words (compound modifiers, some compounds) |

## Dashes and Hyphens

A dash is not the same as a hyphen; each has unique functions, and the two marks of punctuation should not be used in place of one another. A third, related mark is called an en dash. Table A.4 displays the widths and functions of hyphens, en dashes, and dashes.

The rules for dashes and hyphens are extensive, with many exceptions (see Table A.5). Consult a comprehensive style guidebook to ensure complete accuracy. Each rule in this table is identified with a letter (D, for dash; N, for en dash; and H, for hyphen) and a number.

**TABLE A.5**

## Dash and Hyphen Rules

| Rules | Examples |
|---|---|
| **D1.** Use dashes in place of commas for emphasis (often in pairs). | ✔ Google Translate—which supports 59 languages—allows you to translate passages into nearly any language you can imagine. ***Explanation:* Using dashes instead of commas highlights the additional information in a much stronger way.** |
| **D2.** Use a dash in place of a semicolon for emphasis (but not between two independent clauses). | ✔ Google Translate provides fairly good translation—that is, if you consider 70 to 75 percent accuracy as good. ***Explanation:* Substituting a semicolon with a dash emphasizes the closely related afterthought.** |
| **D3.** Use a dash in place of a colon for emphasis. | ✔ Google Translate provides poor translation for most Asian languages—especially Chinese, Japanese, and Korean. ***Explanation:* Substituting a dash for a colon highlights the elaboration in a much stronger way.** |
| **D4.** Use dashes in place of parentheses for emphasis. | ✔ WorldLingo—Google Translate's top competitor—provides the most accurate translation for most European languages. ***Explanation:* Substituting dashes for parentheses highlights the additional information in a much stronger way.** |
| **D5.** Use a dash to emphasize a single word. | ✔ Innovation—that's what Google is all about. ***Explanation:* This dash draws sharp attention to the term *innovation* and defines it as a central feature of Google culture.** |
| **D6.** Use a dash for repetitions and restatements. | ✔ Get a username now—before it's too late. ***Explanation:* The dash restates *now* to reinforce urgency.** |
| **D7.** Use a dash to summarize a preceding list. | ✔ Brazil, Russia, India, China—these countries are the future for market growth. ***Explanation:* This dash separates a series of items with a summary of what they are.** |
| **N1.** Use an en dash to connect numbers or other items in a range. | ✔ Google's headquarters are open for tours 10 a.m.–3:30 p.m. Monday–Friday. ***Explanation:* En dashes are used to separate a range of values, such as these ranges in hours and days.** |
| **H1.** Use a hyphen to connect adjectives that modify a noun. | ✔ Computer programmers have <u>high-pressure jobs</u>. ***Explanation:* An adjective phrase or clause in front of a noun is hyphenated.** |
| | ✘ Her computer programming job involves <u>high-pressure</u>. ***Explanation:* An adjective phrase or clause that does not precede a noun is not hyphenated.** |
| | ✔ Her computer programming job involves <u>high pressure</u>. ***Explanation:* An adjective phrase or clause that does not precede a noun is not hyphenated.** |
| | ✔ One of Google's <u>long-term objectives</u> is to rival Facebook with its social networking services. ***Explanation:* An adjective + noun combination in front of a noun is hyphenated.** |
| | ✔ Over the <u>long term</u> Google seeks to rival Facebook in the area of social networking. ***Explanation:* An adjective + noun combination that does not precede a noun is not hyphenated.** |
| | ✔ The <u>one-way road</u> in the Googleplex campus passes through three parks. ***Explanation:* A compound that includes a number or letter in front of a noun is hyphenated.** |
| | ✔ The road that passes through the Googleplex is <u>one way</u>. ***Explanation:* A compound that includes a number or letter and does not precede a noun is not hyphenated.** |
| | ✔ Larry Page is one of the most <u>well-known business executives</u> in the world. ***Explanation:* An adverb + participle combination in front of a noun is hyphenated.** |
| | ✔ Larry Page is <u>well known</u> around the world for his leadership in the technology business. ***Explanation:* An adverb + participle combination that does not precede a noun is not hyphenated.** |

**TABLE A.5**

(*Continued*)

| Rules | Examples |
|---|---|
| | ✔ Google Docs provides an <u>easier-than-ever approach</u> to team writing. **Explanation: A comparative phrase that includes the word *than* and that precedes a noun is hyphenated.** |
| | ✔ Google Docs makes team writing <u>easier than ever</u>. **Explanation: A comparative phrase that includes the word *than* and that follows a noun is not hyphenated.** |
| | ✔ Larry and Sergey's <u>agreed-upon plan</u> was to sell off Google so that they could focus on their academic studies. **Explanation: A participle + adverb combination in front of a noun is hyphenated.** |
| | ✔ Larry and Sergey had <u>agreed upon</u> a plan that would allow them to sell Google and continue their academic studies. **Explanation: A participle + adverb combination that does not precede a noun is not hyphenated.** |
| | ✔ Google executives have adopted a <u>wait-and-see mentality</u> as far as developing a new social networking platform. **Explanation: A verb + verb (often joined by *and* or *or*) combination in front of a noun is hyphenated.** |
| | ✔ Google executives will <u>wait and see</u> how the market emerges before committing more resources to developing a new social networking platform. **Explanation: A verb + verb (often joined by *and* or *or*) combination that is not in front of a noun is not hyphenated.** |
| | ✔ The <u>break-even point</u> is around sales of $4.3 billion. **Explanation: A verb + adverb combination in front of a noun is hyphenated.** |
| | ✔ We will <u>break even</u> when we reach sales of $4.3 billion. **Explanation: A verb + adverb combination that does not precede a noun is not hyphenated.** |
| | ✔ She sent a <u>thank-you note</u> to each of the board members for their time and contributions. **Explanation: A verb + noun combination in front of a noun is hyphenated.** |
| | ✔ I want to <u>thank you</u> for your time and contributions. **Explanation: A verb + noun combination that does not precede a noun is not hyphenated.** |
| | ✔ Google has made <u>across-the-board cuts</u>. **Explanation: Common phrases used to modify a noun are hyphenated.** |
| | ✔ Google will make cuts <u>across the board</u>. **Explanation: Common phrases that do not precede a noun are not hyphenated.** |
| **H2.** Use hyphens for particular kinds of compound adjectives as described here. | ✔ We take a <u>research-based approach</u> to marketing. **Explanation: A noun + participle combination is always hyphenated.** |
| | ✔ Our approach to marketing is <u>research-based</u>. **Explanation: A noun + participle combination is always hyphenated.** |
| | ✔ We have a <u>long-standing commitment</u> to net neutrality. **Explanation: An adjective + participle combination is always hyphenated.** |
| | ✔ Our commitment to net neutrality is <u>long-standing</u>. **Explanation: An adjective + participle combination is always hyphenated.** |
| | ✔ <u>High-priced products</u> are not part of Google's business model. **Explanation: An adjective + noun + *ed* combination is always hyphenated.** |
| | ✔ Google's business model does not involve any products that are <u>high-priced</u>. **Explanation: An adjective + noun + *ed* combination is always hyphenated.** |
| | ✔ <u>Price-conscious customers</u> tend to use Google Docs rather than Microsoft Office. **Explanation: A noun + adjective combination is always hyphenated.** |
| | ✔ Most customers who choose Google Docs over Microsoft Office are <u>price-conscious</u>. **Explanation: A noun + adjective combination is always hyphenated.** |

**TABLE A.6**

Quotation Mark Rules

| Rules | Examples |
|---|---|
| **Q1.** Use quotation marks to enclose direct quotations. | ✔ As Larry Page stated, "I'm excited about our opportunities to make a big difference in people's lives through technology." ***Explanation:*** **The quotation marks surround the *exact statement* made by Larry.** |
| | ✘ Larry Page stated that "he's excited about opportunities to make a difference in people's lives through technology." ***Explanation:*** **Indirect statements typically begin with *that* and paraphrase a person's statements.** |
| **Q2.** Use quotation marks to indicate the exact words of a source or speaker. | ✔ Larry Page said that Google's technologies "make a big difference in people's lives." ***Explanation:*** **The quotation marks indicate that these are exact words and not paraphrased.** |
| | ✔ Larry and Sergey often say that their ultimate goal is to create the "perfect search engine." ***Explanation:*** **The quotation marks indicate that these are exact words and not paraphrased.** |
| **Q3.** Use quotation marks to enclose titles of articles, presentations, and speeches. | ✔ Randall Stross discussed the culture of education at Google in his recent article "What Is Google's Secret Weapon? An Army of Ph.D.'s." ***Explanation:*** **Quotation marks surround the name of an article.** |
| | ✔ Larry Page's speech, "Don't Be Evil," at the annual convention revealed his basic philosophy about developing products and services for customers. ***Explanation:*** **Quotation marks surround the name of a speech.** |

## Quotation Marks

Quotation marks are used to display direct quotations, exact words, and some titles. Each rule in Table A.6 is identified by a letter (Q, for quotation) and a number.

## Italics

Italics are used to emphasize words and phrases, highlight definitions, and set apart some titles. Alternatively, writers sometimes use underlining in place of italics. Each rule in Table A.7 is identified by a letter (I, for italic) and a number.

**TABLE A.7**

Rules for Italics

| Case | Examples |
|---|---|
| **I1.** Use italics to emphasize a word or phrase. | ✔ The misspelled term *googol* became the name of the company. ***Explanation:*** **The word *googol* is emphasized by use of italics.** |
| | ✔ *To google it* has become part of everyday language much the way *to xerox it* was an everyday phrase in the 1980s. ***Explanation: To google it* and *to xerox it* are italicized to highlight particular terms.** |
| **I2.** Use italics for formal definition. | ✔ The term *cloud computing* refers to using remote servers hosted on the Internet, rather than local servers or personal computers, to manage and process data. ***Explanation:*** **Terms that are formally defined are typically italicized as is the case with *cloud computing*.** |
| **I3.** Use italics for titles of books, newspapers, and magazines. | ✔ Larry and Sergey are featured nearly once each month in *The Wall Street Journal*. ***Explanation: The Wall Street Journal* is a newspaper, so it is italicized.** |
| | ✘ Reports that Larry Page would replace Eric Schmidt as CEO first surfaced in "Bloomberg Businessweek." ***Explanation: Bloomberg Businessweek* is the name of a magazine and should be italicized.** |

**TABLE A.8**

Rules for Parentheses

| Rules | Examples |
|---|---|
| **P1.** Use parentheses to enclose details and explanation. | ✔ All correspondence can be sent to the CEO (Eric Schmidt), the global sales director (Nikesh Arora), or the vice president of public policy and communications (Rachel Whetstone). ***Explanation:*** **By providing names in parentheses, additional details are provided for each position. The use of parentheses rather than dashes or commas emphasizes positions and de-emphasizes names.** |
| | ✔ Google has been identified as the most recognized brand in the world for three of the past five years (2009, 2011, 2012). ***Explanation:*** **Provides additional information about the years.** |
| | ✔ Google's recent acquisitions (AdMob, On2 Technologies, ZAO Begun) show that it is aggressively pursuing new technologies. ***Explanation:*** **Provides additional details about the acquisitions.** |
| | ✔ Please send your comments to Google's cloud computing team within two weeks (by May 29). ***Explanation:*** **Clarifies the deadline.** |
| **P2.** Use parentheses to enclose references and directions. | ✔ Please read my report (attached to this email) about opportunities for Google in emerging markets in Africa. ***Explanation:*** **Parentheses enclose directions to locate the report.** |
| | ✔ My last email to Larry (dated July 15) outlined a plan for Google opportunities in emerging markets in Africa. ***Explanation:*** **Parentheses provide a date as a reference to a prior email.** |

## Parentheses

Although people sometimes use parentheses and dashes interchangeably, they have opposite purposes. Dashes are intended to emphasize and draw attention to the phrase they set off, whereas parentheses are used to set off nonessential elements and are thus intended to de-emphasize the phrase that is contained within them. Each of the rules in Table A.8 is labeled with a letter (P, for parentheses) and a number.

# Numbers, Dates, and Currency

Multiple rules apply to the treatment of numbers in a text. The following ones—in Table A.9—are identified by a letter (N, for number) and a number.

**TABLE A.9**

Rules for Numbers

| Case | Examples |
|---|---|
| **N1.** Spell out numbers one through ten. | ✔ Google's <u>two largest markets</u> are the United States and the United Kingdom. ***Explanation:*** **The number is spelled out since it is ten or less.** |
| | **Exceptions:** When related numbers within a sentence or paragraph are above ten. |
| | ✔ In Google's senior management team, <u>3 of the 15 members</u> are former Microsoft employees. ***Explanation:*** **Since a reference to 15 members is made, any other numbers referring to members should also be written in figure style.** |
| | When referring to figures. |
| | ✔ You can see Google's sales projections in <u>Figure 3</u>. ***Explanation:*** **Any reference to a figure, table, or chart uses figure style.** |

**TABLE A.9**

(*Continued*)

| Case | Examples |
|---|---|
| **N2.** Use numerals for numbers above ten. | ✔ Google has <u>43 major product groups</u>. **Explanation: Numbers over ten are generally written in figure style.**<br>✔ My Gmail account has <u>8,028 messages</u>. **Explanation: Numbers in thousands are generally written in numerals.** |
| **N3.** Spell out numbers when they begin a sentence. | ✔ <u>Eleven members</u> of Google's senior management team are former Microsoft employees. **Explanation: Since the first word is a number, it is spelled out.** |
| **N4.** Use a combination of numerals and words for large numbers (over a million). | ✔ Revenues at Google topped <u>$2 billion</u> for the second consecutive year. **Explanation: Large numbers typically include figures and words to avoid displaying too many zeroes.**<br>✔ The mapping software project required nearly <u>3 million hours</u> of development. **Explanation: Large numbers typically include figures and words to avoid displaying too many zeroes.** |
| **N5.** Use numerals for dates. | ✔ July 3, 2017 **Explanation: Most dates are written with the month in word form to avoid confusion since some countries use a day-month-year format.**<br>**Alternatively:** 2017-07-03<br>**Explanation: The *International Organization for Standardization* has adopted the YYYY-MM-DD format.**<br>**Avoid:** July 3rd, 2017<br>**Explanation: Endings to numbers such as *nd* and *rd* are avoided in most business communication.** |
| **N6.** Use numerals with currency symbols in text. | ✔ On average Google software programmers make <u>$174 per hour</u>. **Explanation: Currency amounts are written in figure form preceded by currency symbols.**<br>✔ Many small businesses spend less than <u>$525 per month</u> on Google Adwords campaigns. **Explanation: Currency amounts are written in figure form preceded by currency symbols.** |
| **N7.** Spell out the word *percent* in text. | ✔ The United States is Google's largest geographic market, accounting for approximately <u>47 percent of total revenues</u>. **Explanation: The word *percent* is typically spelled out within sentences.**<br>**Exception:** Tables, forms, highly statistical documents. |
| **N8.** Use parentheses to indicate precise figures in text. | ✔ Approximately half of Google's revenues (<u>47.3 percent</u>) came from the United States. **Explanation: Precise figures are often placed in parentheses so that readers can process the information more easily.**<br>✔ Nearly all of Google's revenues come from advertising (<u>$2.1 billion in advertising revenue out of $2.3 billion in total revenue</u>). **Explanation: Precise figures are often placed in parentheses in text so that readers can process the information more easily.** |
| **N9.** Spell out fractions in text. | ✔ <u>One-fourth of all small businesses</u> in the United States use Google Adwords for advertising. **Explanation: Fractions are spelled out in text.**<br>**Exception:** Mixed numbers (whole number plus fraction).<br>✔ Each year Google holds a <u>3½-day conference</u> for software developers. **Explanation: Since the number is mixed (whole number, 3, plus fraction, 1/2), the fraction is written in figure form.** |
| **N10.** Clearly differentiate adjacent numbers. | ✔ In 2017, 89 percent of Gmail account holders accessed their email daily. **Explanation: A comma is used to help readers quickly identify that these are two separate numbers.**<br>✔ You can have up to twelve 100MB websites. **Explanation: One of the adjacent numbers may be spelled out to help readers see that they are two separate numbers.** |

## Grammar

Table A.10 presents only a few key rules of grammar among the many that guide written language. Each is identified with a letter (G, for grammar) and a number.

**TABLE A.10**

Grammar Rules

| Case | Examples |
|---|---|
| **G1.** Ensure that pronouns agree with their antecedents in number, gender, and/or person. | ✗ Google supports their employees by providing many professional development opportunities. ***Explanation:* The antecedent, Google, is a singular thing. It should not be referred to as *they,* implying a plural.** |
| | ✔ Google supports its employees by providing many professional development opportunities. ***Explanation:* The antecedent, Google, is a singular thing. Therefore, it is appropriately referred to as *it*.** |
| | ✗ Every employee at Google has their own health plan. ***Explanation:* The antecedent, *employee*, is a singular person. Therefore, it should not be referred to as *they*, implying a plural. Writers sometimes do this incorrectly to avoid using sexist language.** |
| | ✔ Every employee at Google has his/her own health plan. ***Explanation:* The antecedent, *employee*, is a singular person. Therefore, it is appropriately referred to as *he* or *she*.** |
| | **Alternatively:** Employees at Google have their own health plans. ***Explanation:* Changing the subject to a plural form avoids the necessity of using an awkward *he/she* expression.** |
| | ✗ Either Bill Gates or Satya Nadella will deliver their speech at the shareholders meeting. ***Explanation:* Two singular nouns connected by *or* or *nor* are treated with singular pronouns.** |
| | ✔ Either Bill Gates or Satya Nadella will deliver his speech at the shareholders meeting. ***Explanation:* Two singular nouns connected by *or* or *nor* are treated with singular pronouns.** |
| | ✗ I want to express our appreciation to you for your outstanding contributions over the past year. ***Explanation:* The singular pronoun, *I,* should not be the antecedent for a plural possessive pronoun, *our*.** |
| | ✔ I want to express my appreciation to you for your outstanding contributions over the past year. ***Explanation:* The singular pronoun, *I,* is an antecedent for the singular possessive pronoun, *my*.** |
| | **Alternatively:** On behalf of all members of the senior management team, I want to express our appreciation to you for your outstanding contributions over the past year. ***Explanation:* The antecedent for the plural possessive pronoun, *our*, is a plural noun, *members of the senior management team*.** |
| **G2.** Ensure that subjects are paired with the correct verb form to achieve subject-verb agreement. | ✗ Microsoft and each of its partners in the delegation is providing reports about upcoming developments in cloud computing. ***Explanation:* The subject is plural (Microsoft and its partners), so the verb should not be in singular form (is).** |
| | ✔ Microsoft and each of its partners in the delegation are providing reports about upcoming developments in cloud computing. ***Explanation:* The subject is plural (Microsoft *and* its partners), so the verb should be in plural form.** |
| | ✗ The handbook of employee benefits are online. ***Explanation:* The subject is singular (handbook), so the verb should not be in plural form (are).** |
| | ✔ The handbook of employee benefits is online. ***Explanation:* The subject is singular (handbook), so the verb should be in singular form (is).** |

**TABLE A.10**

*(Continued)*

| Case | Examples |
|---|---|
| **G3.** Avoid comma splices. | ✘ Sergey Brin is currently the President of Technology, Larry Page is currently the President of Products. ***Explanation:* Two independent clauses should be separated by a period or a semicolon. They should never be separated by a comma unless a coordinating conjunction is inserted.** |
| | ✔ Sergey Brin is currently the President of Technology. Larry Page is currently the President of Products. ***Explanation:* A period separates two independent clauses that are not separated by a coordinating conjunction.** |
| | ✔ Sergey Brin is currently the President of Technology, and Larry Page is currently the President of Products. ***Explanation:* A coordinating conjunction *and* a comma can separate two independent clauses.** |
| **G4.** Check for vague pronouns and replace them. | ✘ Microsoft and Google are well known for attracting innovative, playful employees. They are also known for creating a work culture where playing practical jokes is common. They even play jokes on the public. ***Explanation:* Some readers will be confused whether the *they* pronoun refers to *Microsoft and Google* or the *employees.*** |
| | ✔ Microsoft and Google are well known for attracting innovative, playful employees. The work culture allows employees to play practical jokes on one another. Sometimes the employees even play jokes on the public. ***Explanation:* By removing so many references to *they*, the meaning becomes much clearer.** |
| **G5.** Check for dangling expressions and misplaced modifiers and rewrite to eliminate them. | ✘ Bill Gates spoke about his experience taking his SAT examination at the local university. ***Explanation:* Dangling expressions create confusion because parts of the sentence are not in the correct order. In this sentence did Bill Gates talk at the local university or take the exam at the local university?** |
| | ✔ Bill Gates spoke at the local university about his experience taking his SAT examination. ***Explanation:* This sentence is clear that Bill Gates spoke at the local university.** |
| | ✘ Scoring 1590 out of a possible 1600, the SAT exam didn't seem difficult. ***Explanation:* Many dangling modifiers occur when an introductory participial phrase lacks a subject or does not clearly relate to the material that follows. This sentence is not clear because an SAT exam cannot score 1590 (rather, a person can score a 1590 on an SAT exam).** |
| | ✔ Scoring 1590 out of a possible 1600, Bill Gates thought the SAT exam didn't seem difficult. ***Explanation:* This sentence is clearer—Bill Gates is the person who scored 1590 out of 1600.** |
| | ***Alternatively:*** Because he scored 1590 out of a possible 1600, Bill Gates thought the SAT exam didn't seem difficult. |

## Commonly Misspelled and Confused Words

Spell-checking software is a good tool for identifying most, but not all, spelling errors. Table A.11 lists some commonly misspelled words. Most of the misspellings that are identified as incorrect in this table would not be detected by spell-checking software. For a comprehensive list, consult a guidebook such as the *Gregg Reference Manual*. An ✘ precedes **incorrect** examples, and a ✔ precedes **correct** examples. Parts of speech are noted where the two cases differ.

**TABLE A.11**

Commonly Misspelled and Confused Words

| Case | Examples | Case | Examples |
|---|---|---|---|
| *Accept:* to receive (verb)<br><br>*Except:* apart from; without (preposition or conjunction) | ✗ We <u>except</u> all forms of payment.<br>✔ We <u>accept</u> all forms of payment.<br>✗ We take all forms of payment <u>accept</u> debit cards.<br>✔ We take all forms of payment <u>except</u> debit cards. | *Apprise:* to inform<br><br>*Appraise:* to assess | ✗ You need to <u>appraise</u> him of the situation.<br>✔ You need to <u>apprise</u> him of the situation.<br>✗ You should <u>apprise</u> his performance.<br>✔ You should <u>appraise</u> his performance. |
| *Advice:* suggestions or recommendations (noun)<br><br>*Advise:* to offer suggestions or to recommend (verb) | ✗ Could you provide some <u>advise</u>?<br>✔ Could you provide some <u>advice</u>?<br>✗ Please <u>advice</u> whether to move forward with this plan.<br>✔ Please <u>advise</u> whether to move forward with this plan. | *Capital:* funds or resources; uppercase letters<br><br>*Capitol:* a government building where the legislature meets | ✗ We lack the <u>capitol</u> to make this investment.<br>✔ We lack the <u>capital</u> to make this investment.<br>✗ Our CEO testified at the <u>capital</u>.<br>✔ Our CEO testified at the <u>capitol</u>. |
| *Affect:* to influence (verb)<br><br>*Effect:* a result (noun) | ✗ This <u>effects</u> our business plan.<br>✔ This <u>affects</u> our business plan.<br>✗ This has an <u>affect</u> on our business plan.<br>✔ This has an <u>effect</u> on our business plan. | *Complementary:* something that fits well with or completes another person or object<br><br>*Complimentary:* free (as in a product or service); giving praise | ✗ We form teams with <u>complimentary</u> skill sets.<br>✔ We form teams with <u>complementary</u> skill sets.<br>✗ You will receive a <u>complementary</u> movie ticket as a show of thanks.<br>✔ You will receive a <u>complimentary</u> movie ticket as a show of thanks. |
| *All ready:* complete; finished<br><br>*Already:* previously; by this time | ✗ The business plan is <u>already</u>.<br>✔ The business plan is <u>all ready</u>.<br>✗ She <u>all ready</u> wrote the business plan.<br>✔ She <u>already</u> wrote the business plan. | *Council:* a group that provides advice or recommendations (noun)<br><br>*Counsel:* to advise (verb), advice (noun), or legal representative(s) (noun) | ✗ We will follow the recommendations of the <u>counsel</u>.<br>✔ We will follow the recommendations of the <u>council</u>.<br>✗ We received <u>council</u> not to provide this information publicly.<br>✔ We received <u>counsel</u> not to provide this information publicly. |
| *Altogether:* entirely<br><br>*All together:* all in one place or in unison | ✗ This report is <u>all together</u> confusing.<br>✔ This report is <u>altogether</u> confusing.<br>✗ We should work on the report <u>altogether</u>.<br>✔ We should work on the report <u>all together</u>. | | |

**TABLE A.11**

*(Continued)*

| Case | Examples | Case | Examples |
|---|---|---|---|
| *Elicit:* to draw or bring out (verb)<br><br>*Illicit:* illegal (adjective) | ✗ We want to <u>illicit</u> their feedback.<br>✓ We want to <u>elicit</u> their feedback.<br>✗ We should avoid any <u>elicit</u> conduct.<br>✓ We should avoid any <u>illicit</u> conduct. | *Moral:* principles of rules of conduct<br><br>*Morale:* cheerfulness, confidence, enthusiasm | ✗ Our company abides by high <u>morale</u> and ethical standards.<br>✓ Our company abides by high <u>moral</u> and ethical standards.<br>✗ Our company enjoys high employee <u>moral</u>.<br>✓ Our company enjoys high employee <u>morale</u>. |
| *Incite:* cause, give rise to (verb)<br><br>*Insight:* novel idea (noun) | ✗ His decisions have <u>insighted</u> a minor revolt among employees.<br>✓ His decisions have <u>incited</u> a minor revolt among employees.<br>✗ The business plan contains many <u>incites</u>.<br>✓ The business plan contains many <u>insights</u>. | *Precede:* to come beforehand<br><br>*Proceed:* continue or move forward | ✗ Typically, the phone interview <u>proceeds</u> a face-to-face interview.<br>✓ Typically, the phone interview <u>precedes</u> a face-to-face interview.<br>✗ In some cases, you <u>precede</u> directly to a face-to-face interview.<br>✓ In some cases, you <u>proceed</u> directly to a face-to-face interview. |
| *Insure:* to provide compensation for damages<br><br>*Ensure:* to make certain | ✗ Let's <u>ensure</u> this against legal liabilities.<br>✓ Let's <u>insure</u> this against legal liabilities.<br>✗ Let's <u>insure</u> a smooth transition to the new executive team.<br>✓ Let's <u>ensure</u> a smooth transition to the new executive team. | *Principal:* primary; a person with authority<br><br>*Principle:* a standard or guideline | ✗ My <u>principle</u> place of work is in my home office.<br>✓ My <u>principal</u> place of work is in my home office.<br>✗ One <u>principal</u> for working effectively at home is to limit distractions.<br>✓ One <u>principle</u> for working effectively at home is to limit distractions. |
| *Its:* possessive for *it*<br><br>*It's:* contraction for *it is* | ✗ The beauty of this plan is <u>it's</u> simplicity.<br>✓ The beauty of this plan is <u>its</u> simplicity.<br>✗ <u>Its</u> rare to have such a detailed plan.<br>✓ <u>It's</u> rare to have such a detailed plan. | *Than:* used with comparisons<br><br>*Then:* used to indicate a point in time | ✗ Gold values have grown faster <u>then</u> stock prices.<br>✓ Gold values have grown faster <u>than</u> stock prices.<br>✗ When gold values start falling, <u>than</u> you should move your funds into stocks.<br>✓ When gold values start falling, <u>then</u> you should move your funds into stocks. |
| *Lose:* to lose or to misplace (verb)<br><br>*Loose:* not tight (adjective) | ✗ We'll <u>loose</u> this opportunity if we do not act immediately.<br>✓ We'll <u>lose</u> this opportunity if we do not act immediately.<br>✗ There is a <u>lose</u> connection between your ideas.<br>✓ There is a <u>loose</u> connection between your ideas. | | |

## Capitalization

This is a short list of several important capitalization rules for business communication. See Table A.12 for these rules and several examples. Consult a comprehensive style guide for all capitalization rules.

**TABLE A.12**

Capitalization Rules

| Rules | Examples |
|---|---|
| **Ca1.** Capitalize proper nouns, abbreviations and acronyms, and brand names. | ✔ Sundar Pichai became CEO in 2015. **_Explanation:_** Sundar Pichai is a proper name. CEO is an acronym. <br> ✘ The name of the company's headquarters is googleplex. **_Explanation:_** Googleplex is a proper noun and should be capitalized. <br> ✔ The company's competitors include Apple and Microsoft. **_Explanation:_** Apple and Microsoft are brand names. <br> ✘ The company is partnering with sprint. **_Explanation:_** Sprint is a brand name and should be capitalized. |
| **Ca2.** Capitalize a person's title when it appears before a proper noun but not when it is used alone. | ✔ The company delegation visited President Obama. **_Explanation:_** The title precedes a proper noun. <br> ✘ The company delegation visited professor Janikowski, an expert in artificial intelligence. **_Explanation:_** Professor should be capitalized since it precedes a proper noun. <br> ✔ Our marketing director visited with Stephanie Larsen, operations manager at Google. **_Explanation:_** The two titles in this sentence, marketing director and operations manager, do not precede a proper noun. <br> ✘ You should direct all questions to our Corporate Communication Officer. **_Explanation:_** This title should not be capitalized because it is not preceded by a proper noun. |
| **Ca3.** Capitalize names of areas and regions. | ✔ Google's headquarters are in Northern California. **_Explanation:_** Northern California is capitalized because it is the name of a region. <br> ✘ Google's headquarters are North of Los Angeles. **_Explanation:_** North should not be capitalized because it refers to a direction, not an area or region. |
| **Ca4.** Capitalize names of ethnic groups. | ✔ The company is seeking to hire a higher percentage of African Americans for entry-level developer positions. **_Explanation:_** _African Americans_ should be capitalized because the term refers to an ethnic group. <br> ✘ The company has tried to attract hispanic americans without much success. **_Explanation:_** _Hispanic Americans_ should be capitalized because the term refers to an ethnic group. <br> Exceptions: The words _black_ and _white_ are usually not capitalized when referring to ethnic or racial groups. |
| **Ca5.** Capitalize titles of books, reports, chapters, and other named documents. | ✔ Google has recently contributed to journal articles such as "Gender Differences in Factors Influencing Pursuit of Computer Science and Related Fields" and "Gender Differences in High School Students' Decisions to Study Computer Science and Related Fields." **_Explanation:_** These articles are appropriately capitalized. <br> ✘ The company recently created a white paper called _data analytics in the era of artificial intelligence_. **_Explanation:_** The title of the white paper should be capitalized (with the exceptions of articles and prepositions). |
| **Ca6.** Capitalize the first word of a sentence, a quotation, and an independent clause after a colon. | ✔ Sergey Brin stated, "We had a simple idea that not all pages are created equal." **_Explanation:_** _We_ is capitalized because it is the first word in a quotation. <br> ✔ Our company's current strategy is straightforward: We must integrate cognitive capabilities into all our products. **_Explanation:_** _We_ is capitalized because it is the first word in an independent clause after a colon. |

# Application Exercises

**Directions:** Place commas and other punctuation marks throughout these passages wherever needed, and name the rule that applies.

*Example:* To develop supply chain software and services Microsoft partnered with Infosys.

*Answer:* To develop supply chain software and services, Microsoft partnered with Infosys. (C7)

## Comma Exercises

1. Bill Gates and Paul Allen who were childhood friends founded Microsoft in 1975. Bill met Steve Ballmer who would later become the CEO of Microsoft at Stanford.

2. Bill Gates met the man who would later become the CEO of Microsoft at Stanford.

3. The two technology companies that consistently have the most brand value are Microsoft and Google.

4. In fact they consistently showed high profits during the recent recession.

5. Microsoft and Google the two companies that consistently have the most brand value showed high profits during the recession.

6. To hire Qi Lu as the new president of the Online Services Division was a masterful move by Microsoft.

7. Microsoft enjoys almost limitless advantages in terms of research and development budgets.

8. Steve Ballmer took a smooth methodical approach to developing the five-year strategy.

9. Microsoft from my perspective gained its market dominance through anti-competitive practices.

10. Microsoft Word if you're looking for maximum functionality in your word processing far outperforms Google Docs.

11. Microsoft Word far outperforms Google Docs if you're looking for maximum functionality in your word processing.

12. Steve Ballmer CEO from 2000 to 2014 was a college classmate of Bill Gates.

13. MS-DOS an operating system developed initially for IBM personal computers became Microsoft's first major success.

14. As a result Bill Gates moved the headquarters to Washington.

15. Bill Gates gave up the CEO position in 2000 but he remained active at Microsoft by taking a position as chief software architect.

16. In the early years of Microsoft Bill Gates spent most of his time conducting business but also stayed involved in programming.

17. Microsoft's product categories include operating systems, server applications, information worker productivity applications, business solution applications, high-performance computing applications and software development tools.

18. In 2008 Microsoft acquired Calista Technologies Kidaro Rapt Fast Search & Transfer Navic Networks and DATAllegro.

19. Most people who know Bill say that he is a stubborn determined executive.

20. After Bill moved to management roles he still read and approved most of the code developed for MS-DOS.

21. Under the new set of human resources guidelines all Microsoft employees must declare whether or not they are smokers.

22. Prior to joining the Microsoft team in 2009 Dr. Lu had worked at Yahoo! for 10 years.

23. By acquiring competitor companies Microsoft gains new customers new technology and new ideas.

24. Often Microsoft acquires competitor companies.

25. In July Bill Gates said that he would no longer focus on the day-to-day business activities at Microsoft.

26. In 1980 IBM agreed to let Microsoft develop an operating system for one of its lines of personal computers.

27. IBM agreed to let Microsoft starting in 1980 develop an operating system for one of its lines of personal computers.

28. The new Microsoft Office Suite will go on sale in July.

29. The new Microsoft Office Suite will go on sale in July 2015.

30. The new Microsoft Office Suite will go on sale on July 15 2015.

31. If you purchase the new Microsoft Office Suite between July 15 2015 and January 15 2016 you will receive a $100 rebate.

32. Microsoft employs more than 89000 employees.

33. The ED division develops and produces products such as the Xbox 360 third-party games and the Zune digital music and entertainment platform.

34. Steve Ballmer recently resigned as CEO of Microsoft, he is now the owner of the Los Angeles Clippers.

## Semicolon, Colon, and Comma Exercises

35. Microsoft faces two major threats piracy and patent lawsuits.

36. Bill Gates focuses on product development and strategy Satya Nadella focuses on operations.

37. Bill Gates focuses on product development and strategy on the other hand Satya Nadella focuses on operations.

38. Microsoft's American offices are in Redmond Washington New York City San Francisco Birmingham Alabama and Phoenix Arizona.

39. Cloud computing involves three possible platforms software-as-a-service (SaaS) platform-as-a-service (PaaS) and infrastructure-as-a-service (IaaS).

## Dash and Hyphen Exercises

40. Microsoft Office the leading business software for over two decades takes a research based approach to identifying new markets.

41. Microsoft's spreadsheet software Excel is preferred by engineers economists and statisticians due to the well known statistical functions.

42. Microsoft's strategy will likely produce positive results over the long term.

43. Managers say the break even point is around $50 million.

44. In the short run Microsoft would like to increase its market share in the search engine market.

45. Microsoft has a short run goal to increase its market share in the search engine market.

46. Microsoft's investment based approach to research and development ensures that it produces highly applied results.

47. Because Microsoft has adopted an approach to R&D that is investment based it tends to produce results that are highly applied.

**Directions:** For each set of choices below (separated by slashes), choose the correct answer and name the rule that applies.

*Example:* Microsoft has a presence in over one hundred/100 countries.

*Answer:* 100 (N2)

## Italics and Quotation Mark Exercises

48. The recent story about Microsoft in *The Wall Street Journal*/"The Wall Street Journal" was called Microsoft's Gamble on Cloud Computing/"Microsoft's Gamble on Cloud Computing."

49. Bill Gates said that he'd like to see the phrase *go bing it*/"go bing it" replace the phrase *go google it*/"go google it."

50. At the luncheon, his speech, titled *The Road to the Future*/"The Road to the Future," laid out his vision for cloud computing over the next decade.

## Number Exercises

51. In 2013, 3/three Microsoft business divisions were combined.

52. Revenues for the last fiscal year were $62,484 million/$62,484,000,000.

53. Revenues rose 28 percent/28% over the past year.

54. Microsoft employs over 89 thousand/89,000 employees.

55. Microsoft has five/5 business divisions.

56. 5/Five Microsoft divisions make up the Microsoft corporation.

57. Microsoft lost money in 3/three of the 17/seventeen product groups.

58. Microsoft's largest division, Microsoft Business, accounts for approximately 31%/31 percent of its revenues.

59. In the search engine market, Google holds 63%/63 percent of the market share, compared to just 13%/13 percent for Microsoft.

60. Microsoft was fined $388 million/388 million dollars for infringing on Uniloc's anti-piracy software.

61. The Washington home of Bill Gates is valued at approximately $125 million/$125,000,000, resulting in annual property taxes of roughly $990 thousand/$990,000.

## Grammar Exercises

62. Microsoft joined with Accenture to create Avanade, an IT consultancy. They/It specialize/s in connecting to consumers through online platforms such as social networks.

63. Neither Yahoo! nor Microsoft has/have increased its/their market share in the search engine market for the past five years.

64. Microsoft hold/s its/their annual shareholders meeting at the corporate headquarters.

65. Every new Microsoft employee should provide copies of his/her/their Social Security card/s at the orientation.

66. The manual about computer programming tips are/is on reserve at the corporate reading room.

67. Microsoft and its competitors in the technology industry is/are constantly changing.

## Misspelled Words Exercises

68. Many of Google's HR policies are aimed at eliciting/illiciting honest feedback.

69. The advice/advise on Microsoft's Help menu is not helpful.

70. All employees should ensure/insure that their LinkedIn pages do not contain any content contrary to the Code of Conduct.

71. This decision affects/effects every aspect of our marketing strategy.

72. Their next step is to identify how to raise enough capital/capitol for the venture.

73. She told me that the two products contain complementary/complimentary features.

74. This search engine is much more reliable than/then Google's.

## Capitalization Exercises

75. Sundar Pichai, CEO/ceo of Google, says that Google is ahead of its competitors in the race to develop artificial intelligence capabilities.

76. We just hired her for a Senior Developer/senior developer position.

77. Google's headquarters are located in Silicon Valley/silicon valley.

78. The headquarters are located just West/west of Sunnyvale.

79. Please contact Eileen Chao, Communications Lead/communications lead, for additional press inquires.

80. Ms. Chao explained, "We/we will invest more than $50 million this year to research and develop artificial intelligence."

# Formatting for Letters and Memos

Although most written business correspondence is sent electronically, memos and letters continue to be used in various business situations. When you do use memos and letters, you should use professional, standard formatting. This appendix contains three examples. You can find additional examples in the online resources, including formats for letters that aren't on letterhead and that are more than one page long.

*Memos* are most often used for formal announcements within organizations (see Figure B.1 for a sample memo). In most cases today, memos are distributed as attachments (usually in .pdf format) by email or other forms of electronic messages. Regardless of how memos are distributed, they contain fairly standard components and formatting. They begin with *To*, *From*, *Date*, and *Subject* lines. Then, they move to the body or message, without a salutation or closing. They end with special notations (see below for common types of notations in memos and letters). In most organizations, you can use standard memo templates, which are often created in-house and stored on corporate intranets. If your organization does not have a standard template, you can choose from dozens of professional ones that come with word processing software.

*Business letters* are written far less today than a few decades ago; however, they are still appropriate for various business situations. When you write a letter on behalf of your organization, use official letterhead and find out if your organization employs a standard format. If it doesn't, you can choose from several options, including block format and modified block format (see examples in Figures B.2 and B.3). Block format is the most common because it is very clean, with flush-left margins for the entire letter.

Memos and letters may contain various notations, including the following:

- *Carbon copy* (indicated by *c:* or *cc:*). This allows primary message recipients to see all individuals who have received a copy of the memo or letter.
- *Distribution list* (indicated by *Distribution:*). When you send a memo or letter to many individuals, you can use a distribution list to ensure everyone knows who received the document.
- *Preparer's initials*. When someone has written the letter on behalf of the sender, the preparer places his/her initials in lowercase text.
- *Enclosure or attachments* (indicated by *Enclosure*, *Enc.*, *Attachment*, or *Att.*). When you are including additional documents or materials, make reference to them with a notation.

## Components of Memos

- To
- From
- Date
- Subject
- Body
- Notations (optional)

## Components of Letters

- Letterhead
- Date
- Inside address
- Salutation
- Body
- Closing/Signature
- Notations (optional)

**FIGURE B.1**

Sample Memo

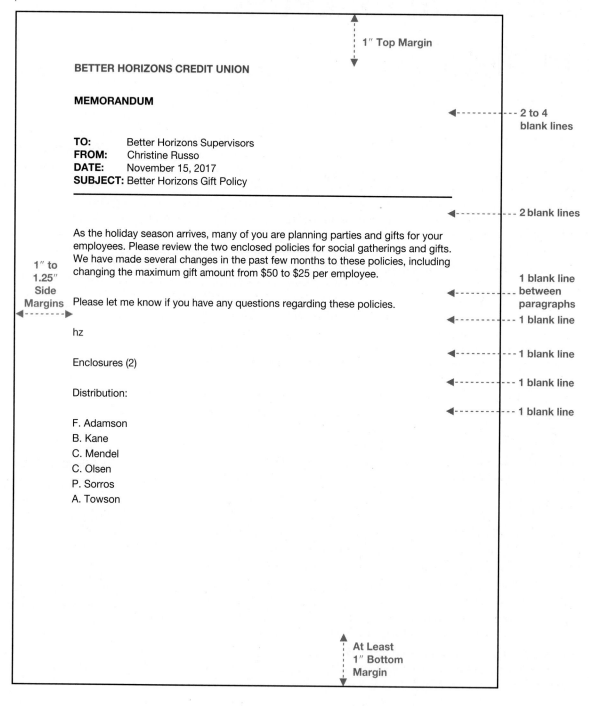

**BETTER HORIZONS CREDIT UNION**

**MEMORANDUM**

1″ Top Margin

2 to 4 blank lines

**TO:** Better Horizons Supervisors
**FROM:** Christine Russo
**DATE:** November 15, 2017
**SUBJECT:** Better Horizons Gift Policy

2 blank lines

As the holiday season arrives, many of you are planning parties and gifts for your employees. Please review the two enclosed policies for social gatherings and gifts. We have made several changes in the past few months to these policies, including changing the maximum gift amount from $50 to $25 per employee.

1″ to 1.25″ Side Margins

1 blank line between paragraphs

Please let me know if you have any questions regarding these policies.

1 blank line

hz

1 blank line

Enclosures (2)

1 blank line

Distribution:

1 blank line

F. Adamson
B. Kane
C. Mendel
C. Olsen
P. Sorros
A. Towson

At Least 1″ Bottom Margin

**FIGURE B.2**

Sample Letter in Block Format Style

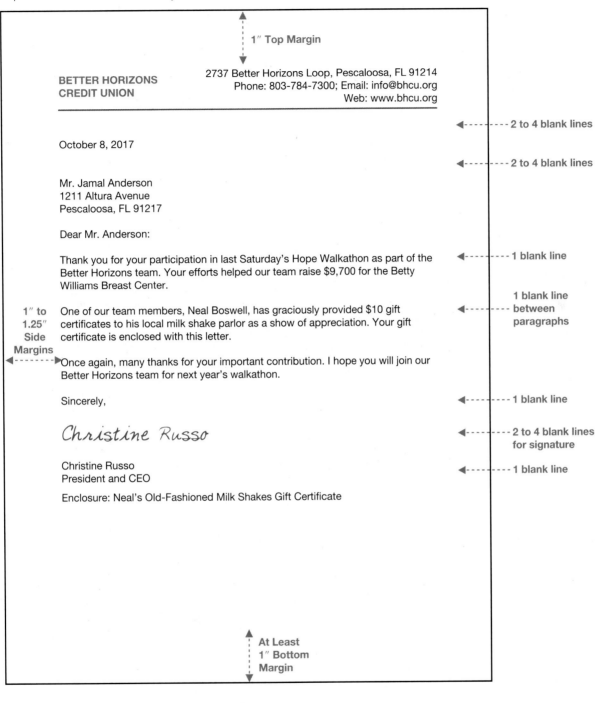

**FIGURE B.3**

Sample Letter in Modified Block Format Style

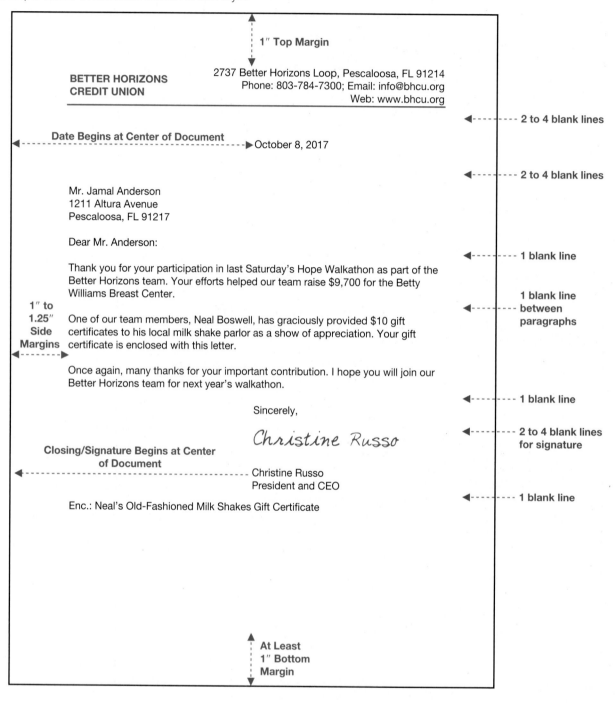

# Index